Memorial Book of the Communities
Dobrzyn-Gollob, Poland

Translation of:
Ayarati; sefer zikaron le-ayarot Dobrzyń-Golub

Editors: M. Harpaz
and
Editorial Committee: Y. Rosenwax, A. Dor and H. Lord

Published by the Association of Former Residents of Dobrzyń-Golub
Published in Tel Aviv, 1969

Published by JewishGen

**An Affiliate of the Museum of Jewish Heritage—A Living Memorial to the Holocaust
New York**

Memorial Book of the Communities Dobrzyn-Gollob, Poland
Translation of *Ayarati; sefer zikaron le-ayarot Dobrzyń-Golub*

Copyright © 2019 by JewishGen, Inc.
All rights reserved.
First Printing: April 2019, Nisan 5779
Second Printing: August 2019, Av 5779

Translator: Allen Flusberg
Layout: Donni Magid
Cover Design: Rachel Kolokoff Hopper

This book may not be reproduced, in whole or in part, including illustrations in any form (beyond that copying permitted by Sections 107 and 108 of the U.S. Copyright Law and except by reviewers for public press), without written permission from the publisher.

Published by JewishGen, Inc.
An Affiliate of the Museum of Jewish Heritage
A Living Memorial to the Holocaust
36 Battery Place, New York, NY 10280

JewishGen, Inc. is not responsible for inaccuracies or omissions in the original work and makes no representations regarding the accuracy of this translation. Digital images of the original book's contents can be seen online at the New York Public Library website.

The mission of the JewishGen organization is to produce a translation of the original work, and we cannot verify the accuracy of statements or alter facts cited.

Printed in the United States of America by Lightning Source, Inc.
Library of Congress Control Number (LCCN): 2019937360
ISBN: 978-1-939561-78-7 (hard cover: 668 pages, alk. paper)

Cover photograph: R. Zalman Rozenwaks (Zalman Hassid). Page 47
Back cover: The poem is from page 7 of the book.
From My Town: In Memory of the Communities Dobrzyn–Gollob, edited by M. Harpaz, (published by the Dobrzyn–Golub Society, Israel, 1969), p. 10.

The Hebrew on the back cover is from page 124 of the book: These words were engraved on the headstone of R. Meir Feivel.

JewishGen and the Yizkor Books-in-Print-Project

This book has been published by the **Yizkor Books in Print Project**, as part of the **Yizkor Book Project** of JewishGen, Inc.

JewishGen, Inc. is a non-profit organization founded in 1987 as a resource for Jewish genealogy. Its website [www.jewishgen.org] serves as an international clearinghouse and resource center to assist individuals who are researching the history of their Jewish families and the places where they lived. JewishGen provides databases, facilitates discussion groups, and coordinates projects relating to Jewish genealogy and the history of the Jewish people. In 2003, JewishGen became an affiliate of the **Museum of Jewish Heritage—A Living Memorial to the Holocaust** in New York.

The **JewishGen Yizkor Book Project** was organized to make more widely known the existence of Yizkor (Memorial) Books written by survivors and former residents of various Jewish communities throughout the world. Later, volunteers connected to the different destroyed communities began cooperating to have these books translated from the original language—usually Hebrew or Yiddish—into English, thus enabling a wider audience to have access to the valuable information contained within them. As each chapter of these books was translated, it was posted on the JewishGen website and made available to the general public.

The **Yizkor-Books-in-Print Project** began in 2011 as an initiative to print and publish Yizkor Books that had been fully translated, so that hard copies would be available for purchase by the descendants of these communities and also by scholars, universities, synagogues, libraries, and museums.

These Yizkor books have been produced almost entirely through the volunteer effort of researchers from around the world, assisted by donations from private individuals. The books are printed and sold at near cost, so as to make them as affordable as possible. Our goal is to make this important genre of Jewish literature and history available in English in book form, so that people can have the personal histories of their ancestral towns on their bookshelves for themselves and for their children and grandchildren.

A list of all published translated Yizkor Books in the project with prices and ordering information can be found at:
http://www.jewishgen.org/Yizkor/ybip.html

Lance Ackerfeld, Yizkor Book Project Manager
Joel Alpert, Yizkor-Book-in-Print Project Coordinator

Yizkor Book Project

This book is presented by the
Yizkor Books in Print Project
Project Coordinator: Joel Alpert

Part of the
Yizkor Books Project of JewishGen, Inc.
Project Manager: Lance Ackerfeld

These books have been produced solely through volunteer effort of individuals from around the world. The books are printed and sold at near cost, so as to make them as affordable as possible.

Our goal is to make this history and important genre of Jewish literature available in English in book form so that people can have the near-personal histories of their ancestral towns on their bookshelves for themselves and for their children and grandchildren.

Any donations to the Yizkor Books Project are appreciated.

Please send donations to:
Yizkor Book Project
JewishGen
36 Battery Place
New York, NY 10280

JewishGen, Inc. is an affiliate of the
Museum of Jewish Heritage
A Living Memorial to the Holocaust

Acknowledgements

Our sincere appreciation to Yad Vashem for the submission of the necrology for placement on the JewishGen web site.

Our sincere appreciation to Susan Dressler for typing up the English section to facilitate its addition to this project.

Acknowledgements and Dedication
By Allen Flusberg, the translator

I would like to acknowledge those who came before me for translating about 10 percent of this Yizkor Book into English. I am grateful to my cousin, Arthur Rones, also a grandson of a Dobrzyner, for suggesting that I should work on translating this Yizkor Book during my retirement. I thank the staff of JewishGen, particularly Lance Ackerfeld, for uploading my translations one by one to the JewishGen Yizkor Books website, and for their patience with my errata. I thank Ania Miler for helping me translate some Polish phrases, and David Jacobson for reviewing my translation of some difficult Hebrew poetry. I am also grateful to my wife, Rosalind Flusberg, for her love, devotion and encouragement.

I dedicate this translation to my grandfather, Abraham Flusberg, who fled from Dobrzyn to the United States in 1928 as a result of a blood libel against him; to my father, David Flusberg, who left Dobrzyn in 1933; and to all my uncles, aunts and cousins who remained behind and perished at the hands of the Nazis.

Summary of the Dobrzyn-Golub Yizkor Book

The Dobrzyn-Golub Yizkor Book evokes both pleasure and pain: pleasure from the nostalgic accounts by the Dobrzyn Jews who emigrated before World War II, and pain from the narratives describing the destruction of all traces of the town's rich Jewish culture. For beginning in 1939 its Jewish population was savagely expelled and murdered, all Jewish institutions were eradicated, and even the Jewish cemetery was obliterated.

This book contains chilling accounts by a handful of survivors who experienced the trauma of the Nazi occupation of the town, the mass-murder of leading Jewish citizens, and the expulsion to ghettos, work camps and death camps. Other essays on prewar personalities describe dreamers, poets, community organizers, scholars and noted rabbis. They tell the story of a multi-faceted prewar Jewish culture: the ardor of religious life and the advent of secular studies, socialism, Zionism, sports, and theatre. The town was home to all the warring Jewish factions of the period: the pious *Hasidim*; the secular socialists; and the Zionists, both secular and religious. Despite their sharp differences they would join hands to provide charity to the needy, and they would be as unified as a close family in the face of anti-Semitism.

The range of topics covered in these essays spans the entire gamut of Jewish experience in the town. There are the adventures of a Dobrzyn Jew in the Czar's army of 1910 and in a World War I German work camp. There is a description of an election of town rabbi in which the two candidates are backed by vying *Hasidic* groups. A scholar living in New York who was raised in Dobrzyn writes how he still yearns for the simple life he led there. An ecstatic poem, written by an ascetic kabbalist who hailed from Dobrzyn, is filled with fury and religious awe. We meet a gabardine-clad *Hasid* who preaches Zionism to his pious fellow *Hasidim* as well as to sophisticated German Jews. And a Dobrzyner, recalling his childhood studies in *cheder*, tells of a prank played by the schoolchildren on their teacher, and the teacher's revenge. The essays also include postwar updates: descriptions and obituaries depicting the lives of those who settled in Israel; and accounts by American Dobrzyners of their *landsmanshaft* fundraising. There are photographs from Dobrzyn in the period 1910-1939, and others from Israel and the US up to the 1960s.

The essays by the American Dobrzyners were nearly all written in Yiddish; those authored by their Israeli counterparts were mostly in Hebrew. The entire set of essays, as well as a map of the town, appear here in English translation, with footnotes by the translator and a Holocaust necrology that has been extracted from the essays.

Explanation of Transliterations in Translations by Allen Flusberg

My transliterations of family names has varied between English spellings, German spellings (e.g. "sch" instead of the English "sh", "Sp" instead of the English "Shp", "z" instead of the English "tz"), and Polish spellings (e.g. "sz" instead of the English "sh", "c" instead of the English "tz"). For example, the same family name is sometimes spelled Tzudkewicz, Zudkevitz, and Cudkewicz, In addition, because this Yizkor Book did not at all vocalize the vowel-letter "aleph" occurring in the Yiddish text, I was forced to make an educated guess as to whether occurrences of this vowel-letter in names were pronounced "a" or "o." Finally, I have endeavored to transliterate proper names and Hebrew words occurring in Hebrew text according to the Israeli pronunciation, but proper names and Hebrew words occurring in Yiddish text according to the Polish Ashkenazi pronunciation.

Notes to the Reader:

We apologize ahead of time for the poor quality of images in the book. Often these images had been scanned from the original Yizkor books which were of poor quality to begin with, being copies of old photographs. Each transfer results in loss of quality. We have done the best we could, given the original material and the resources and technology at hand. Even though images often appear of higher quality on computer screens, that does not transfer to high quality images in print. A reader can view the original scans on the web sites listed below.

Within the text the reader will note "{34}" standing ahead of a paragraph. This indicates that the material translated below was on page 34 of the original book. However, when a paragraph was split between two pages in the original book, the marker is placed in this book after the end of the paragraph for ease of reading.

Also please note that all references within the text of the book to page numbers, refer to the page numbers of the original Yizkor Book.

The original book can be seen online at the New York Public Library site: https://digitalcollections.nypl.org/items/e166de70-6c5b-0133-64a0-00505686d14e

or at the Yiddish Book Center web site:
http://www.yiddishbookcenter.org/collections/yizkor-books/yzk-nybc314178

In order to obtain a list of all Shoah victims from the towns, the reader should access the Yad Vashem web site listed below; one can also search for specific family names using family name option. These lists are continually updated by Yad Vashem, so it is worthwhile to periodically search these lists.

There is much valuable information available on this web site, including the Pages of Testimony, etc.
http://yvng.yadvashem.org

A list of this book and all books available in the Yizkor-Book-In-Print Project along with prices is available at:
http://www.jewishgen.org/Yizkor/ybip.html

Geopolitical Information:

Located at 53°07' North Latitude 19°03' East Longitude

Alternate names: Golub-Dobrzyń [Pol], Dobrin bei Dervents [Yid], Dobrzyń nad Drwęcą [Pol], Dobrin an der Drewenz [Ger], Dobzhin nad Drvents, Gollub [Ger], Golub, Dobzhin, Dobzhin Golub, Dobrzyń-Golub, Golub Dobzhin

Notes: Initially two cities, separated by the Drwęca River. The two cities were united in 1951.

Russian: Голюб-Добжинь. Hebrew: דובז'ין על נהר דריוצה

Before WWI, Golub was in West Prussia (Germany), and Dobrzyń was in Płock gubernia of the Russian Kingdom of Poland.

Between the wars, Golub was in Wąbrzeźno district of Pomorze (Pomerania) province of Poland, and Dobrzyń nad Drwęcą was in Rypin district of Warszawa province.

Jewish Population in 11897: 1,938

Period	Town	District	Province	Country
Before WWI (c. 1900):	Golub / Dobrzyń	Rypin	Płock	Russian Empire
Between the wars (c. 1930):	Golub / Dobrzyń nad Drwęcą	Rypin	Warszawa	Poland
After WWII (c. 1950):	Golub-Dobrzyń			Poland
Today (c. 2000):	Golub-Dobrzyń			Poland

Nearby Jewish Communities:

Wąbrzeźno 12 miles NNW
Lubicz 13 miles WSW
Kikół 15 miles S
Rypin 17 miles E
Brodnica 17 miles ENE
Chełmża 19 miles WNW
Toruń 20 miles WSW
Ciechocinek 20 miles SSW

Map of Poland showing Dobrzyn-Golub

Cover of the Original Yizkor Book

Translation of the Cover of Original Yizkor Book

My Town

Memorial Book of

Dobrzyn-Gollob

Table of Contents

[Hebrew]

With Publication of the Book		1
From the Historical Sources		2
Maps		6
And You Shall Remember (poem)		7
In the shadow of the destruction	The Editor	8
El Male Rachamim		10

The Towns that Were

May My Lot Be with You (poem)	Ch. N. Bialik	13
Dobrzy and Golub on the Drwęca River	Yehudah Rozenwax	13
Dobrzyń, My Town	Dr. Yechiel Lichtenstein	15
My childhood years in Dobrzyń	Yaakov Rimon	36
My town (poem)	Walter Field	40
The town's Rabbi	Mendel Sonabend	41
In My Father's House	Yehuda Rozenwaks	44
Daily Life in the Town	Avraham Dor (Dobroshklanka)	50
The nobility and the inspiration of Dobrzyń's Jews	HaRav Yitzchak Yedidya Frenkel	56
Childhood and Adolescence (Memories)	Zev Lent	58
A few memories…	Dina and Yitzchak Shperling	70

Institutions and Movements

A Vibrant and Active Community	Yehuda Rosenwaks	73
Institutions and Organizations	Avraham Dor (Dobroshklanka)	77
Prayer and Torah institutions and religious ministrants in the town	Yehudah Rozenwax	90
The Jewish education in Dobrzyń-Golub	Shmuel Meiri (Miniwski)	93
The Beginning of the Establishment of the Bund	Yaakov Gorni	97
Hashomer Hatzair	Chaim Lord	98
The Sholom-Aleichem Library	Chaim Lord	110
The Struggle for Education in Our Town	Y. Wrzos	116

Spirit and Vision

On the holidays	Yehuda Rosenwaks	120
A Jewish theatre in Dobrzyń	Avraham Dor (Dobroszklanka)	129
The Idea of Aliya to Israel Strikes Root	Yehuda Rosenwaks	132
The First Dobrzyners in Israel	Yehoshua Eshel (Isaac)	135

From the Horrors of the Holocaust

How Can I Take Pleasure?	Yehuda Halevi	145
The pain in the heart (poem)	Yehudit Golan (Rosenwaks)	147
In the tempest of the war	Zadok Zudkevitz	148
The men left and didn't return	Yehoshua Flusberg	159
Fleeing for Our Lives	Yitzhak Ryż	163
How did we manage?	Yehudit Golan (Rosenwaks)	170
Seven sections of Hell	Gorny Frum	175
In the Extermination Camps	Bracha Rotolski (Goldberg)	189
After the liberation	Gorny Frum	193

Personalities in the Town

Reb Feibush Lipka	Yehezkel Cohen	196
Yosef Chaim Ruda	Eizberg	198
R. Ephraim Eliezer Granat (Rimon), of Blessed Memory	Yaakov Rimon	202
My Dear Mother, May She Rest in Peace	Mendel Sonabend	209
My grandfather's house	Shmuel Meiri-Minisewski	212
Chana Chaya Granat-Katcher, of Blessed Memory	Yaakov Rimon	219
Chaya Shifra Bielawski	Yehuda Rosenwaks	224
My Grandmother's Shloshim Memorial Service…	Moti	227
Shmuel Zeinwil Lipka	Minda Lipka Bornstein	229
The Brothers Mendel and Avraham Hirsh Kohn	Avraham Dor	230
The Dreamer Who Did Not Live to See His Dream Fulfilled	Shmuel Meiri–Minivski	238
A Bunch of Memories about My Brother, the Poet Yosef Tzvi Rimon, of Blessed Memory	Yaakov Rimon	249
Why Do You Weep, My Heart (poem)	Yosef Tzvi Rimon	258
My parents' house	Shmuel Meiri-Miniwski	261
R' Yeshayahu the "Great"	Avraham Dor	264
Tzvi Zev (Hirsh Wolff) Laks	Yaakov Rimon	267
To My Girlfriends Who Did Not Merit…	Rivka Shapira (Horowitz)	269
In Memory of My Parents	Yaakov Kohn	272

In Memoriam

Yehoshua Eshel	Avraham Dor	274
Shoshana Vinkor (Offenbach) of blessed memory	Yisrael Lahav	276
Yehiel Bunim Granat-Rimon	Yaakov Rimon	281
Tova Shivek	Shmuel Shivek	284
My Father's House	Shoshana Vinkor (Offenbach)	286
A man's path	Tzadok Tzvi Florman	289
About Tzvi, For He Is Gone	Yitzhak Sperling	296
To My Very Dear Father…	Chava	299
Chana Rosenwaks	Yehuda Rosenwaks	302

On the Death of Yehuda Sperling	Eliyahu	304
My son, Yehudah, my son	His father, Yitzhak	307
Nisan Fogel	Avraham Dor	312
My husband - Nisan Fogel	Bilhah Fogel	314
Katriel Isaac	Avraham Dor	316
Mordechai Goldberg	Avraham Dor	318
Dov Yalowski	His daughter, Leah	321
Yitzhak Rosenwaks	Ben-Tziyon Epstein	323
Avraham Rosen	Avraham Dor	326
Rosenbaum, Moshe Aharon		328

Personalities and their activities

The poet Yaakov Rimon (Granat)		334
Ask, Jewish people... (poem)	Yaakov Rimon	339
These Days (poem)	Yaakov Rimon	341
The Warshawski Family of New York	Yehuda Rosenwaks	342

[Yiddish]

The Towns that Once Existed		
The Synagogue and Shtiebels in Dobrzyn	An unknown rabbi	347
The Grassroots Jews of Dobrzyn	Shlomo Aleksander	355
My town Dobrzyn	Mechele Platnyarz Schlesinger	359
A Glance at Synagogue Lane	Michl'e Plotniarz-Shlesinger	361
The Synagogue in Dobrzyn	Tuvya Tinski	363
Memories of My Hometown Dobrzyn	Avraham Dor (Dobroshklenka)	370

The Community and its Institutions

The religious life in Dobrzyn	Rabbi Nathan Sanger	375
Institutions and Parties in Dobrzyn	Sara Groner–Krantz	387
The active members of the community	Charles L. Graner	390
The Establishment of the Bund in Dobrzyn	Yaakov Gorny	394
The Struggle for Education in the Town	Yaakov Wrzos	397

Our Landsleit in America		
The brief history of the Chicago Dobrzyn Organization	Ester Graner Rebbe	402
The First Association of Dobrzyners in America	Shlomo Alexander	407

Destruction

Memories from the War Years	Michael Cohen	413
The Twenty Who Were Hanged	Mrs. Degala	420
On the Winding Roads	Yehoshua Goldberg	422
Pain and Suffering of a Family	Gavriel Katcher	426

My Bundle of Troubles in the Russian Military	Yitzhak Rosenwaks	430
Pain and suffering in the Second World War	Elya Tzala	453
After the liberation	Gorny Frum	479
Memories	Yosef Dratwa	485

Personalities

R'Yaakov Leib Graner	Ester Graner Rebbe	489
Bunem Zaklikovski	Shimon Yosef Platnerz (USA)	494
The Rabbi of Dobrzyn	Mendel Sonabend	497
My Beautiful, Loving Mother, of Blessed Memory, the Dobrzyn Rebbetzin	Mendel Sonabend	502
Rivka Aleksander	Avraham Dor (Dobroszklanka)	505
Memoirs Dedicated to My Father R. Feibish Lipka	Yeshayohu Nosson Lipka	507
The "Dreamer" Who Did Not Live to See His Dream Fulfilled	Shmuel Meiri–Minivski	553

From Home to Home

From Home to Home	557
List of Those Who Passed Away in Chicago	568
List of Those Who Passed Away in Israel	571
List of Those Who Passed Away in England and in Germany	573
Commemoration of Parents and Relatives	574
Names of members that are no more with us	584

[English]

My Home Town	Walter L. Field	586
My Mother's Legacy	Walter L. Field	589
Those Terrible Days…	Pozmanter H.	591
The Kristal–Brown Family	Samuel Abraham Meiri	594
Isaac Ryz	Yehuda Rozenwax	597
The Jewish Partisans – Objective and Subjective Difficulties	Shalom Cholawski	598
The Relationship Between the Jewish and the Polish Underground in Nazi–Occupied Poland	Michael Borwicz	602
The Yishuv's Traditional Help to Jews in the Time of Holocaust	Yehuda Slutsky	604
The Uniqueness of Jewish Martyrdom During the Holocaust	J. Gottfarstein	607
List of Names – Golub-Dobrzyn, Poland		613
Index		616

List of the names extracted from the memorial section
Additions to Holocaust Necrology, Extracted from Articles in Yizkor Book
Errata pages: R. Yitzhak Moshe Offenbach (pages 173 of the original book

Family Notes

[Page 5]

With Publication of the Book[1]
By the Book Committee
Translated by Allen Flusberg

After a great deal of labor and continuous effort that has been invested in the gathering and compilation of the material, we are now presenting this Yizkor Book to those who hail from Dobrzyn–Golub.

Through the publication of this book we have sought to erect a memorial to the martyrs of the town, who perished by the hand of the Nazi foe and their henchmen, may their names be blotted out! In these few pages, however, it has not been easy to recreate the memory of this flourishing town—its prodigies, students and ordinary people—especially since only a remnant of its many inhabitants have survived. Nor has it been easy for the few who did remain alive to recall again those days of terror in which their most precious possessions were lost to them—their parents, siblings and children.

Yet we knew how important this undertaking to immortalize our town was, and therefore we insisted on eliciting contributions from our members and encouraging them to write, knowing fully well that they were not skilled at writing.

And indeed we did not toil in vain. In various sections of the book the town has been portrayed in all its richness: its houses and streets; its institutions and organizations; and its prominent figures. And we are inspired again as we recall the activities of the community leaders, whose highest priorities were their concern for the community and their love of humanity.

But how appalling and nerve–racking the descriptions of the Holocaust—accounts written by those of our brethren who experienced its terrors in the flesh. And even if we have heard and read of these things many, many times, our hair stands on end again and we are seized with terror as we contemplate these horrific events. The names of those we grew up with in the town, and whom we knew so well—the names of the martyrs—echo and resonate in our ears, demanding justice for their deaths, for the crime of their murders.

May this book serve as a memorial to the martyred members of our community, and may it provide some comfort, however small, to the remaining Dobrzyn townspeople in both Israel and the Diaspora.

[Pages 6-7]

From the Historical Sources[1]
Translated by Allen Flusberg

Dobrzyn

Until the end of the 13th century, Dobrzyn on the Dreventz[2] River, in the province of Plock, was a suburb of the city of Golub, which was located on the other side of the river, and served as a border-town between Prussia and the Kingdom of Poland.

Only in the year 1684 did the owner of the estate, Zygmunt of Dzialyn[3] (who was also the lord of the church of Dzialyn, the governor of the province of Kalisz, and even the mayor of Inowroclaw[4]), grant the citizens of Dobrzyn the right to choose their own independent mayor, who would serve also as a judge. Alongside him were two of the elders of the town, who together with him made up a court of law. With this he [Zygmunt] provided the residents with several additional rights: the right of residency; the right to build houses, to acquire land, to work the soil, and to plant orchards.

This is the first document that indicates the granting of partial independence to Dobrzyn—a document that was ratified again by his [Zygmunt's] son, Jakob Dzialynski, in the year 1721. Only in the year 1789, after Golub was annexed to Prussia (following the partition of Poland), did Ignacy of Dzialyn, governor of a province of the kingdom of Poland, grant independence to Dobrzyn, bestowing on it the status of a city, with a mayor at its head.

The town, whose buildings were wooden, burned down completely in 1857, after which it was rebuilt with buildings constructed of brick.

The roots of the Jewish community in Dobrzyn are ancient. This community suffered great hardship during the period of the wars between Sweden and Poland. Only a small number of Dobrzyn's Jews were left alive after the cruel riot by the forces of Czarniecki[5] (1656). But despite all this the community continued to exist, and already in the year 1765 the number of Jews within the "synagogue" reached 765, while the total number of Jews in that year within the bounds of Dobrzyn was 1,082.

The nobility ("*szlachta*") of the city often plotted against the rights of the Jews by legislating anti-Semitic laws in the *sejms*[6]. The Church also restricted their movement. Thus, for example, by decision of a high clerical council, all the Jews were concentrated in a special area (1783).

In the year 1857 the town had a population of 2,452, of which 702 were Poles, 140 were German, and 1,610 were Jews. The Jews dealt mostly in crafts and petty trade; a small number of them were employed in agriculture.

At that time the town had a church, a cemetery for each of the communities, a synagogue, a city hall, an elementary school, a customs house, and a post office.

Twice a week there was a market day, and there were fairs six times a year.

Golub

Golub on the Dreventz River was in the province of Chelmno. In earlier times it was also called Golba. It extends along the foot of a mountain on whose peak the nobleman Konrad Sach (or Schach), a Crusader, built a magnificent castle in the year 1300.

Prince Dobrzyn, an estate owner, granted the Crusader order 50 fiefs of land in the vicinity of the castle. In the year 1410, after the defeat of the Crusaders in Grünwald[7], Dobieslaw Puchala established an order of the infantry knights there and conquered the fortress. In the year 1422 Wladyslaw Jagiello took the fortress during a storm, captured the entire region and ordered that the towers should be destroyed[8]. After a peace treaty was signed in the district city of Torun (the birthplace of Copernicus), Golub became a demilitarized city.

In 1605 Zygmunt III[9] transferred authority over the city to his sister Anna, who settled here and even established an orchard of fruit trees near the fortress. She cultivated this orchard exquisitely. (The remains of this orchard, consisting of fruit-bearing trees, were visible until the 1930s.)

The residents were employed mostly in trade of grain and wood. There were two churches in the city, one Catholic and one Protestant. Likewise there were the following: a synagogue, city hall, post office, telegraph station, courthouse, customs office, salt warehouse, and two schools—one for the Catholics and one for the Protestants.

In the distant past all the land was the property of the Church. Two heads of the Church—Simon Gallikus and Loczek of Stolno—handed them over to land tenants to farm. The resident land tenants were forced to pay tribute to the crusaders, as well, and some of them even served as soldiers in the Order of the Knights.

In 1655 the Swedes conquered the city and the fortress. In 1772 Golub was joined to Prussia. In 1781 they began the construction of a Lutheran church there.

In the middle of the 19th century the population was 4,000, of whom about 1,400 were Jews. The first Jews who arrived in this region came after the division of Poland, when the region was annexed to Prussia. They were employed mostly in commerce: textiles, grain, wool and furs.

The Jewish community was organized and well-established. The transfer of the entire region to Poland (after World War I) strengthened ties with the nearby Dobrzyn community.

———

Translator's Footnotes

1. From *My Town: In Memory of the Communities Dobrzyn-Gollob*, edited by M. Harpaz, (published by the Dobrzyn-Golub Society, Israel, 1969), pp. 6-7.

2. Polish: Drwec

3. Dzialyn lies about 10km south of Dobrzyn.

4. Inowrocław, a city lying about 80km southwest of Dobrzyn

5. Stefan Czarniecki, was considered a Polish hero because of his resistance against the Swedish invaders. To the Polish Jews, however, he was viewed as a despicable villain whose forces had massacred the Jews. See the following two links:
   http://en.wikipedia.org/wiki/Stefan_Czarniecki,
   http://www.jewishvirtuallibrary.org/jsource/judaica/ejud_0002_0005_0_04788.html

6. *Sejm* = local parliamentary council (Polish)

7. Also known as the Battle of Tannenberg. See the following link:
   http://en.wikipedia.org/wiki/Battle_of_Grunwald

8. For additional details, see the following link:
   http://en.wikipedia.org/wiki/Gollub_War

9. Zygmunt III, King of Poland. See the following link:
   https://en.wikipedia.org/wiki/Sigismund_III_Vasa

[Pages 8-9]

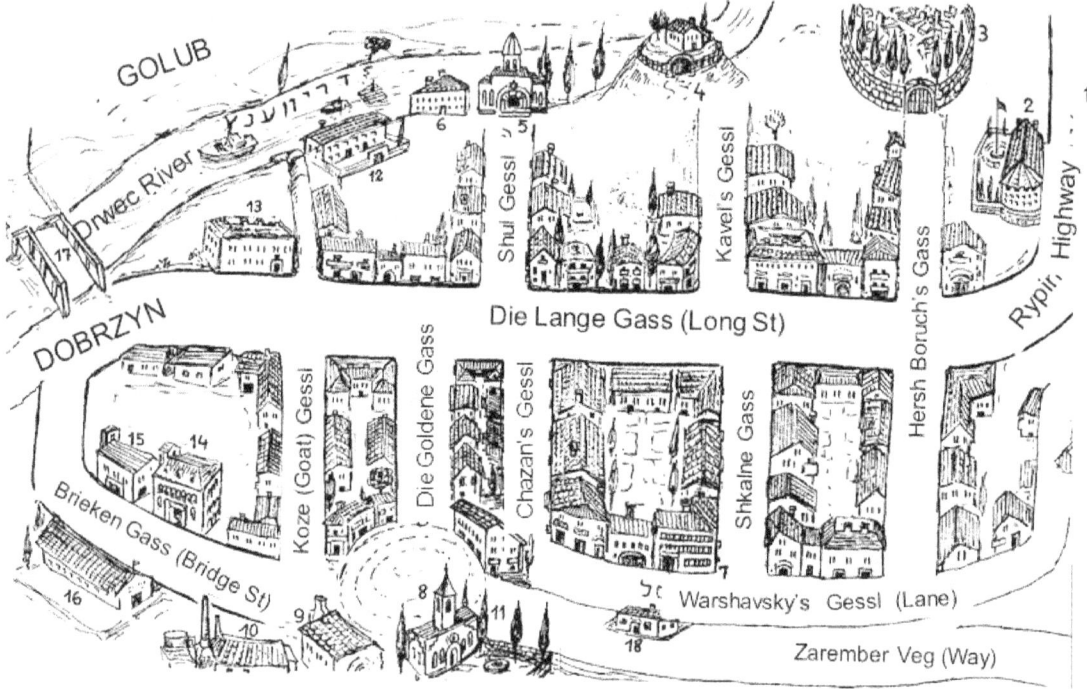

Key to Map
Translated by Allen Flusberg
1. Underwear factory
2. Barracks
3. Jewish Cemetery
4. Roker's Mount
5. Synagogue
6. Bet Midrash (Jewish Study Hall)
7. Government (Public) School
8. Market Square
9. Flour Mill (Isaac)
10. Power Station & Sawmill (Lipke)
11. Polish Church
12. Alexander Cheder
13. "Reformed" (*metukan*) Cheder
14. Fire Station
15. Library
16. Customs House
17. Dobrzyn-Golub Bridge
18. Pharmacy

[Page 10]

And You Shall Remember[1]
Translated by Allen Flusberg

And you shall remember and not forget,
Your eyes always seeing
All that was…
And is no more…
And your heart will pine for them:
For your parents, brothers and sisters,
For your childhood friends,
Killed in the field of slaughter…
And you shall embrace their memory
Forever, for all eternity.

Translator's Footnote

1. From *My Town: In Memory of the Communities Dobrzyn–Gollob*, edited by M. Harpaz, (published by the Dobrzyn–Golub Society, Israel, 1969), p. 10.

[Pages 23-24]

In the Shadow of the Destruction[1]
by the Editor
Translated by Allen Flusberg

About three decades have passed since the terrible Holocaust that utterly devoured the House of Israel. As the Nazi warriors swept across the countries of Europe, they consumed the Jewish communities in the towns and cities, murdering women and children, the young and the old, with a furious hatred; and torturing those left alive with hair-raising torment…

And the enlightened world stood by, washing its hands in innocence, without coming to the rescue of these blameless millions, whose only crime was the fact that they were Jews—members of an ancient people that, to its misfortune, had been forced to live among other nations.

During the Holocaust it became clear to us, more than ever, that there was no one the Jews could pin their hopes on but themselves. It was then, in the face of a hostile world, that the expression "all Jews are responsible for one another" became profoundly meaningful. The expression was articulated most unequivocally in the establishment of the State of Israel and in the displays of devotion and volunteerism by the Jewish people throughout all of their Diaspora.

For a generation we have lived in the shadow of this terrible Destruction, while our brethren, the remnant of survivors of the Holocaust, have dwelled with us and among us, bearing within them the memory of its terror. The pain and agony of that time have not faded away; on the contrary, they have continued to grow deeper.

The significance of what was lost in the Holocaust has become more apparent with the passing years, as our admiration for all that once was and is now gone has been rekindled and has intensified—our esteem for all those communities, poor perhaps in substance but rich in spirit; our reverence for the troops of learned sages who created the idealized image of the [religious] prodigy; and our admiration for the myriads of ordinary folk who displayed devotion to one another and faith in the Destiny of Israel.

The community of Dobryzn-Golub was only one of many, a Jewish community that had spun a rich web of Jewish life as it struggled for subsistence and livelihood while it was maintaining a spirit of transcendence and vision. Among the many memories of this town that survive are some that are heartrending, and yet others that are heartwarming.

Possibly the generation that did not know this community—the children of those who originated from Dobrzyn-Golub—will read this Memorial Book and from it become aware of their parents' roots, lives and dreams. And perhaps this perception will enrich their lives, as well, with deeper meaning.

Dobrzyn was heart. Dobrzyn was feelings, charity, anonymous giving.[2]

[Page 24]

El Malei Rachamim: God, full of compassion, Who dwells above, provide complete rest under the protection of the Divine Presence, within the celestial heights reached by the holy martyrs and pure ones—shining as bright as the firmament—to the souls of the thousands of members of the martyred communities of Dobrzyn-Golub—men, women and children—who were murdered, slaughtered, incinerated, suffocated, or buried alive by the evil ones, Hitler's executioners and their lackeys—may their names be blotted out—during the years 1939 to 1944. May they find rest in Paradise; may the Compassionate One therefore bind their souls in Eternal Life; and may the Lord be their legacy. And may they rest peacefully in their resting place, and let us say Amen![3]

Photograph of memorial plaque memorializing the community of Dobrzyn-Golub[4]

Translator's Footnotes

1. From *My Town: In Memory of the Communities Dobrzyn-Gollob*, edited by M. Harpaz, (published by the Dobrzyn-Golub Society, Israel, 1969), pp. 22-23.

2. From page 22 of reference cited in Footnote 1.

3. Variants of the prayer *El Malei Rachamim*, memorializing departed individuals, groups or entire communities, are recited at gravesides, at various synagogue services and at other memorial services. For alternative English translations see, for example, the following links:
http://en.wikipedia.org/wiki/El_male_rachamim;
http://www.ou.org/yerushalayim/yizkor/emman.htm

4. From p. 25 of reference cited in Footnote 1. The Dobrzyn synagogue is portrayed near the top, between the two eternal flames. The Hebrew text translates as follows: For an everlasting memorial, on Mt. Zion in Jerusalem, to the martyrs of the community of Dobrzyn-Golub and vicinity (located on the Dreventz River, Poland) who were exterminated, incinerated, murdered, or buried alive by the Nazis and their henchmen—may their names be blotted out—in the years 5699 to 5705. Earth, conceal not their blood. And may their souls be bound in Eternal Life. —*The Dobrzyn-Golub Townsmen Organization, in Israel and in the Diaspora. A Declaration of Destruction.*

[Page 26]

May My Lot Be with You[1]
By Ch. N. Bialik[2]
Translated by Allen Flusberg

May my lot be with you, the anonymous
Who shape their lives in secret, modest in thought and deed,
Unknown dreamers, speaking little yet great in glory…

———

Translator's Footnotes

1. From *My Town: In Memory of the Communities Dobrzyn-Gollob*, edited by M. Harpaz, (published by the Dobrzyn-Golub Society, Israel, 1969), p. 26.

2. Chaim Nachman Bialik (1873-1934) was a leading Hebrew-language poet who is viewed as Israel's national poet. See the following web site (retrieved November 2016): https://en.wikipedia.org/wiki/Hayim_Nahman_Bialik

———

[Pages 28-29]

Dobrzyn and Golub on the Drwcca River
by Yehudah Rozenwax
Translated by Sara Mages

The towns of Dobrzyn and Golub were adjacent to each other. They were located on both sides of the Drweca River, Golub east of the river and Dobrzyn to its west. In the past, Golub was within the territory of Germany and Dobrzyn - within the territory of Russia. A short narrow bridge connected the two towns, a German guard stood on one side and a Russian - on the other side. And of course, there were also two separate customs houses, in the two different regions of the bridge.

However, the guards couldn't prevent the smuggling of goods, since the smugglers were able to make their way in secret, when they crossed the shallow narrow river from one region to the other. Therefore, the trading between the two towns flourished, and many Jews, who lived in Dobrzyn and the surrounding area, found their livelihood in it.

The land around Dobrzyn was fertile farmland, and the Christian inhabitants, who cultivated it in the most primitive ways, took out their food from it, though in short supply, but with dignity. There were also those among the Christian residents, who worked at the factories that belonged to the Jews, in the - sawmills, flourmills and more.

Different was the appearance of the town of Golub, which was under German rule until the end of the First World War. The town was transferred to Poland only after it won its independence in accordance with the decision of the League of Nations. It was small, but perfectly groomed: its streets were wide and paved, the houses were pretty, and the shops attracted the eye with their splendor. The appearance - was modern and well maintained, the mountains surrounding the town were covered with greenery, fruit trees and ornamental trees, and the benches beneath them offered rest to the travelers. And indeed, the locals knew how to take advantage of the beautiful mountain scenery: many hotels were built there, and were used as summer resorts during the summer months.

Trains left from the modern train station to all parts of Poland, connected the town with the whole country, and helped with its development. And indeed, the trade flourished in the town and the big shops, including a luxurious department store, were bustling with shoppers.

[Page 29]

A special power station provided electricity to the town twenty-four hours a day, what discriminated the town for the better from many other towns, among them also Dobrzyn. The vibrant urban life characterized Golub and served as a source of attraction to it.

The number of Jews in the town wasn't large, but they stood out with their occupations and their activities. They were good Jews, who aroused respect because most of the factories, shops and hotels were in their hands.

Dobrzyn was poorer: its streets were narrow and neglected, and the buildings - had neither looks nor grace. It was a town like the rest of the towns in Eastern Europe. Large families lived in the small apartments in poor living conditions, something that is difficult to imagine today. The shabby toilet was located in the yard, and only the rich were able to install a washbasin inside their homes. The rest of the people had to settle for a real bath only in the *Mikvah*.

There were many slums in the town, where people lived in poverty and lacked the most basic living conditions. Even the water supply was quite poor: a barrel, which was coated with enamel or tin, stood in the yard and served as a water reservoir. The water was brought by the water drawers, those pitiful figures that are familiar to us from the towns of Eastern Europe.

But even under these conditions, a rich Jewish life was developed, and we continue to draw inspiration from it even today. Some of it will be told on the following pages, pages of memory and testimony to the communities of Dobrzyn-Golub that the hand of the Nazi enemy fell on with full force.

Dobrzyn's Jews were lucky since many of them emigrated from the town ahead of time. The truth is that this migration already started in the 18th century, and grew stronger after the establishment of independent Poland in 1918, because independent Poland was a fertile ground for all forms of anti-Semitism. Most of the young generation left for the United States or to other countries in the world, and some of the young people immigrated to Israel. This migration saved them from the fate of their brothers who perished in the terrible holocaust.

[Page 30]

Dobrzyn, My Town[1]
by Dr. Yechiel Lichtenstein
Translated by Allen Flusberg

Hiding in his room to escape the hustle and bustle of New York, a Jew closes his eyes and gazes far off in both space and time. His spirit crosses rivers and seas, mountains and valleys, days and nights, innumerable weeks and months, decades of years…

Yes, I am that very dreamer. My spirit wanders eastward, crossing the Atlantic Ocean, reaching land: France, Germany under the Kaiser, West Prussia, Bromberg/Bydgoszcz, Thorn/Torun (city of Nicolaus Copernicus and of Rabbi Tzvi Hirsch Kalischer[2], of blessed memory). And soon I get off the train at the Golub station and walk past the remains of the Teutonic knights' castle, up there on the hill. I walk down to the last Prussian town [before the border], and come to the Dreventz (Drevec) River. The building here is the Golub customs house. The bridge is still within the domain of Prussia. But the soldier over there, past the white gate, is already a subject of Nikolay II, and the building next to him is the customs house of Russian Fonya, the first building of my Dobrzyn. Here I was raised and educated during the Russian era of Dobrzyn.

What is this place to me, and whom do I have here? No one of mine is left in this place. Who knows if our enemies left even the graves in their resting places; or my synagogue, my study house, the *shtiebels*[3] of Alexander and Gur[4], the *cheiders*[5] of R.[6] Beryl and R. Nisan of blessed memory—in which I studied? There, on the street leading towards Rypin[7] stood the school of R. Abba Yosef. Has any remnant of it survived?

Half a century has passed since then. I have crossed many borders, visited many large cities, and lived in various countries. Yet my heart returns to impoverished Dobrzyn, to its marshes and dilapidated houses: "The heart is the most deceitful of all and fragile; who can fathom it?"[8]

I was actually a native of Kovel[9], but fate brought me to Dobrzyn. (Footnote: We Jews referred to these two towns by the names Kvohl and Dobjinsk, respectively). I was raised in the home of my grandfather, R. Yisrael Aharon the goldsmith, and my grandmother Etyl, who was known as Etyl'che the bakeress (*lekech-bekeren*[10]). This goldsmith did not have any silver or gold, nor did he even have very much copper. And as for this bakeress of tasty sweets—there was not even very much bread in her home. But out of this poor house came forth Torah and good deeds, just as from one of the large, wealthy homes. I do yearn for it[11], so my heart is not being so deceitful when it brings me back to this humble home and to my little town Dobjinsk. And may these lines serve as a memorial to the members of our family and our town and those that were killed there, those that were buried and those that were not, out there somewhere in Dobrzyn, Lutsk-Slovak and Kovel, and in accursed Chelmno[12]. Let these memories of mine serve as a foundation stone for the monument that was never erected for our fallen. My heart trembles within me, questioning whether I am even worthy of helping to put up a memorial stone for our martyrs.

Was our Dobjinsk any better than other little towns of the same vintage in Poland and Lithuania? I doubt it. However, this question itself is misplaced, being akin to the question "*mah dodech medod*?"[13]. The answer to this question is very simple: "*zeh dodi*"[14], this is my beloved—this is my town, irreplaceable. I will write about it with the hope and prayer that my memory will not mislead me.

The beginning of Jewish life in Poland is steeped in obscurity. Did the very first immigrants come as merchants from the west, by sea or by land? Or did they come from Russia in the east or via Byzantium and Crimea in the south? All this is still unknown. What is certain is that great multitudes of them arrived as refugees fleeing from Germany in the wake of the Crusades. In Poland they were received with open arms by princes and peasants alike. They helped developed the land and were given special privileges. The land of Polska became *Po-lin*[15] for them (and not, Heaven forbid, "Here I will stay because I have desired it,"[16] but rather a kind of Uganda[17], an overnight refuge that lasted 1000 years). Jews stayed over, slept and imagined that they were, more or less, at home and living securely—until Chmelniecki[18] came and woke them up, and Hitler came and wiped them out.

For hundreds of years they considered themselves part of the land, as their names will attest. Among the first great rabbis in Poland we find Rabbi Yaakov Pollak[19], "whose fame extended from one end of the Earth to the other."[20] (The name "Pollak", which was common in the small Jewish towns, became a source of mockery to the Jews of Germany when Polish Jews "returned" to Germany.) Jews used Polish place names but Judaized them. Thus Krakow was converted to "*Kraka dechula bah*"[21], Warszawa to Varsha, Brzszecz to Brisk, Kovel to Kvohl, and Dobrzyn to Dobjinsk. (This name was later transferred to the family name Dobjinski). And we Jews differentiated between Dobrzyn on the Vistula and our Dobrzyn on the Dreventz, referring to them as Dobrin and Dobjinsk, respectively. Indeed, our forefathers treated even the names of the towns of Poland as their own possessions.

Every day a Jew praises the person who "admits the truth and speaks truth from his heart."[22] In order to prevent a historical error, therefore, we must immediately add that Poland was never a Judea. The state was Roman Catholic, and the government, in general, was anti-Semitic. The large cities were at best mixed, and in general Polish. Nevertheless the small town was

Jewish. In our Dobrzyn, the *shamash*[23] would pass through the streets of the town every Friday afternoon, just before sunset, and in a special chant announce, "*L-i-ch-t b-e-n-sh-e-n!*" i.e. "Light candles!" I have heard a public announcement of this type, of the sanctity of the Jewish Sabbath, at only one other time, in Kiryat Shmuel, near Haifa, where one siren blast announces the time to end labor and the second blast indicates the time to light candles. And let us not forget the buses in Jerusalem that also tell all the observant the exact time of candle lighting.

I have not yet had the merit of celebrating the *Yamim Nora'im*[24] in the State of Israel, but I remember the days of *Selichot*[25] recitation in Dobrzyn. When it was still nighttime, that same *shamash* would rap on the doors and windows of our homes, calling out "*kumu la'avoidas haboiray!*"[26] And when Jews are asked to, they act. They awaken the dawn, rather than allowing the dawn to awaken them. Some with lanterns in their hand, and others feeling their way in the darkness, they leave their homes and flock into the synagogue, or into the *beit midrash*[27], or into one of the *shtiebels*. It is Elul![28] The *Yamim Nora'im*! The Days of Judgment! *Selichot*! "Do not forsake us in our old age; do not abandon us when our strength wanes!"[29] These were cries that pierced the Heavens.

A scholar should not go outside alone at night.[30] The Dobrzyn Rabbi did not go outside alone even during the day, and certainly not on the Sabbath. We gazed after him, trembling before his holiness, as the *shamash* accompanied him on his way to the synagogue. It was as if he was a kind of Moses entering the Tent of Meeting[31]. The *dayan*[32], R. Lib'che Hertz, was not any less revered than the town rabbi. All the town residents respected him in a manner that was proper for someone who was a great, God-fearing scholar. The *ne'eman*[33]—who supervised kashrut—was careful not to gaze upon the face of any woman, and primarily not upon the face of a Gentile woman, even when he had to buy eggs from her in the market. R. Beryl did not profane the teaching profession by treating it as a *kardom lachpor bah*[34]. He was tall and round-shouldered; he would look at us with eyes filled with love and softness and say: "I hope for a single reward, that after my life is over you will attest that 'I learned this page under R. Beryl'." R. Nissin was quite different from him. He emphasized the *dagesh*[35]; all his interest was in grammar, in the Hebrew language. People whispered behind his back that he had gone over to Zionism. Abba Yosef—it is appropriate to refer to him as R. Abba Yosef—would teach us reading, writing and arithmetic, that is—general studies—to the extent that it was possible to learn it during the hours of neither day nor night[36]. In actuality Dobrzyn had two additional schools that were not *cheiders*. One was Polish, for the Gentiles, and the second Jewish, but more "modern" than that of Abba Yosef. I don't remember if they taught any Polish in our school on Rypin Street. What I am certain about is that I didn't learn any; what did I need the language of the Poles for? What did I have to do with Polish? A Jew speaks in Yiddish and writes in Hebrew! Nevertheless I do remember that R. Abba Yosef tried to teach us some Russian, the official state language. The teacher did try, but I didn't want to learn the language of Fonya, either. While the other students were reviewing all the adjectives of Nikolai and his wife, Feodorovna[37]—studies that took up an important part in the "program"—I would be leafing through Hebrew books, and in any event to this very day I have remained a complete ignoramus in both Polish and Russian. I learned my limited knowledge of general studies outside the boundaries of Dobrzyn, and even outside the boundaries of Poland and Russia. There was also in Dobrzyn a library where it was possible to obtain the works of Sholom Aleichem and Mendele Mocher Seforim, in both Hebrew and Yiddish, for a small membership fee.

The Jewish character of Dobrzyn was also attested to by the fact that the Jews lived inside the town, while the Gentiles lived outside it, near the fields of Zarembo[38]. The "outsiders" came from the villages on market days—Tuesdays and Fridays. The butter they brought was kept fresh neither in a refrigerator nor on ice, but rather on a large leaf. Before it reached our home and was placed on our table it was already half melted. On Sabbath Eve Jewish men and women would buy a live hen from the outsiders, hurrying to bring it to be slaughtered by R. Yaakov the *shochet*[39]. The Gentiles knew the Jewish calendar very well, raising prices before our holidays—particularly the price of the white roosters which we used ritually for *kapores*[40]. Once when the price of fish rose to an intolerable level, our women outsmarted them by deciding not to put any fish on the holiday table, not even waiting for the local Jewish court to announce that it would be preferable to have a Sabbath without meat and fish than to "fatten up" the Gentiles. A proper boycott!

On those weekly market days my grandfather, Yisroel Aharon, would bring his shop outside. What was his shop? And how did he bring it outside? Nowadays builders take months or years to construct a shop. My grandfather constructed his shop in a few short minutes: a chair on one side, a second chair on the other side, and a shelf between them for the box of merchandise to rest on—there, that was his shop. The merchandise, placed in the box, consisted of spools of white and black thread; packages of needles; kerchiefs;

various spectacles; and all kinds of utensils—sitting and waiting for customers. And the customers were generally Gentiles from outside the town; the Jewish "residents" of the town would buy from an ordinary shop, not just from a temporary Tuesday or Friday shop that stayed open from 8 AM to 2 PM, by which time the outsiders were hurrying to to their homes beyond Dobrzyn. And in this way my grandfather would sit with exceptional patience, waiting for customers, and in the end he would bring home a ruble, one-and-a-half rubles, or even two rubles, making a profit of two or three złoty on an ordinary day. On the days of a fair, when there were numerous customers and it was necessary to very carefully watch the additional customers—who would come intending to buy and to then "forget" to pay—the rest of the members of the family would help do the watching, and the profit may have been an additional ruble.

And why did my grandfather, of blessed memory, need a shop—wasn't he, after all, a goldsmith? He neither bought nor sold silver and gold rings, but rather he repaired them. When a necklace or earring broke, it would be brought to him. However, the male and female residents of Dobrzyn were careful, and rarely broke their rings, necklaces and earrings; it was rare for them to even warp a *Kiddush* or *havdala cup*[41]. As a result, there was little prosperity in our home, and there was a great need to supplement our income. In fact it was not for his own needs that my grandfather needed his shop. All his life he was satisfied with the little he had. Never during his life did he wait for the landlord to press him to pay his rent; he would always pay it on time. He also paid the teachers very punctually. It was not only in the *birkat hamazon*[42] that he pleaded, "And may You not place us in need for either a gift or a loan from another person." This prayer was the guiding light for his life—and for his death. He collected one coin after another until he had amassed enough to cover his burial shroud and the payment to the *chevra kadisha*[43] out of his own money. "And may You not place us in need..."...even after 120 years.[44]

My grandfather was one of the small merchants and dedicated craftsmen who established the economic and social image of the town. The bigger merchants would travel to Wloclavek[45] or to Lodz and Warsaw to obtain merchandise; others crossed the bridge to work and do business in Golub, or traveled to Prussia for the *Yamim Nora'im* to serve as *chazanim*[46] or *klei kodesh*[47].

Our neighbor, R. Mordechai Hartbrod, owned a cigarette "factory" in Golub; I believe he was the only one there. On the Dobrzyn side of the Dreventz he used to wear a "Jewish cap", while on the other side he wore a stiff Western-style hat. On Sabbaths he was customarily the last to leave the *Beit Midrash*, after a long friendly-political-scientific conversation with Rabbi Lib'che the *dayan*.

Our other neighbor, R. Zalman Hassid, was a wagon driver. In spite of the marshes on the Kikół-Lipno-Wloclavek road, he would bring his passengers to their destinations safely. When his "steeds" became tired, he would lead them slowly, then feed them, so as not to violate—Heaven forbid—the prohibition against *tzaar baalei hachayim*[48]. He would comfort the impatient among the passengers with "*gepashet iz oich geforn*"[49] (*l'haachil kinesia damya*[50]). When we had to go up a hill, and it was hard for the horses to fulfill their task on their own, the passengers would get off to make it easier for the horses. In fall and winter, when the marshes expanded, we would tighten our belts and push the wagon until it came out into the wide-open road. The passengers who were in a hurry would be ready to set out early in the morning, but R. Zalman refused to leave with "an empty wagon"; we would wait until additional passengers arrived and the wagon filled up. And meanwhile he would stand and comfort us, "Soon, soon we will set out." And truthfully we would set out and arrive safely, and believe me—no one was resentful. More than just a wagon driver, R. Zalman was a friend and a *Hassid* [a kind, benevolent person].

Yaakov'che, our third neighbor, was a short man, who benefited from the toil of his hands and of his shoulders; he was a porter. And did he have a good life? No! Illness never left his house, so we were doubly connected to him.

The Jews of Poland—among whom a minority was affluent but most were poor, and even desperately poor—were exemplary at establishing charitable institutions, religious institutions, and educational institutions—beginning with the period of independent rule, nearly governmental, during the period of the Council of Four Lands[51], and up to the community and national organizations of the generation of destruction in our own times. Illnesses, too, were visited upon the Jews of Poland in general and Dobrzyn in particular. The town was small and too poor to establish and support a hospital. The hospital that was closest to us was in Wloclavek. The ill among us were treated by our *feldsher*[52], Mr. Russak (a barber who understood medicine, as well). He would transfer them to the local doctor. In serious cases they would go outside the country for treatment, to Thorn, Koenigsberg[53], or to Posen[54] and Berlin. However within the town itself the *bikur cholim*[55] organization sent volunteers and aides to the homes of the ill and to their families. Every Friday the *gabaim*[56] would come by our door, collecting charity for the needs of *bikur cholim, hachnasat orchim*[57], *hachnasat kalah*[58], *linat hatzedek*[59], *gemilut chesed*[60], and *talmud torah*[61]. And the descendants of Abraham, Isaac and Jacob—the wealthy, the middle class and the poor—when they were asked to, they would give. All the various types of people who were in need—those who had been through a fire; those who had been brought down low; parents whose daughters had reached the age of marriage; and ordinary wanderers—all these found helping hands and open hearts. The *gabaim* of the synagogue and *beit midrash* did not home until they had found food and lodging for every guest.

A blessing upon those who are active—as well as on their deeds—in modern charitable organizations: their presidents, their male and female secretaries! They accomplish great things. However, it is worth remembering that today we magnify the role of "charity with one's money" over "charity with one's body". The written check and the brain have replaced the soul and the heart—the personal participation in the grief and joy of another person. We neither wish to, nor are we capable of, returning to the previous situation of a town somewhere in Poland. However we should recognize the sanctity that prevailed in the town. Let us try to rescue from it whatever can be saved! Let our children and grandchildren see what "charity with one's body" is! Let them see and learn from our actions, and those of our forefathers, the attitude of one person to another, to his worries, to his rejoicings, to his spirit: "for you know the spirit of the stranger."[62]

Charity of this type came to life in the form of my grandmother Etyl, of blessed memory—or as she was known in Dobrzyn, Etyl'che. She was short in stature but large in spirit; poor monetarily but rich in soul; weak in body and a heroine in her deeds. She had a "golden heart". Even more: a heart of flesh, a heart of an upright person, of an angel.

Her children: Sarah Brayna, the firstborn, was married to a teacher who supported himself, with difficulty, by giving private lessons in Wloclavek.

Wolff, who sewed shoes—he was a machine manufacturer of shoes—also lived there. All his children perished and were cut off by the accursed ones. It is said that his son Yechiel, a follower of the Gur Hassidim, shortly before his own death handed over his daughter, then a small girl, to a Gentile woman to save her from death. The Gentile woman did save her—but for the Church. "*Chesed le'umim chatat*"![63] A Jewish tragedy! "Christian love"!

The youngest, Esther Yente, was more of a resident of Dobrzyn than any of the other members of the family. She was married to R. Mordechai David Kowalski in Wloclavek. His graciousness, and the graciousness of his father and mother, are deeply engraved in my heart. Only one daughter of theirs was saved; she lives in Bat Yam, Israel.

My uncle, Yaakov Hayyim, was an incidental merchant; in his head, within most of him, and with all his might he was a scholar. He was a close friend of R. Sender Techursh and Rabbi Kowalski in Wloclavek; of Rabbi Brod—of Lipno and then of Antwerp, New York and Tel Aviv; of the Rabbis Herzog—the father, R. Yoel, in Paris, and the son, R. Yitzhak, the chief rabbi of Israel. Together with Rabbi Mordechai Shochetman—who officiated earlier in Soroka, Romania, then later in Paris, and at the end of his life in New York—he established a center for Religious Zionism in France. In his position as secretary of the "Council of Ultra-Orthodox Rabbis in France", which was headed by Rabbi Shmuel Rubenstein, he did great things to help benefit *agunot*[64] that were left in the wake of the War and the Holocaust. In his letter to me (dated 6 Tishri, 5714[65]) he wrote: "I have made up my mind to resign from my rabbinical position here, to emigrate to the Land of Israel, and to spend the rest of my years, that God will grant me, there. All my life I would excuse myself, not wishing to take upon myself ordinary responsibility…and may I perhaps merit reward that after the terrible destruction I did work and inquire and research a great deal into the years of evil, to find redemption and relief for those unfortunate women, and I did everything that I possibly could for this purpose; and with God's help I believe that hundreds, thank God, were saved by us." He is buried with honor in *Har Hamenuhot*[66] in Jerusalem.

My father, of blessed memory, R. Grunem, was exiled to various centers of Torah study. It appears to me that he studied in Lodz, Kutno and Lipno. All his life he was humble and pious[67]. In the beginning of his life he was a Hassid, in the ordinary sense of the term. In his youth he "went" to Alexander[68]—he was unable to actually travel there, and for a very simple reason: where would he get the money from? With the passage of time he distanced himself from formal Hassidism, but he remained a Hassid in his deeds. With all the purity of his soul he was completely sold on the Zionist concept. To indicate very briefly his character, I would say that he was meticulous—meticulous in his writing, as his beautiful letters attest; meticulous in language, particularly with the language of prayer and *Onkelos*[69]: the *siddurim*[70], *machzorim*[71] and *chumashim*[72] that he left behind are full of comments and clarifications. He taught us to not hurry through prayer, but rather to think deeply about it—even if that meant that we would have to skip over some of them—particularly on the *Yamim Nora'im*. And many a time he would review the words he had heard from his teachers against those who fill their bellies with many prayers at the price of *kavana*[73]: "The printer printed it, so they say it." He was also meticulous to a hairsbreadth about *mitzvot*[74] and good deeds. And first and foremost he kept and remembered the commandments of honoring one's father and mother in all its provisions and minutia. And with respect to his hairs, he did not remove a single one of them from his beard even though he spent most of his years living in Western Europe: in Germany, Belgium, France, Austria and Italy[75]. For twenty years he served as a *shochet* and *bodek*[76] in Milan, where he established an exemplary level of *kashrut*. He was also meticulous in ethics: like his mother, Etyl'che, "The teaching of truth was in his mouth, and injustice was not found on his lips; he walked with Me in peace and with fairness, and he turned many away from sin."[77]

From the exile of Rome-Italy he went up to the Land of Israel. There he lived his last years. He did not merit seeing the rebirth of Israel. During the "incidents"[78] that preceded the establishment of the State—when he was more than 75 years old—he was heard to call out in the streets of Tel Aviv, "Give me a rifle and I will go out to fight!" This man of peace, who during his entire life did not lay a hand on his fellow man by even a hairsbreadth, was ready to fight for his people and country. No rifle was given to him, so he never laid a hand on even the enemy. This man of peace died in peace, and was one of the last Jews to be buried on the Mount of Olives, on the 8th of Tammuz, 5707[79].

When my father was forced to wander outside the country, I was left for a while in my grandparents' home. Parting from their beloved son was very hard on them [my grandparents], but no sigh came out of their mouths. He took care of his parents in their old age—in both the physical and spiritual sense, and much more than he could actually afford. But as long as he did not earn enough for his own livelihood and theirs, there was an atmosphere of poverty in the house. In addition to the two beds in the room (which served as a dining room, workroom, bedroom and guest room), there stood in the kitchen a "sleeping bench". What is a sleeping bench? During the day we sat on it; at night one would take off the cover, put a blanket on the "bag of straw" that was in it, and sleep a sweet and pleasant sleep, a sleep following toil in Torah and work[80]. The contents of this bag—that is, the straw—hardened with the passage of time. In honor of the approaching holy day, the straw was replaced between Purim and Passover. I do not remember whether it was also replaced between *Rosh Hashana* and *Yom Kippur*. Whenever a guest or guests happened to come, they would be given the bed or beds, and the members of the household would make their beds on the floor.

Grandmother Etyl was a good cook and an excellent baker. I can still taste the flavor of her *challot*[81]. A good Jew does not fill up his belly and does not wash his hands ritually on Sabbath and holiday eves[82]. In order that we children should not be hungry, we would sometimes get a little fish soup with some dessert, and as a result the *neshama yetera*[83] entered inside us several hours before *Kiddush*.

The fame of our grandmother's baking and cooking was known all over Dobrzyn. They would call on her to cater weddings and circumcisions. She baked cakes and cookies for sale before Passover. If a little dough was left at the edge of the kneading trough, she would prepare from it a small *challah* or a cookie for her little ones, who were proud to have their very own challah in honor of the Sabbath, "like one of the grownups." And if no dough was left, it was enough for us to lick the paper on which the cake had been baked. She never raised her voice except for "a Jewish word," that is, prayer. She was careful not to taste any food before prayers[84]. I think that it was from her that my father inherited his love for prayer and for extra *kavana*. In the women's section of the synagogue she was the *magedet*[85] who read out loud from the *tze'ena ur'ena*[86] and the *techinot*[87] for upright women. Either the small letters of these prayers were not so clear to the other women, or they simply enjoyed the charm of her reading, her way of explaining things, the radiance of her face and the sanctity of her deeds.

Every poor person, every sick person and everyone who was having a hard time was known to her, and she, who was poor herself, stretched a helping hand out to them: to this one she brought a little soup, and to that one a piece of chicken. She also prepared a full pharmacy jar for the ill whom she cared for, and when her own means were exceeded, she knew to whom to turn to provide help for those in need.

The month of Elul was her major month, when Jews, both wealthy and poor, came to "*kever avot*"[88]. The Angel of Death does not distinguish between rich and poor. At that time of year, Jews arise to repentance, prayer and charity. During this month it was as if my grandmother lived among the dead in order to obtain food and medicine for the living. Did she have a special box in which she placed the money she collected? I remember only the knot that was in her kerchief. She let us participate in opening the knot and counting the wealth that she brought home—this time much more than usual.

This is what she was like, this pearl of Dobrzyn and of the world—my world: Grandmother Etyl, may she rest in peace—or Etyl'che the bakeress, as she was called by the people of Dobrzyn.

Who acknowledged her and her deeds when, after my grandfather died, she wandered off to Wloclawek, to the home of her daughter, Esther Yente? Was there anything written on her gravestone to memorialize her righteousness?

And who knows what the wicked ones, members of various nations, did to the cemeteries of our Dobrzyn, Wloclawek and Kvohl? What was the fate of the other holy places: synagogues, houses of study, the various *shtiebels*, as well as the various Jewish schools, community centers and auditoriums? How great was the destruction! What Jeremiah will lament it?

I can still see the new white-stone fence that had been built around the cemetery in Dobrzyn. It replaced the previous wooden fence, for which the portions that were broken through were more numerous than the portions that were standing, and so the bad shepherds would desecrate the graves with their sheep and cattle. It was easy for us to see the fence while we were walking to the synagogue, which was near it. Is the fence still standing? Who knows whether the plowmen ploughed up the very graves? (Indeed I recently found out that the plowmen, *yimach sh'mam*[89], did plough it all up!)

They ravaged our houses and pillaged our communities. They put our families to death, starting with the great and the good. They destroyed the Jerusalem *dil'mata*[90], while the Jerusalem *dil'maala*[91] remains and will remain for us: the memory of our Dobjinsk, as well as that of the hundreds and thousands of other Dobjinsks; the memory of our pious, who were great in their simplicity and giants in their charity.

**R. Shlomo Hertzke,
the *shamash* of the Great Synagogue**[92]

The Great Synagogue. Drawings, works of craftsmanship decorated the ceiling and the walls of the synagogue in Dobrzyn. Colorful stained glass adorned its windows. Its floor consisted of a multicolored mosaic. [93]

Landsberg, the son of the *melamed*[94] Monus, who perished together with his entire family in the Holocaust[95]

Translator's Footnotes

1. From *My Town: In Memory of the Communities Dobrzyn-Gollob*, edited by M. Harpaz, (published by the Dobrzyn-Golub Society, Israel, 1969), pp. 30-40.

2. Kalischer was a nineteenth-century Orthodox rabbi and scholar who championed Jewish resettlement of the Land of Israel.

3. *Shtiebel* = a single-room synagogue, usually Hassidic

4. Alexander and Gur are the names of two Hassidic groups that had many adherents in Dobrzyn. These groups are named after the towns in which they originated, Aleksandrow Lodzki and Gur or Ger (Góra Kalwaria), respectively, both in Poland.

5. *Cheider* = Jewish school for young children, dedicated almost exclusively to religious studies

6. " ר' " has been transcribed as "R." throughout this translation. It can stand for Rabbi but also "Rebbe" or "Reb", the latter being more a title of respect.

7. Rypin is a town located 25 km due east of Dobrzyn. A major street of Dobrzyn led out of the town towards Rypin.

8. Jeremiah 17:9. The wording of this verse is obscure and has been translated in many different ways.

9. Kovel is located in northwest Ukraine, on the border with Poland. Between the two World Wars it was part of Poland, and before that it lay within the Russian empire.

10. *Lekech-bekeren* (Yiddish) = bakeress of pastries

11. *me'ai hamu lo* (Hebrew, alluding to Jeremiah 31:20) = I yearn for it

12. Chelmno, located about 70 km northwest of Lodz, was the site of an extermination camp where about 200,000 people were murdered. In 1942 a Jewish escapee provided the first eyewitness report of the mass killings to the outside world. See the following link: http://www.jewishvirtuallibrary.org/jsource/Holocaust/Chelmno.html

13. *Mah dodech medod* = How is your beloved better than any other beloved? (Song of Songs 5:9)

14. *Zeh dodi* = This is my beloved (Song of Songs 5:16)

15. *Po lin* (Hebrew) = Here stay over. Perhaps because of the play on words, *Polin* became the Hebrew word for Poland, whose name in Polish is *Polska*.

16. Psalms 132:14, the complete verse being "This is my resting place forever; here I will stay because I have desired it".

17. A reference to the Uganda Proposal of the early Zionist period (1903), by which Jews persecuted in Russia would have been settled in Uganda as a temporary refuge. After much discussion, the proposal was rejected by the Zionist movement. See, for example, the following link: http://www.jewishvirtuallibrary.org/jsource/Zionism/Uganda.html.

18. In the mid-17th century Chmelniecki (Khmelnytsky) led a Cossack uprising against the Polish ruling class, during which his followers massacred many tens of thousands (and perhaps hundreds of thousands) of Jews. These events traumatized the Jews of Eastern Europe. See, for example, the following link: http://en.wikipedia.org/wiki/Khmelnytsky_Uprising.

19. Rabbi Yaakov Pollak, who died in 1541, is credited with bringing the intensive study of Talmud to Poland. See the following link: http://en.wikipedia.org/wiki/Jacob_Pollak

20. This is how he was described by later rabbis of Poland. The expression itself parallels similar expressions that occur in Talmudic and Midrashic works.

21. *Kraka dechula bah* (Aramaic) = a city having everything in it

22. This quotation is from the prayer book; it is recited daily at the beginning of the morning service.

23. Synagogue beadle, who sees to it that the synagogue runs smoothly

24. *Yamim Nora'im* = Days of Awe, the ten days beginning with *Rosh Hashana* (Jewish New Year) and ending with *Yom Kippur* (Day of Atonement). Some also include in the *Yamim Nora'im* the days just before *Rosh Hashana* when the *Selichot* prayers (see next footnote) are recited.

25. *Selichot* = special prayers asking God for forgiveness, recited late at night starting from several days before *Rosh Hashana* and, in most communities, until *Yom Kippur*

26. *Kumu la'avoidas haboiray / kumu la'avodat haborei* (Hebrew) = arise for worship (service) of the Creator

27. House of study, where men sit at tables studying Talmud, and prayer services are often also held

28. Elul, the name of the last month just before *Rosh Hashana*, when *Selichot* were first recited

29. A line from the *Selichot* (as well as *Rosh Hashana* and *Yom Kippur*) prayer services, paraphrasing Psalms 71:9

30. Babylonian Talmud, Berachot 43b

31. It was in the Tent of Meeting that God would reveal himself to Moses. See for example Exodus 23:8-11, Numbers 12:4-13.

32. *Dayan* – judge in Jewish religious court

33. *Ne'eman* = trustworthy—someone employed to supervise kashrut

34. *Kardom lachpor bah* = a means of making money (literally, a spade to dig with). The expression derives from Pirkei Avot 4:9.

35. *Dagesh* = emphasis mark, a diacritical mark in a Hebrew letter indicating emphasis.

36. "Hours of neither day nor night" is a reference to the marginalization of secular studies in the schools of the more pious in Eastern Europe. The expression comes from the Jerusalem Talmud (Peah 1:1), which mentions that Rabbi Yehoshua (c. 100 CE) was once asked whether it was permissible to learn Greek philosophy, to which he replied, "During hours that are neither day nor night, since the Bible states that `this book of the Torah shall not depart from your mouth; you shall contemplate it day and night' (Joshua 1:8)."

37. She was actually his mother, not his wife

38. Zarembo is likely Zareby, a rural area 2 km south of Dobrzyn.

39. *Shochet* = Jewish ritual slaughterer

40. *Kapores* (or *kaparot*) is a ritual conducted on the day before Yom Kippur, in which a Jew would wave a purchased rooster around his head, reciting "...let this rooster be my atonement (*kaparati*)..." The rooster would be slaughtered, and either the meat or its monetary value given to charity. See the following link:
http://www.chabad.org/holidays/JewishNewYear/template_cdo/aid/989585/jewish/Kaparot.htm

41. Silver cup or chalice used for wine in the ritual blessings recited at the beginning of the Sabbath (*Kiddush*) and at its completion (*havdala*)

42. *Birkat hamazon* = prayer recited after completion of a meal

43. *Chevra kadisha* = burial society, the people who prepare the body for burial

44. i.e. even after death, "120 years" being a euphemism for the length of one's life

45. A larger town on the Vistula River, 60 km due south of Dobrzyn

46. *Chazanim* = cantors

47. *Klei kodesh* = religious officiators of various types (beadles, prayer leaders, etc.)

48. *tzaar baalei hachayim* = causing living things pain or suffering, such torment being forbidden by Jewish law

49. *gepashet iz oich geforn* (Yiddish) = providing grazing is also part of the ride

50. *L'haachil kinesia damya* (Hebrew-Aramaic) = feeding is equivalent to traveling, a Talmudic-style statement that means that feeding the horses is part of the ride

51. The Council of Four Lands governed the Jews of Poland from 1580 to 1764. It gave the Jews of Poland a degree of autonomy. See the following link: http://en.wikipedia.org/wiki/Council_of_Four_Lands

52. Feldsher = a health-care provider with no degree in medicine. See the following link: http://en.wikipedia.org/wiki/Feldsher

53. A city in East Prussia. After World War II it was annexed to the Soviet Union (later Russia) and renamed Kaliningrad.

54. A city in West Prussia. After World War I it became part of Poland under the name Poznan.

55. *Bikur cholim* = visiting the ill

56. *Gabaim* = synagogue functionaries who were responsible for collecting charity

57. *Hachnasat orchim* = provision of hospitality (food and lodging) for out-of-town visitors

58. *Hachnasat kalah* = bridal fund to provide for the wedding of a bride from a poor family

59. *Linat hatzedek* = charity to provide medical treatment for the needy

60. *Gemilut chesed* = general charity for those in need, e.g. interest-free loans

61. *Talmud torah* = teaching of Torah

62. Exodus 23:9. The entire verse reads: "Do not oppress a stranger, for you know the spirit of a stranger, since you were strangers in the land of Egypt."

63. *Chesed le'umim chatat* (Proverbs 14:34) is here taken to mean "the kindness/piety of the Nations is sinful (being perhaps driven by ulterior motives)", following an interpretation given in the Babylonian Talmud (Baba Batra 10b).

64. *Agunot* = "anchored" wives, i.e. deserted wives, wives of men who have disappeared. In the absence of a divorce, or evidence that their husbands are dead, they are forbidden by Jewish law to remarry.

65. September 15, 1953

66. The major Jewish cemetery of Jerusalem, located at the western edge of the city

67. Here the Hebrew word used for pious is *hassid*, which usage leads into the next few sentences.

68. i.e., he joined the Alexander Hassidim (see Footnote 4). Adherents of a Hassidic group would often travel to the headquarters of the group, where the *Rebbe* of the group resided.

69. *Onkelos* = the Aramaic translation of the Torah

70. *Siddurim* = prayer books for weekdays and Sabbaths

71. *Machzorim* = prayer books for Rosh Hashana and Yom Kippur

72. *Chumashim* = printed versions of the Pentateuch

73. *Kavana* = concentration on meaning during prayer

74. *Mitzvot* = Torah commandments

75. The most pious of Eastern Europe (particularly Hassidim), followed a custom not to trim their beards, even with a scissors, although the latter is permissible according to Rabbinic interpretation of Leviticus 19:27. In Western Europe, where they were more exposed to Western society, this was a difficult custom to maintain.

76. *Shochet* = ritual slaughterer; *bodek* = inspector of slaughtered meat for blemishes that would render it not kosher

77. Malachi 2:6, referring to the ancient *kohanim* (priests)

78. Attacks by Arabs against Jewish civilians

79. June 26, 1947. As the War of Independence approached, the Mount of Olives, located in Eastern Jerusalem, became inaccessible to Jews. It lay on the Jordanian side of the "Green Line" border when an armistice was declared in 1948. It was not until the Six-Day War of June, 1967 that the Jews of Israel regained access to this ancient Jewish cemetery.

80. The word for work, *avodah*, can also refer to religious service (prayer), which is what it often means when "Torah" and "*avodah*" are mentioned sequentially this way.

81. *Challot* = special loaves of bread, usually braided, for Sabbaths and holidays

82. So as to not approach the Sabbath or holiday meal, eaten after sunset, satiated. If whatever was eaten earlier in the day did not include bread, there was no requirement for the hands to be ritually washed.

83. *Neshama yetera* = "additional soul" that provides the proper Sabbath spirituality, said metaphorically to enter a Jew's body at the onset of the Sabbath

84. In accordance with a widespread Jewish custom not to taste any food in the morning until after praying

85. *Magedet* = woman who would read a text as the other women listened

86. *Tze'ena ur'ena* = "Go Out and Gaze," the name of a commentary on the Torah, composed in Yiddish in the 17th century for people who had difficulty understanding Hebrew, and particularly popular among women in Eastern Europe. The name is based on the verse "Go out and gaze, daughters of Zion, upon King Solomon..." (Song of Songs 3:11).

87. *Techinot* = supplications, prayers for women that were written in Yiddish in the 17th century

88. *Kever avot* = graves of forefathers. It was customary for Jews to visit the graves of their departed during the month of Elul, the last month before *Rosh Hashana*.

89. *yimach sh'mam* = "may their names be blotted out", a phrase used after mentioning someone wicked

90. *Dil'mata* (Aramaic) = that is down below, terrestrial, i.e., the physical Jerusalem on Earth, a metaphor here for the physical Jewish presence in Poland

91. *dil'maala* (Aramaic) = that is up above, celestial, i.e. the spiritual Jerusalem. The concept of a terrestrial and celestial Jerusalem is mentioned in the Babylonian Talmud, Taanit 5a.

92. From p. 31 of reference cited in Footnote 1

93. From p. 33 of reference cited in Footnote 1

94. *Melamed* = children's teacher

95. From p. 36 of reference cited in Footnote 1

[Pages 41-43]

My childhood years in Dobrzyn
by Yaakov Rimon
Translated by Sara Mages

My town Dobrzyn and the Drweca River, which ran beside her, are engraved in my memory. In my childhood, I loved to stand by the river, look at its flowing waters and marvel at the beauty of nature. The town's Great Synagogue stood in a courtyard bathed with greenery and grass, and its red roof was visible from a distance. Every Sabbath I came with my friends to sit on the lawn in the synagogue's courtyard. Even then, the greenery attracted my heart, and I loved being outdoors for long hours. I also remember the *Heder* where I learned *Chumash* and Rashi. I especially remember the precious moments in which I learned *Parashat "Vayechi"*[1], and when I reached the verse, "As for me, when I came from Padan, Rachel died to me in the land of Canaan" with the interpretation of Rashi, that Yaakov said that he didn't bury Rachel in the land of Canaan, not even in Bethlehem, but near it, so the exiles, who were expelled by Nebuzaradan[2], will be able to cry on the tomb of our Mother Rachel when they pass by it, and plead for their lives. And then -"A voice is heard on high, lamentation, bitter weeping, Rachel weeping for her children, she refuses to be comforted". And God answered her with words of comfort:"For your work will be rewarded, and your children shall to their own border. "This legend, and the words "And your children shall to their own border" moved the child in me to tears, aroused my national pride, and lit the first Zionist spark in me ... which turned into a burning flame in my heart.

My brother Yehiel told me, that when I was born my father of blessed memory thought of a name to call me. Since *Parashat "Vayechi"* was read from the Torah on that week, he decided to call me Yaakov, as it is written at the beginning of the *Parasha*, "*Vayechi* Yaakov" [and Yaakov lived], a talisman for long life. I also heard from my brother Yehiel that my circumcision turned into a Zionist event. My father of blessed memory bought "Carmel Mizrachi Wine", the drinking of the wine from Eretz-Yisrael increased the joy and gathered the supporters of Zionism in Dobrzyn, who sang songs of Zion and danced to "Next year in Jerusalem".

In my father's home, which was a Zionist home saturated with Hebrew and religious culture, I drew my intense love to Zion, my affection to Hebrew literature and our heritage. My father, who was an ardent lover of Zion and the manager of the Hebrew Library in Dobrzyn, bought, at that time, the book "*Kinor Zion*" [Harp of Zion] which was published by "*Tushia*" [Warsaw]. The book's editor and collector of songs of Zion, was the author and researcher, Mr. Abraham Moshe Luncz of blessed memory. From it, my father taught me to sing the songs of Zion, and I was five years old at that time. I knew these songs by heart, and since I had pleasant voice I sang them at parties, Zionist gatherings, and in the synagogue of the Warka-Otwock Hassidim where my father prayed. In "*Shalosh seudoth*" I sang "*Shir Hama'aloth*" [Song of Ascent] to the melody of "*Hatikvah*", or to the melody of "*Sham Bimkom Arazim*" [Where the cedars grow].

[Page 42]

Between, my mother May she rest in peace and my father of blessed memory, was a Yissachar-Zevulun arrangement[3]: she engaged in trade and my father studied the Torah and also served, for a known period of time, as a *Gemara*, Rashi Commentary, and *Tosaphot* [commentaries on the Talmud] teacher. The main breadwinner was my mother, and the burden of the house lay on her. I will never forget the Thursday evenings, when she was getting ready for the Sabbath after a hard day of work. She sat me on a bench, and while she was working she sang to me, with great emotion, from the national and human songs of the popular song writer Eliakum Zunser, and the labor songs of the song writer Morris Rosenfeld, who lived and died in the United States. The poems of Eliakum Zunser, which he drew from the Bible, captured my heart. His poems about "Yaakov fleeing from Esau on a stormy night, the parting of his mother, Rivka, from him," or "Yosef in the pit, and the selling of Yosef to the Midianim, moved me to tears for fear of their fate. Morris Rosenfeld's poems "I have a little boy" and "Don't search for me where the flowers grow" instilled within me great love, respect and admiration for the working man. This feeling lived inside me, and gave me the power of performance and fulfillment when I participated in the founding of "*Hapoel HaMizrachi*" [Mizrachi Workers] in Israel.

**The Crusader fortress on top of the mountain range
in Golub and the Drweca River at its foot**

[Page 43]

The first six years of my life in Dobrzyn, until I immigrated to Israel, served as the basis for my national, religious and public life, and as a future Hebrew poet. In my father's house in Dobrzyn I drew the beginning of my love for these things.

In my town, Dobrzyn, I received the first reading of Hebrew literature in my father's Hebrew library. There, I was also introduced, for the first time, to the popular composer Goldfaden. Troupes of Hebrew actors came to Dobrzyn and presented Goldfaden's plays: "Shulamit", "Bar Kochba" and others. In the evenings, I stood next to the building where the play was presented, and listened to Goldfaden's supreme music which took root in my heart to this day. Dobrzyn established Zionist homes, and parents sent their sons to study in "*Gymnasia Herzliya*", the Hebrew high school in Tel-Aviv. These sons served as a living bridge between Israel and the Jews of Dobrzyn, who immigrated to Israel and settled there. My father was rewarded, that he and his family were the first to immigrate from Dobrzyn to Israel, and settle there permanently. I wrote my first poem in Jaffa when I was nine years old, but there's no doubt that it was drawn from the Zionist and cultural atmosphere in which I grew up in Dobrzyn, and received more meaning and strength in our country - our Hebrew homeland.

Translator's Footnotes

1. Parashat "Vayechi" - the weekly Torah portion "And he lived".

2. Nebuzaradan was a captain in Nebuchadnezzar's army.

3. "Yissachar-Zevulun" arrangement - is an actual partnership between a person who studies the Torah and someone who financially supports him. In other words, the "Zevulun", who spends his day involved in business, gives "Yissachar", who studies Torah, half of the profits that he earns.

[Page 44]

My Home Town[1]
By Walter Field
Translated by Allen Flusberg

This poem was a translation into Hebrew of the original English version that appeared on pp. 3-7 of the English-language section of this Yizkor Book.[2] The author of the English poem was Walter Field. The Hebrew translation was authored by Chaim Lord.

At the entrance of the Hall of Remembrance in Jerusalem[3]

Translator's Footnotes

1. From *My Town: In Memory of the Communities Dobrzyn-Gollob*, edited by M. Harpaz, (published by the Dobrzyn-Golub Society, Israel, 1969), pp. 44-50.

2. See the English-language section at the end of this volume.

3. From p. 50 of the reference cited in Footnote 1. The "Hall of Remembrance" is the main building of the Yad Vashem Memorial.

[Page 51]

The Town's Rabbi

by Mendel Sonabend

Translated by Sara Mages

My late father, Yehudah Leib Sonabend, was born in Dobrzyn in the Plock Province, and originated from an extensive rabbinical family. Indeed, his father, R' Rafael, was a textile merchant, but he was related to a privileged family of geniuses, and his nickname was - "The sharp-minded". His brother, R' Avraham Sunaban, was the rabbi from Nishava [Nieszawa], his brother-in-law was the rabbi from Gostynin, and his nephew, R' Yisrael Alter Gruberd, was the rabbi from Bendin [Bedzin].

Close to his wedding, my father was appointed as the rabbi of the town of Janów in the Plock Province. Three years later, he received a letter of appointment from the community of Dobrzyn. The preparations for the selection of the rabbi were conducted in a heated struggle between the Gur Hassidim and the Aleksander Hassidim. The struggle was difficult and long. The Gur Hassidim were on my father's side, but the Aleksander Hassidim were on the side of their rabbi's grandson. The struggle took place in the whole town, without finding a solution that will be accepted by all. Only at the very last moment, the town's residents decided to join the Gur Hassidim, and it was decided to nominate my father as the town's rabbi. After the failure of the Aleksander Hassidim, a letter arrived from their rabbi, that he sees in it the will of the Creator.

My parents used to travel together with my grandfather, R' Mordechai Globus, in his elegant carriage. My grandfather was a well known forest merchant and his carriage, which was drawn by four white horses, attested to his upper class. My father came in this carriage to receive the letter of appointment, and a large crowd waited at the outskirts of the town to welcome him. They escorted him to the synagogue, where he was received by the community leaders in festive warmhearted reception. The cantor and the chorus sang the song "*Baruch Haba*" ["Blessed is he who comes"], and the crowd joined them. My father gave a long sermon, which was received with great enthusiasm, and even the Aleksander Hassidim wished him success.

There was a special room in the rabbi's apartment, which was designated for the meetings of the court.

[Page 52]

Shelves filled with the books of the Sages, *Tannaim* and *Amoraim* [teachers of the Mishnah and the Talmud], covered the walls. These books were the present of my grandfather- R' Mordechai Globus. In the court-room stood a long table, two benches, and a tall chair for the rabbi. Many Jews came here to pour out their troubles and to make their claims. After many discussions, when all the sides made their statements, my father considered the matter for several days after he received, in advance, the consent of the litigants to accept his verdict. This agreement was made in a special way, according to the local custom. The rabbi gave them a handkerchief, ordered each side to hold it, and pulled it out of their hands. This act was a "confirmation of an agreement", and everyone pledged to accept the rabbi's decision. Divorces, arrangements for the "*Halizah*" and others were held in this court-room.

On Saturday evening, the respected proprietors gathered in my father's house for "*Shalosh seudot*", and as they sat comfortably, they sang "*Bnei Heichala*" ["The sons of King's Palace"] and also other songs. My mother served herring and a challah to the table, and my father accompanied the meals with "*Diveri Tora*" [commentaries], since it was time for compliance when the gates of heaven opened. When the stars appeared in the sky, the assembled prayed "*Tefilat Maariv*", while my mother's humble prayer - "*Elohai Avraham, Yitzchk VeYaakov*" - came from the next room.

The twilight hour was enveloped with holiness, mystery and elation. It's difficult to describe in words the holiness that descended on the rabbi's house on the conclusion of the Sabbath. The prayers ended with the "*Havdalah*" blessing, when my father held the Spice Box in his hand, and the wineglass, which was filled to the rim, stood on the table. At the same time, all eyes were directed at my father and the lips wished: "*Shavoa Tov! Shavoa Tov!*" [good week].

My father served as Dobrzyn's Rabbi for thirty-four years and died, at dawn, after a short illness. Before his death, he called all of his relatives and laid before them his special request: to protect each yeshiva student, since he took care of their education and their advanced studies in the Torah and the Talmud. He ordered to divide between them the booklet that he wrote, his Torah commentaries, to serve them as guides in their studies. His interpretations and innovations made a lot of impression on his acquaintances and his students. There was an exceptional depth in his writings, and they passed from hand to hand.

My father was known not only as a pious, but also as an educated gifted speaker, whose influence was great on everyone who came in contact with him. His acquaintances and his admirers admired him very much.

The townspeople especially loved to listen to his moral sermons.

[Page 53]

They saw in him not only a rabbi, but a personality that was above it. His profound words brought their hearts closer to the work of the Creator.

My father was one of the enthusiastic supporters of the Hebrew language, which was expressed in his book "*Shirei Tiferet*" [beautiful poetry].

The yeshiva students were every close to his heart, and he dedicated most of his time to them. Twice a week he went out with them for a walk in the nearby forest. He loved them as if they were his sons. He taught them from the ancient works of Judaism, and dedicated all of his life to studying the Torah and its interpretation.

All the members of the town and hundreds of students, small and big, attended his funeral, and all of them felt that an extraordinary Torah scholar was taken from them.

A reception for Mendel Sonabend and his wife from Mexico, which was held by the Association of Former Residents of Dobrzyn-Golub in Israel

[Pages 54-58]

In My Father's House[1]
by Yehuda Rozenwaks
Translated by Allen Flusberg

In and around Dobrzyn, my father was known not as Zalman Rozenwaks—Rozenwaks being our family name—but rather as "Zalman Hassid".[2] He got this nickname because he distinguished himself in the way he lived as a *Hassid*[3]. In every one of his deeds he made sure to go beyond the letter of the law[4], in the way that someone rises above mundane, day–to–day life through benevolence.

I myself was not fortunate enough to have known my grandfather, my father's father. But my father's stories portrayed him as a pure and lofty figure, a Hassid who was devout in his benevolence, someone who had set his mind to perform good deeds. My father inherited these traits from him.

My father was not inclined to serve in any public role. However his heart was open to anyone in need, or to someone who was having a difficult time. He was glad to come to anyone's aid to the best of his ability. And he was particularly joyful whenever he was able to do a good deed.

On Friday nights, after *Kabbalat Shabbat*[5] in the *shtibl*[6] of the Alexander Hassidim, he would hurry to take care of out–of–town guests who were in the town by chance, and he would take much trouble to find them a place to stay over in. In general there was no shortage of Jews who were prepared to open their homes to guests; but when some of the guests were left with no suitable arrangements, our house would always be open to them. For this reason he would be travelling around on the roads four or five days a week, between Dobrzyn and Wloclawek[7], working hard. His hard labor did not, however, adversely affect his spirit. Since he had a good singing voice, he would customarily lead the Friday-evening service in the *shtibl*, and his good voice would give the Hassidim much pleasure.

Even after the evening meal he didn't go into his bed to relax, since Man does not live by bread alone. Rather, he sought the company of his Hassidic friends. And indeed, the Hassidim tended to get together in the home of one of the wealthy Hassidim, usually R.[8] Mendel Kohn, to listen to words of Torah as they sat at prepared tables. And mostly they were accustomed to gather together during the long winter nights, the meetings lasting until the wee hours of the night. And when they would , each to his own home, their spirits had been uplifted, their souls elevated.

But anyone who has never seen the joy of the Hassidim on the Sabbath, the day they hallowed for the study of Torah, has never seen joy of exaltation in his life.[9] Most of the people gathered to pray in the *shtibl* for the *Mincha*[10] service and for the "*Shalosh Seudot*"[11], which they held as a group. Each of them would bring along some food and drink: some would bring *challa*[12], and some would bring liquor or bottles of beer. After the *Mincha* prayer they would wash their hands and sit at prepared tables; they would eat a tiny bit and launch into the *Shalosh Seudot* hymns.

At this time my father would demonstrate his singing power: he would sing in a loud voice, pulling everyone else in to follow along and join him in song. They would all sing devoutly, with my father's voice audible above the rest. Indeed, these were moments when material thoughts were banished and the soul was uplifted. The Hassidim were caught up in their own world, a world of faith and devotion.

After the *Maariv*[13] prayer, the congregation would scatter, each man returning to his home. But they would come back and gather again in the *shtibl* after *Havdala*[14] to complete the Sabbath with a "*Melaveh Malka*"[15] meal. And this meal lasted for many hours as well, not ending before midnight. Indeed, such was the way and custom of the Hassidim, and this is how they lived in those days in the various small towns of Poland.

Their engagement in Torah, prayers and hymns provided to some extent a way to make them forget the hardships of their daily lives, lives that were difficult and ashen, lives in which each of them had to strive to provide for his household. My father struggled to make a living in small business, spending many hours traveling between Dobrzyn and the large city of Wloclawek. He would go in his own wagon, which was hitched to a team of horses, there not being any other means of transportation in the towns in those days. He customarily made the trip to the big city twice a week. There he would purchase various types of merchandise, which he would re-sell to either Jews or Christians. However, like other small-business merchants, he didn't always manage to get paid in cash, since in those days most commerce took place on credit. And, as usual, "the needs of the people of Israel are extensive, but money is tight"[16] ...particularly in a place like Dobrzyn, where the townspeople were not very prosperous...so my father had to trudge after his debtors to collect what they owed him. And many times he had to compromise with a debtor who was unable to pay—and compromise meant a large discount, sometimes fraught with a real loss.

It was hard to do business under these conditions, in which the profit margin was small; and my father could not manage to take the losses. However, he didn't give up, but rather put his trust in the Creator to take care of him as He takes care of all of His creatures. Therefore he didn't despair, and he continued to supply merchandise even to those debtors who didn't pay their debts, always believing, in his naiveté, that they would settle their debts the next time.

And the troubles never ended: sometimes a wheel came off the wagon; or, even worse, sometimes a horse suddenly gave up the ghost and my father would be left on the road, unable to continue going. Truth be told, the townspeople of Dobrzyn did not neglect him, upholding the command "*azov taazov imo*"[17] ...They helped him through his ordeals, making sure that he could continue to make a living.

As time went on the situation deteriorated, going from bad to worse, until finally my father was forced to find a different livelihood. What did he do? He began dealing in the sale of seasonal staples such as dried fruit, citrus fruit, various vegetable seeds, and wine for the holidays—each of which had its own season. The burden for this occupation fell mainly on my mother, and even we youngsters would work along with her in our spare time at our market stand, mostly on Tuesdays and Fridays.

The years passed. One of my sisters immigrated to the Land of Israel. My parents, who remained in Dobrzyn, were growing old. My mother passed away. My second sister remained with my father, to care for him in his old age. My father was elderly and frail then, after my mother's death, and he longed with all his heart to immigrate to Israel in his twilight years. I sent him an immigration permit and he prepared to make *Aliya*, but fate would have it otherwise...Two weeks before his journey was to begin, when everything had already been prepared for the trip, he fell ill and never recovered. He did not merit to realize the objective he had longed for, his great dream—to go to the Holy Land and to be buried in the Land of the Patriarchs.

After my father, of blessed memory, had passed away, my second sister immigrated to Israel; only my oldest brother, Avraham Yaakov and his family (seven children), as well as my oldest sister, Miriam and her family (six children), remained in Dobrzyn. They perished, together with the other six million, at the hand of the accursed Nazi beast...Only two of my brother's children, Yerachmeel and Yehudit, survived: Yerachmeel, who is in the United States, and Yehudit, who is in Israel.

R. Zalman Rozenwaks (Zalman Hassid)[18]

Fine young men in Dobrzyn
Right to left: **Aharon Kohn, Elyakim Rojna, Yaakov Yechiel Bielawski**[19]

Translator's Footnotes

1. From *My Town: In Memory of the Communities Dobrzyn–Gollob*, edited by M. Harpaz, (published by the Dobrzyn–Golub Society, Israel, 1969), pp. 54–58.

2. For more on Zalman Hassid (or Zalman Chossid), see pp. 289–290 of S. Dzialdow and N. Sanger, "Religious Life in Dobrzyn," pp. 284–291; also Y. Lichtenstein, "Dobrzyn, My Little Town," pp. 30–40, both in reference cited in Footnote 1.

3. Here the term *Hassid* denotes someone who consistently demonstrates extreme kindness and benevolence (the usage in Pirkei Avot [Ethics of the Fathers] 5:9: "Someone who says 'Your property belongs to you, and my property belongs to

you' is a *Hassid*."), rather than the more common meaning as a follower of the Hassidic Movement of Judaism.

4. Hebrew: *Lifnim mishurat hadin* = going beyond the letter of the law (with leniency), bending over backwards. See, for example, Babylonian Talmud, Bava Metzia 30b for examples given of this type of behavior in the Talmudic period.

5. *Kabbalat Shabbat* = the Friday–night service to welcome the Sabbath, consisting of psalms and poems that are sung with joyous melodies

6. *shtibl* (alternative spellings: *shtiebel, shtiebl*) = a small prayer house, typically used by Hassidim

7. Wloclawek was a larger town, located on the Vistula River, ~60km south of Dobrzyn

8. R. = *Reb*, similar to English "Mr."

9. Borrowing from the Talmudic statement (Mishna Sukkah 5:1), "Whoever has not seen the Water–Drawing Rejoicing has never seen rejoicing in his life."

10. *Mincha* = afternoon prayer service

11. *Shalosh Seudot* = (literally) three meals, the name used for the last (third) meal of the Sabbath

12. *challah* = a special type of bread that is eaten on the Sabbath

13. *Maariv* = night prayer service

14. *Havdala* = separation (literally), blessings said over wine, spices and fire at the completion of the Sabbath to indicate the beginning of a new week

15. *Melaveh Malka* = accompanying the queen (literally), the queen referring allegorically to the Sabbath

16. A Jewish saying

17. *azov taazov imo* (Ex. 23:5) usually translated as "You shall surely help him", and interpreted to refer to helping anyone in need.

18. From p. 55 of reference cited in Footnote 1

19. From p. 57 of reference cited in Footnote 1

[Pages 59-62]

Daily Life in the Town[1]
by Avraham Dor (Dobroshklanka)
Translated by Allen Flusberg

At first glance the town of Dobrzyn is no different from other small towns of Poland: a town square surrounded by streets and alleyways, filled with large and small houses pressed up against one another, some standing sturdily, and others showing signs of age. The Dreventz[2] River, flowing along the side of the town, constitutes a natural boundary between Germany and Russia. Pedestrians and wagons cross over the bridge spanning the river.

At the entrance to the town, coming along the road from Rypin, one can see, at the top of the mountain, the historical castle from the Crusader period. In it there is a museum that incorporates a collection of valuable artifacts. Villages lie scattered all around the town. They are populated by Polish farmers, who make up the agricultural hinterland that provides for the town.

With the exception of the road to Rypin, all the roads leading into the town are unpaved. For this reason they are difficult to navigate during autumn because of the deep mud that the frequent rainfall brings. And in the town itself, even here are streets that are nearly impassable because of the deep mud. Many a time passersby would leave behind their galoshes, which they had been unable to extricate.

On the cold winter days, when snow fell and covered the streets with a thick layer that reached up to the windowsills, the residents would emerge and try to shovel it aside, toiling until their faces became flushed. Afterwards they would clear the sidewalks so that it would be possible to reach the shops.

The winter season is hard on the ordinary people, who have to use their limited resources to stockpile food and fuel throughout the rest of the year. And when winter finally does end, the town comes back to life, awakening as if from a deep sleep, and begins to resume its normal routine.

For the young people, summer starts with cheerful outings to the nearby fields and forests. They gather strawberries, biting into them passionately and bringing home whatever is left. These "celebrations" are repeated several times during the summer, each one giving everyone great joy.

There are two reasons why most of the young people are unemployed. First, there are practically no sources of employment for Jewish young people. And second, which Jewish boy would be willing to sully his hand with real labor that is considered lowly and contemptible by the community?

And so it is common and accepted that a younger boy, and even an older boy, is taken care of by his father, who toils with all his strength to support him. The father, the head of the family, is the one and only source of livelihood for all of his dependents. Often he is just a wreck, a weak and failing man, who is burdened with a household of more than ten people and is killing himself to support them.

There was no shortage in our town of "pious women", or—as they would be referred to nowadays—community volunteers. Some were concerned with the poor and needy for the sake of fulfilling *mitzvoth*[3], while others were motivated by compassion. In both cases they aided the poor and oppressed, rescuing them from degradation and from the shame of hunger.

The needy of the town fell into two categories: those who were extremely poor—the destitute paupers for whom hunger had always been a constant presence; and those who had only recently fallen on hard times and were ashamed to receive charity. The second category included respectable families—craftsmen, small-time peddlers and businessmen who had lost everything, either because of the boycott or as a result of an economic crisis. These were taken care of by those particular "pious women" who knew them; they saw to their needs in a special, proper manner, doing their good deeds secretly so as not to hurt their feelings.

There were no professional beggars in the town. Even the well-known pair—Leibke and Shimele—who for many years would go from house to house to collect alms, were not viewed as beggars; they were greeted pleasantly, with smiling faces, as if they were visiting guests. During the period of the Czar, a normal donation was a single groshen; and if someone, in a spirit of generosity, allowed himself to hand them a kopeke, they would be indignant, complaining "What, are you trying to make fun of us?!" For dozens of years they would collect the pennies generously given to them on their traditional Friday "rounds" of the town homeowners.

The "large fairs", special market days that were conducted four or five times a year, were like holidays in the town. At these times all the farmers of the region would stream into the town square with their goods. On the previous day the town would awaken as if to a new life, with everyone getting ready to set up stalls for selling merchandise. The stalls would be spread out next to the sidewalks, along "Long Street" (Pilsudski). Here the dealers laid out pants, coats and suits. Even the shoemakers laid their goods out—shoes and boots— in stalls. However the hat makers and the haberdashery dealers brought their goods to the market square itself, where they placed their merchandise on tables.

Thousands of farmers descended on the town on this day, whether to sell their own goods or to buy merchandise that they needed. They would fill the taverns to capacity, drinking beer and whiskey until they were intoxicated. As evening fell and the market day ended, many of them could be found lying along the sides of the streets and on the sidewalks, drunk as Lot, having spent all their money on liquor.

For the children these market days were especially joyous. They would look at the mobs of farmers with great glee, watching them wandering around the town square and the streets with deafening noise. In addition, the children would also get some "fair money" and become "rich" on these days.

And indeed on various other occasions and holidays the children were given many opportunities to play and have a good time, the way children do. Thus, for example, they would go out on *Lag BaOmer*[4] to the nearby forests, carrying bows and arrows and shooting at birds up in the trees. They would spend the entire day there, returning home in the evening, group by group, singing with gusto.

On Purim[5] everyone would be disguised in colorful masks, purchased at Yehoshua Meir Waldenberg's store. Bigger boys, wearing scary masks, would go out of their way to frighten the little children and make them cry.

A "wedding procession" was a particularly spectacular event. It would run from the bride's home to the synagogue. The bride would be accompanied by close relatives and a festive crowd, marching to singing and music. The adults would dance as they walked, and the young people would accompany them with song. Indeed, the following saying was common: when Dobrzyn marries off one of its girls, all of the townspeople are *mehutanim*[6].

There was a long list of customs that were specific to the town. Some had been initiated during periods of joy, others in periods of grief. But with the passage of time, as new ideas made their way into the small towns, including our own, some of these customs fell into disuse. The few customs that were retained had long traditions behind them. However, with the destruction of

Polish Jewry, such unique customs—characteristic of Jews who lived in small towns—disappeared, leaving no trace behind.

May these lines serve as a small remembrance of the lives and customs of the Jews of Dobrzyn.

The western portion of the town square[7]

A group of boy scouts in Dobrzyn[8]

Translator's Footnotes

1. From *My Town: In Memory of the Communities Dobrzyn–Gollob*, edited by M. Harpaz, (published by the Dobrzyn–Golub Society, Israel, 1969), pp. 59–62.

2. Polish spelling: Drwęc (pronounced Dreventz).

3. *Mitzvot* = commandments, in this case the requirement by Jewish law to care for the poor and needy

4. *Lag BaOmer* = A minor holiday on the 33rd day after Passover, celebrated with outings in forests, as well as archery and other sports.

5. Purim = a joyful holiday commemorating the survival of the Jews of Persia after being threatened with destruction by their enemies, according to the account in the Biblical Book of Esther. It occurs in February or March, one month before Passover, and is celebrated with costumes and disguises.

6. *Mehutanim* = in–laws, i.e. partaking relatives.

7. From p. 59 of reference cited in Footnote 1. The German print at the top left reads "Gollub, W. Pr." (abbreviation of *Westpreußen* =West Prussia). The German print at the top right reads "Marktplatz m. Burgruine Golau" = Market square with ruin of Golau castle. The photograph appears to have been part of a pre–World–War–I postcard.

8. From p. 62 of reference cited in Footnote 1

[Page 63]

The nobility and the inspiration of Dobrzyn's Jews

HaRav Yitzchak Yedidya Frenkel

Translated by Sara Mages

It happened on the thirtieth day of the passing of the genius, Rabbi Meir Shapira, the Rabbi of Lublin and the founder of "Chachmei Lublin Yeshiva", when I traveled from Ripin [Rypin] to nearby Dobrzyn to eulogize the same Jewish genius - it was my first encounter with the town of Dobrzyn. Despite the fact, that the distance between Ripin and Dobrzyn wasn't great, the town was considered to be a border town between Germany and Poland. The bridge over the Drweca River, which crossed the town, separated the section that was called Dobrzyn from the sections that was called Golub, meaning - between the Polish section and the German section. Such was the situation until the end of the First World War, when the whole town, with its two sections, was transferred to Poland.

It was possible to distinguish between these two sections because of the major differences in construction, architecture and lifestyle. However, its Jewish residents weren't different from the Jews of other Jewish towns in Poland. The same Jews: Hassidim and men of action, scholars and Cabbalists, merchants and laborers, philosophers and intellectuals, visionaries and pioneers, Beit-Midrash and Yeshiva students. And in addition to this, a special nobility and a respectable lifestyle which characterized the Jews of Dobrzyn.

As mentioned, I arrived to the Great Synagogue, which was filled to capacity, to eulogize the same genius who died suddenly, in his prime. The Jews of Dobrzyn listened to the eulogy with great interest. Tears flowed from the eyes of many, as if the deceased was their father! At the end of my words there were a few calls, which soon caught the entire audience, to maintain the Rabbi's life work - "Chachmei Lublin Yeshiva". Many volunteered on the spot to go to each household in the town and collect donations for the "*Kofer-nefesh*" [charitable] project, which will be used to support the Yeshiva.

At that time, I saw the Jews of Dobrzyn in their characteristic enthusiasm. Jews that a fire blazed in their hearts, even though they looked quiet and reserved from the outside. These Jews were the first to everything that was sacred, and were among the first who immigrate to Zion and loved their homeland.

[Page 64]

It is possible to say, that Dobrzyn was a loyal sister to its neighboring Ripin - in the Torah, Hassidut, nobility, dedication, love of Zion, and all the qualities that characterized this environment - one of the magnificent links of Polish Jewry, which was destroyed by the German "Master race," with the mute silence of the foreign world.

On my bed at night, when my thoughts carry me to my past, Dobrzyn is standing before my eyes as a beloved memento. I see her beautiful nobles Jews, who were satisfied with little. All the grief and sorrow of the word is reflected in their eyes as they march in rows to the center of the fire, to be sacrificed.

The silent scream is ringing in my ears and shakes the heavens...

Dobrzyn's Jews, with their wives and children, I will never, never, forget them!

The town's Great Synagogue

[Page 65]

Childhood and Adolescence (Memories)[1]

by Ze'ev Lent

Translated by Allen Flusberg

Fragments of memories from days gone by, memories of home and of the town—such memories flood my consciousness from time to time. Although they are jumbled and chaotic, they stir up my heart and warm it. They are memories of seemingly trivial things, minor matters that a stranger would not understand and would not find interesting…But someone who once lived in the town of Dobrzyn; someone whose childhood and adolescence were spent in the shadows of its houses, near the river that carries its waters into the earth of the town; someone who has taken a leisurely stroll across the bridge that connects the two towns, Dobrzyn and Golub; such a person will feel it when within him that fire is kindled, when his spirit is flooded with the recollection of small things that transpired in those towns that once were but are no more…

1914

I recall that we were traveling in horse-drawn carriages, along the Lipno-Wloclawek road towards the city of Warsaw[2]. My father was not with us. He had crossed the border to Germany, having not a shred of desire to fight for the Russian Czar—definitely not!

I remember that year only dimly, since I was then a very small child.

1915

The armies of the German Kaiser are entering Warsaw. The Zeppelin hovers over the city, threatening to bomb it. We stand next to the gate of the house and watch, our eyes turned upward to the heavens—the adults with anxiety, and we children with curiosity.

In the streets of the city the German army demonstrates its power: the soldiers are marching, accompanied by a band, as their anthem, "Germany Above All Else", is struck up with pride. To this very day I have not forgotten this event and the singing of the anthem…

...And again we are wandering on the road, except that this time we are returning home, to Dobrzyn. I was a small child when I was first taken along this path, but remarkably I remember the places that we are going past the second time around. Near Wloclawek we cross the river again in a large rowboat, except that this time, unlike the first time, we are no longer afraid of the great waters. Father is waiting for us in Lipno. I am overcome by a strange sensation: it seems that I am shy in front of him. Although I remember what he looked like, I am not able to suppress this feeling. He is a tall, good-looking man, cultivating a beard and mustache in the style of Nikolai II[3]. His clothing is elegant and shiny, and on his head is a black hat. I look at him, and it appears to me that he is someone who has just stepped out of the world of mythology.

1916

I am attending school at a cheider[4] that is located near the shtiebel[5] of the Alexander Hassidim. A sofer satam[6] lives opposite the door of our house. The courtyard of our house overlooks the Dreventz[7] River. Not far from us is a path used by the water-carriers to get to the river. Along this path is a drainage pipe made of concrete; this drainage pipe serves as an attraction for children. We play a great deal at its entry point, especially the bigger children, whom we consider our heroes. Some of them, such as Yisraelik Lipstadt, Tzudek Zudkevitz and Shaya Dobroshklanka, even dare to go all the way through it, along its entire length to its end.

Tzudek was my closest friend. The two of us would do a lot of daydreaming, which we would enjoy a great deal. Each of us would brag to the other about the images he was able to see on an ordinary wall, in the air, or up in the sky. "Here, do you see," I would turn to him to say, "Here is the ladder and there are the angels going up and down on it..." But Tzudek would not be bested for long: "Here is the burning bush," he retorts, "and here is Moses with a lamb in his arms."

It matters little that we both know these things are all made up, nothing more than the fruit of a vivid imagination. Neither of us gets angry at the other or contradicts him, for this is only a pastime, an ongoing form of amusement.

That summer my brother Leibel, who was a year younger than me, passes away of stomach typhus. I am depressed by my mother's constant crying. I have been used to seeing her always smiling. Ill at ease at home, I look for shelter in Tzudek's company. We are in his room. As someone whose brother has just passed away, I don't know how to behave. And in order not to show weakness, I try to make a completely different impression. I stand up and describe to all present how my brother's soul is going up to Heaven, until I am reprimanded by Tzudek's father. I am filled with shame and stop talking.

A different image from that year comes back to me: the eve of the holiday Sukkot. Everyone, me included, is working hard to put up a sukkah[8]. I feel an ache in my head, a particularly sharp pain; but I don't leave until the sukkah is ready, standing in place, completed from top to bottom. Only then do I reveal to my mother that my head aches, and I hurry to lie down. I don't go to synagogue with my father. They promise to wake me later for the festive meal in the sukkah, after they've all returned from synagogue.

When I woke up it was dark everywhere, night time. The house was completely silent. My mother, fully dressed, was asleep at my feet, a frown on her face. "Mother, have they already come back from synagogue?" I asked. "Yes, son, lie down and go back to sleep." I tried to close my eyes, but the fierce pain in my head hadn't yet gone away.

The holiday went by and I was still ill, lying in bed, as the Polish doctor, accompanied by the medic Russik, came to see me every day. Many days passed until I overcame my illness and was finally able to sit near the window, staring at the vast market square opposite me, where German soldiers were training all day.

1917

We would take many strolls around town in those days, drawn to the groves as well as to the more distant forest. One of the charming places that attracted us was the Zaremba farm. This farm, which belonged to Jews whom we knew, and who attended the *shtiebel* that we prayed in, was located not very far from the town.

However, on our traditional Sabbath strolls we didn't go further than half the distance to Zaremba, where there was a sparse grove of pine trees. Opposite the grove there was a slope that went down to the Struga River, with a small wooden bridge over it. Sometimes we continued on our way and reached the farm itself; other times, accompanied by older children, we continued walking up to the Zaremba[9] forest, which extended several kilometers beyond the farm.

I was about eight years old then. My friends were also young, ranging in age from eight to ten. We belonged to a boy-scout group that was led by Fishel Zudkevitz. We were all students at the Hebrew school of Paznewski, located near the fire-station hall "Harmiza". We all knew the Hebrew language, in which we would converse during all our meetings.

I remember how we all went out to spend *Lag BaOmer*[10] in the forest of Zaremba. We sang Hebrew songs along the way, as we walked through the grove and marched over the bridge, until we came to the farm. After a short rest we continued on our way towards the forest, as the farmers, who lived along either side of the dirt path, came out of their houses and looked at the strange Jew boys in wonder and astonishment.

We reached the forest. To this very day I remember the excitement we felt at the moment the sweet, stimulating smell of the forest entered our nostrils. Not lingering for even a moment, we burst in running, and we quickly dispersed among the trees.

Only after we had gone duly wild, we heard the whistle being blown by our supervisor. We gathered together at his call and listened to his orders. He warned us not to disperse and not to go very far, so that we should not get lost in the forest and be unable to find our way out.

We spent several hours within the forest, picking red, juicy strawberries that we devoured passionately, even putting some in our knapsacks. We kept running around, and continued to sing and fool around, while throughout we were gobbling them down.

On the way back we marched one behind the other, single file, making sure that we didn't disperse. While we were walking we kept talking to each other, and so we didn't realize we were going deeper and deeper into the forest. Just as we began wondering whether we were going the right way, we reached one of the tributaries of the Struga, one that we hadn't passed on our way into the forest. Now we knew that we had gone the wrong way. We crossed over the tributary and continued onward, hoping that we would eventually reach the edge of the forest. Walking got harder, particularly since the wooden sandals we were wearing became slippery, and we had to exert ourselves greatly to keep from stumbling.

Suddenly we were overcome with dread: eight young brawny Polish cowherds faced us. They stood looking at us with smiles on their faces. We were afraid that they were planning to do something bad to us, since they were

Gentiles and that is what Gentile boys[11] usually do. Moshe Fishel, our counselor, seemed a bit ill at ease as he took counsel with himself and conferred with us to decide how to get out of this predicament. Finally he decided to suggest giving them some money so that they would agree to let us go and even give us directions. But it turned out we had no money with us. So the counselor stood up and decided that we should take up a collection—pocketknives, whistles, and the like—and hand them over. And so it was: we gave them some "gifts" and then continued on our way, following their instructions. And very soon we found ourselves outside the forest, on the road leading home.

What I remember is that in the end those Gentile boys didn't benefit from the whole affair: some Jewish boys, who were members of *HeChalutz*[12], went out to the forest, accompanied by one of the police. They caught the Gentile boys, took away our "gifts", and dealt them blows appropriately.

1918

We moved out of our spacious apartment that was in Klinowski's house, and we moved into a wooden house on the "Street of Gold"[13]. My mother worked hard to set up a shop with various items for sale, but with no success. Meanwhile my father was appointed a border-guard policeman after the Germans had left Dobrzyn.

I recall how he brought home his rifle, warning me not to touch it, Heaven forbid! Only sometimes, after he had removed the bullets from the cartridge, he did let us play with it. For some reason it occurred to me back then that even my father himself was afraid of it, of the rifle. There were three Jews in the border guard in those days: Yitzhak Rosenwaks, now deceased, Rydz and my father.

1920

After the Germans had left Golub, in the year 1919, the owners of the farms that were on "the other side"[14] began to frequent our town to shop there. At that time our shop re-opened and our situation improved. My father, as well as the other two Jews, quickly quit the border guard.

It was a tense time. Rumors circulated about the Bolsheviks who were getting closer to our town, and even worse, about the Cossacks who were massacring the Jews, and about the Tatars with shaven heads, who had only one eye in their heads[15].

I recall: on one afternoon two horsemen burst into the market square, galloping like a whirlwind. They stopped their horses in the square and then, rearing their horses, turned around and disappeared back to wherever they had come from. Only on the next day, during morning hours, a cavalry unit entered our town without encountering any sign of resistance.

It seems that the days during which the Bolsheviks governed our town was a period of relative calm. In any event, for us children these were pleasant times. The Bolsheviks didn't harm anyone; just the opposite—the "bigger" youngsters among us got a chance to ride on their horses when they brought them to the river for washing.

However, after a few days had passed a group of Polish volunteers deployed on the hills behind Golub and surrounded the town. A hail of bullets fell on the houses. My parents were concerned about the children and hurriedly sent my older brother and me to the home of my uncle Hershel Lent, who lived on the second floor of Zudkevitz's house. Since the bullets were being fired nonstop, my uncle sent us down to the Zudkevitz apartment on the lower floor. We were there together with some other youngsters. We occasionally peeked outside, listening to the noise of the machine guns and trying to imitate them by tapping on the large wall closet.

After some time had passed the machine guns went silent, and a hush fell on the town. It appeared that the battle was over. We left our uncle's house and returned home. In the courtyard we found men, armed with rifles, who were conducting a search of the area. My father had been hiding for some reason, and, finding him, they thought that he was none other than a Bolshevik. Fortunately for my father, at that very time one of the residents of Golub, who knew him very well, happened along. He testified that my father was not a Bolshevik, but—the very opposite—someone who had served in the border guard at the founding of the Polish State. This testimony saved my father's life.

1926

The town's commerce is flourishing. Business in our store is excellent, and we have to expand it at the expense of our apartment. My brother Moshe completed his studies this year at the vocational school located in Warsaw. I myself am already in the fourth and last grade, while my two younger brothers, Nahum and Yitzhak, together with my sister Yehudit, are studying at the general [unaffiliated] school of Dobrzyn. We are coming to the end of summer vacation, a period that is generally one of the most pleasant, except that right now all the people of the town are very apprehensive because of the blood libel[16].

Gypsies, who had pitched their tents outside the town, spread a rumor that a Jew named Flusberg had kidnapped one of the Gypsy girls and had slaughtered her for ritual religious purposes. Very quickly the streets of the town were filled with Christians from Golub, young and old, who roamed around intimidatingly, trying to find some victims. As was usual in such cases, the local police did not make an appearance. My uncle, Hershel Lent, together with several others Jews, rushed out to Rypin[17] to ask for help from the district police. And wonder of wonders: quickly several policemen, few in number but spirited, arrived and successfully ejected the Golub residents from the town.

The danger passed. In the end it turned out that the father of the girl was the one who had killed her with his own hands, and that he had sought to frame the Jews. The next day the Gypsies were expelled beyond the town limits, and some of them were taken away in handcuffs. For the Jews of Dobrzyn it was a time of joy and gladness[18].

1929

I am now in Warsaw. Dobrzyn is too small for me, especially since working in the shop is not to my taste. And here, in the big city, I succeed in working in the profession that I have acquired, as an automobile locksmith; however, this work serves only as a means of subsistence for me, since all my interest is in sports. I belong to the sport organization Maccabi[19], and am practicing swimming a great deal, after I had previously been in boxing. I rapidly make first place in the breast stroke and appear as a representative of Maccabi of Warsaw in the country-wide competition.

In that period, as I am reaping praise as a gifted athlete and am enjoying life in the big city, I run into my good friend Kobe Lipka, who tells me that Monik Fin is immigrating to Brazil, and that he himself is preparing to do the same. He suggests that I join him. At first I am not inclined to; why should I, since I am having a good time in Warsaw and everyone here likes me? But as time passes the idea begins to gnaw at me, and I am overcome by the desire, ingrained in me from birth, to experience adventure. I decide to immigrate to Brazil.

1933

I have recently returned from Brazil. I am sitting with a group of friends in a coffee house in Golub, sipping coffee and listening to the results of the elections in Germany, reported by the minute on the radio. The picture is now absolutely clear: Hitler's party, the National Socialists, is the winner. However, for the time being we don't feel a thing and we are not concerned, even though in Golub itself the young people are organizing in the Hitler Youth[20] movement.

Meanwhile I am not involved in work of any substance, except for helping my parents somewhat in their shop. Business is now very bad; many of the customers are not paying their debts and we are forced to stop giving them credit. I take the responsibility for this task, which is not pleasant at all, upon myself, since I have in the meantime matured and I have obtained some business experience in Brazil. But truth be told, even afterwards we are forced to again give credit to the veteran customers, who still cannot afford to pay.

The customs house near the bridge leading to Golub[21]

Young people of Dobrzyn hiking in the hills of Golub during the winter[22]

**Mr. Abraham Flusberg, the principally
accused individual in the Gypsy libel**[23]

Translator's Footnotes

1. From *My Town: In Memory of the Communities Dobrzyn-Gollob*, edited by M. Harpaz, (published by the Dobrzyn-Golub Society, Israel, 1969), pp. 385-387.

2. From Dobrzyn, the road heads due south for 65km via Lipno to Wloclawek on the Vistula River, then more or less follows the river east for 170km to Warsaw.

3. Nikolai II, Czar of Russia

4. *Cheider* = Jewish school for young children, dedicated almost exclusively to religious studies

5. *Shtiebel* = a single-room synagogue, usually Hassidic

6. *Sofer satam* = a scribe who writes Torah scrolls and Biblical texts (on parchment) that are placed into *tefillin* (phylacteries) and door-post *mezuzot*

7. Drwec in Polish spelling

8. *Sukkah* = a temporary booth for the week-long fall festival *Sukkot* (two weeks after *Rosh Hashanah*, the Jewish New Year). During this period, meals are eaten in the *sukkah*.

9. Written "Zaręba" in Polish, it is located about 2km south of Dobrzyn.

10. *Lag BaOmer* = A minor holiday on the 33rd day after Passover, celebrated with outings in forests, as well as archery and other sports.

11. The word used here is *Shekatzim*, a pejorative for Gentile boys or young men.

12. *HeChalutz* = Zionist youth movement, organized to teach the Jewish youth agricultural skills that would prepare them for immigration to the Land of Israel.

13. This street, called *Die Goldene Gass* (Yiddish for Golden Street or Street of Gold) by the Jews, ran northeast from the main square to *Die Lange Gass* (Yiddish for Long Street), as can be seen from the map appearing on pp. 8-9 of reference cited in Footnote 1.

14. The other (Golub) side of the Dreventz, which had been in Prussia but was now incorporated into Poland.

15. For a reference to myths of the one-eyed Tatars, see the following link: http://www.iccrimea.org/reports/18may2002.html

16. For a history of the blood libel, the false accusation that Jews murder Gentile children for their blood, see the following link: http://en.wikipedia.org/wiki/Blood_libel.

17. Rypin was a larger town, located about 30km due east of Dobrzyn.

18. An allusion to the end of the Purim story (paralleling the language of Esther 8:16).

19. The Maccabi movement was a Zionist gymnastics and sports organization. See the following link: http://www.yivoencyclopedia.org/article.aspx/Maccabi_Movement

20. The Hitler Youth (Hitler Jugend in German) was a paramilitary organization whose members were indoctrinated in anti-Semitism. See the following link: http://en.wikipedia.org/wiki/Hitler_Youth.

21. From p. 67 of reference cited in Footnote 1

22. From p. 70 of reference cited in Footnote 1

23. From p. 72 of reference cited in Footnote 1. As a result of the accusation, Abraham Flusberg immigrated to the US. The photograph was taken in New York in the 1960s, when he was in his eighties.

[Page 73]

A Few Memories...[1]
by Dina and Yitzchak Shperling
Translated by Allen Flusberg

Quietly, reverently, I am attempting to conjure up that Jewish life, with its many manifestations: modest, but with invaluable content. To go back and see, with my inner eye, that little town in Poland: Dobrzyn on the River Dreventz, separated from Golub, the adjacent town in West Prussia, only by the waters of the narrow river.

Beloved Dobrzyn with its beautiful, low houses; its narrow streets, populated by hundreds of Jews: good, pure and honest Jews, both wealthy and poor, whose unique lives were firmly set in Jewish tradition.

Dobrzyn with all its strata, its various affiliations: the unique ferment within it, the never-ending pursuit of livelihood and the struggle for survival. Vibrant Jews, craving to participate in the fascinating community life of the town.

As I recall the childhood that I spent there, I am flooded with memories and a warm, pleasant sensation. After the more than three decades since I left, my memories of the town seem to be enveloped in mist. It is as if it was no more than one large dream; yet I remember almost every single house and every family. When I reflect upon all that has passed, the eras come and go; one event follows upon another...Indeed, the life that was lived there had a singular flavor.

And as long as I am bringing up the memory of the town and all that was in it, I must mention my dear, martyred parents: our father, Moshe Shperling; our good mother, Feyge née Zudkewicz; our brother and our sisters, Reizel and Tzipora, of blessed memory! I recall how they accompanied me, sad yet happy, when I left for the Land of Israel. I still have those memories, but they are only memories...

In the year 1943, at the end of the World War, after the terrible Holocaust, I discovered a single survivor, a brand plucked from a fire[2], my cousin Zudkewicz, of blessed memory, a member of the household of Avraham Zudkewicz.[3] As I listened to his moving, riveting account of what he had gone through, I sensed the magnitude of the disaster that had been visited upon my extended family, on my own family and on the Jews of my town, Dobrzyn. Only a small number of them succeeded in uprooting themselves from there in time and immigrating to the Land of Israel. The vibrant youth, thirsting for knowledge, those who were members of the "Hashomer Hatzair" movement, and those who tried to redeem and be redeemed[4], bringing respect and glory to themselves and to the town: those are the ones who managed to immigrate to the Land of Israel and save themselves.

But alas! The vast majority of the townspeople perished and were lost…uprooted in the horrific storm that descended even upon this lovely town …

Can a small number of words summarize all that was and is gone?! Are they capable of recalling the memory of a glorious past of which nothing remains but memories—memories that will never be obliterated?!

At the ruins of the synagogue
In the photograph: **Leib Szlachter**[5]

Translator's Footnotes

1. From *My Town: In Memory of the Communities Dobrzyn-Gollob*, edited by M. Harpaz, (published by the Dobrzyn-Golub Society, Israel, 1969), pp. 73-74.

2. The expression *ud mutzal me'esh* (= a brand plucked [or saved] from a fire) derives from Zech. 3:2.

3. Zadok Zudkewicz arrived in the Land of Israel in 1943, after traveling through the Soviet Union and various Arab countries with the Polish Anders army. See the article by Zudkewicz, "In the Tempest of the War," pp. 130-136 of this volume (reference cited in Footnote 1).

4. "To redeem and be redeemed" is a line taken from an old pioneer folk song, of unknown authorship: "We have come to the Land to build and be built up in it...to redeem and be redeemed in it".

5. From p. 74 of reference cited in Footnote 1

[Page 76]

Institutions and Movements

[Pages 76-78]

A Vibrant and Active Community[1]

by Yehuda Rosenwaks

Translated by Allen Flusberg

A. Economic Activity

Earlier, Dobrzyn was no more than a town within the province of Rypin; but after the establishment of an independent Poland following the end of the First World War, it became a more independent city because of its unification with Golub.

Railroad tracks and organized transport connected Dobrzyn with the cities Wloclawek, Lodz and Warsaw, aiding its economic development. And indeed, thanks to its convenient shipping connections, it became a thriving commercial city that attracted other residents from the surrounding areas.

The animated economy impacted the social and cultural development of the place. As time passed, a fairly broad class of young intellectuals arose, leaving an imprint on the life of the city.

Thanks to the well–organized transport, many of the townspeople found their livelihood in trade with Germany—in the grain business and in agricultural manufacturing—leading to a boom in Dobrzyn–Golub. Even so, there was no shortage of poor people; but in general the economic situation of the city, as opposed to that of others in the vicinity, was good.

As their economic activity continued to expand, the tradesmen needed additional investment capital, whose absence became more and more critical. And then a few businessmen toiled relentlessly to establish a bank that would be able to provide services to the residents. Indeed this bank, a kind of funding lender, served the townspeople well, and its imprint was rapidly felt in the business life of the place.

The influence of the twentieth century began to be felt in Dobrzyn–Golub not only economically, but in its social-cultural life, as well. As also in the large cities, various political parties with a large number of members arose. Nearly all the young people joined one of these parties. Each group would get together almost every day, particularly on Saturdays, in the movement's meeting hall. At these meetings they would listen to lectures and have discussions and debates with the passion characteristic of youth.

Competition between the parties was fierce as each sought to attract more of the young people. These struggles occasionally led to a great deal of tension and to embittered relations between some of the young people.

B. Educational Activity

As was usual in most of the towns of the House of Israel in the Diaspora, Jewish children in the past received their initial education in the "*cheder*"[2], where the "*melamed*"[3] taught his young students religious texts, often with the aid of a strap.

This education was restricted to boys; parents didn't actually give much thought to their daughters' education. It sufficed that a girl should know how to read the prayers, so that she would not need to have the prayers read to her out loud by another woman in the women's section of the synagogue. Parents sought to educate daughters to make them suitable as mothers who knew their place and their role in life. Their entire education did not have to go beyond an ability to read the *siddur*[4] and the *machzor*[5], without even understanding the meaning of the words. The more liberal parents made certain that their daughter would learn to read and write Yiddish, and would even be able to recognize the letters of the Latin alphabet, so that she could address envelopes in the official language of the country. And in those days that was the sum total of a girl's education.

In the 1920s the first cracks in the rigid walls of tradition began to appear. Secular schools with modern methods and goals were established, and libraries containing books in different languages were founded. The young people, who were no longer willing to follow their elders' dictates verbatim, began to make their own way. Many streamed into the new schools, seeking to acquire knowledge of various cultures. Some continued their studies in high schools and even in universities.

The cultural activities and the spread of the secular schools also significantly influenced traditional education. Recognizing that they could no longer remain isolated from the demands of the times, traditional schools were forced to introduce secular learning within the framework of Jewish studies. Indeed, the reformed *cheder*, which broke open a window to secular culture, continued to enroll a large number of students. They emerged enriched by both Judaism and general culture.

It should be noted that Zionist activity also began in this period. It was expressed in the study of the Hebrew language and in the departure for Zionist pioneer training camps in agricultural farms, to prepare for *aliya* to Israel. Jews who owned farms were found; they agreed to make their farms available for this purpose, greatly assisting not only the training of the youth in agriculture, but also enhancing the influence of Zionism on the town. It is fitting to mention the following farm owners who helped found the training camps and encouraged the young people: Yitzhak Yaakov Szmiga, Yaakov Rojna, Poleder, and Hershl Dobrzinski. The training camps served as greenhouses for Zionist pioneers from all over Poland who then immigrated to the Land of Israel and were rescued from the bitter fate of their brethren in the Diaspora.

Translator's Footnotes

1. From *My Town: In Memory of the Communities Dobrzyn–Gollob*, edited by M. Harpaz, (published by the Dobrzyn–Golub Society, Israel, 1969), pp. 76–78.

2. *cheder* = boys' school, where the curriculum was dominated by religious studies

3. *melamed* = teacher of small children

4. *siddur* = Jewish prayer book

5. *machzor* = special prayer book for Rosh Hashana and Yom Kippur. The prayers and liturgical poems that are recited on these holidays are numerous, requiring a special book.

6. From p. 78 of reference cited in Footnote 1.

Delegates of the Zionist Organization in Dobrzyn–Golub, headed by Mr. Yitzhak Moshe Offenbach (first row, second from left)[6]

[Pages 79-86]

Institutions and Organizations[1]

by Avraham Dor (Dobroszklanka)

Translated by Allen Flusberg

For as far back as I can remember, Dobrzyn, the town in which I was born and raised, was a quiet, peaceful corner of the western part of Congress Poland[2]. When I think back to the days of my childhood and adolescence, trying to recall memories from the remote depths of my past, images of Dobrzyn come back to me: Dobrzyn, with its houses, alleyways and courtyards, with its good, compassionate people, with its distinguished, welcoming Jews who were well known throughout the surrounding area as affable, hospitable people. Many times I happened to overhear people from other towns conversing, extolling the townspeople of Dobrzyn for their benevolence. And from various itinerant Jewish preachers[3], who used to make the rounds of the towns of Poland, I have heard remarks of praise for the philanthropy of my townspeople.

An image comes back to me from the days of World War I, a period in which a great famine raged throughout the large cities of Poland. Thousands of Jews, most of them miserably poor, descended upon the towns and villages of the country to find food and satisfy their hunger. Dobrzyn was one of the first towns to come to the aid of these refugees. The soup kitchen that was right next to the "Otwock *shtiebel*"[4] gave meals out all day to all who asked for them. The women of the town toiled to prepare these dishes and to distribute them among the needy. How wonderful it was to feel the great animation affecting all the townspeople; all were happy to partake in this mitzvah[5], and the most dedicated were the women volunteers, the pious women who did not spare themselves any labor or toil to provide a bit of joy to those in need.

When the war ended and life began to get back to normal, most of the refugees returned to their places of origin. However, some of them, captivated by the town, were unwilling to leave, and they settled there. These were mainly craftsmen who had managed to make a good living among us. Many years later, after they had become respectable residents, they lauded the many acts of generosity that the townspeople had done for them while they were impoverished, miserable refugees, penniless and starving.

Indeed, the words of Mendel Sonabend, who was the son of the town rabbi, Rabbi Judah z.l.[6], were particularly succinct when he spoke in memory of our town and of its residents, saying: "Dobrzyn was heart, Dobrzyn was feelings, charity, anonymous giving…In Dobrzyn there were no wretched or deprived people, because all the people who lived there were like a single family." (Footnote: These words are excerpted from a speech he made in a general meeting, held in Tel Aviv, of Dobrzyners in Israel.)

[Page 80]

The Community Council

As in other Jewish communities throughout the Exile, The Community Council of Dobrzyn was a particularly respected institution whose influence was discernable not only in the religious domain but also in other areas of life. Thus it is not surprising that many a time attaining representation in it led to bitter struggles. It was customary to appoint the members of the Council from among the elders and wealthy of the city, who would decide among themselves who would be selected. Generally they held sway and remained in office for an unlimited length of time.

After World War I ended, the influence of the newly wealthy and powerful, who had made their money during the war, was on the rise. Supported by the Hassidim of the *shtiebels*, they were able to impose their authority on the veteran members of the community.

The elections for the Community Council were an important event in the life of the town. These elections were accompanied by an enormous ruckus as each side tried to prevail over the other, whether in the synagogue, the *Beit Midrash*[7], the *shtiebels*, the streets, and even the *mikva*[8].

At the end of World War I a group of young people from among the members of the World Zionist Organization of the town organized themselves, attempting to take an active role in the life of the community. The following were in this group: Lemel Rojna, Klein Lichtenfeld, Kutner, Perger, as well as others. Of course these young people had to struggle to obtain appropriate representation in the Community Council. The veteran members as well as the rich and the powerful were not overjoyed to fulfil the desire of the young people; it was only after a lengthy struggle, and after more democratic elections were held, that these young people managed to get a single one of them, Lichtenfeld, on the Council. The *"Bund"*[9] and *"Poalei Tzion"*[10] also tried to expand their influence via representation on the Council, but in spite of all their efforts they were unable to do so. Their ideologies were still much too novel for the townspeople to accept.

The rabbi of the town, Rabbi Yehuda Leib Sonabend, who was considered a great scholar, had an especially lofty and respectable standing. He distinguished himself not only in his vast and wide-ranging knowledge, but also in his compassion and other noble qualities that made him a popular leader. With his amicable, popular approach, he was able to bring all the residents of the town—people of all persuasions —closer to him. He would lead the community with the wisdom and humility that was so very characteristic of him. For the townspeople he was not only a spiritual and religious leader, but more than that—a father...

And indeed, after he passed away, the town remained without a rabbi for a long time, in spite of all the attempts to find someone to replace him. Of course there was no shortage of candidates. Rabbis from as far away as Lithuania applied, but none was judged to be suitable to inherit Rabbi Yehuda Leib Sonabend's position. In this period the "*Dayan*"[11] filled in for the rabbi who had passed away; he tried to continue the tradition of good relations with the townspeople. And indeed the *Dayan* was a God-fearing Jew, a seeker of justice who was well liked by the people.

[Page 81]

Movements, Organizations and Parties

Parties and movements did not arise in the town all at once; rather, they developed fairly slowly, concentrating around either a single figure or a group of people who were dedicated to a particular idea and who tried to find members who would be faithful to it. I recall that this is how R. Feibush Lipka z.l. and R. Hirsh Wolf Laks initially represented the movements "Hibbat Tziyon"[12] and "Hamizrachi"[13], respectively. Small groups represented the "Poalei Tziyon" party on the one hand, and the "Bund" on the other. It was only after World War I ended that the activities of these movements and parties intensified and their membership increased.

The Balfour Declaration served as a stimulus to organize a large Zionist movement, headed by R. Yitzhak Moshe Offenbach z.l., a prominent figure in Dobrzyn; the Zionist concept was deeply ingrained in it. Zionist activity was concentrated in the club "*Hatechiya*"[14], which had been organized in

Shperling's house. In this club the elite of the young people of the town got together. On Sabbaths they would listen to the lectures of R. Yitzhak Moshe Offenbach z.l., mainly on Herzl-type Zionism, but also on various other topics. And similarly they would listen to the overviews presented by Aharon Zudkewitz, the representative of the young people. Every now and then invited speakers, including some from the Warsaw Center, would also appear in the club. In addition, the members took an active role in working on behalf of the Zionist funds: the Jewish National Fund and *Keren Hayesod*[15].

Another important activity that was conducted in the "*Hatechiya*" Club was familiarizing the young people with the Hebrew language. Among those who taught night courses was Mr. Shaul Blum, the son-in-law of R. Nisan Melamed. (Later on he taught Hebrew to the well-known Polish writers Pszuwieszewski and Zeromski[16], who lived in Danzig.) The living spirit behind this education of the youth was Mendel Sonabend, who dedicated his utmost energy and talent to enhancing the prestige of the Zionist youth of the town. His good humor and skill were deeply appreciated by the young people with whom he toiled to prepare performances, particularly just before the traditional holidays. Standing at his side in this praiseworthy work was Esther Kranz-Groner.

In that period a scout movement was also organized. It was led by Shmuel Baruch Rusk. After a short period of activity Rusk left Poland, and the scout movement was transformed into the "Hashomer Hatzair"[17] movement. I recall the first "*ken*"[18] that was set up in Elka-Chana's house. Here we gathered together, mainly on Sabbaths, for various cultural activities: group singing, talks led by Hirsh Hartbrot z.l., and other things. The hall was always too small for everyone to fit into, and many of us wound up standing outside. Other movements that grew out of this one included "Hechalutz"[19] and later the sports club "Hakoach"[20].

[Page 82]

Hechalutz

In the early 1920s, with the spread of the "Hechalutz" movement throughout all of Poland, a branch of the movement was also set up in Dobrzyn. The beginning of its establishment is connected with the lecture by Pinchas Rashish, from the Warsaw Center, who passed through the towns of Poland lecturing on the political platform of "Hechalutz" and working to establish branches of the movement. (Footnote: P. Rashish later served for many years as the mayor of Petah Tikva, Israel.) The response was strong, and many joined the movement as members. The main activity of "Hechalutz" was preparing the young people for Aliya and ensuring that they obtain entry visas ("certificates") to the Land of Israel. Later, *Hachshara*[21] centers were established for those who were candidates for Aliya. (Footnote: The first group from Dobrzyn that immigrated to the Land in the early 1920s did not actually have the opportunity to go through the "melting pot" of *Hachshara*. Was the failure of some of them to take root in the Land possibly attributable to the fact that they did not experience *Hachshara*?!)

The members of the branch in Dobrzyn took part in all the activities of "Hechalutz", carrying out all the instructions they received from the Center in Warsaw. We were always alert to take action, and we followed the instructions that we were given swiftly and precisely. I recall how we were once given a difficult mission: collecting a large sum of money for the Center (500 zloty, an enormous amount of money for our small branch[22]), and we were able to do so, although not very easily. We invested a great deal of hard work to come up with schemes to collect the requisite money. During our committee meeting one of the members suggested that we invite Kipnis and Zeligfeld, a pair of folk singers who were popular in our community and who were then living in the resort city of Czechocynk, to perform in the town. We worked very hard to organize this event, calculating the revenues and expenses, and distributing the tickets. It was with a great deal of trepidation that we took on this very serious obligation of bringing the pair of musicians to the town. But our great enthusiasm and confidence in the reputation of these singers throughout Poland served us well. And indeed our hopes were not dashed. The tickets, which had been given out to be distributed by representatives of the various organizations, were already sold out several days before the performance.

I recall how the town was decorated for this event as if for a holiday. The townspeople came to the evening performance dressed in their finest clothing.

The firemen's hall, an auditorium containing more than 600 seats, was completely full for the show. The performance by these artists was a great success, and we emerged rewarded: we covered the expenses, we sent the Center the requisite sum, and quite a respectable amount of money was actually left over for our own treasury. This successful activity was met with great approval in all the surrounding towns.

Among the other acts to benefit "Hechalutz", we should also mention our activity in organizing *Hachshara*. When the Warsaw "Hechalutz" Committee made the decision to establish centers of *Hachshara*, training camps for pioneers who intended to immigrate to the Land of Israel, the estate owners of Dobrzyn, influenced by our local branch, were the first to provide places on their land for young pioneers. May R. Yitzhak Yaakov Szmiga be remembered favorably for allowing pioneers from all over Poland to be sent to his estate "Szitna"[23]. His concern and that of his family for these young people was not forgotten by them even many years later, when I ran into them in Israel. They remembered very well the sympathetic attitude that they got not only from the owners of the estate, but from the all the people of Dobrzyn.

With the development of the pioneer movement in Poland the number of members of our branch rose, and with it also the demand for entry certificates to the Land. Obviously it was not possible to satisfy the increasing demand for certificates, especially after our branch's standing was somewhat weakened with the failure of some of our first pioneers to acclimate and be absorbed. I myself was already in the Land then, and although I did my best to try to dissuade these comrades from their hasty step, I was not successful; they returned to Poland, and they were among the millions who were cut down.

[Page 84]

The Sports Club "Hakoach"

In the early 1920s a group of young people took the incentive to lay the foundation for a sports club in our town. Within a short period of time dozens signed up for membership, and football [soccer] players were selected from among them. Very quickly these players learned the rules of the game, and they distinguished themselves in their ability to score a goal. Their first win against the veteran local Polish team was a surprise to the spectators. Our team continued to improve, and it was considered one of the best in the entire area; nevertheless, it had to struggle hard to endure, since initially all its revenues derived from membership fees only. Its survival was ultimately ensured by money raised from Chanukah and Purim parties that were very popular in the town.

[Page 85]

Education

Until the early 1920s, no substantial educational institutions had been generated in our town, with the exception of several "*cheders*"[24], run by "*melamdim*"[25] who taught the little children to read at an early age; and then, as the children grew older, the *melamdim* taught them *chumash*[26] with Rashi's commentary. They were taught each word of the text followed immediately by its translation, the translation being, of course, into Yiddish. Among the students, there were those who continued their education by studying *gemara*[27] with renowned *melamdim* who were sharp and proficient; among them were: R. Nissan Melamed, R. Tanna Levinson, R. Yisrael Shimon, R. Beryl, and others. On Sabbaths the rabbi of the town, together with several of the esteemed members of the community—men learned in the study of Torah—would test the achievement level of these students. The names of those who excelled were on everyone's lips, the townspeople being extremely proud of them.

There was a school for studying the Yiddish language and arithmetic; it belonged to R. Abba Yosef, a dedicated teacher and a very likeable person, who provided his students with the basic knowledge of reading and writing in Yiddish. For many years this school was located in the home of Rachel Leah Cohen. After World War I ended, a reformed[28] *cheder* was established by the brothers Mendel and Avraham-Hirsh Kohn; it introduced a variety of new teaching methods.

At the beginning of the 1920s the first elementary school, with all eight grades, was established under the administration of Hartman, a teacher from Warsaw. Many of the graduates from this school continued their education in high schools outside Dobrzyn; and some of them even succeeded in studying in universities and in obtaining degrees far beyond the borders of Poland.

Trade and Craft

As in most of the towns of Poland, trade in Dobrzyn was concentrated in Jewish hands. The Jews dominated here in the trade of wheat, textiles, wood and leather, and in the trade of grocery items. The Gentiles stayed away from these sectors, shying away from competing with Jews who were experienced in them. The farmers of the area, who came to the town on market days, went to the Jewish stores to shop, trusting those merchants with whom they had established connections of friendship. This tradition of connections with merchants was passed down from father to son within the farmers' families, who knew the shopkeepers by their special nicknames. When—after Poland achieved its rebirth[29]—a business boycott against Jewish merchants was proclaimed and anti-Semitism spread throughout the entire country, the farmers from the area tried to maintain business connections with the Jews, in spite of threats made by Polish vandals.

The Jewish wagon drivers, who delivered supplies from far away, played a special role in the business of the town. To sustain their families, they wound their way along the roads for days and weeks on end, transporting their heavy loads, whether during the deep winter frost or in the blazing summer sun. How truly noble these simple Jews were: when, completely exhausted after their long journeys, they would bring their heavily loaded wagons back on a Friday afternoon, they would still take the trouble to change out of their unattractive clothing and put on their Sabbath best, rushing to the synagogue or *shtiebel* for *Kabbalat Shabbat*[30].

The number of craftsmen in Dobrzyn was small. Blacksmithing, locksmithing and carpentry were almost not at all within the line of work of the Jews of the town. Because of their contempt for these professions, Jewish parents avoided sending their children to serve as apprentices to Polish craftsman. The lines of work that were acceptable to the Jewish middle class were watchmaking, sewing, and silversmith work. There were also professions that were considered less desirable and that were adopted by the poorer people who were part of the working class. If indeed the latter may have been viewed as a specific group from a social standpoint, in their day-to-day lives they were not set apart from the other residents of the town. Reuven the shoemaker and his children; Sina the tailor and others—may they be remembered favorably, for they were well liked by the townspeople for their honesty and integrity. They and their children were happy with their lot and lived peaceful lives in the town. One generation followed another, yet the town practically did not change its appearance: the quiet and tranquility so characteristic of the town were reflected in its inhabitants' way of life.

Many generations could have recounted stories about figures who worked for the public benefit in various ways, whether in maintaining the ethics of the town or in ensuring mutual aid; so too they could have told about the pious women who oversaw the anonymous giving of charity. The women volunteers who worked at the beginning of the twentieth century to help the poor and needy of the town deserve much appreciation; they include: Rivka Aleksander z.l., who passed away in the United States, and Sarah and Chana Lichtenfeld, z.l., who did not spare themselves any toil in their concern to provide clothing and money for the needy. Their dedication to those who were suffering and in need was boundless. Much more could be recounted about the self-sacrifice of these two wonderful individuals, who during their lives made a name for themselves by supporting the impoverished of the town. May the memory of their deeds endure forever.

The town of Dobrzyn was not one of the larger towns, and its Jewish community was not one of the most distinguished among the Jewish communities in the Exile; yet even in it exemplary Jewish lives existed, lives full of activity and charm, of which a great deal could be recounted.

The end descended upon the town, sealing it like a grave. But under the ashes of destruction the coals of remembrance are still glowing: a memory of a past spanning hundreds of years, a memorial that will last forever and will never be left abandoned.

A "Poalei Tzion" group[31]

The football team "Hakoach"[32]

From right to left and back to front: Row 1: **Aharon Zudkewitz, Menashe Dobroszklanka, Hersh Topol, Nisan Fogel, Giorg Riesenfeld, Avraham Lipka**

Row 2: **Yosef Turkewitz, Leib Szeinbart, Avraham Dor (Dobroszklanka)**

Row 3: **Aharon Lipka, Yosef Shperling, Mordechai Goldberg**

Translator's Footnotes

1. From *My Town: In Memory of the Communities Dobrzyn-Gollob*, edited by M. Harpaz, (published by the Dobrzyn-Golub Society, Israel, 1969), pp. 79-86.

2. "Congress Poland" was the unofficial name of the semi-autonomous Kingdom of Poland that was part of the Russian Empire during the period 1815-1915. The appellation "Congress" originates from the Congress of Vienna (1814-15),

in which the partition of Eastern Europe was decided upon. See the following Web site (retrieved August, 2015):
https://en.wikipedia.org/wiki/Congress_Poland

3. Hebrew: *maggidim* (itinerant preachers who castigated their audiences for unethical behavior, and often accompanied their reproaches with terrifying descriptions of punishment in the afterlife) and darshanim (preachers who specialized in Midrashic interpretation and allegory). The two terms were sometimes used interchangeably. The preachers would receive donations from the townspeople for their lectures. See the following Website (retrieved August, 2015): https://en.wikipedia.org/wiki/Maggid

4. A small prayer house of the Otwock Hassidim

5. Mitzvah = good deed (literally the fulfilment of a [Torah] commandment)

6. z.l. = abbreviation for *zichrono livracha* (= of blessed memory)

7. *Beit Midrash* = usually a study hall for religious study; in Dobrzyn there was a Beit Midrash that was used exclusively for prayer services.

8. *Mikva* = ritual bath

9. The *Bund* was an evolving Jewish socialist/Marxist organization that supported cultural autonomy for the Jews within the countries of Eastern Europe, rather than a homeland in Palestine. It also favored Yiddish, rather than Hebrew, as the cultural language of the Jews.

10. *Poalei-Tzion* = Workers of Zion, or Zionist Workers, a Jewish Marxist-Zionist party. See the following Web site (retrieved August 2015) for more information: https://en.wikipedia.org/wiki/Poale_Zion.

11. *Dayan* = judge in legal disputes.

12. *Hibbat-Tzion* = Love of Zion, also known as *Hovevei Tzion* = Lovers of Zion, Jewish religious groups organized in Eastern Europe in the late 19th century to promote Jewish immigration to the Land of Israel. They are considered the forerunners of the Zionist movement. See the following link (retrieved August, 2015): https://en.wikipedia.org/wiki/Hovevei_Zion

13. Mizrachi = the religious Zionist movement and party. See the following link (retrieved August, 2015):
https://en.wikipedia.org/wiki/Mizrachi_%28religious_Zionism%29

14. *Hatechiya* = the revival

15. *Keren HaYesod* = The Foundation Fund, a Zionist fundraising organization established in 1920 to support the immigration of Jews to the Land of Israel. See the following link (retrieved August, 2015):
https://en.wikipedia.org/wiki/Keren_Hayesod#The_pre-state_era

16. The second writer referred to is probably Stefan Żeromski (1864-1925), a Polish novelist. See the following web page (retrieved September, 2015): https://en.wikipedia.org/wiki/Stefan_%C5%BBeromski.

17. *Hashomer Hatzair* = The Youth Guard (Hebrew). See the following link (retrieved August, 2015): https://en.wikipedia.org/wiki/Hashomer_Hatzair. See also C. Lord, Hashomer Hatzair, pp. 95-101 of this volume (reference cited in Footnote 1).

18. *ken* = literally nest (Hebrew), equivalent to a local branch of the Shomer Hatzair movement

19. *Hechalutz* = the pioneer

20. *Hakoach* = the force

21. *Hachshara* = training in work to prepare for the move to Palestine

22. In c. 1930, 500 zloty was worth US $130, which, taking inflation into account, would be equivalent to approximately US $2000 in 2015.

23. On Szmiga and his Szitna estate see "The Synagogues and Shtiebels in Dobrzyn", pp. 264-269; also Dzialdow and Sanger, "Religious Life in Dobrzyn," pp. 284-291, both in this volume (reference cited in Footnote 1).

24. *cheder* = boys' school, where the curriculum was dominated by religious studies

25. Plural of *melamed* = teacher of small children

26. *Chumash* = Pentateuch

27. *Gemara* = Talmud

28. Hebrew *metukan*, i.e. revised to be more modern

29. Around 1920

30. *Kabbalat Shabbat* = the synagogue service consisting of hymns and poetry, recited around sunset Friday evening, to welcome the Sabbath

31. From p. 81 of reference cited in Footnote 1

32. From p. 84 in reference cited in Footnote 1

[Pages 87-93]

Prayer and Torah institutions and Religious Ministrants in the town

by Yehudah Rozenwax

Translated by Sara Mages

A. The Synagogue

The synagogues, Batei HaMidrash, and the assembly of scholars were the glory of each Jewish town, and each and every member of the community was blessed with them. Indeed, in the harsh Diaspora, which sated her Jews with bitterness even during their so called days of "tranquility," the synagogues and Batei HaMidrash were a place of "spiritual importance," and every person poured his bitter words and his prayers in them.

Gathering next to the synagogue

Dobrzyn was also blessed with a big and handsome synagogue, which was the glory of the community. It was built in the 18th century, but for another purpose - a factory. The members of the community, who purchased it, gave it a grand look, as befits a Jewish synagogue.

Paintings, the work of artists, decorated its ceiling and its walls, and colorful stained glass windows, which drowned it with splendor of sacred tradition, adorned its windows. The colorful mosaic floor was very nice and was considered, at that time, to be a masterpiece. Above all stood the big and beautiful *Aron Hakodesh*, which was the focus of the worshipers' hearts.

[Page 88]

Also the women's gallery, which ran along three walls - south, west and north - was tastefully built and decorated with crystal lamps, as befits a modern synagogue.

The building itself stood on a high elevation, near the river, and was surrounded on all sides by a stone fence. The entrance leading to the synagogue was wide and astonishingly pretty.

The wedding ceremonies were held in the synagogue's courtyard, opposite the grand entrance, and the bride and groom were brought there from their homes accompanied by a large crowd. A band delighted the celebrators and a comedian scattered his sayings and jokes. Also the cantor didn't sit idle and sang in honor of the couple.

There was also a choir in the synagogue that accompanied the cantor in his prayer, and as it was proper and required, a conductor conducted it. I now recall two members of the choir who were its pillars: Moshe Schlesinger who now lives in the United States, and my late brother Yitzchak of blessed memory.

B. Beit HaMidrash

Beit HaMidrash served as a place for prayer and a place to study the Torah and the Gemara. They gathered there three times a day to pray, and studied the Torah in the hours between *Mincha* and *Ma'arive*. Most of those who came to Beit HaMidrash were craftsmen and just Jews, who came to pour their emotions, listen to a commentary on the Torah in order to forget their poverty, sufferings, and daily concerns.

On the Sabbath, the preachers preached before the congregation. Many times, preachers and scholars, who weren't local, appeared in Beit HaMidrash and managed to gather a large crowd who drank their words of wisdom and their teachings.

Indeed, the religious subjects that were studied together, were seasoned with words of morality. They pulled the hearts, warmed them, and awakened the community members to perform good deeds - to take care of the poor and the weak.

Beit HaMidrash was a gathering place not only for prayer and Torah study, but also a place for secular conversations, when everyone sought the closeness of the other and natured together their confidence and faith.

Beit HaMidrash, like the whole town, was erased from face of the earth by the malicious hand of the wild beast, Hitler's soldiers and their defiled helpers. The magnificent synagogue was also destroyed, and the cruel hand didn't skip the cemetery. Again, there is no marking on the graves of our beloved parents, brothers and sisters...

[Page 89]

C. Rabbis and Slaughterers

The Rabbinate was a very respectable position in the Jewish towns, and the rabbi had a significant influence on the community's life. Therefore, it is not surprising, that the election of a rabbi served as a debatable ground between the various sectors of society - especially among the Hassidim who belonged to different rabbinical courts.

And so it was in Dobrzyn that her Hassidim belonged to various rabbinical courts: Gur, Aleksander, Otvosk and more. Each group wanted to appoint one of its members as a rabbi, and that caused quarrels, strife and hatred, and soured the atmosphere in the town.

I remember the running around and the intensified struggle in our community after the death of Rabbi Sonabend, the righteous of blessed memory. Various rabbis appeared before the public with their sermons, to show their strength and their knowledge, because this is how a rabbi was examined. Due to these quarrels, the town was left for a long period of time without a leader. In addition, it wasn't easy to find someone worthy to assume the high office after HaRav Sonabend, who was one of the great Torah scholars of his generation.

The situation worsened when two rabbis, who didn't receive the community's appointment, settled in Dobrzyn. Even when I left the town, in 1925, on my way to Israel, there was still chaos in the town and a new rabbi wasn't elected.

Also the appointment of the slaughterers was accompanied by a struggle between the various Hasidic groups, each seeking to appoint one of their members. Indeed, tempers flared, from time to time, because of such natters, as if the members of our nation didn't lack worries, troubles and suffering, that were their lot in the Diaspora...

[Page 90]

The Jewish Education in Dobrzyn-Golub

(The "*Heder*", the "*Melamed*"-the Rabbi, and the advanced teacher)

Shmuel Meiri (Miniwski)

Translated by Sara Mages

"If you have learned much Torah, do not take credit for yourself---it is for this that you have been formed" [Ethics of the Fathers: Chapter 2:8]. This view, which saw the highest value of Torah study, was the guideline for the Hassidic education that grew and developed in Poland in the first half of the 19th century.

The teaching language in the old "*Heder*" was Yiddish, and the Hebrew language - the "Holy Language" was only a secondary study, because it was only intended for prayers by the "ordinary people," and for understanding the writings of the Holy Scriptures. The girls didn't go to school, and only later a separate school, "*Beit Yaakov*," was established for them.

Dobrzyn was renowned for its large number of old style "*Hadarim*," which were intended for students from prestigious rich families, or for students whose parents belonged to the "*Shtiebelekh*" of various rabbis.

A daring step to change these "long-standing practices" and the ancient tradition, which took root in the old "*Heder*," with all its faults and benefits, was done at the beginning of the 20th century with the establishment of "*Heder Metukan*" ["Reformed *Heder*"] by a small group of dignitaries from the city of Golub. This "*Heder*" was much more advanced, the study of the Hebrew language was added to its curriculum, and the teachers paid attention to the national-religious education. However, the existence of "*Heder Metukan*" was a bone of contention between the city treasurers and its leaders. Many of them saw it as a "dangerous *Heder*," improper, wasteful and non-Jewish in its nature. They boycotted it and fought against it with bigotry, war to the death…No wonder that the "*Heder Metukan*" couldn't hold out, and again, the old "*Heder*" for the children of the poor and the needy, remained in control.

According to tradition, at the end of the "period," during the intermediate days of Passover or Sukkot, the rabbi ran around, knocked on the doors of the parents, the masters and the benefactors, to get new students. The "*Melamdim*" [teachers] received tuition for each "period," and extra gifts for the holidays and festivities. The sons of the rich studied individually, sometimes with teachers in their own homes. However, the primary educational institute was the "*Heder*," which was located in the rabbi's home. The studies started early in the morning and continued until nightfall. The rabbi maintained a strict discipline and used punishment to deter those who violated the discipline, without all the educational measures that are in effect today.

[Page 91]

However, when we look back at the education in the old "*Heder*," which have become the laughingstock of the intellectuals of the previous generation, we have to admit that this "*Heder*," with all of its faults, was the forefather of the new school, in all of its forms and phases, in the Diaspora and in Israel. After all, it was the very basic concept of the elementary school. If not for this "*Heder*," the children of the ordinary people wouldn't have studied the Torah. As it is says in the Gemara about Yehoshua ben Gamla who ruled: "There should install teachers of small children in every district and town, and they should bring him at the ages six or upward…at the beginning, the one who has a father learns the Torah from him, and the one who has no father, won't learn the Torah…"

The old style "*Hadarim*" were located in the various Batei-HaMidrash of the Alexander and Gur rabbis, next to the synagogues, and mostly - in the rabbi's house. From early morning, young children, destitute children, and just Jewish children sat and learned the Torah and the prayers from the "*Melamed*" [teacher]. The textbook was the *Siddur*, and the studies merged with the prayers, which were said on the spot. It was a traditional religious education, in the holy language which was translated to Yiddish.

The students of the "*Heder*"- "*Yesod Hamala*"

From the right: Schlechter, Yehoshua Flusberg, Alter Piaskowski, and Avraham Natan Postolsky

[Page 92]

It is my duty to mention one old "*Heder*," the exemplary "*Heder*" of my relative, Rabbi Meir Fajwel, son of Yehudah Bromberg of blessed memory, who was a biblical scholar and an inspiration. He had a deep and sincere love for the abandoned, lonely, and the orphaned child. Innocence, nobility and greatness merged in him, in the modest R' Meir Fajwel, who taught the Torah in his "*Heder*" to the children who came from poor homes, and if not for him, they wouldn't have learned the Torah at all.

The headstone on his grave, in the old cemetery, is unique in its Hebrew style and content, kind of a tender elegy written in the language of our ancestors. It testifies to the magnitude of his soul, and the modesty of a person who dedicated his life to teach the Torah to the children of the poor.

The wife of Rabbi Meir Fajwel, Rachel Leah the "*Melamedet*" [female teacher], was a special person in the history of female teachers. She was endowed with special lofty qualities, and was her husband's helper. Indeed, she rewarded him well all of her life and it can be said that: "Her value is far beyond pearls, her husband's heart relies on her and he shall lack no fortune…" She divided her food between the hungry school children, who crowded in the room, dressed them and fed them.

I remember the time when the rabbi called his wife, the "*Melamedet*," to help a slow student. She sat him down at the table, that a Siddur was placed on, and whispered in a calm motherly voice "My child, if you learn well, the good angels will come to serve you! And now repeat *Aleph-Bet-Gimel*."

After the death of her husband she continued his life work as a "*Melamedet*" with great success.

Her three daughters; who absorbed the value of Judaism and love of humanity in their home, took care of sad incurable women, who were left widowed and lonely.

Their daughter, Pessie Bromberg, married the teacher Yitzchak Yaakov Lewiston, a progressive teacher who taught in the Polish State School (a great achievement for a Jew in those days). He taught the Russian and the Polish languages to the Jewish children, and also taught various religious and secular subjects to the students who came to his home in the afternoon.

[Page 93]

He used to open the school day with the song: "Children, we have gathered at school…" Of course, he was an excellent teacher, who projected his charming personality on his students. His body was weak, but his teaching ability was excellent. He wore a modern hat on his head and a small thin beard covered his pale face.

Many of his students are in Israel today, and some of them immortalized the community in this memorial book. Even today, they still remember his lovely, gentle and charming image and remember him with admiration, because his heart and his home were always open for them.

These teachers, and others like them, laid the foundation for the progressive schools. Afterwards, these schools were a source of inspiration for Judaism, and undaunted faith in the Jewish nation and the Land of Israel.

A class at school

[Page 94]

The Beginning of the Establishment of the *Bund*[1]

by Yaakov Gorni

Translated by Allen Flusberg

Note by translator: in the original, this article appears to be a translation, into Hebrew, of the Yiddish article appearing on pp. 298-299 of the reference cited in Footnote 1.

Translator's Footnote

1. From *My Town: In Memory of the Communities Dobrzyn-Gollob*, edited by M. Harpaz, (published by the Dobrzyn-Golub Society, Israel, 1969), p. 94.

[Page 95]

Hashomer Hatzair[1][2]
by Chaim Lord
Translated by Allen Flusberg

Our town was never considered a large residential area; after all, it numbered only a few thousand Jews. It was surrounded by mountains—the mountains of Golub—as well as by woods and forests. The Dreventz[3] River traversed it, adding a lovely touch of tranquility. Nevertheless, even this small town was not a greenhouse, isolated from the winds and storms that were raging through the world. The new ideas that were spreading like wildfire between the two World Wars—the period during which our/my generation grew up—reached and penetrated into our little town, as well.

From a social standpoint, the Jews of the town had never been divided by class, as determined by property ownership, but rather by their viewpoints and beliefs: that is, their ideologies. Thus our parents' generation was split between the Hassidim of Gur[4] and those of Aleksander[5], or between those who attended prayer services in the synagogue and those who attended them in the *Beit Midrash*[6].

Nor were the secular of the town all cut from the same cloth. On the contrary—they were a veritable rainbow of opinions and beliefs: Folkists[7], Bundists[8], General Zionists[9] and even Communists. Many a time the struggle between the various ideological groups stirred the town up, shaking it awake from its tranquility and serenity.

When I was very young, I myself found my way to the Hashomer Hatzair movement. The year was 1929, and I happened to attend a Purim[10] party given by the movement's *ken*[11]. The party took place in Goldman's house, which was located not far from the Prum bakery.

That year is engraved in my heart not only because it was then that I joined the movement, but also because it was the very year of the shocking massacre of the Jews of Hebron[12]. I remember, as if it happened just yesterday, how the Jews of our town gathered in the synagogue to pray, all together, in solidarity with the souls of those who had been slaughtered.

What was the experience like of being in the *ken* in those days? What did we do when we used to regularly get together? Generally we spent the time singing as a group—sitting around and singing songs of the Land, songs of longing for youngsters who were dreaming about Aliyah and about a very different life. The *Oneg Shabbat*[13] parties were particularly charming, as were the games we played and the many outings we took. These activities would unify and embolden us.

We received a great deal of support and encouragement from several patrons. Their outlook may actually have been very different from ours, but that did not stop them from standing up for us and helping us out in various ways. It is likely they preferred to see the young people of the town spending their time in the Hashomer Hatzair movement—dedicating their free time to thought and to Jewish/Israel activities, looking forward to immigrating to the Land—rather than wasting their time.

I would like to mention here that among these patrons were the following families: Offenbach, Ruda[14] and Riesenfeld[15]; and especially the youngest among them, Meir Kszeczanowski and his family. Indeed it is hard to imagine how the Shomer *ken* would have persisted without Meir Kszeczanowski's help; he stood at our side with advice and guidance and never ceased to encourage us. He was frail in body; but that did not prevent him from being dedicated, with all his might, to the activities of the movement. And throughout he was longing to fulfil his dream of going on Aliyah to the Land of Israel.

The 1930s were difficult years for the Jews of Poland, a period during which anti-Semitism was intensifying, casting a shadow of fear and terror over the Jewish communities—particularly after Hitler's rise to power in Germany.

This was reflected in Golub, where a flag bearing a swastika flew over the German school, portending dark troubles for us...In Dobrzyn itself the *Endek* (ND[16]) movement spread; their members had no compunctions about conducting pogroms against the Jews. Thus, for example, [in Dobrzyn] they went out to demonstrate in a procession after the events of Przytyk[17]; this procession ended with the smashing of shop windows of Jewish-owned businesses.

I still recall this pogrom, as if it happened just yesterday: The *Endek* procession passed along the "Street of Gold"[18], where the Jewish shops were located; they smashed the shop windows one after another, terrifying the Jews. And indeed, the Jews were at that time holed up in their own houses, afraid to show their faces outside.

The only ones who were not intimidated by the *Endek*s and who were not hiding in their houses were the members of Hashomer Hatzair, who still gathered together in the *ken* and continued to engage in their educational–cultural activity. We were prepared to display our might to the *Endek* hooligans and to use additional methods of self–defense; we were determined to not shut ourselves up in our houses.

Even graver and particularly depressing was our feeling that we teenagers had no future in our town. Children of the wealthy families, only few in number, left for the nearby cities to study in high school. Others, whose parents could afford to help them out, immigrated to countries on the other side of the ocean: the United States and Canada. Meanwhile, the rest of us, the ordinary people, were forced to join our parents' meager businesses after we completed elementary school. These businesses consisted of shops and open stands in the marketplace. Some of us continued on in their fathers' professions: tailoring, shoemaking, painting and carpentry.

One of the principles on which we were educated in the Hashomer Hatzair movement was that of productivity—that is, acquiring productive professions that had the potential to change the economic–social structure of our people. However, it was particularly difficult to find someone skilled in a profession who would accept Jewish apprentices for training. I remember once going out of my way to approach an exceptionally good, non–Jewish professional painter, requesting that he would take me on to teach me the trade. But he refused to accept me.

In the Jewish town they looked upon professional workers with disdain; as a result, those young people who sought to learn a profession found the path they were on to be laden with hardships. I recall how Yosef Siskind's mother, Chana of blessed memory, approached me, pleading that I should convince her son to give up his intention to learn to be a shoemaker. At the time her son Yosef was about to leave for *hachshara*[19]. She was quite puzzled by this aspiration of his, which she viewed as inappropriate for their well–off family. In those days laboring with one's hands was considered a stain on a family's reputation.

I will not forget the bold impression made on us by the *hachshara* members of Kibbutz "Hayotzrim"[20]. Today some of them are to be found in Kfar Masaryk[21], and among them: Yitzhak Sperling, as well as Nechama and Tzadok Zudkewitz. However, the members of this *hachshara* group spent only a very short time in our town, since it was difficult for them to find work there. But even their short stay in the town aroused excitement and pride in us. It was no small matter to see Jewish young women toiling at sawing logs in the courtyards of houses that belonged to Jews.

Our instructors were, of course, the backbone of the movement and the guiding spirit of the ken. Several of them had a profound influence on me. I am very pleased that, although not all of them are in Hashomer Hatzair kibbutzim, all are living in Israel.

I vividly remember Shoshana Offenbach, whose maternal attitude to us members of the "Kfirim" troop is engraved deeply in my heart to this very day. She was always there for us with an attentive ear and a sensitive heart, and so her very presence would make us feel good.

Years later, when I got older and became the administrator of the *ken*, I once happened to be leafing through old meeting minutes and found that when Shoshana was responsible for the secretariat everything was extremely organized. Indeed, she was not only sympathetic and maternal, but also well organized, wise and responsible.

When I think back about Avraham Rosen, memories of the *Oneg Shabbat* parties come back to me. During these parties, which took place at dusk, he would sing Hassidic melodies in a pleasant, passionate voice that would overwhelm even us youngsters.

Each of us would usually bring fruit or candy to this party from home, according to his means; and afterwards we would sit down for a common "meal". These parties implanted in us the first seeds of cooperative living, since each of us was taught to bring whatever food he had available to the "table" we shared.

We were very fond of Yaakov Lipka for his likeable temper and for his riveting stories about the Shomer in the Land. I remember these stories to this very day. He got special affection from us for the lumber yard owned by his parents. He gave us permission to use it, and there we were able to engage in various outdoor sports.

The very first flag of the group was embroidered by Minja. It was a red, silk flag embroidered with sheaves and below them the name "Ruth". How enchanted we were by this flag, and how we were filled with pride whenever we waved it!

There is no doubt that the graduates' leaving for *hachshara* and their immigration to the Land had a definitive influence on the formation of our personalities. Personal example served as the most powerful educational factor.

I recall how great the influence on us was of the bon–voyage parties that we made for the group leaders when they left for *hachshara*, or when they left for Aliyah to the Land of Israel. Afterwards we would read their letters with excitement and jealousy, since we were filled with the desire and anticipation of being just like them. Their tribulations through *hachshara*, their meanderings on their way to the Land of Israel, their adventures in Aliyah Bet[22] or during the World War that had broken out, all fed our imaginations for a long time.

It would be difficult to describe the ideological convergence of the members of our *ken* without mentioning the welcome influence of Yisrael Shleifstein (now known as Lahav), currently a member of Kibbutz Mizra[23], who was sent to us in the role of a *shaliach*[24] and as a Hebrew teacher. His serious attitude to our studies and his in–depth approach to ideological problems awakened in us a strong desire to increase our knowledge, so that we could use our critical approach on contemporary issues. And indeed this preparation helped us afterwards when we had to take part in stormy debates with members of other movements, particularly non–Zionist leftists.

The Zionist activities of our *ken* were extensive. We participated in all the activities of the Zionist movement: organizing meetings for *Keren Hayesod*[25]; selling "shekels"[26]; and collecting money for the Jewish National Fund, something we always excelled at and invariably led in.

I recall those conferences that we helped organize; crowds of Jews of the town attended them to find out what was going on in the Land of Israel. And among the noteworthy speakers were: Bialopolski[27], Dr. Schiper[28] and Gross–Zimmerman[29].

We worked hard to distribute the newspaper of *Eretz Yisrael Haovedet*[30], and we did much to support the existence and expansion of the Shalom Aleichem town library. Indeed, I spent a good deal of my adolescent years in this library, expanding and improving my knowledge.

It is fitting to mention here those who aided us in founding and developing the library: Eliezer Zaklikowski (Lozar)[31], Aharon Holtz, the Fein family, as well as others. Within the framework of the library there were also cultural evenings that were dedicated to various literary topics.

Organizationally our *ken* belonged to the Mława[32] regional branch; we obtained our educational directives from both the regional administration and from the head administration in Warsaw.

Some of our members were sent to summer camps in the vicinity of Ciechanow[33], where they spent several weeks in the forests. These get-togethers contributed greatly to expanding their horizons and their idealistic base, as well as to creating ties with new comrades. And most important, we returned afterwards with renewed energy to being active in the movement.

I myself also participated in a national seminar for instructors near Warsaw. Janusz Korczak, the renowned educator, the children's friend, took part in this seminar. Later, during the Holocaust, he refused to abandon the children he was responsible for and went up into the train cars of death with them.[34]

In this seminar there had gathered together those who were expected to take the reins of leadership into their hands just before the war broke out. Among them were the comrades of Mordechai Anielewicz[35], the hero of the Warsaw Ghetto. They headed the people's struggle until the very last moments of their lives.

The members of my group were drafted into the [Polish] army the year before I was drafted. They were in active service when the war broke out. Nearly all of them were killed on the battlefields.

Just before the war broke out, I myself left for *hachshara* in Rovno[36], a city in the Wolyn district, on the Russian–Polish border. The war found me there when I felt its impact as we were being bombarded from the air by the Germans. Hundreds of thousands of refugees with just the shirts on their backs flocked to the city, terrified and desperate. Among them was our comrade Shimshon, who was so completely worn out and exhausted that it was difficult to even recognize him.

Then the eastern region of Poland was occupied by the Russians, and the local inhabitants welcomed the Red Army with joy. But I was concerned throughout about the fate of my family and sought ways to immigrate to the Land of Israel as soon as possible. I believed that if I could steal across the border to Romania I would find a way to continue on from there.

Days of wandering south, in trains and even on foot, ensued. I travelled via Lwów[37], Stanisławów[38] and Kołomyja[39]. One rainy autumn night I somehow managed to reach Romania via back roads in the Carpathian mountains.

I stayed in Romania an entire year, leading the life of a refugee. I was thrown into prison, threatened with being drafted into the Polish army, and lived in dread of the Germans, who had already made their appearance at the outskirts of Bucharest. Finally, at the very last moment, just before Romania was conquered by the Germans, I was able to get away and immigrate to the Land.

Nor did my aliyah take place smoothly, "in tranquil waters"[40]...The ships of the Italian navy were already dominating the Mediterranean Sea, while the British ships were retreating towards Alexandria from their bases in this area. After two weeks of sailing in cargo ships within a British military convoy, we reached the port of Alexandria, and from there to the port of Haifa in the Land of Israel.

Leaders of Hashomer Hatzair
On the left: **Meir Kszeczanowski (head of the *ken* [local branch])**[41]

The Keren–Kayemet [Jewish National Fund] committee of Dobrzyn

Standing: **Florman, Yaakov; Rosen, Avraham; Kszeczanowski, Meir; Lipka, Meir**
Sitting: **Florman, Menashe; Bielewski, Yaakov; Waldenberg, Yehuda**[42]

Graduates of Hashomer Hatzair of Dobrzyn[43]

Translator's Footnotes

1. From *My Town: In Memory of the Communities Dobrzyn–Gollob*, edited by M. Harpaz, (published by the Dobrzyn–Golub Society, Israel, 1969), pp. 95–101.

2. *Hashomer Hatzair* = The Youth Guard (Hebrew). See the following link (retrieved May, 2015): http://en.wikipedia.org/wiki/Hashomer_Hatzair

3. Polish Drwęc (pronounced Dreventz)

4. Ger = a Hassidic group that had many adherents in Dobrzyn ("Ger" being Hebraicized to "Gur"). See the following link (retrieved May, 2015): http://en.wikipedia.org/wiki/Ger_%28Hasidic_dynasty%29

5. Aleksander (or Alexander) is the name of a Hassidic group that had many adherents in Dobrzyn. See the following link (retrieved May, 2015): http://en.wikipedia.org/wiki/Aleksander_(Hasidic_dynasty)

6. *Beit Midrash* = study hall, where men sit to study religious books, and prayer services are sometimes held, as well. In Dobrzyn there was one *Beit Midrash* that was used exclusively for prayer services.

7. The Jewish *Folkists* (sometimes spelled *Volkists*) supported a Jewish cultural nationalism, with Yiddish as the national language of the Jews, within the

countries of Eastern Europe. Unlike the *Bundists* (whose platform was otherwise similar), they opposed Marxism and socialism. See the following link (retrieved May, 2015): http://en.wikipedia.org/wiki/Folkspartei

8. See previous footnote; also the following link (retrieved May, 2015): http://en.wikipedia.org/wiki/Bundism

9. *Tzioni–Klali* = General Zionist, a Zionist party that was not affiliated with either the Social Zionists or the Religious Zionists. In the 1930s it split into two factions, one favoring cautious cooperation with the British in Palestine and the other advocating stronger opposition. See R. Medoff and C. Waxman, *The A to Z of Zionism*, "General Zionists" (Scarecrow Press, 2009).

10. Purim = a joyful holiday commemorating the survival of the Jews of Persia after being threatened with destruction by their enemies, according to the account in the Biblical Book of Esther. It occurs in February or March, exactly one month before Passover, and is often celebrated with costumes and disguises.

11. *ken* = literally nest (Hebrew), equivalent to a local branch of the Shomer Hatzair movement

12. See the following link (retrieved May, 2015): http://en.wikipedia.org/wiki/1929_Hebron_massacre.

13. *Oneg Shabbat* = a celebration at the conclusion of the Jewish Sabbath (Hebrew: Sabbath delight)

14. For a biography of Ruda, see article on pp. 171–173 of reference cited in Footnote 1.

15. For biographies of Riesenfeld, see articles on pp. 193–200 and 439–442 of reference cited in Footnote 1.

16. ND = *Narodowa Demokracja* = National Democracy, an anti–Semitic Polish political party. Its members and followers were referred to as Endeks (equivalent to 'NDers').

17. Przytyk is a town in central Poland, about 300 km southeast of Dobrzyn. For more information on the pogrom and riots that took place there in March, 1936, see the following link (retrieved May, 2015): http://en.wikipedia.org/wiki/Przytyk_pogrom. The pogrom was viewed by the *Endeks* as violence that had been instigated by the Jews.

18. Golden Street, or Street of Gold (called *Die Goldene Gass* in Yiddish). See map of Dobrzyn–Golub, pp. 8–9 of reference cited in Footnote 1.

19. *Hachshara* = training in work to prepare for the move to Palestine

20. Kibbutz Shomrat (~3km north of Akko, Israel) occupies the original site of Kibbutz Hayotzrim.

21. Kfar Masaryk is a kibbutz in the Western Galilee in northern Israel. See the following link (retrieved May, 2015): http://en.wikipedia.org/wiki/Kfar_Masaryk

22. Aliyah Bet (i.e., Aliyah 'B') = illegal immigration to British Mandate Palestine beginning in 1934. See the following link (retrieved June, 2015): https://en.wikipedia.org/wiki/Aliyah_Bet

23. Kibbutz Mizra, founded in 1923, is located in the Jezreel Valley in Northern Israel. See the following link (retrieved June, 2015): https://en.wikipedia.org/wiki/Mizra. The following link (in Hebrew), retrieved June, 2015, contains a short biography of Yisrael Lahav (Shleifstein): http://mizra.org.il/he/content/318

24. *Shaliach* = a delegate from the Land of Israel sent to educate the local Jewish population

25. *Keren HaYesod* = The Foundation Fund (Hebrew), a Zionist fundraising organization, established in 1920, to support the immigration of Jews to the Land of Israel. See the following link (retrieved April, 2015): http://en.wikipedia.org/wiki/Keren_Hayesod#The_pre-state_era

26. The "shekels" referred to here were symbolic banknotes that were sold throughout all Jewish communities. Purchasers obtained the right to vote for delegates to the Zionist Congress, while the number of delegates from each country was determined by the number of shekels sold there. The money raised by the sale supported Zionist activities. See, for example, JTA, "Election Day in Palestine: Thirty Thousand Shekel Payers Electing 30 Delegates to Zionist Congress," (May 26, 1931), available at the following link (retrieved April, 2015): http://www.jewishgen.org/yizkor/ostrow/ost298.html http://www.jta.org/1931/05/26/archive/election-day-in-palestine-thirty-thousand-shekel-payers-electing-30-delegates-to-zionist-congress

27. Abraham Bialopolski, a Zionist leader in Poland. See "The Poale Zion (Z. S.) party as depicted in the party newspapers," by M. Hamfer., p. 263 of Bedzin, Poland Yizkor Book (*Pinkes Bendin*, Edited by A. Sh. Stein, Association of Former Residents of Bedzin in Israel, Tel Aviv, 1959); English translation by Lance Ackerfeld reproduced in the following link (retrieved June 2015): http://www.jewishgen.org/Yizkor/bedzin/Bedzin.html#TOC-part

28. Yitzchak (Ignacy) Schiper or Schipper (1884–1943), a Jewish historian and Zionist who served as a representative in the Polish parliament. He perished in Majdanek in the Holocaust. See the following link (retrieved June 2015): http://www.yivoencyclopedia.org/article.aspx/Schiper_Ignacy

29. Moshe Gross–Zimmerman, a Polish–Jewish (later Israeli) writer on the subject of Yiddish and Hebrew literature. See the following link in Hebrew (retrieved June, 2015): http://www.tidhar.tourolib.org/files/tidhar/index/assoc/HASH019c.dir/images/V05_178.jpg

30. *Eretz Yisrael Haovedet* = Working Israel (Hebrew), a general term used for the Jewish labor movement and its institutions in British Mandate Palestine

31. Zaklikowsli's photograph appears on p. 301 of the reference cited in Footnote 1.

32. Mlawa is located ~100km east of Dobrzyn

33. Ciechanow is located ~130km east of Dobrzyn

34. See the following website (retrieved June, 2015) for more information: https://en.wikipedia.org/wiki/Janusz_Korczak

35. For more information see the following website (retrieved June, 2015): https://en.wikipedia.org/wiki/Mordechai_Anielewicz

36. Równe, Poland; now (2015) Rivne, in Ukraine, a town about 700 km southeast of Dobrzyn. It was occupied by the Russians in 1939.

37. Lwów (then in Poland) is presently (2015) known as Lviv, Ukraine

38. Stanisławów, Poland, present–day (2015) Stanislaviv, Ukraine, located ~130km south of Lviv

39. Kołomyja, Poland, present–day (2015) Kolomyya, Ukraine, 60km southeast of Stanislaviv. From there the Romanian border, via the Carpathian mountains, lies about 100km further south.

40. Hebrew *al mei menuchot* = by tranquil waters (paraphrasing Psalm 23:2)

41. From p. 96 of reference cited in Footnote 1. Caption written on photograph reads: Dobrzyn–Golub, 1933.

42. From p. 98 of reference cited in Footnote 1. Caption written on photograph reads: Keren–Kayemet Committee, Dobrzyn, 1930.

43. From p. 100 of reference cited in Footnote 1. Caption written on photograph reads: "Massada". With the first *Olim* [those who went on Aliyah]. Dobrzyn on the Dreventz, December 24, 1934.

[Page 102]

The Sholom-Aleichem Library[1]
by Chaim Lord
Translated by Allen Flusberg

The library in Dobrzyn, which was named after Sholom-Aleichem[2], served as the cultural and social center of the town. Several evenings every week, when the library was open, the young people would gather there. Sometimes it was just to spend time together and have friendly conversations; at other times it was to browse through books in the reading room; and at still other times it was to attend either a lecture or a debate on some contemporary issue.

However, it is difficult to describe the cultural and social activity of the young people in the town without referring to the library. It was there that they got together during evenings; it was also there that those who thirsted for knowledge—but did not have the means to study in a large city—acquired their education.

The library began as a covert facility in a time when libraries were regarded with suspicion by the Czarist regime of Russia. And indeed, in those days nationalist and social activity was associated with acquisition of knowledge, with reading the works of thinkers and revolutionaries whose writings were forbidden throughout the Russian empire.

At first the books were collected from various donors, particularly from the *Folkists*[3] and members of *Poalei-Tsion*[4], who had purchased them in Warsaw and Lodz and had contributed them to the library. As time passed the number of books ballooned. Most of them were in Yiddish and Polish, and later many were in Hebrew as well.

Fein, who was one of the Jewish communist activists in the town, ran the library, organizing it into various departments and guiding the readers with his advice. Sitting nearby to help him were: Menashe Florman (a *Tsioni-Klali*[5]), Meir Kaszczenowski and Shimshon Abramowitz (of *HaShomer HaTzair*[6]), and Eliezer Zelikowski (of *Poalei-Tsion*).

The library relied on a monthly membership fee, which gave members the right to borrow books and to participate in the various cultural activities that took place in the library auditorium. In addition, there were donors who supported the library with their contributions.

When I took over the administration of the library it already had more than 3,000 books and dozens of daily newspapers, as well as weekly and monthly magazines, that we received from various cities and countries. There were more than 100 members—a substantial number for such a small town—who were paying the membership fee every month.

Within this collection one could find works by the Yiddish writers Mendele Mocher-Sforim[7], Sholom-Aleichem, Peretz[8], and others. There were also translations into Yiddish of books on political economics, Marxism, etc.

I recall the library auditorium that was decorated with photographs of Sholom-Aleichem, Mapu[9] and Bialik[10]. This auditorium had about 200 seats in it. Here—particularly on Saturday nights—we held cultural evenings that were dedicated to book reviews or to literary discussions. For example, one evening was dedicated to Peretz Markish[11], while another was dedicated to Oscar Wilde's work, *The Picture of Dorian Gray*.

In the auditorium we also had many meetings that were dedicated to Zionist activity, whether to organize the distribution of shekels[12], or to hear a report from the Zionist congresses, or to hear from a delegate who had recently been in the Land of Israel what was happening there.

No one knows what became of the library during the Holocaust period. Most certainly it was destroyed, sharing the fate of the synagogues and Houses of Study of the town.

Movie night to benefit *Keren Kayemet*[13]

Right to left: **Yechiel Fogel, Freida Gorny, Tziporah Alberg, Azriel Dobraszklanka, Itta Rappaport, Lidzberski, Shmil-Baruch Rusk, Esther-Freida Prum**[14]

A letter sent by the administration of the Sholom-Aleichem Library in Dobrzyn to Wolff Lichtenfeld in Chicago[15]

Translator's Footnotes

1. From *My Town: In Memory of the Communities Dobrzyn-Gollob*, edited by M. Harpaz, (published by the Dobrzyn-Golub Society, Israel, 1969), pp. 102-104.

2. *Sholom Aleichem* was the pen name of the famous Yiddish author Sholom Rabinowitz (1859-1916).

3. The *Folkists* supported a Jewish cultural nationalism, with Yiddish as the national language of the Jews, within the countries of Eastern Europe. Unlike the *Bundists* (whose platform was otherwise similar), they opposed Marxism and socialism. See the following link:
http://en.wikipedia.org/wiki/Folkspartei.

4. *Poalei Tsion* = Workers of Zion, a Zionist Marxist-socialist organization and party (Labor Zionists). See the following link:
http://en.wikipedia.org/wiki/Poale_Zion.

5. *Tsioni-Klali* = General Zionist, a Zionist party that was not affiliated with either the Social Zionists or the Religious Zionists. In the 1930s it split into two factions, one favoring cautious cooperation with the British in Palestine and the other advocating stronger opposition. See R. Medoff and C. Waxman, *The A to Z of Zionism*, "General Zionists" (Scarecrow Press, 2009).

6. *HaShomer HaTzair* = The Youth Guard, a secular socialist-Zionist party that encouraged Jewish immigration to Palestine and communal living in kibbutzim. See the following link:
https://en.wikipedia.org/wiki/Hashomer_Hatzair

7. Mendele Mocher-Sforim =Mendele the Book Peddler, the pen name of Sholem Yaakov Abramovich (1835-1917), the first Yiddish novelist. See the following link: http://en.wikipedia.org/wiki/Mendele_Mocher_Sforim

8. I. L. Peretz (1852-1915) was a Yiddish-language author and playwright. See the following link: https://en.wikipedia.org/wiki/I._L._Peretz.

9. Abraham Mapu (1808-1867) was a Lithuanian Jewish author who wrote the first Hebrew novel. See the following link:
http://en.wikipedia.org/wiki/Abraham_Mapu.

10. Chaim Nachman Bialik (1873-1974) was a poet who wrote primarily in Hebrew. See the following link: https://en.wikipedia.org/wiki/Hayim_Nahman_Bialik.

11. Peretz Markish (1895-1952) was a Yiddish poet and playwright who lived in the Soviet Union. See the following link:
http://en.wikipedia.org/wiki/Peretz_Markish.

12. These "shekels" were symbolic banknotes that were sold throughout all Jewish communities. Purchasers obtained the right to vote for delegates to the Zionist Congress, while the number of delegates from each country was determined by the number of shekels sold there. The money raised by the sale supported Zionist activities. See the following link:
http://www.jewishvirtuallibrary.org/jsource/Zionism/shekel.html

13. *Keren Kayemet* (Hebrew) = Jewish National Fund, an organization that purchased and developed land in Palestine for the settlement of Jews there. See the following link: http://en.wikipedia.org/wiki/Jewish_National_Fund

14. From p. 103 of reference cited in Footnote 1.

15. From p. 104 of reference cited in Footnote 1. The letter, handwritten in Yiddish, reads as follows: Sholom-Aleichem Library, Dobrzyn on the Dreventz, August 8, 1922, to Mr. Wolff Lichtenfeld, Chicago. In the last committee session of the Sholom-Aleichem Library, we passed a resolution to contact members of ours who are now in America. We are now suffering a severe financial shortfall, which is making it difficult for us to develop the library, the only cultural institution in Dobrzyn, without support. We are therefore kindly requesting that you collect donations from among our members and other sympathizers whom you know, and that you send this money to us as quickly as possible at our address. We are arranging that you may also send it to the address "Riesenfeld Golub", for the "Dobrzyn Sholom-Aleichem Library". With the hope that you will fulfill our request as quickly as possible, respectfully, (signature).Secretary, Sholom-Aleichem Library.

[Pages 105-110]

The Struggle for Education in Our Town[1]
By Y. Wrzos
Translated by Allen Flusberg

Note by translator: in the original, this article appears to be a translation, into Hebrew, of the Yiddish article appearing on pp. 300-304. The following photographs appear within the pages of the Hebrew translation:

[Page 106]

Representatives of the town preparing for the Polish senate elections
In center: **Bolislav Warszawski and Henech Pinczewski**[2]

[Page 109]

Dobrzyn Land-of-Israel Office

Standing, from right: **Aharon Zudkiewic, Menashe Dobraszklanka, Shlomo Holtz**
Seated: **Aharon Holtz, Lemel Rujna, Yaakov Yechiel Bielowski, Mendel Prum, Nissan Fogel, Mordechai Goldberg**[3]

Young members of the Maccabee movement[4] in the town[5]

[Page 110]
Translator's Footnotes

1. From *My Town: In Memory of the Communities Dobrzyn-Gollob*, edited by M. Harpaz, (published by the Dobrzyn-Golub Society, Israel, 1969), pp. 105-110.

2. From p. 106 of reference cited in Footnote 1. The Polish caption reads: "Participants in a senate election. Dobrzyn on the Drwęc, 25 August 1935."

3. From p. 109 of reference cited in Footnote 1

4. Maccabee was a Zionist sports organization

5. From p. 109 of reference cited in Footnote 1

6. *Poalei Tsion* (Hebrew) = Workers of Zion, a Zionist Marxist-socialist organization and party (Labor Zionists). See the following link: http://en.wikipedia.org/wiki/Poale_Zion.

7. Dov Ber Borochov (1881-1917) was a Marxist Zionist. He was a founder and leader of the *Poalei Tsion* Labor Zionist movement. See the following link: http://en.wikipedia.org/wiki/Ber_Borochov

8. From p. 110 of reference cited in Footnote 1

A group of *Poalei Tsion*[6] members
(with a photograph of Borochov[7] at the center)[8]

[Page 112]

Spirit and Vision

[Pages 112-116]

On the Holidays[1]

by Yehuda Rosenwaks
Translated by Allen Flusberg

When the month of Elul[2] arrives, you immediately sense the special atmosphere that has enveloped the town, the atmosphere of the approaching *Yamim Noraim*[3]. The blasts of the shofar emerge and rise up out of the prayer houses, announcing the Day of Judgment[4] and encouraging the Jews to repent.

As yet there is no discernable change in the behavior and practices of the townspeople; all are still acting the same way they do the rest of the year. But once the days of the short *Selichot*[5] arrive, that apparent indifference melts away and disappears, and dread of Judgment Day places its mark upon every single person.

At the start of the third night-watch[6] the *shamash*[7] begins to drag his feet from one house to the next, tapping his small hammer on the walls to arouse the Jews and get them out of bed, as he announces in the traditional tune: "Awaken, awaken; rise up for *Selichot*!"

Even those shopkeepers who are busy all year round in their shops and don't usually tear themselves away for the *Mincha* [Afternoon] or *Maariv* [Evening] Prayer Service—even they now leave their wives in their shops to take over for them and free themselves up from all business to participate in public prayer in the synagogue.

The sense of a Judgment Day engulfs the synagogue on Rosh Hashana, especially when the prayer "*Unetaneh Tokef*"[8] is recited and one comes to the fear-inspiring lines: "Who shall live, and who shall die…" Even those who do not know the meaning of the Hebrew words and don't quite understand the import are praying with complete devotion, appealing to the Master of the Universe to grant them a favorable judgment.

And those who have prayed are not in a hurry to return home on this day [Yom Kippur Eve]; even during the break they remain in the synagogue, crowding around the tables. Some are listening to talks on Torah and ethics, while others are studying a chapter of *Mishna*[9], and still others are reciting chapters of *Tehillim*[10].

The day after Rosh Hashana arrangements begin to be made for *kapparot*[11]: the heads of households make sure to purchase chickens for *kapparot* for all members of the family, according to what they can afford. And already on Yom Kippur Eve, beginning with early morning hours, just after the morning prayers have been completed, a sense of reverential awe encompasses everyone, and the townspeople begin to recite *hatarat nedarim*[12]. Since it is permissible for a court consisting of three men to nullify a Jew's vows, everyone is rushing to find three men who can serve as his court judges, so that he can declare before them the customary request that his vows be nullified. And these three respond accordingly, nullifying his vows, as they wish one another a good year and a *chatima tova*[13].

During the afternoon, around one o'clock, the daily *Mincha* prayer service begins. One group of ten men completes its prayer service and another group of ten immediately starts theirs. Later, when it is time for the *Maariv* service, on Yom Kippur Eve, every single Jew of the town will participate; not a single one will be absent.

This was also the opportunity for the *gabbaim*[14], who throughout the year customarily collect whatever donations the congregants pledge, to ask for any outstanding pledges. The money collected on this day usually covers most of the expenses of the previous year.

On Yom Kippur Eve the various institutions, "*Chevrat Bikur Cholim*"[15], "*Kupat Gmilut Chassadim*"[16], the Jewish National Fund and others would customarily place bowls in the synagogue for the collection of contributions. All those attending services on that day would tend to contribute generously, each according to his ability.

Those who have attended the afternoon prayers would have serious expressions on their faces when they return home to sit down with their families for the last meal before the fast. The meal passes without small talk; the atmosphere of Judgment Day is palpable throughout the home. After the meal the children approach their father for him to bestow on them the traditional blessing: May you be inscribed and sealed with a good year!

The head of the household then stands up, wearing a while *kittl*[17], and with great emotion he spreads his hands on the heads of the children while his lips murmur a long prayer. Standing opposite him is his wife, the mother, bent over the candles, tears running down from her eyes as she prays in a whisper, requesting that her husband and children should be inscribed and sealed for a good life.

These moments are deeply ingrained in the souls of the children. Many years have passed since I, too, was one of the children in my father's house, but I still recall this experience with reverence and awe, as if it had just happened yesterday.

And when we leave the house after the pre-fast meal, everywhere in the street the atmosphere of the holy day is noticeable. People are streaming to the synagogue, wishing one another a good year.

The synagogue, too, has changed its appearance: on the right, at the entrance, there is a crate of sand sitting on a table, with memorial candles stuck in it. Fresh, fragrant hay, with the scent of the outdoors, has been spread on the floor, to make it comfortable for the people to take off their shoes[18] and not be bothered by the cold of the floor.

The adult men praying are all wrapped in *talitot*[19], and many of them are also wearing white *kittls*. The tension reaches a crescendo when the Torah scrolls are removed from the Holy Ark, and two distinguished members of the congregation stand on either side of the cantor as he recites the agitating verses: "With God's permission and with that of the congregation…"[20]

And then, when the cantor begins to recite the *Kol Nidre* prayer, one can hear the sound of weeping from the women's section; with their tears they are seeking to relieve their worries and concerns about the Day of Judgment. And at that moment the sense of holiness and awe intensifies throughout the entire synagogue…

And when the fast day is over, at the end of the *Ne'ila*[21] prayer service, the mentality of those who are praying changes: the melancholy expression on their faces has faded away and has been replaced by a feeling of confidence, so characteristic of Jews. Their hearts have been filled with faith, with the belief that their community prayers have been accepted and that they will merit a good and blessed year.

And it is as if even the street looks different: the light of a full moon casts a glow over it, chasing the shadows away, as if it wishes to announce a renewed life.

The adults are still not hurrying home in spite of the difficult fast. Instead they are lingering outside the synagogue in order to sanctify the moon in its renewal[22], so that they can, through this prayer, fulfil their very first mitzvah for the new year.

And similarly there are those who have the custom of erecting a tent peg at the anticipated location of their *Sukka*[23] right after the meal eaten when the Yom Kippur fast day ends.

And anyone who has not seen *Simchat Torah*[24] being celebrated in the town has never seen true joy[25]. On the eve of the holiday the synagogue is crowded with people, their eyes aglow with the joy of the holiday. All anticipate being involved in the circular processions, during which everyone, from young to old, is given a turn to carry a Torah. The singing begins, rising up to heaven, and the dancing rattles the foundations of the synagogue. And the longer the processions last the more intense the jubilation becomes.

The following morning the prayer service begins early, to make it possible to have a celebratory holiday *Kiddush*[26]. This custom has been practiced by the townspeople for generations, and each of them tries to bring along and contribute some small portion of food according to what he can afford. Meanwhile people of means prepare a meal that is fit to be called a *Kiddush*, inviting the entire congregation to their homes. These *Kiddush* celebrations last until noontime, it being easy to see that, were they to continue longer, the congregants would have a hard time enjoying the meals that await them in their own homes. Truly a day that is all joy and delight.

> מקונת כאול, ולמכוותיך אשון, לרבים קפו ונכבדי
> אקף יש, ובים בצב, ורבבים קן, ולא ה'
> על רבים צרת כאוו, ורבכת האל אחי נשומ
> כ"פ ב' יולי, כ' לכאורו לא ופני
> שמת מאצלו, והאות עלוו אווי נפשכה
> וכי מאיר פייב ל יהודה בכורו לאכלה
> טון לפני פני ומרום פט. ואושר ויהלוך
> את ועמו לגביו פנגוי ורוים ארצה נכונה
> בכ' כלום ק' יב אאכ תפנה כלה וכלוה ואני
>
> תנצב"ה

These are the words that were engraved on the headstone of R. Meir Feivel, words of eulogy that are stylistically unique: a kind of tender lament, written in the phraseology of our ancient ancestors, and attesting to the modesty and greatness of spirit of a person who dedicated himself selflessly to teaching Torah to children of the poor (see p. 95)[27] [28]

A group of young people in the Schutzen-wald woods

Bottom center: **Bertcha Holz**[29]

Young people of Dobrzyn

In the center of the second row from below: **Hersh Hartbrod**[30]

Translator's Footnotes

1. From *My Town: In Memory of the Communities Dobrzyn-Gollob*, edited by M. Harpaz, (published by the Dobrzyn-Golub Society, Israel, 1969), pp. 112-116.

2. Elul = Hebrew month corresponding approximately to September, the last month before the New Year

3. *Yamim Noraim* = Days of Awe (Hebrew), i.e. Rosh Hashana (New Year) and Yom Kippur (Day of Atonement), which are 9 days apart.

4. Day of Judgment: a reference to the tradition that God passes judgment on all of mankind once a year, on Rosh Hashana, and seals their fate on Yom Kippur

5. *Selichot* = prayers for forgiveness, recited at night, beginning several days before Rosh Hashana

6. Approximately 4 hours before sunrise

7. *Shamash* = beadle (Hebrew), who is responsible for running the daily prayer services of a synagogue or prayer house

8. *Unetaneh Tokef* = the first two words of a Hebrew liturgical poem, more than a thousand years old, recited on both Rosh Hashana and Yom Kippur, relating how God judges mankind on these days, as He decides "who shall live and who shall die…"

9. *Mishna* = book of Jewish law, written down circa 200 CE.

10. *Tehillim* = Psalms, recited for special merit.

11. *Kapparot* (Hebrew: atonements), a ritual carried out on the day before Yom Kippur, in which a Jew would wave a purchased chicken around his head, reciting "…let this chicken be my atonement (*kapparati*)…." Males would wave a rooster, while females would wave a hen. The chicken would be slaughtered, and either the meat or its monetary value given to charity. See the following link (retrieved June, 2014):
http://www.chabad.org/holidays/JewishNewYear/template_cdo/aid/989585/jewish/Kaparot.htm

12. *Hatarat nedarim* = nullification of vows (Hebrew), a ceremony customarily conducted on Yom Kippur Eve, in which a person "convenes" a "court" of 3 men and requests them to nullify past vows he may have made in error, as well as any vows that he might make throughout the following year. Generally such a procedure is considered to apply only to vows the person has made to impose restrictions on himself, such as not eating a particular food that is permitted by Jewish law. See the following link (retrieved July, 2015):
http://www.jewishcontent.org/cgi-bin/calendar?holiday=tishrei402

13. *chatima tova* (Hebrew) = (literally) a good sealed inscription, i.e. a favorable judgment by God in His "Book of Life"

14. *Gabbaim* (plural of *gabbai*) = synagogue treasurer functionaries, who, among other duties, collected contributions and organized the provision of charity to the needy

15. *Chevrat Bikur Cholim* = Association for Visiting the Sick

16. *Kupat Gmilut Chassadim* = Benevolence Fund

17. *kittl* = loose white robe, tied at the waist, customarily worn by men on Yom Kippur. See the following Web site (retrieved August, 2014):
http://en.wikipedia.org/wiki/Kittel

18. Wearing leather shoes is prohibited on Yom Kippur.

19. *Talitot* = prayer shawls (singular: *tallit*)

20. See the following link (retrieved July, 2015) for more details on the *Kol Nidre* prayer and the verses recited before and after it:
https://en.wikipedia.org/wiki/Kol_Nidre

21. *Ne'ila* = the closing prayer service of Yom Kippur, which is completed about 40 minutes after sunset

22. For details on the ritual sanctification of the moon (*kiddush levanah*) see the following link (retrieved July, 2015): https://en.wikipedia.org/wiki/Kiddush_levana

23. *Sukka* = temporary dwelling erected for the one-week celebration of the Sukkot holiday, which begins five days after Yom Kippur.

24. *Simchat Torah* = a joyous holiday of dancing in a procession in which Torahs are carried around; it is celebrated 8 days after the beginning of the Sukkot holiday.

25. Paraphrase of statement in the Mishna (Sukkah 5:1; Babylonian Talmud Sukkah 51a): "Whoever has not seen the Celebration of the Water Drawing has never seen true joy."

26. *Kiddush* = (literally sanctification) food and drink eaten to sanctify and celebrate a Sabbath or holiday, in this case immediately after the morning prayer service ends

27. From p. 112 of reference cited in Footnote 1.

28. An English translation of the Hebrew inscription follows:

"Here lies buried Meir Shraga, son of Yehuda the Kohen. May his soul be bound in everlasting life. Call the dirge-singing women and send for the skilled women to arouse crying and wailing; Together with them let our tears run down, and let us weep with a wailing sound. For the crown of our head has fallen, our dancing turned into mourning. Our hands are all weakened, for we have been left desolate and solitary. The gladness of our heart has been stilled by the death of our father, a precious soul, Rabbi Meir Feivel son of Yehuda of blessed memory. May his great righteousness in teaching Torah accompany His soul, keeping it bound in heights above, concealed, in perfect peace. At the age of 52, on the 9th of Adar 5658, he passed away and is gone."

The poem is a double acrostic. The abbreviation for "Here lies buried:" at the very top of the inscription are continued by the first and last letters of each line, the first letters spelling out "Meir Shraga, son of", and the last letters spelling out "Yehuda, the Kohen". In the first two lines of the poem the reference to dirge-singers who arouse weeping is an allusion to Jeremiah 9:16-17. The date of death corresponds to March 3, 1898.

29. From p. 115 of reference cited in Footnote 1.

30. From p. 116 of reference cited in Footnote 1.

[Page 117]

A Jewish Theatre in Dobrzyn[1]
(A Tribute to Yaakov Baruch Degala)

by Avraham Dor (Dobroszklanka)
Translated by Allen Flusberg

The unfavorable view of the small Jewish towns of Eastern Europe—which was adopted predominantly by the Enlightenment Period writers, and then later by the leaders of the pioneer-oriented movements—has long since faded away. Today we have learned to discern the extent of the hyperbole that was present in their criticism, and we have come to value the coping skills and morale of our forefathers who lived in these towns. Nowadays we marvel at the unglorified courage and unpraised valor of the many Jews who lived in small towns and were able to withstand the persecution they were suffering and, in effect, outsmart the Gentiles by defiantly fashioning a thriving Jewish milieu.

Life in the town was indeed vibrant, not only within the realm of Torah, but in ordinary, daily life as well. The town had a way of life of its own that differentiated it from its Gentile surroundings and set it apart.

There is no doubt that the Jewish theatre played a particularly important role in this Jewish milieu. For it was here, on the stage, that we had an opportunity to express what was in our hearts, to soar on the wings of our imagination and to dream…

In Dobrzyn, as well, there was a theatre that belonged entirely to one person, Yaakov Baruch Degala. For who, other than Degala, was ready to devote his days and nights to stage a play, in difficult circumstances and with amateur actors—actors who, with his guidance, were just beginning to learn how to enunciate correctly and how to position themselves on the stage?

I can still see him: a man of average height, his long hair hanging down over the nape of his neck, and a smile on his clean-shaven face. That smile never left his face; he always greeted people cheerfully, and he was always ready and willing to tell a colorful joke.

He was the son of the town cantor, a bachelor who continued to live at his parents' house. There was not a single performance in the town that he did not take part in, whether as director or as one of the organizers. He encouraged the amateur actors with his inexhaustible energy. He would first read the play out loud to the actors and elaborate on the personalities of the characters. Many of the young people in the town were among his student actors. I, too, was fortunate enough to take part in one of the plays, *Reb Aba'le Ashkenazi*, written by Z. Anchi.

He found these plays in the stories and skits of Yiddish writers: Shalom-Aleichem, Peretz, and others, arranging them for the stage. The plays were performed in Morzanski Hall, which had about 300 seats and specialized in performances.

How much toil and trouble Yaakov Baruch Degala took to bring these plays to the stage, not only in selecting suitable actors and directing them, but also in bringing in costumes and other stage accessories that he did not have in his possession!

At first the Hassidim of the town did not look favorably upon this theatrical activity, but as time passed they adapted to the idea, particularly since the plays were staged during the Jewish holidays, when Jewish hearts crave for a bit of pleasure.

But we, the young people of the town, were very attached to him and were enchanted by his cheerful personality. We remember him as someone who contributed a great deal to the social and cultural life of Dobrzyn.

Translator's Footnotes

1. From *My Town: In Memory of the Communities Dobrzyn-Gollob*, edited by M. Harpaz, (published by the Dobrzyn-Golub Society, Israel, 1969), pp. 117-118.

2. From p. 118 of reference cited in Footnote 1.

Performance of "God, Man and the Devil" in the amateur theatre of Dobrzyn[2]

[Page 119]

The Idea of Aliya to Israel Strikes Root[1]

by Yehuda Rosenwaks

Translated by Allen Flusberg

The spread of the Zionist idea among Polish Jewry and the strengthening of the yearning for the Land of Israel did not skip over Dobrzyn and Golub. I recall, from the time of my youth, the first Zionists in the town. The fire of the Zionist idea was kindled in their hearts by the sight of the destruction wreaked during the pogroms and the accompanying cries of despair by the Jewish masses; and from that day and on they did not cease, even for a single moment, encouraging their people to leave the Exile.

The shock of the pogroms opened the eyes of many who had until then viewed the Zionist endeavor as a false illusion, a chimeric vision. Now they felt they had reached a crossroad, and a number of them began to ask themselves: what is this place to me, and whom do I have here?

The verses that had so often been repeated as an afterthought: "And may our eyes behold Your merciful return to Jerusalem"… "And may You build up the Holy City of Jerusalem speedily in our time"[2]…began to receive a new, fuller meaning as an imperative. And thus as they sought to fulfil this idyllic aspiration of generations of Jews, many of the young people were brought closer to the Zionist idea.

There was, of course, no shortage of parents who tried to prevent their children from immigrating to the Land; but in this matter the children were no longer fulfilling the commandment to honor the desire of their fathers and mothers. Many of the townspeople joined the pioneer movements, went off to *hachshara*[3] locations, and prepared themselves for Aliya.

Seeing various categories of anti-Semites flourishing, and their influence intensifying, only made the longing to leave the Exile grow by leaps and bounds. Gangs of anti-Semites would often rampage through city streets, harassing Jews. The young people of the town felt that the ground was burning under their feet, and that they no longer had any future in this blood-soaked land. The decision crystalized in their minds that they had to immigrate to the Land of Israel and to help build and resurrect the old-new homeland.

However, there were many whose eyes were unable to see clearly, and who ignored the harsh, dismal reality; they did not discern the political changes and did not sense the reverberating enmity against the Jews. Like ostriches, they hid their heads in the sand, waiting out the storm…until the terrible storm came and swept them away…

Among the first to immigrate to the Land, at the beginning of the nineteenth century, was the family of R.[4] Ephraim Eliezer Granat; and after them the first pioneers, who arrived when they were very young: Shlomo Hartbrot and Yehoshua Isaac[5] of blessed memory.

Mention must be made of the Zionist R. Feibish Lipka,[6] a great Torah scholar who was an Otwock Hassid[7]. By 1913 he had already begun to preach the idea of redemption. His enthusiasm increased even more after he made a visit to the Land and observed with his very own eyes the great desolation and the generation of the *Magshimim*[8] who were struggling against the desolation and managing to overcome it. After he returned to Poland he traveled from one city to another and encouraged his fellow Jews to arise, to immigrate to the Holy Land and rebuild its ruins.

His toil was not in vain. The Zionist movement in Dobrzyn and Golub grew and expanded as the members of the passionate youth movements rose up to fulfil their dream, leaving their parents' home behind as they immigrated to the Land of Israel.

The youth movements that arose intensified the Zionist activity and won the people over. Many began to learn the Hebrew language and to study the doctrines of Zionism, which were capturing the hearts of the people.

As stated above, Sh. Hartbrot and Y. Isaac were the first of the *Magshimim*. They had been educated in and graduated from the "Herzlia" high school. The former was killed at a young age at the end of the First World War, when the Germans invaded the Land. The second, Y. Isaac, joined the "*Hashomer*"[9] organization, which had as its goal the defense of the Jewish settlements against Arab bandits. He was one of the founders of the Hebrew Defense Forces and served from the days of "*Hashomer*" until the rebirth of the State of Israel, by which time he had risen to the rank of lieutenant colonel in the Israel Defense Forces.

Those who were the first to arrive did not remain alone: many others followed in their footsteps, contributing their talents and their youthful enthusiasm to the rebuilding of the Land.

Translator's Footnotes

1. From *My Town: In Memory of the Communities Dobrzyn-Gollob*, edited by M. Harpaz, (published by the Dobrzyn-Golub Society, Israel, 1969), pp. 119-120.

2. These are quotations from the *Amida*, the silent prayer recited three times daily.

3. *Hachshara* = training in work to prepare for the move to Palestine.

4. R. = *Reb*, an honorific similar to English "Mr."

5. Yehoshua Isaac (later Eshel), 1900-1966. A short biography of him can be found in this volume: A. Dor, "Yehoshua Eshel," pp. 218-219 of reference cited in Footnote 1. Eshel was also the author of the next article, "The First Dobrzyners in the Land of Israel," pp. 121-126 of reference cited in Footnote 1.

6. For more details on R. Feibish Lipka, see Y. Lipka, "Memoirs Dedicated to My Father, R. Feibish Lipka," pp. 404-438 of reference cited in Footnote 1.

7. Otwock (pronounced Otvotsk) is the name of a town in Poland (located ~30km southeast of Warsaw) that the leaders of this Hassidic group were associated with. See the following links (retrieved August, 2015): http://en.wikipedia.org/wiki/Amshinov_%28Hasidic_dynasty%29, http://www.yivoencyclopedia.org/article.aspx/Vurke_Hasidic_Dynasty

8. *Magshimim* = those who fulfil (the dream)

9. For more details on *Hashomer* (= the Watchman), see the following link (retrieved August, 2015): https://en.wikipedia.org/wiki/Hashomer

[Pages 121-126]

The First Dobrzyners in Israel[1]
by Yehoshua Eshel (Isaac)
Translated by Allen Flusberg

I recall that I was still a little boy in Dobrzyn when an event occurred that shook me up and agitated all the townspeople: one day an ordinary Jew, the baker Mordechai Glitzenstein, picked himself up, took his entire family, and immigrated with them to the Land of Israel. This event took place in 1908 (or 1909). I don't remember how many years that ordinary Jew remained in the Land—two or three years; I don't know what kind of work he tried to do when he was here; nor do I know why he returned to Dobrzyn.

Two or three years later, the entire family of Ephraim Eliezer Granat (Rimon) immigrated to the Land.[2] Granat had run a "reformed" *cheder*[3] in Dobrzyn, the first of its kind in the town; in it they taught *ivrit be'ivrit*[4]. My older brother, Yaakov z.l.[5], studied with him and was actually enamored by Zionism. I once visited that *cheder* together with my now deceased brother, and I remember very well its appearance and the atmosphere that prevailed in it.

In 1913 I immigrated to the Land in order to study in the "Herzlia" *Gymnasia* [high school] (inspired by my brother Yaakov and with the support of my father z.l. and all of our family). While my family was not Zionist, it did have deep Jewish roots and a clear nationalist consciousness. As a family that lived by agriculture (we had an agricultural farm located about 15 km from the town), we had many discussions about what was going on in the Land of Israel, and we knew all about the beginnings of intensive agriculture there. My uncle on my mother's side, Mendel Baum z.l. of Wloclawek[6], was a "fiery" Zionist, and he was the one who gave me the final "push" to immigrate to the Land. I came on Aliya as a student, and I was a member of the seventh class of the "Herzlia" *Gymnasia*.

Once I was in the Land I met up with the Granat family—traditional people who were careful to properly fulfil all the religious precepts. Their home was on the main street of Neve-Shalom[7], where they also had a grocery store. A Dobrzyn spirit—in its full, best sense—held sway throughout their home. They enveloped me with great warmth. I continued to meet with them during the first years of World War I, until the expulsion from Yafo and Tel Aviv (1916)[8].

Already at the outbreak of the war my connections with my parents' home had been severed, and my financial situation, like that of my other friends, became particularly difficult. I recall that Mrs. Rimon made a pair of sandals for me out of cords, since I had no shoes to wear. Several times I met the poet Yosef Tzvi Rimon z.l., who was widely acclaimed in those days.

In the beginning of 1914 Shlomo Hartbrot, someone I knew from Dobrzyn, arrived in Israel. He was already speaking Hebrew from back home and was well prepared for his Aliya; he was a pioneer, an idealist, and the epitome of the type of person who came in the Second Aliya[9]. Naturally, he went off to do agricultural work, going up to the Galilee and the Jezreel Valley. He also lived in Merhavia[10] for a while. In 1915 the Germans set up an airfield in Afula for their warplanes. Hartbrot happened to be there for something connected with his work, and he was killed when the airfield was bombed by English pilots. He was buried in the Merhavia cemetery, at the foot of the mountain Givat-Hamoreh (now right near Afula Illit [Upper Afula][11]). His grave is located among those of the pioneers of the [Jezreel] Valley and the members of "Hashomer"[12]. We had met several times. He worried about the things that used to be of concern to the members of the labor movement[13] of the Second Aliya. With his death by happenstance, before his time, we lost one of the most outstanding of our townsmen. He never made it to the last meeting we had arranged. May his memory be preserved in our hearts.

In the spring of 1914 my cousin (second cousin once removed), Asher Dobrzynski, the son of Bina and Hershel Dobrzynski of Dobrzyn, arrived in the Land. He had graduated from an agricultural school in Germany, and he came to the Land for the purpose of settling here as a farmer. In Germany (in Stonehurst) he had studied together with several Israelis, children of farmers here; among them was someone from Rishon-Letziyon[14]—a member of a family who were among those who had founded the village, people from the First Aliya[15]. He [my cousin] was invited to live and work with them. He went to work in their field and in their almond orchard. One day I received word from him that he was ill, and when I came to see him I found him lying in bed with a high fever. I was told that he had malaria; many of the people in the settlement were then coming down with malaria, and it would have been natural that as a new, unimmunized immigrant, he would have come down with it, too. And the only medication for malaria was quinine, quinine and more quinine. When he didn't improve, he was brought to a sort of clinic—a separate room in one of the houses—and I stayed with him to take care of him. I slept on the floor of his room. That was during the very beginning of

World War I. When his condition worsened, we brought him to the hospital in Yafo/Tel-Aviv, which was then located in Neve-Shalom, on the coast. In the meantime I was told that when he was in the orchard Asher had gone down into the well to fix the pump. It appeared that going into the well was what had caused his illness—it was not malaria, but rather typhus; and in the hospital they were already treating him as someone who had typhus.

This was during the summer vacation. I was off from school and went to Kfar-Saba to work on the farm of my uncle's son-in-law, Nelkin, who owned a plot of land there. One day I went off to Yafo riding on a donkey, to visit Asher. Just as I left the village I had a bad feeling, and my heart told me that something bad had happened. And apparently I was right. When I reached the hospital, Asher was no longer alive. He had died at the very moment when that strange feeling had come over me, when I was on the road. Asher was buried in the cemetery of Tel-Aviv, the Old Cemetery on Trumpeldor Street.

In the First World War, we joined the Jewish Brigades of the British Army. There were three brigades of this type: one made up of Jews from the Land of Israel, a second with British Jews, and a third with American Jews.[16]

When the war was over, in 1919, a large muster took place of several divisions from the Palestine front that had fought against the Turks. In my brigade I had served as a sergeant of Division 16, the last division of the brigade. I was standing in the rear of my division during the muster; other units were standing behind us.

During the muster, while we were standing at ease, someone put his hand on my shoulder. I turned my head and saw, to my delight, a young man from Dobrzyn, Yitzhak Yeshayowitz, who was a young cousin of the deceased Shlomo Hartbrot. It turned out that he was in one of the American brigades. But how surprised I was that he had spotted me from far away— while I was standing among about 100,000 soldiers—and had recognized me even though we had not seen each other for several years. Our meeting didn't last very long, only a few moments.

In the year 1921, while I was a member of Degania[17], I was called up, as a security guard, to serve in the "Hagana"[18]. I was appointed commander of the Jerusalem district and the surrounding area. During the events of November 2, I was in command in the battles in the Old City (details can be found in "Sefer Hahagana" [Book of the Hagana]).[19]

During one of the musters of the "Hagana", after the battles were over, someone came running over to me—against all of the rules of discipline, and to the bewilderment of those who were there. It was someone sturdy and radiant—Yitzhak Rosenwaks, the son of Zalman Hassid from Dobrzyn. To the great delight of those who were present, we embraced each other (and certainly that embrace rescued him from disciplinary action).

I met with him many times afterwards, almost always concerning security matters. He was the superb embodiment of the plain people—an individual with a generous, compassionate heart: a Jewish heart. He passed away at an advanced age in Kibbutz Dovrat[20], surrounded by his daughter and grandchildren. May his memory be a blessing![21]

After the "events" of Jerusalem, at the end of 1921, I was one of the first of the settlers at Ein-Harod[22], and afterwards I lived in Tel-Yosef[23]. In 1924 my brother, Yehuda (Isaac), who is now deceased, arrived here. He was sent as a pioneer, coming ahead of his family (his wife, Tzipora z.l., daughter of Avraham Hersh Kohn) to set up an economic, agricultural foundation for his entire family. And indeed, for this purpose he had bought 1000 hectares[24] of land in the Arab village of Sulam, near Merhavia (a purchase that was rescinded for political reasons). He also acquired land—several hectares—on the Carmel, where he put up a shack for living quarters. Similarly he bought about 30 hectares of sand dunes near Akko to set up a factory for making silicate bricks. After some time had passed his wife, Tzipora z.l., also immigrated to the Land, together with their little boy, my nephew Yitzhak Isaac (who came [again] to the Land from Cyprus around the time of the establishment of the State, establishing a home and raising a family here).

Meanwhile the machines for the factory arrived, and Yehuda, together with his family, moved to Akko. While he was waiting for the machinery to arrive, he had had enough time to be a member of the Heftziba agricultural cooperative[25] in the Jezreel Valley for an entire year.

Once the foundations for the factory building had been laid, Avraham Hersh Kohn came to the Land for several weeks; with him was Dobroszklanka of Dobrzyn, who came as the manager of the factory, and a Polish Gentile, a mechanic, whose job was to assemble the machinery. Meanwhile a severe economic crisis suddenly occurred in the Land (1926), and it became pointless to continue setting up the factory. It was all abandoned in the sand dunes near Akko. To pay for all the travel expenses, Yehuda was forced to sell the land on the Carmel; he and all the members of his family went back to Poland.

For many years he looked for ways to immigrate again, but he was not able to; and he did not get to continue taking part in the building up of the Land.

In that period another Dobrzyner, Menashe Gutglaz arrived in the Land. He became a member of Kibbutz Nes-Tziyona, but returned to Dobrzyn after several years. I heard about his attempts to return to the Land again—but he, too, did not manage to…

From that point on additional Dobrzyners began to arrive in the Land from time to time; but they are not part of this story, the story of the first arrivals.

Shaya Natan Lipka and Avraham Dor (Dobroszklanka), during the period in which they were counselors in the youth movement of the town.[26]

Female members of "Poalei Tziyon"[27]

Committee of Emigrants from Dobrzyn in Berlin[28]
The writing in German translates as follows:
Committee of the Association of Dobrzyn *Landsleute*[29] of Berlin. 10 November, 1920

Administration of the Sports Group "Hakoach".[30]
Sitting, right-to-left: **Lipman Rebe, Adam Sterling, Avraham Dor (Dobroszklanka)**
Standing: **Leib Szeinbart, Menashe Dobroszklanka, Mordechai Goldberg, Nisan Fogel and Aharon Lipka**

Translator's Footnotes

1. From *My Town: In Memory of the Communities Dobrzyn-Gollob*, edited by M. Harpaz, (published by the Dobrzyn-Golub Society, Israel, 1969), pp. 121-126.

2. See Y. Rimon, "R. Ephraim Eliezer Granat (Rimon) z.l.", pp. 176-179 of this volume (reference cited in Footnote 1).

3. *Cheder* = school for young boys, in which studies were dominated by religious subjects. The "reformed" *cheders* tried to introduce new teaching techniques and a more modern curriculum.

4. *Ivrit be'ivrit* = Hebrew in Hebrew, a technique in which the Hebrew language (and sometimes other subjects, as well) is taught in spoken Hebrew, with virtually no translation to one's native language.

5. z.l. = abbreviation for *zichrono livracha* (of blessed memory)

6. Wloclawek is a city located about 60km south of Dobrzyn.

7. Neve-Shalom was one of the first Jewish neighborhoods established outside the walls of Yafo, in what is now part of Tel Aviv.

8. The Granats were expelled as enemy nationals. See Footnote 2.

9. Second Aliya = immigration to Land of Israel, predominantly from the Russian Empire, in the period 1904-1914. See the following Web page (retrieved September 2015): https://en.wikipedia.org/wiki/Second_Aliyah

10. Merhavia was then an agricultural settlement located on the eastern outskirts of Afula.

11. Afula Illit is located ~5 km northeast of Afula.

12. *Hashomer* (= the Guard, or Watchman) was a Jewish defense organization during the period 1909-1920 whose purpose was to provide Jewish security guards to Jewish settlements. See the following Web page (retrieved September 2015): https://en.wikipedia.org/wiki/Hashomer

13. Hebrew: *anshei ha'avoda*

14. Rishon-Letziyon is located ~10km south of Yafo

15. First Aliya = wave of Jewish immigration (1882-1903) to the Land of Israel under Ottoman rule, predominantly from Eastern Europe and Yemen. See the following Web pages (retrieved September 2015):
https://en.wikipedia.org/wiki/First_Aliyah,
http://www.jewishvirtuallibrary.org/jsource/Immigration/First_Aliyah.html.

16. See the following Web pages (retrieved September 2015):
https://en.wikipedia.org/wiki/Jewish_Legion;
http://www.jewishvirtuallibrary.org/jsource/judaica/ejud_0002_0011_0_10141.html.

17. Degania, the first cooperative settlement (a form that served as the model for what was later called a kibbutz) was located at the southern tip of the Sea of Galilee. Since 1920 it has been known as Degania Aleph. See the following Web page, retrieved September 2015: https://en.wikipedia.org/wiki/Degania_Alef.

18. Hagana (= Defense), a Jewish paramilitary organization, established in 1920 as a defense force against Arab rioters. See the following Web page (retrieved September 2015): https://en.wikipedia.org/wiki/Haganah

19. In May, 1921, there were a series of attacks and massacres by Arab rioters on Jews in Yafo and elsewhere. As a result, the Hagana leadership began organizing armed defense forces in various Jewish communities. On November 2, 1921, Arab mobs attacked the Jewish Quarter of the Old City of Jerusalem, but were successfully repulsed by the Jewish defenders with the backing of the Hagana. See the following Web page in Hebrew (retrieved September 2015): http://lib.cet.ac.il/pages/item.asp?item=2039.

20. Dovrat is in northeastern Israel, ~10km southeast of Nazareth.

21. For more on Yitzhak Rosenwaks, see his autobiographical essay describing his service in the Russian army before World War I and his labor in German work camps during World War I, pp. 332-353; a photograph from the early 1920s, p. 353; and a biographical essay, pp. 246-247: all in this volume (reference cited in Footnote 1).

22. Ein-Harod is in Northern Israel, ~20km southeast of Nazareth. See the following Web page (retrieved September 2015): https://en.wikipedia.org/wiki/Ein_Harod.

23. Tel Yosef, located in northeastern Israel, was founded in 1921. See the following Web page (retrieved September 2015): https://en.wikipedia.org/wiki/Tel_Yosef.

24. 1 hectare = 10,000 square meters (~2.5 acres)

25. Hebrew *kevutza*, the forerunner of the kibbutz

26. From p. 122 of reference cited in Footnote 1

27. From p. 125 of reference cited in Footnote 1

28. From p. 126 of reference cited in Footnote 1

29. *Landsleute* = immigrants who hail from the same place (Yiddish: *landsleit*)

30. See Dor, "Institutions and Organizations", pp. 79-86 of present volume (reference cited in Footnote 1).

[Page 128]

From the Horrors of the Holocaust

How Can I Take Pleasure?[1] [2]

by Yehuda Halevi

Translated by Allen Flusberg

…How can I take pleasure in food and drink as I behold
Dogs dragging away your mighty lions?
Or how can the light of day be sweet to my eyes, while I still see
Your eagles' corpses in the mouths of ravens?…

The expulsion of the townspeople by the Nazis[3]

Translator's Footnotes

1. From *My Town: In Memory of the Communities Dobrzyn-Gollob*, edited by M. Harpaz, (published by the Dobrzyn-Golub Society, Israel, 1969), p. 128.

2. These lines are excerpted from a poem by Yehuda Halevi (~1075-1141), *Tziyon Halo Tishali Lishlom Asirayich* (=Zion, Do You Not Inquire After the Welfare of Your Captives). This poem is recited in synagogues on the Fast Day of the 9th of Av, commemorating the destruction of the two Jewish Temples in Jerusalem and other calamities that befell the Jewish people throughout the ages.

3. From p. 128 of reference cited in Footnote 1

[Page 129]

The Pain in the Heart (Poem)[1]

By Yehudit Golan (Rosenwaks)

Translated by Allen Flusberg

Twenty years have passed and are gone,
But my heart cannot comprehend:
How nations stood by in silence
As my people were ravenously devoured.

I cannot forget, never, not ever,
The atrocities, the genocide.
I know neither peace nor rest,
I cannot, I cannot forget.

Not one moment do the sights depart from my eyes
The terror at night and by day;
My brethren brought to crematoria
Going up as sacrifices like innocent lambs.

Can there be vengeance for such bloodshed?
Is there balm for my mournful heart?
The pain within will forever be raw,
As I struggle, a captive in a world of nightmares.

Translator's Footnote

1. From *My Town: In Memory of the Communities Dobrzyn-Gollob*, edited by M. Harpaz, (published by the Dobrzyn-Golub Society, Israel, 1969), p. 129.

[Pages 130-136]

In the Tempest of the War[1]

By Zadok Zudkevitz

Translated by Allen Flusberg

The year is 1938. Fascism is raising its head and is being rewarded with many successes; its influence is growing steadily in Europe. With it anti-Semitism is on the rise as well, obtaining support, encouragement and a "scientific" foundation from Nazi Germany.

The anti-Semitic parties of Poland are no longer satisfied with the economic-cultural war [against the Jews] that is supposedly being conducted by the ND party[2]. Instead, they are making an effort to catch up to their Hitlerite neighbors…The OZN party[3] is endeavoring to uproot the Jews and expel them from Poland—and all this systematically, with a diabolical plan to make the Jews loath their own lives, to bring them to despair. But most terrible of all, there is nowhere to flee to; all the gates are closed to the Jews!

Even in our small town the signs were recognizable, signs portending disaster. Significant changes had occurred in the composition of the city administration: a former general, a well-known anti-Semite, was appointed as mayor. To replace the priest who had passed away—and who had been known for being friendly to the Jews—a new religious leader was sent to the town. This new priest had published in *Slovo Pomorskie* articles filled with hatred for the Jews, articles in which he tried to blame the Jews for all the failings and shortcomings of the Polish state: the economic crisis, the absence of jobs, the hardship and the poverty[4]. This is how anti-Semites operate, transferring the anger of the masses from those who are truly blameworthy to the Jews…

OZN thugs attack unsuspecting Jewish passersby in the street—they rain down blows, break windows, and scatter the merchandise of Jewish shopkeepers, who stand by helplessly. The situation continues to worsen, with dark clouds gathering in our skies. We are full of trepidation and worry.

But all this was nothing compared to what happened to us on [the day we later referred to as] *Black Sunday*. That day large crowds gathered in the church, where they listened to a speech of incitement by the priest. Afterwards an incited, aroused mob ran through the streets of the town, going wild and attacking the Jews. A sight like this had never been seen before in our town:

the rioters attacked women walking with their babies, tossing them and their baby carriages off the sidewalk; they uprooted fences and broke windows. All this took place under the auspices of the police, who stood by to prevent any attempt by the Jews to fight back.

We were at a loss at what to do. This time [even] the young people—who had previously always stood up to rioters-thugs—were forced to shut themselves up in their homes. [Meanwhile] a speaker who was supposed to lecture that evening in the auditorium of the Peretz Library managed, with great danger, to finally reach the train so that he could hurry back to his home in Warsaw.

The next day all of the Jewish press was filled with horrible descriptions of what had taken place in the town. Another Jewish community had been struck—joining those that had previously experienced the taste of riot's, in Paszitik[5], in Mińsk-Mazowiecki[6] and others. All the efforts by the Jewish leaders in Poland for help from government authorities ended with absolutely nothing...The riots continued for several days. Then, even after they ended, the situation did not return to what it had been before...The rift that had opened remained a threat...

Even those Poles who had been friends with Jews (and I, too, had several such friends, who had studied with me in school) now tried to distance themselves and to hide their relationship as friends because of their fear of the anti-Semites, who were accusing them of treason to the homeland. Indeed there were here and there Poles with socialist consciousness who attempted to stand by the Jews and to struggle jointly with them against the rioters—but to no avail. Even they were forced in the end to worry about themselves, their livelihood and their safety...

This situation continued almost to the start of World War II, when the persecuted Jews were joined by members of the "Master Race"—the Germans who lived near us. The attitude of the Polish people toward the Germans was no better than their attitude to the Jews. On the insulting signs, hung in front of cafes and hotels in Torun[7], proclaiming "No entry to dogs and Jews", the word "Germans" was now added...Jews and Germans were now in the same boat!

The irony of it! How ludicrous it was to see these Germans—the very same Germans from whom the Poles had received their tenets of racism—in their humiliation, as they sought refuge, bowing and begging for their lives...

August 14, 1939

Already at dawn Katarzynska Street[8] is teeming with men. These are the days just before war. Many of the men have already received their mobilization order, while others are waiting to receive theirs. All are conversing and arguing and trying to guess what awaits us...They've just called me to come home to tell me that I, too, have received a conscription order—I have to report to my army unit in Torun in two hours.

The recruiting office is crowded with men who have streamed here from both near and far. There is an atmosphere of disorder and panic; things are not organized. Rumors are going around about German espionage taking place from within our ranks.

We are already in our uniforms, carrying arms. Since the barracks are too crowded, schools and public auditoriums have been commandeered to house the conscripts. On that very same night we go out for maneuvers near the German border.

August 30, 1939

Everyone senses that war is inevitable. The men are called up to again take an oath of allegiance to the homeland...At night we are stationed near the border, in a state of readiness. Suddenly the air is pierced by the sound of sporadic shooting...As morning approaches the firing becomes steadier. The attack is joined by machine guns and cannons, and heavy bombers make their appearance. The attack is now at full intensity. The Second World War has begun! The Nazi army is piercing our lines and enveloping us with all its strength. It is trying to deliver a heavy, overwhelming blow by using the blitzkrieg method that had been talked about all the time. We, who have trained with antiquated tactics, following the rules of the First World War, are beaten back and are caving in under their powerful strikes. After only two hours of standing up to the enemy, our front is broken through, and a panicky, disorganized retreat begins.

September 15, 1939

We are near Lubicz[9]. Three divisions in this vicinity have surrendered. White flags are fluttering over the houses in the towns and villages. Here and there some attempts at defense have been made, but with no success. The Germans are scattering fliers that call for the Polish army to put down its weapons and surrender.

On that very day the Germans transport about 20,000 prisoners of war on the road leading to Lubicz. Among them are several fellow townsmen: Avrohom Yizchak Schlachter, Avrohom Kuzak, Leib Ulstein and others.

September 20, 1939

After much wandering and unending suffering, we reached the city of Kalisz[10]. Here we were brought to a synagogue. The synagogue, the adjoining *beit midrash*[11] and the orphanage were transformed into a prisoner camp, surrounded by a fence, with machine guns stationed at its corners. (This orphanage was large; the contributions for maintaining it had been coming in from all parts of Poland and even from outside it; there had been about 400 orphaned children living there.) Even though prayer verses were still fluttering here and there, it was hard to imagine that there had ever been a synagogue and *beit midrash* in this place…

How terrible the spectacle! Whatever the Germans had left intact, the Poles had completely finished off: they tore up the *parochet*[12] to use as rags for shining shoes; *tallitot*[13] were employed as towels…Only the Torah scrolls, which the Jews [of the town] had managed to take out early enough, were saved from the unclean hands of the desecrators.

Every now and then we peeked outside from the *Ezrat Nashim*[14], and our hearts sank seeing the torment of the Jews of Kalisz as they were being pursued by the Germans, who were humiliating them beyond words and cruelly beating them senseless.

September 30, 1939

After being freed from the prison camp we arrived in Torun in freight trains. From there we set out on foot to our homes via roundabout ways, fearing the Gestapo. Although we were carrying release documents, these had no value in the eyes of the Gestapo; they tended to destroy such documents, in many cases together with those who were carrying them. Leib Ulstein was in the group walking with me; the others in the group were Poles from Golub.

At dusk we reach Golub. We are careful to make our way quietly. We meet a Polish woman and ask her what has gone on in the town. Is it possible to cross the bridge?[15] (The original bridge has been blown up by the Germans; in its place there is now a very narrow temporary bridge.) The woman reveals to us that incidents have already occurred, in which captured Polish soldiers who had been released have since been arrested. What she is telling us is not very encouraging...We decide to make our way to one of the Jewish families living in Golub, the Fein family. It is a lucky decision—they are still in their house. We now realize that most of the Jews of Golub have been expelled to Dobrzyn.

There is an atmosphere of depression in the house. Everyone is fearful, not knowing what will happen next. Shmuel Hersh Riz is sleeping in one of the secluded rooms, but they are not letting us go into that room. They say he has suffered a nervous breakdown after being held for several hours by the Gestapo. Leib decides to spend the night here. But placing my trust in the darkness of the night and in the rainy weather, I quietly make my way to my house, making sure that the enemy does not detect me. I reach my house. But is it still my house?

November 9, 1939

We still don't know about what is actually taking place in the town. We work at dismantling the bridge that had been blown up—labor that has been imposed on all the Jews, five days a week. Our group consists of ten Jews of various ages.

Suddenly one of the children comes over and tells us that they are about to expel all the Jews from the town. Only when we return home for a lunch break do we find out all the details. On that very morning several of the Jews, among them Hershel Linet of blessed memory, were invited to a meeting with the occupation authorities, where they were told that an explicit order had come down to expel all the Jews of the town to Warsaw. Nonetheless, if the Jews would prefer that the expulsion should take place in an orderly, proper fashion, they must bring valuables—gold, silver and jewelry—as payment.

The representatives of the Jews naively believed that this order was nothing but an excuse to extort money, and that with sufficient ransom they would have it within their power to cancel the expulsion decree. They therefore worked quickly and brought two buckets filled with silver and gold jewelry to City Hall. But their hopes were dashed. All the Jews were ordered to gather in front of City Hall. Here documents were distributed to them, and they were categorically ordered to leave town within two hours.

And in fact, within only two hours armed policemen made their appearance in the streets. They stood there, urging the Jews to quickly vacate their homes and depart. They accompanied their words of encouragement with blows.

The Jews abandon their homes and set out in one convoy after another, carrying on their backs the few possessions that they could manage to bring along. Most go on the main road leading to Rypin[16]. They take one last look toward their town…Is this a nightmare? Many generations lived here, experiencing joy and grief—one generation following another…Here their days of childhood and youth passed, here they grew up and became adults…But the end has come! They are being chased out like dogs, as curses rain down on them, "Away from here, you leprous Jews!"

The sun has set, and darkness descends on the world. Jewish families find spots for themselves in the ditches along the edges of the road, and sprawl down there on the ground. It was only yesterday that they still had a home, a bed and a slice of bread…The men are at a loss. The weeping of the children and of the women weighs heavily on their hearts. A hell on earth!

We continue to march to Rypin in the darkness of night, some of us in vehicles and some on foot (there were some who manage to rent wagons from farmers). I, too, am able to rent a wagon together with David Pienek. We seat members of our families in the wagon. With me is my wife and her relatives; I have lost track of my own parents and my other relatives along the way, just as we were leaving Dobrzyn. There is not enough room for everyone in the wagon. I take our baby carriage, fill it with some possessions and march on foot, pushing it along in front of me.

In one of the ditches along the way I found my mother, may she rest in peace, and my sister-in-law, Zelda Krajank (my brother Aharon's wife), together with her little children. I discovered that my father and brother Aharon had gone on ahead to one of the villages to look for a wagon [to rent]. I followed after them, but was not able to find them. I have never had the privilege of seeing them again. In the end they apparently managed to get to Plock[17] — while I wound up instead in Warsaw.

*

On November 30th I crossed the border into Russia...I went through many hardships there, getting a taste of Russian prison and of an internment camp in the remote north...Only after joining the Polish Anders army[18] and then, after much wandering on the byways of Russia and in the Arab countries, did I reach Palestine in the year 1943. Of all the members of my family I am the only one who survived.

Yehuda Rosenwaks, representing the Jews of Dobrzyn, lights a candle in the Chamber of the Holocaust[19] in memory of the martyrs[20]

On the ploughed–up earth of the Jewish cemetery (of Dobrzyn)[21]

Zadok Zudkevitz (author of this article) together with his friends [22]

Translator's Footnotes

1. From *My Town: In Memory of the Communities Dobrzyn-Gollob*, edited by M. Harpaz, (published by the Dobrzyn-Golub Society, Israel, 1969), pp. 130-136.

2. *Narodowa Demokracja* = National Democracy, a well established Polish political party

3. *Obóz Zjednoczenia Narodowego* = Camp of National Unity, a Polish nationalist party founded in 1937

4. The new priest referred to is probably Father Charczewski, who in 1938 wrote an article in the periodical *Chronicles* entitled "Was There a Ritual Murder in Dobrzyn?" In it he accepted the blood libel against the Jews as historical fact, although he also concluded that the Jews of Dobrzyn were probably not guilty of the 1926 incident in which a Gypsy girl was found near death in the Jewish cemetery.

5. A town in Poland where anti-Jewish riots had taken place in March, 1936. See Abba Kovner, *Scrolls of Testimony*, translated into English by Eddie Levenston, JPS, 1993; reproduced in the following link: http://www.worldcat.org/wcpa/servlet/org.oclc.lac.ui.DialABookServlet?oclcnum=44681771.

6. A town 40 km east of Warsaw (about 250 km southeast of Dobrzyn), the scene of a series of anti-Jewish riots in April-May, 1936 in which many Jews were wounded and some killed (see: http://www.sztetl.org.pl/en/article/minsk-mazowiecki/5,history/?print=1)

7. A city in Poland, about 40 km southwest of Dobrzyn

8. A street in Dobrzyn, running northeast out of the main square

9. A town located 30 km southwest of Dobrzyn.

10. A city in Poland, about 200 km south of Dobrzyn.

11. Study hall

12. Curtain, usually elaborately embroidered, hung over the door of the ark that houses Torah scrolls

13. Prayer shawls

14. Women's section of the synagogue, usually in a balcony

15. Golub was connected to Dobrzyn by a bridge spanning the Drevęc River.

16. A town 25 km due east of Dobrzyn

17. A town on the Vistula River, about 100 km southeast of Dobrzyn

18. The Anders army, named after its commander, Władysław Anders, was the "Polish Armed Forces in the East" that was organized within the Soviet Union after the Germans invaded it. After filling its ranks with former Polish prisoners of war, the Anders army made its way to Palestine via Iran and Iraq. See the following link: http://en.wikipedia.org/wiki/Anders%27_Army.

19. *Martef haShoah*, the first Holocaust museum established in Israel (1948). It is located on Mount Zion in Jerusalem. Its walls are covered with hundreds of plaques, each of which memorializes the Jewish victims of a European community. The plaque at the lower left is a memorial to the Jews of Dobrzyn-Golub.

20. From page 132 of Ref. 1.

21. From page 134 of Ref. 1.

22. From page 136 of Ref. 1.

[Pages 137-138]

The Men Left and Didn't Return [1]

By Yehoshua Flusberg, 1969

Translated by Allen Flusberg

It was now two weeks that the Germans were in our town. First, even before they entered it, we had fled, following the retreating Polish army, and we had reached Skempenu[2]. But then the Germans also came there.

I remember that it was the time of *Selichot*[3], and my uncle, Mr. Getzel-Meir Horowitz, poured his heart out in prayer, asking Almighty God to have mercy on his people And there was at that time a special meaning to his request.

I was very young then when the first German soldiers appeared, only 13 years old, but to this very day I have not forgotten the fear that seized us all. We felt that the Day of Judgment was indeed near. Those days outside our town were very hard on us, particularly with *Rosh Hashanah*[4] approaching. So we decided to return to our home in Dobrzyn, and we got back on the eve of the holiday.[5]

We were afraid to pray communally in the synagogue, and so we gathered on the eve of *Rosh Hashanah* in the home of the *Moreh Horaa*[6]. But the next day we discovered that a communal service had taken place in the *shtiebel*[7] of the Ger Hassidim, and all had passed quietly. My father was filled with courage, and he decided that he, too, would pray in the shtiebel, come what may This walk to the *shtiebel* had become an expression of great devotion and a *kiddush hashem*.[8]

Even in ordinary times a great fear enveloped those praying on *Rosh Hashanah*. But this time the fear was even greater. A heavy silence descended on everyone at the moment Mr. Yehoshua Rosenthal, who had a *chazaka*[9] on leading the *shacharit*[10] service, raised his voice in prayer.

Suddenly an alarmed whisper swept through the congregation: the Germans had surrounded the *shtiebel*. The great silence was torn by a sharp command: "Come out!"

We were surrounded by German soldiers. A light rain began to fall. I slipped away from the Germans and ran home to bring coats for my father and my brother David. When I returned as quickly as I could to the *shtiebel*, all the women of the town were already there, carrying coats and bundles, and trying to press close to their loved ones and hand over to them what they had brought them. I, too, pushed my way through and was able to hand the coats to my brother. Afterwards I got away from there and began, for some reason, to walk through the streets of the town.

After some time had passed I found myself again standing near the *shtiebel*. The sight that revealed itself to me was shocking: the Holy Ark was broken into, and the Torah scrolls were rolling on the floor, torn and defiled. With tears in my eyes, I gathered the books and put them back in the Holy Ark.

That day the men were ordered to assemble for muster. The order was brief and concise: "Every Jewish man who does not appear in the next ten minutes will be shot!"

How sad was the look of the men who began to come out of their hiding places to obey the order. I remember how my aunt Chana pleaded with her husband, Mr. Mendel Gurfinkel, the *shochet* and *bodek*[11], that he should not put his life in danger, God forbid, but rather that he, too, should hurry to appear. And Moshe Rudzink ran as fast as he could after the buses, begging that they should agree to take him, too.

On that day, Jewish Dobrzyn was emptied of all its men.

A period of anxiety and anticipation descended on us. When it became clear that the men were in Bydgoszcz[12], Mrs. Stoltzman gathered up her courage, rented a wagon and went there, carrying many packages with her. But when she got there she was unable to find them.

The men had indeed been there for about two weeks, but then they disappeared. The (much later) investigations and the requests for information from the Red Cross turned nothing up.

The only one who came back from there was Mr. Yisrael Miller, who was freed by the Germans in return for a huge sum of money, and was brought home ill in an ambulance. But the Angel of Death descended even on him: after several days the heads of the 35 wealthy families, with him among them, were sent to a place from which they never returned.

A single "regards" from the heads of the families reached us via a German newspaper that was published either in Torun or Bydgoszcz. In the newspaper there appeared a picture of Jews who were quarrying stones. The picture was accompanied by the headline "Jews Being Trained for Work." In the group of four Jews, all with beards and *peyot*[13], and appearing to be holding each other up, was my father.

Except for this "regards," no additional information on their fate ever reached us. They disappeared and are no more.

But the forests of Bydgoszcz hide the secret within them, a secret of days of terror and atrocities.

Family of Eliyahu Flusberg[14]

And cursed be he who says: Avenge!
Vengeance of this sort, blood revenge for a small child
The Devil has not yet created…

— H.N. Bialik[15]

Translator's Footnotes

1. From *My Town: In Memory of the Communities Dobrzyn-Gollob*, edited by M. Harpaz, (published by the Dobrzyn-Golub Society, Israel, 1969), pp. 137–138.

2. Skępe, Poland, about 40 km southeast of Dobrzyn

3. Late-night prayers for forgiveness, recited in synagogues on several nights before *Rosh Hashana*

4. Jewish New Year

5. Wednesday, September 13, 1939

6. A distinguished rabbi and expert on Jewish law, probably serving as the head rabbi of the town

7. Small synagogue, usually Hassidic

8. Sanctification of the Name of God by fulfilling a commandment in spite of risk

9. Priority, i.e. he had led this prayer for many years

10. Morning

11. Ritual slaughterer and inspector of meat for kashrut

12. A larger town, about 80 km west of Dobrzyn

13. Side-curls

14. Yehoshua Flusberg (second from right), his father Eliyahu-Mordechai (far right), his mother Esther-Leah (nee Lesznik), and his older brother David (far left), circa 1938

15. From Hayim Nachman Bialik's poem "On the Slaughter," written in 1903 in reaction to the pogrom against the Jews that had just occurred in Kishinev, Bessarabia (presently in Moldova).

[Pages 140-144]

Fleeing for Our Lives[1]

By Yitzhak Ryz

Translated by Allen Flusberg

When the war broke out on the 1st of November [sic][2] 1939, I was in Dobrzyn. I recall that from the moment the German forces penetrated into Poland, a universal flight began: everyone was running away, fleeing for their lives from the enemy. On that very day all the Jews of Dobrzyn escaped to Sitno[3], but even there we stayed over for only a single night. On the next day we continued to run away, trying to get as far away as we could from the foe. After several days we reached Wloclawek[4]. When we had just crossed the bridge over the Vistula River, the Poles blew it up to try to prevent the enemy's progress.

We rested for a few hours in Wloclawek, but rest was actually well beyond us. We continued our flight day and night until we reached Sochaczew[5], which is near Warsaw[6]. By then bitter battles were taking place there, as enemy planes swooped down in one wave after another, dropping destructive, fiery bombs.

Fleeing with all our might we managed to get far away from the combat zone, running with all our strength without any clear destination…seeking to escape from the inferno of gunfire pouring in from every direction. The people who had come from Dobrzyn scattered in all directions as each of them tried to save himself.

The villages of Gostynin and Gabin[7], which we finally reached, were already in the hands of the Germans. Everything had been consumed by fire; the enemy left nothing behind. I lost track of my brothers, who had been with me until then, as each of them looked for a hiding place for himself. We tried to hide in the cellars of houses or in bunkers—anyplace a person might be able to crawl into…

But all these attempts were futile. The Germans located those who were in hiding and ordered everyone, Jews and non-Jews alike, to come out into an open field. Tens of thousands of people were there with me. We were ordered to move arms and heavy equipment from some other place to the field in which these tens of thousands of people were being held.

We did the work, our knees buckling and our thoughts full of fear that these were to be our last hours. And when we completed the work our nerves were completely frayed, as if we were on the brink of a breakdown. Alas, many times we were to experience terrifying moments like these, as we stood at the edge of an abyss, seeing death in front of our eyes, and struggling, even at such moments, to escape with our lives...

To our great surprise the Germans ordered all of us to return to our homes. We turned away from there with great trepidation and began to walk, without knowing where we were going. We didn't ask any questions...We walked without any destination, with our last strength, as if there was a way that this trek could somehow rescue us. When we reached Wloclawek we found signs of destruction everywhere: the houses were in ruins and the bridge had been destroyed. Knowing we could not stay there, we searched for ways to continue on towards our town. After a great deal of effort we succeeded in crossing the Vistula, and finally we reached our town, Dobrzyn.

How depressing and frightening was our return to our home town, the place where we had spent our childhood. And how shocking were the stories that we heard from those who had stayed behind in Dobrzyn—those that the Germans had so far not harmed. We heard that all the men who had not been able to flee had been taken by the Germans and transported somewhere, a place from which they had not returned again. We didn't know what exactly had happened to them, but beyond the shadow of a doubt they had been executed...The cantor of the town, together with Avraham Makowski and Frenkiel had been executed by the Germans near the Golub fortress on that very same day of retribution, when all the men had been taken away from the town and transported to a place from which they never returned.

We stayed in town for 3-4 weeks, sustaining ourselves by selling some of the few items that were still in our houses, until a Nazi arch-murderer, accompanied by some officers, appeared in the town, and proclaimed that all the Jews must vacate the town within three weeks. Three days later the son of a Dobrzyn German came by, explaining that he wanted to let us know that the Germans were going to expel all of us in two days. He advised us to hurry and leave even sooner.

We left our homes again and set off, leaving behind my mother, who was confined to bed, together with my youngest brother, who would take care of her while she was ill.

When we arrived in Wegiersk[8] at dawn, most of the Jews of Dobrzyn were already there. We continued going, walking with no destination, desperate and weary…Among those who were walking I met my uncle Yisrael Asher and his family. I told them I was returning to Dobrzyn. I couldn't go on walking while knowing that my mother and younger brother were left by themselves in the town, at the Germans' mercy.

I returned along back roads. I was actually risking my life, but I was propelled by an overpowering force. Finally I was in Dobrzyn again, in my very own house. And there was my mother, still lying in bed, ill, with my brother at her side, tending to her.

I knew that we had to leave this place at any price. After a great deal of effort, I managed to buy a horse and wagon, and we set out on our way—my ill mother, my brother and I—traveling without any food or water; I struggled to obtain at least enough food for the horse, so that it would have the strength to continue dragging the wagon loaded with its passengers.

We wandered along roads for weeks, hungry and tired, just a few refugees fleeing among thousands of others. Finally we reached Ostrołęka and Łomża[9]. Here my mother, brothers and sisters parted from me. And I have never seen them again; they shared the fate of all our other Jewish brethren…

In Łomża I met up with Yechiel Lipstadt. We decided to make our way together to the Russian border, which was not very far from Ostrołęka. Near the border we conducted some business to sustain ourselves, until we managed to cross the border. We stayed there for a while, waiting to see what would happen.

After several days an announcement was published, ordering all foreigners to have their passports available and to register, indicating where they were headed. We, together with many others, stated that we were on our way to Israel. Well, we were much too naïve: instead of Israel, they sent us deep into Russia, to labor in the forests. We joined tens of thousands of others who were sent to do this work—approximately 300,000 men, women and children.

We were sent to Murmansk[10], but along the way more than half of the men died of hunger, while those who were still alive were sent to Midozh-Gorsk[11], which is near Finland. I didn't see any trace of Yechiel Lipstadt there. I remained in this place about one and a half years, working as a mechanic. Then war between Germany and Russia broke out, and another period of wandering, suffering and hunger began for me.[12]

We were sent to Ural in a large boat that sailed along the Onega, Volga and Kema Rivers until we reached our destination. I will never forget this terrible journey, five thousand of us men crowded together with no food and no water for about forty days. It seemed to us that this journey would never end and that only a small number of us would survive it. And indeed, many perished along the way. Those who survived were helped a great deal by Russian citizens, who were also sent along with us on the journey to Ural.

Even in the Ural camp our situation did not improve very much. In order to keep ourselves alive, I and another fellow I met there became entertainers—he played the violin as I sang along. And so, by making an effort to bring a smile to the faces of the other residents of the camp, we were rewarded with a few crumbs from our brothers in misery.

When the Polish Anders army[13] began to organize, new possibilities opened up for us. The Jews were released from labor. We were now free to travel anywhere we wished. We chose to go to Uzbekistan, where we managed to find work mixing concrete. Although the work was difficult the compensation we received was enough for only a slice of bread. From there we were sent to Kazakhstan. To my great delight I met up again with Yechiel Lipstadt, and together we began planning our future. We decided to jump off a moving train. After innumerable hardships we were able to get to Samarkand.

And again we began looking for a way to keep ourselves alive. We started trafficking in bread, but very quickly we were caught and jailed. The verdict, 10 years of prison for bread trafficking, was not considered a very harsh sentence in that period. After I had been in prison for three years, I sent a written request to the government in Moscow, asking for a pardon; in my defense I claimed that everything I had done was done only to keep myself alive. I was given the pardon.

The war was ending. After I was freed from prison I began planning my return to Dobrzyn. Finally, after several months of torment—utmost suffering and agony—along the way back, I reached our town. There, to my delight, I found Yisrael Yitzhak Nussbaum, Shmuel Rebi, Shemaya Prum, Yehuda Kopland, as well as Manya Kowalski.

I did not stay in Dobrzyn very long, however. Thoughts about my parents, sisters, and brother hadn't let up for even a moment during all my hardships and wanderings. Now I decided to try to follow their trail and find out what had become of them. After several days of searching, I was able to find only my brother Yaakov in Szczecin. We decided to cross over to the American-occupied part of Germany. From there I later immigrated to the United States, where my brother Avraham Moshe was already located. Another brother, Leyb Shmuel Hirsh, had immigrated to England before the war. All the others—my parents, my oldest brother, my youngest brother, Meir, and all five of my sisters—were exterminated by the Nazi foe.

These recollections are just a tiny fraction of the heavy burden of memories that I carry from the period of the Holocaust. I have successfully established a home and a family in the US, but I can never forget those horrific days that have been engraved deep into my heart.

Can there be any balm for this great pain? We can draw a small bit of consolation from the State of Israel, seeing as we recently did here—during a trip in which we traversed the country from one end to the other—our brothers and sisters laboring to build the country up and to watchfully protect our people's existence.

> And I will return the captivity of my people Israel,
> And they will rebuild desolate cities and settle them,
> And they will plant vineyards and drink their wine
> And they will cultivate gardens and eat their fruit.

—Amos 9:14

Translator's Footnotes

1. From *My Town: In Memory of the Communities Dobrzyn-Gollob*, edited by M. Harpaz, (published by the Dobrzyn-Golub Society, Israel, 1969), pp. 140-144.

2. This should read "September".

3. Sitno is a village located 9km southeast of Dobrzyn.

4. Wloclawek is a city 60km south of Dobrzyn, on the Vistula River.

5. Sochaczew is a city 150km southeast of Dobrzyn, a bit south of the Vistula. It can be reached from Wloclawek by going eastward along the southern bank of the Vistula.

6. Warsaw is ~50km east of Sochaczew.

7. Gostynin and Gąbin are two villages 20km apart and south of the Vistula, about 50km northwest of Sochaczew.

8. Węgiersk is located about 5km south of the center of Dobrzyn.

9. Ostrołęka lies 220km east of Dobrzyn, and Łomża 30km further east.

10. Murmansk, Russia, is near the Barents Sea, some 1300km north of St. Petersburg.

11. The reference is probably to Medvezhyegorsk, which lies along the Murmansk railway at the northern end of Lake Onega; it is about 100km east of the Russian-Finnish border. See the following link: http://en.wikipedia.org/wiki/Medvezhyegorsk.

12. During the second half of 1941, shortly after Germany invaded the Soviet Union, Finland also invaded the Soviet Union and occupied Medvezhyegorsk and the surrounding areas, pressing the Russians to evacuate the region.

13. The Anders army, named after its commander, Władysław Anders, was the "Polish Armed Forces in the East" that was organized within the Soviet Union after the Germans invaded it. After filling its ranks with former Polish prisoners of war, the Anders army made its way to Palestine via Iran and Iraq. See the following link: http://en.wikipedia.org/wiki/Anders%27_Army.

14. The Chamber of the Holocaust, a museum established in 1958, is located on Mount Zion in Jerusalem. See the following link: http://en.wikipedia.org/wiki/Chamber_of_the_Holocaust.

15. From p. 141 of reference cited in Footnote 1.

A memorial service in the Chamber of the Holocaust[14][15]

[Page 145]

How did we Manage?[1]
by Yehudit Golan (Rosenwaks)
Translated by Allen Flusberg

As I take pen in hand to write of my bitter memories of the Holocaust period, my hair stands on end again, and my entire body trembles…I feel as if my heart is about to go into shock…

I see them again, my Dobrzyn kindred: men, women and children, on the day of terror when they were expelled, destitute, from their homes—pursued like beasts of the forest, with no protection and no shelter; isolated and desperate in a cruel world.

Starting from that bitter and fateful day, the day the Germans entered Dobrzyn like ravenous, wild beasts—taking the men, and among them my dear father, and sending them away, never to return—my heart is continuously torn with the question: how was I able to take all this? How did I, a young, frail girl, manage? How did I survive the frightful catastrophe? How was I able to live through all the ordeals and afflictions, all the horrific sights?

How did we human shadows manage all this, transported in the train cars of death, crammed in together with no air to breathe? How did we not lose our humanity? Can it be that a Higher Power watched over us and accompanied us, those few who were saved, in our many wanderings from one village to another, from one city to another, via the Warsaw and Lodz ghettos to the crematoria of Auschwitz and Mathausen?

Who has ever been able to probe the mysteries of Providence? We, the few who were rescued from the furnaces, do not have any answers. We have been left with only the memories that inundate us every day, every night…

***

Already for several years before World War II broke out we had felt that the ground was slipping out from under our feet. In our town, too, anti-Semitism continued to grow more intense: a boycott against Jewish merchants, pogroms…In the evenings we did not step outside, fearing that we would be attacked by anti-Semitic agitators. Still, even in this somber period it did not occur to any of us that a frightening catastrophe might be hanging over our heads…

The persecutions and murders began as soon as the Germans entered the town. A. Riesenfeld of blessed memory, the owner of the Golub pharmacy, was the first victim. He had a noble character and was loved and respected by all. He was a devoted, passionate Zionist. His murder was a terrible blow to all of us, portending that worse was to come.

Afterwards the expulsions began. First they took all the men of the town on *Rosh Hashana*,[2] transporting them away. To this very day we don't know where they brought them and exactly how they were killed. The mystery of this atrocity will apparently never be solved...Several days before the total expulsion they came to take away the wealthy townspeople, transporting them as well to some place they never returned from.

My thoughts turn to the daughter of Mayor Berka, the mayor of the town at that time. Is she now living in peace and security somewhere in Germany? How this murderous woman had rejoiced at our misfortune as she took an active role in the persecution of the Jews! May she be damned!

When the general expulsion order was given, we were already broken in body and spirit, apathetic to what was happening to us. We left everything behind, unable to take along even the minor objects that every person requires. It was hard to get a horse and wagon in that period. We all went on foot, a long procession of men, women and children, exhausted and at a loss, sighing and weeping, none of us knowing what the morrow would bring...walking without knowing where we were going...

***

How frightening and sad was my meeting with my oldest brother, Chaim of blessed memory, who lived in Lodz before the war. When he heard that we had arrived in Warsaw after much wandering, he hurried to come to us. My father and my brother Hersh (Zvi) of blessed memory were no longer alive at that point. He brought me with him to Lodz. After that I didn't see any of my other relatives again.

I stayed with my brother, his wife and small child until the ghetto was liquidated. Certainly it was not easy to hide a small child while the accursed Nazis were spying on every corner, every hiding place. It seemed as if even he understood that something terrible was happening around him, and he adjusted to the circumstances that we were in. As a result, we were able to hide him from the eyes of the murderers until [as we thought] the troubles would end.

After the ghetto was liquidated we were brought to Auschwitz. Even there we continued to believe that we would be rescued; we were unable to imagine that this was the very end…

After three weeks they brought me, together with some others, to Germany. I worked hard there, exhausted and hoping to die, until I had no strength left. What reason was there to continue living? I knew I was the only one left from my entire family. I was as desolate as a juniper in the wilderness[3], with no one to look out for me[4]…

Only the yearning to see the defeat of the Germans kept me alive, encouraging me and giving me strength to tolerate the immense suffering. And indeed, while still on German soil, I did have my revenge: the sight of Germans bombed by the Allies, running for their lives, filling all the roads, their eyes wide with terror…

Even then, on the verge of defeat, they did not let us alone. Instead, they dragged us in train cars for three weeks, with nearly no food and under inhumane conditions, to bring us to Mathausen.

We sensed that the war was nearing its end, and that the Nazi beast was gasping its very last death spasms. And we were then all filled with an intense desire to remain alive and be able to see their downfall.

I don't know how I found the courage, but at the first opportunity I jumped from the train.

I was free, but where might I go back to? Did I still have a home?

An unconscious force drew me, as if against my own will, to return to see the town. I wandered around in it as if in a phantom world, searching for a past that was no more; searching for my father's house, my relatives, the members of the community, and for all that had been dear to my heart here.

All had vanished. I was walking around in a desolate town. Where was the synagogue? Where was the "Street of Gold"[5]? Where were the Jews who once filled the streets, and where were the little ones, engaged in mirth and mischief?

I could not remain in Dobrzyn. I left my town, ruined and devoid of Jews. I was headed for the old-new homeland, the land of Israel. But even now our hardships were not over. The British blockaded the country; we were taken by force and sent to Cyprus, where we stayed for eight solid months, until we were freed and immigrated to Israel. We merited to come to our own country and even to participate in the War of Independence.

My long journey had ended. My heart grieves for the millions who did not make it, who were felled by the hands of the murderers. But we look ahead with the hope that succeeding generations will know lives of freedom, peace and security in our homeland.

> Woe, culture of cowards, woe to the mighty deeds of haughty rabbits!
> That a thousand burly Gentiles should chase after one tiny Jew,
> And myriads of evildoers after two plundered exiles.

(—*From "And the Middle Ages Have Returned", by Z. Shneour.*)

Mrs. Yehudit Golan (née Rosenwaks), a Holocaust survivor, lighting a flame to memorialize the martyrs.[6]

The cemetery, devoid of headstones.[7]

Translator's Footnotes

1. From *My Town: In Memory of the Communities Dobrzyn-Gollob*, edited by M. Harpaz, (published by the Dobrzyn-Golub Society, Israel, 1969), pp. 145-148.

2. Jewish New Year, which falls in September.

3. Allusion to Jeremiah 17:6.

4. Literally "with no kin or redeemer", alluding to Ruth 2:20.

5. This street, called *Die Goldene Gass* (Yiddish for Golden Street or Street of Gold) by the Jews of Dobrzyn, ran northeast from the main square to *Die Lange Gass* (Yiddish for Long Street), as can be seen from the map appearing on pp. 8-9 of reference cited in Footnote 1.

6. From p. 146 of reference cited in Footnote 1.

7. From p. 148 of reference cited in Footnote 1.

[Page 149]

Seven Sections of Hell[1][2]
by Gorny Frum
Translated by Allen Flusberg

November, 1939. Nazi Germany has conquered Poland. The Jews are subject to persecution, with stories of atrocities growing more numerous from one day to the next. We are full of trepidation and at a loss; we do not know what the morrow will bring. We are holed up, hiding indoors, wrapped in winter coats because of the cold, and trembling with terror from the rumors we are hearing.

From the day the men of the town were kidnapped from the prayer houses on *Rosh Hashanah*[3], we have been living in perpetual fear; we have a feeling that a bitter fate is awaiting us, as well. At times we console ourselves, thinking that perhaps we will get lucky and they will let us be.

On November 9, 1939 the dignitaries of the town were asked to report to the Nazi commander. Gravely he ordered them to collect and bring him gold and silver with a total value of 50,000 zloty[4] in the next few hours. He did not forget to warn them that only by paying this ransom could they cancel the decree to expel all the Jews from the town.

All the Jews were seized with fear and terror. We all hastened to bring our valuable objects: silver candlesticks, goblets, gold watches, coins, rings, and even wedding bands. However, we were about to realize the maliciousness of the commander, whose only intention was to rob us of our possessions. We were given travel documents and ordered to leave the town within an hour.

How immense was the blow that had fallen on us, and how great the pandemonium at that moment, as everyone began scurrying about in terror, searching for close relatives, gathering some belongings and preparing to depart. We left the town fearful and in despair, embittered and crying.

The sight was appalling: weeping, overwrought mothers carried their infants in their arms, walking with difficulty on the road leading to Rypin[5]. The mournful convoy extended over several kilometers, with even the elderly and the children forced to go on foot. After a great deal of effort we did manage to rent several wagons from some farmers, and in them we seated the children and the infirm.

We had not yet come to terms with the calamity that had befallen us. From time to time we looked back toward the town we had grown up in, refusing to believe that we had indeed been uprooted from it. The thought gnawed at us: will we return there again someday?

The road from Dobrzyn to Rypin was full of refugees, Jews who just yesterday had sat around their ovens in their very own homes, refusing to believe, until the very last moment, that a terrible calamity was approaching.

The lot of the elderly was the most difficult. They were forced to stop to rest from time to time to catch their breath and recover their strength. How my heart went out to our acquaintance, the tailor Hersh Baruch Boretka, who was disabled and yet tried, in vain, to keep up with the others. Finally we found him a seat in a wagon that had been intended only for toddlers and children.

During that entire day the little children did not stop crying. The sound of their cries was mixed with that of their parents' sighs, as they continued walking without knowing where they were headed. From time to time people looked at one another with a silent question, "to where?"

The sight of the women whose husbands had been taken away by the Nazis on the eve of Rosh Hashanah was particularly painful. They walked along with their children—widows with no breadwinner to support them, their eyes full of sorrow.

[Page 150]

*

I was only sixteen years old when I left Dobrzyn, and my younger brother was thirteen. We marched along together on the road leading to Rypin. After innumerable hardships we reached Plock[6] together with our mother. But as soon as we heard how the Nazis had abused the Jews there we quickly left the city, deciding to make our way to our father's birthplace, Minsk Mazowiecki[7].

Along the way we reached Warsaw and decided to visit our aunt, our father's sister, for a few hours. Our mother, who was exhausted and frail, decided to stay at her sister-in-law's home, and there she passed away shortly thereafter. My brother and I continued on our way, hand in hand. As we walked we met several families from our town, among them: Sali Pieniek, his sister Rochtsa and her husband Mordechai Lipka; the Pozmanter family; the

Goldfinger family—sisters and their parents. Together we reached Minsk Mazowiecki. After a short time, Franya and Tova Dobraszklanka arrived there as well.

It appeared that we had gone from bad to worse. The Jews here had been ordered to wear a white band with a blue star, which the ravenous beasts referred to as a "lanta". Each and every Jew had to wear this badge, and woe to anyone who was caught without one on his clothing. He could expect to be imprisoned; or, even worse, to be sentenced to death by firing squad.

As was done in many other cities, a ghetto was established in Minsk Mazowiecki. Thousands of people were brought there, crowded into a small area, hungry and freezing. Every day orders were given whose only purpose was to make the lives of the Jews miserable; even without these orders the Jews were reeling under the burden of their torment.

As the war widened and the Germans needed more and more metal, the Jews were ordered to bring silver, copper and steel to a central location that had been set up by the Nazis. The other residents were also ordered to support the war effort, but the main demands were imposed on the Jews.

I had in my possession two candlesticks that I had carried along the entire way, wrapped in a blanket so that no one would see them. They were an heirloom from my grandmother and so were precious to me. I remembered how my mother used to light Sabbath candles in them. After spreading a white tablecloth over the table she would place the candlesticks on it. She would cover her eyes with the palms of her hands, whispering a prayer. As the glow of candlelight flooded the house, my mother's sad eyes would sparkle with joy.

I couldn't bring myself to hand these precious candlesticks over to the Nazis. I decided to bury them in the ground, in a hidden place, until that day when I would be able to come back to retrieve them…

Later on, during the summer of 1941, a command was given to hand over fur—even torn bits of fur and fur buttons—to the occupying administration. Whoever had any fur in her possession quickly buried it in the ground, and only scraps of fur were brought over and handed in to the Germans. We understood that the Germans must be becoming well acquainted with the Russian winter, given that they were in such need of fur. The following saying was going around among us: "Hitler, you won't win the war, even in a warm Jewish fur."

In the summer of 1942, rumors were beginning to reach us from Warsaw, and also from the outlying towns—rumors of Jews being murdered in extermination camps that had been established for this very purpose. Filled with fear that our fate was also about to be sealed, we endeavored to be taken on in German factories; we hoped that if we could show that we were of some benefit they would let us be and not harm us.

My brother managed to get a job in a carpentry shop, and as a result his situation improved; he was entitled to a larger food ration and to a permit allowing him to leave the ghetto. But this improved situation did not last very long. On August 21, 1942, Lithuanian and Ukrainian gangs, accompanied by the German military police, raided the streets of the ghetto, and began to cruelly beat—and even murder—the Jews. Children and the elderly were murdered then and there, while all others were brought to the market square, from which they were transported to extermination camps.

Hearing the shouts of people being tormented and murdered, we were all looking for some way to save ourselves. Many people hid themselves in attics or cellars. I saw my chance to slip out of the ghetto. Once outside I came upon some farmers who were going back to their villages, returning from market day; I joined them and tried to make myself look like one of them.

As night fell I found myself a place to lie down in a nearby forest. I was shivering from both cold and terror as I lay there, listening to the sounds of shots and shouting. The hours passed very slowly as I waited for morning and daylight.

In the morning I discerned a group of Jews, brethren in sorrow, who had also escaped from the murderers. I came over to them, and we conferred among ourselves. We decided to wait out the storm and remain in the forest for now. But after two days had passed we were extremely hungry and thirsty, and so we were forced to return to the city. We also felt a strong desire to know what had happened to our relatives and friends.

We made our way cautiously, trying not to fall into the hands of the military police. Here and there we observed Jewish workers engaged in various types of labor. From them we found out that the Germans left about 250 Jewish workers in the town, among them carpenters, tailors and mechanics. All of them were being housed in a school building, the Kopernik School. The rest of the Jews of the ghetto had been murdered or had been sent in train cars and trucks to extermination camps. Only a small number of Jews had managed to escape and save themselves during the pandemonium.

We continued on our way, our destination now the Kopernik School. There we found some workers, whose faces told the story of the terrible calamity that had been visited on the Jews. Their eyes were sunken with grief. Choking back tears, they told us about the horrifying acts of murder in the ghetto and how their close relatives had died.

We stayed there until nightfall, when other workers began returning from their jobs. My brother was among them. When he saw me he was so overcome with joy that I became concerned that he was losing his mind. He had been so certain that I had been murdered or that I had been sent with the others to an extermination camp.

The next day many more of those who had escaped to the forests, or had hidden out in various hiding places, began returning. To a large extent they were motivated by the information that had reached them that nearly all the Jews who had been in the Kopernik School had survived. Within only a single week the number of people in the camp increased to about 800. Among those who came back were Sali Pieniek, his wife, and children; Ruchtza Lipka and Franya Pieniek, who had hidden for several days in a nearby dung heap.

The school was too small for all of us. Some of us slept in the courtyard, while others slept in a sitting position. When SS men came by, which was often, we had to quickly hide from them. For the time being they let us alone, thinking that there were very few of us.

Two weeks after the mass murder SS men again raided our camp, surrounding the school from all sides. They ordered us to kneel down and began shooting indiscriminately. We were terrified.

Then silence reigned. An SS officer appeared before us and read out loud names of workers from a list that had been prepared in advance. Those whose names were called out were ordered to return to the school building. I was very glad when I saw my brother among them; at least he would survive…

The rest of us were surrounded by SS men. Threatening us with their weapons, they led us away, but we had no idea where they were taking us. We believed this was going to be the end, that they were about to shoot us then and there, or send us to extermination camps. The passing minutes seemed like an eternity…

Finally we were brought to an abandoned house. Only a small number of SS men stayed behind to guard us. We were permitted to move around within the house, but they warned us not to go near the door or any of the windows.

How difficult and dreadful the suspense is when you can't tell what is about to happen. Only the children quickly adapt to the situation, as if no danger is hanging over their heads. But we adults are steeped in fear; we sense something bad is coming.

Hunger is gnawing at us. We haven't tasted any food for an entire day and night. Nor do we have any food to give the children. The bolder among us are trying to think of ruses to escape from this place, but they are afraid to get close to the door.

On the second day of our stay here an SS company appeared, accompanied by several civilians. We were ordered to go out to the courtyard. There we were told that they needed 100 men and 80 women in good health with no children. And so, as we stood before them, they selected those they needed from among us. Whoever received the lash of a whip on his back was fortunate—for this was the sign that he had been selected. Franya Pieniek and I were among the few fortunate ones who were included in the group of women.

On the spot we were assigned workplaces. I was in a group who worked in the forest. The job I had been given was to strip the bark off the trees. It was particularly difficult work, but I carried it out in a manner that satisfied my taskmaster. That most intense desire to remain alive gave me the strength to overcome all hardships.

Every day we rose at dawn for work. After roll call we received a bowl of nothing but soup, without any bread. At noon as well we received nothing more than some soup cooked with coarse flour. Only in the evening were we granted 100 grams of bread with jelly. Yet we were given a salary, 20 zloty each and every week. How bitter and ironic that at a time when we were on the verge of being exterminated they were bestowing a salary on us...

The days are passing. It is already December. The cold is at its worst. Still wearing summer clothing, we are shivering from cold. Only after some time passes do we receive blankets. At least we will be warm at night.

The information reaching us is appalling: mass murder of the Jews in the nearly towns. Again Jews are streaming into Minsk Mazowiecki, to the Kopernik School, mainly those who managed to slip away from the transports to the extermination camps. Among those who return are Sali Pieniek and his daughter Ruth. Sali's wife and sister have been brought to the extermination camp in Treblinka.

Sali's situation is especially difficult, since sheltering children in the Kopernik School is forbidden. Mornings, as we leave for work, we hide her [Ruth] between the mattresses, where she stays until we come back. But our concerns about her fate and that of all of us never let up, not for a single moment.

Finally we decide to contact the partisans, thinking that perhaps they can rescue us. We get together with their leaders and propose to them that about 40 of us should join them, as a first preliminary group, joining others who were setting out on this very day to the forests. I was quite sorry that I wasn't one of those who were selected to be in this first group. I was jealous of them that they were already about to leave the Kopernik School.

How horrible was the information that came back to us the next day, concerning the bitter fate of that entire group. It appears that the Polish police ambushed them and killed them all.

I continue strategizing, knowing that our days are numbered...With the help of some acquaintances I succeed in obtaining passports for my brother and myself, but we can't use them, since we have nowhere to go. So we stay in Kopernik. Someone suggests that I should go to work in Germany, in a place where no one knows me, since young women can easily find positions there. However, I cannot agree to leave my brother behind by himself. And we are thinking positively, since in the meantime rumors are circulating that with the advent of spring the war will be over.

To our misfortune a typhus epidemic has broken out in our camp. Almost half of the population comes down with it. However, many of them are making the effort to go out to work, in spite of their high fever. The Polish doctor from Minsk Mazowiecki, who has been invited for a visit, hurries to report the situation to the German commander, warning him of the danger to the city inhabitants.

And indeed, his warning found a sympathetic ear. On December 24th SS men raided the camp and began killing those who were ill. Sali Pieniek was also among them. We hid his daughter, Ruth; but when the girl heard the sound of the shooting, she understood that something terrible was going on, and she burst into tears, shouting: "I want to live together with my father; I don't want to be left alone!" When she came out of her hiding place a bullet fired by the murderers struck her, and she was killed on the spot.

When the killing was over, a new count was made of the inhabitants of the camp. Then 218 men and women who looked weak to them were taken to the local cemetery, where they were ordered to dig pits. After that they were all shot. One of them was Franya Pieniek.

We burst into bitter tears, lamenting all our dear ones who had fallen by the hands of the murderers. We wept until no more tears could come, knowing that a similar fate was in store for us...

Now they are no longer taking us out to work; we are inside the camp, surrounded by a very heavy guard. They have given us the job of erecting a barbed-wire fence around the entire camp. This work intensifies our speculation that our end must be near. We decide we will not allow the murderers to lead us away like sheep to the slaughter. We start collecting whatever we can find: scrap iron, stones and bricks; and we resolve to avenge our own deaths. The camp is completely sealed—no one can enter or leave. We listen for the slightest rustle that might indicate that they are coming for us, to take us away and put us to death...

Those with whom I share a room do not cease encouraging me to leave this place. They castigate me, telling me I should not deprive myself of life, that I have every chance of saving myself, and that I should not be seeking a hero's death. But how can I go away and leave my brother behind—the brother who is the only member of my family still left alive?

I remembered a Polish friend who was living in Warsaw. On a recent visit to the camp she had promised that she would stand behind me if I needed her. So I decided to slip away from here, together with my brother, and somehow try to reach Warsaw.

We are in a frenzy of preparations for our escape. I put red coloring on my pallid face, gather my hair into two long braids, and cover my head with a red scarf—all of this to make myself look like a *shiksa*[8]. My brother, however, is wearing a cap. On January 6, 1943 we slip past the barbed wire surrounding Camp Kopernik and wend our way to the train station, from which we wish to get to Warsaw. We proceed cautiously: we don't go to the nearest train station, but instead walk to the next one, several kilometers away. There we get on the train and go to Warsaw.

At evening we reached the big city and went straight to my friend. She and her husband gave us a warm reception, promising to provide all the help they could give us. Her brother, who introduced himself as Ukrainian, also lived in the same house.

On the very day after our arrival my brother became ill. His fever rose to a temperature above 40 degrees C. He needed a doctor but I was afraid to get one, since he might be able to recognize my brother as Jewish. On the third day red blotches appeared on my brother's body, a clear indication of spotted typhus.

We are in a very unpleasant and—even dangerous—situation, since concealing the illness from the government health department is a severely punishable offense. I am at a loss, especially since the Ukrainian brother's attitude towards us has begun to change. Apparently he is pressuring his sister to send us away. I myself hear him threaten her that if she doesn't send us away he will throw my brother out into the street. Fearful, I give the Ukrainian brother a watch the next day as a present. He calms down somewhat and I no longer hear him making threats. However, I sense that we cannot stay in this house anymore—that we have to leave as soon as possible.

Several times it occurs to me that we have no alternative but to return to Kopernik. But one day I get hold of a flier from the Underground, which reports that the Kopernik Camp has been liquidated—the camp has been burned down with everyone in it. I can hardly believe what I have read, but there is no reason for me to doubt the veracity of this report.[9]

I was shocked. My closest friends—together with whom I had experienced so much suffering and hardship—had been devoured by fire...My throat was choked with tears, but I had no more strength to weep. Nor was there anyone there who could comfort me in my great mourning for the death of my comrades, with whom I had been linked with every fiber of my soul, with whom I had shared my bread and water, and with whom I had woven dreams and hopes.

Meanwhile no improvement in my brother's condition has occurred; he is moaning and burning up with fever. The house we are in looks to us like a trap, since the Ukrainian brother is still plotting to get rid of us. Perhaps I might have overcome my concerns and gotten a doctor, but I am deterred by the frowns on the brother's face. I am at a loss, and I have no one to talk to about my anxiety.

In the end I decided to turn to someone who used to visit the house regularly—an elderly man, the very same man who had handed me the

Underground flier. He seemed to me to be a good person, a gentle soul. I told him all about my troubles, and he promised to do his best to help me. And already on the very next day he happily informed me that he had been able to find a suitable place for us to live—in the house of an elderly widow, in one of the nearby villages.

How happy I was when we put my brother, wrapped in a blanket, into the carriage we had ordered to take us to the village. The elderly lady was waiting for us along the way to bring us to her house. After I had told her in a long conversation all about the events of the last few years, I was glad to see that she was an honest, good-natured woman.

It was only at nightfall that we reached our destination. Quickly we put my brother to bed, covering him with blankets to keep him warm. At the same time the old woman revealed to me that two Jews were already hiding in her house. They were two brothers, Feivl and Shlomo Bronstein, from the town of Planitz[10] that is near Warsaw. They had managed to slip away from a group of Jews that had been sent to an extermination camp.

My trust in the elderly woman grew stronger, especially when I saw with what great care she had prepared a suitable hiding place for us outside the rooms that were actually part of the house. She had told her village neighbors that her sister's children, from the city of Zamosc[11] had come to visit. To prevent anyone from becoming suspicious, I accompanied her to church on Sundays, and I even did some work in the garden and within the house.

The days went by. My brother recovered and began to walk around in the house. But now a new matter began to irk us—our money had run out, and we no longer had any means to pay for our lodging and food. Although the good-natured old woman never even mentioned it, we felt uncomfortable. She was a masseur by profession, and she often made trips to work in Warsaw. She would bring back various staples. She didn't even forget to bring us books to read, knowing how we longed for reading material during the long hours in which we sat around idle.

In this manner spring and summer passed. Then we found out that a rumor was going around in the village—that the old woman was concealing Jews in her house. One of the neighbors had said that with her own eyes she had seen a bearded man walking around inside the house. Another neighbor had added that for a while she had been wondering why the old woman was emptying her waste pails during nighttime only, and why she was cooking so many potatoes.

We knew that danger was looming over our heads, so we began looking for a suitable hiding place; after all, the farmers do not have a great love for Jews...The Bronstein brothers had hidden themselves in an attic, and I was also seeking a hiding place of this type for my brother. I was very glad when I did find a hiding place in an attic—a narrow, small area that was like a dungeon cell, so confined that no one could even stretch out in it to lie down. To reach it one had to climb up a ladder and then crawl over to its opening. We had no other alternative. My brother had to move there, while I remained very fearful for him. I continued to sleep in the same bed with the elderly woman.

One night the police knocked at the door to the house. The old woman, who was half asleep, opened the door and stood trembling before the military police. They began shouting at her, accusing her of concealing Jews in the house. Without waiting for a reply they went down to the cellar, looking for Jews in hiding. When they didn't find anyone there they turned to the attic, the clatter of their boots as they climbed the stairs audible at a distance. Our hearts stood still; we thought the end had come. However, they didn't find the hiding place. The men in hiding held their breath in fear as they listened to the policemen threatening to set the house on fire. But finally the police, having given up, left the house.

From that day onward we became much more cautious. The men hardly ever left their hiding place. For two-and-a-half years we remained this way, imprisoned in our hideout, as from time to time the police visited us, turning the house upside down as they looked for Jews.

A few weeks before the Liberation we were in bad shape. The little food that we had was running out, and the elderly lady, whose health had been affected, could no longer travel to Warsaw for work. There was no money, and we were starving for some bread.

With her remaining strength, the elderly woman made an effort to take care of us. She went to the houses of the wealthier farmers and gathered old bread and a few potatoes, explaining that they were for the goats that belonged to her sister, who lived in the vicinity. We toasted the bread and ate it to satisfy our hunger.

Rumors of impending liberation lifted our spirits, while at the same time we observed the airplanes flying overhead and heard the bombs exploding. How happy we were when the old woman came to us with the news that the

German army was retreating in panic and that the Red Army was rapidly approaching our village.

In August 1944 we left our hiding place for the first time, going out into daylight after having hid for about three full years[12]. We looked half dead, yellow and gaunt, like human shadows. We continued to stay at the elderly woman's house, first because we were afraid of being attacked by the local people, whose hatred for Jews was intense, and second because we didn't really know where we could go. And she, that noble woman who had saved our lives, continued to stand at our side, guiding us with her advice.

It is actually hard to appreciate how noble-minded this elderly lady showed herself to be as she endangered her own life to rescue us. From that time onward her image stayed with us as we continued to keep in touch with her by mail. From time to time we sent her money, packages, and crates of oranges.

When I stood under the *huppa*[13] [at my wedding ceremony] she was my chief *shushvinit*[14], for it was only thanks to her that my brother and I had remained alive.

Twenty years have passed since then. My son is about to complete his service in the Israel Defense Forces. However, to this very day I have not been set free from the terrors of the Holocaust, which have left their deep marks on my heart. And how could it be possible to forget those terrible, dark days, during which we drained the bitter cup of suffering to its dregs!?

—Translated from Polish [into Hebrew] by Avraham Dor (Dobraszklanka)

Mrs. Degola, a survivor of the Holocaust, lighting a candle in memory of the martyrs[15]

Translator's Footnotes

1. From *My Town: In Memory of the Communities Dobrzyn-Gollob*, edited by M. Harpaz, (published by the Dobrzyn-Golub Society, Israel, 1969), pp. 149-160.

2. Hebrew *shiva medorei geihinnom* = "Seven Sections of Hell", i.e. extreme, unending suffering. The original expression comes from a statement in the Babylonian Talmud (Sotah 10b) that Purgatory contains seven sections; to complete its expiation, the soul passes through each section, one after another.

3. *Rosh Hashanah* = Jewish New Year. The men were seized during the morning prayer service of the first day of the two-day holiday, Thursday, September 14, 1939. See Y. Flusberg, "The Men Left and Didn't Return," p. 137 of the reference cited in Footnote 1.

4. 50,000 zloty was equivalent to US $9,000 in 1939. Taking inflation into account, it would be equivalent to approximately US $150,000 in 2013.

5. Rypin lies 25km east of Dobrzyn.

6. Plock is 90km southeast of Dobrzyn.

7. Minsk Mazowiecki is a Polish town that is located some 200 km southeast of Dobrzyn, about 40km east of Warsaw.

8. *Shiksa* = young Gentile woman

9. For more details, see entry "Minsk Mazowiecki" in the *Encyclopedia Judaica*, vol. 12, pp. 59-60; also the following link: http://chgs.umn.edu/museum/responses/benezra/relics.html; also *Sefer Minsk-Mazoviecki, Yizkor Buch noch der Choruv-Gevorener Kehilla Minsk-Mazoviecki*, edited by Ephraim Shedletzki, Jerusalem, 1977, article [in Yiddish] on p. 465, "Kopernik in Flames," by E. Shedletzky (accessible via the following link: http://yizkor.nypl.org/index.php?id=2050).

10. Possibly the town of Połaniec is meant. But it is fairly far from Warsaw, 240km south.

11. Zamość lies 250km southeast of Warsaw.

12. Since she came to the village in January, 1943 (see above), it appears that it had been only one-and-a-half years since her arrival.

13. *Huppa* = wedding canopy

14. *Shushvinit* = woman who leads the bride to the *huppa* (see previous footnote), usually the bride's mother if she is living

15. From p. 160 of reference cited in Footnote 1

[Page 161]

In the Extermination Camps[1]
by Bracha Rotolski (Goldberg)
Translated by Allen Flusberg

November, 1939. With the outbreak of war, Dobrzyn was bombed from the air. We were terrified. Hurriedly the men left the town, leaving only women and children behind. Quickly the Germans appeared. They broke into the houses and stood us up against the wall; threatening us with their weapons, they demanded that we hand over our silver and gold.

Trembling with fear we acceded to their demand, handing over to them whatever we had in the house. But this was not good enough for them: we were asked to fill out questionnaires that they had given us, listing all the goods that we had in our shops. The next day they were back to retrieve the forms and to demand the keys to the shops and apartments.

Everyone began hastily leaving the town. We went toward Lubicz[2], where we had relatives. We stayed there only a single week, fearful and anxious, until leaving. The Germans sent us towards Warsaw in a freight train, without food or water. There, in the big city, German soldiers were waiting for us, to beat us mercilessly.

We barely managed to reach the home of our relatives in Warsaw. It was perilous for us to walk through the streets; the German soldiers were attacking any Jews they ran into and beating them cruelly.

The men were in even greater danger: they were snatched away to concentration camps, where they were cruelly tortured. Whoever had the courage tried to flee east, toward the Russian border. However, any such attempt was at the risk of one's life, since those who were caught were shot dead on the spot.

We were in the Warsaw Ghetto. At first it was possible to sustain ourselves in the ghetto, whether by working or by selling a few belongings and some jewelry. We were able to buy and sell to Christian city residents who would find a way to get into the ghetto. We were forced to hide not only from the Germans, but from the Jewish police as well, who were charged with supplying, on a daily basis, a quota of men, women and children to be sent to extermination camps.

When the policemen came into our house, they broke down doors and shattered windows as they searched for people to fill the quota demanded of them. Trucks were waiting outside to transport this live cargo. Feeling my end was near, I decided to run away and try to save myself. I moved away from the truck that I was already standing next to and went back into the house, running; I had decided to flee, come what may. I hid behind the entrance door of the house. A Jewish policeman chased after me to bring me back to the truck. I was lucky: he searched through the entire house, but it never occurred to him that I was hiding right near him, behind the iron door.

How appalling it was to see people following behind the policemen without trying to resist, even though they clearly knew that the trucks were about to transport them to extermination camps. It was a miracle that I found the courage to run away and hide. Meanwhile my two brothers were also rescued, thanks to the fact that they were working in a carpentry shop and were considered professional workers.

We hid in a bunker that we had built by hand in the ghetto, a strong bunker in which ten families were living. As night fell some more people would join us. Among them were those who during the day were involved in planning the resistance against the Nazi foe.

We believed that we would be able to sustain ourselves in this bunker until the liberation would come. However, our bunker's location was discovered by the Germans. They sent soldiers to get us out, but we shot dead any German soldier who got near the entrance to the bunker.

The Germans then decided on a cunning scheme. They sent members of the Jewish police to persuade us to leave the place. The policemen convinced us to leave the bunker, explaining that the Germans were determined to blow the place up. Seeing that there was no hope left, we came out into the street. The Germans quickly blew the bunker up.

Afterwards they put us into a truck and sent us to an extermination camp. Those for whom there was no room in the truck were shot on the spot. Among them was my brother Yosef Gershon. My other brother, Yaakov Moshe, was [later] executed by hanging after he was caught trying to escape from a death camp.

As for me, I was sent to Birkenau[3], to a work camp. Life here was like an extended, slow death… I recall one occasion when I dozed off, from weakness, and did not report at roster. When they realized one person was missing, they sent agents out to search the camp. It was clear that, once caught, that person would immediately be executed. Fortunately, when my friends found me asleep they managed to sneak me into the head count, and thanks to that I remained alive.

In the Birkenau labor camp they mistreated us abominably in order to sap our strength. They made us go out to work no matter what the weather—in rain, cold and snow. The work was difficult and grueling, enough to overwhelm even the sturdy who were used to hard labor. When the guards observed that we were unable to lift large logs or heavy stones, they brought us elsewhere, where they made us lift logs that were even larger…On a daily basis several of the laboring women collapsed from exhaustion. The entire intention of all this work was to torture us as much as possible, to make us die from the severe and cruel torment, with no food or water.

But that wasn't all. Near our camp there was a large house, where Jewish children were brought to be put to death. All day we would hear terrifying, heart-rending screams coming from there. We knew they were being horrifically tortured to death. Only once evening came did the screaming abate.

The wailing of children as they were being put to death and the spectacle of caravans of people being brought to the crematoria—these were our daily bread. Only God knows how we survived all of this, how our hearts did not burst.

The cries of the young children still ring in my ears, demanding retribution!

Translator's Footnotes

1. From *My Town: In Memory of the Communities Dobrzyn-Gollob*, edited by M. Harpaz, (published by the Dobrzyn-Golub Society, Israel, 1969), pp. 161-163.

2. Lubicz is a small town located ~25km southwest of Dobrzyn.

3. For additional information on Birkenau, see, for example, the following links (retrieved May, 2014):
http://www.jewishvirtuallibrary.org/jsource/Holocaust/auschbirk.html,
http://en.wikipedia.org/wiki/Auschwitz_concentration_camp

4. From p. 162 in reference cited in Footnote 1

Nachman Freilich (right) visiting the Jewish cemetery in Dobrzyn[4]

[Page 164]

After the Liberation[1]
by Gorny Frum
Translated by Allen Flusberg

Note by translator: in the original, it is stated that this article is a translation by Avraham Dor (Dobroszklanka) from Polish into Hebrew. A Yiddish version of the same article appears on pp. 381-384; see the English translation of that article, in which any differences from the Hebrew version have been highlighted in the footnotes.

The following photographs appear within the pages of the Hebrew translation:

Mrs. Sonabend (first on left), daughter of Tuvya Pieniek, visiting the grave of her father in Dobrzyn[2]

The bank administration of Dobrzyn
In center, at table: Tuvya Pieniek, Tzvigil, and Yosef Chaim Rojna[3]

Dobrzyn townsmen in Berlin on the their way to new lands of refuge[4]

Translator's Footnotes

1. From *My Town: In Memory of the Communities Dobrzyn-Gollob*, edited by M. Harpaz, (published by the Dobrzyn-Golub Society, Israel, 1969), pp. 164-168.

2. From p. 166 of reference cited in Footnote 1

3. From p. 168 of reference cited in Footnote 1. The author of the English translation has been able to identify one additional person: Jacob Fogel (seated, second from left).

4. From p. 168 of reference cited in Footnote 1

[Page 170]

Personalities in the Town

Reb Feibush Lipka

by Yehezkel Cohen
Translated by Jerrold Landau
Donated by Steve Bolef

The influence of my grandfather Feibush Lipka of blessed memory (my mother's father) upon me was very great not only during my childhood, but also as I matured and became independent. His patriarchal personality and refined spirit always accompanied me. He was a scholar as well as a dedicated Zionist in his heat and soul, who infected others with his enthusiasm.

His refined and enlightened personality served as a symbol for the Zionist movement in the town, where he radiated his personality primarily upon the Zionist youth. I recall how I enjoyed sitting with him for hours on end, as he told me about his trip to the Holy Land before the war, about the holy places that he visited and the sights that he saw. At such a time, his eyes burned with the fire of enthusiasm, as his words expressed his great love for the Land of Israel.

His emotional words penetrated deeply into my heart, the heart of a youth, and influenced me for a long time. He was the one who planted in me, and in the friends of my age, the love for Zion and the faith in the return to Zion. Under his influence, many youths became enthusiastic Zionists, who were no longer satisfied in following the normative path paved by their fathers.

I recall how he worked for the election of Rabbi Brod of Lipna, the candidate of the Zionists, for the Polish Sejm (parliament). The religious circles supported the candidacy of my father to the Sejm, whereas the Zionists, including me, fought for our candidate. My grandfather Feibush Lipka supported us with his whole heart, and utilized all of his powers of persuasion to that end.

His influence in town was great, and was recognized in all spheres of life. He had a great deal of property: sawmills a flourmill, lumber warehouses, land, and an electric generator that provided electricity to the entire town. Nevertheless, his great wealth did not blind his eyes and did not harden his heart. His headed the charitable institutions and supported his poor brethren with his money and advice.

He visited the Holy Land twice. The first time was in the 1880s, and the second time in 1914, at the eve of the outbreak of the First World War. He returned from these visits enthused, and urged the townsfolk to make *aliya* to Zion.

[Page 171]

Feibush Lipka merited to have sons and daughters who followed his path and took part in communal affairs. He also had a great deal of satisfaction from his grandchildren who were affected with his love of Zion and stood at the helm of Zionist activities in the town.

He passed away full of activity and full of years.

Reb Feivush Lipka

Yosef Chaim Ruda[1]

by Eizberg

Translated by Allen Flusberg

Yosef Chaim Ruda was an active community leader who had a particularly significant impact on the Dobrzyn community. Always empathetic to all that was happening among his Dobrzyn brethren, he devoted a great deal of his time to community affairs.

It would take too long to go into all the details of what he did for dozens of years, working tirelessly for the sake of the town with no expectation whatsoever of reward. To this very day, many of those who emigrated from Dobrzyn long ago remember him and his many good deeds.

During World War I the number of townspeople in need escalated sharply. Yosef Chaim Ruda came to their rescue, seeing to it that free groceries were distributed to them. In this project he found loyal, dedicated assistants in Avraham Hirsh Kohn, z.l.[2], and Yaakov Bielawski, may he live long[3], who lives among us in Israel.

The First World War uprooted a large number of Jews from various towns. Some of them made their way to Dobrzyn, where they found a temporary refuge to wait out the storm. Chaim Ruda came to their rescue with great passion, working day and night to take care of them. He was always thinking about "the poor among your people"[4], and he took care of them the way a father looks after his children.

He was also one of the founders of the Cooperative Jewish Bank and continuously headed its administration. He considered it a very important institution and worked hard to expand its activity. And indeed, this bank helped many of the people of Dobrzyn with both large and small loans, its central goal being to be able to provide firm support for the "little guy".

Ruda also served as a member of the committee that assessed taxes, which met right next to the income–tax office. In this role as well he revealed his humane approach and his great dedication.

However, most of all Ruda stood out in his Zionist activism, for he was a Zionist in every fiber of his being. He did all in his power to instill the concept of Zionism among his brethren and to help build up the Land, even though he himself was living far away, in Dobrzyn.

When Yitzhak Moshe Offenbach and Adolph Riesenfeld were officiating as the heads of the Zionist *Histadrut*[5] in the town, Yosef Chaim Ruda and Yaakov Bielawski, may he live long, served as deputies, together carrying the burden of operations. The two of them were also members of the local committee of *Keren HaYesod*[6].

Like many other people his age, Chaim was, in his youth, a yeshiva student who studied Torah day and night. Once he grew up he became secular and Zionist, bringing down upon himself the wrath of the ultra–Orthodox. On one occasion they even got up and threw him out of the synagogue. None of this was enough to prevent his extensive activity in support of Zionism, for which he travelled a great deal to Warsaw to attend Zionist conferences and various meetings that were convened in the city.

Ruda practiced what he preached. Under the influence of his relative, Shmuel Zanwil Pozner z.l., a Zionist activist who was well–known in his times (and who immigrated to Israel from Rypin before the war and passed away here), he sent two of his daughters to the Land of Israel. Although he himself longed to come on *Aliya*, as well, it was not meant to be.

Yosef Chaim Ruda, his wife Rivka, and their daughter Esther Yehudit (Yudka), perished in the Holocaust. So too also his only son, Pinchas, who lived with his wife in the city of Kutno[7], where he worked growing flowers on a farm that belonged to Katriel Isaac. Ruda's oldest daughter, Perl Leah, did not escape this fate, either, even though she immigrated to Vienna several years before the war to acquire property she had inherited from her grandfather, Rabbi Avraham Fuchs, z.l. She stayed there, and when the Germans seized Vienna she was caught and sent to a concentration camp.

Yosef Chaim Ruda's wife, Rivka, managed to escape to Warsaw after undergoing an extremely arduous journey that was the lot of all the refugees who were running away. In her testimony before someone from the Social Department, she related the story of the liquidation of the Dobrzyn community and told about the death of her husband. He, too, had fled with all the others from the town, carrying with him only a single suitcase containing his clothing. The tribulations of the journey and the deathly terror that he had experienced had sapped what little strength he had had left. During their wanderings he and his wife had hid out in a farmer's house, but he had fallen ill there and had never recovered.

The name of Yosef Chaim Ruda, who was among the active leaders of the community of Dobrzyn, is unalterably bound up with the community life of the town. His image and his activities are indelibly imprinted in the minds of those who came from the town; they recall his benevolence and kindness, as well as his great devotion to the Zionist ideal.

**Yosef Chaim Ruda,
one of the leading Zionists of Dobrzyn**[8]

Translator's Footnotes

1. From *My Town: In Memory of the Communities Dobrzyn–Gollob*, edited by M. Harpaz, (published by the Dobrzyn–Golub Society, Israel, 1969), pp. 171–173.

2. z.l. is an acronym for "*zichrono livracha*" = of blessed memory

3. "May he live long" is often appended to the name of a living person who is mentioned in the same sentence as someone who has passed away.

4. "The poor among your people" is a paraphrase of Deut. 15:7, following Babylonian Talmud, Baba Metzia 71a.

5. *Histadrut* = Jewish socialist–Zionist party in Poland

6. *Keren HaYesod* (literally "The Foundation Fund"), a Zionist fund founded in 1920 to support the establishment of a Jewish State in Palestine. See the following Web site (retrieved June, 2014): http://en.wikipedia.org/wiki/Keren_Hayesod

7. Kutno is a city in Poland, located ~100km south of Dobrzyn

8. From p. 172 of reference cited in Footnote 1

[Page 176]

R.[1] Ephraim Eliezer Granat (Rimon), of Blessed Memory

(His Life and Actions)[2]

by Yaakov Rimon
Translated by Allen Flusberg

My father and teacher[3], Ephraim Eliezer Granat, z.l.[4], was born in the town of Biezun[5], in the province of Plock, Poland, on the 10th of Tevet, 5629 (1869 [sic])[6], to his father, Rabbi Yosef Tzvi, and his mother, Chana Chaya. (He was their twelfth child; his mother was 55 years old when she gave birth to him.) He was educated in the bosom of Torah and Hassidism, but he was also interested in modern Hebrew literature. While he was still young he moved to the town of Dobrzyn on the Dreventz River, where he lived and was active for many years, until he immigrated to the Land of Israel.

Already in his youth he was drawn to *Hibbat–Tzion*[7], and he joined the Mizrachi movement[8] when it was just getting started. He wished to attract the Hassidim to the religious–Zionist movement and to the redemption of the People and the Land; since he was an author and a poet, he published an article entitled "On Zionism and Hassidism" in the monthly "Hamizrachi", which was published under the editorship of the author and historian Rabbi Zeev Yavetz[9]. He signed the article Ephraim Eliezer Even–Shayish[10]. He was active in and around Dobrzyn, supporting the settling of the Land of Israel, and he ran a campaign to favor citrons from the Land of Israel and "Carmel–Mizrachi" wine produced in the Land of Israel. He supported the Jewish National Fund in fundraising for the redemption of land from ownership by foreigners in the Land of Israel. On Yom Kippur Eves he would struggle with and fight against the fanatical Hassidim, placing a contribution–bowl in the synagogue for the benefit of the Jewish National Fund; he was persecuted by these fanatical[11] Hassidim because of his Zionism. He established a charity association in Dobryzn, and in addition energized his friends and acquaintances to participate in groups that were dedicated to the study of Talmud or Mishna. He served as a Talmud teacher in Dobrzyn; and since his love for the Hebrew language was boundless, he established a Hebrew library in Dobrzyn. As its administrator, he toiled to bring the young people closer to our national language.

While he was still undergoing persecution by the Hassidic fanatics for his Zionism, his older sister, who was also opposed to Zionism, aligned herself with the fanatics and decided to "sit Shiva"[12] for him on the basis of the rumor that he and his family were preparing to immigrate to the Land of Israel. And not only that, she actually traveled to Otwock to speak to the elderly *rebbe*[13] of Warka[14], *Rebbe* Simcha Bunim[15]—may the memory of the righteous be a blessing—and told him about the rumor. The elderly Hassidic leader sent a message to my father, telling him to come to him. When he asked my father his intentions, my father answered: "It is true: we are immigrating to the Holy Land." The *rebbe* spoke to my father, who was a beloved follower of his, privately, for many hours. But in the end when my father left the *rebbe*'s study, his face was glowing as he reported, "The *rebbe* gave me his blessing and even promised to follow me to the Holy Land"...And indeed, since the *rebbe* did not merit to immigrate to the Land of Israel during his lifetime, he stipulated, before his death, that his body be buried in Tiberias.[16] The Torah scrolls and sacred books that were in the *rebbe*'s house are presently located in the synagogue "Kehal Hassidim" that my father established in the neighborhood of Neve Shalom[17], in Yafo.

In the year 5667 (1907), my father overcame material hardships and immigrated to the Land of Israel. He settled in Batei-Varsha[18] of R. Shaul Fenigstein[19] z.l., and served as a Talmud[20] teacher for R. Shaul's children. After two years, in the year 5669 (1909), my mother, Esther Chava the daughter of R. Yechiel Bunim Elstein, z.l., immigrated and joined him. With her came two of her sons, Yechiel Bunim and Yaakov, may they live long.[21] My sister, Chana Chaya Katcher z.l., the wife of Moshe Yaakov Katcher z.l., remained in Dobrzyn together with her husband and their children; and my brother, the well-known poet R. Yosef Tzvi Rimon z.l., who came before any of us, was already living in Jerusalem at that time.

As stated above, my father settled in Yafo. He and my mother had an agreement that was like that of Issachar and Zebulun: she conducted business and my father studied Torah.[22] My mother had a grocery store, and every day my father would come for an hour or two to do the bookkeeping.

In Neve Shalom that was in Yafo, my father established a Beit-Midrash[23] for Hassidim who had emigrated from Poland. It is in existence to this very day, under the name "Kehal Hassidim", on Baal Shem Tov

Street.[24] Since he was affable and spoke knowledgeably and intelligently, my father became well–liked not only by the Hassidim, but also by the "*Perushim*"[25], and even by the free–thinkers; and many benefited from and were helped by his good advice. Our grocery store became a meeting place for immigrants from Poland, who used to come to my father for guidance just after they arrived in the Land. Among them also were Jews from Dobrzyn who immigrated to the Land at that time. The "Kehal Hassidim" synagogue served as a center for the Polish Hassidim who came on Aliya and settled in Yafo.

My father was also an expert in modern [Hebrew] literature, and he published several articles, lists and poems in the Hebrew newspapers of that period: "Moriah" and "Herut". In Yafo he initiated the founding of an association for purchasing plots of land to expand Jewish settlement on the basis of mutual aid, and he published a passionate leaflet on this subject.

My father authored four books: (1) *Pelach Harimon*[26]: interpretations of various place–names that appear in the Bible, Mishna and Talmud; (2) *Hadat Vehadaat*[27]: questions and answers between a father and his son on the subject of faith and religion; (3) *Michteve Tzair Shehizdaken*[28]: ideas and thoughts on the revival of Israel and Judaism; and (4) *Nachalat Ephraim*[29]: a compilation of articles on the subject of religion and faith. I am sorry to say that because of a lack of funds the only one of these books that appeared in print was *Nachalat Ephraim*, a book describing a father's testament to his son. It was published by Pinchas Ben–Tzvi Grayevsky, Jerusalem; it was widely acclaimed, and the author Eliezer Steinman incorporated three of its chapters in his book *Sefer Hamaala*, which includes a selection of testaments throughout the generations, up to the present time. Since I feel that because of my impaired vision I will regrettably not be able to do anything with my father's manuscripts, I have transferred them to be preserved for all time in the manuscript department of the Religious–Zionist archives, which is near the Rav Kook Institute in Jerusalem. It is my hope that perhaps these manuscripts will someday see the light of day.

When the World War broke out in the year 5674 (1914), my father and his family were supposed to be deported from the Land as "enemy nationals." However, my father chose to accept upon himself all the tribulations of the war; he clung to the Land, hoping he would not be wrested away from it. Together with his family he went through the torments of the expulsion from Yafo and suffered for several months in the deportee camp located in Kfar Sava[30], where they lived in open tents built of eucalyptus wood. The main food there was sorghum seeds that are used as poultry feed. Under these harsh, morbid conditions, while he was suffering hunger, my father wrote his book *Nachalat Ephraim*. The expulsion remained in force, bringing the family to Samaria[31], where my mother passed away during a typhus epidemic on the 1st of Nisan, 5678[32]; she was buried in Zichron Yaakov[33]. My father dedicated his book *Michteve Tzair Shehizdaken* to her memory. After the expulsion ended my father returned to Yafo, where he fell ill from all the hardships he had experienced. He passed away on the 2nd day of Adar II 5679[34] and was buried in the Old Cemetery[35] on Trumpeldor Street in Tel Aviv.

R. Ephraim Eliezer Granat (Rimon)[36]

Esther Chava Granat (Rimon)[37]

Translator's Footnotes

1. R. = Reb, an honorific similar to English "Mr."

2. From *My Town: In Memory of the Communities Dobrzyn–Gollob*, edited by M. Harpaz, (published by the Dobrzyn–Golub Society, Israel, 1969), pp. 176–179.

3. Here "teacher" (Hebrew: *mori*) is written as a token of respect to a parent; except for this first occurrence, it has been omitted in the translation.

4. z.l. is an acronym for *zichrono livracha* (= of blessed memory)

5. Polish spelling: Bieżuń, located ~70km east of Dobrzyn and ~60km north of the city of Plock

6. 10 Tevet 5629 = 24 Dec 1868 (12 Dec 1868 according to the Julian calendar then used by Russia)

7. *Hibbat–Tzion* = Love of Zion, also known as *Hovevei Tzion* = Lovers of Zion, Jewish religious groups organized in Eastern Europe in the late 19th century to promote Jewish immigration to the Land of Israel. They are considered the forerunners of the Zionist movement. See the following link (retrieved August, 2015): https://en.wikipedia.org/wiki/Hovevei_Zion

8. Mizrachi = the religious Zionist movement and party. See the following link (retrieved August, 2015): https://en.wikipedia.org/wiki/Mizrachi_%28religious_Zionism%29

9. Yavetz (1847–1924) was a prolific writer and historian. See the following link (retrieved August, 2015): https://en.wikipedia.org/wiki/Ze'ev_Yavetz

10. *Even–Shayish* = marble (Hebrew), perhaps an echo of the name Granat (= granite)

11. i.e. zealously anti–Zionist

12. *Shiva* = seven–day mourning period for an immediate relative who has died

13. *Rebbe* = religious spiritual leader of a Hassidic group. The Hebrew word *Admor* used here instead of *rebbe* is a contraction of *Adoneinu Moreinu Verabeinu* (= our master, teacher and rabbi), the Hebrew title of a Hassidic spiritual leader.

14. Warka, Poland, is a town located some 300km southeast of Dobrzyn, and about 60km south of Warsaw. A dynasty of Hassidic *rebbes*, known as Varker or Vurker, originated in this town.

15. Simcha Bunim Kalish (1851–1907), who resided in Otwock, Poland for much of his life and was descended from the Warka (Varka) dynasty of Hassidic *rebbes*.

16. Other accounts state that in 1905 he immigrated to the Land of Israel unaccompanied, with neither his family nor Hassidic entourage, and that he died in 1907 in Tiberias, Israel, where he was buried. See the following links (retrieved August, 2015):
http://www.yivoencyclopedia.org/article.aspx/Vurke_Hasidic_Dynasty;
https://he.wikipedia.org/wiki/%D7%A9%D7%9E%D7%97%D7%94_%D7%91%D7%95%D7%A0%D7%99%D7%9D_%D7%A7%D7%90%D7%9C%D7%99%D7%A9

17. Neve Shalom, established in 1890, was the second neighborhood that was settled by Jews just outside the walls of Yafo (Jaffa).

18. Batei–Varsha (= houses of Warsaw) was a Jewish agricultural settlement established within Yafo in 1871. See next footnote.

19. Shaul Fenigstein, a Ger Hassid who hailed from Varsha (= Warsaw), was the founder of Batei–Varsha.

20. Here written "g.f.t.", a Hebrew acronym for Gemara (=Talmud), *Perush* Rashi (=Rashi's commentary on the Talmud) and *Tosafot* (additional medieval commentary on the Talmud).

21. "May they live long" is added as a descriptor of living people mentioned together with those who are no longer alive. Yaakov is the author of this article.

22. Issachar and Zebulun were two tribes of ancient Israel that shared a common border. According to the Midrashic interpretation of Gen. 49: 13–15, the tribe

of Issachar chose Torah–study as their calling; they were financially supported by the neighboring tribe of Zebulun, who thereby received the same credit as Issachar for the study of Torah (Bereishit Rabba 99:11).

23. Beit–Midrash = study hall (for studying Torah)

24. In the late 1970s the Neve Shalom neighborhood deteriorated and the Kehal Hassidim synagogue was abandoned. Around 2000 it was sold in a public auction by the city of Tel Aviv and was rebuilt by the purchaser as an upscale new home in what had become a gentrified neighborhood. See the following Web site (retrieved August, 2015):
http://www.nrg.co.il/online/54/ART2/295/003.html

25. *Perushim* = members of the non–Hassidic ultra–religious Ashkenazi community of Israel, whose ancestors had arrived from Europe during the 18th and 19th centuries. Members of this group who remained behind in Eastern Europe were known as *Mitnagdim* (= opponents [of Hassidism]).

26. *Pelach Harimon* = The Slice of Pomegranate

27. *Hadat Vehadaat* = Religion and Knowledge

28. *Michteve Tzair Shehizdaken* = Letters of a Youth who Grew Old

29. *Nachalat Ephraim* = Inheritance of Ephraim

30. Kfar Sava is located ~20km northeast of Yafo. A Jewish settlement founded in 1898, it was destroyed during World War I in the fighting between the British and Turks. In 1917 about 1000 residents of Tel Aviv and Yafo were brought there as deportees, where they lived in huts made of eucalyptus branches until the British victory of 1918. See the following Web sites (retrieved August 2015):
https://en.wikipedia.org/wiki/Kfar_Saba#Ottoman_era;
https://he.wikipedia.org/wiki/%D7%9B%D7%A4%D7%A8_%D7%A1%D7%91%D7%90#.D7.9E.D7.9C.D7.97.D7.9E.D7.AA_.D7.94.D7.A2.D7.95.D7.9C.D7.9D_.D7.94.D7.A8.D7.90.D7.A9.D7.95.D7.A0.D7.94_.D7.95.D7.A4.D7.A8.D7.95.D7.AA_.D7.AA.D7.A8.D7.A4.22.D7.90

31. Samaria (Hebrew *Shomron*) is the mountainous region lying ~50km northeast of Yafo.

32. 1 Nisan 5678 = 14 March 1918

33. Zichron Yaakov was a Jewish agricultural settlement that had been founded in 1882. It is located near the Mediterranean coast, ~70km north of Yafo.

34. 2 Adar II 5679 = 4 March 1919

35. For more details on this historic cemetery, see the following Web site (retrieved August 2015): https://en.wikipedia.org/wiki/Trumpeldor_Cemetery

36. From p. 177 of reference cited in Footnote 2.

37. From p. 178 of reference cited in Footnote 2.

[Page 179]

My Dear Mother, May She Rest in Peace[1]

by Mendel Sonabend

Translated by Allen Flusberg

My departed mother, the Dobrzyn *Rabbanit*[2], studied during her youth in the Plock *gymnasia*[3] together with the future Zionist leader, Nahum Sokolow[4]. She knew four languages well: Yiddish, Hebrew, Polish and German.

She was well educated and quite intelligent; she would always be reading works of Tolstoy, Turgenev, Gorky, Mickiewicz, Heine, Bialik[5] and Peretz[6]. The Dreyfus trial caught her interest, and she followed it on a daily basis, reading in particular the reports by Max Nordau[7]. She was also interested in music and art, to which she dedicated much time.

She ran her household with modesty and good taste; she dressed nicely and properly, and dressed her children well, too. She did not leave concerns for running her household to the housemaid only, but rather gave thought to every detail, like someone who wanted to leave the stamp of her personality on everything. Her esteem and fulfilment came from her husband and children.

No sigh ever crossed her lips; her face always glowed with a loving smile, and nothing was ever lacking in her home. We children wondered where she got it all from, as we knew full well that the salary of the town rabbi was not particularly high.

In spite of our great economic hardship, she did not hesitate to help all who were in need; she was willing to share her last slice of bread with others. I recall how she once stood on a Friday, as the Sabbath was approaching, in front of the candles she had just lit, covering her gleaming eyes with her hands and then passing them over the flames as she blessed the God of Abraham, Isaac and Jacob. And while she was quietly murmuring the words of the blessing, she burst out in heart–rending sobs. At that moment I saw before my eyes a Jewish mother who was asking God for health and success for her family members and for all the Jewish people. I got up on a chair and embraced her; I kissed her and comforted her, saying: "Right away Father will be coming home from the synagogue; he will greet us with the blessing of 'Shalom Aleichem'[8], so please don't let your face show signs of sadness." Immediately the sadness disappeared, her face lit up, and she stood ready to greet my father.

And indeed at that very moment the door opened. Our father came in with his face shining, cheerfully declaring: "A Good Sabbath! A Good Sabbath!" Two guests came in with him, Russian Jews who were about to cross the border on their way to the United States.[9] My mother hastened to bring the gefilte fish to the table as she labored to make the guests' Sabbath as pleasant as possible.

My father noticed the sadness on the guests' faces. They were probably thinking about their families and were worrying about what would happen to them. My father quickly cheered them up, assuring them that everything would work out well. "Don't worry, fellow Jews, don't worry!" he said over and over. He poured some wine into their cups and toasted them, "*Lechaim*[10], fellow Jews, *lechaim*!"

Observing that the guests were wearing light clothing, my mother hurried over to the closet and took out some warm clothing. She gave it to them and wished them a safe trip, saying "Go in peace and arrive in peace!"

This is what my mother the *Rabbanit* was like, a modest and pure woman, whose heart was devoted to her children, her husband, and to all who were in need or were experiencing difficulties.

Translator's Footnotes

1. From *My Town: In Memory of the Communities Dobrzyn–Gollob*, edited by M. Harpaz, (published by the Dobrzyn–Golub Society, Israel, 1969), pp. 179–180. See also the English translation of the Yiddish version of this essay (similar but with some differences) by the same author, on pp. 401–402.

2. *Rabbanit* = Rabbi's wife (Hebrew)

3. *Gymnasia* = high school

4. Sokolow (1859–1936) was a Zionist leader and author. See the following link (retrieved June, 2015): https://en.wikipedia.org/wiki/Nahum_Sokolow

5. Ch. N. Bialik (1873–1934) was a poet who wrote primarily in Hebrew. See the following link (retrieved July 2015):
https://en.wikipedia.org/wiki/Hayim_Nahman_Bialik

6. I. L. Peretz (1852–1915) was a Yiddish–language author of fictional stories and plays. See the following link (retrieved July 2015):
https://en.wikipedia.org/wiki/I._L._Peretz

7. Nordau (1849–1923) was a Zionist leader and author. See the following link (retrieved June, 2015):
https://en.wikipedia.org/wiki/Max_Nordau#Dreyfus_affair

8. *'Shalom Aleichem'* = "Welcome, angels of peace...", A Hebrew poem recited or sung just before the Friday–night Sabbath meal, welcoming the angels who bring with them the tranquility of the Sabbath

9. Until 1920, the border between the Russian and German empires ran along the Dreventz River that separated Dobrzyn (in the Russian Empire) from Golub (in the German Empire). Smuggling people across the river border was common, and this is likely what the border crossing is referring to. See p. 415 of Y. Lipka, "Memoirs Dedicated to My Father", R. Feibish Lipka, pp. 404–438 of reference cited in Footnote 1; also p. 270 of S. Aleksander, "The Grassroots Jews of Dobrzyn," pp. 270–272 of reference cited in Footnote 1.

10. *Lechaim* (Hebrew) = to life, a Hebrew toast

[Page 180]

My Grandfather's House[1]

R.[2] Ber, son of Shmuel Kristal, a Torah Scribe

by Shmuel Meiri-Minisewski

Translated by Allen Flusberg

Our large family, as I look back on it, left indelible marks in my heart and became part of my substance, my very being. I remember it for the idyll that it was; I recall the serenity and quiet that encompassed it, as well as the modest conduct and atmosphere of sacred spirituality that held sway.

The town of Dobrzyn-Golub on the Dreventz River was the cradle of my extended family on my mother's side. My mother, Beila of blessed memory, was the daughter of the Torah scribe Ber Kristal. The many families of the house of Kristal were indeed endowed with something "crystal-like": they were imprinted with a unique mental substance that expressed itself with singular characteristics of humility, modesty and tranquility. These qualities distinguished the sixteen Kristal families that were headed by my grandfather, R. Ber Kristal.

He was handsome and noble, and he imparted his gentility to his progeny. His face, encompassed by a long, white beard, expressed majesty. His intelligent eyes, thirsting for knowledge, radiated wisdom. And all of his being emanated holiness, giving him an aura of charm and inspiring respect.

Patriarchal attitudes, which were common in those days, did not hold sway in my grandfather's home, for all of his being was devoted to writing religious scrolls and studying Torah unselfishly, for its own sake. He would separate himself from everyday matters in order to concentrate on his sacred labor with all his might, to purify himself and to dedicate himself to writing Torah scrolls, *tefillin*, *mezuzot*[3], charms, etc.

This sacred labor produced a deep, melancholy look on his face. And if he felt that his concentration and devoutness were not complete enough for his task, or if he was fearful that he might be disturbed by profane thoughts, he would fast, study the Zohar[4] and read from *Tehilim*[5], until he became confident that he could commence working. Only then did he dare take up the feathered writing quill and reverently begin his service to the Creator with trembling hands and an anxious heart.

How great was the contrast between his everyday life, his conduct with ordinary people, the joy and happiness he shared with his family, and the way he distanced himself from any extraneous thoughts or from the tiniest of pleasures while he was working. It was as if there were two worlds within his soul: one, a warm heart, devoted to his family, open to others and especially affectionate to children, to whom he would endear himself with little jokes as he pinched their cheeks; and the other, a heart zealous for the tradition, an extreme zealousness deriving from love for the Creator and from studying the sacred: learning for its own sake, without allegiance to any of the Hassidic courts.

He was certainly reclusive, closed up in his own world, with no dependence on anyone else. And for this reason people from all strata of the community liked him, viewing him as a dignified personality who was fit to judge between a man and his fellow, whether for criminal or civil matters.

I recall that once, when I was a child, he sat me down on his lap, swinging me up with ease as he smiled endearingly. He tested me on the weekly Torah portion[6], on Mishna[7] and Gemara[8], treating me with singular gracefulness and tenderness. He encouraged me, refreshing my memory with a simple hint and a pat, making comments as his penetrating smile made my eyes light up. He was making sure I did not fail, since I was his pampered grandchild, the only child of my parents. And in his heart he carried the hope that I would someday be given the title of "Rabbi in Israel", a wish that was somewhat fulfilled when I became a student at the Warsaw rabbinical school *Tachkemoni*[9], under the training of the prodigy, Rabbi Soloveichik[10], and Professor Balaban[11].

He barely eked out a living, but he overcame the bleak reality of his circumstances through his virtue and the purity of his soul. I will never forget how he would sometimes secretly collect food to distribute to the poor of the town; or how, despite the exasperation of our family members, he once wrote a *mezuza*[12] for a poor woman without taking any payment.

Within our home an atmosphere of tranquility and joy is present; all is arranged properly in its place, with a palpable feeling of sanctity in the air. In a corner, next to a wide table, my grandfather is stooped over the holy books, laboring at writing. He is completely unaware of the mundane world, for he is immersed with all his heart and all his might in a world of radiance and holiness.

And when a mundane thought did pass through his mind, he would quickly put his feathered quill down on the parchment he was writing on. Sighing deeply, he would go out to immerse himself in the *mikve*[13] to purify himself. Only then would he return and go back to his corner, purified and at peace, fit to continue his holy work.

Members of the family were careful not to interrupt him, to allow a deep, inner connection between him and the sacred letters to be formed; for they would be united by signs[14] and twiddles[15] into something resembling a pastoral composition. I used to imagine hearing the beating of wings of angels as they hovered over him, rising up from the squeaking noise of the quill. At those times the veins in his forehead would bulge from great concentration and mental exertion; and from his mouth there emerged a silent prayer of the signs, based on hidden, mystical teachings, the prayer of a kabbalist who was overpowering the *Mastin*[16].

How his face would radiate as he labored, and how great his joy was when he completed the writing of a Torah scroll. He felt that the work had been done through the inspiration of God's Presence, like a priest who was engaged in the sacred. And indeed he was a priest, a *kohen* directly descended from Aaron the Priest[17].

And if you would like to know from where he drew the power to concentrate so completely, with no fatigue, throughout a period spanning more than two generations—then go to the *Beit Midrash*[18] that is located right near the old cemetery. There you will find him sitting by himself, wrapped in his *tallit*[19], his gaze fixed on the tiny letters of rare holy books. In the margins of their pages he is adding his own novel ideas and *pilpul*[20], marginal notes of reflection and insight, words whose liberating power make his spirit soar.

To this very day I still have my little sack with *tefillin*[21] inside it that are written in his crystal-clear handwriting, *tefillin* that he dedicated to me when I reached the age of responsibility to fulfil the commandments[22]. I recall how his face radiated when he saw the *tefillin* straps wrapped around my arm.

It is fitting that as we bring up the memory of my grandfather, with his many virtues, we should also mention his wife Freida Michla of blessed memory. Small in stature, she knew how to create a peaceful atmosphere around my grandfather, who was so different from other people. She was a pleasant and humble woman, whose entire dignity was within her. To her daughters she bequeathed true religion, righteous conduct and charity, which left an everlasting imprint on them.

Once the Kristal-Brauns were the family with the largest number of branches in Dobrzyn. With the passage of time, however, and because of the difficulty finding means of support at the beginning of the twentieth century, many of them immigrated to America, on the other side of the ocean. Today the family has branched out even more, its various parts scattered among several lands. But to this very day the unifying connection, following family tradition, has not been severed; it is a particularly powerful link, for all the good qualities that were acquired in their town, Dobrzyn, still live on among the family members.

The many large families often gather together, particularly on the holidays. At the Passover Seder they sit together, nearly 300 people, in one of the halls. This custom has become a holiday tradition and an opportunity for socializing get-togethers of the family. The "Association of Families" publishes a pamphlet called "Kibbitzer", with advertisements for family events: celebrations, births and birthdays, weddings, blessings, letters and announcements—that is, all that has transpired during the year within the extended family—not only the American contingent, but also those that live in other countries, particularly in Israel. The pamphlet is called "News of the Kristal-Brown Family", and it is published by New York family members Tilly Sperling and Ira Kay. The goal of this welcome enterprise is to collect and publicize every news event that is connected to the large, widely scattered family.

The "Kibbitzer" is distributed among all the branches of the family. It is published in a fine, cultured format that demonstrates the good taste of the publishers, who are filled with deeply rooted Jewish culture and consciousness. So also a "Blue Book" called "Family Tree of the Kristal-Brown Family" has been published. It lists all the members of the family branches, and shows how they have branched out from one another over the generations. And this common thread continues up to our own time: members of the extended family visit one another and make sure to remain in close contact with one another. And all this thanks to the activities of the above-mentioned family members, two intelligent and noble ladies.

The great effort that is being invested in gathering and editing material, done purely voluntarily, strengthens the family link, which is expressed via family gatherings and mutual support, both spiritual and moral, in a time of need; all is done unobtrusively, with minimal fanfare. This family-cultural enterprise has preserved the family connection down to the seventh generation, and through it has greatly influenced Jewish feeling and consciousness. And all this is connected with the genealogy of the house of my grandfather, R. Ber the son of Shmuel Kristal, and the house of my grandmother, Freida Michla née Braun. The bond between the generations has not been severed; for it is connected to the noble image of my grandfather and to the tradition of his modest, sacred deeds, which has been passed down orally like a legend.

The tight family bond expresses itself in various memorial services, gatherings, and retrieval of memories, a kind of conversation between generations. The flame that the scribe R. Ber lit in our hearts has not died out, and the young generation of Kristal-Braun descendants is being educated by its glow.

Indeed, the link has not been severed, nor has the Jewish-Zionist fountain of faith dried up. A testimony of this is the work of Sidney (Shmuel) Danziger[23], son of Sheine Kristal, daughter of Shmuel of blessed memory, and his wife Gloria. They are among those who head the United Jewish Appeal, and they contribute their own strength and capital to the success of this enterprise. The energetic Sidney Danziger is very close in his heart to Zionism, and he has been utilizing his great influence within the centers of government in his country to move the hearts of those who shape American policy and persuade them to favor Israel. There was a time when he was close to the late Senator Robert Kennedy; in his letters to him he expressed his positive attitude to the policy of the State of Israel.

When the Six-Day War broke out, he published an appeal to the Jews of America, urging them to contribute to the "Emergency Fund". He had inherited his affinity for Zionism from his mother, Sheine Kristal-Danziger of blessed memory, who hailed from Dobrzyn. He also inherited his noble spirit from her. She had once articulated the idea of visiting the Land of Israel and settling there. However, Sheine Kristal did not live to fulfil her aspiration to settle in Israel. She died in America in 1959, leaving four children: Henry, Benjamin, May (Ida) of blessed memory, and Sidney. All her life she was a person of simple faith who educated her children to be good and compassionate.

*

In this article I have sought to highlight the spiritual strength that has distinguished our family. I am emphasizing it especially now, when materialism is spreading and dominating everywhere. I have also endeavored to highlight the importance and value of the family, which also continues to lose its value and influence in the era of technology.

It is my hope that these recollections, which have left their stamp on me, will serve as a valuable legacy to the members of my family and to future generations, as the image of my grandfather, R. Ber the son of Shmuel Kristal of blessed memory, from the town of Dobrzyn, Poland, hovers before their eyes always.

Translator's Footnotes

1. From *My Town: In Memory of the Communities Dobrzyn-Gollob*, edited by M. Harpaz, (published by the Dobrzyn-Golub Society, Israel, 1969), pp. 180-184. See also the parallel English-language article by the same author, "The Kristal-Brown Family", on p. 13 of the English section of this Yizkor Book. The spelling "Brown" is American; the name would have been spelled "Braun" in Poland. Both spellings appear in this translation.

2. R. = *Reb*, a title similar to "Mr." in English.

3. *tefillin* = phylacteries, which are bound on the arm and placed on the head, contain handwritten parchment scrolls; mezuzot (plural of mezuza) = handwritten parchment scrolls mounted on doorposts. Tefillin and mezuzot fulfil the commandments of Deut. 6:8-9.

4. Zohar = a mystical, kabbalistic book written in Aramaic. See the following Web page (retrieved June, 2016): https://en.wikipedia.org/wiki/Zohar.

5. *Tehilim* = Book of Psalms

6. Weekly Torah portion = section of Pentateuch read on Sabbath, the entire Pentateuch being read section by section over a period of a year

7. Mishna = the concise book of Jewish Law written down in Hebrew in ~200CE. See the following Web site (retrieved June, 2016): https://en.wikipedia.org/wiki/Mishnah.

8. Gemara = literally "study by tradition" (Aramaic), the detailed analysis and discussion of Jewish Law based on the Mishna and additional traditions, completed in Babylon ~500CE, and written in a mixture of Hebrew and Aramaic. The Mishna and Gemara are the two components of the Talmud. See the following Web site (retrieved June, 2016): https://en.wikipedia.org/wiki/Gemara.

9. *Tachkemoni* = a rabbinical seminary with secular studies

10. Rabbi Moshe Soloveichik (1879-1941), who served as rosh yeshiva [rabbinical dean] of the Tachkemoni school in Warsaw in the 1920s.

11. Meir Balaban (1877-1942), a Polish Jewish historian who administered the Tachkemoni seminary in the 1920s. See the following Web site (retrieved June, 2016): https://en.wikipedia.org/wiki/Meir_Balaban.

12. See Footnote 3.

13. *Mikve* = ritual bath. Customarily, a scribe immerses himself in a mikve to be ritually pure before engaging in writing sacred scrolls.

14. Signs (Hebrew: *simanim*), probably a reference to the decorative crowns that adorn many of the characters in handwritten scrolls. Their form is regulated by tradition.

15. Twiddles (Hebrew: *tagim*), a reference to the decorative twiddles adorning characters in handwritten scrolls. Their form is regulated by tradition.

16. *Mastin* = accusing angel

17. Aaron, brother of Moses, was the first priest (kohen) of Israel. All Jewish kohanim are patrilineally descended from him.

18. *Beit Midrash* = Study House

19. *Tallit* = prayer shawl

20. *Pilpul* = casuistic commentary

21. *Tefillin* = phylacteries (See footnote 3). They are usually stored in a small sack that can be kept closed.

22. i.e. the age of 13 years, when Jewish boys begin wearing tefillin during morning prayers

23. See the 1991 New York Times obituary for Sidney Danziger, retrieved June 2016: http://www.nytimes.com/1991/03/12/obituaries/sidney-danziger-executive-87.html.

[Page 185]

Chana Chaya Granat-Katcher, of Blessed Memory[1]

(Dobrzyn—Yafo—New York—Bronx)

by Yaakov Rimon

Translated by Allen Flusberg

My sister, Chana Chaya, the daughter of R.[2] Ephraim Eliezer and Esther Chava Granat of Dobrzyn, was the wife of Moshe Yaakov Katcher of Dobrzyn, who passed away in the Bronx, New York. From childhood on she was educated in the bosom of Religious Zionism. Her love for the Land of Israel knew no bounds. Already in the year 1910—several years after my father z.l.[3] immigrated to the Land of Israel—she and her husband, as well as their baby boy, came on Aliya to the Land [of Israel] with the intention of settling there. But fortune did not smile on them. Her husband became ill with pestilential fever[4], and the doctors were unable to find a cure for him. Having no alternative, my sister and her husband had to go back to Dobrzyn, Poland. Just before she left she visited the holy places of Jerusalem. She collected small stones and grains of sand in a little sack; these she kept all her life and even left instructions to bury them with her in her grave. Her letters to our father were full of yearning for the Holy Land. All her life she dreamed to return and settle in the Land, but she did not merit it.

Several years before Hitler y.m.sh.[5] rose to power, my sister and her husband were able to immigrate to the United States with their five children. They were accepted for immigration by virtue of a document that I obtained from Rabbi Kook[6], z.tz.l.[7], certifying that my brother-in-law was a religious functionary; and as such his entry to America was approved.

In New York my sister dedicated herself to community work. She collaborated with the *Landsmanschaften* Supporting Israel[8]. She was active as a member of the committee of the Dobrzyn townspeople[9], and she greatly aided the transfer of clothing and food to Israel. Two years after the establishment of the State [of Israel], she and her husband made a trip to Israel. They brought with them a Torah scroll that had been rescued from Dobrzyn, the town she had been born in; it was brought into *Bnei Tzion*, the central synagogue of the Montefiore neighborhood, with great pomp and ceremony. The committee of immigrants hailing from Dobrzyn held a country-wide meeting of Dobrzyn townspeople to honor my sister and her husband. The meeting between the townspeople and my sister was dramatic. Many wept with joy for having lived to see her again. From all the speeches that were given in her honor she enjoyed the great recognition that so many had shown her and their appreciation for her character.

Again she wished to settle in Israel. She traveled throughout the entire country, visiting the house of the first president, Dr. Weizmann z.l.; but unfortunately the president was ill and she was received by one of his aides, who carried on a long conversation with her. She tried hard to persuade her husband to settle in the Land, but his business affairs required him to return.

I will never forget the moments when we parted, as the taxi that was going to take her to the airfield in Lod stood waiting. She was helped into the taxi weeping silently and faint, as if her heart was telling her that she would never again see the land of her childhood dreams. After she had returned to the United States she spoke often in meetings and gatherings about the State of Israel and her experiences there…

After a difficult illness of paralysis, lasting two years, death came and released her from her harsh agony.

She was a well-educated woman; in her youth she had studied Mishna[10] and Bible with our father. She could read Hebrew, and she wrote comments and responses on various topics in the Yiddish press. In all her responses she defended Israel with warmth and zeal. The wound she carried in her heart, for not being able to settle in the Land, did not ever mend completely, not even up to the very last moments of her life. She died at home on 1 Elul 5717[11], as her husband, her four sons and her daughter stood gathered around her bed.

May her memory be preserved forever in the hearts of all who loved and cherished her.

Chana Chaya Granat-Katcher[12]

R. Moshe Yaakov Katcher[13]

Translator's Footnotes

1. From *My Town: In Memory of the Communities Dobrzyn-Gollob*, edited by M. Harpaz, (published by the Dobrzyn-Golub Society, Israel, 1969), pp. 185-186.

2. R. in this context stands for Reb, an honorific similar to the English "Mr."

3. z.l. is an acronym for *zichrono livracha* = of blessed memory

4. Hebrew *kadachat mameret* = pestilential fever (probably typhus)

5. y.m.sh. is an acronym for *yimach shemo* = may his name be blotted out, an epithet generally appended to the name of someone heinous

6. Rabbi Abraham Isaac Kook (1865-1935) was the first Ashkenazi Chief Rabbi of Mandatory Palestine. See the following link (retrieved September 2016): https://en.wikipedia.org/wiki/Abraham_Isaac_Kook

7. z.tz.l. is an acronym for *zecher tzadit livracha* = may the memory of the righteous be a blessing

8. *Landsmanschaften* were beneficial societies organized by Jews hailing from various towns in Eastern Europe. They collected dues to support members who had fallen on hard times. Surplus funds were donated to other charities, particularly various funds supporting the State of Israel. See the following Web site (retrieved September 2016):
https://en.wikipedia.org/wiki/Landsmanshaft

9. i.e. the Dobrzyn *Landsmanschaft*. See Footnote 8.

10. Mishna = the concise book of Jewish Law, written down in Hebrew~200CE. See the following Web site (retrieved September 2016):
https://en.wikipedia.org/wiki/Mishnah.

11. Jewish date 1 Elul 5717 corresponded to 28 August 1957.

12. From p. 185 of reference cited in Footnote 1.

13. From p. 186 of reference cited in Footnote 1.

Page 187]

Chaya Shifra Bielawski[1]

by Yehuda Rosenwaks
Translated by Allen Flusberg

The Bielawski family was known in Dobrzyn for its devotion to the Zionist ideal and to all that was connected with the Land of Israel. Their house was always open, and in it all those whose hearts burned with a love of the people and the Land used to come together.

As for Chaya Shifra: even though she was the daughter of R.[2] Hersh Ber Berman, an ardent Ger[3] Hassid, she soon became one of the leading activists supporting the Zionist ideal; together with her husband, she devoted her energy and her time to every activity that was connected with the Land of Israel.

In spite of the opposition of the Hassidim, who still viewed the Zionists as heretics, deniers of the belief in the coming of the Messiah, Shifra and her husband were not deterred from transforming their home into a center for every Zionist activity: every evening they would hold meetings and gatherings, with the aim of boosting and intensifying Zionist activity.

Shifra, of blessed memory, was a wonderful, noble person: a personality who stood out within the town for her dedication to community affairs and for her great concern for anyone in need. This community activity kept her extremely occupied and robbed her of much free time; nonetheless she was able to be an extraordinary spouse, mother and grandmother who influenced her family members with her devotion and love.

Once the Bielawski family had immigrated to the Land [of Israel], their home continued to serve as a center for people hailing from Dobrzyn; these fellow townspeople flocked to their home, whether to experience the warmth permeating it or whether to receive advice and guidance.

Once the Dobrzyn Townsmen Organization had been established, the Bielawski couple, with their characteristic enthusiasm, joined, and provided their home for Committee Member meetings. Here, during our many meetings, we felt ourselves completely at home, with Shifra glowing with joy as she hosted her fellow townspeople and again brought back memories of the old days.

She dealt with the townspeople like a wise and devoted mother, concerned most with the most recent arrivals, those who had survived the Holocaust, who found in her a sympathetic ear and an understanding heart.

Even in the last few years, when she was already ill, she did not cease providing for the needy; she conducted this sacred work incognito, toiling tirelessly under her final moments.

With her death we lost a wonderful, gentle person. Her husband, daughters and grandchildren have been bereaved; and the Dobrzyn–Golub Townsmen Organization has become bereft of a loyal member, who did so much for her fellow townspeople.

Her altruism and devotion to her townspeople will succor us always!

Mrs. Chaya Shifra Bielawski, of blessed memory[4]

Translator's Footnotes

1. From *My Town: In Memory of the Communities Dobrzyn–Gollob*, edited by M. Harpaz, (published by the Dobrzyn–Golub Society, Israel, 1969), pp. 187–188.

2. R. stands for *Reb*, an honorific similar to "Mr." in English.

3. Ger = a Hassidic group that had many adherents in Dobrzyn. At that time most of them opposed Zionism.

4. From p. 187 of reference cited in Footnote 1.

[Pages 188-189]

My Grandmother's *Shloshim* Memorial Service...[1] [2]

by Moti

Translated by Allen Flusberg

Stunned, gloomy and silent we stand over your grave, my dear one. Thirty days have passed since that bitter morning on which you closed your eyes forever, leaving behind wretched, wounded hearts throughout the land; people who refuse to believe that this was indeed what fate had demanded. Even the heavens wept and raged on the day of your death, when we were all bereaved of Grandmother.

You were and will remain for us a symbol and ideal of a "*Yiddishe* grandmother", overflowing with compassion, integrity, modesty, frugality, altruism—and above all, a pure faith in the Creator.

Never again a warm, encouraging caress at a moment of crisis; never again hot stew in honor of a holiday; never again an *afikomen*[3] present on Passover; only a cold, silent gravestone and a great many stories, memories of an era that will never come back again.

I recall one cold, rainy Friday when I came by to see you, and I observed several beggars sitting on the stairs as you brought them hot soup and meat, and as you gave them clothing and candy for their children…Only after a lengthy interrogation did you admit, with a modesty that was so characteristic of you alone, that they came by every week.

When we came to visit you in the hospital, the nurses asked us why you had not requested anything, and we found it hard to explain to them that you did not want to trouble them, so you were suffering silently. And indeed, who among us knew how much you had suffered during all that time when you were being moved from one hospital to another and from there home. And only the powerful desire to live and to see the good fortune of the family were able to strengthen your heart and lengthen your life.

Your tears were the only thing that revealed from time to time what it was that you were keeping to yourself as we stood around helplessly, hoping that perhaps a miracle would take place, and you would recover...

Your house on Yehuda Halevi had always been a residence for all of us, a warm home from which caring and love radiated out to members of your family, wherever they were, and in which everyone gathered on holidays to celebrate together joyfully.

We remember that you were always ready to be a loyal advocate, with no limits and no compensation, for your sons-in-law and your grandchildren; and even when we were to blame you knew how to come to our defense, in your own special way, with forgiveness and understanding. And just a few weeks ago, on some Friday, when you were in crisis and terribly weak, you refused to light Sabbath candles in bed; but instead, overcoming your frailty, you put on your Sabbath clothing and your white apron, so that you were prepared like a queen to greet the Sabbath; and you rose, leaning on the table for support, to make the blessing over the candles.

We who are standing here will not ever forget what you imparted to us during your lifetime: the values that you bestowed on us as you served as a personal demonstration of a life of purity and faith, kindness and love, able to live in harmony with happiness, satisfaction and enjoyment of life.

You were a woman of valor, and in our eyes you shall remain a woman of valor forever. On your grave we promise to continue in the path that you delineated for us, as your image continues to walk before us.

Translator's Footnotes

1. From *My Town: In Memory of the Communities Dobrzyn-Gollob*, edited by M. Harpaz, (published by the Dobrzyn-Golub Society, Israel, 1969), pp. 188-189.

2. *Shloshim* = thirty. The *Shloshim* memorial service is conducted at the gravesite, after the inscribed gravestone has been put in place over the grave, typically (in Israel) 30 days after the death and burial.

3. *afikomen* = a portion of matzah (unleavened bread) set aside to serve as the last dish to be eaten at the Passover Seder meal. Since the *afikomen* is an integral part of the ritual, the Seder cannot continue until it is consumed. In many families the children "steal" it and hold it hostage to trade for gifts, one of the many traditions that have been introduced over the centuries to keep the children awake and involved throughout the entire Seder.

[Page 189]

Shmuel Zeinwil Lipka

by Minda Lipka Bornstein
Translated by Jerrold Landau
Donated by Steve Bolef

My late father was born in Dobrzyn. He served as the communal administrator (*parnas*) and was active in the *Chevra Kadisha* (burial society). He concerned himself with the *Yeshiva* students and supported them with his money. His home was open to those passing through the town.

His sons Wolf and Aharon Lipka, as well as his sons-in-law Wolf Szeinbart and Aharon Szlechter continued in the traditions of their father.

His memory will never depart from my heart!

His daughter: Minda Lipka Bornstein

[Page 190]

The Brothers Mendel and Avraham Hirsh Kohn[1][2]

by Avraham Dor

Translated by Allen Flusberg

The Kohn family was considered one of the longstanding, venerable families of Dobrzyn; its name had already appeared in community records dating from the beginning of the nineteenth century. It was a very extended family with numerous branches and households that were concentrated in and around Dobrzyn.

The family included many scholars and prodigies who brought it respect and glory. One of them, from the previous generation, was R.[3] Meir'l[4] z.l.[5], the father of R. Mendel and Avraham Hirsh. R. Meir'l became famous as a great Torah scholar, and many of the townsmen would come to him, to be in his presence and to hear his penetrating *drashot*[6].

The brothers Mendel and Avraham Hirsh absorbed Torah and wisdom in their father's home, and they were well versed in Talmud and *Poskim*[7]. Yet they also turned out to be successful businessmen who proved to be the financial base of the family.

At the beginning of the 20th century, a company called "Meir Kohn and Sons" was established. Its business partners were R. Meir'l and his sons, R. Mendel and Avraham Hirsh. Very quickly it became renowned in the nearby towns and villages for both its vast wealth and its many extensive businesses. It owned agricultural farms, forests, factories, and a great deal of cattle. In addition it owned a shop for farm machinery and work tools, machines and tools that landowners and farmers considered indispensable.

And indeed the shop expanded, its storerooms extending over a continuously widening area. From dawn until dusk, farmers flocked to it from near and far to buy whatever they needed for their work.

The brothers invested their energy and talent in the development of the shop, laboring hard and witnessing the great success of their handiwork.

Their financial success did not blind the eyes of the Kohn family, nor did it distance them from their impoverished brethren. On the contrary, their home served as a charity center for the poor; the wife of R. Mendel z.l., the now deceased Tzivya, orchestrated the charity operation with the help of women volunteers[8] who sought to ease the plight of the town's needy.

Tzivya Kohn z.l. was a modest, agreeable woman who invested all of her passion into her concern for the needy. She carried out her work in a pleasant, delicate manner so as not to hurt the feelings of those families that had become impoverished and were endeavoring to hide their bitter fate from other people.

Various community matters were also decided in the home of R. Mendel Kohn. Here members of the Community Council met to consider various problems that had arisen in the town; and here also they convened for a *din torah*[9], with the spacious house serving both the litigants and the judges. I recall a famous *din torah* between R. Yitzhak Yaakov Szmiga[10] and Yosef Ruina, which was held in R. Mendel's house and lasted many months. Many townspeople came to listen to the proceedings, and all were served tea and cake.

R. Avraham Hirsh z.l. distinguished himself in public service. He was considered one of the leading members of the Aleksander Hassidim[11]. He was also once a candidate for the Polish senate, at the side of Tuvya Bialer[12] of Lodz, to represent the *Agudat Yisrael*[13] party.

The Kohn brothers also did much to advance education in the town, which until then was limited exclusively to study of the Torah, Mishna[14], and *Gemara*[15], with the children learning from the *melamed*[16] in the *cheder*[17]; the *melamed*'s knowledge was limited entirely to the religious sphere. They [the Kohn brothers] and many others felt that there was a need to also provide the children with secular studies side–by–side with religious studies. In their endeavor to help establish a *cheder metukan*[18], the Kohn brothers contributed a plot of land that was adjacent to the Dreventz River, in order to build an appropriately large building on it. With the passage of time an elementary state school wound up situated there; it was designated for Jewish students only.

The Polish tax authorities, who were never particularly friendly to the Jews, fixed their gaze on the Kohn brothers' huge property, which had aroused the jealousy and enmity of many of the wealthy of Poland. Harsh taxes were imposed on them [the Kohn brothers], without any attempt to make a fair assessment, until they [their assets] dwindled and collapsed, especially as the years 1929–30 were years of a severe economic crisis throughout the entire world.

To save the little that could still be rescued, the brothers transferred part of their capital to Israel, investing it in the completion of a building that would house a silicate–brick factory in the port of Akko [Acre]. Construction of that building had actually begun in 1925. However, they were not successful in this endeavor either, whether because of a crisis in the construction business at the time, or because of the negligent way they were treated by officials of the Jewish Agency.[19]

As compensation for the loss that they had sustained, they agreed to accept a plot of land in Kiryat Binyamin[20] from the Jewish National Fund. One of the brothers, R. Avraham Hirsh, who came on Aliya to the Land in 1933, settled there with his family members and became a farmer.

Even here he showed that he was still quite capable: his farm became one of the nicest in the entire vicinity. Although he was already middle–aged, he managed to adjust to the conditions in the Land; nor did he let go of the shovel and the hoe until his dying day.

The Kohn family and the memory of their good deeds will not be forgotten by their townspeople.

Family of Avraham Hirsh Kohn[21]

Mrs. Tzivya Kohn, z.l.[22]

R. Mendel Kohn, z.l.[23]

Tzipora Kohn, mother of Mendel and Avraham Hirsh Kohn[24]

Translator's Footnotes

1. From *My Town: In Memory of the Communities Dobrzyn–Gollob*, edited by M. Harpaz, (published by the Dobrzyn–Golub Society, Israel, 1969), pp.190–193.

2. The family name "קאהן", here transliterated as "Kohn", may be pronounced either Kahn or Kohn; the translator is not certain which pronunciation or spelling was used by this family.

3. R. is an abbreviation for *Reb*, a title similar to "Mr." in English. It can also denote "Rabbi".

4. "Meir'l" is a diminutive form of "Meir"

5. z.l. is an acronym for *zichrono livracha* (= of blessed memory)

6. *Drashot* = analytical Torah homilies

7. *Poskim* = post–Talmudic literature settling Jewish law (literally adjudicants, referring to the authors of these works)

8. Hebrew *nashim tzidkaniot* (literally righteous women)

9. *Din torah* = legal dispute judged according to Torah law (i.e. Jewish law)

10. A photograph of Szmiga appears on p. 316 of reference cited in Footnote 1. More details on his life and death at the hand of the Nazis can be found in the following articles: "Religious Life in Dobrzyn", by Dzialdow and Sanger, pp. 284–289; also "The Synagogues and Shtiebels in Dobrzyn", pp. 264–269, both in reference cited in Footnote 1.

11. Aleksander (or Alexander) is the name of a Hassidic group that had many adherents in Dobrzyn. It originated in the Polish town Aleksandrow Lodzki, hence its name. See the following link (retrieved June 2016): http://en.wikipedia.org/wiki/Aleksander_(Hasidic_dynasty).

12. A textile manufacturer who accompanied the Hassidic *Rebbe* of Ger on his visit to Palestine in 1924.

13. *Agudat Yisrael* (or *Agudas Yisroel*, *Agudath Israel*) = the ultra–orthodox organization that was established in 1912 to strengthen Orthodox institutions independent of the religious Zionists. In Poland between the two world wars it spawned a political party with the same name. See the following link (retrieved June 2016): http://en.wikipedia.org/wiki/World_Agudath_Israel.

14. *Mishna* = book of Jewish law, written down circa 200 CE

15. *Gemara* = the detailed analysis and discussion of Jewish Law based on the Mishna and additional traditions, completed in Babylon ~500CE. The Mishna and *Gemara* are the two components of the Talmud. See the following Web site (retrieved June 2016): http://en.wikipedia.org/wiki/Gemara.

16. *melamed* = children's teacher.

17. *cheder* = religious elementary school, where secular subjects were generally not taught.

18. *cheder metukan* = a "reformed" *cheder*, in which both secular and religious subjects were taught.

19. For a parallel account, see Eshel, "The First Dobrzyners in Israel", pp. 121–126 in reference cited in Footnote 1.

20. Kiryat Binyamin is located at the southwestern edge of Kiryat Atta, about 10km east of Haifa.

21. From p. 190 of reference cited in Footnote 1

22. From p. 191 of reference cited in Footnote 1

23. From p. 192 of reference cited in Footnote 1

24. From p. 193 of reference cited in Footnote 1

[Page 193]

The Dreamer Who Did Not Live to See His Dream Fulfilled[1]

by Shmuel Meiri–Minivski

Translated by Allen Flusberg

At times history favors us with multi-talented individuals who are also men of action; in spite of their many nuances and the richness of their spirit they are consistently true to their own ideals. And they are thus able to project their strength and light upon everything around them.

Perhaps this was the true meaning of the words "the man Moses"[2]: Moses the leader, the lawgiver who battled and struggled to fulfil a lofty ideal—an individual who was multi-faceted yet was true to his own ideals, and was therefore "unique in his generation".

Adolf Riesenfeld (Avraham son of Pesach) was such a person. He was born in the year 1878 in Silesia[3]. He grew up in a village among Gentiles and achieved his successes among Gentiles, but remarkably he never forgot his brethren, his people.

The love for his people, the persecuted Jews, lit a spark in his warm heart. The glow of the flame that it ignited radiated out beyond him, illuminating everything around him. The German expression he constantly used, "*mein Volk*", i.e. my people, had a profound significance, attesting to an unbreakable bond with his brethren and with their glorious humane and universal history.

Jewish Destiny endowed him with many treasured talents, virtues of the Treasured People.[4] By viewing him from many different perspectives, one can appreciate how numerous his qualities were. He could have been noteworthy and made a name for himself in any single one of them.

Thus Riesenfeld was: the pharmacist; the Zionist; the intellectual; the leader; the man with unique Jewish rootedness; the tutor who coached others in his hobbies, particularly the game of chess; the humorist; the community activist; the benefactor of the needy; the "physician" who had no diploma; the writer; the gifted speaker; the dedicated father and faithful husband; the paragon who served as an inspirational model for everyone…

I can still see him: his tall, imposing figure, the ever-present laugh that he retained even in difficult moments of struggles within the community; for indeed he had many critics and enemies who did not properly understand him.

His primary activity was his enthusiastic, tireless labor in the Zionist Movement, which was his crowning achievement. It is this work that I will endeavor to describe with the greatest of reverence and awe, as is deserved by one who dedicated himself entirely to the Zionist cause, devoting days and nights to bring about a radical change in the exilic views of his brethren, his people.

His path was not easy, no bed of roses. The very opposite: on a daily, even hourly basis he had to wrestle tempestuously with fierce opponents and commit himself completely to convincing and influencing them, whether with pleasant words or with passion and rage.

He did not isolate himself in an ivory tower, nor did he view himself as being on a higher plane than everyone else. On the contrary, he dedicated a good deal of his time and energy to small details and day-to-day issues, knowing full well that sometimes the supposedly minor matters determine the fate of great issues.

He was ready to help every single person; not only with advice, but also with his own money—albeit with great delicacy. I recall how once, in my presence, he provided some medication to an elderly woman. After she had paid him, he returned her money with a warm blessing and words of encouragement for a speedy recovery. He did not forget to invite her to come back if she needed more.

His pharmacy was called *Apteka Pod Orlem,* Polish for "The Pharmacy Under the Eagle". But the truth was that the eagle was located not above the pharmacy, but rather inside it: an eagle that watched over its wretched, deprived chicks with its sharp "claws", defending them against their enemies, German and Polish alike. With his "beak" he gnawed and scratched to find "breadcrumbs" for the poor among his people, so that they would not starve from hunger…Within the pharmacy the blue charity box of the Jewish National Fund was located in a prominent, conspicuous place. All were asked to place their generous contributions into this box. Indeed, Riesenfeld collected respectable sums for the redemption of the Land.

His home was a meeting place for those active in the community and for the youth, whether to consider community matters or to debate political and party issues. It was as if it was a mini–parliament, where people discussed and debated, with Riesenfeld conducting with a baton, his magic wand.

Agents of the Jewish National Fund and *Keren HaYesod*[5], as well as various envoys from the Land of Israel, frequented his home, where they always found a sympathetic ear and a readiness to help them do their job.

Nor did he ignore the impoverished of his town, doing as much as he could for them, trying to rehabilitate them. For this purpose he used his own money and funds he collected from affluent fellow–townsmen, who put their trust in him. Any families that had gone bankrupt when their fortunes dwindled were helped by him clandestinely and anonymously, so as not to humiliate them.

He helped many families pass between Dobrzyn and Golub and vice–versa, when the two towns were under the rule of two different regimes, being on opposite sides of the border between Germany and Russia.[6]

His concern for the poor knew no bounds, as is evident from the letter he sent in 1939 to his fellow townsman, Jacob Foge [sic][7], who was living in the United States. In emotional language he asked him not to forget the people of Dobrzyn. He demanded that he should support them generously, since they were facing economic collapse and were on the verge of perishing.

For this reason Riesenfeld could not bring himself to abandon the town when it was still possible for him to do so. For how can the shepherd leave behind the flock that follows him around with faith, affection and hope…

In the above–mentioned letter he grumbled that because of the hard times the townsmen had no sources of livelihood, and only 200 shekel–payers purchased shekels.[8] Indeed, I can say that the Dobrzyn townspeople were similar to Mendele Mocher Sforim's poor, hungry, emaciated horse[9]. Like that horse they were pitifully wretched and emaciated, but nonetheless they had a strong sense of conscience and morality, and so their impoverishment never made them lose their way.

Riesenfeld's favorite hobby was chess, which he indulged in during his leisure time—at home and even in his pharmacy. Many times I had the opportunity to play against him and to observe from up close his great acuity and the strength of his perseverance, which were reflected by his use of classical "openings". His openings had the potential to surprise and crush his opponent.

While playing he was always cheerful. He would joke around a great deal as he explained his moves. He used to enjoy the game itself, rather than the anticipated victory. Usually he would gain the upper hand, since he tended to be inventive and his moves were surprising; but when he did lose he knew how to take it in stride. The occasions that I spent with him, listening to him talk as we played, gave me great pleasure and were imprinted deeply within my heart.

At times he left his home and travelled to give lectures on Zionism and to collect contributions for the [Zionist] funds. On these trips he reached as far as Danzig[10]. He succeeded in influencing his audiences with his attractive appearance, his well-considered words, and the cultured German that he was fluent in.

He participated in several [Zionist] Congresses—the fifth, the eighth, and the twelfth, which took place in Basel and Vienna. His family accompanied him: his wife, and his daughter Ruth (may she live long[11]). At these Congresses he was able to make contact with many of the Zionist leaders and thinkers. And indeed he corresponded with many of them, including: Nordau[12], Gruenbaum[13] Rytov, Rosenbaum[14], Ussishkin[15], Motzkin[16], and others.

He was good at writing, and in his letters one can find his principal sentiments, which mostly concerned the fate of his people. His faith in Zionism was complete, and he saw in it the only solution for his people, whom he loved so dearly.

Several times he visited the Land of Israel. He aspired to go on Aliya and settle in Jerusalem, where he would establish a pharmacy. However, he did not manage to fulfil his dream. Bound to his townsmen with every fiber of his being, he could not leave them behind. In addition, he did not believe that a war would break out. He remained there with his flock until the bitter end, and he perished together with them in the horrific Holocaust.[17]

How he aroused his listeners when he returned to the town in 1925 after a visit to the Land to commemorate laying the cornerstone of the Hebrew University on Mount Scopus![18] He was very strongly impressed by this lofty event, and when he spoke about it his eyes sparkled and there was a thrill in his voice. Tears welled in many of the listeners' eyes when he described to them all that he had seen and heard. Many were influenced by his account and some even immigrated to the Land.

His exciting accounts that were expressed so intensely lit a spark in many a heart; they were like a breath of fresh air for their confused, wavering hearts. Members of all the factions respected him greatly, starting from the Hassidim who were waiting idly for the Messiah to come, and ending with the various leftists who were swept up in their multitude of denominations with alien ideals. His great sincerity, integrity and enthusiasm won over even his foes.

He was a paragon for many with the truth that burned in his very being and his relentless devotion to the Zionist cause. He saw Zionism not as an abstract entity but rather as an attainable vision—something that one should arise and act upon, rather than waiting for the End of Days.

It was difficult to be around him without binding to the passion of his vision and to his great love for his people and his land. These are the things he thought about constantly and dedicated all his time to. Everyone sensed that he was good not only at preaching, but also at practicing—prepared to make any sacrifice…

He was chairman of the Zionist Federation of the town. He did not hold this title in vain, but rather he demanded more from himself than from others. He carried out deeds and made others do them, inspiring them to arise and act for the sake of their people.

Riesenfeld the person—he who loved all human beings, especially children—could not imagine the depth to which the Teutonic–German hatred was liable to degenerate, nor that of their Polish collaborators. For this reason he did not anticipate the Holocaust that was coming…

He had a religious consciousness, even though he was forced by the law to open his pharmacy on Sabbaths and holidays. On Rosh Hashana[19] and Yom Kippur[20] he would attend the synagogue located near the bridge connecting Dobrzyn to Golub. For it was among his people that he dwelled[21], and it was to them that he devoted all of his life and his thinking.

His enthusiastic, uncompromising Zionism was a riddle to his contemporaries. Even his closest friends were puzzled, not knowing where he drew this faith from. For some unknown reason he did not strive to integrate into the Gentile society around him; yet he had not been brought up in the bosom of Jewish, national–religious culture or in Hebrew literature. For what reason did he did not aspire to the respectable positions that he turned down when they were offered to him? Why did he prefer to live in a remote, impoverished town, struggling together with his brethren until the end of his life? And from where did he draw that endless inspiration for his strong faith in Zionism and the Land of Israel?

The answers to these questions lie within the remarkable personality, full of inspiration, that was granted to him like the charm of the treasured additional soul[22]—a soul devoid of any selfish motives, dedicated completely to Zion.

His childhood and youth were spent in a village, in the company of Gentiles, but he distanced himself from them, always proclaiming to them, proudly and vehemently: "I am a Hebrew!" Herzl's writings had a profound influence on him. When he contemplated them it was as if he were listening to the beating of angels' wings.

The Dreyfus trial shocked him, too, and served as a turning point in his perspective. He came to the realization that there was only a single path for him—dedicating his life to the Zionist idea and to the Zionist movement.

As a student of pharmacology—for a period of seven years, until he received his degree—he excelled in the sciences, while the humanities were not to his liking and had no influence on him. Nor did he get any Jewish education in his parents' home. That is why it seemed that his Jewish awareness and his Zionist consciousness penetrated into his heart from some hidden, higher Power that shook him out of his tranquility.

It is difficult to analyze his personality dispassionately, for there was much of the irrational in his shift to Zionism and to his people. There were factors that were essentially emotional, unknown even to him and difficult for everyone else to comprehend.

It is a sacred duty for us to immortalize this man, who more than many others sacrificed his entire life on the altar of Zionism and the Land into which he himself did not live to enter. His life should be an instructive example to the younger generation, for it was the life of a noble spirit who was devoted to his people.

May his name be engraved in the annals of our people, among the names of those who paved the way for the establishment of the State of Israel.

Adolf Abraham son of Pesach Riesenfeld[23]

Mrs. Johanna Riesenfeld[24]

**Riesenfeld's house in Golub.
Below: the pharmacy**[25]

Translator's Footnotes

1. From *My Town: In Memory of the Communities Dobrzyn–Gollob*, edited by M. Harpaz, (published by the Dobrzyn–Golub Society, Israel, 1969), pp. 193–200. A parallel version of this article, written in Yiddish, appears on pp. 439–442 of this volume.

2. "And the man Moses was very humble, more than any person on earth" (Num. 12:3)

3. Silesia was a province of Prussia (part of the German Empire) until after World War I.

4. Treasured People = the Jews, following Deut. 7:6.

5. *Keren HaYesod* = The Foundation Fund (Hebrew), a Zionist fundraising organization, established in 1920, to support the immigration of Jews to the Land of Israel. See the following link (retrieved April, 2015): http://en.wikipedia.org/wiki/Keren_Hayesod#The_pre-state_era

6. Before 1920, after which the two towns were merged within independent Poland.

7. Jacob Fogel, a native of Dobrzyn, had immigrated to the US in April, 1939. The spelling "Foge" is probably a printer's error. See the parallel Yiddish-language article, cited in Footnote 1.

8. The "shekels" referred to here were symbolic banknotes that were sold throughout all Jewish communities. Purchasers obtained the right to vote for delegates to the Zionist Congress, while the number of delegates from each country was determined by the number of shekels sold there. The money raised by the sale supported Zionist activities. See, for example, JTA, "Election Day in Palestine: Thirty Thousand Shekel Payers Electing 30 Delegates to Zionist Congress," (May 26, 1931), available at the following link (retrieved April, 2015): http://www.jta.org/1931/05/26/archive/election-day-in-palestine-thirty-thousand-shekel-payers-electing-30-delegates-to-zionist-congress

9. The reference is to an allegorical story, *Di Klyatshe*, (The Nag), written in 1875 by Mendele Mocher Sforim (Sholem Yankev Abramovich). In it the horse, who represents the downtrodden Jewish people, is actually a prince who, through a spell, has been turned into a horse. See the following links (retrieved April, 2015):
http://www.yivoencyclopedia.oCrg/article.aspx/Abramovitsh_Sholem_Yankev; http://en.wikipedia.org/wiki/Mendele_Mocher_Sforim

10. Danzig is the German name of the port city now known as Gdansk, Poland.

11. This phrase is often appended to the name of a living person who is mentioned in the same sentence as someone who has passed away.

12. Max Nordau (1849–1923), a Zionist leader. See the following link (retrieved April, 2015): en.wikipedia.org/wiki/Max_Nordau

13. The reference is probably to the Zionist leader Yitzhak Gruenbaum (1879–1970). See the following link (retrieved April, 2015): http://en.wikipedia.org/wiki/Yitzhak_Gruenbaum

14. The reference is probably to the Zionist leader Dr. Shimshon Rosenbaum (1859–1934).

15. Menachem Ussishkin (1863–1941), a Zionist leader. See the following link (retrieved April, 2015): http://en.wikipedia.org/wiki/Menachem_Ussishkin

16. Leo Motzkin, a Zionist leader. See the following link (retrieved April, 2015): http://en.wikipedia.org/wiki/Leo_Motzkin

17. In the autumn of 1939 Riesenfeld was singled out, arrested and murdered by the Nazis, shortly after they occupied Dobrzyn. See the article "How Did We Manage?" by Yehudit Golan (Rosenwaks), pp. 145–148 of the reference cited in Footnote 1.

18. The Hebrew University of Jerusalem was officially opened in 1925. See the following link: http://en.wikipedia.org/wiki/1925_in_Mandatory_Palestine (retrieved April, 2015).

19. Jewish New Year

20. Day of Atonement

21. Paraphrasing II Kings 4:13

22. Hebrew *neshama yeteira*, a personification of the additional spirit experienced, for example, during observance of the Sabbath

23. from p. 194 of reference cited in Footnote 1

24. from p. 197 of reference cited in Footnote 1

25. from p. 199 of reference cited in Footnote 1

[Pages 200-205]

A Bunch of Memories about My Brother, the Poet Yosef Tzvi Rimon, of Blessed Memory[1]

Yaakov Rimon

Translated by Allen Flusberg

My father and teacher[2], Rebbe[3] Ephraim Eliezer Granat z.tz.l.[4], who was a writer and poet, worked as a teacher. One time he was staying at a large estate to teach the owner's children Talmud[5]. He had taken along my brother, Yosef Tzvi, so that he could study with him. The adolescent Yosef Tzvi became very impressed by the natural beauty of the estate. The house he used to study in stood at the edge of the forest. The youth took many walks on the estate, looking at the fauna and flora; and that was when he began to write his first poems.

After my father returned from the estate to his permanent residence in Dobrzyn on the Dreventz River in Poland, he established and ran a Hebrew-language library, with the purpose of disseminating the Hebrew language in the Diaspora. It was then that the gates of Hebrew literature were opened to my brother Yosef Tzvi; he read a great deal and became proficient in our literature.

When he was 17 years old, my father sent him to study in the Yeshiva of Lida[6], which had been established by Rabbi Reines[7] z.tz.l., the founder of Mizrachi, the Religious Zionist movement. My father, who was an ardent follower of Chovevei Tzion[8], was one of the first to join him and stand at his side. At that time my brother Yosef Tzvi published his first poem in Perachim, a monthly publication for young people, edited by Y.B. Levner[9].

From Lida my brother traveled to Warsaw, where he first met the well-known writer and thinker R.[10] Hillel Zeitlin[11] h.y.d.[12] In one of his letters to me, the poet Aaron Zeitlin[13], who now lives in New York, has described the very first meeting between my brother and his father. One day a shy young lad, a dreamer, comes up to R. Hillel Zeitlin, h.y.d., holding a notebook of poems in his hand. With great modesty and humility, the lad hands the notebook to R. Hillel, who reads it and is impressed with my brother's writings, and from that time onward he kept close with him. The poet Aaron

Zeitlin establishes in his letter that that particular meeting became deeply engraved in his heart.

From Warsaw my brother the poet came on Aliya in 1908 to the Land of Israel, where he was appointed to the position of secretary of "Kollel Varsha"[14] in Jerusalem. Mrs. Leah Zeliger, the wife of Rabbi Yosef Zeliger z.l.[15], helped my brother publish his first collection of poems, "Leket", which made a great impression at that time; and Eliezer ben Yehuda[16], who had brought the Hebrew language back to life, praised it and devoted several enthusiastic lines to my brother in his newspaper.

Being a secretary did not satisfy my brother; the poetry within him burst out of its confines and demanded more space. He moved from the capital city to Yafo and was given a position as a teacher in the religious elementary school "Tachkemoni". In the publications of the school library two booklets appear: one is the first booklet of his poems; and the second, "Chalomot Hayaldut"[17], contains stories by Hermann Schwab[18], translated by him [my brother] from German.

One day he was called to Haifa to administer the municipal Hebrew library there, and during this period my father sent him letters concerning the ethics of Judaism and the essence of faith and religion. These letters later served as the first book by my father z.tz.l., "Nachalat Ephraim", which was published by Pinchas Ben-Tzvi Grayevsky in Jerusalem. This book by my father received a special citation, including the reprinting of several of its chapters, in the book "Sefer Hamaalot" by Eliezer Steinman.

These letters strengthened religious sentiments in my brother's heart, deepening and reinforcing them. At that time my brother published his poem "Echad" in "Hatarbut Hayisraelit", which was edited by the writer A.Z. Rabinowitz[19], who liked him and became very close with him. This poem, which incorporated a poem of praise to the Oneness of the Holy One, Blessed be He, is reminiscent, in its expressive power and its religious-intellectual perception, of Rabbi Shlomo Ibn Gabirol, the author of the poem "Keter Malchut"[20]. Yosef Chaim Brenner[21] was very moved and impressed by this powerful work; he asked my brother over and they collaborated on "Achdut", which he edited. My brother wrote a second poem, "Halevana Hameta", which was published in the literary collection "Jezreel", edited by A.Z. Rabinowitz. Readers of Hebrew poetry were impressed by this one, as well, and my brother became famous as a poet of mysticism.

From Haifa my brother moved to Petah-Tikva, where he was given a position as a teacher in the school "Netzach Yisrael", under the administration of Rabbi Dr. Auerbach. It was then that he published his third booklet of poems, "Bamachazeh".

During the Incidents of 5681[22] he was gravely wounded by Arab rioters while he was traveling on foot from Petah-Tikva to Tel-Aviv. Since then he remained disabled, suffering in tremendous pain. He began roaming around the country, going from one end of the Land to the other. He wandered from kibbutz to kibbutz and from one agricultural settlement to another, communing along the way with beautiful vistas of the Land, the land of his life. And it was then that he wrote and published his marvelous poems on the sights of the Land, with much descriptiveness and with a feeling of unbounded love for the homeland.

During that period he told me the following story: On one of his hikes in the mountains of Upper Galilee, while he was lost in contemplation of the ancient poet's feelings, "Hadur Naeh, Ziv Haolam, Nafshi Cholat Ahavatecha"[23]—and he was utterly elevated by the towering splendor of the Living God, Fashioner of Creation—he came upon an Arab horseman[24] along the way. The sun was setting, and there was no one there except for the two of them. My brother Yosef understood the precariousness of his situation, and this is what he told me: "I thought I would end up like Rabbi Yehuda Halevi, who was trampled by an Arab horseman, and I prepared to die. I raised my hands and waved them towards Heaven. My lips did not cease praying to my Father in Heaven. As my heart burnt with love of Heaven I became immune and strengthened, and I cried out from the depths of my heart, 'Hear O Israel, the Lord is our God, the Lord is One!' And wonder of wonders: the Arab horseman remained where he was, not approaching me, and called out 'Allah Akbar' (Great God), 'Nabi' (prophet). Off he went, into the mountain ranges, and in this manner I was saved from death."

In his wanderings he reached Safed, city of the kabbalists, where he secluded himself in the "Ari" synagogue[25] for three years, not once stepping outside into daylight. During this period he went through the entire Zohar and the Talmud, and he published mystical poems under an additional name "Eliyahu" [Elijah], signing them "Yosef Tzvi-Eliyahu". And at the end of the three years he stopped using this added name.

Like an ancient poet he traveled through the country; like the author of "Yedid nefesh, av harachaman, meshoch avdach el retzonach"[26] he fulfilled, with awe and deep meditation, the concept of "yarutz avdach kemo ayal, yishtachave el mul hadarach"[27]; like a hart he ran through the expanses of the country, living within the panoramas of the Land of Israel, and all for a single intended purpose: to bow before the Splendor of God, before the Majesty and Name of the world's Creator.

The poems that my brother published, after his tragic calamity, in the magazine "Hedim", edited by Asher Barash and Yaakov Rabinowitz, are the inalienable assets, with unalterable value, of lyrical Hebrew poetry and intellectual-religious philosophy. He weeps over his fate, but without any complaints against God Above. He accepts his destiny—all the evil and suffering that has been visited upon him—with love, with the fervor of faith and the strength of trust in God, from Whom all things originate.

In his longing for Zion, in his poems that are filled with messianic yearnings, my brother was, in our generation, like Rabbi Yehuda Halevi[28] in his generation; in his intellectual-religious outlook he was like Rabbi Shlomo Ibn Gabirol[29]; and in his mysticism, solitude and seclusion, he was like a spark of Rabbi Moshe Chaim Luzzatto[30].

Within the choir of Hebrew poets, he stands alone and apart with a tone that is unique. His poetry is ardent in its intense, pure faith in the God of Israel, and in devotion to the world's Creator.

As fate would have it, my brother's religious poems were adopted by the secular and not by the religious community, which is mainly concerned with Torah literature and has not yet felt free to adopt religious poetry of our times. It was "Am Oved"[31] that published my brother's poems, arranged and concentrated in a single volume, under the name "Ketarim"; the introduction was written by the deceased writer Yaakov Rabinowitz and the poet Avraham Kariv.

When my brother left the Ari Synagogue in Safed, after he ended his three years of seclusion, he headed for Jerusalem and frequented the house and Yeshiva of Rabbi Kook z.tz.l., Chief Rabbi of the Land of Israel. Rabbi Kook, who greatly esteemed my brother for his poetry and his persona, induced him to write about the Bible; and as a result of this influence, my brother wrote his Biblical commentaries, which have appeared in several published booklets.

Already during his youth I was fortunate enough to observe him on many occasions during his moments of creativity. When he was a young man he would come to my room and seclude himself there. He would compose his poem while the paper was in place on the table and the pen was in his hand, as he walked back and forth in the room, humming an original tune that had been fashioned on the spot for the purpose of writing down the poem; the tune was filled with fervor and utmost devotion. Every now and then, as he was pacing and humming, he would go over to the table and write down another poetic line, until he completed the entire poem. I would sit in a corner, observing and listening. During the moments of composition my brother's face would radiate with happiness; his eyes, glowing like lamps, were illuminated by a fervent heart and flooded with a brilliant galaxy of poetic emotion. And then he would read the poem back to himself, and once he saw that what he had constructed was good, his face radiated with the joy of creation. At that time the spectacle would give me intense spiritual pleasure, and the glow of my brother's image during his moments of composition have remained engraved on my heart. My brother composed many tunes for his poems, the work of an anonymous, improvising musical composer—tunes that came and went, never to return, yet had generated lofty creations that will endure for generations.

My brother Yosef Tzvi was taciturn: all closed up within himself, completely bound up under the wings of the Divine Presence, absorbed in thought, shut up within the sanctuary of his vision. He hardly ever spoke, as if he had taken a vow of silence. When someone asked him a question, he would answer it directly; and then he would enclose himself once more in his silence.

In the last few years my brother returned to his family nest: to his wife, his daughter and his only son; and since then he found rest for his spirit that had been wearied by his extensive wanderings. He moved in with them in the Yad-Eliyahu neighborhood of Tel Aviv, where he was appointed a Bible lecturer in the "Ateret Zekenim" Yeshiva, located in the largest synagogue of the area. His grandchildren gave him great pleasure and were a source of encouragement.

When I would open the door to his room and he would notice me, he would greet me by calling out my name with an inner joy; he would ask how my family and I were doing, and then he would sink back into silence. And when I succeeded in eliciting a response, his words were balanced and gentle, spoken with pleasure and graceful humility, with simplicity and purity of heart. His words would touch my heart like the dew of life as I sat before him like a student before his rabbi, with veneration and reverence.

In his life and deeds he was a hidden saint. His agony purified him and made him holy. His poetry—filled with holiness, sanctified completely to God—

elevated him to the highest Spheres of Heaven, in the ladders of the Zohar and mysticism; for he was indeed one of the most remarkable individuals of our times. May the memory of the righteous be a blessing.

The poet R. Yosef Tzvi Rimon[32]

President Y. Ben Tzvi Prize is awarded to poet Yosef Tzvi Rimon[33]

Translator's Footnotes

1. From *My Town: In Memory of the Communities Dobrzyn-Gollob*, edited by M. Harpaz, (published by the Dobrzyn-Golub Society, Israel, 1969), pp. 200-205.

2. "Teacher" here is a term of respect for a parent.

3. *Rebbe* = teacher of older children

4. z.tz.l. is an acronym for *zecher tzadik livracha* = may the memory of the righteous be a blessing

5. Here written "g.f.t.", a Hebrew acronym for *Gemara* (=Babylonian Talmud), Perush Rashi (=Rashi's commentary on the Talmud) and Tosafot (additional medieval commentary on the Talmud). All three appear together on each page of the Talmud.

6. Lida, Belarus, is located ~500km east of Dobrzyn. In the period of this narrative both Dobrzyn and Lida were in the Russian Empire.

7. Yitzhak Yaakov Reines (1839-1915) is viewed as a founder of Modern Orthodoxy. He supported the incorporation of secular studies into the school curriculum, side-by-side with religious studies; and he was an ardent supporter of Religious Zionism. See the following link (retrieved September 2016): https://en.wikipedia.org/wiki/Yitzchak_Yaacov_Reines

8. *Chovevei Tzion* = Lovers of Zion, a movement, begun in 1884, that is considered the forerunner of Zionism. See the following link (retrieved September 2016): https://en.wikipedia.org/wiki/Hovevei_Zion

9. Yisrael Binyamin Levner (1862-1916), an educator, editor and writer of Hebrew books for children.

10. R. stands for *Reb*, a title similar to "Mr." in English.

11. Hillel Zeitlin (1871-1942) was a Hebrew and Yiddish writer.

12. h.y.d. is an acronym for *hashem yikom damo* = May God avenge his blood. Zeitlin was murdered by the Nazis during World War II. See "Hillel Zeitlin", in *Encyclopedia Judaica*, vol. 16, pp. 974-975; also the following link (retrieved September 2016): https://en.wikipedia.org/wiki/Hillel_Zeitlin

13. Aaron Zeitlin (1898-1973). See "Aaron Zeitlin", in *Encyclopedia Judaica*, p. 975; also the following link (retrieved September 2016): https://en.wikipedia.org/wiki/Aaron_Zeitlin

14. *Kollel Varsha* = Warsaw Community, an organization, based in Warsaw, Poland, that supported the poor of Israel who had come from Poland and Lithuania with donations from abroad

15. While still in Eastern Europe, Zeliger (1872-1919), had already championed Hebrew as a spoken language. See the following link (in Hebrew, retrieved September 2016): https://he.wikipedia.org/wiki/זליגר_יוסף

16. Ben Yehuda (1858-1922) was a fiery proponent of spoken Hebrew; he is credited with the revival of Hebrew as a spoken language, a mission he undertook virtually single-handedly.

17. *Chalomot Hayaldut* = Dreams of Childhood

18. Herman Schwab (1879-1962) was a Jewish German journalist and publisher. In 1911 he published a book of stories for children, *Kinderträume* = Dreams of Childhood. See "Hermann Schwab", in *Encyclopedia Judaica*, vol. 14, pp. 1013-1014.

19. Alexander Siskind Rabinowitz (1854-1945) was a scholar closely aligned with the pre-state Labor Movement of Israel; he sought to bridge the divide between secular and religious Jews. See "Alexander Siskind Rabinowitz", *Encyclopedia Judaica*, volume 13, pp. 1474-75; also the following link (in Hebrew, retrieved September 2016):
https://he.wikipedia.org/wiki/%D7%90%D7%9C%D7%9B%D7%A1%D7%A0%D7%93%D7%A8_%D7%96%D7%99%D7%A1%D7%A7%D7%99%D7%A0%D7%93_%D7%A8%D7%91%D7%99%D7%A0%D7%95%D7%91%D7%99%D7%A5%27

20. Gabirol was an 11th-century Jewish philosopher and poet who lived in Spain. The poem *Keter Malchut* (= Crown of Kingship) describes—in 40 stanzas of concise, simple Hebrew—the author's reflections as he comes before God's judgment. See the following link (retrieved September 2016):
https://en.wikipedia.org/wiki/Solomon_ibn_Gabirol.

21. Brenner (1881-1921) was a pioneer of Hebrew literature. He was murdered in the "Incidents" of 5681 (see below, Footnote 22). For more details, see the following link (retrieved September 2016):
https://en.wikipedia.org/wiki/Yosef_Haim_Brenner.

22. The "Incidents" or "Events" of 5681 (1921-1922) are the Arab riots that took place that year. See the following link (retrieved September 2016):
https://en.wikipedia.org/wiki/Jaffa_riots.

23. "Hadur Naeh…" can be loosely translated as "Splendid, Beautiful, Light of the universe, my soul is lovesick for You." This is a line from the mystical liturgical poem Yedid Nefesh, recited in most synagogues in Israel at the start of the Sabbath service on Friday evening. It has been attributed to the 16th-century poet Azriki, among others. See the following link, retrieved September 2016:
https://en.wikipedia.org/wiki/Yedid_Nefesh.

24. Yehuda Halevi (~1075-1141) was a philosopher and poet who lived in Spain and wrote of his yearning for the Land of Israel. He died during his pilgrimage to Israel; according to legend, he was trampled by an Arab horseman. See the following link (retrieved September 2016):
https://en.wikipedia.org/wiki/Judah_Halevi#Journey_to_Israel

25. The "Ari" synagogue, dating from the late 16th century, was built and named in memory of the "Ari" (Rabbi Isaac Luria), a famous 16th-century kabbalist of Safed. See the following link (retrieved September 2016):
https://en.wikipedia.org/wiki/Ari_Ashkenazi_Synagogue.

26. This first line of the mystical poem *Yedid Nefesh* (see Footnote 23) can be loosely translated as: Soul-Mate, Compassionate Father, draw Your servant toward Your Will.

27. This second line of *Yedid Nefesh* (see Footnotes 23 and 26) can be translated as: May Your servant then run like a hart to bow before Your Splendor.

28. See Footnote 24.

29. See Footnote 20.

30. Luzzatto was a prominent 18th-century rabbi, kabbalist and philosopher who was born in and raised in Italy. See the following link (retrieved September 2016): https://en.wikipedia.org/wiki/Moshe_Chaim_Luzzatto

31. *Am Oved* (= A Working People) is a secular pubishing house, founded in 1942 "to meet the spiritual needs of the working public." See the following link (retrieved September 2016): http://www.am-oved.co.il/page_23079; https://en.wikipedia.org/wiki/Am_Oved.

32. From p. 201 of reference cited in Footnote 1

33. From p. 205 of reference cited in Footnote 1

[Pages 206-208]

Why Do You Weep, My Heart[1]
(by Yosef Tzvi Rimon)
Translated by Allen Flusberg

1

Why do you weep, my heart, for your sanctuary's ruins?
The tempest was great—did the tempest enrage you?
The *Shekhina*[2] sheared the hair of Her head from sorrow,
Calling you too for rebuke as Her anointed.[3]
She took hold of you like a thief on Her mountains,
She tormented you, saying, I too am tormented.
She raved when you looked and shouted
From anger, from pain; and did you not know how to betray?
Woe! Darkness from day to day, and under
God's wings; where can I find refuge from the storm?...

He casts reproach upon his angels[4], and I in his bosom
Dwell, the whirlwind rips my flesh
And my harp strings have been torn, and my lip
Has been violated. Why do you gaze at me, astonished?
Has not the splendor of God been upon me from the beginning
And the glow of the end…has been upon me in evening,
By night my God She[5] hovers over the chasm of tears
And soars over a wing of light…
The storm struck, and She became wretched, and called Her anointed
For rebuke…Woe, for night, for day
Man creates them…And no compassion for God's seer!

2

Did You fall ill like a human, O God,
That You fashioned
Your creations of Genesis slowly?
You designated the days: good,
And one of them: very good,—[6]
And Man betrayed…
Wisdom, which is a song, was violated,
And chaos surrounded life![7]
The Woman's cherubic image, violated;
No water and no ark,
And the world is weary…

No redemption for the light,
Nor does the world enter wisdom's gates:
There is no measure for the evil in it,
And God's curse in Satan's apparel
Walks about wearily...
Desire, Man, and betray!
Or please desire and love!...
Discipline not to be spurned[8]
Is surely spurned,
Even the land is not to be built—
Evil, evil, evil...

3

In vain heaven's blue was poured out,
My agony is mute,
The prophetic hummingbird[9] foretold falsely—
My day accursed!
Trees bewildered by the tempest—
My soul weary.
Who will give me light, console me—
I am faint.

Play, my harp, play, musician!
I have become wretched.
Rise up, my soul, in the tempest,[10] rise up in the vision!
I am in tears.

The moon concealed in me its venom,
All radiance—deceit,
I walk in gloom, tottering, falling—
Upon hills of a dream.

Translator's Footnotes

1. From *My Town: In Memory of the Communities Dobrzyn-Gollob*, edited by M. Harpaz, (published by the Dobrzyn-Golub Society, Israel, 1969), pp. 206-208. The translator acknowledges insightful comments and suggestions by Professor David Jacobson of Brown University.

2. *Shekhina* = Divine Presence of God. The term "*shekhina*" is feminine in Hebrew. Midrashic sources refer to the Shekhina as suffering and weeping upon the destruction of the Temple and mourning with the Jewish People in their exile (e.g. *Eicha Rabba, Petihatot*, Section 25, "...Thus when the *Shekhina* left the Temple She was caressing and kissing its walls, weeping..."; *Yalkut Shimoni, Exodus, Parshat Bo*, Section 210, "...whenever Israel is enslaved the *Shekhina* is enslaved with them...").

3. The ideas expressed here recall Isaiah's "suffering servant" (Is. 53), interpretable as suffering of either (1) the Jewish people personified; or (2) the seer / poet / messianic figure. This ambiguity is present in Is. 53.

4. After Job 4:18

5. Given its feminine form, "She" is translated here as referring back to the *Shekhina*.

6. See Genesis 1, especially 1:31

7. This verse echoes a statement in the Zohar (87b, *Tikuna* 54) that eating from the Tree of Knowledge of Good and Evil (Gen. 3) confounded good and evil; as a result, the righteous sometimes experience evil.

8. Phraseology based on Prov. 15:32, 13:8

9. See previous article by Yaakov Rimon, "A Bunch of Memories about My Brother, the Poet Yosef Tzvi Rimon, of Blessed Memory," pp. 200-205 (in reference cited in Footnote 1). The poet would hum a tune, composed on the spot, to inspire him as he wrote his poetry.

10. See II Kings 2:1, 2:11

[Page 209]

My Parents' House[1]
(In memory of my son Meir z.l.[2], whose life was cut short)
by Shmuel Meiri (Minivski)

Translated by Allen Flusberg

My mother, Beila, who was the daughter of: R. Ber Kristal, a torah scribe from Dobrzyn[3], was married to my father, Meir Minivski z.l. of Rypin. Together they established a faithful household in the spirit of Jewish-Zionist tradition. My father, who excelled with the industriousness of a working man, established a flourishing household for his four daughters: Fradl, Sarah Leah, Esther Devora z.l., and Ruhama; and for his only son Shmuel Avraham, may he live a long life[4]. My father was a visionary who viewed religious Zionism as paramount, and it was in this spirit that he educated the members of his family.

I can still recall that day when members of the community gathered together in the synagogue of Rypin[5], during the massacres of 1921[6], how my father cried bitterly, moaning and speaking broken-heartedly…and how he read the Scroll of Destruction[7] at home, sitting on an overturned mourning stool, as I listened to his reading with misty eyes…

My father's house was open to many guests, to lecturers and speakers of the Religious-Zionist "Mizrachi"[8] of those days: the rabbis Kowalsky from Wloclawek[9] and Broida from Lipno[10], z.l., who ceremoniously assembled a large crowd in our house, to work for the success of Zionist fundraising and to encourage Aliya to the Land [of Israel]. My father, in whose heart there burned a fire of love for his homeland and people, lit the flame of longing for the Land in the souls of his household members, as well. And our hearts did indeed languish for a Zionist-Pioneer fulfillment.

With all his might, my father passionately dedicated himself to organizing a Hebrew school, in the spirit of the Jewish-Zionist tradition. His entire ideal was to educate us in the bosom of the pure spirit of the Jewish people: Torah and Destiny.

He was a hard worker, imbued with the recognition of the value of labor; a person of great inspiration and national vision, who had the courage to send his only son, when he reached the age of 13, to the Rabbinical Seminary in Warsaw, and later to the Hebrew University in Jerusalem. He did not live to see me become an educator and principal of a *mamlachti*[11] school in Israel, the fulfillment of his ideal.

I remember how my mother Beila z.l. would wave her gentle, pure hands while she lit the candles on Sabbath Eve. She would move her hands in circles around the flames and reverently insert pennies into the blue charity box of the Jewish National Fund.

How fervently and with what trepidation did she study *Tze'ena Ur'ena*[12], immersing herself completely in the legendary stories and the homilies, encompassed by a spirit of holiness. It was a legacy from her father, the scribe.

My sisters: Fradl the eldest, with her two little children and her husband; and also Sarah Leah and Esther Devora, trainees in the *Shomer Hatzair*[13], z.l., all perished in the Holocaust…

…For this reason does my soul grieve with sorrow, and there is no one to comfort me. Let these pages therefore be a selflessly established monument, preserved for future times:

"And I shall give them a memorial in My house and within My walls…an everlasting name shall I give them that shall not be cut off."[14]

[Page 210]

The Meiri (Miniwski) family: his parents and sisters[15]

Translator's Footnotes

1. From *My Town: In Memory of the Communities Dobrzyn-Gollob*, edited by M. Harpaz, (published by the Dobrzyn-Golub Society, Israel, 1969), pp. 209-210.

2. z.l. stands for *zichrono livracha* (= of blessed memory)

3. See Meiri, "My Grandfather's House", pp. 180-184 of the reference cited in Footnote 1.

4. This phrase is often appended to the name of a living person who is mentioned in the same sentence as someone who has passed away. In this case the author himself is the living person.

5. Rypin is a city located approximately 25km east of Dobrzyn.

6. See for example the following link (retrieved June 2016):
   http://kehilalinks.jewishgen.org/tetiev/massacresoftetiev.htm
   This assumes the reference is to the massacres that had taken place in Ukraine. Alternatively the author is referring to the "Incidents of 5681", the massacres that took place in Israel during the Arab riots of 1921. See the following link: https://en.wikipedia.org/wiki/Jaffa_riots

7. Presumably the Book of Lamentations

8. Mizrachi = the religious Zionist movement, founded in 1902. See the following link (retrieved June 2016):
   https://en.wikipedia.org/wiki/Mizrachi_%28religious_Zionism%29

9. Rabbi Judah Leib Kowalsky (1862-1925), a leader of the Mizrachi movement. See the following link (retrieved June, 2016):
   http://www.encyclopedia.com/article-1G2-2587511534/kowalsky-judah-leib.html. He was the Rabbi of Wloclawek, Poland during much of his career.

10. Probably a reference to Rabbi Shmuel Brodt (1885-1963) of Lipno, Poland, who became a leader of the Mizrachi movement. See the following article: "Brodt, Shmu'el", in the Yivo Encyclopedia of Jews in Eastern Europe, available at the following link: http://www.yivoencyclopedia.org/article.aspx/Brodt_Shemuel (retrieved June 2016).

11. *Mamlachti* school = state school

12. *Tze'ena Ur'ena* (sometimes written *tzena urena*) = "Go Out and Gaze", the name of a commentary on the Torah, composed in Yiddish in the 17th century for people who had difficulty with Hebrew, and particularly popular among women in Eastern Europe. The name is based on the verse "Go out and gaze, daughters of Zion, upon King Solomon..." (Song of Songs 3:11)

13. *Hashomer Hatzair* (= the Youth Guard) was a youth movement whose purpose it was to prepare people for agricultural work in Israel

14. Isaiah 56:5

15. From p. 210 of reference cited in Footnote 1.

[Page 211]

R. Yeshayahu the "Great"[1]
(The *Nistar*[2])
by his Nephew, Avraham Dor (Dobroszklanka)
Translated by Allen Flusberg

R.[3] Yeshayahu "the Great" (the Great R. Shaya [in Yiddish]), or "the *Nistar*"—this was his nickname in our town. He was known by this name even in the surrounding areas near and far. He owned a store for buying and selling metal; it was managed by his sons, but he himself sat day and night studying Torah. He submerged himself in the Talmud and the *Poskim*[4]. He was writing emendations and comments, as we later discovered in the margins of his various volumes of Talmud. He was an avid Hassid in the court of Warka[5]. He would spend much of his time near the *Rebbe*[6], in his court for months at a time, discussing the foremost religious issues of the day with him.

Accepted as he was by the people of Dobrzyn as the local rabbinic authority, he had set up a kind of rabbinical seat; many of the townspeople would come to him frequently [for religious advice]. When Rabbi Yehuda Leib Sonabend[7] was appointed Rabbi of Dobrzyn, he [Yeshayahu] was also appointed a member of the religious court; and there was no *din-Torah*[8] or religious meeting that he did not participate in.

He was very concerned about proper family life. When a case of a family quarrel was brought before him, he would invite the two sides over to him, not letting them leave until he had made peace between them. And under his influence they put an end to the town card game that had had an especially damaging effect on family life.

He had a wide following of admirers among the townspeople, particularly from among the various groups of Hassidim. They used to come to listen to the religious talks and Talmud classes that he gave on a weekly basis in his *shtibl*[9].

To this very day the memory of R. Yeshayahu "the Great" accompanies his descendants, who recall him with pride and veneration. His image is bound up with the town of Dobrzyn, whose best and finest have been wiped out.

The son of R. Yeshayahu "the Great", R. Zalman Dobroszklanka[10]

The daughter-in-law of R. Yeshayahu "the Great", Malka Dobroszklanka[11]

Translator's Footnotes

1. From *My Town: In Memory of the Communities Dobrzyn-Gollob*, edited by M. Harpaz, (published by the Dobrzyn-Golub Society, Israel, 1969), pp. 211-212.

2. *Nistar* = Hidden: an extraordinarily righteous person who is not recognized or appreciated as such. Additionally, since kabbalah is termed *torat hanistar* ("hidden teaching"), the term *nistar* also hints at a mystic.

3. R. = *Reb*, an honorific similar to the English term "Mr.". R. can also stand for Rabbi.

4. *Poskim* = post-Talmudic literature settling Jewish law (literally adjudicants, referring to the authors of these works)

5. Warka is a town located about 300km southeast of Dobrzyn (about 60km south of Warsaw). A dynasty of Hassidic *rebbes*, known as Varker or Vurker, originated in this town.

6. *Rebbe* = leader of a Hassidic group

7. See articles by M. Sonabend, "The Rabbi of Dobrzyn", pp. 51-54 and 397-400 of the reference cited in Footnote 1.

8. *Din-Torah* = case or dispute judged according to religious Jewish law

9. *Shtibl* = small prayer room, usually Hassidic

10. From p. 211 of reference cited in Footnote 1

11. From p. 212 of reference cited in Footnote 1.

[Page 213]

Tzvi Zev (Hirsh Wolff) Laks, of Blessed Memory[1]

Yaakov Rimon

Translated by Allen Flusberg

One of the distinguished Jews of Dobrzyn, a lover of Zion, active in Zionism and community affairs. The administration head of the charity funding of Dobrzyn; the *gabbai*[2] of the synagogue of the Hassidim of Warka-Otwock[3]; a dauntless warrior for the Zionist funds. Every Yom Kippur Eve he fought to put up a donation bowl to benefit the Jewish National Fund. An honest man, modest and humble. All his life he yearned to go on Aliya to the Land of Israel, and after the events of 1921[4] he went on Aliya with his daughter. For several weeks he was a guest at the apartment of Yechiel Bunim Granat-Rimon, and afterwards he moved into a large house that he bought, located on Gedud Haivri Street in Tel Aviv. One of his sons, who is now abroad [outside Israel], ran his household. May his memory be a blessing!

Translator's Footnotes

1. From *My Town: In Memory of the Communities Dobrzyn-Gollob*, edited by M. Harpaz, (published by the Dobrzyn-Golub Society, Israel, 1969), p. 213.

2. *gabbai* = synagogue treasurer functionary, who, among other duties, collected contributions and organized the provision of charity to the needy

3. Warka and Otwock were towns in Poland from which Hassidic dynasties originated. See the following link (retrieved July, 2016):
https://en.wikipedia.org/wiki/Amshinov_(Hasidic_dynasty).

4. See for example the following link (retrieved June 2016):
http://kehilalinks.jewishgen.org/tetiev/massacresoftetiev.htm

5. "R." stands for *Reb*, an honorific similar to the English "Mr." It can also stand for "Rabbi".

6. Mizrachi = the religious Zionist movement and party. See the following link (retrieved July, 2016):
https://en.wikipedia.org/wiki/Mizrachi_%28religious_Zionism%29

7. From p. 213 of reference cited in Footnote 1.

R.[5] Laks, Hirsh Wolff, one of the founders of the "Mizrachi"[6] in Dobrzyn[7]

[Page 213]

To My Girlfriends Who Did Not Merit...[1]
Rivka Shapira (Horowitz)
Translated by Allen Flusberg

I will never forget the friends that I grew up with in our town, and how we spent time together dreaming about *aliya*[2] to the Land of Israel. I will never forget how we girls would gather together every evening in the "Beit Yaakov" building, in the presence of Pesya Gutmorgen, our lovely, modest teacher, whom everyone in the town was fond of. How we enjoyed those meetings—whether it was a Bible class, an open discussion, or a game. And sometimes we would sit around, singing late into the night; or we would carry on, the way young girls do.

Every Sabbath we would gather before evening for "*Shalosh Seudot*"[3]. We would sit around a table, set appropriately with an abundance of delicacies and treats. Pesya Gutmorgen sat at the head of the table, giving a talk on "*Parshat Hashavua*"[4], while we girls lapped up her words with relish. We felt engulfed with peace and serenity. We would start singing as soon as her talk ended, and then we would finish by dancing. It was a kind of harbinger of a good week to come.

Whenever my thoughts turn to my childhood I recall these friends of mine, envisioning them before my eyes. One in particular stands out, a close friend whose image has been with me all these years since I left Dobrzyn—Chana Kadecki.

She was the daughter of wealthy parents. We were bound together in a very close, devoted friendship. When they began distributing *aliya* certificates to the *Agudat Yisrael*[5] girls, they set up *hachsharot*[6] for girls in Warsaw and Lodz. Chana Kadecki also wanted to go on *hachshara*[7], but only if we would be together. And indeed in the end we did go to Lodz together. However, when it actually came to immigrating, I wound up going to Israel by myself; it was not possible to obtain two travel visas, nor were her parents in a hurry to agree to let her go.

After that she wrote me a great deal, letters abounding with love for the Land of Israel. To prepare for aliya she went to learn needlework, wishing to find means to support herself by working. She believed that she would join me in a matter of a few months. She believed it, but did not merit it...How unhappy I was! For together the two of us had dreamed about *aliya* to Israel as we strolled through the streets of the town, our thoughts taking us far, far away…

I left Dobryn in 1936, on a Sunday in the month of Tammuz[8]. Very early that morning we strode towards the Golub train station, a distance of several kilometers. I was accompanied by my dear family members and by my many girlfriends, tears in their eyes. The tears were tears of joy that I was going up to the Holy Land, and tears of sadness that they were remaining in the Exile. We parted, using the word *lehitraot*[9] to say goodbye; it did not occur to any of us that we would not see each other ever again…

May these words constitute an everlasting testimony for my family members and for my friends:

Family members	**Friends**
My father, Elyakim Meir Horowicz	Altyna, Bina
My mother, Bayla Frumit	Groner, Tultza
My brother, Yaakov	Grosman, Sara
My brother, Avraham Yosef	Goldbruch, Hinda
My sister, Hinda	Goldbruch, Yente
My brother, Baruch Mendel	Kadecki, Chana[10]
My sister, Hinda[11]	Frajlich, Esther
My aunt, Chana	Rosenwaks, Gela
My uncle, Mendel Gurfinkel	Szlachter, Neche
	Szlecka, Henye

Translator's Footnotes

1. From *My Town: In Memory of the Communities Dobrzyn-Gollob*, edited by M. Harpaz, (published by the Dobrzyn-Golub Society, Israel, 1969), pp. 213-214.

2. *Aliya* = immigration to Israel

3. *Shalosh Seudot* = the festive third Sabbath meal, eaten Saturday evening, shortly before the Sabbath ends

4. *Parshat Hashavua* = the weekly section of the Torah (read in the synagogue that Sabbath)

5. *Agudat Yisrael* = name of ultra-Orthodox religious movement

6. *Hachsharot* = Training camps for work in Palestine (see next footnote)

7. *Hachshara* = Training in work to prepare for the move to Palestine

8. June-July

9. *Lehitraot* = See you again

10. According to a written eyewitness account, Chana Kadecki was in the group of 35 wealthy families of Dobrzyn that were taken away by the Nazis in November, 1939, shortly before all the Jews of the town were expelled. No member of this group of families was heard from again; it is believed that they were all murdered almost immediately. Written in Warsaw in 1941, the account was preserved there in the Ringelblum archive. See the following link, which contains a copy of the original document in Yiddish with an English translation by Frank Dobia:
http://home.connexus.net.au/~fdobia/TwoLetters.htm

11. Here the name "Hinda" is apparently a typo in the original Hebrew text, since it already occurs above as that of an older sister. The actual name of the youngest sister was Sheina.

[Page 216]

In Memory of My Parents
R. Mordechai Mendel and Chaya Tzivya Kohn[1]
by Their Son, Yaakov Kohn

Translated by Allen Flusberg

I recall that I was a small child when the First World War broke out. At that time we were staying in the summer home that was on my grandfather's property, Kwasno, which is near Sierpc[2]. By disposition my father was fond of fields and trees, and so we would usually spend the summer months in Nature's bosom.

It was a time of war, and the information we were getting was frightening. The battle lines, which continued to move around, were approaching our vicinity. Several Jews from Dobrzyn were then staying with us on the farm: Isaac Shochet and his son-in-law Daniel; R. Yisrael Karpa the *melamed*[3] and his son Yosef Chaim; Januar and his wife; as well as others. Grandfather Meir'l and Grandmother Michle also joined us. Grandfather was a distinguished farmer; he had transferred his shops for construction materials and farming equipment to his sons, Mendel and Avraham Hirsh, while he himself was managing the Kwaśno and Kowiziniec farms.

What we were dreading came to pass! The war came closer, disturbing the bucolic serenity with terrifying reverberations of shots and explosions. We were frightened for our lives. To avoid being hit by bullets we stretched out on the floor, eating just the small portions of food that one of the workers was risking his life to bring us.

The farm passed back and forth between the two sides: first the Russians seized the area, but very quickly they retreated and the Germans took their place. We tried to maintain good relations with each of them, making sure to provide food to the hungry soldiers.

But one cannot maintain immunity indefinitely! In the end my father was accused of espionage. This took place during a *seudat mitzvah*[4] that my father gave, as he usually did, on the Yahrzeit[5] date of *Rebbe* Yismach Yisrael[6], an Aleksander Hassid; for our family also belonged to this group. Suddenly Russian soldiers, headed by an officer, came in. They accused my father of spying for the Germans, which was a wicked slander. Our miller, Shevikowski, who wanted to get back at my father, was the one who had slandered us. After a great deal of effort we were able to get my father released. And once the Germans returned and conquered the entire area, we all went back to our town, Dobrzyn.

Translator's Footnotes

1. From *My Town: In Memory of the Communities Dobrzyn-Gollob*, edited by M. Harpaz, (published by the Dobrzyn-Golub Society, Israel, 1969), p. 216.

2. Sierpc is located ~50km southeast of Dobrzyn and ~125 km northwest of Warsaw

3. *melamed* = teacher of young children

4. *seudat mitzvah* = a ceremonial meal with religious imperative

5. Yahrzeit = anniversary of death

6. *Yismach Yisrael* (or *Yisroel*) = Yerachmiel Yisrael Yitzhak Dancyger (1853-1910), an Aleksander *rebbe*, whose nickname derives from his most famous book, entitled *Yismach Yisroel*. See the following link (retrieved June, 2016): http://en.wikipedia.org/wiki/Aleksander_%28Hasidic_dynasty%29. "Aleksander" is the name of one of the many Hassidic movements; "*Rebbe*" is the title given to the leader of such a movement.

[Page 218]

In Memoriam

Yehoshua Eshel[1]

by Avraham Dor (Dobroszklanka)
Translated by Allen Flusberg

Even back in our town, Dobrzyn, Yehoshua Eshel distinguished himself with his talents and his courage. Young and energetic, he decided to leave the town to broaden his horizons and acquire knowledge. And since he was already then a Zionist with every fiber of his being, he went off to the Land of Israel, where he was one of the first students at the Herzliya *Gymnasia*[2].

Although I was only a child then, I can still remember how he left the town for the Land of Israel. The town was in an uproar: was it a small matter that a young person, a member of a prosperous family, was leaving for a faraway country, Israel, on the other side of the sea? Many of the townspeople, astonished that his parents had agreed to this bold journey, kept pestering them with questions.

I saw him again a year later, when he came back for summer vacation after his classes had ended. That was about a year before World War I broke out. We were all jealous of him that he was living and studying in the Land of Israel.

When all ties with the East were severed during the war,[3] no one, of course, received any letters from him, which certainly must have worried his parents more than just a little. But once the war had ended they received a picture from him that turned into the talk of the town. It was a photograph of Yehoshua in the uniform of a sergeant of the Jewish Brigade[4]. Indeed, the picture of a Hebrew soldier, full of courage and valor, with an insignia inscribed with a menorah on his hat, was no small matter in the town. It was particularly impressive from our perspective, that of the young people who yearned to immigrate to the Land of Israel.

In the year 1921, when I was in Kutno[5], acquiring expertise in the rose farm that belonged to Katriel (Yehoshua's brother), a rumor was going around that Yehoshua Eshel was in Danzig[6] and that all of his family was getting ready to travel to see him. And indeed he was outside Israel then; he was evading the British forces that were trying to arrest him as well as other young Hebrews, the leaders of the Hagana[7]. He and his comrades had taken part in the defense of Jerusalem during the events of May, 1921.[8] Already then he was one of the main active members of the Hagana, and he had been forced to defend his brethren against Arabs who had been incited to riot. He stayed abroad for a while, waiting for the storm to pass. And once things calmed down, he hurried to return to the Land.

When we arrived in the Land, at the end of the year 1925, Yehoshua Eshel was already a well-known, prominent personality, one of the leaders of the Hagana, who had contributed to organizing and establishing it. From then until the end of his life, his days and nights were dedicated to defending his homeland and his people. During the War of Independence we would see him in the uniform of a lieutenant colonel, devotedly continuing his actions to keep the State secure.

After his brother Katriel arrived in the Land, in the beginning of the 1950s, we met him again at the yearly gathering of the Organization of Dobrzyners. As occupied and busy as he was, he paid attention to what was going on among those who hailed from his town; and when he heard about the preparations for the publication of a Yizkor Book, he encouraged those who were organizing it and promised to participate.

He did not live to see the publication of the book. During a memorial service for a comrade that took place in the Hagana Building, he collapsed just after he had delivered a eulogy. How characteristic indeed his death was in view of his lifelong path, a life of untiring activity and unending devotion to his people.

He carved out for himself a place of honor on the Eastern Wall[9] of the founders of the Hagana and those who shaped its image—among those who built up the Israeli Defense Forces and the elite of its officers, the individuals who dedicated their lives to building up and defending the homeland.

May his image be with us for all time!

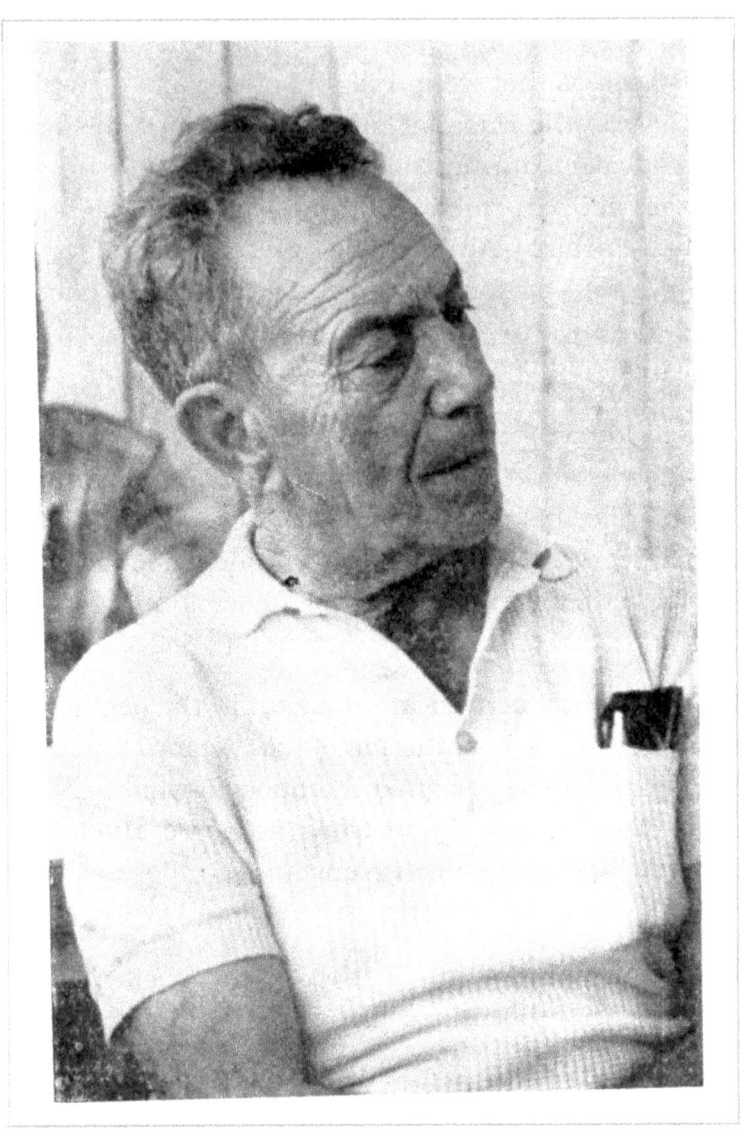

Yehoshua Eshel, one of the heads of the "Hagana", and one of those who shaped its image[10]

Translator's Footnotes

1. From *My Town: In Memory of the Communities Dobrzyn-Gollob*, edited by M. Harpaz, (published by the Dobrzyn-Golub Society, Israel, 1969), pp. 218-220.

2. *Gymnasia* = high school

3. Dobrzyn was in the Russian Empire, which in World War I was at war with the Ottoman Turkish Empire that Palestine was part of.

4. The Jewish Brigade, referred to in Hebrew as the *Gedud Ivri* = the Hebrew Brigade, was part of the British army in World War I. See the following Web pages (retrieved September 2015):
https://en.wikipedia.org/wiki/Jewish_Legion;
http://www.jewishvirtuallibrary.org/jsource/judaica/ejud_0002_0011_0_10141.html.

5. Kutno is a city in Poland, located ~100km south of Dobrzyn

6. Danzig = Gdansk, Poland, located on the Baltic coast, ~150km north of Dobrzyn.

7. Hagana (= Defense), a Jewish paramilitary organization, established in 1920 as a defense force against Arab rioters. See the following Web page (retrieved September 2015): https://en.wikipedia.org/wiki/Haganah

8. See the article by Yehoshua Eshel, "The First Dobrzyners in Israel", pp. 121-126 of this volume (reference cited in Footnote 1).

9. The term "Eastern Wall" here indicates the highest and most desirable place of honor. In countries lying west of Israel (e.g. in Europe), Jews turned towards the eastern wall of the synagogue when they recited the *amida*, the silent prayer (to follow the practice of facing towards Jerusalem during this prayer). As a result, the eastern wall became a desirable location, and it was where the dignitaries usually sat. See the following Web site (retrieved September 2015): https://en.wikipedia.org/wiki/Mizrah.

10. From p. 220 of reference cited in Footnote 1.

[Pages 221-222]

Shoshana Vinkor (Offenbach) of Blessed Memory[1]

by Yisrael Lahav
Translated by Allen Flusberg

Shoshana is gone: what a shock this news has been to us. The heart refuses to believe it. It was just a short time ago that we met, albeit on her deathbed. However, her strong will to live and her desperate struggle to hang on to her family, her spouse, the kibbutz home: all these promised to put off the evil decree. But her luck did not hold out, and her fate has been determined.

I had known Shoshana for several decades, from a time when she was still young, one of those who managed the *ken*[2] of the *Hashomer Hatzair* Movement[3] in Dobrzyn, the town situated on the banks of the Dreventz River. In spite of the distractions, her bearing the burden of her family, she devoted all her time, energy and concern to organizing groups of young people; to changing their exilic way of life; to supporting the life of a youth movement that was preparing itself for the fulfilment of the dream of pioneering creativeness, of a new Jewish society in the long-awaited Land of Israel.

Shoshana was not only someone who preached to others: she was also one of the first members who imposed the duty of fulfilment on themselves. As the leader of an educational group, she knew how to reach the wavering younger generation. Modest and quiet, she did not like parading around or being conspicuous. But whoever looked at her during the *ken* evenings—during the youth dances; during the passionate singing filled with longing; on the winter hikes, filled with laughter and boisterousness, in the snowy mountains and the unending forests—would see how her eyes sparkled and glowed, how she was slowly but surely joining in the inordinate ardor of the young people.

I found myself in her home town just before the rise of Nazism. Anti-Semitism in Poland was growing, and the ground was burning under the feet of the Jews of Poland; but it had not yet sunk in to the minds of all the Jewish youth that it would be necessary for them to change their way of life. We knew that it was imperative for us to have a period in which we could organize ourselves to shift the young people away from exilic life and toward pioneer fulfilment. Shoshana, together with a handful of adult members, had decided to struggle against the complacency, and she was devoting all her energy and strength to organizing the *ken* of the *Shomer Hachalutzi*[4]. She set up an evening school in Hebrew and helped establish summer camps and ideological groups.

I remember how—just before I completed my mission in the town, when the local *ken* summer camp had ended—we marched in full scout ceremony, singing passionately. Shoshana marched at the very front in scout uniform, surrounded by a group of young members of the *Shomer Hachalutzi*. She whispered to me that these were the most beautiful and best years of her life. She evidently saw that what she was doing was working. But a concern gnawed at her heart: would it be possible to bring all of these young people to the shores of the homeland? Could we manage to take them away from their complacent families, and wouldn't they be scattered like chaff before the storm? Would we be able to bring them to *hachshara*[5] and Aliya? Yet she did indeed do it, for most of the members did reach the Land [of Israel]. And a significant number of them have continued on in communal life, scattered in every corner of the Land.

The time came, and Shoshana left her family nest and immigrated to the Land. We met again. She was now a member of Kibbutz Tel-Yosef[6], working in the agricultural branch, in the cowshed. I was surprised to see how a comrade who had never experienced physical labor had immersed herself in hard, backbreaking work with such zeal. The pains of her absorption into kibbutz life were difficult, engendering doubts that stayed with her until the end of her life. But below the layer of her troubles and the criticism that weighed down on her, you could find a warm heart with appreciation for the kibbutz that she was living in, the place where she had established her family nest. She was able to create for herself many companions and close friends; and on that bitter day that arrived so quickly they were orphaned from a comrade in life and in the struggle.

Shoshana not only knew how to maintain friendship with members of the kibbutz community, but also to keep her bonds of friendship with her trainees and friends, who are scattered throughout the entire Land.

With Shoshana's passing, we have been deprived of a comrade for life, for joy, for friendship and for difficult decisions. A vacuum has been left behind.

The thread binding the community of dispersed comrades has been severed. For her family, for Eliezer and her children, who can find words of comfort?

We shall be able to preserve her beautiful comradely devotion, a bond of many years of friendship. We will bind her soul into the tradition of our lives, and we shall never forget her.

Yisrael Lahav, Mizra[7]

Translator's Footnotes

1. From *My Town: In Memory of the Communities Dobrzyn-Gollob*, edited by M. Harpaz, (published by the Dobrzyn-Golub Society, Israel, 1969), pp. 221-222.

2. *ken* = literally nest, equivalent to a local branch of the *Shomer Hatzair* movement, where members got together for meetings and activities.

3. *Hashomer Hatzair* = The Youth Guard or Young Guard, a socialist-Zionist movement. See the following link (retrieved September 2016): https://en.wikipedia.org/wiki/Hashomer_Hatzair

4. *Shomer Hachalutzi* = the Pioneer Guard

5. *hachshara* = training (for labor, usually agricultural)

6. Tel Yosef is located between Afula and Beit Shean, about 15km southeast of Afula.

7. Mizra is a kibbutz in Northern Israel, about 5km north of Afula. Although there is some ambiguity and possibly a typesetting error at this point in the original Hebrew, the translator believes that the intention was to state that the author (Lahav) lived in Mizra.

[Pages 222-223]

Yehiel Bunim Granat-Rimon[1]

by his brother, Yaakov Rimon

Translated by Allen Flusberg

He was born in Dobrzyn on the Dreventz River to his father Ephraim Eliezer and his mother Esther Chava. He was educated in a *cheder*[2].

In the year 5669[3], at the age of 16, he came on Aliya to the Land of Israel together with his mother and his brother Yaakov y.b.l.ch.a.[4] When he arrived in Yafo [Jaffa] he studied in the Histadrut trade school "Hamizrachi" in Neve Shalom[5]. When my parents opened a grocery store on the main street of Neve Shalom, my mother worked behind the counter, and my brother Bunim helped her out in the store, while my father sat and studied Torah.

Like all the new immigrants of those days, all of us became ill with fever and malaria. In the year 1914, when the First World War broke out, they began seizing young men for the "ferer" (the forced draft into the Turkish army), and he, too was caught. With the last of his strength he went on foot with the army from Yafo to Jerusalem[6], carrying on his back a rucksack that contained *tefillin*, a *siddur*, and a book of *Tehillim*[7]. From there he was sent on a caravan with camels to the vicinity of Shechem and Jenin[8], over hills and through valleys, over desert sand that was hot by day and cold at night. For many months he tended the camels; and like all the Turkish soldiers of that time his clothing became ragged and patched, and he hungered for bread. And whenever he became very embittered he would make the camels lie down; he would then sit down and read *Tehillim* as tears fell from his eyes, and that would make him feel better. And sometimes he would recite a prayer of his own making, and he would feel that he was not alone in this world, for there was an Eye that saw and an Ear that heard his words.

After being in the army for a while he came down with dysentery. He kept walking behind his camels until he finally collapsed, helpless. And a miracle occurred: an Arab who was passing by on his donkey brought him to a Jerusalem hospital, where he lay sick for six months. After that the medical team released him for four months, but he never went back to the Turkish army.

Since the Turks had expelled the Jews from Yafo[9], he moved to Tel Aviv at the end of the war and opened a vegetable store there. And afterwards he built a house in the Montefiore neighborhood and moved into it, opening a vegetable shop in his house. He passed away in Tel Aviv at the age of 75, on the 4th of Shvat 5726[10].

Yehiel Bunim Granat (Rimon)

Translator's Footnotes

1. From *My Town: In Memory of the Communities Dobrzyn-Gollob*, edited by M. Harpaz, (published by the Dobrzyn-Golub Society, Israel, 1969), pp. 222-23.

2. *cheder* = Jewish school for young boys, where religious subjects were taught and secular learning was usually marginal.

3. Jewish year 5669 corresponds to the secular years 1908-1909.

4. y.b.l.ch.a. is an acronym for *yibadel lechaim arukim* = may he live a long life (literally, may he be distinct with a long life), a phrase that is appended by some to the name of a living person who has been mentioned in the same sentence as one who passed away. In this case the mentioned living brother is the author himself.

5. Neve Shalom, established in 1890, was the second neighborhood that was settled by Jews just outside the walls of Yafo.

6. The distance from Yafo to Jerusalem is ~65km (almost totally uphill), a total walking time of ~15 hrs.

7. *tefillin* = phylacteries; *siddur* = prayer book; and *Tehillim* = Psalms.

8. Shechem (Nablus) is located ~70km north of Jerusalem, while Jenin is ~30km north of Shechem.

9. While Turkey was at war with Russia, Jews of Yafo who had emigrated from the Russian Empire in Eastern Europe were considered enemy nationals by Turkey and were expelled from Yafo. See Rimon,"R. Ephraim Eliezer Granat (Rimon)", pp. 176-179 in this volume (reference cited in Footnote 1).

10. 4 Shvat 5726 = 25 January 1966.

[Page 224]

Tova Shivek, of Blessed Memory[1]

by Shmuel Shivek
Translated by Allen Flusberg

She was born in Dobrzyn on the Dreventz River to her father R.[2] Wolff Lipka and her mother, z.l.[3]

Her father, R. Wolff z.l., was a grain merchant in Dobrzyn, an enthusiastic Zionist and a community functionary. The love for the Land of Israel burned fiercely in him, and he was dedicated, heart and soul, to affairs of the Land. He supported the Zionist funds with kindness and generosity.

In her father's house, Tova Shivek a.h.[4] was brought up on love for the Land of Israel. She married R. Shmuel Shivek y.b.l.ch.a.[5] of Lipno[6]. She was endowed with a kind heart filled with human compassion, and she performed charitable acts with an open hand.

After her marriage she lived in Lipno, where her home was a gathering place for Zionist leaders from all over Poland, as well as for members of "Maccabee"[7], since her husband served as vice-chairman of the "Maccabee" board in Lipno.

She immigrated to the Land of Israel in 1936, together with her husband and daughter. Their absorption was a difficult and painful adjustment.

In 1952 she passed away in Tel Aviv, on the 13th day of Tevet, 5713[8].

Her daughter Miriam is married to Arye Simchoni of Ashdod.

Her grandchildren are named Yafa and Dalia.

Tova Shivek z.l.[9]

Translator's Footnotes

1. From *My Town: In Memory of the Communities Dobrzyn-Gollob*, edited by M. Harpaz, (published by the Dobrzyn-Golub Society, Israel, 1969), p. 224.

2. "R". is an abbreviation for *Reb*, an honorific similar to the English "Mr".

3. z.l. is an abbreviation for *zichronam/zichrono/zichrona livracha* = of blessed mcmory

4. a.h. is an acronym for *aleha/alav hashalom* = peace be upon her/him, equivalent to "may she/he rest in peace".

5. y.b.l.ch.a. is an acronym for *yibadel lechaim arukim* = may he differ with a long life, appended to the name of a living person who is mentioned in the same sentence as people who have died. In this case the author himself is the living person.

6. The city of Lipno, Poland is located about 30km south of Dobrzyn.

7. "Maccabee" was a Zionist sports organization

8. Corresponding to December 31, 1952.

9. From p. 224 of this volume (reference cited in Footnote 1).

[Pages 224-226]

My Father's House[1]

by Shoshana Vinkor (Offenbach)

Translated by Allen Flusberg

When I try to recall memories of my parents' home, I have trouble, not knowing where to begin. My father's house! And who did not know our house and our parents? Who did not know my energetic father, and my mother who was active in many various spheres?

My father, the ardent Zionist, educated us and everyone around us in the spirit of Zionism. Community leaders, members of the movement and anyone who had ties to the Land of Israel stayed over in our house as honored guests. My father's life was not so easy, for he toiled, together with his children, to make a living for the family; but he dedicated the main part of his energy and time to the Zionist program. And whenever there was some money available at home, we would first donate some of it to the Jewish National Fund, to *Keren HaYesod*[2], and to other funds.

I remember that when I was still a child how much my father would travel, disappearing from home on various missions for the town. They used to tell me that even on the day that I came into this world my father was not at home, but rather, on one of his usual trips. He was then traveling to Plock[3] to take care of erecting a large fence around the Jewish cemetery of the town.

This was the way we grew up, with our father devoting most of his time to the general good. Yet our lives were very interesting, since our home was a meeting place for community leaders and guests. Many meetings took place in our house, and we were always listening to stories about the Land [of Israel].

I remember with what excitement my father accompanied the first groups that immigrated to the Land. I don't remember everything, since his extensive activity began even before I was born. But we grew up in this atmosphere of Zionist-nationalist activism. And from it we also drew the force of will to continue in the Land.

My father took care of everything. I remember the Sabbath Eves [Friday nights] in our home. All members of the family are seated around the table, with some guest always there, as well: the kindergarten teacher who worked in the culture kindergarten of the town, or some emissary from the movement, who is recounting what is going on in the Diaspora. Sometimes, when he [my father] was reading a Hebrew-language newspaper, he would quickly translate into Yiddish for us, since we were not yet fluent in Hebrew.

I remember especially the atmosphere of freedom in the house. We could always meet with whomever we pleased, or bring home our friends. My mother and father received them with open arms, making an effort to make them feel at home.

Every single event that took place in the Land was close to my father's heart. I remember how emotional he became when we became aware of the events that took place in the Land in 1929[4]. Every Jew in our town was filled with anxiety about the *Yishuv*[5]. We already had so many friends living in the Land, many of them close friends. In the morning, once the newspapers arrived, a protest meeting against the pogrom was held right away.

We gathered in the synagogue. The congregation was standing, waiting expectantly. My father hadn't yet arrived. My mother was ill and so he had been delayed, but he was supposed to speak. And then he came in and gave his speech. Imagine the pain…the feeling of a common destiny…He spoke with emotion and excitement. Suddenly he became speechless and could not continue. He burst out crying and fainted. I remember this as if it happened yesterday. With great effort they brought him home.

Indeed, I could easily tell much more about my father's devotion to the Land of Israel. I believe that many Jews, among those who are now in the Land, immigrated here thanks to the seed of Zionism that he planted in their hearts; yet he himself did not live to immigrate. When I immigrated to the Land with my brother I went to a kibbutz, where I continue to live to this very day. At first all my thoughts were about my family: I tried to bring them here, but my father didn't make it.

I will never forget how proud he was when I told him about the cows that I was milking. People wrote to me that he used to tell every Gentile who happened to come into his store how much milk his daughter was milking.

About half a year after we had come to the Land the tragedy occurred: my father passed away. The blow was hard; but we then decided that we had to do everything to rescue our mother and our two younger brothers—and we were successful. Our mother lived to spend many years with us in the Land, but the rest of the family members and the sisters did not manage to leave. Hitler's cruel hand reached them.

And our mother: how happy she was in the Land. She lived the rest of her life here in the kibbutz. She was full of enthusiasm, seeing all that was taking place. She was proud and happy the first time she went to vote for the Knesset. She was proud that she had lived to merit this day.

Yes, many lovely, beautiful things took place in our house. I believe that this was the correct path, one that was right for all of us.

May these words be a small memorial to all those that did not live to reach the Land.

Translator's Footnotes

1. From *My Town: In Memory of the Communities Dobrzyn-Gollob*, edited by M. Harpaz, (published by the Dobrzyn-Golub Society, Israel, 1969), pp. 224-226.

2. *Keren HaYesod* = The "Foundation Fund", a Zionist fundraising organization, established in 1920, to support the immigration of Jews to the Land of Israel. See the following link (retrieved September, 2016):
http://en.wikipedia.org/wiki/Keren_Hayesod#The_pre-state_era

3. Plock (pronounced "Plotzk"), Poland, is a town on the Vistula River, about 100 km southeast of Dobrzyn.

4. The reference is to the Arab massacre of the Jews of Hebron in 1929. See the following Web site (retrieved September 2016):
https://en.wikipedia.org/wiki/1929_Hebron_massacre.

5. *Yishuv* = the Jewish population of the Land of Israel

[Page 226]

A Man's Path[1]

by Tzadok Tzvi Florman

(In Memory of Tzvi Zudkevitz)

Translated by Allen Flusberg

A hill overlooks the Dreventz River, a tributary of the Vistula. The river flows across the region of Pomerania, cradle of the Crusaders. The northern side is in Prussia; the southern part is land belonging to Czar Nikolai II, ruler of Greater Russia. The town of Dobrzyn is ancient, mentioned in chronicles of the Polish people from the period of the Crusader Wars. On the other side of the river lies Golub, a typical provincial Prussian town with narrow streets and ancient houses. In the distance, a 13th-century Crusader castle rises on an opposite hill.

The house of our common grandfather, Tzadok Hirsh Zudkevitz, was located on the hill of Dobrzyn. A traditional Jewish home, it radiated warmth to everything nearby. Children grew up in it, boys and girls. The head of the household was a skilled furrier and tailor. Among his customers were Polish nobles, owners of nearby estates, members of the local administration and even the priest. Two of his sons and a daughter immigrated to the distant land of America.

One of the sons, Avraham, was diligent in both religious and secular studies. He also spent several years in a yeshiva[2]. He served in the Czar's army for three years. I recall the picture of Avraham Zudkevitz and Moshe Sperling, Yitzhak's father, in Russian army uniforms. They served in the same battalion in the 1890s. Avraham married a woman who was from Brodnica, on the other side of the border[3]. He settled down as a man of prominence and took up his father's profession. He developed a reputation as an honest, intelligent man, becoming one of the community leaders. His home was wide open not only to members of his extended family, but also to anyone in need. During the First World War he served as mayor. The residents, both Jewish and Christian, treated him with respect. He built himself a large house in the center of town.

[Page 227]

Childhood and Adolescence

Tzvi spent his childhood in his parents' affluent home during the First World War. He studied in a *cheder*[4]. He absorbed the tradition of his father's house. The calm atmosphere, the peaceful, untroubled way of life had a great influence on him. As a child he was favorably disposed toward religion. Even while attending a secular public school he would put *tefillin*[5] on every day, and we considered him a boy who was bound up with religious values. We liked him for his integrity.

During his adolescent years, like most of the boys who came from traditional homes, he found himself at a crossroads between the past and the allure of the present. He read a great deal and became familiar with the classic works in the Yiddish language. Enamored of the progressive world, and searching for truth and justice, he skipped over even the Zionist youth movement and became a leftist. And just as much as he had been a faithful believer in religion in his childhood, he now devoted himself passionately to Communist ideology.

But this was just at first sight. Whoever knew Tzvi well knew that within this young man there beat a warm, Jewish heart. In the Capital [Warsaw], the fellow thirstily drank up whatever was available to learn and become familiar with. With great reverence he would go over to the Writers' Association that was located on Tłomackie Street. He would listen to lectures and follow public debates between writers. He greatly extended his knowledge. He was very well liked in society. He could sing Yiddish songs well.

[Page 228]

At the Decisive Moment

He settled in Dobrzyn and served in the army. His battalion was camped in Pomerania. He was a good, disciplined soldier, well-liked by his comrades in arms.

Echoes of the changes that had taken place in Germany with Hitler's rise to power made their mark on Poland[6]. Anti-Semitism intensified. The anti-Jewish laws, and later the pogroms against the Jews of Germany, unleashed the Poles' enmity towards the Jews. The Jews suffered, but they accepted these occurrences as something that would run its course. People did not believe that Hitler would dare attack Poland.

On the day the war broke out, the entire area near the border was overrun by Hitler's troops. Although Tzvi had been conscripted he did not get to fight very much. The lines of defense of the Polish army quickly collapsed. The Nazi conqueror imposed himself with harshness on the Polish populace, especially on the Jews. The entire northern and western parts of Poland were annexed to Germany. The Jews were served with a first course of persecution and humiliation. They were not permitted to walk along sidewalks, but rather had to walk along the edges of the streets and take off their hats before every German they passed. Bearded men were taken out of their homes to toil cleaning streets and clearing trash, work that was accompanied by curses and blows.

After a few weeks had passed, expulsion orders were issued. From cities and towns, human caravans made their way to the center of the country. These people left behind homes with all their possessions, the product of generations of toil. Tzvi observed all of this with his own eyes.

Tens of thousands of Jews fled eastward, to Russia. Among them were Tzvi and my brother Mordechai Yisrael y.b.l.ch[7]. They reached the city of Vileyka[8], somehow establishing themselves there. Tzvi worked and, being among family members, was satisfied with the place. However his yearning for the town he was born in and his concern for the fate of his family, now displaced from Dobrzyn, bothered him. Once permission was granted to submit requests to return to Poland in order to bring family members to Vileyka, Tzvi applied to the local authorities, just as many other Jews were doing. But permission to make these requests was a hidden trap: All applicants for the trip to Poland were arrested, convicted of attempting to leave Russia for the purpose of espionage, and sent to labor camps.

[Page 229]

In the Distant Russian North

Tzvi was in one of the camps in the distant Russian north. Camps like it were scattered over vast areas. Within them, hundreds of thousands of exhausted people from many nationalities were wandering around, dressed in rags. Living conditions were terrible. They worked clearing land and felling trees in forests. Scant clothing, limited food, and arduous work twelve hours a day; frost in winter down to [minus] 50 degrees; living in wretched shacks. Tzvi's resistance steadily weakened. He lost his strength and lost weight. He became thin and frail.

And then one day, in the year 1942, he was suddenly freed without any advance notice, together with a large group of Polish citizens. General Sikorski had reached an agreement with Stalin, according to which they had to release all the Polish citizens from the camps[9]. Permission was granted to establish a Polish army in Russia.

In the Polish Army in Exile

Tzvi volunteered in the army that had been established by the Polish general Anders[10]. In the barracks that had been provided he quickly recovered. The army was trained by Polish officers and sergeants. At that point echoes of what had been transpiring in Poland reached them. They knew about sealed Jewish ghettos and about inhuman persecution by the Nazis. All the conscripts, and particularly the Jews among them, waited impatiently for the great moment when they would be able to stand up to the Nazi enemy. According to the agreement, this army was supposed to fight on the southern front, North Africa and Italy.

The troops climbed onto trains that were going south. One battalion after another, the Polish army left Russian soil and made its way to Persia, Iraq and to other countries of the Near East. Tzvi was in Baghdad for several weeks. It was during the autumn of 1942. There were a considerable number of Jews in the Anders army. During the holidays the Jewish soldiers streamed into the synagogues. Tzvi led the services. The education he had received in his father's house served him well in distant Baghdad. The young men from Poland and Lithuania prayed according to the Ashkenazi custom, following the ways of their ancestors[11].

[Page 230]

The New Life

When he reached Tel Aviv he sought out old friends. He found friends and even relatives. Only then did he find out about the great calamity that had been visited upon the Jews of Poland. His emotion and yearning knew no bound. His world had gone dark. He suffered a mental breakdown. He realized that for a Jew life has value only on the soil of the Land of Israel. He decided not to continue on, and so remained in Israel.

Zvi's life from that point onward is known to all his friends. He was known as an affable person, serious mannered, at peace with his new way of life. He knew how to laugh and joke around. He was a likable person, a good husband and a devoted father.

However, deep within him there remained a wound that did not heal until the end of his life. When he spoke about the Holocaust of the Jews of Poland and Lithuania his face would become serious; grief and pain could be seen in his eyes. Who knew the secrets of his heart as well as I did…His parents, two brothers and two sisters had been residing in the Warsaw Ghetto together with their families. His father died of a stroke in the summer of 1942. All the rest of his family perished in the crematoria of Treblinka.

I had seen him in Warsaw in November, 1939. He was all set to cross the border into Russia in the vicinity of Bialystok[12], hopeful that the war would end quickly. And back then we were simply wearing white ribbons with blue Stars of David on our right arms. No one had yet thought about setting up ghettos. Crematoria and gas chambers did not occur to anyone, not even to the bleakest prophets of doom.

When we met again in the year 1950, it was a different Tzvi from the one from 1939. This man had been swept up in a maelstrom of powerful forces that had picked him up and carried him all the way here, to a safe harbor.

Tzvi has left us, the last of his family household: one of the few who saw the war in its savage ferocity and yet remained whole and honest in every way.

It is hard to get used to the thought that Tzvi is no longer with us, for we spoke to him only two days before his death; it was just now that he was still walking among us. And whenever memories came back to him, he would launch an inexhaustible spring of stories about the past. It was with pleasure that he visited relatives who lived in cities. He drew work colleagues close to him through his good conduct and unblemished integrity.

How can it be within my power to tuck his rich life, full of hardship, into a few pages? May these words of mine therefore serve as a clod of earth, saturated with tears, on his fresh grave.

To the bereaved Sarah, Chava, David and Avraham, may you never again experience grief and sorrow.

Tzvi Tzadok Zudkevitz[13]

Translator's Footnotes

1. From *My Town: In Memory of the Communities Dobrzyn-Gollob*, edited by M. Harpaz, (published by the Dobrzyn-Golub Society, Israel, 1969), pp. 226-230.

2. Yeshiva = Jewish religious school for older boys

3. Brodnica is located 30km northeast of Dobrzyn. Before 1920 it was part of Prussia.

4. *cheder* = a Jewish elementary school for boys, where religious studies were taught intensively, while secular subjects were usually marginalized.

5. *tefillin* = phylacteries, worn on the arm and head during weekday morning prayers

6. See the autobiographical account by Tzvi Zudkevitz, "In the Tempest of the War", pp. 130–136 of this volume (reference cited in Footnote 1).

7. y.b.l.ch. is an acronym for *yibadel lechaim* = may he differ with life, a phrase that is appended by some to the name of a living person who has been mentioned in the same sentence as one who passed away. Apparently the author's brother was still living.

8. The city of Vileyka (in Belarus) lies 300km northeast of Bialystok, Poland.

9. Władysław Sikorski (1881-1943) was a Polish military and political leader. In 1941 he was the prime minister of the Polish Government in Exile and Commander-in-Chief of the Polish Armed Forces. After the German army invaded the Soviet Union in 1941, Stalin, who in 1939 had allied the USSR with Germany and presided over the Soviet invasion of Poland, chose to make an alliance with the Polish Government in Exile. See the following link (retrieved July, 2016):
https://en.wikipedia.org/wiki/W%C5%82adys%C5%82aw_Sikorski..

10. The Anders army, named after its commander, Władysław Anders, was the "Polish Armed Forces in the East" that was organized within the Soviet Union after the Germans invaded it. After filling its ranks with former Polish prisoners of war, the Anders army made its way to Palestine via Iran and Iraq. See the following link (retrieved July, 2016):
https://en.wikipedia.org/wiki/Anders%27_Army.

11. The Ashkenazi (European) Jewish versions of prayer differ somewhat from those of the Jews of Middle Eastern countries in pronunciation, wording and style, sufficiently for Ashkenazi Jews unacquainted with the prayer services of Middle Eastern Jewry to feel uncomfortable and find themselves unable to follow.

12. The city of Bialystok, Poland lies about 300km due east of Dobrzyn. The border between German-occupied and USSR-occupied Poland was about 50km due east of Bialystok.

13. From p. 227 of reference cited in Footnote 1.

[Page 231]

About Tzvi, For He Is Gone[1]
by Yitzhak Sperling
Translated by Allen Flusberg

Death came abruptly. The tragic fate of my dear cousin Tzvi was sealed in only a few terrible seconds.

We have been orphaned—both the immediate family and the extended one. A devoted wife and good, precious children have been left behind…

It would never have occurred to me that in these difficult times that I am experiencing I would have to eulogize you, my dear relative. I have never called you Tzvi. This is the name that he picked up here. His real name was Tzadok. By this name I saw him frequently within our extended family.

He was born in the town of Dobrzyn. He was a member of an affluent family that owned a fur store and a workshop. It was a privileged, respected family, the most illustrious of the town. His father was one of the community leaders who for a while even served as mayor. Who was there who did not know or know of the family of Avraham Tzudkovich, this proud and active Jew?

It was in this atmosphere that the three brothers and two sisters were educated. All of them studied, acquiring knowledge in other cities. One of the brothers was an enthusiastic Zionist. Tzvi's oldest brother spent two years in the Land [of Israel] in the 1920s. But because he had trouble adjusting he returned to his town.

Tzadok was the youngest of the brothers. Already as a child he aspired to study in order to accomplish something, and in fact he did. He was integrated into all areas of life; he learned and read a great deal, especially Yiddish literature. In spite of the prosperousness of his home, his views were leftist. He was considered a Communist, or, as they called them where we lived, "Stalin-Communist".

In the years before the war we would freely come and go into his home, and we would often discuss the course of the Jewish youth. Although he did not share our views, he always expressed a deep appreciation for *Hashomer Hatzair*[2] and for its educational values.

And in this manner he led his life in prosperity in our town. Until the year 1939 came, the year in which the Second World War broke out. That year anti–Semitism rose up in the towns of Poland. The Jewish population suffered greatly.

Once the war broke out all communications between us were severed. And then, at the end of 1943, as we were overcome with anxiety because of the Holocaust that had descended upon our people, my cousin Tzadok appeared in my kibbutz[3]. Looking at him was like seeing the mournful Jewish people and my extended family. The vast majority of our relatives and friends were already no longer alive.

Tzvi had a unique talent to recount and then tirelessly tell again of devastation and hardships: the expulsion of the Jews of our town, the looting and the humiliation. He pointed out all the details, like an artist who can make you envision living images: he was rescued from the Holocaust and wandered from one land to another, getting as far as distant Siberia. He was a political prisoner. When he was informed of the possibility of fighting against the Germans, he felt he should volunteer in the Polish army, under the command of General Anders, and in this manner he reached the Land [of Israel][4]. Here he came to the conclusion that after the crematoria and gas chambers we could no longer permit ourselves to graze in strangers' pastures. He decided to leave the Polish army, and he joined us. He changed his name to "Tzvi" and quickly integrated into kibbutz life.

Once he had established his family he moved to Kibbutz Dan[5], but after a short time he came back to us.

Since his return he was an industrious, active and conscientious member. He struck roots not only at work but also in various tasks assigned to him by the kibbutz.

He was a quiet individual who was well liked, cultural and refined: someone with values. He will be remembered as one of the best and most dedicated members that we have ever had.

Translator's Footnotes

1. From *My Town: In Memory of the Communities Dobrzyn–Gollob*, edited by M. Harpaz, (published by the Dobrzyn–Golub Society, Israel, 1969), pp. 231–232.

2. *HaShomer Hatzair* (= the Youth Guard) was, in this context, a Jewish youth movement whose purpose it was to prepare young people for agricultural work in Israel.

3. The name of the kibbutz is not provided in this article. It was Kfar Masaryk (located about 10km north of Haifa), as is documented in a short biography of Tzvi Zudkowitz (1911–1963), written by his daughter, and available in Hebrew at the following link: http://www.kfar-masaryk.org.il/viewpage.asp?pagesCatID=3866&MemorialPage=1&Personkey=gf85g4g873878397832178321vx1&siteName=masaryk. As mentioned in that biography, he died of a stroke.

4. For more details see previous article in this volume: Florman, "The path of a man", pp. 226–230, and references cited therein.

5. Kibbutz Dan is located ~10km northeast of Kiryat-Shmona, near the northern border of Israel.

[Page 232]

To My Very Dear Father...[1]
by Chava[2]
Translated by Allen Flusberg

Suddenly, on a clear summer day, on the morning of a bright day full of joy, I have been struck by a hammer blow: for me the heavens have darkened. The sun has just risen, but it is already dark: gloom, darkness in everything. Gloom in my heart.

...Is it really true? ...Has your voice actually been stilled, Abba[3], and will I never hear it again? Suddenly we will no longer see you among us, so cheerful, so kind and so devoted?...

Dear, beloved Abba: Is what the comrades[4] and Mother are saying true, that I will never see you again? Is it correct, that you have left us this way, without a single parting word, without saying goodbye?

Many times you and I have parted from each other, but this is a different kind of parting; this is a very long separation, an eternal parting...and so it is the cruelest one of all.

Ah...cruel fate. You have left me orphaned of a father, and I had no inkling, you gave me no advance warning.

"Abba": this word will accompany me for the rest of my life.

You never permitted me to call you by your name, "Tzvi".[5] You wanted to feel there was someone who called you "Abba"...

...For a long time you wandered among various peoples; you felt in the flesh what not many have felt or will ever feel. To us, you children, you recounted what had happened to you through rose-colored glasses, but I, Abba, saw and felt what these tales reflected. I looked into your glistening eyes that had seen so much, had observed so much.

And yet you came to the Land [of Israel], you found a wife, and then, and only then (when you were no longer young), you began to establish your home, your family, which was your only solace after all you had lost in the war.

...You, Abba, you had gone and left everything behind, but not of your only volition, Abba. You were not one who disliked life. Just the opposite, you have always loved whatever life you had. You loved work and you carried it out with modesty and devotion. You loved the people around you; you never aspired to greatness…you did what you were supposed to do discreetly, quietly, but with great reliability and dedication.

You left everything behind. Even so, nothing has changed, nothing has happened. Life goes on as usual, just as it was…

But I—I do not believe it. I look again and again; perhaps I will see some tiny change—it does not make sense that everything remains as it was…but Abba, you did leave everything as it was, you did not shake anything up, nor did you wreck anything. It is only our hearts that you have racked and broken. Our spirits are low, torn to pieces. A vacuum has been created in my heart, a giant rip…

Is it possible, conceivable that the right to say "Abba" once more in my lifetime has been taken away…Can this be?

Can anyone believe that my right to be in your company again, even only one more time, has been taken away, the right to get even a single fatherly kiss from you?

Will I not sit with you again in the twilight of evening, listening to the stories that you knew how to tell so well, that you loved to tell?…

I am proud of you that you were a good father to me: a concerned, devoted and loyal father. You were ready to give anything up as long as you knew that you were doing it for the sake of your children:

"What care I for silver and gold

What care I for precious objects and pearls

If I am far from my children?"

Yes, Abba, this is what you were like, and as such you will remain in my memory all my life.

I am different from others, dissimilar from all my friends. They have *parents*, the most precious thing that a person can have. I am not like them: I have been destined to continue on with only "half". Can a person walk on only one leg? Can he brace himself with only one of his arms?…

…I still do not believe it. Every day I still expect you at the time of day when you usually return from work. I see your figure before me, coming back from work, exhausted and tired (but even when you are tired you are not irritable).

So I can almost hear your cordial "hello". I want to reply, "Hello, Abba"; but all at once all my illusions are shattered.

You do not come. I wait for you until evening. The sun has just set in the west. Darkness covers the face of the Earth, but still you do not come...and you—so people are saying—will never come again...

Should I trust what they say, my father? Are they right?...

No, no, no, I cry out inside, within myself: I do not want to believe it. But reality reveals all and forces me to stand before it, face to face.

How can I, when it is so cruel?

Translator's Footnotes

1. From *My Town: In Memory of the Communities Dobrzyn-Gollob*, edited by M. Harpaz, (published by the Dobrzyn-Golub Society, Israel, 1969), pp. 232-234.

2. Chava Zudkewitz was 17 when her father, Tzvi Zudkewitz, passed away suddenly in 1963, at the age of 52, in Kibbutz Kfar Masaryk. See the following articles appearing in this volume (reference cited in Footnote 1): Sperling "About Tzvi, For He is Gone," pp. 231-232; Florman, "The Path of a Man", pp. 226-230; Zukdewitz, "In the Tempest of War," pp. 130-136. See also the following article written years later by the same daughter, available in Hebrew at the following link (retrieved September 2016): http://www.kfar-masaryk.org.il/viewpage.asp?pagesCatID=3866&MemorialPage=1&Personkey=gf85g4g873878397832178321vx1&siteName=masaryk. According to this last article, Tzvi died of cardiac arrest.

3. Abba = father, daddy (Hebrew)

4. Hebrew *chaverim* = comrades (fellow members of the kibbutz)

5. In many kibbutzim it was customary for children to call their parents by their first names.

[Page 234]

Chana Rosenwaks[1]
by Yehuda Rosenwaks
Translated by Allen Flusberg

My sister-in-law, Chana Rosenwaks (née Bern) of blessed memory, was the granddaughter of R.[2] Avraham Neiszt, and was greatly influenced by his personality. Since she was orphaned from her father at a tender age, she spent much time at the house of her grandfather, the father of her mother Rivka. Her grandfather was a multifaceted personality who was well known not only for his wealth, but also for his Torah erudition; he was also enlightened and an enthusiastic Zionist.

Her mother, who was a magnanimous and pleasant woman, devoted to her home and children with all her heart, also greatly influenced the molding of Chana's personality. Her very close relationship with her mother and grandfather strengthened in her the sense of family bonds, a deep and fine sentiment that never left her.

When she married my brother Yitzhak of blessed memory, she quickly got close to our family, and she became like one of us, influencing us young children with her love and gaiety.

She was aware of everything going on around her, and once she sensed the continuous growth of anti-Semitism, she spurred my brother to leave everything behind and go on Aliya to the Land of Israel. It actually did not take much of a struggle to convince him. He too was fed up with the Poles and all that was theirs, especially after having tasted anti-Semitism during his service as a soldier among the Poles[3]. So he arose and came up to the Land, with Chana's encouragement. After several months she joined him, together with their four-year-old son.

Although conditions in the Land were difficult then, Chana was happy, and she did not cease rousing family members in Dobrzyn to follow in her footsteps. Her letters had the intended effect: my two sisters, my older brother's daughter and I—and also her sisters and her brother—all of us came on Aliya to the Land of Israel, and as a result we were rescued from the bitter fate of all those who had remained behind in Europe.

Throughout the years she remained a faithful source of support to my brother Yitzhak, inspiring all in her household with her personality. When my brother retired I encouraged him to come and settle in Kibbutz Dovrat[4] so as to remain near his daughter and grandchildren.

And even here, in kibbutz society, she quickly found her niche as a pleasant, cultured and industrious woman. Members of the kibbutz and the children, many of whom were wearing sweaters that she had made by hand, bonded with her in friendship and love.

Chana and Yitzhak passed away in the kibbutz and were buried there. May the clumps of earth of the Dovrat farmstead remain a pleasant resting place for them.

Translator's Footnotes

1. From *My Town: In Memory of the Communities Dobrzyn-Gollob*, edited by M. Harpaz, (published by the Dobrzyn-Golub Society, Israel, 1969), pp. 234-235.

2. R. stands for *Reb*, a title similar to "Mr." in English.

3. See autobiographical essay by Yitzhak Rosenwaks, "My Bundle of Troubles in the Russian Military", pp. 332-353 in this volume (reference cited in Footnote 1).

4. Dovrat is in northeastern Israel, ~10km southeast of Nazareth.

[Pages 235-237]

On the Death of Yehuda Sperling
Born 17 September 1940
Died 29 October 1963[1]

by Eliyahu

Translated by Allen Flusberg

An Elegy for My Brother

The days pass, yet it seems as if the tragedy took place just yesterday.

We have been left in a state of complete confusion over the emptiness, and we ask: is it possible to speak of you in past tense: can I say of you that I had a brother, but no longer have him?

Seemingly these are ordinary days; all goes on just as in the past. Yet you are missing in all of it. In all moments of life, it is as if someone is shouting: how is it you are not with us?

At the time that I write these lines, at the time that I try to find words to express myself, your radiant image stands before me; and as I look upon it, a smile rises up on my lips, unintentionally. It is so pleasant to go back to those years, those happy years of childhood: walking at your side, my hand held in yours, as I gaze on you with a thrill in my eyes. And there are too many memories to count; they rise up in me and then sink back into the recesses of the past.

You were an incomparably devoted and kind brother to me.

I remember the days when our mother was ill, when our father was not at home. You knew exceptionally well how to fill in what was missing. You were a sort of inexhaustible source of stories, legends and magical entertainment, with which you knew how to enchant the heart of a little boy.

As the years passed I was always wondering: from where did you draw the strength to take it all? How did you overcome your physical limitations and yet were still able to lend a helping hand? And this is what you were like until your very last day: always struggling, always striving to be like everyone else, and never giving up.

You did not ever experience a moment of boredom. With unending devotion you invested all your strength in your work, and no one could stand in your way. We saw the expression of satisfaction on your face. We saw how anxious you were to do manual labor, and we did not have the heart to tell you to stop.

When you were late coming home and we were worried, we stood at the window, watching for your approaching figure. Suddenly we saw you on the tractor, with a line of wagons behind you, as you brought in the fruit of your labor. I saw our mother's eyes radiating, and a feeling of pride swept through all of us.

It seems to me that you never experienced more happiness among us than those last few years brought you. You reached the goal you were striving for: you were just like everyone else. And therefore you marched unafraid toward that large building, from which you never returned.

We became very close during your last days. I would walk over to you and suddenly feel a strong desire to grasp you with both hands. However, I saw the look of confidence and calm that was spread across your face, and so I held back.

I will never forget the day we parted. I accompanied you part of the way. A warm handshake; and my extensive gaze followed your figure as it moved into the distance, my heart fluttering and my entire body trembling. In spite of the fear and concern, we were full of hope and faith. When I got the news that the surgery had been successful, I wanted to shout for joy. I felt a feeling of release after so long a period of nerve-racking tension. However those hours of gladness did not last very long. Like thunder the news came that your heart had stopped beating and you had lost your life. With that our happiness was lost, and we were left immersed in depression and enveloped in darkness.

Dear Yehuda! As we carried you to your grave, we were steeped in bitter pain yet determined to continue struggling and to remain faithful to your memory.

Your bright gaze stays with me whichever way I turn. The kibbutz that you loved so much followed everything that happened to you and now grieves for your loss.

May we maintain the strength to continue on, with only memories in our hearts.

Goodbye my brother, goodbye for all eternity.

Yehuda Sperling

Translator's Footnotes

1. From *My Town: In Memory of the Communities Dobrzyn-Gollob*, edited by M. Harpaz, (published by the Dobrzyn-Golub Society, Israel, 1969), pp. 235-237.

[Page 237]

My Son, Yehuda My Son[1],[2]
by his father, Yitzhak
Translated by Allen Flusberg

For evermore: two ordinary, simple, words, embodying within them eternity—life and death. This eternity created an abyss out of a beautiful, young and pure life, that of a blossoming youngster, whose plans for life were aborted, with cruel suddenness, at a time when the future had begun to embroider his heart's mysteries together…The thread of his life ended! The heart! Alas for the heart! It betrayed him, not holding up against the chisel of life—and it was cut down.

Is any consolation possible? No, forever no! The heart does not believe, nor can the hand write about this bitter truth.

Several times I began to write and to immortalize your name, our dear, beloved son. Is such a thing possible? Our home is filled with mourning and sorrow. We are still living with you, and we always will, as if you are still walking around among us, thinking with us. Is this at all possible? A young lad, sparkling with young life? To write about, to immortalize forevermore! A good-natured, gentle and pure son.

Many days have passed, long, restless nights, even months have passed—and it is true that you are not among us. I must overcome, grow strong, and bring back memories, chapters of your beautiful, peaceful but short life.

*

The end of the year 1940, the Second World War. Haifa is being bombarded by the Italians. Rommel is at the gates of the western desert. The German war machine is aiming to approach us. The kibbutz[3] is considering an evacuation. We have to evacuate the female kibbutz members to the agricultural settlements of the Valley[4]. The time came…and you were born, in Afula[5]. From your very first moment you were afflicted with a heart defect. Your development was difficult and slow, causing us worry and anxiety. Your build was weak, somewhat sickly, but your head of hair was blond, amazingly beautiful, filled with curls. A face that expressed gentle feelings: smiling, with good eyes, as if you already understood then what you were up against. You caught all the childhood ailments. Slowly you created a path unique to you among the children who were close to you. They showed you affection and love every step of the way. You grew up—and the defect with you.

And your mother! She gave you everything, all of her life! She ran back and forth from one doctor to the next, from one expert to another. Is it even possible to express what your mother gave you during the first half of your life? But when you reached the age of 12, your mother collapsed on that wintry evening when you had fallen off your bicycle and injured your lip...

*

You studied in grade school and high school, and you acquired knowledge. You knew what had happened at home and you were a great help. You had a great power of understanding, and a profound heartfelt desire to help others. You loved the kibbutz and all that was in it. You loved music. When you listened to concerts, your face took on a serious look that was particularly beautiful, expressing sublime feelings.

You grew up, and the defect with you. You went to register for military service; and when you returned home, with tears in your eyes, I understood our tragedy...You are not fit for the military. How and when will it be possible to build a life in the future? There ensued a long silence between the two of us. I encouraged you! Our mutual tears sealed a chapter in our lives...

Every year you went for an examination to get a diagnosis—until you reached the age of 23. Only twenty-three years and no more!

*

You were an unusually responsible individual. You fulfilled the Ten Commandments of *Hashomer Hatzair*[6], especially that of "Achiezer and Achisamach"[7]. You could not conceive how it might be possible not to help others. You liked to work, even the hardest work. You were among the first to go wherever you were needed.

I remember how when you were eight years old, you were walking on the lawn, crying bitterly. "What happened, my dear child?" I asked you, and the answer was: "The children's farm hens have run away, and I haven't got anyone who can help me." I lifted you up onto my shoulders. The two of us took care of this and your beautiful face showed great happiness.

And you continued on from there: in the library, in the institute, the administrative office, in caring for the kibbutz archives, in the orchard sector that you got very involved in, with a special love.

You read and became well educated; you had a thirst for knowledge, in spite of your limitations. You communicated with children from abroad. You won many prizes, excelling in various crossword puzzles; you completed studies in accounting, which you did not like. Courageously you carried the burden of labor.

*

You had a good, healthy sense of humor. Your comments were witty and poignant. In spite of your great fatigue, you had a fresh spirit. You were a modest person, satisfied with even a little, and you stuck to tasks. You participated vigorously in the life of the youth unit of the kibbutz. You responded willingly to every kibbutz member. At a young age you were a public figure who maintained contact with the entire kibbutz. You got involved with all your heart in the orchard sector, and you became the one who was responsible for it. You willingly burdened your weak shoulders with tasks, and you held your own.

I recall our conversations, at home, on this subject. With great respect you spoke of the relationship to work and to that of the orchard sector in particular. You were full of excitement and energy. You loved your family—you brought it much respect. You repaid your mother with a love that was accompanied by twice as much concern and worry—and so also to other members of the family. You were shy and timid, but the look in your eye always reflected a sense of calm and great responsiveness. This is what you were like, our dear son.

*

Your last weeks with us were a special chapter in our lives together. When we were informed that there was no way to avoid this fateful step, we were struck with great anxiety. Yet we knew of no alternative, and with a heavy heart we decided on the fateful step.

We were very tense the entire time. Just two weeks earlier we had mourned our dear cousin Tzvi[8], of blessed memory. I said then: I am going through crazy times…as our son walked around in the hospital, waiting for what fate has in store.

*

We will never forget your last days in the hospital. You did not surrender. Your face was fresh, calm and smiling. You sang beautiful melodies, one after another. When we walked together, I did not have the courage to talk about what was about to happen, except on the last evening. You insisted that I be strong, that everything would be all right. You ate your last meal peacefully and quietly. And early the next morning I stood next to your white bed. I caressed you...you were already asleep. I came along with you to the surgery room, our hearts full of anxiety, anxiety...

On your deathbed, moaning deeply, you asked: How is it going? And who could imagine that your hours were numbered and that these were your last moments. The entire kibbutz, all of them were anxious for you. Members rushed to donate blood to save you. You greeted them with a smile befitting your nature and you good spirit. What affection the people in the hospital, who got to know you, showed. Many people conversed with me, praising your character. Nothing helped; nothing, our dear one!

When, the next morning, weary and frightened, I came to you again, to see you, to hug you—my eyes grew dark...They held me up...Yehuda is no longer with us! Not anymore!

*

From the wall your beautiful picture gazes upon us. Memories encompass us—memories of our lives together in our good, warm home.

We have been left without you...

We have been left mourning and bereft. You have been interred in the ground of our agricultural community, the place where you had hoped to build your future. Clumps of earth cover you. Your spirit lives on among us, and will continue to always!

May your memory be a blessing, our dear son.

Translator's Footnotes

1. From *My Town: In Memory of the Communities Dobrzyn-Gollob*, edited by M. Harpaz, (published by the Dobrzyn-Golub Society, Israel, 1969), pp. 237-240.

2. The subject of this article is Yehuda Sperling (1940-1963). See the previous article, "On the Death of Yehuda Sperling, by his brother Eliyahu, pp. 235-237 in this volume (reference cited in Footnote 1). Note that the title "My son, Yehuda my son" is written in the style of King David's lament for his son Absalom (II Samuel 19:1), which reads "My son, Absalom, my son, my son, Absalom, if only I could have died in your place."

3. The kibbutz, whose name is not mentioned here, is Kfar Masaryk, located about 10km north of Haifa. See the following Web page (retrieved November 2016) for a short biography (in Hebrew) of the author of this article: http://www.kfar-masaryk.org.il/viewpage.asp?pagesCatID=3866&MemorialPage=1&Personkey=gf45g6g870878327832108321vx2&siteName=masaryk. See also C. Lord, "Hashomer Hatzair", pp. 95-101 in this volume (reference cited in Footnote 1).

4. Valley of Jezreel

5. Afula is located in the Jezreel Valley, ~10km south of Nazereth.

6. *Hashomer Hatzair* = the Young Guard, a socialist-Zionist movement which many kibbutz communities in Israel were part of..

7. "Achiezer and Achisamach" are Biblical names that can be translated as "my brother helps" and "my brother supports". In its original (1916) version, the "Ten Commandments" of the *Hashomer Hatzair* movement included one of helping and supporting one's comrades; it was known as "Achiezer and Achisamach". See the following Web site (in Hebrew, retrieved November 2016): https://he.wikipedia.org/wiki/%D7%94%D7%A9%D7%95%D7%9E%D7%A8_%D7%94%D7%A6%D7%A2%D7%99%D7%A8

8. The reference is to Tzvi Zudkewitz. See the article "About Tzvi, for He Is Gone," by Yitzhak Sperling, pp. 231-232 (in this volume, reference cited in Footnote 1).

[Page 240]

Nisan Fogel[1]
by Avraham Dor (Dobroszklanka)
Translated by Allen Flusberg

We were childhood friends. We studied together under Manus[2], who taught the smallest children, and later under R.[3] Nisan Melamed[4]. We lived not far from one another, and we met almost every morning on our way to the cheder[5]. Since school studies continued until evening, we spent our time together until the day ended.

Once we grew up, the bond between us grew stronger, since we were both members of the "Hakoach" Sports Club[6], and we would meet almost every day for football [soccer] practice on the sports field.

We excelled in the sport, and we were both on the first team. We appeared together in competitions in Dobrzyn as well as in inter-town matches.

He was a good, loyal friend, a good-natured person. How sorry we were when he left our town to go to the United States at the request of his oldest brother, Yechiel. But this was an unfortunate journey: because of a technical flaw in his immigration papers, he was sent back to Poland by the American authorities. How disappointed and depressed he was when he returned, how hurt and embarrassed.

After the branch of "Hechalutz"[7] was set up in our town and several entry visas (certificates) for immigration to Palestine were allocated to us, Nisan and I were among the first to receive certificates. I came on Aliya at the beginning of 1925, and Nisan arrived a short time later. Again we would meet, although now only on rare occasions, since we lived in different cities: he in Haifa and I in Tel Aviv. But when he occasionally came to Tel Aviv to take care of various things he used to come over to see me.

After establishment of the State we managed to meet more often. During these meetings we would usually reminisce about our youth. Just a week before he passed away I met him in his home on the occasion of publication of the Yizkor Book, a project we had worked on.

How shocked I was to hear from a relative of his, Asher Graner, about his death. A feeling of melancholy descended on me while his casket was being borne during his funeral, as I realized that with his end another of the good people of Dobrzyn had left us.

May his memory be preserved in our hearts forever!

Nisan Fogel, of blessed memory[8]

Translator's Footnotes

1. From *My Town: In Memory of the Communities Dobrzyn-Gollob*, edited by M. Harpaz, (published by the Dobrzyn-Golub Society, Israel, 1969), pp. 240-241.

2. Manus Landsberg, a teacher of small children. See the list of Dobrzyn townspeople on p. 447 of reference cited in Footnote 1.

3. "R". stands for *Reb*, an honorific similar to the English "Mr".

4. Nisan Kutner. See the list of Dobrzyn townspeople on p. 450 of reference cited in Footnote 1. Townspeople would append the title *Melamed*, meaning teacher of small children, to the first name of a teacher, as if it was his family name.

5. *Cheder* = Jewish school for young boys, where religious subject were taught, and secular learning was usually marginal.

6. On *Hakoach* (= the Force) see p. 84 of: Dor, "Institutions and Organizations", pp. 78-86 of reference cited in Footnote 1.

7. "Hechalutz" (= the Pioneer) was an organization that prepared its members for Aliya to the Land of Israel. See p. 82 of: Dor, "Institutions and Organizations", pp. 78-86 of reference cited in Footnote 1.

8. From p. 241 of reference cited in Footnote 1.

[Page 241]

My Husband, Nisan Fogel, of Blessed Memory[1]

by Bilhah Fogel

Translated by Allen Flusberg

He was born in 1903, in the town of Dobrzyn, Poland. In his youth he joined the *Hashomer Hatzair*[2] movement, and he immigrated to the Land of Israel in 1925. Like many other *chalutzim*[3], he suffered for the first few years, being unemployed. His family urged him to return home, but he would not agree to it. On the contrary: he did as much as he could to overcome the difficulties.

His good temperament did not leave him even in difficult times, nor did he lose hope. As a result his friends liked him and were bound to him. He was dedicated to his friends and worried about them quite a bit, particularly when one of them was in distress.

As soon as he came to the Land he joined the ranks of the *Hagana*[4], and he was active in it until the day he died, volunteering for every settlement and defense activity. He was among those who were engaged in "occupation jobs"[5] in Akko [Acre] and other places; and even later, when his lot improved and he was one of the regular workers of *Solel-Boneh*[6], he was among those workers who would go out to work in dangerous places.

With the outbreak of the Second World War he was sent to work in Safed, to construct the police building in Canaan[7]. He brought his family with him to Safed so that they would be nearby. When he was asked to go to work in Abadan, Persia [Iran][8], far from home, he did not hesitate very long, understanding that it was an hour of need; and he was one of the first to take the assignment on.

He did not tend to complain; always content, he filled our home with his cheerfulness and warmth. Indeed, he was dedicated to his family. He passed on to his children the values of the pioneer movement; and in actuality his children followed this path and established their homes in kibbutzim[9].

Nisan Fogel was fortunate enough to see the establishment of the State, something he had dreamed about so much.

One day, after he returned home, he felt unwell, and he expired. He died an easy death, only 49 years old.

May his memory be blessed!

Translator's Footnotes

1. From *My Town: In Memory of the Communities Dobrzyn-Gollob*, edited by M. Harpaz, (published by the Dobrzyn-Golub Society, Israel, 1969), pp. 241-242.

2. *Hashomer Hatzair* (= the Youth Guard) was a socialist-Zionist youth movement that trained young people in agricultural work. See the following link (retrieved July 2016): https://en.wikipedia.org/wiki/Hashomer_Hatzair. The activities of this organization in Dobryzn are described in: C. Lord, "Hashomer Hatzair", pp. 95-101 of references cited in Footnote 1.

3. *Chalutzim* (= pioneers), term for the early Jewish immigrants to the Land of Israel.

4. Hagana (= Defense), a Jewish paramilitary organization during the British Mandate in Palestine, established in 1920 as a defense force against Arab rioters. See the following Web page (retrieved July 2016): https://en.wikipedia.org/wiki/Haganah.

5. Hebrew: *avodot kibbush*, day labor paving roads, erecting wire fencing, operating cranes, etc.

6. *Solel-Boneh* (= Paving and Building) is a large construction and public works company in Israel, founded in 1921 as a cooperative organization and reorganized as a business corporation in 1923. As early as the 1920s it employed thousands of workers. See the following (retrieved July 2016): https://en.wikipedia.org/wiki/Solel_Boneh.

7. Mount Canaan in Safed, where a fortified British police station was constructed. (In 2016 the building is near the intersection of HaGalil and Lamed-Aleph Streets).

8. During World War II (beginning in August, 1941) Iran was occupied by Allied forces. A crucial oil refinery, owned by a British company, was located in Abadan. For details see the following website (retrieved July, 2016): https://en.wikipedia.org/wiki/Anglo-Soviet_invasion_of_Iran

9. Kibbutzim (plural of kibbutz) = collective communities in Israel.

[Pages 242-243]

Katriel Isaac[1]
by Avraham Dor (Dobroszklanka)
Translated by Allen Flusberg

I knew the family of Hirsh Isaac of Dobrzyn; and I got to know their son, Katriel, when I went out to his flower farm in the outskirts of the city of Kutno[2], for a year of field work.

How glad I was when, on one of his visits to Dobrzyn, at the end of 1922, he agreed to take me on in his farm as a student specialist. I had just completed my studies in a horticultural school that was in Tsenstichov[3], and I was seeking to utilize my education in a practical manner. Once he agreed I went out to the farm and began working.

Here I had an opportunity to appreciate several of Katriel's characteristics: his diligence, organizational capacity, wisdom and love for his work. At dawn he used to go out to the fields, to keep track of the growth of the plants and trees whose planting and growth duration he recorded very carefully. He would check the trees after they had been grafted, the roses as they grew and flowered, and most of all the vegetables: cucumbers and onions—produce that he sent to the central market in Lodz three times a week.

He was always trying to extend his knowledge of his profession. For this purpose he stayed in contact with the school that he had studied in, and with managers of the large flower gardens of Europe.

He became famous in the entire vicinity as one of the great experts in growing roses. Grafting was his strong point, and indeed he sometimes succeeded in obtaining new varieties that were not yet known.

He never tired. He labored from dawn to dusk, doing his work happily without losing interest. He was severe with anyone who was negligent on his job, demanding from each worker that he do the best he could.

The years of World War II, which he spent in exile in Russia, left its marks on him. They could be seen in his tired face and the melancholy in his glances. Having lost his wife and children in the ghastly Holocaust, he married again, seeking to reconstruct his life and start life over.

He immigrated to the Land of Israel and went back to his previous line of work on a farm and nursery in Ganei-Yehuda[4]. With his great diligence he succeeded in establishing here, as well, flower nurseries and magnificent fruit trees, serving as an example for his neighbors. It appeared that he had found himself again; he was active in his profession and was joyfully spending time with the son born to him.

Yet he was completely worn out after the horrors of the war and his years of suffering in the Russian Steppes. His heart failed him and gave out. Now the flowers and plants that he loved so much decorate his grave; with their blaze of colors they shelter the man who dedicated the best years of his life to them.

Translator's Footnotes

1. From *My Town: In Memory of the Communities Dobrzyn-Gollob*, edited by M. Harpaz, (published by the Dobrzyn-Golub Society, Israel, 1969), pp. 242-243.

2. Kutno, Poland is located ~100km south of Dobrzyn.

3. Częstochowa, Poland, a city located approximately 300km south of Dobrzyn.

4. Ganei Yehuda is a moshav (agricultural community) that was incorporated into Savyon (near Petah-Tikva) in 2004.

[Pages 243-245]

Mordechai Goldberg[1]
by Avraham Dor (Dobroszklanka)
Translated by Allen Flusberg

One of the modest, shy people, who devotedly, very quietly do what they are supposed to, without trying to earn any laurels: this is what Mordechai Goldberg, of blessed memory, was like. I knew him from childhood—his family and him. He was always a devoted, loyal friend who was willing, with all his soul and all his might, to help anyone.

Their house was located in the market square of the town; I went over there often, for we had become very close friends, heart and soul. And also for a while we were in school together, taught by the same *melamed*[2], R. Mendel Holtz.

When I was about to go away to study gardening in the school in Tsenstichov[3], he divulged to me that he, too, wanted to go there. At his request I approached his mother, who made all the decisions at home, to try to get her to send him with me; but for various reasons she wished to put the matter off. Unfortunately for him, and also for me, no opportunity for him to leave for studies ever came up again.

When I returned from my studies in Tsenstichov, we renewed our friendship and worked together in the town branch of the organization "Hechalutz"[4]; we also became members of the sports club "Hakoach"[5]. We met often, since we played on the same team and spent time together in various events.

We were active together a great deal in the "Hechalutz" movement, taking part in organizing various parties and performances that served as an important source of revenue. I remember Purim and Chanukah balls that we held in Golub, parties that drew large crowds. We transferred a major part of the revenues to the "Hechalutz" Center in Warsaw.

He played an active role in all these activities, performing his duties punctually and with dedication. For a while he served as treasurer of the "Hechalutz" movement, and on many occasions he would cover a shortfall by lending his own money to the cashbox.

We planned our *aliyah* to the Land [of Israel] together, hoping to get immigration visas (certificates). And indeed, when the two of us were among the first to obtain them, our joy knew no bound. For various reasons we did not immigrate together, but when he did come, following in my footsteps several months after I had gone, we began meeting and hanging around together, just like in the old days.

At the end of a day's work, in the evenings, he used to come over to my room, and together we would go out to take a walk along the Tel Aviv shoreline, or, as was customary back then, in the square next to *Mitbach Hapoalim*[6] on Allenby Street, where we would meet up with some people we knew and with immigrants who had just arrived.

After some time had passed, he got a position as a laborer to put up telephone lines, and he moved to Haifa for his work. Our paths separated, but we continued to meet from time to time. These were happy meetings in which we used to bring up memories of our childhood.

In the beginning of the 1930s he got married and also had a son, Noah. But a short time later he became ill, and his condition continued to worsen. He travelled to Heliopolis in Egypt for medical therapy, but did not find a cure there, either. Shortly after coming back to the Land he became ill again. He was brought to the hospital in Afula, where he passed away.

His untimely death was a hard blow to all the friends that he had been devoted to, heart and soul.

May his memory be a blessing!

**Mordechai Goldberg,
of blessed memory**[7]

Translator's Footnotes

1. From *My Town: In Memory of the Communities Dobrzyn-Gollob*, edited by M. Harpaz, (published by the Dobrzyn-Golub Society, Israel, 1969), pp. 243-245.

2. *melamed* = teacher of small children

3. Czestochowa, Poland, a city located approximately 300km south of Dobrzyn.

4. "Hechalutz" (= the Pioneer) was an organization that prepared its members for Aliya to the Land of Israel. See p. 82 of: Dor, "Institutions and Organizations", pp. 78-86 of this volume (reference cited in Footnote 1).

5. On *Hakoach* (= the Force) see p. 84 of: Dor, "Institutions and Organizations", pp. 78-86 of this volume (reference cited in Footnote 1).

6. *Mitbach Hapoalim* = the Workers' Kitchen, a cooperative

7. From p. 244 of reference cited in Footnote 1.

[Pages 245-246]

Dov Yalowski[1]
by his daughter, Leah
Translated by Allen Flusberg

When I recall my father as he was in those days when we were still living in the town of Dobrzyn, the image of our home immediately comes back to me: a home that was filled with a Zionist atmosphere and with activism for the Land of Israel. And above all else I remember my father's many activities, his tireless work to instill the Zionist idea in the hearts of the townspeople. Nor was it all preaching: he took his entire family with him and immigrated to the Land in the year 1933 as many of his friends looked on, shaking their heads and viewing this act of his as extremely impetuous.

More than anything he was aware of the suffering of other people and was ready to help them with all his might. In the early 1930s, when we were living in Bydgoszcz[2], his devoted himself entirely to taking care of Jewish soldiers who were serving in the Polish army and whose regiments were stationed in our town. He worked hard organizing a communal "seder"[3] for all the Jewish soldiers who were going to remain on their base during the days of Passover. He refused to disperse them among Jewish families as holiday guests, so as not to give them the sense of being charity cases…The communal "seder", to which he devoted so much effort, was one of the most beautiful events in our town. And in addition we adopted two or three soldiers; they became close to us and used to stay over when they had leave.

When we arrived in the Land we went through the pains of adjustment that were the lot of many other new immigrants. Nevertheless, even here he attempted to live up to, in practice, the same ideas that he had always championed: He took his family, with all his many children, and settled in a completely desolate area, where he tried to establish an agricultural farm and to live by the toil of his own hands. Since he had neither experience nor knowledge of agriculture, this move of his had aspects of both pioneering and audacity.

He raised his children in a Jewish-Zionist atmosphere that has influenced their paths more than just a little. He lived to see grandchildren who continued to follow the very ideas that he had bequeathed to his children:

whether in cities or in settlements, in education or in security. To his very last day he remained bound to his farmland.

May his memory be a blessing!

Translator's Footnotes

1. From *My Town: In Memory of the Communities Dobrzyn-Gollob*, edited by M. Harpaz, (published by the Dobrzyn-Golub Society, Israel, 1969), pp. 245-246.

2. A city in Poland, about 80 km west of Dobrzyn

3. *Seder* = Passover meal, during which the story of the Exodus from Egypt is ritually recounted

[Pages 246-248]

Yitzhak Rosenwaks, of Blessed Memory[1],[2]
by Ben-Tziyon Epstein (of Dovrat)
Translated by Allen Flusberg

I knew Yitzhak from the time he came to the meshek[3] of Dovrat[4], since he got here only a short time before I did.

In 1954, when he had reached the age of sixty-five, Yitzhak and his wife Chana decided to leave Jerusalem and come to the Dovrat meshek. They wanted to be close to their children in the twilight of their lives, so that they could enjoy being near their children and grandchildren and have a warm relationship with them. And indeed their children knew well how to fulfil the commandment of honoring their father and mother.

Yitzhak and Chana had no trouble getting involved in kibbutz life and adopting a lifestyle that was completely different from that of the city. They struck roots in their new home very quickly, without any trouble. On the contrary, they very rapidly sensed the pulse of life in their new society, adapting and becoming part of it.

Certainly what helped them along was their Zionist education, which had brought them to the Land [of Israel] when they were still young, in the year 1920. They also knew how to guide their children toward pioneering undertakings, starting from a young age. And indeed to this very day their son and daughter are among those who have fulfilled the kibbutz ideal.

What I saw of Yitzhak in the meshek was his great diligence in work, his enthusiasm and persistence. Every day he sorted the mail and hurried to bring it to the post office in Afula; in addition he would take upon himself setting various matters in order for the meshek. And when he returned from the city he would fully immerse himself in the completion of work-related errands that had accumulated.

He was aware of everything that was happening in the meshek and participated in addressing all its problems. At the same time he did not sever his previous ties, and he very capably continued to nurture his connections with friends and family members in the Land and in the Diaspora.

With his great energy he succeeded, after the State was established and after the siege of Jerusalem was lifted, in setting up a charity and free-loan fund for people who hailed from his town. The fund developed well and it served, and continues to serve, as a great help to those who are in need of it, mainly new immigrants and survivors of the Holocaust. This project filled his heart with joy, and he told me about it with great pride.

He was among the active and energetic pioneers from the period of the beginning of the New Yishuv[5] in the Land, and he made many friends over a period of many decades, years of labor and participation in the Hagana. He loved to tell all about the days of the Hagana[6] in Jerusalem, in which he had been quite active during the 1920s and 1930s.

While he was living in the meshek he had to undergo surgery, and in spite of much suffering he continued his regular work, sitting at his work desk in the administrative office every morning, during the sweltering days of summer and the harsh days of winter. Nevertheless he was never in a bad mood; on the contrary, he greeted the early-rising kibbutz members with a cheerful good-morning. For this reason the kibbutz members liked him very much and appreciated him.

His life with his wife Chana could serve as a model for happy family life; his son and daughter appreciated him and reciprocated love to him. Often they would gather in his room during the evening, together with the grandchildren, giving him great pleasure.

Nor did Chana sit idle. She knitted for the children and the kibbutz members. During the sweltering days of summer she sat in the shade of the trees, working on her craft, her face radiant as she conversed with anyone that happened by, young and old, members of the meshek.

She very much liked to read books written in Yiddish. Many times she liked to talk about the books she had read, and in these conversations she demonstrated a deep understanding. She had found these books in the libraries of members of the meshek, who greatly valued the interest she showed in the writers and their works.

To this very day people mention Savta[7] Chana with great esteem. And is it any wonder? Many of the children and members of the meshek are still wearing the warm sweaters, her glorious handiwork.

Yitzhak and Chana struck roots in the meshek, and it seemed as if they had been among its founders. Their fluency in the Hebrew language, their positive attitude in every matter, their awareness of all that was going on, provided them with a special status as members' parents who had successfully been integrated into kibbutz life.

Yitzhak and Chana were laid to rest in the cemetery of the Dovrat meshek. Their memory remains engraved in the hearts of their children, friends and relatives in the Land and the Diaspora.

May their memory be a blessing!

Translator's Footnotes

1. From *My Town: In Memory of the Communities Dobrzyn-Gollob*, edited by M. Harpaz, (published by the Dobrzyn-Golub Society, Israel, 1969), pp. 246-248.

2. See also the following: Y. Rosenwaks, "Chana Rosenwaks", pp. 234-239; autobiographical essay by Yitzhak Rosenwaks (describing his service in the Russian army before World War I and his labor in German work camps during World War I), "My Bundle of Troubles in the Russian Military", pp. 332-353; Y. Eshel, "The First Dobrzyners in Israel", pp. 121-126, all in this volume (reference cited in Footnote 1).

3. *Meshek* = agricultural community or farmstead

4. Dovrat is a kibbutz located in the Galilee, ~8km northeast of Afula and ~10km southeast of Nazareth

5. *Yishuv* = Jewish population of the Land of Israel. The "new" Yishuv refers to those Jews who arrived after ~1880 with the desire to work, rather than to live off charity from the Diaspora.

6. *Hagana* (= Defense), a Jewish paramilitary organization, established in 1920 as a defense force against Arab rioters. See the following Web page (retrieved October 2016): https://en.wikipedia.org/wiki/Haganah

7. *Savta* = grandmother, a title of respect for an elderly lady

[Pages 248-249]

Avraham Rosen, of Blessed Memory[1]
by Avraham Dor (Dobroszklanka)
Translated by Allen Flusberg

I knew Avraham Rosen when I was still a youngster in Dobrzyn. And around the time I was about to leave for the Land of Israel I saw him together with other children, exuberant, completely carefree. And then I met him again in the mid-1930s, this time in the Land, when he was a new immigrant looking for a job.

It was not easy in those days to find work, and it was only after much effort that he was able to get a job involving hard manual labor. Yet very soon he adapted to the situation in the Land of Israel of those days, striking roots and trying to make an independent living for himself.

And indeed, as time passed, he got himself onto the "main highway": his economic situation improved; he set himself up and was able to establish a nice home, filled with cheerfulness and innocence. Although it appeared that this man had achieved peace and prosperity, it was not meant to be.

His faithful wife, a devoted mother, came down with a malignant disease, and the doctors were unable to save her. He walked around sorrowfully as his wife's life faded away before his very eyes. I met him then, and although he did not recount his troubles to me, I was able to see the depth of his misery in his sunken eyes, his gloomy face. His wife was forty-eight when she died.

How morose it was in his house when I came to visit, during the "Shiva"[2], to comfort him while he was in mourning. Already then he confided in me about a weakness that he was experiencing and pains that he was feeling every now and then. Some time afterwards, I found out the bitter truth from one of his friends. I visited him again shortly before he passed away, when his illness had already almost completely consumed him…In torment and anguish he closed his eyes for all eternity.

How great was the grief over the untimely deaths of these lovely and pleasant individuals, an inseparable couple. The children were left orphaned; and even his friends, those who hailed from his town, felt an overwhelming sense of bereavement, as if they, too, had been orphaned.

Avraham was gone forever—a son and grandson of noble-minded parents and a grandfather—a member of an extensive family that had been the pride of the town.

Woe for the loss!

Translator's Footnotes

1. From *My Town: In Memory of the Communities Dobrzyn-Gollob*, edited by M. Harpaz, (published by the Dobrzyn-Golub Society, Israel, 1969), pp. 248-249.

2. *Shiva* = seven-day mourning period, during which visitors come to comfort the bereaved

[Pages 249-252]

Rosenbaum, Moshe Aharon[1] [2]
Translated by Allen Flusberg

The son of Menahem Ben-Tziyon and Feige Mindel, he was born on 11 Nisan 5680 (March 30, 1920) in the town of Dobrzyn, Poland. His parents were veteran Zionists. His father was active in the "Poalei-Tziyon" movement[3].

When he was 11 months old his parents immigrated to the United States. The family settled in Brooklyn, where he grew up and completed high school. Educated in the spirit of Zionism, he was proud of his Jewishness and glad of the atmosphere of freedom in the country that he lived in. For him Chaim Weitzmann[4] and Abraham Lincoln served as representatives of twin ideologies.

When the Second World War broke out, he was a student at a college in central New York. Immediately he left his studies to volunteer in the US Air Force. After graduating from a 9-month course with honors, he was appointed navigator with the rank of second lieutenant. Sent overseas, he joined the Allied Air Force in the Mediterranean region. He was based in Italy, where he met soldiers of the Jewish Brigade, became good friends with them, and decided to go on Aliya to the Land of Israel when the time was ripe.

He was a bombardier, and during his 13th action, over the oil fields of Romania, his plane went down and he was taken prisoner. He spent 13 months in a prisoner-of-war camp in Germany, near Dachau, until May 1945, when the camp was liberated by Allied forces. While he was still a prisoner an Air Force medal had been awarded to him and delivered to his father.

When he returned to his university studies he registered in the department of mechanical engineering, intending to graduate in a profession that would be suitable for a future position in the Land of Israel. He studied for two-and-a-half years. He had only one month of studies to go to receive his degree in engineering, but he chose to put it off in order not to delay, even for a single day, volunteering in the Israeli Air Force during the War of Independence.

During his years of university study he was active in "Bnei Brith" (the Hillel Institute) and in "Habonim"[5]. He excelled in several sports, and he was awarded a prize as the best, most skillful boxer in the student class of 1947-48. He liked art, participating especially in painting; his paintings of scenery, in particular, drew much attention. He also excelled in singing and in meditation.

He served in the Israeli Air Force for only a short time. He died a hero near Hulda[6] on May 30, 1948 and was buried in Hulda on June 1, 1948.

Cornell University of New York posthumously awarded him a degree in mechanical engineering.

By an Israel Defense Forces Chief-of-Staff Order of the Day, dated September 29 1949, he was posthumously promoted to Flight Commander.

Rosenbaum, Moshe Aharon[7]

Family of Avraham Yaakov Rosenwaks[8]

Chaim Rosenwaks and his wife[9]

Yaakov Dratwa[10]

Chana Dratwa[11]

Translator's Footnotes

1. From *My Town: In Memory of the Communities Dobrzyn-Gollob*, edited by M. Harpaz, (published by the Dobrzyn-Golub Society, Israel, 1969), pp. 249-252.

2. See also the following Web site (retrieved November 2016), commemorating non-Israeli volunteers in the Israel Defense Forces who fell in battle; it contains very similar material, but adds a description of how Rosenbaum was killed: http://www.machal.org.il/index.php?option=com_content&view=article&id=445&Itemid=767&lang=en; also the corresponding, but slightly different, Hebrew version (retrieved November 2016) at the following Web site: http://www.machal.org.il/hebrew/index.php?option=com_content&view=article&id=168&Item

3. *Poalei-Tziyon* = Zionist Workers, a Jewish Marxist-Zionist party. See the following Web site (retrieved November 2016) for more information: https://en.wikipedia.org/wiki/Poale_Zion.

4. Weitzmann (1874-1952) was a Zionist leader in Israel who, after the establishment of the State, became its first president. See the following Web page (retrieved November 2016): https://en.wikipedia.org/wiki/Chaim_Weizman

5. *Habonim* = The Builders, a Socialist-Zionist movement. See the following Web page (retrieved November 2016): https://en.wikipedia.org/wiki/Habonim_Dror

6. Hulda is an Israeli kibbutz located about 10km southeast of Rehovot.

7. From p. 249 of reference cited in Footnote 1. The caption, missing on p. 249, is given in the list of photographs that immediately follows the Table of Contents.

8. From p. 251 of reference cited in Footnote 1.

9. From p. 251 of reference cited in Footnote 1.

10. From p. 252 of reference cited in Footnote 1. See also photograph on p. 359.

11. From p. 252 of reference cited in Footnote 1.

[Page 254]

Personalities and their activities

The Poet Yaakov Rimon (Granat)
His Life and Activities[1]

(Excerpted from the Encyclopedia of the Pioneers and Builders of the Yishuv[2], by David Tidhar[3])
Translated by Allen Flusberg

He was born in the town of Dobrzyn in Poland on the 3rd of Tevet, 5663 (beginning of 1903)[4], to his father R.[5] Ephraim Eliezer[6] and his mother Esther Chava (Granat) Rimon. In Dobrzyn he attended a cheder[7]; and by the age of five he had acquired the Hebrew language from his father. His father even taught him to sing Songs of Zion from Kinor Tzion by the writer and researcher R. Avraham Moshe Luncz[8], a blind resident of Jerusalem. At the age of six he immigrated to the Land of Israel with his entire family, settling in Yafo [Jaffa]. Here he attended the Torah-Cheder "Tachkemoni"[9], the Talmud Torah[10] and the Yeshiva Shaarei-Torah that is in Neve Shalom[11]. And afterwards he attended the Tachkemoni school in Tel Aviv. He left Yafo with the other people expelled by the Turks to Kfar Sava and from there to Samaria. During these wanderings he lost his mother Esther Chava, who died in Zichron Yaakov on 1 Nisan 5678[12] from the typhus epidemic of the First World War; and only a few short months after they had returned to Jaffa he lost his father, as well.[13]

In the year 5679 [secular year 1918-19] he founded a student association called "Bonei-Haaretz"[14] to promote using products produced in the Land. This association lasted for several years, and in its name he edited two promotion pamphlets: "Paamon"[15] and "Tuv Haaretz"[16]; and he also worked on distributing them from house to house.

In 5681 [1920-21], he was accepted as an official of the Jewish Communal Council of Yafo and Tel-Aviv; afterwards he was transferred to the Department of Social Welfare of the community. He worked for many years as department administrator, and upon the merger of the community with the municipality of Tel Aviv he served for 11 years as secretary of the United Department of Social Work. Because of a serious eye disease he left this position and transferred to the position of Administrator of Economy and Supplies in this department.

He married Bracha, who was a daughter of Shmuel Halevi-Lezkovski and Miriam Esther (née Walter) from Kutno, Poland.

In his social work, routine office activity was not enough to satisfy him; but rather he invested heart, emotion and enterprise into his work. He also contributed a great deal of enterprise and activity to organizing and promoting work, outside the framework of the department, to support individuals who started associations and institutions for assisting those in need. Among the institutions that he participated in founding and administering were: "Ezrat Cholim" of the Sefardi Jews, and its infirmary; "Bikur Cholim veLinat Hatzedek"; "Beit Hachnasat Orchim"; "Beit Hamachsah Lenechim"; "Beit Hahavraah Shalva", named for Yehoshua and Olga Henkin; and others.

He participated in the founding of "Hapoel Hamizrachi in the Land of Israel", and he was active in it as a member of the local and land-wide administrative committees, as well as a speaker, lecturer and essayist for the party newspapers. He also participated in the founding and editing of the ultra-Orthodox weekly "Hayesod".

In 5687 [1926-27], he headed the Hebrew Youth Association of Unaffiliated Young People. In 5695 [1934-35] he participated in the founding of the Association of Religious Writers in the Land of Israel, and he was active in the leadership of its Tel-Aviv branch. In 5690 [1929-30] he joined the Association "Bnei Tziyon", and he was active in its leadership and in its cultural work. For years he served as president of the "Moshe" bureau, and also as the secretary of the board of "Bnei Tziyon" in Tel Aviv. In addition he joined the "Bnei Hayishuv" association, and he was selected to its leadership; he was active in the Organization of Young People for the Study of Judaism in Tel Aviv.

In the year 5690 [1929-30] he established his house in the Montefiore neighborhood near Tel Aviv, and he participated in activities, in founding and managing community institutions in the neighborhood (the state-religious school named for the official D. Tz. Pinkus of blessed memory; a kindergarten; the "Amen" gardening of the Mizrachi Women; the parents' committee; the infirmary; the neighborhood committee; the cultural committee; the review committee; and others). Likewise he founded and administered a branch for the association "Bnei Hayishuv" in the Montefiore neighborhood, a branch for the sports union "Elitzur", a branch of Poel Hamizrachi, and others. Similarly he founded a league advocating annexation of the neighborhood by the municipality of Tel Aviv, and he successfully administered its activities until it was victorious.

He had already begun his literary work at a young age. He started with publication of articles in the daily newspaper "Doar Hayom". And then he published articles and literary notes, poems, liturgical sketches, and stories in newspapers, both in Israel and abroad.

Works of his that have appeared in print are as follows: His first book, Sultana (5684 [1923-24]); a collection of liturgical poems "Hishtapchut" (5685 [1924-25]); a collection of poems "Artzi" (5688 [1927-28]); "Artzenu Hakdosha", a collection of stories and sketches (5694 [1933-34]); a book of poems "Sneh", which was published by "Bnei Tziyon" on the 25th anniversary of his literary work; and the collection of notes "Yeladim Beoni", published by David Tidhar. This collection contains the impressions experienced by a kindly social worker during his office work. "Chulyot Basharsheret" (5717 [1956-57]) consists of stories and legends, and "Shachar Ran" (published by Mordechai Newman, Jerusalem -Tel Aviv) contains poems for children and youngsters. And in addition a monograph about Rabbi Benzion Meir Chai Uziel, the Chief Rabbi of the Land of Israel, z.tz.l.[17]; "Hanetziv Hayehudi"; and "Yehudei Teiman beTel Aviv".

Several of his poems, put to music, have been distributed throughout the community. About sixty-two poems were recorded by the "Kol Yisrael" Radio, with various interpretations and musical composers. So also some of his songs were recorded in "Hed-Artzi". Popular songs include the songs "El haNegev", "Haroeh Bagalil", "Nerot Shabbat", "Horeh Birushalaim", "El Hakfar", "Tirtzah", "Rina Bat Harim". He published several pamphlets on topics of public interest. His literary poems and notes are continually published in "Hameasef" of the Association of Hebrew Writers in Israel; "Moznaim", a monthly of the Writers' Association "Hatzofeh"; "Hatzofeh Liladim"; "Shearim" (an organ of the Municipality Workers of Tel Aviv-Yafo); "Hadoar"; "Hapoel haTzair" (Tel Aviv); and in the monthly "Sinai", which had been founded by Rabbi Y.L. HaKohen-Maimon z.tz.l., and others.

**The poet Yaakov Rimon
(Granat)**[18]

Translator's Footnotes

1. From *My Town: In Memory of the Communities Dobrzyn-Gollob*, edited by M. Harpaz, (published by the Dobrzyn-Golub Society, Israel, 1969), pp. 254-257.

2. *Yishuv* = Jewish population of the Land of Israel

3. This source is available (in Hebrew) at the following link (retrieved August 2016): http://www.tidhar.tourolib.org/tidhar/view/1/103. Although the text of the Yizkor Book article is not identical, there are a large number of excerpts.

4. 3 Tevet 5663 corresponds to 2 January 1903 in the Gregorian (present-day) calendar used by the Poles. The corresponding date in the Julian calendar, still in use then by Russia, was 20 December 1902. Thus some sources give the year of his birth as 1902.

5. "R." stands for *Reb*, an honorific similar to "Mr." in English.

6. An article written by Yaakov Rimon about his father Ephraim Eliezer Granat appears on pp. 176-179 of this volume (reference cited in Footnote 1).

7. *cheder* = Jewish elementary school for boys with intensive religious study and little, if any, secular learning.

8. Avraham Moshe Luncz (1854-1918) was a prolific author and geographer of the Land of Israel. His published songbook *Kinor Tzion* (=Harp of Zion) contained 50 Hebrew-language songs, full of yearning for the Land and promoting Jewish nationalism. See the following links (retrieved August 2016) for more details: https://en.wikipedia.org/wiki/Abraham_Moses_Luncz (in English); https://he.wikipedia.org/wiki/%D7%90%D7%91%D7%A8%D7%94%D7%9D_%D7%9E%D7%A9%D7%94_%D7%9C%D7%95%D7%A0%D7%A5 (in Hebrew, with additional details).

9. *Cheder-Torah Tachkemoni* was a boys' elementary school in Jaffe (and in a branch in Jerusalem) with an emphasis on Jewish religious studies; secular subjects were taught as well. See the following link (in Hebrew, retrieved August 2016): http://www.jerusalem-love.co.il/?page_id=10126.

10. *Talmud-Torah* = a religious boys' high school. In the present context "yeshiva" refers to a school of advanced religious study. Shaarei-Torah was extended to Yeshiva (post high-school) study for the brightest students. See the following link (in Hebrew, retrieved August 2016): https://he.wikipedia.org/wiki/%D7%A9%D7%A2%D7%A8%D7%99_%D7%AA%D7%95%D7%A8%D7%94_(%D7%AA%D7%9C%D7%9E%D7%95%D7%93_%D7%AA%D7%95%D7%A8%D7%94_%D7%91%D7%99%D7%A4%D7%95)

11. Neve Shalom was a Jewish neighborhood that had been established outside the walls of Jaffa in 1890; it was later incorporated into Tel Aviv.

12. 1 Nisan 5678 corresponds to 14 March 1918.

13. For more details, see the article in this volume cited in Footnote 6.

14. *Bonei Haaretz* = Builders of the Land.

15. *Paamon* = bell

16. *Tuv Haaretz* is roughly equivalent to "the fat of the Land"

17. z.tz.l. = *zecher tzadik livracha* = may the memory of the righteous be a blessing

18. From p. 255 of reference cited in Footnote 1.

[Pages 257-258]

Ask, Jewish People...[1],[2]

by Yaakov Rimon

(Excerpted from "Sneh"[3])

Translated by Allen Flusberg

Ask, forlorn Jewish People[4], whither the Eternal People are headed,
Where Moriah's light shines not upon the wounds of your despairing sons,
Sinai's radiance does not illuminate their gloomy lives bereft of salvation,
The lawgiver's covenant stays not the scythe of death as it reaps outside…
Terrifying darkness has covered all the demolished Jewish homes,
And the pathways to life are sealed, shut within the prison of evil,
Martyrs are burned upon Torah scrolls,[5]
Scorched with tufts of wool in a fiery burial.
Akivas and Tradyons in the killing fields
With *tefillin*[6] straps on the severed arm and split skull…
In torn *tallitot*[7], Death walks about as if in shrouds,
And books by seers lie stinking on dung of the uncircumcised…
An infant's entrails co-mingle with its mother's upon mutilated breasts
And corpses of great sages, luminaries of Torah, are vultures' feed.
With his own hands a son buries his father alive before the savage oppressor's eyes
And a mother casts her children into the pouncing beast's mouth…
Somewhere lies a head severed from its body, with lopped-off beard and sidelocks,—
What does it whisper in the pools of blood, what does its tongue utter
As it licks the dust? And he who hisses toward heaven, his laughter pierces
The Almighty's throne and the tears in the gouged-out eyes congeal
In refuse, from which dogs lick up the remaining blood.
Ask, oppressed Jewish People, where are the boundaries of Man in the dark gloom,
What is the sword driven into her heart, which could not bear it…
And still Sabbath candles are lit on ground red with blood—
Memorial candles for human skeletons, shadows of the terrifying atrocity…
Ask, Jewish People, consumed by all the fiends' fire
When will it be that dawn appears on Mount Horeb[8],
And God's light blazes in the soul of all mankind,
And from Mounts Amana, Senir and Hermon[9] the Almighty's call
Rings out to redeem the world's heart, crushed in blood?

Translator's Footnotes

1. From *My Town: In Memory of the Communities Dobrzyn-Gollob*, edited by M. Harpaz, (published by the Dobrzyn-Golub Society, Israel, 1969), pp. 257-258.

2. This poem, apparently an elegy for victims of the Holocaust, echoes language of *Shaali Serufa Baesh* (= Ask, You Who Has Been Consumed by Fire), a medieval poem lamenting the public burning of Talmud manuscripts by French authorities in 1242 CE. *Shaali Serufa Baesh* is in turn modeled after an earlier poem by Yehuda Halevi, *Tziyon Halo Tishali Lishlom Asirayich* (= Zion, Do you Not Inquire After the Welfare of Your Captives). For many centuries both of these medieval poems have been recited in synagogues on the public fast day of the 9th of Av.

3. *Sneh* (= Bush), a collection of poetry by Rimon, published in 1946 (see entry "Jacob Rimon" in *Encyclopedia Judaica*, vol. 14, p. 187).

4. Hebrew *Knesset Yisrael*, literally Assembly of Israel, i.e. the Jewish people personified, here translated as "Jewish People"

5. Beginning with this line many images echo the medieval poems *Eile Ezkera* (=These I shall Remember) and *Arzei Halevalon* (= Cedars of Lebanon), elegies on the martyrdom of leading rabbis at the hands of the Romans in the 1st and 2nd centuries. Among the rabbis were Akiva and Chananya son of Tradyon; both are referred to here. These medieval poems are recited in synagogues on the fast days of Yom Kippur and the 9th of Av, respectively.

6. *tefillin* = phylacteries

7. *tallitot* = prayer shawls

8. Horeb is another name for Sinai.

9. Amana, Senir and Hermon are Lebanese mountains mentioned in the Song of Songs 4:8. This verse is interpreted allegorically as referring to messianic redemption.

[Pages 259]

These Days (Poem)[1]

(From "Sneh"[2])

by Yaakov Rimon

Translated by Allen Flusberg

Human traces are obliterated, the world transformed into a dense forest.

Every house looks like a tree, and between them—beasts burst forth.

City streets—just trails of forests and wilderness,

Extending from desolation to desolation within the green wasteland…

When a car passes by somewhere, the horn sounds

Like an angry spirit, slicing the expanse with its sorrowful call…

And the newspaper vendor who goes by wearily, advertising the paper,

Sounds to me like an angry lion, roaring fearsomely, blood seeping…

In each tree with peeling bark, I see in its bareness the untended wounded,

And in every chimney on a roof—the muzzle of a thundering cannon…

The days are strung together link-to-link, like on a rusty chain,

Soon they will break apart, in a moment be as naught…

And the skies look like a can full of explosives,

Just touch it and it blows up, destroying all…

These days the beast, with its black fright, is pouncing on Man,

As if from hidden caves, like a terrifying monster, a world to devour!

Translator's Footnotes

1. From *My Town: In Memory of the Communities Dobrzyn-Gollob*, edited by M. Harpaz, (published by the Dobrzyn-Golub Society, Israel, 1969), p. 259

2. *Sneh*, a collection of Yaakov Rimon's poems, was published in 1946 (see Encyclopedia Judaica, vol. 14, p. 187, "Rimon, Jacob").

[Pages 260-262]

The Warshawski Family of New York[1]

Zippora Warshawski, Daughter of Daniel Itche's (Kohn) of Dobrzyn
And Her Husband, Nachum Yisrael Warshawski, Born in Rypin[2]

by Yehuda Rosenwaks

Translated by Allen Flusberg

At first sight, what do Zippora Warshawski and her husband have to do with a Yizkor Book? They have, after all, been living in New York for ages—and may they continue to until a hundred and twenty. But in fact this book would not be complete without celebrating their great devotion, as well as their many actions, in support of the State of Israel and their brethren who hail from Dobrzyn and Rypin.

Already in her youth Zippora stood out in Dobrzyn as a lively and active Zionist. In the household of Daniel Itche's (Kohn)—a Zionist, intellectual home that was warm and open to anyone interested—she, the eldest child, was the spirited one. She did not spare any effort to win people over to the Zionist idea.

In those days the Zionist movement of the town was still in its infancy. It was a time when the heads of the religious community alienated themselves from it and were even persecuting it. They viewed the young people, who were taken with the Zionist idea, as heretics, may the Merciful One save us[3]—unbelievers who were denying the pure faith and were trying to bring about the End of Days before its appointed time[4]. But their struggle did not have the power to keep the young movement away; it continued to capture more and even more hearts, ceaselessly. In spite of, and in defiance of those who opposed it, the Zionist movement of the town was gathering strength, capturing the elite among the young people and even some of the adults. The contribution of Zippora Warshawski to this state of affairs was significant.

Some 50 years ago she and her husband immigrated to the United States; but even there, in the New World, they did not forget their people: they continued, and still continue, to this very day, working for and remaining active in support of the Land of Israel.

Success smiled on them in the United States: they did well and are considered to be among the wealthiest people of their community. However, wealth did not blind them and make them forget, even for a moment, those who hailed from their towns, Dobrzyn and Rypin, and now live in the State of Israel.

I had the opportunity to meet them during their visits to Israel; and I was glad to see for myself, once again, how very interested they were in the people from their towns, and particularly in the State of Israel and its development.

And indeed, the Warshawski family is among the honored benefactors who are dedicated to all the funds that raise money for the State of Israel. Only very recently, during the Six-Day War, they contributed the sum of $110,000 to the Emergency Fund.

We are glad to know that Zippora and Nathan Warshawski, originally from Dobrzyn and Rypin, have continued along the path that they had started on in the town, with a love for and devotion to their people still burning in their hearts.

Mrs. Zippora Warshawski (née Kohn), New York[5]

Reception for guests from the United States. Center: Max Goldfeder[6]

Mrs. Milka Plotnirsh (née Shulsinger) of Chicago speaking during the reception[7]

Translator's Footnotes

1. From *My Town: In Memory of the Communities Dobrzyn-Gollob*, edited by M. Harpaz, (published by the Dobrzyn-Golub Society, Israel, 1969), pp. 260-262.

2. Rypin is a town 25 km due east of Dobrzyn

3. Aramaic *rachmana litzlan*, an expression that might have been appended by an opposition figure mentioning heretics

4. Hebrew *lidchok et haketz*, from Babylonian Talmud, Ketuvot 110b-111a. The rabbis who opposed Zionism interpreted this Talmudic passage as an admonition against trying to reestablish a Jewish State in Israel before the miraculous advent of the Messiah.

5. From p. 261 of reference cited in Footnote 1

6. From p. 262 of reference cited in Footnote 1

7. From p. 262 of reference cited in Footnote 1

[Page 264]

The Towns that Once Existed

The Synagogue and *Shtiebels* in Dobrzyn[1]

By an Unknown Rabbi

(submitted by Engineer Davidovicz)

Translated by Allen Flusberg

Only a bridge over the little river separates one town from the other. But in fact it is a single community with one rabbi—in spite of the fact that each town has its own synagogue and *beis medrash*[2] and also a separate cemetery. For in times past these were two separate towns, with separate communities, located on either side of a border. Today, however, it is a single community.

The Jewish community of Golub is very old, with an ancient walled synagogue, an old *beis medrash*, and an old cemetery. In this cemetery a local rabbi who was a great prodigy and a student of Rabbi Akiva Eiger[3] lies buried. In the *beis medrash* there was a trove of valuable rare religious books.

The Jewish community in Dobrzyn is also old, but not as old as that of Golub. The synagogue, which is constructed of wood, is about one hundred years old. The cemetery, however, is older than the synagogue. There Rabbi Toib, a student of the old Alexander[4] *Rebbe*[5], Rabbi Yechiel[6], had been laid to rest.

Rabbi Toib was supposed to be Rabbi Yechiel's successor, as had been requested by the older, highly regarded Hassidim. But Rabbi Toib categorically refused the position; he himself began traveling to see[7] Rabbi Yechiel's son, Rabbi Yisroel Yitzchok (the author of the book "Yismach Yisroel").

There were 15 Torah scrolls in the synagogue and 5 in the *Beis Medrash*. In the *Beis Medrash* there were also several sacred silver vessels.

In January, 1939 Dobrzyn became famous throughout all of Poland with the terrible pogrom incitement that the local *Endekes*[8] carried out against the

Jews. It resulted in a boycott and in picketing, and it ended with an actual pogrom, during which many Jews were wounded and very seriously stabbed; 70 windows were shattered in Jewish dwellings, and merchandise was robbed and destroyed.

The local priest, Barszewski, stood at the head of the pogrom incitement. He was a well-known anti-Semite and enemy of the Jews. He was the author of the well-known inciting work "Shadow", which was circumspectly polemicized in his newspaper. These events in Dobrzyn were echoed by an interpellation by Rabbi Rubenstein[9] in the Polish *Sejm*[10].

Immediately after the outbreak of the war, in September 1939, hordes of German soldiers descended on the town. Right after their arrival they began to seize Jews for various types of labor, at the same time beating them cruelly. One day later a series of beard shearings began. Nearly all the Jewish men were left with no beards, and during the beard shearings the beatings and torment were repeated.

Four days later they sealed all the Jewish houses and businesses. Additionally they began to inventory Jewish homes and simultaneously confiscate their property—all their meager belongings and merchandise.

Not far from Dobrzyn there was an estate, called Szitna, which belonged to a Hassidic Jew named R.[11] Yitzchok Yaakov Szmiga, a rare, generous person, a philanthropist and a prominent social leader. In spite of the fact that a terrible anti-Semitic incitement had gone on for an entire year in Dobrzyn and in the surrounding area, Szmiga had not been affected by it. With a generous hand he had distributed various products, as well as cash, to needy Jewish families. But at the same time he had provided for the peasant farmers and farmhands; for this reason he was well liked by them, as well. The landowners also liked him very much.

During the massive bombardment, hundreds of Jews and Christians fled to Szitna. Szmiga allowed them access to the manor, which had dozens of rooms; he himself spent each night in the barn. He opened the granaries that were full of food, and from them he distributed flour, kasha and potatoes to the people; the cows were milked and the milk was distributed; the refugees also ate the many geese, chickens and turkeys that were on the estate. He did not hold anything back, but in spite of everything a bitter fate awaited him. One fine day several SS members came in and took him away. He disappeared forever without a trace, and no one even found out how and where he had met his death.

Another sorrowful event took place on the first day of Rosh Hashana 5700[12]: two huge trucks filled with a large number of police drove onto the main street of the town, and went after the synagogue and the Ger[13] shtiebel[14], taking out 230 Jews who were wrapped in their *taleisim*[15] and dressed for the holiday in their silk *kapotes*[16]. Among them were elderly men, in their eighties, as well as some children ten to twelve years old. They loaded them into the trucks and took them away in an unknown direction; and to this very day no one even knows what became of their bones.

This transport contained the finest and most prominent personalities of the town: party leaders and socially active people, community representatives, municipal councilmen, etc.

Here we provide a partial list of the most prominent of those who were seized: (1) Avrohom Gurfinkiel; (2) Yechiel Zissholtz, a community representative and municipal councilman; (3) Oizer Kohn, 64 years old; (4) Yosef Binyomin Gasior, 60 years old; (5) the *chazzan*[17] Zylberberg; (6) the *shochet*[18] Mendel Gurfinkel; (7) Itzik Shamash; (8) Cudkiewicz; (9) Flusberg[19], 59 years old, an ill, broken-down man; (10) Yisroel Muller; (11) Frenkiel; (12) Dentist Blauzeg; (13) Moishe Pozmanter; (14) Dzialdow; (15) Mordechai Salomon, chairman of all the social institutions in the town; (16) both sons of Chayim Yanuar; (17) Sztetyn; (18) Eliezer Zaklikowski; (19) Kalman Arfa, administrator and leader of the *Poalei-Tzion*[20]; and many others.[21] [22],

The same fate awaited the Golub pharmacist, Riesenfeld, a distinguished person who was a great philanthropist, a great contributor to Zionist funds, and who was beloved by the people of Dobrzyn-Golub. He was arrested by a Gestapo officer and was taken away accompanied by him; and to this day no one knows where he took him.

Later they emptied the synagogue and the *beis medrash* of their benches, tables and *Aron Koidesh*[23], converting both of these sacred places into a stable. The local Poles gathered around for this particular "Culture Action" and took away much of the furniture that had been left outside.

It is worth noting how the Dobrzyn anti-Semitic priest Barszewski behaved in this case. When he became aware that the Poles were dragging away the furniture that the Germans had brought out of the synagogue and *beis medrash*, he quickly came running. He demanded of the Poles gathered there not to dare touch those objects that had been held sacred by the Jews; and, for those who had already taken some of these things, to immediately bring them back.

They demolished the synagogue in Golub, as well, replacing it by a stable.

On the 6th of November 1939, thirty-five of the most distinguished families in Dobrzyn, consisting of approximately 100 people, received an urgent request to appear at City Hall. There they handed them written instructions that they were permitted to take along in the transport; the transport consisted of several vehicles that were already waiting for them at City Hall. The men, women, children and elderly were separated from each other, and they were placed separately in three vehicles. They were driven away in an unknown direction, and to this very day no one knows what became of them.

Among the 35 families were: (1) Shlomo Yosef Lipski; (2) Yisroel Muller, a family of 11 people (not the same Muller who was on the previous list); (3) Lemel Lewin; (4) Mendel Sapersztajn; (5) a woman and child named Dzialdow (see Footnotes 21, 22).

On Thursday, November 9th, early in the morning, the head of the Jewish council was called in to appear before the Chief of Police, who told him the following: Since all the Jews are being evicted from the town today, he has a proposition with respect to this expulsion. If the Jews will deliver a total of 40,000 zlotys during the next three hours, they will be permitted to take small essential items with them.

A terrible panic ensued, and the Jews began to collect money from every direction. But in spite of the best of intentions it was not by any means possible to collect this much cash. Altogether 20,000 zlotys were collected; the remaining 20,000 zlotys were brought in the form of various valuables, including a basket full of gold and silver objects.

As requested, the Jews gathered at City Hall at the appointed time, each of them carrying a bundle on his shoulders and waiting for the police's order. In the meantime some of the policemen went after the unfortunate people gathered there, beginning to cruelly beat them left and right, not even discriminating with respect to gender or age. They did not let anyone get away, and everyone was badly beaten. Then the Jews were told to leave the town in the direction of the "General Government"[24] but not in the direction of the Reich—for obvious reasons.

As we now know, the sacred buildings, such as the synagogue and the *beis medrash*, were later set ablaze; and the Torah scrolls were damaged and torn up. The cemetery was plowed up and turned into a park. The Golub synagogue and *beis medrash* also suffered the same fate. There, too, the cemetery was plowed up.

This is how the Jewish community in these two most beloved towns, Dobrzyn and Golub, ended its physical existence, concluding a living history that had endured for hundreds of years.

*The author is an unknown rabbi; [article] submitted by Engineer Davidovicz.

Mendel Kohn's children (wearing caps) with their friends[25]

No caption[26]

Translator's Footnotes

1. From *My Town: In Memory of the Communities Dobrzyn-Gollob*, edited by M. Harpaz, (published by the Dobrzyn-Golub Society, Israel, 1969), pp. 264-269.

2. *Beis medrash* = study hall, where men sit at tables to study Talmud, and prayer services are sometimes held, as well.

3. Rabbi Akiva Eiger (or Eger), who died in 1837, was a foremost scholar and rabbinical leader of West Prussia, which Golub was part of.

4. Alexander (or Aleksander) is the name of a Hassidic group that had many adherents in Dobrzyn. See the following link: http://en.wikipedia.org/wiki/Aleksander_(Hasidic_dynasty)

5. *Rebbe* = religious leader of Hassidic group

6. Yechiel Dancyger (1828-1894)

7. i.e., to pay homage to Yisroel Yitzchok and support the latter as Yechiel's successor

8. *Endekes* = ND'ers, followers of the ND political party. ND stood for *Narodowa Demokracja*, Polish for National Democracy. This party had an anti-Semitic platform.

9. Rabbi Yitzchok Rubinstein, Chief Rabbi of Vilna (then in Poland), was a member of the Polish parliament. See the following link: http://www.eilatgordinlevitan.com/vilna/vilna_pages/vilna_stories_rubenstein.html.

10. *Sejm* = lower house of Polish parliament

11. "ר'" has here been translated "R.", which likely stands for "*Reb*" (a title of respect), rather than Rabbi.

12. Jewish New Year, Thursday, September 14, 1939

13. Ger = a Hassidic group that had many adherents in Dobrzyn

14. *Shtiebel* = a small synagogue consisting of a single prayer room, usually Hassidic

15. *Taleisim* = prayer shawls

16. *Kapote* = kaftan, long black coat worn by some Eastern European Jews, particularly on special occasions

17. *Chazzan* = synagogue cantor

18. *Shochet* = Jewish ritual slaughterer

19. Eliyohu-Mordechai Flusberg (see essay by Yehoshua Flusberg, "The Men Left and Didn't ," pp. 137-188 of reference cited in Footnote 1). His son, David, was also seized and taken with him.

20. *Poalei-Tzion* = Socialist-Zionist party

21. More complete lists (and accounts) exist in the Ringelblum archives in Warsaw. Handwritten in Yiddish in 1941 in Warsaw, these accounts by two refugees from Dobrzyn were unearthed after the war. They list most of the men taken away on September 14, 1939, as well as most of those persons who were taken separately on November 6, 1939.The names of Szmiga and Riesenfeld, mentioned here as being taken away separately, also appear at the end of the first Ringelblum list. The accounts are reproduced and translated into English in the following website: http://internex.net.au/~fdobia/TwoLetters.htm.

22. Nearly all these names appear in the more complete 1941 lists found in the Ringelblum archives (as cited in Footnote 21). For all those that do, the family names have been spelled here according to the Polish spelling used in those lists. Most would be transliterated differently into English according to their Yiddish spelling; e.g. "Cudkiewicz" might be spelled "Tzudkevitch" in English.

23. *Aron Koidesh* = Holy Ark, in which the Torah scrolls were kept

24. The General Government was the name given to the part of Poland that was administered by Germany during World War II as a territory separate from the Reich. Dobrzyn was located outside (northwest of) the General Government. See the following link: http://en.wikipedia.org/wiki/General_Government.

25. From p. 265 of Reference cited in Footnote 1

26. From p. 269 of Reference cited in Footnote 1

[Page 270]

The Grassroots Jews of Dobrzyn[1]

By Shlomo Aleksander

Translated by Allen Flusberg

Perhaps I am not able to convey with my humble pen the depth of the heartache I feel as I look back at the enormous destruction of our beloved town Dobrzyn. During its hundreds of years of existence a great deal of history had transpired there; and all at once the accursed German murderers arrived and wiped out Jewish Dobrzyn, leaving behind not a trace of its rich past.

Dobrzyn was renowned for its good people: when it unfortunately happened that a Dobrzyn Jew lost his money in business, or a wagon-driver lost his horse and was left without any livelihood—then the dedicated volunteers would immediately take up a collection to put that Jew back on his feet. And all of this was done covertly, "*matan besayser*"[2]. If a Jewish young man did not wish to serve in the Russian army then he would come to Dobrzyn, where the benevolent Jews—a people excelling in compassion[3]— would ensure that he crossed the border to Golub. And from there the Jews of Golub would transport him further, whether or not he had the financial means. I recall once going into the Beis Medresh[4], where I found that there were more than ten Jews who needed to cross the border. The issue was not only bringing them across, but also giving them the capability to continue their journey beyond Golub. Those who were engaged in the needs of the community turned to the wealthy people of the town, and by the time I returned to the Beis Medresh the next day not a single one of those ten Jews was still there—that is, they were all already on the other side of the border.

The list of prominent philanthropists of the town was a long one. Everyone considered it an obligation to do favors for others, and it was not merely for esteem. People would spend their valuable time helping those who were suffering. Whether it was late at night, in rain or in snow, they would hurry to fulfill the sacred duty of "*ozoiv taazoiv imoi*"[5].

The aid institutions that existed in this small town were very active. I will mention only a few of them: the "*gmilas chasodim*[6] fund", "*hachnosas orchim*"[7], "*hachnosas kalla*"[8], "*bikur choilim*"[9], etc. Noble Jewish housewives donated their most precious time to ensure that these institutions could carry out their normal activities. There were pious women who by Thursday would already be making certain that needy families did not lack anything on the Sabbath, Heaven forbid. And who in fact can enumerate all the good deeds that the people of the town accomplished?

***

Dobrzyn also had its political parties, comparable to those of all the large cities of Poland. Foremost was the Zionist organization, which led a great deal of activity for the Land of Israel. Everything was present in this very town, but unfortunately this is all history now. Together with the annihilation of six million Jews, our precious beloved town was destroyed, as well; even the Jewish cemetery, where our dear parents had found their eternal rest, was destroyed—as was also the Beis Medresh with our beautiful synagogue, where for generations Jews had presented their supplications before the Master of the Universe. May the curse of " I will surely blot out the memory of Amalek"[10] accompany our enemies for generations to come.

Our only comfort has been the building up of our beloved Land of Israel, which feels like home to every Jew throughout the world. Today every Jew takes pride in the State of Israel, knowing that it elevates the dignity of each and every one of us. No sacrifice is too great for the sake of our state, which has made it possible for millions of Jews to build their home and presence here.

Let this Yizkor Book serve as an everlasting monument to our fallen parents, sisters and brothers who gave their lives as martyrs—may God avenge their blood.

Mr. Chayim Kaczor and His Family[11]

Translator's Footnotes

1. From *My Town: In Memory of the Communities Dobrzyn-Gollob*, edited by M. Harpaz, (published by the Dobrzyn-Golub Society, Israel, 1969), pp. 270-272.

2. *Matan besayser* = anonymous giving (based on Prov. 21:14). The Talmud describes *matan besayser* as a high form of charity in which the donor and recipient are unknown to one another (Baba Batra 9b). The recipient is spared the embarrassment of accepting charity from someone he knows, and the donor cannot expect future compensation from a recipient who does not know his identity.

3. *Rachmonim bnei rachmonim* (Hebrew), literally the merciful descendants of the merciful

4. *Beis Medresh* = study hall (for religious studies)

5. "*Ozoiv taazoiv imoi*" (Exodus 23:5) = you shall surely help him (as interpreted here). This verse is understood as a commandment to help anyone in need.

6. *Gmilas chasodim* = general charity for those in need, e.g. interest-free loans

7. *Hachnosas orchim* = provision of hospitality (food and lodging) for out-of-town visitors

8. *hachnosas kalla* = bridal fund to provide for the wedding of a bride from a poor family

9. *Bikur choilim* = visiting the ill

10. Exodus 17:14. Jewish tradition views those who attempt to annihilate the Jewish people as Amalek.

11. From p. 271 of reference cited in Footnote 1.

[Page 273]

My Town Dobrzyn[1]

by Mich'le Plotniarz-Shlesinger, Chicago
Translated by Allen Flusberg

It was a lovely, gentle town, with warm and cordial people living in it. In my youth I left to immigrate to America, but I never forgot it. A mystical force had bound me to it and to its inhabitants. Many times my rest would be disturbed when my thoughts turned to the fate of those dozens of families, blessed with many children, as I wondered whether they could satisfy their daily needs. Were they healthy? I can still see their pained faces and sorrowful eyes as they accompanied me when I departed. And to this very day their warm wishes ring in my ears.

With a heavy heart I left them, wondering whether I would ever see them again, whether I would someday return on a visit in the dark nights, slogging through the deep mud to see their sad faces, with not even a feigned smile, always fearful for the morrow. How difficult my first years away were as I adjusted to the reality that we had become separated by a vast ocean, and that we could be together only in our thoughts. We shed many a tear in those days, a generation back, when we arrived in the Golden Land to seek a way to support ourselves under difficult circumstances, while at the same time we carried with us plans to organize help for the needy of the town. At first it was very hard for us to do so, but we did not shirk our duty to those we held dear.

When I visited Israel I attended a meeting at which I spoke of some of my memories from those days. I was pleased to be able to share these memories with my friends in Israel, memories of an era that had passed. Those generations who knew of the greatness of the town in that era could relate anecdotes exemplifying the kindheartedness of individuals there to one another.

Now it has all been destroyed: the town is no more; for us it no longer exists. But the spark of its rich history will remain in the hearts of our fellow townsmen wherever they are, and, with the appearance of this Memorial Book, it will also be passed on to future generations.

Translator's Footnote

1. From *My Town: In Memory of the Communities Dobrzyn-Gollob*, edited by M. Harpaz, (published by the Dobrzyn-Golub Society, Israel, 1969), pp. 273-274.

[Page 274]

A Glance at Synagogue Lane[1]

By Michl'e Plotniarz-Shlesinger
Translated by Allen Flusberg

I can still see Jews, residents of the *Shul Gessl*[2], walking to prayer services in the morning, some to the synagogue and some to the *beis medresh*[3]. I can still see children with chickens under their arms, hurrying to the slaughterhouse. I see Jews on Friday afternoon, going to the *mikve*[4]; and hundreds of children scurrying along during the morning so as not to be late for *cheider*[5]. Most of these *cheiders* were concentrated along the *Shul Gessl*. It was almost impossible to avoid the *Shul Gessl*, the throbbing hub of life in the town, with its synagogue and the *beis medresh*; *shtiebls*[6] and *cheiders*; slaughterhouse and butcher shops; and [places to] heat vessels red hot[7]. In addition those who wished to go down to the Dreventz River, whether to wade or bathe, would access it by walking along the *Shul Gessl*.

Now for the panoramic view: the *gessl* ended at a tall mountain, on the top of which stood a dilapidated house. For dozens of years the shoemaker Moishe Reuven Krajanek, a long-bearded, lanky man, lived and worked there. He was the first to arrive at the synagogue for morning prayers, but he was also the first to leave, even before the prayer service ended. He would say that his stomach was growling, that he was hungry. His four sons were also shoemakers, but in later years they sought various opportunities to free themselves from their calling. Overall, this was a quiet, respectable family.

The majority of the residents of the *Shul Gessl* were members of the working class, but several wealthy families, whose homes and shops had been passed down as an inheritance, lived there as well. At the beginning of the twentieth century the bookstore of Mr. Efraim Eliezer Granat (Rimon) was also located on the *Shul Gessl*.

During the summer months, every passerby's shoes would be covered by dust from the unpaved *gessl*, while during the winter months their shoes would be covered with mud instead. The city council—which was dominated by Poles even though most of the population was Jewish—never found it necessary to pave the *Shul Gessl* with paving stones. But the total destruction has solved all these problems ...Dobrzyn is no more; the *Shul Gessl* no longer exists.

Translator's Footnotes

1. From *My Town: In Memory of the Communities Dobrzyn-Gollob*, edited by M. Harpaz, (published by the Dobrzyn-Golub Society, Israel, 1969), pp. 274-275.

2. *Shul Gessl* = Synagogue Lane. As can be seen from the map, (pp. 8-9 of reference cited in Footnote 1), the synagogue was located at the end of this street.

3. *Beis Medresh* = Study Hall, which in Dobrzyn was located right next to the synagogue (see map, pp. 8-9 of reference cited in Footnote 1).

4. *Mikve* = ritual bath

5. *Cheider* = boys' schoolhouse, where studies were almost exclusively religious

6. *Shtiebl* = small prayer house, usually Hassidic

7. Yiddish: *keilim glien*. This may possibly have been a service to cleanse ("*kasher*") metal vessels by heating them red hot, e.g. to make a vessel that had previously been used by non-Jews kosher, i.e. suitable for preparation of kosher food (based on Numbers 31:23 and Babylonian Talmud Avoda Zara 75b). Red heat may also have been used to patch or mend metal vessels.

[Page 275]

The Synagogue in Dobrzyn[1]

By Tuvya Tinski

Translated by Allen Flusberg

Just like all the other towns of Poland, our town had a synagogue, as well. Ours was known throughout the surrounding towns for its artistic paintings. Landscapes of the holy places in Jerusalem, such as the Western Wall, Rachel's Tomb, the Tower of David, and Absalom's Pillar adorned the walls and ceilings. Whoever saw them for the first time would be quite enthralled. The town also contained a *Beis Medresh*[2] and many *shtiebls*[3], such as the Ger[4], Alexander[5], Otwock[6], and others. When I was already a grown young man, I preferred to attend prayer services in the synagogue, even though I favored Hassidism. I would also enjoy going to the synagogue when I was a little boy. On Sabbaths and holidays I would bring my mother's *siddur*[7] to synagogue for her.[8] It was a thick *siddur*, heavy and large, and I could barely carry it. The *siddur* contained all the prayers with a Yiddish translation, as well as parables and *techines*[9] in Yiddish for the Blessing of a New Month[10] and for *Yizkor*[11]. Many of the women used to listen to my mother praying out loud, and then repeat her words verbatim. Probably a good number of them didn't even know the [Yiddish] alphabet and were pleased to have my mother lead them in prayer. Many times, when I went inside the women's section of the synagogue to carry my mother's *siddur* home, I would listen to the women crying while my mother was saying the prayers from her Yom Kippur[12] *machzer*[13]. For my mother this was both a *mitzvah*[14] and a pleasurable act that she continued to observe for many long years.

When I turned nine and began studying *gemoro*[15] with Mr. Nissan Melamed, he gave me warning that from now on I was no longer to carry my mother's *siddur* home on the Sabbath.[16] Of course I complied with my teacher's demand, thereby bidding adieu to the women's section of the synagogue.

Later I began to sing in the choir led by Cantor Degola, who had influenced my father to let me participate in it. At that point I became a more frequent visitor to the synagogue—but now, of course, in the men's section. Here I also had the opportunity to get to know all the functionaries of the synagogue: the *shamash*[17], the *gabais*[18], and the vested prayer leaders. These functionaries held sway not only over the large synagogue itself, but also over the small *shtiebls* that were located alongside its entrance. The town's skilled workers attended services in them; and in one of them members of the *chevra kadisha*[19] attended weekday services. We young men, a group called "*Loimdei Torah*"[20], also took over one of these *shtiebls*; in it the Mieszaniec Rabbi, who in those days pretended he was the official rabbi of Dobrzyn, used to give lectures.

One *shtiebl* was taken over by the members of the organization *Bikkur Choilim*[21] and *Hachnosas Kalla*[22]. They had their own Torah reader, Moishe Leib Gutglass. Each *shtiebl* held approximately four *minyans*[23], and so on Sabbaths and holidays all these little synagogues were full of men attending the prayer service.

On a slope leading down from the synagogue was the Dreventz[24], a small river with a powerful current. There the pupils who attended the various *cheders*[25] located nearby would bathe in the summer. On Rosh Hashana[26] crowds would throng both banks of the river: the German Jews from Golub[27] on one side, and the Dobrzyn Jews on the opposite bank, both at *tashlich*[28].

To the right of the synagogue stood the tall "Rokers" Mount with its white sand. This sand was used by the housewives as scouring material, and also to sprinkle onto freshly washed wooden floors.

There were beautiful, plastered stones about 20 meters in front of the synagogue, and the entryway was lined on both sides with iron chains. The windows of the synagogue cellar were visible from the courtyard of the synagogue; people were afraid to look down through them because of legends about demons and swooping evil spirits. And for this very reason the bier that was used to carry dead bodies to the cemetery was kept there.

Within the synagogue, everyone instinctively raised his eyes towards the tall *aron koidesh*[29] with its beautiful *poroiches*[30], and also towards the multicolored stained glass windows. The glass tower at the very midpoint of the ceiling was particularly impressive, and everyone was always stealing glances at the beautiful artwork just below it. Even the *bima*[31] for the reading of the Torah was unusual for its esthetic beauty; it was quite different from *bimas* in the synagogues of other small Polish towns.

On Sabbaths and holidays the prayers were led by the cantor, accompanied by a choir.

Every prayer of the *Yomim Noiroim*[32] affected the congregation in its own unique way. They would be gripped by fear when the cantor and choir sang the verses of "*Unesaneh Toikef*"[33]: "And as a great trumpet sounds, a small, silent voice is heard; the angels scurry, seized by fear."[34] The motif of the singing was one the elements used to arouse emotion. The prayer "Man is derived from dust, and his end is dust"[35] gave us pause for thought and soul-searching; at that moment one could hear a quiet, deep wail, as tears appeared on many a face.

Years of joy and sorrow accompanied the synagogue during its many years of existence, until the Destruction.

May these lines of mine serve as a reminder of that lovely, architectural building, the Dobrzyn synagogue, which was destroyed by the Nazi murderers.

Mr. Yaakov Tinski, of blessed memory[36]

Wife of Mr. Yaakov Tinski[37]

Yosef Alterowicz and his wife Tserl[38]

Translator's Footnotes

1. From *My Town: In Memory of the Communities Dobrzyn-Gollob*, edited by M. Harpaz, (published by the Dobrzyn-Golub Society, Israel, 1969), pp. 275-278.

2. *Beis Medresh* = Study Hall, where Jewish religious texts are studied and prayer services are held, as well

3. *Shtiebl* = prayer house—a small, single-room synagogue, usually Hassidic

4. Ger = Hassidic group that followed a rabbinical dynasty whose founder originated from Góra Kalwaria, a town 25km south of Warsaw that the Jews of Poland referred to as Ger. See the following link:
http://en.wikipedia.org/wiki/Ger_%28Hasidic_dynasty%29

5. Alexander (or Alcksander) – Hassidic group that followed a rabbinical dynasty whose founder originated in Aleksandrow Lodzki, a Polish town located near Łódź. See the following link:
http://en.wikipedia.org/wiki/Aleksander_%28Hasidic_dynasty%29.

6. Otwock = A Hassidic group, followers of the Hassidic *Rebbe* Simcha Bunim of Otwock (1851-1907). See the following link: http://www.yivoencyclopedia.org/article.aspx/Vurke_Hasidic_Dynasty

7. *Siddur* = prayer book containing daily and Sabbath prayers

8. By Jewish law an adult may not carry any burden outdoors on the Sabbath and Yom Kippur, unless special provision (an *eruv*) is made to establish a larger area as an extended common dwelling. In the absence of an *eruv*, it is common for young children, who are not subject to this restriction, to carry prayer books to and from the synagogue for their parents on the Sabbath.

9. *Techines* = supplications—prayers in Yiddish that were geared to women. See the following link: http://jwa.org/encyclopedia/article/tkhines

10. The blessing of a New Month is recited in the synagogue on the Sabbath that immediately precedes the beginning of a Jewish-calendric month. Its inclusion of a prayer for health and sustenance for the coming month gives it popular appeal.

11. *Yizkor* = "May God remember...", special prayer for the souls of departed relatives, recited on Jewish holidays

12. Yom Kippur = Day of Atonement, which falls on the 10th day after the beginning of the Jewish New Year (Rosh Hashana, see Footnote 26 below)

13. *Machzer* = prayer book for Rosh Hashana and/or Yom Kippur (as distinct from the *siddur*, the prayer book for all other days of the year)

14. *Mitzvah* = fulfillment of a religious commandment; by extension, a good deed

15. *Gemoro* = Talmud

16. See Footnote 8. By the age of nine a child might begin practicing for the legal obligations of adulthood even though they do not actually come into force until the age of thirteen.

17. *Shamash* (often pronounced "shammess" in Yiddish) = beadle

18. *Gabbai* = synagogue treasurer functionary, who, among other duties, collected contributions and organized the provision of charity to the needy

19. *Chevra kadisha* = burial society, whose members prepare bodies for burial

20. *Loimdei Torah* (Hebrew) = those who study Torah

21. *Bikkur choilim* = visiting the ill

22. *Hachnosas Kalla* = bridal fund to provide for the wedding of a bride from a poor family

23. *Minyan* = ten men (minimum number to form a quorum for a public prayer service). What may be meant is that for each of the daily prayer services each *shtiebl* had four sequential services, each attended regularly by about 10

distinct men; therefore on Sabbaths and holidays, when there was only a single service for the same number of men, the *shtiebls* were crowded.

24. Polish spelling: Drwęc

25. *Cheder* = school for young boys, whose curriculum consisted almost entirely of religious subjects

26. Rosh Hashana = Jewish New Year, which falls in September to early October

27. See map on pp. 8-9 of the reference cited in Footnote 1. The river separated the two towns, Golub on the Prussian ("German") side of the border and Dobrzyn on the Polish (Russian) side. In 1920 the two towns were united within the new Polish state.

28. *Tashlich* = a prayer recited near a body of water on Rosh Hashana (Jewish New Year). While reciting this prayer one symbolically casts one's sins into the water. See the following link: http://en.wikipedia.org/wiki/Tashlikh

29. *Aron koidesh* = Holy Ark, in which the Torah scrolls are stored, and from which they are removed to be read from during certain parts of the prayer services

30. *Poroiches* = curtain covering the ark, usually embroidered with artistic designs

31. *Bima* = synagogue platform from which the Torah is read, often located near the middle of the synagogue

32. *Yomim Noiroim* = Days of Awe, Rosh Hashana and Yom Kippur

33. *Unesaneh Toikef* = the first two words of a Hebrew liturgical poem, more than a thousand years old, recited on both Rosh Hashana and Yom Kippur, relating how God judges humanity on these days, as He decides "who shall live and who shall die..." See next two footnotes.

34. Hebrew "*Uveshoifor godoil yitoka...*". These are successive lines of the pocm *Unesaneh Toikef* (see previous footnote). The "small, silent voice" refers to the presence of God (see I Kings 19:12).

35. Hebrew "*Odom yesoidoi meofor vesoifoi leofor.*" This phrase is part of the poem *Unesaneh Toikef* (see previous two footnotes).

36. From p. 275 of reference cited in Footnote 1

37. From p. 277 of reference cited in Footnote 1

38. From p. 278 of reference cited in Footnote 1

[Page 279]

Memories of My Hometown Dobrzyn[1][2]

by Avraham Dor (Dobroszklanka)

Translated by Allen Flusberg

To the ruins of my birthplace Dobrzyn, which once was, but no longer exists, I dedicate the following memoir…

At first glance the town of Dobrzyn is no different from the many other provincial towns of Poland: a town square surrounded by streets and alleyways, densely built up, filled with large and small houses, some standing sturdily, and others on the verge of collapse. The Dreventz[3] River, flowing along the town's edge, constitutes a natural boundary between Germany and Russia. Pedestrians and wagons cross over the bridge spanning the river.

At the entrance to the town, coming along the road from Rypin, one can look up to see the historical Crusader castle that is located on the mountaintop. In it there is a museum that contains a collection of ancient objects having significant archeological value.

Villages, some tiny, lie scattered all around the town. They are populated by Polish farmers, who constitute the agricultural hinterland of the town, i.e. those who provide it with a livelihood.

With the exception of the road to Rypin, all the roads leading from the tiny villages into the town are unpaved. For this reason they are difficult to navigate during autumn because of the deep mud that the frequent rainfall brings. And in the town itself there are some small streets that are nearly impassable because of the deep mud. Many a time passersby would leave behind their galoshes, which they had been unable to extricate.

On the cold winter days, when snow fell and covered the streets with a thick layer that reached up to the windowsills, the residents would emerge to shovel the snow away from around the houses. Afterwards they would dig out a path to the shops, incidentally clearing the sidewalks of snow.

The winter season is hard on the ordinary people, who have to use their limited resources to stockpile food and fuel throughout the rest of the year. And when winter finally does end, the town comes back to life, awakening as if from a deep sleep, and begins to resume its normal routine.

For the young people, summer starts with *Majówka*[4], that is, May 1st, when they go on outings to the nearby forests. They gather strawberries, eating as many as they can and bringing home whatever is left. These outings are repeated several times during the summer.

Most of the young men of the town were unemployed. There were two reasons for it: First, there were no opportunities for work in the town. And second, even if there had been such opportunities, would it have been appropriate for a *balabatish*[5] Jewish boy to labor? In any event, this was the psychology of the parents in our small town 50 years ago.

And so it was a common occurrence in the small towns in general, and in Dobrzyn in particular, for families blessed with many children—some of whom were already grown up—that the adult children were living off their fathers. The father was the one and only source of livelihood for his entire family. Often he was just an ill and broken man, barely able to keep struggling, who was nevertheless carrying the burden of a household of more than ten people.

In our town there were "pious women," or—as they would be referred to nowadays—community volunteers, who helped the needy. Some were doing it for the sake of fulfilling a *mitzva*[6], while others were simply motivated by compassion. In both cases the main goal was the same, helping those in dire need.

The needy of the town fell into two categories: those who were known as poor people and took charity; and those who were still very far from even asking for charity. The second category included respectable families, craftsmen, small-time peddlers and businessmen who had become impoverished, either because of the boycott or as a result of the generally difficult economic situation. These were taken care of by a specific group of women who approached them in a tactful, honorable manner.

There were no professional beggars in the town. Even the well-known pair—Leibye and Shimye—who for many years would go from house to house on Fridays to collect alms, were greeted by most of the families in the town with smiling faces and sincere warmth. During the period of the Czar, a normal donation was a single groshen; and no sooner than someone handed them a kopeke would Leibye say, "What, are you trying to make fun of me?" For years on end they made their traditional Friday rounds of nearly all the houses of the town.

Typically, special market days—fairs— took place four or five times a year. At these times all the farmers of the region would stream into the town square with their goods. A day earlier the town would already be full of commotion, with everyone getting ready for the coming day. The used-clothing dealers would set up their stalls at the edge of the sidewalk, taking up a large fraction of the *Lange Gass*[7]. Here they would sell pants, coats and suits. The shoemakers also would lay their goods out for sale in the town square on this day on special tables that had been prepared a day in advance.

Thousands of farmers descended on the town on this day, some to sell and others to buy merchandise. They would fill the inns and bars; beer and vodka would flow like water. As evening fell and they began to leave town, many of them could be found lying drunk along the sides of the streets and on the sidewalks. Sometimes they had drunk away the entire sales price of a horse or a cow.

For the children these market days were especially joyous, since they could observe this great commotion that they would otherwise seldom see, and particularly since they would also get some "fair money".

And indeed on various other occasions and holidays the children were given many opportunities to play and have a good time. On Purim[8], for example, they would all be disguised in masks—"*Larves*"[9] as they were known in Dobrzyn—which could be purchased only at Yehoshua Meir Waldenberg's store. On *Lag BoOimer*[10] they would march around in the nearby forests, carrying bows made of branches, pulled taut with some string and supplied with a few wooden arrows. They would return home joyfully towards evening.

It was particularly interesting to see a wedding procession moving through the streets of the town as the bride and groom were led to the *huppa*[11] that was usually set up in the synagogue courtyard. Those accompanying them would be carrying lit candles, the children would be singing, and the adults would be dancing. As the saying went, when Dobrzyn makes a wedding all of the townspeople are *mechutonim*[12].

There was a long list of special town customs, specific to periods of joy and of grief, but with the passage of time many of them fell into disuse. There were those who saw this as progress, but traditions should, to some extent, be preserved.

Of course, with the destruction of Polish Jewry, the way of life of the small-town Jews disappeared, together with their customs and long traditions.

May these lines, dedicated to the town of Dobrzyn, remain as a memorial for future generations.

**Henya Drogen,
one of the first female socialists in Dobrzyn**[13]

Translator's Footnotes

1. From *My Town: In Memory of the Communities Dobrzyn-Gollob*, edited by M. Harpaz, (published by the Dobrzyn-Golub Society, Israel, 1969), pp. 279-282.

2. Note by translator: A Hebrew version of this Yiddish article appears on pp. 59-62 under the title "Daily Life in the Town"; see the English translation of that article. The Hebrew appears to be a translation of the Yiddish. The small differences between the two articles are reflected in the two English translations.

3. Polish spelling: Drwęc (pronounced Dreventz)

4. Majówka = Polish holiday (May Day) at the beginning of May. See the following link (retrieved May, 2014):
http://en.wikipedia.org/wiki/Public_holidays_in_Poland

5. *balabatish* = respectable (Yiddish)

6. *mitzva* = commandment, in this case the requirement by Jewish law to care for the poor and needy

7. *Lange Gass* = "Long Street" (official Polish name: Pilsudskiego), the main street of the town. See map on pp. 8-9 of reference cited in Footnote 1.

8. Purim = a joyful holiday commemorating the survival of the Jews of Persia after being threatened with destruction by their enemies, according to the account in the Biblical Book of Esther. It occurs in February or March, one month before Passover, and is celebrated with costumes and disguises.

9. *Larve* (German) = mask

10. *Lag BoOimer* = A minor holiday on the 33rd day after Passover, celebrated with outings in forests, as well as archery and other sports.

11. huppa = wedding canopy

12. *Mechutonim* = in-laws, i.e. partaking relatives.

13. From p. 280 of reference cited in Footnote 1

[Page 285]

The Community and its Institutions

Religious Life in Dobrzyn[1]

by Rabbi Shlomo Dzialdow and Rabbi Nathan Sanger
Translated by Allen Flusberg

Jewish social life in the Polish cities and towns was generally multi-variegated and also quite dynamic. There were factions, parties and social institutions, around which the various groups of Jewish society were concentrated.

In some cities, for example, the Zionist movement made its imprint, thereby affecting a large fraction of the Jewish population; whereas in other places, especially the smaller cities, religious life influenced the local Jewish inhabitants. Clearly in the latter case the individual who stood at the forefront of the religious camp—first and foremost the rabbi, who had to be the spiritual guide of the people of the community—played a major role.

In the last few decades great Torah scholars officiated as rabbis of Dobrzyn. The first of them was Rabbi Dovid Ber Toib[2] z.tz.l.[3], author of the book *Binyan Dovid*. After the death of their previous *rebbe*, *Rebbe*[4] Yechiel[5] z.tz.l., the Aleksander[6] Hassidim asked him to be *Rebbe* Yechiel's successor, but he did not come forward to fulfill their request.

After Rabbi Toib came Rabbi Sonabend. After Rabbi Sonabend passed away the office of rabbi was not occupied for a long time. Instead the position was taken by the *dayan*[7], Rabbi Hertz z.l.[8], a native of Dobrzyn, who was the author of the books *Minchas Yehuda* and *Yehal-Or*.

After his death Rabbi Blumberg arrived. He was the last rabbi of Dobrzyn.

And because great Torah scholars served as rabbis of Dobrzyn, the city attracted young scholars from the surrounding cities, thereby becoming a center for Torah study and Hassidism.

There, in Dobrzyn, there were Hassidim who had actually journeyed to see[9] the first *rebbe* of Ger[10], Rabbi Yitzchak Meir Alter[11], the "*Hiddushei HoRim*"[12]. After him the Hassidim journeyed to see the *rebbe* Rabbi Arye-Leib[13], the *Sefas Emes* (the name of his book, which is also now the name borne by the Ger Yeshiva in Jerusalem). And still later, they journeyed to see his son, Rabbi Avrohom-Mordechai[14], who, incidentally, was involved, in his own way, in building up the Land [of Israel][15].

Other Hassidim had made the pilgrimage to see the older Varker [*rebbe*], Rabbi Yitzchak Kalish[16], who had once been a student of *Rebbe* Bunim of Pshiskhe[17]. The Varker was a lyrical-wistful *rebbe*; his type of Hassidism relied on pure human love, which necessarily leads to love of fellow Jews[18].

[Page 286]

Synagogues and Hassidic Prayer Houses

The following Jewish Houses of Worship were located in Dobrzyn: (1) the Large Synagogue; (2) the *Beis Medresh*[19]; (3) the Large *Shtiebl*[20]; (4) the Small Ger *Shtiebl*; (5) the Aleksander *Shtiebl*; and (6) the Otvotzke[21] *Shtiebl*.

After World War I there was also a yeshiva in Dobrzyn. The students were from Dobrzyn and from the surrounding cities, as well: Rypin, Szeps, Lipno, and Lubicz. The yeshiva students who were not from Dobrzyn were provided with meals[22] in the homes of various Dobrzyn residents. The day the yeshiva opened its doors was very emotional. The yeshiva, which started with 11 students, was named "Yavne"; one of the speakers at the inauguration of the school stated, among other things, that the name "Yavne" signified "Eleven boys were sanctified today", for which "Yavne" was an acronym.

We have heard that before World War I there was also a large yeshiva in Dobrzyn (details of which can be obtained from members of the older Dobrzyn generation, such as R.[23] Yaakov Wrzos and Yechiel Bielawski in Israel). [In addition there was] a large, beautiful yeshiva "Yesoidei HaToirah" with a large number of classrooms, in a building of its own, where they studied secular subjects, as well. There was also a Jewish public school that had a building of its own; there they attended school on Sunday instead of on the Sabbath. The

"Yesoidei HaToirah" yeshiva had been established immediately after World War I, when the "*Tifferes Shmuel*"[24] was summering in Dobrzyn; on his incentive money was raised through his two Hassidic followers, the brothers Mr. Mendl and R. Avrohom Hirsh Kohn[25], h.y.d.[26]. The last principal of "Yesoidei HaToirah" was R. Yechiel Meir Gutmorgen h.y.d.; his wife h.y.d. was the head of the beautiful, large girls' school "Beis Yaakov", with many classrooms—also in Dobrzyn.

In the vicinity of Dobrzyn there were numerous estates that were owned by Jews. On one of the estates there was a training camp for the pioneers who immigrated to our Holy Land. The owner of this estate was R. Yitzchak Yaakov Szmiga[27], a dedicated Aleksander Hassid. Here it should be pointed out what he used to customarily do with his wealth: every year, immediately after the holidays[28], wagons of his, loaded with potatoes, grain and firewood, would quietly enter Dobrzyn, where their contents were distributed to the needy. From his family his daughter Genya has survived; she lives in Argentina with her husband, Yechiel Lopata, and their children.

As can be seen, Dobrzyn was a city of institutions of Torah and charity. These institutions required member volunteers to faithfully take care of the needs of the community[29]. And we see it as our duty to recollect, to the best of our memories, those particular people and to mention them by name; for with their communal work they raised our city of Dobrzyn to a high spiritual level.

In the Large Synagogue, which stood at the edge of the city, they conducted the morning prayer service daily at dawn; on Sabbaths and holidays it was packed. The *gabbai*[30] of the synagogue was R. Binyomin Yosef (Yosef Binyomin) Gonsher[31]. The cantor of the synagogue was Rabbi Dialap, who at the same time was also a *shochet*. Aside from R. Binyomin Yosef there were two other slaughterers: R. Nesanel Sochaczewski h.y.d., from Czechoczinek, who was the son-in-law of the previous *shochet*[32], R. Yaakov Rozental z.l.; and R. Mendl Garfinkel z.l., who was the son of R. Yitzchok Meir Garfinkel z.l.

In the *Beis Medresh*, which was located not far from the *mikve*[33] and the slaughterhouse, numerous *minyonim*[34] met for prayer on a daily basis. The gabbai of the *Beis Medresh* was Mr. Freilich (a tailor). In the synagogue and in the *Beis Medresh* they would hold prayer services only. But by contrast in the Hassidic *shtiebls* they not only held daily prayer services, but also studied. This was a place of Torah; studying Torah developed there as an activity because many of those attending the services were learned. They set up daily classes where they studied various Talmudic tractates in depth, including also the *daf yomi*[35].

The *gabbai* of the Large Ger *Shtiebl* was R. Hillel Ovadya Goldbrach h.y.d. The learned men who took turns leading the classes were: R. Yaakov Rozental z.l., a *shochet* and *bodek*[36]; R. Elly Yosef Dzialdow z.l. (his son, Rabbi Shlomo Dzialdow, lives in Frankfurt, where he works as a *shochet*); R. Itsche Meir Garfinkel z.l.; R. Hersh Ber Berman h.y.d.; R. Meir Henich Teitelboim h.y.d.; and others. The Torah reader was R. Yisroel Asher Wrzos z.l., and after his death R. Yaakov Henich Dratwa h.y.d. Those who led the services on the High Holy Days were the following: for the *Musof*[37] service, the *shochet* R. Yaakov Rozental z.l.; later R. Avrohom Flusberg[38] n.y.[39]; and last R. Yisroel Miller h.y.d. Those who led the *Shacharis*[40] service were: Mr. Avrohom Yitzchok Holtz z.l. (who died in America). R. Elly Flusberg[41] h.y.d. had the task of calling men up to the Torah[42] (his son, R. Boruch Mendel Flusberg n.y., resides in Israel with his wife Henye, daughter of R. Chayim Yanuar h.y.d.).

Incidentally it is worth noting what an exceptional memory R. Elly Flusberg h.y.d. had. In the Large Ger *Shtiebl* about 8 *minyonim* met for prayer services every Sabbath, and he remembered the *Yahrzeit* of each and every one of the participants. When it was time to call people up to the Torah he knew who had precedence to be called up, i.e. he knew who was going to observe a *Yahrzeit*[43] during the following week[44]. When I observed a *Yahrzeit* for the first time for my departed father z.l., the 4th of Tammuz, 5685[45], he [Flusberg] informed me that the anniversary of this date would never fall on a Sabbath, Tuesday or Thursday[46].

In the Small Ger *Shtiebl* the *gabbai* and Torah reader was R. Shoul Prager h.y.d. (Until half a year ago his son, Nachum [Norbert] Prager, who left Dobrzyn for Germany 50 years ago, lived in Hanover, where he served as head of the congregation, cantor and Torah reader.)

The people who prayed in the Ger *Shtiebl* were not involved in Torah and Hassidism only; they were active in social and political life, as well. Thus, for example, the highly regarded community volunteer R. Yechiel Meir Gutmorgen h.y.d. was the director of the Agudah Bank, the manager of the Yesoidei HaToirah yeshiva, and the chairman of Agudas Yisroel[47]. The *shtiebl* youth organized themselves in the "Young Agudas Yisroel," in which they were vigorously active. Their secretary was the young man Yisroel Meir Piechotke h.y.d., and the following were among those who served on the committee:

Boruch Goldfinger, Mendl Lewkowicz, Zalman Yendziewicz, Moishe Icze Miller, as well as others.

The *gabbai* of the Aleksander *Shtiebl* was R. Yaakov Yehoshua Kufler h.y.d. Among those that prayed there the following were particularly conspicuous: R. Yehoshua Chaim Minsky z.l., a *shochet* and *bodek* (he passed away in Jerusalem, where he last resided); R. Zalman Chossid Rozenwaks z.l.; R. Leibl Lipsztadt (within his family his daughter Manya survived; she lives in America with her husband, Bolek Zeidner from Lipno, and their child); and R. Chaim Yanuar h.y.d. R. Meir Kohn z.l. was a very interesting figure who was very learned. He began his Hassidic life as a follower of the younger Vurker *rebbe*[48] Z.tz.vk.l.[49] and at the end he was a follower of the "*Yismach Yisroel*"[50] Z.tz.vk.l. Despite the fact that he was constantly sitting and studying—and quite literally his Torah study never left his lips[51]— he raised his two sons to be in his business under the name *Meir Kohn and Sons*. It is noteworthy that the "*Yismach Yisroel*" said of him that he clearly knew the entire *Mogen Avrohom*[52] by heart. His son, R. Mendl Kohn h.y.d., who was known in the Hassidic world as R. Mendl Dobzhinsker, was also a great personality. He truly fulfilled "let your home be freely open,"[53] and he merited Torah and greatness in a single place—his business expanded, and yet he did not neglect "you shall contemplate it day and night."[54] He also played a major role in community work: he was the *parnas*[55] of the community, a court alderman and at the same time an alderman of the city council. His bearing and his bearded countenance[56] elicited great respect, even from the Gentiles. From his family[57] only two sons survived, Yechezkel and Yaakov Kohn, who today live in Israel. R. Mendl Kohn's son-in-law, Rabbi Nathan Sanger, drained the bitter cup to the dregs. He lost his wife Nentshe and his two sons, Yitzhak Dov and Meir h.y.d.

His [Mendl Kohn's] brother, Avrohom Hirsh Kohn[58] z.l.—despite his Western dress and his wide connections in the business world, on a colossal scale—was a fiery and dedicated Aleksander Hassid; he never missed accompanying the Aleksander *rebbes* when they travelled abroad for treatment. In the years 1924-25 the Agudas Yisroel nominated him as a candidate for the Polish parliament. In 1925 he took his first trip to Israel, where he immediately founded a company to build a large factory for the manufacture of bricks. He merited immigrating there with part of his family before the Destruction.

Other very interesting figures among the Aleksander Hassidim were: R. Yehoshua Waldenberg h.y.d., the head of the Jewish community of Dobrzyn;

and the *mohel*[59] R. Shmuel Moshe Roine h.y.d. They occupied a respectable place in Jewish society and were worthy defenders of Jewish dignity. A son of R. Zalman Chossid Rozenwaks z.l. is in Israel—he is R. Yehuda Rozenwaks, who lives in Holon. A son-in-law of R. Hirsh Ber Berman h.y.d. is also in Israel—he is R. Yaakov Yechiel Bielawski of Tel Aviv.

[Page 290]

*

September, 1939. The German forces crossed the border. The Polish skies were filled with Hitler airplanes, sowing death and destruction. The first victims were the Jews who were on the German-Polish border.

Very soon after the occupation, on *Rosh Hashana*, a portion of the Jewish population of Dobrzyn was seized and sent away towards Germany. And on *Sukkos* 40 distinguished families from among those who remained were rounded up; they, too, were taken out of the city by the murderers. After that at first glance it did get quieter; Jewish life was becoming stable again a little at a time. But no—immediately afterwards, on the 11th of November, 200 members of the Gestapo appeared and gathered in the town square, their guns loaded. The provincial government ordered the leader of the Jewish community to appear and then demanded that the entire Jewish population vacate the city immediately. Among the Jews a panic ensued. To reverse the evil decree a group of Jews went out into the city, going from door to door to collect money, silver candlesticks, wedding rings and other valuables; they brought all of it to the Gestapo. The Hitler-murderers gladly appropriated it, but all of this did not prevent the expulsion from Dobrzyn. Several days later the city had become *judenrein*.

The Jewish population of Dobrzyn shared the bitter fate of all the Jews of Poland.

[Page 291]

*

May this humble account serve as a monument upon the sown graves of the great Torah scholars, their disciples, those who were active in the community, and the entire Jewish population.

There was once a vibrant Jewish town of Dobrzyn that is...no more.

A group of young men, who were from Dobrzyn, in America[60]

Talmud-Torah school in Dobrzyn-Dreventz[61]

Translator's Footnotes

1. From *My Town: In Memory of the Communities Dobrzyn-Gollob*, edited by M. Harpaz, (published by the Dobrzyn-Golub Society, Israel, 1969), pp. 284-291.

2. In the following link he is referred to as "David Dov Ber Taub, who from 1880 served [as rabbi] in Dubzhin (Dobrzyn)," and was also rabbi of a town named Koniecpol. The link is: http://www.jewishgen.org/yizkor/pinkas_poland/pol1_00233.htm.

3. z.tz.l. = *zeicher tzaddik livrocho* (Hebrew) = may the memory of the righteous be a blessing

4. *Rebbe* = religious spiritual leader of Hassidic group

5. Yechiel Dancyger (1828-1894)

6. Alexander (or Aleksander) is the name of a Hassidic group that had many adherents in Dobrzyn. See the following link: http://en.wikipedia.org/wiki/Aleksander_(Hasidic_dynasty)

7. *Dayan* = judge in Jewish religious court

8. z.l. = *zichroinoi livrocho* (Hebrew) = of blessed memory

9. "Journeying to see" refers to a trip taken by a follower of a *rebbe* to the *rebbe*'s court, to be exposed to his preaching and obtain a private interview—often to ask for a blessing and for personal guidance.

10. Ger = a Hassidic group that had many adherents in Dobrzyn

11. Yitzchak Meir Alter (1799-1866) was the first *rebbe* of Ger. See the following link: http://en.wikipedia.org/wiki/Yitzchak_Meir_Alter

12. *Hiddushei HoRIM* (= Innovations of the RIM, acronym for Rabbi Itzchak Meir). For many generations it has been common for a respected rabbinical author to be renamed, by popular acclaim, after the title of his best work, which often contains an allusion to his name.

13. Arye Leib Alter (1847-1905), who succeeded Yitzchak Meir Alter as *rebbe* of Ger

14. Avrohom Mordechai Alter (1866-1948), who fled from Poland to Palestine in 1940, after the Nazi invasion of Poland. See the following link: http://en.wikipedia.org/wiki/Avraham_Mordechai_Alter.

15. After visiting Palestine several times in the 1920s, he began encouraging his wealthier followers to immigrate there. His son-in-law (and devoted follower) Yitzhak Meir Levine was a signatory of Israel's Declaration of Independence and served in the Knesset for the first few years of the State.

16. Israel Yitzhak Kalish of Warka, 1779-1848. He was called the Varker (or Vurkcr) *rebbe*. Scc thc following link: http://en.wikipedia.org/wiki/Israel_Yitzhak_Kalish

17. Rebbe Bunim died in 1827. Pshiskhe is the Yiddish name of the Polish town of Przysucha.

18. "Love of fellow Jews" in the sense of the commandment "Thou shalt love thy neighbor as thyself" (Lev. 19:18).

19. *Beis medresh* = study hall, where men sit at tables to study religious books, and prayer services are sometimes held, as well. But see below, where it is stated that this *Beis Medresh* was actually used exclusively for prayer services.

20. *Shtiebl* = a small synagogue consisting of a single prayer room; usually Hassidic

21. Otwotzke = from the town of Otwock in Poland. See the following link: http://en.wikipedia.org/wiki/Amshinov_%28Hasidic_dynasty%29

22. Yiddish *gegesen teg*. They would follow a weekly schedule, going from one home to another for meals.

23. The abbreviation 'ר, here translated as "R.", usually stands for *Reb*, meaning "Mr."., although it can also stand for Rabbi.

24. "*Tifferes Shmuel*" = Shmuel Tzvi Dancyger, an Aleksander *rebbe*, who died in 1924. *Tifferes Shmuel* is the name of a book he wrote (see Footnote 12). See the following link:
http://en.wikipedia.org/wiki/Aleksander_%28Hasidic_dynasty%29

25. A photograph of Avrohom Hirsh Kohn, together with his family, appears on p. 190 of the reference cited in Footnote 1. For a photograph of Mendl Kohn, see p. 192 of the same reference.

26. h.y.d. = *Hashem yikoim domoi/domo/domom* (Hebrew) = May God avenge his/her/their blood, referring throughout this article to victims who were murdered in the Holocaust

27. A photograph of Szmiga appears on p. 316 of reference cited in Footnote 1

28. *Rosh Hashana* (New Year), *Yom Kippur* (Day of Atonement), *Sukkos* (Tabernacles), and *Shemini Atzeres/Simchas Toirah* (8th-Day Assembly/Rejoicing of the Law) occur one after the other during a period of 3 weeks in September-October.

29. *Oiskim betzorchei tzibur be'emuno* (Hebrew). A special prayer for these community volunteers, utilizing this Hebrew phrase, is recited in the synagogue every Sabbath.

30. *Gabbai* = synagogue treasurer functionary, who, among other duties, collected contributions and organized the provision of charity to the needy

31. Polish spelling: Gąsior

32. *Shochet* = ritual slaughterer

33. *Mikve* = ritual bath

34. *Minyen* (plural *minyonim*) = quorum of at least 10 men coming together for prayer service

35. *Daf yomi* = "daily page" of the Babylonian Talmud, studied by all participants worldwide on the same day, so that study of the entire Talmud is completed by them in unison every seven years.

36. *bodek* = inspector of slaughtered meat for blemishes that would render it not kosher

37. *Musof* = supplemental prayer service for holidays, recited after completion of the *Shacharis* (morning) service

38. A photograph of Avrohom Flusberg appears on p. 72 of the reference cited in Footnote 1.

39. n.y. = *neroi yoir*, equivalent to "may he live a long life", often appended when others who have died are mentioned in the same context

40. *Shacharis* = morning prayer service

41. A photograph of Eliyahu (Elly) Flusberg and his family appears on p. 139 of the reference cited in Footnote 1.

42. Each man called up recites blessings before and after his Torah section is read

43. *Yahrzeit* = anniversary of death of close relatives

44. By custom, precedence to be called up is given to those who are about to observe a *Yahrzeit* for a close relative, with the closest departed blood relatives (e.g. either parent) providing the greatest precedence.

45. Summer of 1925

46. The Jewish calendar's rules of intercalation prevents the 1st of Tishri from occurring on a Sunday, Wednesday or Friday. The number of days between the 4th of Tammuz and the following 1st of Tishri is always 85 days, i.e. 12 whole weeks and 1 day. Therefore the 4th of Tammuz always occurs on the weekday preceding that of the following 1st of Tishri and can never fall on a Saturday, Tuesday or Thursday.

47. Agudas Yisroel = the ultra-orthodox organization that was established in 1912 to strengthen Orthodox institutions independent of the religious Zionists. See the following link: http://en.wikipedia.org/wiki/World_Agudath_Israel

48. Menachem Mendel Kalish (died 1868), a son of the "older" Vurker *rebbe* (see Footnote 16). See the following link: http://solitude-hisbodedus.blogspot.com/2009/10/meaning-of-echad-oneness.html.

49. z.tz.vk.l. = *Zeicher Tzaddik Vekodoish Livrocho* (Hebrew) = may the memory of the righteous and holy man be a blessing

50. *Yismach Yisroel* = Yerachmiel Yisroel Yitzhak Dancyger (died 1910), an Aleksander *rebbe*, whose most famous book was entitled *Yismach Yisroel*. See Footnote 24 for link to a more detailed account.

51. *Lo pasak pumay migirsa* (Aramaic) = his mouth never ceased reciting what he had been studying

52. *Mogen Avrohom* = a 17th-century commentary, written by Abraham Gombiner, on the 16th-century code of Jewish law, the *Shulchan Aruch*.

53. *Pirkei Avot* (Ethics of the Fathers) 1:5. The adage means that one should allow people (particularly the poor) to come and go freely into one's home.

54. Joshua 1:8. The verse reads "This book of the Torah shall not depart from your mouth, and you shall contemplate it day and night, so that you will take care to do all that is written in it; for then you shall be successful..."

55. *Parnas* = well-to-do lay leader

56. Yiddish / Hebrew *hadras ponim.* His photograph appears on p. 192 of the reference cited in Footnote 1.

57. A photograph of his sons appears on p. 265 of the reference cited in Footnote 1.

58. See Footnote 25

59. *Mohel* = One who performs Jewish ritual circumcision professionally

60. From p. 284 in reference cited in Footnote 1

61. From p. 291 in reference cited in Footnote 1

[Pages 292-294]

Institutions and Parties in Dobrzyn[1]

By Sara Groner–Krantz

Translated by Allen Flusberg

A warm–hearted, good town with benevolent, kindhearted people, devoted to one another heart and soul. Never envious, nor begrudging each other. Mutual help was one of the highest qualities of the town. Everyone was glad to be able to do someone a favor. For example, only a small number of people in the town had newspapers, but whoever didn't could borrow one from someone else at home; and it would even come with a small glass of tea and a slice of cake.

There were no great scholars in the town, but the generation after the First World War looked for ways to improve themselves in middle and higher education. The most important cultural institution of the town was its library, which had been founded covertly during the Czarist regime and continued to exist in secret until the outbreak of the war in 1914; it was not officially sanctioned until the German occupation. There were thousands of books, both fiction and nonfiction, in the library. After finishing reading the first volume of a novel, many a reader would wait impatiently for the second volume that was still in someone else's possession. There was generally a great thirst for culture among the working young people, who strove to broaden their knowledge and horizons in various directions, so that they could take part in discussions or scientific talks that were often held in the library or in the workers' clubs. The members of these clubs were extremely interested in these discussions and talks, and the circle of participants and audience continued to expand.

With the outbreak of the First World War the general situation in the town declined. The Germans were not so cruel in those days; still, they did not have good relations with the populace. They took men for forced labor and sent them far away; the burden of supporting their wives and children fell on the town, which was, as is natural in a time of war, in difficult economic straits. True, no one died from hunger, Heaven forbid, but the repressive inclination of the German regime towards the Jews put the town in a state of fear that was palpable in daily life.

The famous expulsion of 1914, the first year of the World War, was accompanied by earnest threats of mass murder. Even before the expulsion the Jewish populace had felt the heavy-handed pressure of the German occupation, but the expulsion shattered their morale and broke them physically and economically. We then lived through several difficult months, kept far from home under harsh economic conditions. Only after the first "pioneers" went back to Dobrzyn and gave us a feeling of relief did a large number of us begin to return home. And after a short time the town more or less went back to normalcy.

Dobrzyn was blessed with parties, the largest and strongest of which was the Zionist party, which already before the First World War had delegated Mr. Feibish Lipka as its elected representative to the Zionist Congress. Other parties were very active as well, among them the *Poalei–Tziyon*[2], which also had a youth organization, "Borochov"[3]. The activity by the "Bund" was more limited. Each of these parties followed its own ideals, but all had one objective in common: forging a fully conscious youth.

After the First World War a powerful movement— or more properly stated, pressure —to emigrate began. Some of the youth, as well as entire families, that already at the beginning of Polish rule foresaw the difficulties in making a living under this regime, sought to leave the little town. The deeply rooted Polish anti–Semitism began producing more and more enmity of the Jews, expressing itself in a general boycott that robbed dozens of families of their livelihood.

One of these was my own family: we felt as if the rug was being pulled out from under us. At our first opportunity we left the town and went to America. Several other families left at the same time, among them Shlesinger, Plotniarz, and others.

In this way the Dobrzyn era of my life came to an end. I departed from Dobrzyn with a heavy heart, shedding many tears as I left behind my best and closest friends. I left the town I loved and held dear but have never seen again. All signs of its Jewish presence have been erased forever.

May these lines serve as a memorial over the ruins of erstwhile Dobrzyn.

The "Shamna veSolta"[4] of the Dobrzyn youth.
Center: Mendel Sonabend.[5]

Translator's Footnotes

1. From *My Town: In Memory of the Communities Dobrzyn–Gollob*, edited by M. Harpaz, (published by the Dobrzyn–Golub Society, Israel, 1969), pp. 292–294.

2. *Poalei–Tzion* = Workers of Zion (Hebrew), or Zionist Workers, a Jewish Marxist–Zionist party. See the following Web site, retrieved July 2014, for more information: http://en.wikipedia.org/wiki/Poale_Zion.

3. Named after Ber Borochov, a founder of the *Poalei–Tzion* party who died in 1917. See the following Web site, retrieved July 2014, for additional information: http://en.wikipedia.org/wiki/Ber_Borochov

4. *Shamna veSolta* (Hebrew), literally "its oil and its flour", expression (based on Lev. 2:2) loosely translated as "the best and finest"

5. From p. 294 in reference cited in Footnote 1

[Pages 295-297]

The Active Members of the Community[1]

by Charles L. Graner, New York
Translated by Allen Flusberg

Memories from more than 50 years ago take me back to Dobrzyn, and I find myself leafing through the history of the former community and its leading active members.

In that period the most distinguished community leaders of the town were R.[2] Feibish Lipka and R. Chanina Sender Graner. Since the former was a very wealthy person whose many businesses kept him very occupied, the entire burden of community work fell upon R. Chanina Sender, who, by contrast, was not preoccupied with business; he had no concerns about his livelihood, since he had a great deal of rental income from several houses that he owned.

He was not a Hassid; he attended the synagogue, where every single Sabbath he stood on the *bima*[3] and distributed *aliyes*[4] to the congregants in some sequential order, following his own system. He was not influenced by anyone, and in this way he held sway over his empire in the synagogue for years without any controversy or disagreements, having behind him the full backing and support of the congregants.

For many years the wooden fence encompassing the Jewish cemetery had served as a source of heating fuel for the local Polish population, to warm their homes, so that over the years it was almost completely demolished. Cattle were coming in to graze around the graves. The Jews of the town viewed this as disrespectful, a disgrace to the dead, and they demanded of the community leaders that they do something to end this sorrowful situation. Thanks to the initiative of R. Chanina Sender Graner, a fund was established to erect a new fence around the cemetery, a brick wall. Every day, over a period of a full year, he would walk over to the cemetery right after morning prayers to check the workmanship and make sure that it was being done properly. At this opportunity a connecting room was also constructed for *tzidduk hadin*[5], and a place was built for the cemetery watchman to live in.

R. Chanina Sender Graner fashioned many other things that the town needed. In his old age, when he was no longer able to be active, his son, Yaakov Leib Graner, acted as his representive. Yaakov Leib was already more limited. He was a flour merchant, well known among the merchants, and he supplied flour to a large fraction of the town's bakeries. He, too, was devoted to the community, just as his father had been in earlier times. With his effective help the *Chevra Kadisha*[6] was established; it was headed by R. Eliyohu Scheinbart, a well-known merchant who exported grain to Germany. The head *gabbai*[7] was Hershke "R.Wolf's". His actual family name was Landau, but no one knew him by that name. (In those days there were many townsmen who were known by their nicknames; not many people even knew what their official family names were.)

R. Yaakov Leib Graner helped found the institute "*Hachnosas Kalla*"[8], which helped many poor families of the town marry off their daughters. It was chaired by R. Yaakov Kirschner, and the second *gabbai*[9] was R. Leib Schlachter, a refined, modest resident of the town. The members were Tzodoik Hersh Tzidkewicz, Shlomo Elya Plocker, Avrohom Mendel Shefer, Tuvia Wolf Pieniek, Yitzchok Kohn, and Shimon Graner. The latter was also a *baal koirei*[10]; he read the Torah in the *polush*[11] located at the entrance to the Large Synagogue.

At the synagogue there was an association called "*Chevra Bachurim*"[12]. Its members were organized by profession: shoemakers, tailors, hatmakers, and others. Their mission was to provide the poor of the town with fuel for the winter. Sometimes they also provided food for the wandering poor. It is worth noting that not a single poor person of Dobrzyn ever left the town to seek his bread somewhere else; the town provided him with the basic necessities. The kindheartedness of the Dobrzyn Jews has been spoken of for generations, and this benevolence has not been extinguished to this very day.

**Shimon Yosef Plotniarz, Chicago,
during the speech he made at a reception in Tel-Aviv**

Translator's Footnotes

1. From *My Town: In Memory of the Communities Dobrzyn-Gollob*, edited by M. Harpaz, (published by the Dobrzyn-Golub Society, Israel, 1969), pp. 295-297.

2. R. = *Reb*, an honorific, comparable to the English "Mr."

3. *Bima* (Hebrew) = synagogue platform from which the Torah is read, often located near the middle of the synagogue. The person who distributes aliyes (see next footnote) stands on the bima next to the Torah, calling up each recipient of this honor by name just before a section is read.

4. *Aliye* or *Aliya* (Hebrew) = being "called up" to the Torah to recite blessings before and after a section of the Torah is read. Every Sabbath, 8 men (and sometimes a few more) are called up for an *aliye*. Determining who is selected to get an aliye on any given Sabbath and which *aliye* he gets can become a bone of contention.

5. *Tziduk hadin* = (Hebrew: justification of the [Divine] decree), a prayer recited by the bereaved mourners immediately after the deceased is buried. For details see the following link (retrieved July, 2015): http://www.jewish-funeral-guide.com/tradition/justification.htm

6. *Chevra kadisha* (Aramaic) = burial society, whose members prepare bodies for burial

7. *Gabbai* = usually the synagogue treasurer functionary; but here the term appears to refer to a secondary functionary of the organization

8. *Hachnosas kalla* (Hebrew) = bridal fund to provide for the wedding of a bride from a poor family

9. See footnote 7.

10. *baal koirei* (Hebrew) = the person who every Sabbath chants the appropriate section of the Torah as he reads it from a Torah scroll, a difficult task that requires memorizing and practicing, since the words are written with no punctuation, no vocalization marks, and no chanting notes.

11. *Polush* = antechamber or vestibule, here used as an additional prayer room in which an independent prayer service is conducted

12. *Chevra bachurim* (Hebrew) = Society of Young Men

[Pages 298-299]

The Establishment of the *Bund* in Dobrzyn[1]

By Yaakov Gorny
Translated by Allen Flusberg

In 1916, while the First World War was raging, a group of comrades came up with the idea to organize a *Bund*[2] party in Dobrzyn. Comrade Hersh Asher Gottlieb, who was known for his socialist leanings, approached me with a proposal to take part in the establishment of a *Bund* party in Dobrzyn. I agreed, and soon we were covertly contacting additional comrades, whose outlooks were known, to invite them to a meeting.

The meeting place was in Kalinowski's house, in a tiny room up in the attic that served as Hersh Asher's bachelor apartment. In this room there stood a wooden chest, an iron bed with a straw mattress, a bench, and a little chair—this, more or less, was all the furniture in the room.

The following seven comrades attended this meeting: Yechiel Zisshoif [sic][3], Yechiel Krulik, Chaim David Braun, Meir[4] Mendelson, Binyamin Isser Nowalski, Fishel Baruch Smuzyk, and Moshe Golomb.

Since everything was being done secretly and conspiratorially, we were compelled to make sure that the neighbors would not notice us as we entered the little room. This was not so easy—one at a time we had to climb up a ladder to another attic, from which we entered the room one by one.

After we had covered the small window with a blanket, Hersh Asher bent down over the bed and pulled a written proclamation out from under the mattress. With great reverence he proceeded to read it out loud slowly, word for word, as we all listened attentively. And afterwards Hersh Asher added some remarks of his own.

On the spot we elected a committee, with Hersh Asher Gottlieb as chairman, Yechiel Zissholtz—secretary; and Yaakov Gorny—in charge of organization and finances.

We immediately began trying to influence the cultural institutions of the town, especially the library, in a positive way. Indeed, our membership expanded rapidly, and in a short time the *Bund* became a force of consequence.

Once Poland achieved independence, the *Bund*, now a legal party, became active in uplifting the impoverished masses of the town. It provided them with an elementary education and with social support. It was the *Bund* that established the town's first drama group, which often performed classical Yiddish plays.

The activity of the *Bund* was received well and was a boon to the indigent masses of the town.

Golda Tinsky together with her children[5]

Translator's Footnotes

1. From *My Town: In Memory of the Communities Dobrzyn-Gollob*, edited by M. Harpaz, (published by the Dobrzyn-Golub Society, Israel, 1969), pp. 298-299.

2. The *Bund* was an evolving Jewish socialist/Marxist organization that supported cultural autonomy for the Jews within the countries of Eastern Europe, rather than a homeland in Palestine. It also favored Yiddish, rather than Hebrew, as the cultural language of the Jews. See the following links: http://en.wikipedia.org/wiki/Bundism; http://www.yivoencyclopedia.org/article.aspx/Bund.

3. The spelling "Zisshoif" appears to be a misprint. Below and throughout the Hebrew translation of this article (p. 98 of the reference cited in Footnote 1) his name is given as Zissholtz.

4. In the Hebrew translation of this article (p. 98 of the reference cited in Footnote 1), his first name is given as "Yair", rather than "Meir".

5. From p. 299 of reference cited in Footnote 1.

[Pages 300-304]

The Struggle for Education in the Town[1]

By Yaakov Wrzos

Translated by Allen Flusberg

In the following I would like to transcribe some of my memories from my youth in Dobrzyn—various episodes of events, facts and experiences that are deeply ingrained in my memory.

I recall that around the time that we founded an association in Dobrzyn, *Tifferet Bachurim*[2]—which dealt primarily with religious renewal—we celebrated the completion of a Torah scroll at the home of Mr. Yitzchak Lichtenfeld. The principal participants were: Azriel Elya Lichtenfeld, Daniel Miller, Avraham Yaakov Rozenwaks, the Fogel brothers, and the author of this article.

Once the very last letter had been handwritten on the scroll, off we went to the synagogue, where hundreds of Jews were already gathered. The choir and the orchestra greeted us with "Halleluya", as the audience sang along; we drank a *l'chayim* toast, followed by some cake; and then we proceeded to dance joyfully, as is customary everywhere by Jews on such an occasion.

Several years later we founded a different association, for social welfare: its function was to support the needy of the town. We compiled a list of about 200 households that we taxed at a monthly rate of 25 kopeks. We, the members of the association, collected this payment every month. With this money we bought potatoes and heating coals. Every needy family received a monthly stipend of 50 kg of potatoes and 50 kg of coal during the winter months. Clearly this particular form of support did not go very far in addressing the general issue of the prevailing social conditions, but to some extent communal volunteers and charitable housewives were providing for the needy in other ways, thereby supplementing our effort.

At the beginning of the 20th century a thirst for culture inspired a group of us young men—among them Azriel Sachs, Shlomo Hartbrot, Shmuel Prum, Avraham Zudkewicz, Chaim Wolf Rappaport and the present author—to involve ourselves in making it possible to found a library in Dobrzyn. In those days this was not a very easy task. The Russian regime was trying to avoid as much as possible the spread of education and culture—especially via an authorized library—within the non-Russian provinces of its large empire. Although each of us did have a few books, which we would exchange with one another, that did not weaken our resolve to familiarize ourselves with modern literature—particularly the Yiddish classics that were being published at the time. I myself was a member of the Lipno[3] library, and Shmuel Prum was a member of the Sierpc[4] library, but we were not always able to get the books we wanted. So it was natural and understandable that we young people should aspire to obtain a legitimate library in Dobrzyn.

The first request, in the name of Azriel Sachs, was sent to the governor of Plock[5], whose answer was a categorical refusal. As we later found out he had reacted by sending an investigating commission made up of secret police [to Dobrzyn].

A second request to the same governor was sent in the name of Yosef Chaim Ruda, but this time, too, the response was negative. Then we tried to authorize a private library through a Dobrzyn teacher who originated from Lipno; we motivated the request as being for the purpose of his livelihood. But after a short time this request was also turned down.

Once we realized that we would not get permission by following this approach, we decided to try alternatives. We wrote to *Chevrat HaZamir*[6], an organization that had a library in Mława, and we asked them to open a branch in Dobrzyn. But unfortunately the reply that we received was not encouraging, and we decided to delegate our member Eliezer Zaklikovski to meet with the representative of *Chevrat HaZamir* in Mława[7]. He [Zaklikovski] happened to be the cousin of the head of that organization, the well-known author Yakir Warszawski. But after some brief negotiations in Mlawa, Zaklikovski was told that opening a branch would not be possible. We therefore began searching for a still different approach.

Chevrat HaZamir was active in Warsaw, as well; there, the head of the organization was a certain Dr. Levin, a fine, liberal man. Our committee held a brief consultation and decided to delegate me to approach the Warsaw *Chevrat HaZamir*, with the hope that we could get permission to open a branch of theirs in Dobrzyn. When I reached Warsaw I went directly to their address, where I found them holding their weekly committee meeting. After they had greeted me warmly, the president, Dr. Levin, gave me an appointment to meet him the very next day at his own home. We had a very cordial discussion at the meeting, but unfortunately nothing came of it, either. He simply noted that the only Jewish institution that could possibly help in these circumstances was the *Chevrat Mefitsay Haskala*[18] in St. Petersburg, where our current president, Zalman Rubashov-Shazar[9], was then one of the active members. We wrote to them, explaining all the details, but after a short time they replied that they could not help us in this matter.

Having exhausted all these alternatives, we decided to set up an unauthorized library.

We held a meeting, at which we detailed the lengthy trials and tribulations of our committee as it had tried to set up an authorized library in Dobrzyn and ultimately found that there was no way to do it. On the spot we took up a collection to purchase books that we had already made a list of, and we then ordered the books from an agent who was about to travel to Warsaw, where he could purchase them. After a few days we received the books that we had ordered and immediately brought them to the home of Azriel Sachs. The books were lent out to the subscribing members twice a week, Mondays and Thursdays, during the hours of 6 to 9 pm.

During these lending hours we took security measures, posting two of our members at the building entrance to monitor the passersby. Then one day our sentries became suspicious of two policemen who had been seen going past Sachs's house during lending hours. Since discovery of the library would have meant a 3-month prison sentence [for Sachs], we packed the books up in several boxes and moved them to my attic.

This was shortly before the First World War broke out. During the war, when the Germans occupied Poland, they created a civil administration in our town; it was headed by a German lieutenant named Schade who served as mayor. We asked him for permission to open a library. He immediately complied, and after several weeks we opened the library in Nowalski's house. Already at its inception the library contained more than two thousand books, and little by little the number of books continued to grow.

The committee members included (1) Dov Jalowski, (2) Yaakov[10] Pieniek, (3) Chanoch Pinczewski, (4) Yosef Waldenberg, (5) Meir Cohen, (6) David Cohen, (7) Bunem Zaklikowski, and (8) Eliezer Zaklikowski. In its first meeting the committee decided to name the library *Sholom Aleichem*[11] and to keep it out of any conflicts that might arise between political parties.

As time passed we set up literature evenings in the spacious sitting room of the library. These attracted a large audience.

I would like to note the exceptional service of the following members in developing the library: (1) Moshe Sonnabend, (2) Yosef Chaim Ruda, (3) Hirsh Wolf Rusak, (4) Nachum Frager, (5) Moshe Chaim Cierklorsz, and the present writer. Also the following women—Hendel Dobrzynski, Esther Wrzos and Chaya Miller—gave much of their free time to benefit the library.

The library also held evening language courses in Yiddish, Polish and German, led by Yaakov Isaac and Dov Jalowski. A bit later language courses in Hebrew were also offered in the library. If for any reason the teacher could not be present, either Cierklorsz or I would substitute.

This was one of the finest periods of cultural development in Dobrzyn.

Eliezer Zaklikowski, of blessed memory[12]

Translator's Footnotes

1. From *My Town: In Memory of the Communities Dobrzyn-Gollob*, edited by M. Harpaz, (published by the Dobrzyn-Golub Society, Israel, 1969), pp. 300-304

2. *Tifferet Bachurim* (Hebrew) = Young Men's Glory

3. Lipno is located ~35km south of Dobrzyn

4. Sierpc is located ~55km southeast of Dobrzyn

5. Plock, a city ~90km southeast of Dobrzyn, lends its name to the province in which Dobrzyn was located

6. *Chevrat HaZamir* (Hebrew) = Songbird Society, founded to spread an appreciation for the arts among the Jews

7. Mlawa is located ~100km east of Dobrzyn

8. *Chevrat Mefitsay Haskala* (Hebrew) = Society for Dissemination of Knowledge

9. Zalman Rubashov [after 1949: Shazar] (1889-1974) immigrated to Palestine in 1924 and served as president of the State of Israel from 1963 to 1973. He resided in St. Petersburg during the years 1908-1912. See the following link: http://en.wikipedia.org/wiki/Zalman_Shazar

10. First names of Pieniek and Pinczewski do not appear in the original Yiddish article, but have been taken instead from its Hebrew translation (pp. 105-108 of reference cited in Footnote 1), in which they do appear

11. *Sholom Aleichem* was the pen name of the famous Yiddish author Sholom Rabinowitz (1859-1916)

12. From p. 301 of reference cited in Footnote 1

Page 307]

Our Landsleit in America

[Pages 307-311]

The Brief History of the Chicago Dobrzyn Organization

By Esther Graner-Rabbe
Translated by Pamela Russ
Donated by Steve Bolef

To the Yizkor Book that our Dobrzyn friends in Israel are publishing, I would like to contribute a brief overview of the work that the Dobrzyn *landsleit* (referring to people from the same town) in Chicago did to help our tragic Dobrzyner during the time of the destruction of Europe, and what they did for the few that survived after the death of our loved ones by the hands of the Nazi bandits. At the same time, I would like to give an accounting of the thousands of dollars that the Dobrzyn *landsleit* collected in Chicago.

I would like to give a clear explanation to each and every Dobrzyner wherever he may be about the devoted work that the Chicago *landsleit* did for our few surviving sisters and brothers who are now spread across the world.

The history of the Chicago Dobrzyn Organization begins in the year 1917 when it was established as a result of the terrible reports in the American press about the situation of the Polish Jews. At that time, a group of Dobrzyner *landsleit* in Chicago formed together as an organization to be able to assist those who were in the town of Dobrzyn and needed help. Europe then was terribly impoverished, and it was the Jews in the small towns who suffered most. In the years 1919-1920, we sent many thousands of dollars to Dobrzyn. At the same time, our organization also helped a group of Dobrzyn youths who were in Berlin. After that, we sent smaller sums regularly each month to individual families in our town, understandably, to those who most needed the support. In the year 1923, the Dobrzyn women in Chicago took over this assistance work and they immediately sent notices for money –

according to a list – to about 150 families. The need for help was tremendous and many times we were simply unable to meet those needs. In that situation, we women of the organization would borrow larger sums just to satisfy the needs of the community.

[Page 308]

In the mid-1930s, the economic situation in the town worsened because of the anti-Semitic movement that incited a boycott. Then the men's union became more involved in active assistance. They organized themselves to send packages and clothing, shoes, and food. Help was sent for children in the schools and Talmud Torahs, and special help for the library, and a sum of money for the community charity fund (*gemilas chesed*) so that it would be able to help those who presented themselves for immediate help. In the year 1939, with the outbreak of World War II, the assistance stopped completely. The Chicago organization then was flooded with letters that reached out to us, but unfortunately there was already no possibility of sending help. Among us friends the collection of monies did not stop in order that there would be money in the fund, and so that when the opportunity would arise we would immediately be ready to send help. But the realities were not as we had imagined. The destruction of our brothers in Poland in general and in Dobrzyn specifically, undid all our plans.

Only in the year 1948 did we finally have the opportunity to connect with all kinds of centers in Europe, and through them we found out about scores of Dobrzyn refugees that survived the massive destruction. Slowly, we began to receive letters from them in which they asked for help. We immediately undertook massive assistance activity.

[Page 309]

In our correspondence we were in touch with several countries in Europe, and through messengers and through the mail we sent larger sums of money as well as clothing and food. The joy and comfort that our help brought our letters brought to the survivors, was heard in their heartfelt thanks from the pained hearts that lived through the war, some in bunkers in Europe and some in the vast wasteland of Russia. Their joy was enormous and with doubled efforts we threw ourselves into more collection activities. To our great joy, everyone doubled their contributions and money flowed in from all sides. Often we organized lunches where we would read the letters from our dear survivors. When we would read these letters, a quiet weeping could be heard among those gathered together. We looked for any opportunity to support our dear ones not only materialistically but also in morale through sending them pictures and letters that, as soon as they were received, evoked tremendous joy. They didn't feel abandoned, God forbid, knowing that there were still devoted family members who would make sure that these survivors would be able to get on their feet again and build their lives.

Mrs. Zbicki from New York at a welcoming in the hall of the Keren Kayemet in Tel Aviv

[Page 310]

Our help reached each person wherever he would be, even in China. We sent all kinds of medicines, blankets to cover themselves, and help for those with lung problems so that they could cure themselves. Also, through our intensive correspondence, we brought together families that were spread apart, family members that didn't know of the others' existence. We busied ourselves with making sure they would be able to rebuild themselves as quickly as possible. Because of that, many of them left Europe as soon as they could, and many of them immigrated to Israel, as well as many to America. When they arrived in Israel we received mail from them very often and upon their request we sent work materials that would help them with their livelihoods -- machines for example, etc. We responded to each request according to our possibility, and I think no one was wronged and everyone was treated fairly.

Among all the letters of pain, we received a request from one of our Dobrzyn survivors, a man that lost his entire family. The author of the letter was a *chassidic* Jew and he said he would be very grateful if we would send him a *talis* (prayer shawl). Of course we immediately sent him a *talis,* and the letter of thanks that we received from him completely touched our hearts. He wrote:

> "Dear friends,
> When I received the *talis*, I cried deeply from great joy. The *talis* will serve as a valuable garment for my life and I will ask that I be buried with this *talis* upon my death. When I wrap myself in this *talis* my Jewish soul sings and I remember the heartfelt folksong, 'The dear *talis*, the dear *talis*, my only joy and comfort.' Be well and be blessed for your esteemed gift.
> Your friend who will never forget you,
> Mordechai Eliezer Tinski"

A half a year after we received this letter of thanks, we received a letter from a friend of Eliezer telling us that Eliezer had died in Poland and was buried wrapped in the *talis* that we had sent. In that way we knew that we had done a true kindness for the dead (*chesed shel emes*) for a religious Jew who after terrible pain and suffering merited at least to be buried in a Jewish grave.

[Page 311]

Now, dear friends, we will stand shortly at the publication of the Yizkor Book – a book that must serve as a holy tombstone for our Dobrzyner martyrs. In this should also be remembered the important activities of our friends in Chicago, many of whom are already in the Next World, for what they organized and did for our suffering brothers who came out with their lives from the horrific destruction. And when we will assemble at a meeting and open the Yizkor Book, with our heads bowed, we will say Yizkor from the deepest sorrows in our hearts for our dearest and most devoted parents, brothers, and sisters, and all the other millions of Jews and our innocent children, the future of the Jewish nation. A holy *kaddish* for all the martyrs of all generations.

Yisgadal ve'yiskadash shemai rabboh

Family Lurd

[Pages 312-316]

The First Association of Dobrzyners in America[1]

by Shlomo Aleksander
Translated by Allen Flusberg

The history of the settlement of Dobrzyn Jews in America began at the moment when the first few dozen immigrants from Dobrzyn reached the shores of the New World, approximately in the first half of the nineteenth century. The hardships of earning a living on the part of the Jewish masses, in Poland in general and in the small towns in particular, motivated many of them to look for a way to settle across the vast seas. By then America had made a name for itself as a land of unlimited possibilities; immigrants from all over the world were streaming to the Golden Land in waves of tens of thousands, to seek and find a source of subsistence. They began their new lives under rather harsh conditions: whether as peddlers or by putting in a hard day of work, often beyond their strength. But the stubborn will to stay in the new country and to create a means of support for themselves overcame all the obstacles. Most of them stayed, and with the passage of time acclimated and adjusted themselves to the conditions of the land.

It with some satisfaction that we call attention to the intimate, fraternal solidarity and cohesiveness among the Dobrzyn immigrant *landsleit*[2]. They were concentrated for the most part in the Lower East Side of New York, which in those days generally served as a mecca for all the Jewish immigrants from the Eastern European countries. In that very district the day-to-day lives of the few Dobrzyn immigrant–*landsleit* were fashioned. First and foremost, the boundaries that had existed among them because of pedigree, station and class fell away. Unified in purpose, like siblings of a single family, they gathered together, after a hard day of labor, on a cold winter night of the year 1870, at the home of one of their members, whose name was Braun; and they established the modest foundation of an association that they called "*Doresh Tov Dobrzynsk*"[3]. The association began its activity with limited means along the lines of a *gmilas chasodim*[4] fund for making loans, supporting the sick, and ensuring a cemetery plot *noch hundert un tsvantsig yor*[5]. With the passage of time and with the steady growth in the number of immigrants from Dobrzyn, the association expanded and branched out in its activities, and thus became a significant force for helping those new immigrants who were in need. At the same time it contributed to various prominent charitable institutions. Among these institutions were HIAS[6] and the JOINT[7], which already at that time—and especially after the First World War—had expanded their activities throughout the entire Jewish world in support of the oppressed, defenceless Jewish masses, whom they were literally rescuing from ruin.

The warm, close relationship that had existed among the Dobrzyn Jews within the town, and which had served as an example for many other Jewish towns in Poland, was brought with them to America by the immigrants. And now that they were settled in their new homeland, they did not forget their needy families and friends from their old home town; on all occasions, whether those of joy or sorrow, they remembered the poor and unfortunate people there and provided for them. However, because of the distraction of their own day-to-day concerns, it was better and more constructive for them to organize this aid. We must call attention, with the greatest of respect, to a group of women volunteers of the Dobrzyn Association for their tireless years of effort and toil and for their achievements fulfilling the relief program. The most active members of this group were the following: Mrs. Rivka Aleksander, Mrs. Goldfeder, Mrs. Garber, Mrs. Zaklow, Mrs. Francis Gorski, and Mrs. Mary Zabytski.

It is no secret that the impoverished families of the town viewed their American friends—who continued to display yearning and sympathy for their unforgotten families and friends in the old homeland—as a life raft for a sinking ship. It would be superfluous to point out the empathetic attitude and benevolent acts of individual members to benefit various families of the town. While the association was generally concerned with assisting the very neediest, they also did not forget to donate in the form of *matan besayser*[8], so as to ensure respect for the dignity of the recipient families.

Decades passed in hope and nostalgic longing. "*Doir hoileich vedoir bo*"[9]; but the Association continued its regular relief activity for the benefit of the needy of the town. Even for the second generation it was like a sacred, though unwritten, testament. And they, too, fulfilled their obligation with distinction. At the most critical moment, the town was threatened with hunger because of the Polish anti-Semitic and hooligan-like bands that ran amuck in the town, cutting the Jews off from the very last sources of their difficult and harsh livelihoods and thereby actually leaving dozens of families destitute, with no food. At that critical moment their relief arrived and prevented those dear to them from hungering.

The tragic fate that befell Polish Jewry in general did not skip over our town, either. The Second World War signified the end of the history of Dobrzyn, a history that had lasted hundreds of years.

When the first reports of the brutal calamity reached us, we still questioned and thought that perhaps these reports were exaggerated. But very soon the reality of the horrific catastrophe became clear to us. Only after the war had ended did we fully realize that what we were seeing was the destruction and doom of Polish Jewry and the dire loss of our forlorn people, who were almost totally eradicated throughout Poland. Receiving the first reports of refugees from Dobrzyn in various countries of Europe, the *Landsleit* Association of New York immediately undertook a large aid campaign: it contacted the few remaining refugees and sent aid, money, food, shoes and clothing.

After some time had passed, when a large fraction of the refugees were now concentrated in Israel, and the drive for constructive loans grew on a daily basis, our Association reinforced the money shipments by creating a matching fund for this important purpose. The committee in Israel stays in close contact with our American members and sends us reports from time to time.

Our main goal at the present time is to speed up publication of the Yizkor Book that is dedicated to the martyrs of Dobrzyn–Golub—a sacred memorial to our martyrs.

Yitzchok Yaakov Szmiga, his wife and grandchild[10][11]

The Zaklikowski brothers, children of Berish Zaklikowski[12]

Translator's Footnotes

1. From *My Town: In Memory of the Communities Dobrzyn–Gollob*, edited by M. Harpaz, (published by the Dobrzyn–Golub Society, Israel, 1969), pp. 312–315.

2. *Landsleit* (singular: *landsman*) = compatriots, Yiddish term for Jewish immigrants who hailed from the same town or region.

3. *Doresh Tov Dobrzynsk* (Hebrew) = seeking the good of Dobrzynsk (paraphrasing Esther 10:3), i.e. Benevolent Society of Dobrzynsk. It should be noted that the Jews of Dobrzyn called their town Dobrzynsk (pronounced Dubjinsk). See Y. Lichtenstein, "Dobrzyn, My Town", p. 30 of reference cited in Footnote 1.

4. *Gmilas chasodim* = general charity for those in need, e.g. interest–free loans

5. *noch hundert un tsvantsig yor* (Yiddish) = literally, after 120 years, i.e. upon one's eventual death. 120 years was the age that Moses lived to; the mention of one's future death is transformed into a blessing of sorts by suggesting a longevity surpassing that attained by ordinary mortals since Moses.

6. HIAS = Hebrew Immigrant Aid Society. See the following link (retrieved July, 2015): http://www.hias.org/history.

7. JOINT = American Jewish Joint Distribution Committee. See the following link (retrieved July, 2015): https://en.wikipedia.org/wiki/American_Jewish_Joint_Distribution_Committee.

8. *Matan besayser* = anonymous giving (based on Prov. 21:14). The Talmud describes *matan besayser* as a high form of charity in which the donor and recipient are unknown to one another (Baba Batra 9b). The recipient is spared the embarrassment of accepting charity from someone he knows, and the donor cannot expect future compensation from a recipient who does not know his identity.

9. *Doir Hoileich vedoir bo* = a generation goes and a generation comes (Hebrew, Ecl. 1:4)

10. From p. 316 of reference cited in Footnote 1.

11. On Szmiga see "The Synagogues and Shtiebels in Dobrzyn", pp. 264–269; also Dzialdow and Sanger, p. 286 of "Religious Life in Dobrzyn," pp. 284–291, both in reference cited in Footnote 1.

12. From p. 316 of reference cited in Footnote 1.

[Page 318]

Destruction

Memories from the War Years[1]

By Michael Cohen
Translated by Allen Flusberg

For many long years we lived in my birthplace Dobrzyn, where I was brought up until the second decade of my life. For various reasons we left the town in 1929, and my family settled in Zgierz[2], an industrial town not far from Lodz. However, we kept up our connection with our friends and acquaintances of Dobrzyn for many years, and whenever one of them visited Lodz he would also often be a guest at our home.

I recall an accident that David Pieniek had when he was driving to Lodz in a truck, loaded with cartons of eggs and butter to bring to a major wholesale dealer. He was accompanied by Yaakov Yechiel Bielowski, y.b.l.h.[3] Several kilometers before they got to Lodz the truck overturned. Bielowski managed to get out unharmed, but Pieniek was injured badly. Since they weren't very far from Zgierz, Bielowski ran over to Zgierz to get us, leaving Pieniek in the field with the damaged merchandise. When I heard what had happened, I immediately took a car and two workers and drove over to the site of the accident. First I brought Pieniek back to our place and gave him first aid after calling in a doctor. After that I went back to the site of the accident. I collected the merchandise, which was not in good condition, and brought it to the dealer in Lodz. David Pieniek stayed at our home for several days, and when he began to feel better he went home to Dobrzyn.

*

In 1932 my older brother, Oizer Ber z.l.[4] left Poland to set out for Israel during *Aliya Bet*[5]. His journey was organized by Betar[6]. In Israel the first place he lived in was Petah Tikva, and he wound up remaining there. He was a dedicated member [of Betar], and was also in the underground. He was willing to do a favor for anyone anytime, which is how all his friends remembered him. Unfortunately he died young in a tragic accident: while riding his bicycle to work he was hit by a truck and was killed on the spot. He was only 26 years old.

From the moment this sad news reached us, my parents began considering building our home in Israel to implement the plan that my brother Oizer z.l. had devoted so much time and thought to right after he arrived in the Land, but which he unfortunately was not privileged to fulfil. My parents made an effort in various ways to obtain a certificate [of immigration], which was not very easy to obtain in those days. But that didn't prevent my sister Chava from joining an illegal *aliya*, and in this manner she reached Israel in 1935. But my parents had various formality difficulties; also the events of 1936 in Israel[7] prevented them from achieving their life's dream. In the end they perished in the Holocaust together with my youngest sister, Ita. I have never succeeded in obtaining details about [what actually happened to] my parents and sister; I know only that they were deported from the Warsaw Ghetto to a Death Camp.

I was mobilized several days before the war began. We were not very far from Lodz while the German Luftwaffe was bombing the city unremittingly, murdering hundreds of innocent people, mainly those who lived near strategic points. The Germans knew the precise locations of these points thanks to betrayal by the Germans—Nazis—of Lodz. We fled in the direction of Warsaw; along the way we saw towns and villages in flames. The population was fleeing in all directions, not knowing where to go.

In this enormous din of fire and flame we arrived in Warsaw–Praga[8], where we were put up in private homes for the time being. When we found out that it was Rosh Hashana[9], we went out into the street, weary and covered with dust, where we saw Jews, dressed up in holiday clothing, streaming by the hundreds to synagogues, as well as to services being held in private homes. We—that is, I and the one other Jewish soldier—went into a private home where a few dozen people had gathered to pray. When they saw us they were at first quite frightened, but they calmed down as soon as they heard that all we wanted was to participate in their communal prayer. One could sense the disaster that was approaching in the sorrowful cries of the people as they prayed.

As we left the service we saw a huge line of people waiting for bread in front of a bakery. Suddenly a German fighter plane, a Messerschmitt, came swooping down, and in a few seconds half of the people were mowed down, staining the street with their blood.

That year Yom Kippur[10] fell on a Sabbath, and we were then holed up in trenches not far from Warsaw. The incessant bombardment was deafening, and we knew that Warsaw's days were numbered. That Tuesday Warsaw surrendered, and the Germans marched in freely, illuminated by the flame and fire that had engulfed almost all of Warsaw. With the fall of Warsaw our company was sent to Skierniewice[11].

Altogether we were the only two Jews in our company. After the Germans captured our company the two of us were very fearful that they might find out our secret—that we were Jewish.

One day they brought us to the train station to send us to Germany, but the train didn't show up and they brought us back. On the way back we saw a German policeman cruelly tormenting a defenseless religious Jew dressed in a *kapote*[12].

Using some subterfuge I managed to get a pass, and so I made my way back to Zgierz. Once there I found out that my parents had been hidden away in the home of a family, and I went straight over to see them. I am incapable of describing the convulsion that gripped both me and my parents during this short meeting. I had to part from them in silence and sorrow, with a deep lament in my heart, as I imagined the fate that was awaiting them—as well as me.

After a difficult, dangerous journey I reached Bialystok[13]. I immediately signed up with the Russians for work, believing that by doing so I would survive, at least for the time being. But already then the Russians were conducting mass arrests of the Jewish refugees in Bialystok, sending them to labor deep within Russia. As much as I tried to hide away to avoid being arrested, I was forced, in the end, to make my peace with it, and I joined the large number of those who were transported away.

After a long journey we arrived in Russia—in the city of Arsha[14]. Right away the NKVD[15] began to come after us. They searched under every little button and tore the soles off our shoes. After that they put us up in a large prison under a heavy guard, with big dogs monitoring us. There were about 150 of us in each room, and there was simply not enough room to put one's head down—never mind the unimaginable sanitary conditions.

After some time they transported us to a camp in Finskiy Zaliv[16], on the sea, not far from the border with Finland. There I came across Kasriel Isaac; we were delighted to see each other. Right away he told me how the place operated, and specifically about the bread rations, which were the major problem of all the refugees in Russia.

Kasriel was receiving packages of food from his brother Yehuda, who was still in Bialystok. But as quickly as a package would reach him it would be taken away. This was the work of a group of underworld gangsters who were in the camp. As soon as I intervened with the gang leaders, however, their thievery ended.

Kasriel was generally very apathetic about life as he observed how deadly the troubles we were having were.

One day, with no forewarning, I was sent with a group far to the north. There we started new lives at a temperature of 40 degrees below zero. Many of us got frostbite in our noses and ears. The Russian work supervisor assured us that they would be finishing us off the same way the Arabs had taken care of the Jews in the Land of Israel in 1929[17]. This was at the time[18] that Hitler's army was approaching Moscow. We submitted a complaint to the commanding officer and requested an investigation. The work supervisor disappeared, and we never saw him again. Later, however, it turned out that they had transferred him to a different camp where he was given a higher position.

One day—a short time before we were liberated—when we had just completed our work in the forest and began to leave, one of our group lingered behind; he was picking a few berries to satisfy his hunger. The soldier who had accompanied us trained his rifle on him and shot him dead on the spot. Shouting and wailing, we tore up our bread ration cards in protest and demanded an investigation. Right away an officer arrived on horseback. He was accompanied by several soldiers, who surrounded us. The soldier [we were protesting against] claimed that he had shot the worker for attempting to escape. The officer accepted this explanation; he told us that if we did not line up in orderly rows he would shoot every second man. We complied, of course, and the officer, in his great mercy[19], gave each of us a piece of bread without the ration cards.

After we were liberated, when we were already on our way back to Poland, we came across many Russian Jews, and we thus had the opportunity to observe the extent of their ignorance: they were completely unaware of how the Jews were living worldwide.

During *Chol HaMoied*[20] of Passover we arrived in Warsaw. At the railway station we were met by representatives of the Jewish community, and among them I found one of my parents' acquaintances. He wanted to help me get settled in Warsaw, but I had my sights set on Israel. Before continuing on my journey, however, I took a little free time that I had left to go for a walk in the area that had been the Jewish part of Warsaw. But to my sorrow all I saw there was rubble and burned walls.

I took the first train to Kutno[21] to visit the brothers Kasriel and Aharon Isaac. I left my wife and child there and travelled to Zgierz, hoping to find out something about my family. I found our house, plundered and in ruins. I wanted to have a look inside the mill, thinking that I might come across someone there. But a Polish worker standing at the entrance said to me very plainly: "You have nothing to look for here." This was my welcome back to liberated Poland.

Shortly thereafter I joined up with "*Bricha*"[22]. When I got to Germany, I ran into Yehoshua Goldberg and his wife. Together we made inquiries in Bergen-Belsen about his sister Brocho, whom we were searching for.

Broken in body and spirit, we finally reached Israel, where we began to build our home anew. After the great destruction in Europe, this is our only comfort—that we are living in independence in our own state.

Hirsch Arnow, grandson of R. Zalman Chossid [23]

Translator's Footnotes

1. From *My Town: In Memory of the Communities Dobrzyn–Gollob*, edited by M. Harpaz, (published by the Dobrzyn–Golub Society, Israel, 1969), pp. 318–323.

2. Zgierz, Poland is located ~13km north of Lodz, some 200km south of Dobrzyn.

3. y.b.l.h. = acronym for *YiBodel LeHaim* = may he be set apart to live; appended to the name of a living person mentioned in the same sentence as that of someone who has passed away.

4. z.l. = acronym for *Zichroinoi Livrocho* = of blessed memory

5. *Aliya Bet* = name of a wave of *aliya* (immigration of Jews to Israel) during the British Mandate, starting in the 1930s and ending with the independence of the State of Israel in 1948. This immigration was illegal or restricted by British law at the time. See the following web site (retrieved June, 2014): http://en.wikipedia.org/wiki/Aliyah_Bet

6. Betar was a non–socialist Zionist youth movement, founded by Zeev Jabotinsky, that organized illegal Jewish immigration to Palestine in the 1930s and 1940s in violation of British Mandate immigration quotas. See the following web site (retrieved June, 2014): http://en.wikipedia.org/wiki/Betar

7. In 1936 a revolt of the Arab population of Palestine began. It led to further limitations on Jewish immigration by the British. See the following web sites (retrieved June, 2014): http://israelipalestinian.procon.org/view.answers.php?questionID=506, http://en.wikipedia.org/wiki/1936%E2%80%9339_Arab_revolt_in_Palestine.

8. Praga is a borough of Warsaw that is located on the east bank of the Vistula River. See the following Web site (retrieved June, 2014): http://en.wikipedia.org/wiki/Praga).

9. Rosh Hashana = Jewish New Year, which in that year (1939) fell on Thursday and Friday, September 14–15.

10. Yom Kippur = Day of Atonement (Jewish Fast Day), which that year fell on Saturday, September 23.

11. Skierniewice is located ~80km southwest of Warsaw.

12. *kapote* = caftan, the coat worn by devout Jews

13. Bialystok, Poland lies ~300km east of Dobrzyn. It was then (1939–1941) in the Soviet–controlled zone of Poland. See the following Web site (retrieved June, 2014): http://en.wikipedia.org/wiki/Bia%C5%82ystok.

14. Arsha, Russia, lies ~2000km northeast of Bialystok, Poland.

15. NKVD = Soviet secret police

16. Finskiy Zaliv, Russia, lies ~1400km northwest of Arsha, Russia. It is on the coast, ~100km northwest of St. Petersburg, Russia.

17. The reference is to the massacre of the Jews of Hebron in 1929. See the following Web site (retrieved June, 2014):
    http://en.wikipedia.org/wiki/1929_Hebron_massacre.

18. Late 1941

19. Hebrew: *berov chasdo*, a term taken from a line in the 14th–century Hebrew poem *Yigdal* (incorporated into the Jewish prayer book), "In his great mercy, God will make the dead come back to life."

20. *Chol HaMoied* = intermediate days (Days 3–6 of the 8–day Passover festival)

21. The city of Kutno, Poland, lies ~120km west of Warsaw.

22. *Bricha* = Escape (Hebrew), a group that organized the illegal transport of Jews from Europe to British Mandatory Palestine immediately after World War II. See the following Web site (retrieved June, 2014):
    http://en.wikipedia.org/wiki/Berihah

23. From p. 321 of reference cited in Footnote 1. For more on R. Zalman Chossid (or Hassid), whose family name was Rozenwaks, see pp. 289–290 of S. Dzialdow and N. Sanger, "Religious Life in Dobrzyn," pp. 284–291; also Y. Lichtenstein, "Dobrzyn, My Little Town," pp. 30–40, both in reference cited in Footnote 1.

[Pages 324-225]

The Twenty Who Were Hanged[1]

By Mrs. Degala

Translated by Allen Flusberg

It was during the month of August, 1942, in the Tschenstochau[2] Ghetto, that suddenly, quite unexpectedly, several dozen police burst in. A terrible panic ensued. After a few minutes they led 20 men out of the ghetto, bringing them into a nearby cellar that they then encircled with police. For three weeks they held them in the cellar under barbaric conditions, barely giving them anything to eat. Once when we did see them we could not even recognize them: they were emaciated, pale, and completely indifferent, knowing as they did what awaited them.

Several days later a car arrived in the camp bringing a group of Gestapo members with prefabricated gallows for the twenty arrested men. The entire camp of men, women and children were ordered to assemble in the main square, where the executions were to take place. Men were ordered to dig a long pit as the twenty for whom the gallows had been prepared looked on. As they led them to the gallows, there was dead silence, everyone choking back tears, for an order had been given for us not to scream or cry. Among us stood policemen, their guns drawn, ready to shoot anyone who dared open his mouth.

For eight hours, on a very hot day, the men were left hanging, until the smell of death began to be noticeable. Only then was the order given to cut them down. One at a time the bodies were carried to the large pit, and all were buried together in the common grave.

Only then, once the Nazi beast had satisfied its thirst with the blood of the twenty who had been hung, was it quiet in the camp for some time.

Translator's Footnotes

1. From *My Town: In Memory of the Communities Dobrzyn-Gollob*, edited by M. Harpaz, (published by the Dobrzyn-Golub Society, Israel, 1969), p. 324.

2. Tschenstochau is the German name given to the town of Czestochowa during World War II. The Jewish ghetto was established in April, 1941, and the Jews were forced to work as slave laborers in the armaments industry. See the following links: http://en.wikipedia.org/wiki/Cz%C4%99stochowa_Ghetto, https://en.wikipedia.org/wiki/Cz%C4%99stochowa#World_War_Two.

[Page 325]

On the Winding Roads[1]

By Yehoshua Goldberg

Translated by Allen Flusberg

Our little house had stood for generations in the famous market square of Dobrzyn on the Dreventz River, my birthplace. There my family lived; and we also worked there in our business and clock-repair shop, which was the destination of hundreds of Dobrzyn families when their clocks didn't work right. For everyone in town knew that whatever Shmuelik the watchmaker repaired was guaranteed for some time—and it was really true.

Not far from us was the well-known passageway to the *Lange Gass*[2]; this passageway, known as the "Lik", served as a shortcut from the *Lange Gass* to the town square—and back again. People avoided the passageway because of the unpleasant odors wafting up from behind the "Lik", odors that were caused mostly by those who took the shortcut. But the smell wasn't very much of a deterrent, and passersby made use of the "Lik" from sunrise to late at night.

One of the town's most highly regarded assets was the Dreventz River, which separated two nations from each other: Russia on one side and Germany on the other side of the river. Until the outbreak of the First World War hundreds of families in the town made their living from the riverbanks. Thousands of young men from various locations in Poland who were obliged to serve in the military, but were not too excited about putting on Russian uniforms, found their way to Dobrzyn ahead of time. There those of our brother Jews[3] who specialized in this calling made sure to transport them not only across the river to Golub, but often all the way to the Golden Land[4], as well. Traffic also flowed in the other direction: dozens of small boats, laden with German merchandise, crossed the narrow little river to the Dobrzyn side; from there the merchandise was transported to various cities and towns in Poland. It is worth mentioning that the Russian officers of the border watch didn't suffer any loss from this business—none whatsoever—and meanwhile the Jews of Dobrzyn enjoyed flourishing livelihoods from it.

The river also provided the inhabitants of the town with a place of recreation in both summer and winter. In the summertime people—especially young people—would go to the Dreventz shore, which in some places was overgrown with small trees. There they would spend many hours, quietly reading books, or carrying on conversations with friends, while they snacked on tasty delicatessen that they had brought along from home.

On hot summer days many groups of young people would congregate in the shade of the thick wooded areas. In winter you would see them skating on the frozen river. Setting out in groups, wearing iron skates, they would skate several kilometers along the length of the river. This sport was repeated year in and year out. And there were hardly any young people in Dobrzyn who didn't know how to skate or to swim.

Often we would visit the famous castle, visible from afar, that stood on a high mountain in the neighboring town of Golub. In it was a museum with many artifacts that were ancient, hundreds of years old. On each of our visits we would learn something new about these artifacts, each of which had its own particular meaning.

The contrast between the two towns, Dobrzyn and Golub, was significant. For the most part it was noticeable in organizational life: in Dobrzyn there were Zionist and Socialist parties, sports associations and various youth clubs; whereas in Golub there was only a single, nonaligned party—and not because Golub was smaller than Dobrzyn, but simply because the German Jews of Golub had no interest in such things. They were interested in family, business, and entertainment. As a result any affection between the Jews of Dobrzyn and Golub was very subdued; the young people of Dobrzyn lived in their own secluded domain and made no attempt to approach the German young people, in spite of the richer culture of the latter.

The library with its beautiful reading room, the Zionist club "*HaTechiya*"[5], the theatre performances—these were things that the Golub Jews almost never visited or attended. Even lectures on all kinds of subjects, given by renowned invited speakers who had been brought in for this purpose, did not interest them. Only in 1918, when Poland achieved its independence and Pomorze[6] became part of Poland, only then did the Golub Jews become closer with the East European Jews. One who helped this process along was the Golub pharmacist Dr. Riesenfeld, who was also a dedicated Zionist. But the majority of the Golub Jews left for Germany.

The first time the two towns felt a bitter taste together was during the Bolshevik invasion of Poland in 1920. The Russian soldiers did not physically terrorize the inhabitants of Dobrzyn–Golub. Economically, however, they impoverished the local businesses by appropriating the best goods from the merchants in return for rubles that even at that time had no effective value.

In the late 1920s, when the economic conditions in Dobrzyn grew worse, several Dobrzyn families moved to Pomorze. Although the sympathy of the Polish population there for Jews was not satisfactory, economically the situation was considerably better [than in Dobrzyn]. We were one of the families that lived in Chelmza, Pomorze[7] for many years. Our relationship with the local Polish population was no bed of roses, but we did endure there until shortly before the war. Seeing what was taking place, we understood that the sooner we left Chelmza the better. And so we returned to Dobrzyn.

Several days before the war broke out, as sometimes happens in moments like these, it came back to me how I had accompanied my brother Mordechai, of blessed memory, when he began his journey to Israel together with a group of pioneers from Dobrzyn in the early 1920s, and how during all that time our dream had been to unite with him again. And even after his death in the early 1930s we had not given up our longing for the Land of Israel. But practical difficulties made our dream unattainable.

Together with tens of thousands of other refugees we tasted the dark exile of Russia with all of its ramifications, but miraculously we did survive. And finally we reached the Land of Israel. Here we established a family and began a new life, leaving behind the brutal past of the war.

May these lines of mine serve as an eternal monument memorializing my beloved and faithful ones who perished.

Translator's Footnotes

1. From *My Town: In Memory of the Communities Dobrzyn–Gollo*, edited by M. Harpaz, (published by the Dobrzyn–Golub Society, Israel, 1969), pp. 325–328.

2. *Lange Gass* = Long Street, the Yiddish name for the street officially known as Pilsudskiego in Polish. See map on pp. 8–9 of reference cited in Footnote 1.

3. Yiddish text: *acheinu bnei yisroel* (Hebrew) = our brethren the Children of Israel

4. Golden Land = America

5. *HaTechiya* (Hebrew) = Revival. See E. Tzala, "Pain and Suffering in the Second World War", p. 356 of reference cited in Footnote 1

6. Pomorze = Pomerania, the district that Golub was in.

7. Chełmża is located ~40km west of Dobrzyn.

8. *mikvahnik* = *mikvah* attendant who is in charge of the *mikvah* (ritual bath)

9. From p. 326 of reference cited in Footnote 1

Left: Yisroel Szaijnbart, the *mikvahnik*[8] of Dobrzyn[9]

[Page 329]

Pain and Suffering of a Family[1]

by Gavriel Katcher
Translated by Allen Flusberg

At the outbreak of the war, I was with my sister, brother-in-law and their five small children in the Polish port city of Gdynia[2]. When the Germans began bombarding the city and dozens of people were killed, I understood that we must find a way to flee. At first I was concerned for my sister, brother-in-law and the children—how was I going to rescue them from Gdynia? Our goal was to transport them back to their birthplace, Dobrzyn. The trains were packed, and it was almost impossible to get any space in them. I began by bringing the most necessary items, which were already packed, to the train station. After that we all ran together to the station, where we waited for a train that was supposed to arrive one hour later. It is impossible to imagine the crush of people—three times as many as the train should have held. The sound of the women and children crying and screaming was deafening; as thousands of people pushed from all directions to get into the train, many were being trampled underfoot. Everyone wanted to leave the city—the target of bombardment—as quickly as possible, although danger was in fact lurking in every corner of Poland. To this very day I do not know how I found the strength to push them onto the train—first my sister and her husband; and then afterwards the children, whom I got in through a window.

After the train had begun to move I went back to my apartment, unable to stop worrying about them, wondering whether they would manage to make it to Dobrzyn. But a day later I received word that they had arrived safely.

Meanwhile I remained in Gdynia, trying to decide what to do next. When I realized that there was no alternative, I reported to duty in the Polish army and was sent straight to the battlefield. After 19 days of battle, my entire outfit was taken prisoner. Right away they interned us and sent us to hard labor. I destroyed my passport and indicated that I was a Christian. In the barrack I was the only Jew among sixty Poles. One day, while I was standing outside, a Pole came over and said to me in a loud voice: "But you are a Jew—what are you doing here?" On the very next day the Gestapo officer had already found out that I was Jewish. He began to carefully watch every single move I made. The same Polish soldier had recounted, in the presence of the Gestapo officer, that when the German military had marched into Poland the Jews had thrown stones at them and had poured boiling water on them.

The next day I was ordered to appear before the commandant. When I came into his office—he was an older officer, who had already been a soldier in the First World War—he straightaway asked me, "*Bist du Jude?*"[3] I told him that I was Jewish. He then said: "See to it that you get out of here as quickly as you can," adding, "It was your comrades who informed on you that you are Jewish." I went back to my barrack, tormented by the realization that they were keeping an eye on me.

From fright I came down with a high fever, and the next day was not able to go out to work. The supervisor who counted the workers every morning and noticed that I was missing came straight into my barrack. Seeing me lying in bed, he warned me that if I did not go out to chop wood he would send for the Gestapo police, who would finish me off on the spot. Ignoring my high fever—and in spite of the weak condition I was in—I picked myself up and went out into the courtyard. I stood there in the bitter cold chopping wood, and it was really a miracle that I was able to endure it.

Aside from the difficult conditions we also suffered in the barracks from bedbugs and lice, and so we were not really able to sleep. This motivated several prisoners to run away. We saw them going out a window; immediately we woke the supervisor up and told him what we had seen. He quickly reported it to the Gestapo, who, with several tracking dogs, followed the escapees; but they lost their tracks in a nearby forest. They returned and began investigating us—particularly me, since I understood German. They beat me very hard with a rubber truncheon, demanding that I tell them the truth. But of course they couldn't get anything out of me, and eventually they freed me from the interrogation.

I was imprisoned as a forced laborer in Germany until the end of the war. When liberation came I was a sick, broken man. After a short investigation I found out that I was the only survivor of my entire family. My older brother, Zalman Boruch, his wife Tsirl and five children; a second brother, Avrohom Yisroel, his wife Miriam and five children; my two sisters, Zisl and Perel and the latter's husband, Avrohom Shafran, also with five children—all of them had perished.

After marrying in Germany in 1947, I left immediately for Israel, where my wife gave birth to our two children. In 1959 we immigrated to America, where we still live.

Mordechai Lipka, *Reb* Feibish's son[4]

Translator's Footnotes

1. From *My Town: In Memory of the Communities Dobrzyn–Gollob*, edited by M. Harpaz, (published by the Dobrzyn–Golub Society, Israel, 1969), pp. 329–331.

2. Gdynia is on the northern coast of Poland, approximately 200km north of Dobrzyn.

3. *Bist du Jude* (German) = are you a Jew?

4. From p. 331 of reference cited in Footnote 1. See also articles beginning on p. 170 and p. 404.

[Page 332]

My Bundle of Troubles in the Russian Military[1]

by Yitzhak Rosenwaks, Z"L[2]

Translated by Allen Flusberg

I Am Mobilized

I am writing my memoirs some forty-odd years after my return from the Russian military as a veteran soldier in the year 1914. For more than three years I served the Czar Nikolai II. It is possible that by using standard means to create a deformity in an arm or in some other part of my body I could have avoided military service, but for understandable reasons I was completely unwilling to do so. Deserting was also unthinkable because of the severe monetary fine (300 rubles) that the Russian regime imposed on the parents of a deserter. Therefore I made the firm decision to present myself for military service and to actually serve.

In the small towns of Poland there was a strange custom: before leaving for their service recruits would carouse for a night or two, conducting various pranks in the town. For example: breaking down fences, removing wagon wheels, and the like. And I, too, carried out this "*mitzvah*"[3].

There were three of us Jewish recruits from Dobrzyn: Yaakov Krystal, Baron and I. We rode by wagon to Ostrolenka[4], and from there by train to Warsaw. This was the first time I had seen Warsaw. In Warsaw I visited acquaintances and my cousin, Yossel Atlasberg; and from there I continued on by train to reach the place where I was to serve.

After three days we reached Tula[5], far beyond the Pale of Settlement[6] of those days. There we went out into the street to meet the local Jews. From the announcements we had read we had found out that on that evening a large dinner sponsored by the *chevro kadisho*[7] of the city was to take place. Understandably, we went straight over there, and we had a reasonably good time. On our way to the dinner we met some *passek* players. Yeshayowitz from Rypin, who was with us, got the urge to play with them, and in this way, within only a few minutes, he lost the 10 rubles that he had had in his possession. The fellow was quite upset afterwards, but we calmed him down, telling him we would make sure that he would get his money back. At the dinner they honored us with all the best food. We told them the story of what had happened to Yeshayowitz, and immediately taking up a collection from those present, they collected 25 rubles. Yeshayowitz got his money back, but with a warning not to do this again.

After a few days in Tula we continued by train for several weeks, until we reached Barnaul[8]. There they temporarily split us up and apportioned us among the local peasant farmers, who did not know enough to distinguish between a Jew and a Gentile. I actually fell in with a good peasant who treated me courteously, but two days later I was already in the military barracks.

[Page 334]

We Reach Siberia

When I had signed up in Plock[9], I had described my vocation as saddlery. But since there were no horses at the place where we were being divided up, the orderly sergeant, a Jew, advised me to say that I was a tailor. I did so, and right away I was assigned to a tailor workshop. I did know how to sew by machine. Since Shloimo Yakir, a friend of mine who was a good tailor, was working right near me, he would do the most critical part of the job and I would finish up. In the course of time I learned how to sew well, and I truly became a full-fledged tailor, even sewing for the officers. The soldiers who had arrived in the camp together with me quite simply were jealous of me. While they were going out on maneuvers in heavy snow during the cold winter days, I was sitting in a warm room, working slowly. Meanwhile I learned drilling exercises from a book that I had already bought in Warsaw. In it there was also a section on how to handle arms. Even as a tailor I had to know all these things.

Shortly before Passover we received three packages from home. An officer sent one of the soldiers to the post office to retrieve them. The soldier returned with three wooden boxes that contained sausages, sardines, and, most importantly, bottles of vodka. The latter were immediately opened, and with the help... of the officers emptied on the spot.

In the course of time Yeshayowitz became ill. They took him to the hospital, and after some time he was released from military service. This event irritated the Jewish soldiers a bit, who began looking for possibilities... of becoming ill in order to be released. It is to be understood that this was not an easy thing to do, since even under normal circumstances the Jewish soldiers who originated from Poland were treated with suspicion.

[Page 335]

The First Passover

In the meantime, Passover was approaching, and we Jewish soldiers were looking for a way to be at a *Seder*[10] in the city. Permission for something like this could be obtained from someone with the authority of our captain; he was not a Jew-hater, but to get permission one of the soldiers would have to go to his office and hand him a request. Since at that time I had given the officer some vodka as a gift, the burden fell on me. I did my duty and I succeeded in obtaining the permission we had requested, but on condition that the soldiers behave properly in the city, that they not get themselves drunk, and that they return on time. To some extent he had made me responsible for them.

A group of us Jewish soldiers marched into the city, in the direction of the synagogue, where we also encountered a large number of other Jewish soldiers. When the prayer service ended we wished one another a happy holiday, sat down in sleds and were off to the Seder, somewhere far away from the synagogue. As soon as I arrived there, however, I decided that we would not celebrate the *Seder* in this place, because members of the underworld were gathered there. Bread and sausages, together with other similar *treif*[11] dishes, were spread out on the tables. A gramophone was playing, and disreputable couples were dancing to the music. I immediately declared that my soldiers would return to their barracks unless the tables were cleared and the unsavory people would leave. My words were effective: the disreputable element was expelled from the hall, and we went in. But it was dark in the hall, so we lit two lamps. Sitting down at the tables, we wept somberly as we recalled the Seders back home. We didn't stay there very long; we drank a toast, ate some *matzo*[12], completed the *Haggada*[13], and returned to the barracks.

The next day we again went into the city and made our way to the synagogue, where we met a large number of people attending the service. Our friend Zeinwill, who had a beard[14], was with us, too. The local residents wanted to invite him home for a meal. However, he demurred, telling them he had heard about their "good deeds" against the *shochet*[15] and *baal-tefillah*[16]:

they had turned them in to the police, who then had them imprisoned for not having city-residency permits[17].

Approximately 800 [Jewish] families lived in the city, among them a large number of wealthy people: merchants, officers, and people with high salaries. Among them were also intermarried couples. Most of them came to the synagogue for *hazkoras neshomos*[18] or to say *Kaddish*[19], at the same time contributing money or candles to the synagogue. The money or the candles were handed over to the old *gabbai*[20], who would give them a receipt in return.

Passover ended. I was back in the barracks, but right away a new trouble began: the time for the soldiers to be sworn in was approaching. The soldiers had to be ready and had to know this very "torah"[21] well enough to answer questions that were going to be asked by the general who was to swear us in. Understandably, these questions were not so easy for us recruits to answer. But presently we had some luck: the swearing-in day arrived, and the general—an outspoken anti-Semite—arrived with his entourage, and began asking the questions of each soldier individually. To my great joy I answered all the questions precisely as required, and I was now a full-fledged soldier.

Maneuvers began, but truthfully I didn't have a very strong desire for them. What I wanted was to get into the "*shvalnie*" (new workshop) and there engage in tailoring work as I did previously; thereby I would be saved from maneuvers. I was successful in this business after I provided the officer with a small "gift" and promised him that I would sew him a nice pair of trousers.

My future brother-in-law, Baron, had signed up for officer school. With the passage of time he received a rank and was appointed head quartermaster. His job was to supply the soldiers with food and drink, as well as to take care of their cultural interests. He had 30 men under him who conducted the physical labor in the storerooms; they also helped prepare banquets that the officers had arranged for their civilian guests. As an observant Jew, my brother-in-law did not taste any of these foods[22].

At one of these banquets we met a prominent Jew, who told us that on Passover they had collected a nice sum of money for the soldiers and that a committee was involved in all these matters. Right away we sent a delegation, consisting of two soldiers, to the head *gabbai* to find out what was going on. He didn't receive us particularly well, and as soon as we explained the reason for our visit he began shouting at us. However we were not intimidated; we immediately contacted a different *gabbai*, a Polish Jew, who sympathized with our request and treated us well. He declared that on the following Passover they would arrange a *Seder* for all the soldiers, and that we would be able to bake our own *matzos*. Expressing our gratitude, we left the *gabbai*'s home with satisfaction, being certain that we were already ensured with a *Seder* for the following Passover.

We were also concerned about the hundreds of arrested Jews, among them political prisoners, who were languishing in prisons. Many times I had been given the job of transporting arrested Jews from one prison to another. On these occasions I would treat them to cigarettes and various treats. We received a promise from the *gabbai* that they would ensure a *Seder* for the prisoners, as well.

A short time before Passover, the *gabbais* sent us several wagonloads of flour for matzos, but when we opened the first sack it turned out not to have any flour in it, but actually bran. Our baker reacted, telling the *gabbai* who was present that we would not bake any *matzos* from this flour. The gabbai got upset, but a second gabbai got involved, promising that the bran would immediately be exchanged for fine, white flour. The first *gabbai*, who had expressed himself by saying that our soldiers were "*shnorrers*"[23], was struck by one of our soldiers, whom he then threw out of the synagogue building. After this incident he was not selected to be a *gabbai* anymore.

For the night of the first *Seder*, we invited our colonel, whose wife was Jewish. He came with his adjutant. He ate gefilte fish with us; he thanked us properly; and he gave us his best, heartfelt wishes. The next day, his visit was described in the official daily regiment report. On the second day of Passover, as well, we conducted a *Seder* in the synagogue building with many invited guests from Barnaul. We were warmly welcomed by a well-respected resident, and we finished up with a tasty meal. Late in the evening we returned to the barracks—calm, quiet, and sober—all the Jewish soldiers together, not a single one having remained behind in the synagogue building.

Several days later the Christian holiday of Easter was observed. At that time they gave all the Christian soldiers leave, allowing them to march to a prayer service in a church. On the first night 20 soldiers went missing. And when on the next day they sent out 100 soldiers to look for them, ten more went into hiding. This made the company captain very angry. The next day he gathered many hundreds of soldiers into the main hall of the barracks and gave them a speech. In it he said: It is well known that Jews avoid military service as much as possible, but it is also clear that once they are in the military they are serious, proper, and dedicated. "Just take, for example," he continued, turning to the Christian soldiers, "the behavior of the Jewish soldiers on their holiday, Passover. With all due respect, not a single one of them went missing; not one of them got drunk; and they completed their holiday without any scandal. From among the Christian soldiers, on the other hand, we have only disgrace and shame from their behavior in Barnaul: drunkenness, beatings, people with knife wounds, and, finally, 30 soldiers who have disappeared. Those that did return came back in tatters and barefoot."

The soldiers that the military police had been looking for were severely punished. For a period of 20 days they were forced to stand in the blazing sun carrying a full military backpack that weighed 25kg. They were not allowed to move at all, and whoever did move was forced to stand an additional two hours.

[Page 339]

Military Maneuvers

Some time afterwards the entire regiment was taken out on a difficult maneuver in heavy rain. During the maneuver, one of the soldiers fired live ammunition, and one of the bullets happened to pass through the colonel's hat as he was riding on his horse. He immediately suspended the maneuver, saying, "I will give a reward of 50 rubles to the soldier who will tell me the reason for the sudden suspension of the maneuver." No one answered. Then, with tears in his eyes, he said: "Someone wanted to pick me off, but God was watching over me. I will not neglect my military duty on that account; I have already served our Czar for 30 years and I will continue to safeguard the glory of the Russian crown." With that he ended his message to the troops and rode off back to the barracks. Afterwards an order came down that we should all return to the barracks. As soon as we got back, the barracks were occupied by military police, and each person's personal storage case was inspected. It was clear that the bullet had come from one of the 30 soldiers who had been severely punished for being absent without leave. Later the colonel was transferred to a different regiment.

Because of the bad attitude of one of the senior officers I requested a doctor's appointment, so that I should be hospitalized for an illness that I was feigning. I was given an appointment with a *feldsher*[24] that I was acquainted with, and he sent me to the hospital. A few days later a lady invited me to a party for civilians, and with the doctor's help I left the hospital and went to the party. But suddenly I was astonished to see my colonel walking into the hall as a visitor. I immediately fled via a side door back to the hospital, but it turned out that he had already noticed me. Just as I lay down in my bed, telling the doctor what had happened, the colonel arrived at the hospital. He asked the doctor how many patients he had in his department. When the doctor told him the number, he said: "You are mistaken; there is one less." The doctor immediately took the lantern and went through the department with him, showing him that all the patients were present. Realizing that he had failed, the colonel remained silent and left.

But then he encountered me in the workshop, where I had gone because I had to prepare a pair of trousers for an officer. Here too I seemed to get away. Soon after that incident I left the hospital, and immediately afterwards I was given a month of house arrest, which meant not leaving the barracks for an entire month. I told one of the distinguished ladies of the city, who used to visit us, about this. She was sorry, but said nothing. Several days later they transferred the colonel to a different regiment in Omsk[25], and several weeks later they moved our regiment to Omsk.

[Page 340]

In Omsk

We knew that Omsk was a place where soldiers were released, and we hoped that we would be released from there. But as it later turned out, we were still far from being released, even though we had already served out our three years.

Arriving in Omsk, a large city with a fairly small number of Jews, we immediately made the acquaintance of the local Jewish functionaries: the rabbi, the *gabais* of the synagogue and the heads of the community, who generally had a very good attitude to the Jewish soldiers—the members of the two regiments, Regiments 42 and 43, which were stationed there. When we reached the barracks we were immediately given different outfits, and in general we were treated like new recruits. We attempted to get information about our release, but we were completely unable to find out the truth. There were no newspapers, but from the local soldiers we found out that in connection with the strained political situation all releases had been suspended.

In Omsk I immediately set myself up in my trade, in the tailor workshop. Via the workshop I became acquainted with the officer corps, for whom I sewed trousers or made alterations. At that time new soldiers arrived in the city; among them I met my friends, those with whom I had traveled from Poland to Russia. It was a joyous moment, and later we became close friends, maintaining a certain connection with one another.

The colonel of the regiment, Feinburgmeister, a German, loved to hold a parade, at the front of which he would always ride on his horse. Knowing that he had experienced soldiers who knew how to march, he would from time to time take us out to parade in the city. In general the Barnaul regiment was renowned for its excellent soldiers.

In the meantime information about the murder in Sarajevo[26] reached us, and we understood that from now on it would be much more difficult to be released from the military.

Meanwhile we had to participate in some exercises arranged by a new officer who wanted to utilize our experience to aggrandize himself. He was actually making us miserable, but since he was an elderly man we quite simply felt sorry for him. When we did in fact get our revenge, it was serendipitous. One day several hundred soldiers of the 4th Regiment arrived. Almost all of them were drunk, and each had an extra bottle of vodka in his pocket. The depravity and brawling were spreading through all the barracks. Our commanding officer ran from one barrack to the next, bewildered, but was completely unable to calm them down. With no alternative, he turned to us, asking us to quiet them down one way or another. Right away we—who were experienced soldiers—separated out the ones who were the most intoxicated and put them to bed, giving them at the same time three days' leave. There was a bit of a ruckus, but we succeeded in establishing order.

Among the drunk soldiers there was also a Jew from Zuromin[27], an unsavory character—a drunkard, a thief, and furthermore a bully. Once, when he was on night watch, he took his dozing companion's gun away. When the other soldier woke up and couldn't find his gun, he straight away ran to report it to his officer. An investigation was initiated, and it was concluded that this was the work of the fellow from Zuromin, who was immediately arrested and threatened with 10 years in prison. As a representative of the Jewish soldiers I turned to a Jewish lawyer in Omsk, asking him to take the case as defense attorney; meanwhile I had to pay the lawyer 25 rubles out of my own pocket. When the day of the trial came the defense was prepared: we had already bought off the sergeant whose testimony was the most critical, and the young man was declared innocent. It is worth noting that later, shortly after the outbreak of the First World War, the fellow deserted; when he was caught he was brought before a military field court and was shot.

Aside from the usual day-to-day troubles that most of the Jewish soldiers experienced in the Russian army, there was no shortage of other troubles in my regiment. I recall the troubles we went through when a Jewish soldier had an argument with a Kavkaz[28] officer.

[Page 343]

For the Sake of a Dagger

In our regiment there was a fellow from Lomzh[29] who was a good dancer. Once he was invited to an officers' evening to demonstrate his skill. His repertoire also included a Kavkaz dance, for which he needed the costume of a Kavkaz officer, as well as a belt with a dagger. After managing to obtain all these things, all borrowed from a Kavkaz officer, the fellow succeeded in doing his dance. Afterwards he returned the outfit to the Kavkaz officer's orderly. A short time later he was summoned by the Kavkaz officer, who called his attention to the fact that the dagger was missing from among the items he had returned. The fellow from Lomzh swore that he had returned everything, but it did him no good. The officer gave him warning that he would kill him if he did not return the dagger within 14 days. Now the fellow was walking around worried, looking for a way to influence the orderly to return the dagger; but the orderly claimed he had never received any dagger. So the fellow turned to us for help.

I took this matter into my own hands. First, together with a companion, I went to see the Kavkaz officer and told him that if there was anyone at all to blame it was his orderly. We also proposed monetary compensation, but the officer explained that since the dagger was an antique—an heirloom passed down for many generations—and was about 300 years old, it was not a question of money; he must get his dagger back unconditionally. I left the officer with a heavy heart, not knowing what to do or where to turn to. But then I remembered something I had once been told: if a Gypsy cheats you, ask another Gypsy how to handle him. So we decided to turn to a Kavkaz attorney to ask for his advice. We promised him a nice sum of money for his trouble, on the condition that he should extricate our fellow from his plight.

And the Kavkaz attorney actually did find a way to reveal the theft. He engineered a brawl in which the officer's orderly would also participate, and in a moment of anger the orderly pulled out his dagger to stab his opponent. Then, with the help of two soldiers, he was tackled, and his dagger was taken away from him. It turned out that this was the Kavkaz officer's dagger. The dagger was immediately returned to the officer, the orderly was arrested, and our fellow was saved from serious trouble. Understandably this business cost us a lot of money, but we—the Jewish Soldiers' Committee—always had a sum of money set aside for when we would need to get a Jewish soldier out of trouble.

[Page 344]

My Release from Military Service

The day on which I would be released approached, and quite unannounced they called me into the regiment office and stated that in three days I had to be ready to leave the barracks; after returning all military items in my possession I would be free to return home. During those three days I made all my preparations, and in the course of a month I was already back in Dobrzyn.

In those days making a trip from Omsk in Siberia to Dobrzyn in Poland was not one of the easiest things to do. Nevertheless I did get back to Dobrzyn, healthy and cheerful. The joy at my homecoming was indescribable. The entire town gathered together in my house, and everyone shook my hand. For weeks on end the neighbors didn't stop visiting us, asking me various questions. Additionally relatives from various other places, outside Dobrzyn, came to greet me. It took quite a bit of time before I again became a resident who was no longer greeted by the word "welcome".

[Page 345]

The First World War

For a short while I worked in Dzalin, an estate that belonged to Jewish landowners. When the rumors of mobilization became more earnest, I returned to Dobrzyn. I no longer slept at home because I didn't want to be up against a fait accompli. Meanwhile the Russian soldiers that made up the border guard left the town one at a time. On the other side of the border, i.e. in Golub, one could discern a concentration of German soldiers, and it was nearly certain that this meant war.

In the meantime hundreds of refugees arrived in Dobrzyn. They came from all corners of Poland, looking for a way to cross over into Germany. Among those that did cross, most were immediately interned and sent deep into Germany to work camps; only a small fraction returned to Dobrzyn.

A few days later, on a Sunday at 12 PM, the German army entered Dobrzyn, first a few dozen riders and afterwards hundreds carrying heavy weapons. They quickly spread out through the town, searching for Russian soldiers or officials. The few Russian officials that had apparently not fled were at first taken into custody, but later they were freed.

After a few weeks of occupation, the town residents began to feel the flavor of the German conquest. Every day the inhabitants were assembled in the town square, where those among them who were most fit for labor were selected and sent to dig trenches. Those who had horses and wagons had to work along with them. Those who hid, whether they were Jews or Christians, were severely beaten when they were found, and only then were they sent to do the hardest labor.

As time passed thousands of captured Russian soldiers were transported through the town on their way to Germany. They had been captured in the first large battles near Plock.

The general situation in the town became worse than ever. No supplies of food were brought in, and there was no way to make a living. Those whom the Germans took for labor did receive food, but their families at home went hungry. I once had an opportunity to travel around in the vicinity of the town, and together with my older brother I paid visits to peasant farmers whom I knew in the villages surrounding Dobrzyn, in order to acquire food from them; some of them even refused to be paid for it. Towards evening, when I returned to the town, my father assembled needy Jews, and, sharing the small amount of food that my brother and I had brought back, kept almost nothing for himself.

When the economic situation became even worse, deteriorating on a daily basis with no solution in sight, people in the town began to look for ways to feed their families. Many put knapsacks on their shoulders and filled them with of all kinds of fine merchandise that they could barter in the villages for a bit of food. They were pleased if they acquired a few potatoes or a little flour during the course of a day.

[Page 346]

Away at Work in Germany

As time passed, the Germans let us know that whoever wanted to register for work in Germany would be able to get work with good terms. Young, healthy people signed up immediately, and I was one of them. A few days later they assembled us in the square, brought us over to the Golub train station, and from there transported us deep into Germany.

The crying of the elderly and relatives when we parted from them is hard to describe in writing; heartrending scenes transpired. But there was nearly no other solution: we were looking for a way to avoid starving, and it seemed to us that this was the way.

It was a pleasant afternoon when our train left for Torun. At the Torun train station people were actually throwing stones at us, swearing at us and cursing us: "Damned Russians! Filthy Russians!", etc. So we were pleased when the train started moving out. But at all the other stations the same thing happened again and again, until we reached the Holstein station. There they ordered us to leave the train cars. It was already late at night.

Frozen and tired from the difficult journey, we were led for several kilometers on foot to the camp. One of us, Leib Ruska-Bulka, didn't feel well and wasn't able to tolerate the march. A soldier came over to him and hit him on the head with his rifle, and an officer who was right there didn't say anything to the soldier.

Finally we arrived to our destination, which was surrounded by barbed wire. Forests were all around it. We were quartered there in long barracks, 60 men to a barrack. Right away they gave us tattered military uniforms and old felt boots. They made us shower and cut off our hair. Putting us together with prisoners and foreign citizens who had been interned in Germany, they brought us into the barracks. There were 800 of us men, with no food and not even any water. An armed German soldier stood in every corner. At the same time they gave us notice that everyone must turn in any matches or cigarettes, as well as pocket knives or other tools that we might have in our possession. If any of the above items were found on someone, the penalty was going to be death, with no trial.

For a short time we were in the camp, busying ourselves with setting things up, digging, cleaning up, and other similar labor, meanwhile not receiving even minimal portions of food. Later we were split up to either work for farmers or to work in factories. I was assigned to a large carpentry workshop. There were 12 of us workers there. When we complained to the owner that we were hungry he immediately sent his young son to get us some food. After we had eaten our fill we thanked him and got down to work.

After a few months a series of wandering around began again. We were sent to a different place. We traveled for several days, circling around all of Germany, stopping finally in the town of Friedland, near the border with Holland. There were 63 of us Jews. The people working there, who had been sentenced to hard labor, were digging a canal. Here, too, they quartered us in barracks, again giving us notice about the death penalty for not turning in the above-mentioned items that we might have in our possession. In any event, the food they gave us was superior to that of the previous camp. The Jewish butcher who supplied meat for the camp promised us that he would see to it that we 60 or so Jews would be provided with kosher meat for the holiday—it being shortly before Rosh Hashana—and he would also take care of getting us *machzorim*[30]. But then afterwards we didn't see him again.

After two days in the camp they led twelve of us men out to the train station, where several train cars stood waiting. On one of the platforms of the cars about ten engineers and German mechanics were standing. We twelve had to push the train car, there not being any locomotive present. It took us two hours of pushing to reach the destination.

[Page 348]

Cruel Treatment

At the destination, giant machines were digging the canal. With us were several Poles who did not understand the German language, and they were immediately given a few blows by the supervisors. In contrast the Jews, who understood what was being demanded of them[31], obediently did their work... In general the local mechanics treated the laborers very poorly. They didn't take weakness or illness into account; everyone had to do his work even if, while working, he collapsed from exhaustion. We tried to intervene with management, but it didn't help at all. Then we decided that as an attempt at protest we would not go out to work on the Sabbath. When we presented ourselves Saturday morning, about to go out to work, I came forward and declared that, in the name of the 63 Jewish laborers, I was asking that we be given off from work on Saturday. I had barely completed my statement when I received a blow on my face from the work supervisor, and my blood dripped down like water. I raised a terrible cry, all the workers threw their tools down, and a ruckus started. Immediately they quieted us down; a junior officer stated that he was not authorized to give us off from work on Saturday, but that he would ask a higher authority. Meanwhile we did go to work, and when we got to the work place they separated us Jews from all the other workers and assigned the hardest labor to us.

In the meantime we were forced to work on Sabbaths and holidays, but after various twists and turns the entire matter came before the court. We declared before the judge in good German that we were not Russians, but rather came from a town near the German border; that we possessed German culture; and the like. The verdict was that on the Sabbath and Jewish holidays we could have off from whatever work there was, but that we would all have to work on Sundays instead. In connection with this verdict they increased our food rations, and our supervisors' attitude towards us improved. But the general conditions of the prisoners and forced laborers worsened.

In the vicinity of where I was, there were more than 60,000 prisoners, most of them Russians. The hygienic conditions were actually intolerable, with a typhus epidemic prevailing in nearly all the prison camps. Every day a large number of dead bodies were taken out of our camps, although all measures to treat erythema were being given in the hospitals. I myself was then working as a hospital orderly, and I had the opportunity to observe the methodology used by the German doctors. This was in the year 1916. The battles on the various fronts were in full swing, and Germany was simply unable to satisfy the needs of the German army. For this reason even the least of our needs were not satisfied, and yet to some degree we had to remain silent. Still some circles of the camps showed signs of an uprising as a result of desperation, not seeing an end to the troubles that spread from one day to the next.

I recall that on one of the Sabbaths most of the forced laborers from Dobrzyn gathered in an open field far from the barracks, looking for a way to free ourselves from this hell and return home. As far as I can remember, the following men were present there: (1) Hirsh Wolf Russik; (2) Nachum Frager; (3) Shmerl Bramberger; (4) Mendel Lent; (5) Shlomo Neumann; (6) Yaakov Gornie; (7) Yechiel Zissholtz; (8) Chaim David Broyn; (9) Yaakov Wier; (10) Binyomin Isser Nobleski; (11) Shlomo Lasher; (12) Mordechai Zilberman; (13) Fishel Boruch; (14) Shloimo Yakir Landberg; (15) Binem Bich die Zodektes; (16) Chaim Patchek, a grandson of Nachum Milifyes; (17) Henech Katcher; (18) Lipman Dratwa; (19) Henich Chamand; (20) the blind Yitzchok; (21) Iksya, a relative of the cantor's; (22) Shiya Katz; (23) Chona Zaklikowski; (24) Leib Ruska-Bulka; (25) Michael Dratwa; (26) Hillel Dratwa; (27) Yisroel Kankowalski; and myself.

At that time, Abraham Hirsh Kohn was the representative of the Dobrzyn Jews to the German authorities. We decided to appeal to him in writing, asking him to intervene in favor of the Dobrzyn forced laborers and to have them released. As it later turned out, however, he had been trying to intercede all along, but to no avail.

[Page 350]

My Liberation from the German Camp

And thus I languished under the severe yoke of the German regime until 1917. Then by happenstance I was liberated, while all my friends had to remain as prisoners longer. As the first one liberated, I was received with great joy by all the residents of Dobrzyn, Christian and Jewish alike, particularly by the families whose children or parents had remained in the camps. Among these my homecoming renewed the hope that they would soon also merit being reunited with their loved ones.

I didn't stay in Dobrzyn for very long. I went for a long visit to my sister in Szrensk[32]. There I had the opportunity to utilize my capabilities and experience as a hospital orderly when a typhus epidemic broke out near the place I was visiting.

In some instances I gave hygienic help that succeeded in localizing the illness. In Dobrzyn, as well, they utilized my techniques for cases of typhus. Here I would like to point out with joy that in many instances this helped.

Some time passed. The war ended. Poland obtained its independence, and new troubles began. To a certain extent the transition from German rule to that of an independent Poland threatened the security situation. Polish drunkards and pogrom inciters were able to go around unhindered. They would beat people up a bit, trying to plunder from Jews in a gentle fashion. After an appeal was made by the Jewish representative to the temporary Polish authority, a militia consisting of Poles and Jews was organized. To them was assigned the task of guarding the town. I was one of the members of the militia, and it happened many times that I was put in the position of defending a Jewish citizen whom Polish militia members intentionally wanted to harm.

Shortly thereafter, when also a portion of Pomorze [Pomerania] went over to the Poles, we suffered from the well-known Hallercheks[33] that used to beat Jews up, cut off their beards, and also do some plundering.

I must note here that authority had not yet been established in Poland; there were then two camps: the socialist PPS[34] and the extremely nationalist party ND[35]. The subject of the conflict was who should take over authority. But meanwhile the Jews, not having anyone to protect them, suffered from excesses. From time to time various unsavory military and police officials would descend on the town. Their function was singular: to make the lives of the Jewish population miserable, to confiscate merchandise, and to limit trade.

They reached a record during the Bolshevik invasion, in the year 1920. They accused the town's Jewish population of aiding the Russian soldiers, of pointing out to them where the Polish military positions were, and of giving them food and merchandise. Understandably the result was arrests and never-ending troubles. Only after intervention with the military authorities by the central Jewish Community Representatives of Poland did the incitement against the town's Jews slowly die away.

[Page 352]

*

When the Balfour Declaration was issued, a lively Zionist movement was launched in the town; the dream and aspiration—primarily of the Zionist youth—was to leave darkly anti-Semitic Poland as quickly as possible. My family and I were one of the first to immigrate to the Land of Israel. In spite of the fact that our economic situation had been good, we did not want to remain in Poland, and in the year 1921 we reached the Land of Israel.

Photographs Appearing in This Article

[Page 333]

Chana and Yitzchok Rosenwaks and their children

[Page 337]

Shmuel Prum and his son, Shemaye

[Page 346]

Yaakov Yosef Lichtenfeld reading *Tehillim* [36]

[Page 352]

**Yaakov Yosef Lichtenfeld with his
wife and daughter, Sarah Wechne**

[Page 353]

Yitzchok Rosenwaks, one of the first Dobrzyn *olim*[37] in Israel. One of the dedicated battlers for the security of Jerusalem in the early 1920s.

Translator's Footnotes

1. From *My Town: In Memory of the Communities Dobrzyn-Gollob*, edited by M. Harpaz, (published by the Dobrzyn-Golub Society, Israel, 1969), pp. 332-353.

2. Z"L = *zichroinoi livrocho* = of blessed memory, i.e. the author was already deceased at the time of publication.

3. *Mitzvah* = a religious commandment or good deed; here used facetiously to denote an immutable custom

4. Ostrołeka, Poland, which lies 200km due east of Dobrzyn. Warsaw is 120km south of Ostrołeka.

5. Tula, Russia lies about 1500km northeast of Warsaw.

6. Pale of Settlement = area within the Russian Empire where Jews were permitted to reside legally. Outside the Pale Jews required special government authorization for residency. See the following link: http://en.wikipedia.org/wiki/Pale_of_Settlement.

7. *Chevro kadisho* (Aramaic) = Jewish burial society, whose members prepare the body and ensure a proper burial. In some places these societies also took on the function of fraternities.

8. Barnaul, Russia (in Siberia) is located about 4000km due east of Tula.

9. Plock is a city on the Vistula, about 90km south of Dobrzyn.

10. *Seder* = Passover meal, during which the story of the Exodus from Egypt is ritually recounted

11. *Treif* = non-kosher. In particular, ordinary bread is strictly forbidden on Passover.

12. *Matzo* = unleavened bread, eaten on Passover instead of ordinary bread

13. *Haggada* = ritual recounting of the Exodus story, traditionally read from a book called a *Haggada*

14. His beard indicated he was more religiously observant, hence the invitations by the locals

15. *Shochet* = ritual (kosher) slaughterer

16. *Baal-tefillah* = synagogue prayer leader

17. See Footnote 6

18. *Hazkoras neshomos* = prayer for the dead souls, recited in the synagogue on holidays, and associated with giving charity in their memory; the prayer is also known as Yizkor (after the first word of the prayer)

19. *Kaddish* = prayer recited in the synagogue by mourners; also by relatives on the death anniversary of their loved ones. Their selective attendance for these prayers indicates they were not very knowledgeable.

20. *Gabbai* = synagogue treasurer functionary, who, among other duties, collected contributions and organized the provision of charity to the needy

21. "Torah" used figuratively here to signify a complex subject that requires study to master

22. Since they were not kosher

23. *Shnorrers* = moochers or spongers (literally, beggars who go from door to door asking for alms)

24. Feldsher = a health-care provider with no degree in medicine. See the following link: http://en.wikipedia.org/wiki/Feldsher.

25. Omsk is about 1000km west of Barnaul.

26. The June, 1914 murder of Archduke Franz Ferdinand of Austria in Sarajevo, which sparked the beginning of World War I

27. Żuromin, Poland, lies 60km east of Dobrzyn.

28. Kavkaz = Caucasus, southern part of the Russian empire that included Chechnya, Dagestan, Armenia, Azerbaijan, and Georgia

29. Łomża, Poland is situation about 200km east of Dobrzyn.

30. *Machzorim* = prayer books for the High Holidays (Rosh Hashana and Yom Kippur)

31. German being intelligible to the Jews, whose native language was Yiddish, a sister language of German

32. Szrensk is located 90km east of Dobrzyn.

33. Hallercheks = members of the Polish militia that was commanded by Jozef Haller. See the following link: http://en.wikipedia.org/wiki/J%C3%B3zef_Haller

34. PPS stands for *Polska Partia Socjalistyczna* = Polish Socialist Party

35. ND stands for *Narodowa Demokracja* = National Democracy

36. *Tehillim* = Biblical Book of Psalms

37. *Olim* = immigrants to Israel

[Page 354]
Pain and Suffering in the Second World War[1]
by Elya Tzala
Translated by Allen Flusberg

My Home

Dobrzyn on the Drevęc—that is the name of my little town, the place where I was born and was brought up, and where I also spent the years of my youth. Across the Drevęc is the neighboring little town of Golub. In reality they are like a single town, separated from each other only by the Drevęc River.

My name is Eliyohu Tzala, born on the 19th of September, 1917. I am a son of Yosef Wolff and Miriam, of blessed memory—the third of five children, all of whom were still living until the Second World War broke out.

My oldest sister, Rochel, was one of the most interesting and intelligent young girls in the town, and furthermore also very pretty. Even back then she knew the Hebrew language well and participated in various types of volunteer social work. And after she was married to Avi Stoltzman they built their home in Bydgoszcz[2], Pomerania. Many years later they helped many Dobrzyn families set themselves up in Bydgoszcz.

My parents, of blessed memory, tended toward traditional Judaism. They conducted themselves tactfully and were low-keyed about their attitudes; and they were known for this in our town. They were devoted heart and soul to their children, giving them everything they could, ensuring that they had a decent education, and striving for us to grow up honest, respectable people, to both Man and God. Their love for their children knew no bound. We repaid them with our own immature love, respecting them for their good parenting. We were always sensitive to their feelings and sympathetic with them, whether in moments of joy or pain.

I recall my father's daily schedule, especially that of the cold days of winter. I can still see him getting up very early, when it was still pitch black outside, taking his *tallis* and *tefillin*[3] under his arm, and – wrapped in a heavy overcoat and with a lantern in his hand – leaving with measured steps, on his way to the synagogue for the Morning Prayer service. I can see him coming back after our mother had already prepared breakfast, as all of us were sitting around the table eating.

Only after we had left our apartment – some of us to school and some to *cheider*[4] – only then did our father sit down to do his work, which he continued to do diligently until late in the day. As the sole support of the entire family he carried a heavy burden on his shoulders. There was no shortage of friends who visited him while he was working, unintentionally distracting him somewhat from work. But he took everything in stride, and as a result was very well liked.

In spite of his serious worries about making a living he also found time for volunteer social work. He was the chairman of the "Bikur Cholim"[5], an organization whose objectives were to take care of the impoverished ill, to give them medical help and to make it possible for someone who needed an operation to undergo surgery. Many a time he would sit at the bedside of someone who was seriously ill. His devotion to help the needy was admirable. Often he would neglect his own daily work, the source of his own livelihood; but for him it was the greatest joy to have someone that he could help. He was also a member of the *chevro kadisho*[6]. All this charitable work was conducted mostly at the expense of his livelihood. But he didn't take that into account, believing that one must not miss out on a single *mitzvo*[7]. With respect to this *Yid fun a gants yor*[8], what was most noteworthy was his devotion, how much of his heart and soul he put into helping those who suffered, how he sympathized with the oppressed, and how he was always ready to help out, even with his limited means.

He himself was the type of person who was satisfied with the little he had. He hoped and dreamed to see his children grown up and successful. But unfortunately he did not live to see it. He passed away after a short illness – at the young age of 52. Our family experienced a difficult grief. The entire town shared our sorrow as well. People would converse about the admirable virtues of our devoted father, who was a dedicated member of the Dobrzyn community.

[Pages 356-357]

Childhood in Dobrzyn

When I look back on my past in Dobrzyn, I see before me the good-looking young people, most of whom tended toward Zionism.

I recall the Zionist club "HaTechiya"[9], to which I belonged. There we would get together often to study the Hebrew language, to sing, to participate in dances from the Land of Israel, and to discuss various issues. On nationalistic celebrations, such as Lag BaOmer[10], Chanukah[11], or Herzl's *Yahrzeit*[12], etc., we would march through the streets of Dobrzyn, carrying blue-and-white flags and singing nationalistic songs that expressed our great longing for the Land of Israel.

While among themselves they did disagree about many things, the Jewish youth of Dobrzyn lived like a single family that did not take class or status into account. We provided help to each other on a daily basis. Everyone understood that we had to be united against the Poles of the town, who were always looking for opportunities to do us harm.

In general the youth of Dobrzyn had plenty to do in their free time. In the summer we would go on various excursions and play soccer. We spent winters skating on a frozen part of the Drevęc River, several kilometers away. The summer excursions were dedicated to meeting up with young people from neighboring towns, sometimes in Rypin[13] and very often in Mlawa[14]. Even years later, when we were already grown-up young men and many of us had left our town to look for a livelihood in the larger cities—or even abroad—this friendship was not broken; we wrote to each other, keeping alive the spark of our old relationships.

That is what Dobrzyn was like.

[Pages 357-360]

In the Polish Military

Meanwhile anti-Semitism had been going on a rampage in Poland, and we young people were suffering a great deal because of it. I recall that when my younger brother, Sho'ul, left to serve in the Polish army, he suffered greatly from Polish soldier hooligans who used to look for ways to make the lives of Jewish soldiers harder. Even worse was the situation of the Jewish soldiers in the Polish army during the period in which Hitler took control of Germany. The state of security in the small towns also worsened, and no Jew felt safe when he left his home at night. Jews were constantly being beaten up by Polish thugs.

When I was mobilized by the Polish military I made up my mind not to let the anti-Semitic Polish soldiers push me around. More than once I was insulted as a Jew, not only by ordinary soldiers but also by officers. But I always stood up to them, not taking the consequences into account; in the same way I even helped other Jewish soldiers out.

In the year 1939, when there was already a whiff of war in the air, I was on maneuvers in a forest near Dobrzyn. At that time I asked my commanding officer to give me leave to go home for a day or two, giving him as a reason that my mother was ill. Although he really wasn't allowed to, he granted my request. Apparently there were still some fine Poles, even in the military. I would like to point out that thanks to this visit I had the opportunity to see my mother for the last time before she passed away.

The war began shortly after my visit to Dobrzyn. The Germans bombed us incessantly. We lay in the trenches that we had previously prepared, but in reality we had nothing to defend ourselves with. The few cannons that we had were not capable of standing up against the organized German military might. Quickly most of the army fled, leaving behind its weapons and looking for a place where they could hide out and protect themselves from the German bombs. I myself took cover underneath a cannon, laying there for a long time until the bombing stopped.

After that the Polish soldiers regrouped and began wandering through forests and fields, but with no destination, since we didn't know where to head for. Meanwhile bridges that had been destroyed by Polish sappers were impeding the Polish military no less than the German one.

Not until the third day, as we arrived in the vicinity of Kutno[15], did they tell us that we would mount our resistance when we got closer to the Vistula River. But soon afterwards it turned out that we were encircled on three sides. An order was given to open fire with all the weapons we had. Thousands of soldiers fired rifles and cannons all night, but with no objective. Then at daybreak we saw that we were already surrounded on all four sides, and that German airplanes were flying overhead.

We ceased firing, and tens of thousands of our soldiers began running away. I grabbed a horse and started riding in a completely unfamiliar direction. I wanted to get as far as I could from the large military camp. On the way I came across thousands of soldiers, most of whom were fleeing in the direction of Warsaw. But also along the way German airplanes reached us and bombed us unmercifully.

I hid out in a forest, but after two days of not eating I started to look for a bit of bread to still my hunger. I went into a village farmyard and there noticed a familiar face—it was Nachman Engler of Dobrzyn. His helmet had been shot through by a stray bullet. Even before we got a chance to speak to each other properly, I had already lost sight of him and didn't see him anymore. (Later I found out that he, together with dozens of other Jewish soldiers who had been in the Polish army, was shot by the Germans in a prisoner camp.)

Meanwhile tens and hundreds of soldiers arrived, and the camp grew from hour to hour. When their number reached a couple of thousand, the order was given to break through the front and to try to reach Warsaw at any price. We marched through fields, but the German airplanes bombed us incessantly. Dozens of soldiers fell down dead around me. I was actually stepping on their bodies, but I had no alternative. I had to keep going, since the officers had adopted the tactic of circulating among the soldiers with their revolvers drawn to make sure we didn't run away and didn't turn ourselves in to be taken prisoner.

[Pages 360-362]

In Captivity

In this manner we walked through a thick fog, but as it got light outside we could make out from far away German artillery spread out across the fields. At this point the soldiers didn't wait for any more orders. Hundreds of them hung white handkerchiefs on their rifles to signify that they were surrendering. Needless to say the Germans surrounded us, taking away our weapons as well as various other items of even minimal value. They crowded us into an open field. Around us were a few dozen armed German soldiers who continually threatened to shoot us for the terrible sin of having wounded—in the midst of battle – a German officer as well as several soldiers. As a Jew I understood the implications of the threats. But I was a prisoner; my fate, as well as that of the other Jewish soldiers, was dependent on [the whim of] each German soldier that guarded us. They gave an order that all Jewish soldiers who were in the large camp – consisting of thousands of Polish soldiers – should come forward to identify themselves, but very few did. Later they led us, one group at a time, to a large outdoor area that was surrounded by barbed wire.

It began to dawn on us what power the Germans had over the Polish territory. I was thinking: Poland wanted to wage war against this military and against such weapons!

We have now been staying in the field for two days, and we are overcome by extreme cold. Having nothing at all to cover ourselves with, we lie right up against each other to keep somewhat warm. Others among us walk around all night, since they feel the cold even more strongly when they lie down. Also we are not given enough food to still our hunger. Women from a nearby little town throw some bread and other food, such as sausages and the like, over the fence to us. Occasionally some bread gets caught in the barbed wire. Any soldier that rushes over, reaching into the barbed wire to take out the bit of bread, gets a bullet fired at him by the German guard, and he falls down dead. These are daily occurrences. This is how the German soldiers treat Polish prisoners of war in the camps.

After we had been in the camp for a week, an order was given to bring us to a different camp. We went on foot for several hours, and then found ourselves in a place where there were barracks. They divided us up – officers separate from regular soldiers – but in general the new prisoner camp was no better than the previous one…Cold and hunger, with no possibility for anyone to acquire anything to buy from anywhere…Once imprisoned soldiers who assaulted a wagon full of bread that was meant for the camp prisoners were shot. The Jews, who were confined in special barracks, were forced to do the filthiest work. I was still hiding myself among the Polish soldiers and was considered a Pole – all thanks to my corporal, who asked the Polish soldiers among whom I stayed not to inform on me.

One day several dozen prisoners, I among them, were called out to come to the central area. The announcement was as follows: "Each of you must bring five horses to a certain location that is about 200 km away from the prison camp. Each of you who succeeds will be freed and will be allowed to return home." Although the task to be carried out was not very easy, I was overjoyed.

We set out, and one time after another it appeared to us that we would not be able to reach our goal. As tired as we became, the horses suffered even more fatigue, and several of them collapsed along the way.

I recall that as we went along our long journey we passed through Lodz. Seeing us in our Polish uniforms—blackened and worn out—dozens of women brought us bread with sausages, as well as candy and other things to eat.

The last day of our march I felt as if it was all over – my feet were full of blisters, and I couldn't really take another step. But my desire to live was so strong that I overcame all my pain and finally reached the designated place. Of the five horses that I had taken with me, only two were left.

Along the way we would pass German soldiers, and I would eavesdrop on their conversations. Each of them was bragging about the number of Jews he had slaughtered.

Those horses that couldn't keep going were shot by the Germans. The remaining horses were distributed by the Germans among the farmers who lived in the vicinity.

On the second day after I had arrived, a German soldier realized, just by chance, that I was a Jew. He started shouting and telling everyone that they had to get me. I hid, and nothing came of it.

[Pages 362-364]

On the Path Home

The next day they announced to us that all those who had brought the horses were being liberated and could go home. My joy was unbounded.

Meanwhile I found out that dozens of Jews had been segregated in one of the barracks. I looked for a way to communicate with them. I thought that they might have some messages they would like to have delivered, and in any event I figured that there must be some way to get to talk to them. After a couple of hours I was already in their barracks. A few of them recognized me; they were very glad to see me and asked me to tell their parents that they were here.

I went straight to Lodz, where I still hoped to meet up with my sister. When I first got to Lodz I went over to a friend of mine with whom I had worked for the last three years before the war broke out. This person was now completely desperate. The situation in Lodz was getting worse from one day to the next. And this was even before the ghetto was established. I went out into the street to buy a loaf of bread, which was already somewhat difficult to obtain. Long lines of people stood in front of the shops to buy a little food. I got in line with everyone else. A police corporal who was maintaining order immediately recognized me. He was a friend that I had worked with before the war. He was actually German, but he was far removed from doing any harm to Jews. As a sign of good friendship he immediately provided me with some slices of bread. Thanking him profusely I paid him, and went back to my friend.

The very next day I found out that my dear brother Sho'ul had arrived from Bydgoszcz and was staying with the Kirstein family on Pomorska Street. I went straight over to him. When he saw me he could hardly believe his eyes, since everyone had been sure that I had perished in the war. He had a chance to tell me all about the entire family...the misfortune that befell my younger brother, Shloime, who was shot in a Bydgoszcz street by an SS officer...My sister Rochel and her husband, Avrohom Stoltzman, had gone to Kutno, to Isaac.

Without much thinking I made my way to Kutno, but unfortunately I didn't meet up with them there. People there explained to me that they had gone off to Warsaw, hoping they would make it to Russia from there. I thought I would try to get to Warsaw, but as I reached the train station I saw that it would be impossible – the train was full of soldiers, and they weren't letting any private passengers on. At that moment I made the decision to go home.

As I traveled past the town of Krosniewice, 9 kilometers from Kutno, I remembered that an uncle of mine lived there, and I went over to see him. When I came into his place I noticed an air of sorrow in the house—they had taken my uncle away to work at hard labor. It had already been two days since he had last been seen. A German officer who observed that I was in their apartment – dressed in my Polish military uniform – immediately ordered me to leave. I got out of there as quickly as I could. Only later did I find out that the Germans shot my uncle in the middle of the town square.

On my way to Dobrzyn I stopped in various little towns, where I witnessed the misery the Jews were in. Everywhere the same destruction: they were beating and murdering Jews – never mind the hunger and hardship.

It was evening when I arrived in Dobrzyn. I went over to Hersch Boruch Dratwa, who lived at the edge of town. As soon as I got there he let my uncle Mechel Tzala know, and my uncle immediately sent me civilian clothes. I changed my clothes, but after I had heard about the "good deeds" that the Hitler bandits had been doing in Dobrzyn I didn't leave the house.

One day followed another and various rumors were going around, but no one knew what the morrow would bring. I heard about the bitter fate of the Jews in Bydgoszcz, and therefore didn't go there. Wives were waiting for their husbands—and parents for their children—to return from the unknown place the Germans had taken them away to "work"[16]. But the relatives' hope was only a false illusion. These men were long gone from this world. Two days after they had taken them out of the synagogues and houses they killed them in a forest near Inowroclaw[17]. The few men who were left in the town had been mobilized to labor daily.

[Pages 364-366]

We Flee from Dobrzyn

I didn't dare step outside the house until the 9th of November, 1939, when the grievous order was given to expel all the Jews from the town. This occurred two weeks after I had gotten back to Dobrzyn. Without much thought I joined the large number of Dobrzyn Jews traveling on the highway to Rypin. We traveled by day, and at night we stayed over at the homes of local farmers, who gave us a place to sleep. We purchased a horse and wagon in which we could put the small children and elderly people, who no longer had the strength to walk. After several days of travel we reached the Russian border. But the Russian army would not under any circumstances let us cross the border. In our group we were two men, four women and five children. After enduring two days and two nights of cold weather, we, being families with small children, were forced, with no alternative, to turn back onto the same path we had come on. Traveling back the other way, we entered Plonsk[18]. The condition of the Jews who had remained there was terrible, and we discovered that there was no place for us there.

Continuing on our way we arrived in a small town called Drobin[19]. Although here too it was not easy to find a temporary place for ourselves, we decided to stay here. My uncle and I took the initiative to take the horse and wagon out in the vicinity to make some food for ourselves and to obtain some wood that we could use for a fire to warm it up. We slept in a cold house that we happened upon, and we made sure that at least the children were warm. My uncle was with me, together with his elderly mother whom he had taken out of Rypin and brought over to us under very dangerous circumstances. A couple of weeks later she died in Drobin and received a proper burial there in a Jewish cemetery.

As time went on it became very hard to get even a little food to buy, because the Germans took everything away. We were literally starving. But through happenstance we succeeded – thanks to my uncle – to settle ourselves in a village near Drobin. My uncle was a tailor, and the local farmers were interested in having him sew for them. So they provided him with a room, and all of us took advantage of the opportunity. We now had a place to lay our heads down, and we had no lack of food. And this is how we spent the harsh winter of 1939-40.

[Pages 366-368]

They Persecute Us

Later on an order was given to present ourselves to work for the Germans. I should emphasize that each order to present ourselves to work was accompanied with a warning that anyone who would not come forward to work was under a threat of execution. It goes without saying that almost everyone came forward. I left to work at a German company that constructed roads. The advantage of working was that we were paid and could buy ourselves food.

They never seized me to do any other kind of work, and in this manner several months passed quickly, until a new order was given – that all Jews who had not been living in Drobin before the beginning of the war had to report to the market place. My uncle Mechel and I came from the village to present ourselves. As we stood in the square, a German soldier who had come over to pick on me tried to knock my hat off my head. When I didn't let him, he beat me till he drew blood. Fortunately for me the trucks that were supposed to take us away were already there and began leaving immediately – otherwise who knows how I would have ended up. They took us away in dozens of trucks, and we had no idea where we were going.

Finally we were let off in a camp near Dzialdowo[20]. There we already saw from far away the accursed members of the SS, their whips extended to provide amusement for themselves over our bodies. They were lined up in two rows, and we had to pass through these two rows to get into our barracks. The cries and screams of the unmercifully beaten men were indescribable. Dozens of bleeding men, and those who couldn't even stand up anymore, particularly elderly men, remained laying on the ground at the entrance to the barracks. I landed only a few harsh, dry blows, but I felt them for quite a long time afterwards.

The camp that we had gone into was a transit camp. After a few days they put us in a train that brought us to Piotrkow Trybunalski, not far from Lodz[21], where they gave us neither the means to live nor a place to live. My uncle, Mechel, looked up an acquaintance, who provided him with a sewing machine and a corner to work in. Generally the camp in Piotrkow was not a very good place. All kinds of diseases were going around, and as a result many of the people caught them and died. There wasn't any food. So I decided to leave Piotrkow as quickly as possible. (As I found out later on, my uncle Mechel and my entire family [who had stayed behind] were sent to Treblinka, where they all perished.) One evening I took off the blue-white stripe, went off to the train station, bought a ticket to Warsaw, and with it ended my stay in Piotrkow.

The trip to Warsaw was very dangerous for a Jew at that time, but as it turned out I made it there. It was evening when we arrived. All the passengers stayed in the train station and took the opportunity to get some sleep. I was sitting in a corner with my head down, so that the German police should not take much notice of me.

I went out into the street at dawn and took a taxi to get over the bridge to Praga[22]. From among the group of taxi drivers one of them shouted "But this is a Jew, don't take him—he'll cause you trouble!" However my cab driver didn't pay any attention to this comment, and so luckily I crossed over the bridge and arrived in Praga. Interestingly, the driver didn't demand any more than I offered him, so he got paid for the ride only.

One hour later I was already sitting on a train that was headed for Mława[23]. To play it safe, I didn't get off at the Mława station, but instead one stop before. At this village station I met Polish farmers, who warned me not to go to Mlawa, where, they said, the Germans seize Jews and either send them away or shoot them on the spot. Therefore I set off in the direction of Ciechanów[24]. That day was Sunday, and I went along with the farmers as if I was one of them. After a tiring trip I arrived in Ciechanów.

I found out that there was a *Judenrat*[25] in Ciechanów. I was looking for some way to get in contact with them when a commotion broke out. The Germans had blocked off several streets to look for Jews who were in hiding. I hid in an abandoned house, where I stayed until it got quiet. Later I heard footsteps of people walking nearby, but since I could see that these were *undsere*[26] I came out. They explained to me how to get to the *Judenrat*. When I got there one of the *Judenrat* told me that harboring an illegal Jew in Ciechanów would be dangerous; they advised me to go to Mława, where there was a Jewish ghetto in which I would be able to hide out. They also helped me solve the problem of how to get into Mława. They secured a place for me among the boxes in one of the trucks that transported vegetables and potatoes. In this way I arrived safely in Mlawa and entered the ghetto after much effort, fatigue and fright.

[Pages 368-372]

In the Mlawa Ghetto

Despite my difficult situation it gave me a real fright to see the state of the Jews in the Mlawa Ghetto. The hunger was extreme. In each home one or more people lay ill. The sanitary conditions were not tolerable. And in addition every day the Germans gave new orders designed to shorten our lives even more. As a means of provocation the Jewish police were ordered to guard the periphery around the ghetto, so that no one could enter or leave. At the entrance they hung large signs with the word "typhus" on them. Regardless, the terror continued to grow.

One day they demanded that all the Jews of the ghetto report to the market place. It turned out that they had caught two Jewish boys with several potatoes, accused them of stealing, and sentenced them to death. As we arrived at the square we saw four gallows that had been prepared, and immediately they brought the four victims: the two boys, the father of one of them, and some other Jew. We were surrounded by soldiers, and the order had been given that anyone who showed any sign of grief by crying or shouting out would be shot. With pain and anger we watched the terrible tragedy unfold, and with heads bowed we returned to the ghetto.

One day a notice appeared in the ghetto that all men capable of labor should present themselves at the work office. I was one of the first to get there.

They sent us out to build roads in the nearby village of Czernice. They put us up in barracks, and we were allowed to go back to the ghetto once a month.

Not far from our camp was a prisoner camp for Russian soldiers, whom we saw almost every day marching in groups of tens. They looked terrible—thin, pale, barely able to stand. The Germans were letting them starve. They did get some food from some Polish farmers who were transporting stones in their wagons, to be used to pave the road. Risking their lives, the farmers managed to find ways to give these prisoners small amounts of food to eat. But two of the farmers did pay for this with their lives. When the Germans caught them they took these farmers to the nearby town of Prosnicz, assembled the entire town in a place where two gallows had already been prepared, and hanged them.

The situation in the Mlawa Ghetto worsened from day to day. There was just no food at all. So each time we returned to the ghetto we would collect some clothing or shoes, and on the way back to work we would barter with the farmers who were there. We would give them a pair of pants, a skirt or a pair of shoes, and we would receive some food in exchange. The day on which we would bring some of this food back to the ghetto was celebrated like a holiday.

One day when I was returning from work to the ghetto I developed a high fever. They brought me to the hospital, where I received the appropriate remedy, the application of *bankes*[27]. When the nurse lit the alcohol she accidentally spilled a little of it on the bed, setting it on fire, and I myself was also badly burned. It took a long time, but my wounds did heal, thanks to the devotion of the Jewish doctor in the ghetto, who soon thereafter died of typhus. When the weather got a little warmer I started going outside again.

Meanwhile the Germans intensified the terror in the ghetto. Once they called the *Judenrat* representative to the commandant's headquarters. He never returned. They sent a coffin with his dead body back to the ghetto, with an order not to open it, but rather to bury it immediately. Later they arrested the Jewish police who guarded the ghetto periphery and murdered them all. Aside from this they once took away 50 young Jews together with 50 elderly Jews, ordered them to dig a long pit, and then sent them back into the ghetto. That night it rained very hard, filling the pit with water. But this didn't bother the Germans, and before daybreak they led the same 100 Jews back out, shot them all and tossed their bodies into the water-filled pit. Their blood mixed with the water, forming a large lake of blood.

The Germans began to visit the ghetto more frequently, with the intention of murdering the people one by one. The summer of 1942 had almost passed when the Germans suspended the road-building work and split us up to work in the fields that belonged to the farmers from the surrounding villages. Suddenly an order was given that all the Jews had to return to the Mlawa Ghetto. So within a day or two all the Jews who had been working in the vicinity were gathered together in the ghetto. One rumor followed another, and no one knew what the morrow would bring.

One day an order was received that all the Jews of the ghetto must gather in the market place. After the square had filled up they conducted a selection, separating the young people from the elderly. At that time we already knew to some extent of the existence of death camps for Jews, and the rumor was that the Germans were preparing to send some of the Jews to a death camp. During the selection various interpretations of what was going on were circulating. One person would say that being on one side was good, while another argued that being on the opposite side was better. People were running back and forth. In the turmoil the Germans began to fire their weapons, and a young woman fell down, shot dead. When things quieted down they registered everyone who was in the square, and we were told to be ready to be called back at any time.

Two days later they called us back to the square. Nearly all of the residents of the ghetto – the young, the old, women and children – they registered us all and sent us to the train station. There they locked us inside freight cars, first taking away from each of us whatever he had: gold, money or other valuables. No one tried to hide anything. One woman had hidden a ten-mark note, and she was immediately shot.

Since we already knew about the death camps Treblinka and Auschwitz, we could, as the train moved, tell from the stations that we were on our way to Auschwitz. The train stopped after two days of travel, and we were ordered out of the cars. After walking for several minutes we found ourselves in front of a high barbed-wire fence with a large inscription, "Work makes one's life free". We soon found out that this was Auschwitz.

[Pages 372-373]

In Auschwitz

It was the 18th of November, 1942. An officer stood at the gate of the camp, and with a short stick indicated who should go to the left and who to the right…Women, children and the elderly on one side; and healthy, young people on the other side. The implication of the directions was clear.

It would be superfluous to describe the camp with its gray atmosphere…The high barbed-wire fence with the giant light tower, the shouting and screaming and just plain tumult was deafening. They locked us up in a large barrack and immediately tattooed us with numbers on our left arms. My number, 76249, accompanied me [as an identification number] all the way to the liberation.

The first few days we hardly did anything. We stood around outside, and we saw the half-dead people who worked in the camp as cleaners and garbage collectors—pale, emaciated, and dressed in striped prison clothing. Several days later they took us away to another camp, about 7 kilometers away from Auschwitz. This was a camp that they had just begun to build: a total of 6 large barracks with 800 prisoners; knee-deep mud; a fence with towers, like that of Auschwitz, but with fewer people moving around. They gave us a place to sleep in one of the barracks, and slowly I began to get used to camp life. Our work was to build new barracks, which were soon filled up with people, mostly Jews whom they had brought from various ghettos. There I recognized several Jews from Dobrzyn and Rypin, but most of the Jews were from Holland and Germany. They also brought in German criminals who served as camp guards. There were also Christians from the German-occupied countries —those whom the Third Reich considered undesirables.

[Pages 373-376]

In a New Work Camp

After we had finished putting up the barracks, they attached us to the building commando, whose mission was building factories and refineries to extract gasoline from coal. This was in a giant area of greater than 20 square kilometers. We dug kilometer-long lengths where they placed electrical cables. We also dug trenches for pipes, and we built bridges. Hundreds of laborers were employed to set up the giant plant. But the work was not conducted as envisioned by the engineers, simply because the laborers didn't get fed.

We would get up while it was still dark, in cold weather when the temperature would drop to -5°C. We stood around for a half hour until the camp director arrived and counted us, and then we received a small slice of bread and a cup of black coffee – at least it was referred to as coffee. After that we marched off to work in a place located not far from the camp. We marched in groups of 30-50 workers, each of which was headed by a *kapo*[28]. At noon we received lunch, a grassy soup containing biscuits. This lunch was supposed to sustain us until dinner, which we received after returning from work. Dinner consisted of a thick soup with a small slice of bread, not enough to even satisfy the hunger of someone who was not working hard. It goes without saying that under such conditions of sustenance many of us became ill and unfit for the work after several days. Once the camp director observed that a particular worker was not capable of labor, that worker was not seen again.

The winter of 1942-43 was characterized by severe cold. The striped camp clothing that we wore at work provided the body with minimal protection from the cold, and many times one of the laborers' limbs became frostbitten. The cold prevented many of the laborers from properly carrying out their duties. The German supervisor would take note of such a laborer, and on the way back to the barracks he would knock that worker's hat off his head and tell him to go back and pick it up. We would then hear a shot ring out and the worker would fall down, dead. The report that the supervisor would give the commandant stated that the worker had tried to escape. The next morning the supervisor would receive a commendation. The cruelty of the supervisors was so extreme that they would severely punish us for wrapping small bags of cement onto our bodies for insulation on very cold days. Daily one could see the diminishing number of laborers who went out to work. The weak and ill were being taken away and murdered.

By chance I got acquainted with a Czech *kapo*, who was in charge of high-elevation construction work. He himself was a political prisoner. He arranged for me to be in the group under his command, and I worked there for almost two years. The supervision of the work was in civilian hands, and in any case we felt freer. The work was not so easy because of the cold that we felt more strongly higher up than on the ground. But they let us warm our hands around a fire, and they provided us with other similar comforts that made the day's work easier. We also found a way to get food for ourselves. I would just bring the *kapo* a shirt, and in return he gave me bread several times. All the supervisors were civil and, seeing our bitter fate, were sympathetic to us.

Meanwhile a new class of Jews arrived from all over Europe: Poland, Lithuania, Hungary, Holland, etc. They were brought in special trains. They were ragged, but they didn't look that bad. Needless to say, however, they became weak, pale and emaciated after a short time in the camp. Mostly this happened to the middle-aged people, who couldn't adapt to the difficult living conditions in our camp. Every day they took away dozens of the ill, and we never saw them again.

There was no shortage of tragic events in the camp. The Germans accused a young Jewish boy from Lithuania of trying to smuggle arms into the camp. To carry out the verdict—death by hanging—they brought in a German officer from Auschwitz, a specialist in this profession. They ordered everyone to come to the place of execution, and before the eyes of thousands of spectators they hanged him. It should be noted that hangings were very common occurrences in the camp. Once when some *kapos* got into a fight with each other, they were put on trial and sentenced to hang.

Reports from the Russian front began to worry the German forces, and their behavior became more erratic from day to day. Their treatment of the Russian prisoners became more brutal after the latter had organized several escapes. The workers and also the supervisors didn't suffer any less: they had been negligent at completing the great plant in which the Germans were supposed to extract gasoline from coal. And slowly they were beginning to feel the shortage of gasoline. Rumors about their downfall on the Russian front also began reaching them. One could see it from their fallen faces.

One day, as I was leaving my barrack, I heard a whistling sound, and suddenly several bombs fell not far from the camp, towards where we had been building the great plant. In this manner several airplane sorties passed over, continually bombing the great plant. On that first day 30 British prisoners who had been living in a particular barrack were killed. More than 100 laborers on the great plant, where 30,000 workers had labored, were also killed. The great plant, which had almost been completed—and whose construction had been going on for more than two years with the help of tens of thousands of workers—was completely destroyed; it burned for weeks, and no one even tried to put the fire out. We were all happy about the downfall, but at the same time we were mourning for our 100 innocent victims who were killed in the bombing, nearly all of them Jews.

The Allies' planes paid us visits almost every day, and the panic that ensued as they approached was awful. The German experts and the engineers began leaving one by one, and we began to think about what might become of us. The German downfall was now already certain. Information reached us that Krakow had already been taken by the Russians. The German civilians began treating us in a very fawning manner, but we didn't trust them.

In the meantime a group of Russian prisoners succeeded in constructing an escape tunnel. The Germans found it, and only a few days before the liberation they shot them all.

Daily the German decline became more noticeable. The trains were now fueled by wood, and one automobile was forced to tow another – all these were signs showing that the war was ending and the downfall of the Germans was certain. But the question that the Jewish prisoners now had was whether they would live to see this downfall.

[Pages 376-379]

We Leave the Work Camp

One day we were given an order that we were all to leave the camp and to be brought in the direction of Germany. I provided myself with enough food. This was on the 20th of November, 1944, just two years after my arrival in the Boyna[29] camp. Accompanied by older soldiers – the young soldiers were all on the front – we began to march until we got to the train station at Gliwice[30]. There we were [about to be] loaded into freight cars, but just then airplanes appeared high above us, lighting up the sky with their incessant bombing. We were gripped with fear; many ran away, but no one knew where they had gone. On the way I had met someone from Dobrzyn, Yitzchak Nussbaum, but right away I lost track of him.

Even though I was wearing civilian clothes, I had been afraid to run away. We sat in an open field and waited to see what would happen. Then an order was given to load us into the freight cars. We stood inside them, pressed right up against one another. Those who were unable to stand and tried to sit down were trampled to death. The train went slowly in the terribly cold winter night; we were without food and even a little water. People died like flies. Every morning, when the train stopped for fuel and water, we found dozens of dead bodies, which we simply tossed out of the car. We arrived at the Mauthausen[31] station and they wanted all of us to get off there, but the German military forces didn't allow it. They said they didn't have any room for us. We continued onward in the direction of Oranienburg, near Berlin. The entire path to Berlin was covered with dead bodies from our train, which we were tossing out every day. When we got out in Oranienburg, after 11 days of travel[32], we were a total of 3,000 people who were left from the 10,000 that had started out in Boyna.

We were in the Oranienburg camp for only a few days, since Berlin was being bombed continuously. An order was given to bring us to the Flossenbürg[33] camp, which was located on a mountain. This was a camp that Hitler had constructed in 1933, soon after he came into power. The situation there was very difficult. There was nothing to sleep on, nor was there any food. Even worse, dozens of dead bodies lay around the barracks. They couldn't bury them because the mountain was made of stone[34].

I was lying on some boards, engrossed in thought, when suddenly I heard someone calling my name. It was two fifteen-year-old boys who had travelled with me the entire way. They had brought me some food, but I didn't want to take it from them until they assured me that they had enough food for themselves, as well.

I started thinking about how to get out of this camp, and when I became aware that they were preparing a new transport to bring us to a different camp I immediately signed up and attached myself to the group that was going to the new camp. As I was leaving, I noticed one of those two boys waving to me through the window to say goodbye. To this very day I don't know what happened to those two boys.

We went inside sealed train cars and arrived at Lansburg[35], near Stuttgart. This was a small camp with a few barracks near a large tunnel. Within the tunnel we worked in an aircraft plant. The Americans were bombing it incessantly, yet weren't able to do it any harm. We worked the night shift. Weak and exhausted, I was hardly able to stand. Knowing the Americans were already not very far away, the Germans had placed explosives along the walls of the plant, so that if the Americans approached they would be able to blow it all up.

Meanwhile the order was given to take us away from there. This was already in March, 1945. In the darkness of night we got together and began marching. We got onto a train and got off after one hour. As we exited the cars we found ourselves surrounded by soldiers. We all sat down. Meanwhile it started to rain. Some of us tried to stand up, but were immediately given a warning that whoever tried to stand up would be shot. We sat this way until morning. Wet to the bone, we were led to a camp named Kaufering[36]. There were no barracks there, only bunkers under the ground. We found out that not long before, several thousand prisoners died here of an illness that the Germans had not at all been interested in diagnosing.

After a few days they loaded us into train cars again and took us away, but with no destination. The Germans simply didn't know what to do with us.

During this trip I began to feel unwell. Unable to hold my head up, I fell asleep. The German soldier who came through the train car hit me in the head with his rifle. As the blood dripped down my face, my friends bound the wound.

Shortly afterwards we got off the train again, this time in a camp called Ganacker[37]. Here there was an airfield in which airplanes were parked, but with no fuel to make them go. I was ill and weak. My friends brought me some water with a little sugar. This was the aid that I received, while next to me lay a Russian prisoner who was near death.

Meanwhile the British had bombed the airfield, and all the airplanes in the airfield were burning brightly. The Germans fled. Left to ourselves, we used the opportunity to look for food.

Eventually SS police arrived and ordered us to march. Those among us who were too weak to walk were immediately shot by them. After 26 km of walking we came to a village named Arensdorf. There they didn't guard us very well. A few of us went into a barn full of bundles of hay and straw, hiding between the bundles. I had decided that, come what may, I would not go any further. Knowing that the day of liberation was just around the corner, we were willing to take our chances.

But when the police came back and saw that eleven prisoners were missing they began searching, and among other places they also searched inside the barn. They stabbed at the straw with their bayonets but didn't find anyone. They then took a group of 10 prisoners and shot all of them. This somewhat defused their murderous feelings, and thanks to that we were saved.

[Page 380]

The Liberation

After some time had passed, when we felt that things had quieted down outside, all eleven of us crawled out. The Americans hadn't yet arrived, but the Germans had organized a civil police force that protected us to make sure no one would cause us any harm. This was in April, 1945.

Meanwhile a German man who owned an estate appeared and invited us to come over to work for him. When we arrived he served us the best of food at his table. In this way he wanted to rehabilitate himself with his good deeds for what he had done to Polish and Russian prisoners during the war years.

A few days later, while we were sleeping in the barn, we heard a commotion, followed by the firing of machine guns. We understood that the war had ended and we were free. It was the 1st of May, 1945.

Although we felt as if we were newly born, we could not forget the thousands of victims whom we had lived with in the Boyna camp for two years, and who did not merit to see the downfall of Hitler, *yimach shemoi le'oilomim*[38].

Weak and broken, I began to establish my life anew, but with a bitter feeling—knowing that I was the only survivor from among my large extended family.

Let these lines serve as a memorial to my dear unforgettable parents, Miriam and Yosef Wolff Tzala of blessed memory; my sister Rochel with her husband Avrohom Stoltzman; my dear brothers Sho'ul, Shloime and Avigdor Tzala; and my uncles and aunts together with their families.

Yisgadal veyiskadash shemay rabbo[39].

Eliyohu Tzala, in garments of a death-camp inmate[40]

Yaakov Dratwa, in uniform of a Polish soldier[41]

Directors of Dobrzyn Association in *Yaar HaKedoshim*[42]
Right to left: **Avraham Dor (Dobroszklanka), Yehuda Rosenwaks, Yehudit Polinicki (Lipka), Yaakov Cohen, and Yaakov Yechiel Bielawski** [43]

Translator's Footnotes

1. From *My Town: In Memory of the Communities Dobrzyn-Gollob*, edited by M. Harpaz, (published by the Dobrzyn-Golub Society, Israel, 1969), pp. 354-380.

2. Bydgoszcz is a large town located about 80 km west of Dobrzyn, in the Polish province of Pomerania.

3. Prayer shawl and phylacteries

4. Jewish religious school for small children

5. *Bikur cholim* (Hebrew) = visiting the ill

6. *Chevro kadisho* (Aramaic) = Jewish burial society, whose members prepare the body and ensure a proper burial

7. Good deed (literally, a Torah commandment)

8. *Yid fun a gants yor* = a Jew who is careful to observe both the ritual and ethical precepts of Judaism, and who is involved in religious observance all year round, not just on major holidays. (literally, a year-round Jew)

9. *HaTechiya* (Hebrew) = the revival or renaissance

10. 33rd day after Passover, celebrated with archery and other sports, possibly in commemoration of a military victory during the Bar Kokhba rebellion in Israel in ~135 CE

11. 8-day winter holiday, celebrating military victory of Maccabees in 165 BCE that later led to an independent Jewish state in Israel

12. Anniversary of death

13. A town 25 km due east of Dobrzyn

14. Mlawa lies 100 km due east of Dobrzyn.

15. Kutno lies about 120 km south of Dobrzyn.

16. See the article by Yehoshua Flusberg, "The Men Left and Didn't Return", on p. 137 of the Dobrzyn Yizkor Book (cited in Footnote 1).

17. Inowroclaw lies 40 km south of Bydgoszcz.

18. Plonsk lies about 115 km southeast of Dobrzyn.

19. Drobin lies on the road back from Plonsk towards Dobrzyn. It is some 25 km northwest of Plonsk and about 90 km southeast of Dobrzyn.

20. Dzialdowo is about 80 km north of Drobin.

21. Piotrkow was a ghetto for Jews, located 26 km south of Lodz, in central Poland. See the following link:
http://www.deathcamps.org/occupation/piotrkow%20ghetto.html.

22. Praga is a borough of Warsaw that is located on the east bank of the Vistula River (see the following link: http://en.wikipedia.org/wiki/Praga).

23. The town of Mlawa lies about 130 km north of Warsaw and about 100 km east of Dobrzyn.

24. The town of Ciechanów is located about 35 km south of Mława.

25. *Judenrat* = German word for Jewish Council—a governing body, made up of Jews, set up by the Germans to administer a Jewish community in the German-occupied territories.

26. *Undsere* = [some of] ours—a Yiddish expression for Jews.

27. *Bankes* = suction cups placed on various parts of the body, a folk remedy commonly used in Eastern Europe. The variant used here appears to have been "fire cupping", in which a cotton ball that has been doused in alcohol is lit and placed inside the cup for a short time to heat the cup and the air inside it. The cup is then pushed firmly onto the patient's skin in the desired location to make an airtight seal, and as the air cools a vacuum forms inside. See the following link: http://en.wikipedia.org/wiki/Cupping_therapy .

28. A "prisoner functionary", a prisoner who was assigned to supervise forced labor. See the following link:
http://en.wikipedia.org/wiki/Kapo_%28concentration_camp%29

29. The name of the plant was "Buna Werke". See the following link, which describes the history of this camp:
http://en.wikipedia.org/wiki/Monowitz_concentration_camp

30. The Buna Werke site in Monowice was about 6 km away from the main camp of Auschwitz. Gliwice is located about 60 km northwest of it.

31. Mauthausen is in Austria, about 500 km southwest of Gliwice, Poland. The train from Gliwice would probably have passed through Slovakia to get there.

32. Oranienburg, Germany is about 700 km north of Mauthausen. The entire trip from Gliwice, Poland to Oranienburg (via Mauthausen) would therefore have been about 1200 km long.

33. Flossenbürg is 450 km south of Oranienburg, back in the direction of Mauthausen.

34. The Flossenbürg camp slave laborers quarried stone from the mountain.

35. What is probably meant is Leonberg, the site of an aircraft plant hidden in the Engelberg tunnel, where slave labor was used extensively during World War II. It is located near Stuttgart, about 300 km west of Flossenbürg. See the following link for its history: http://en.wikipedia.org/wiki/Engelberg_Tunnel

36. The Kaufering concentration camp (near Munich) lies 200 km east of the Engelberg tunnel that is near Leonberg. See the following link for its history: http://en.wikipedia.org/wiki/Kaufering_concentration_camp

37. Ganacker is located 200 km northeast of Kaufering.

38. = "May his name be blotted out forevermore", a Hebrew expression used to curse the memory of someone particularly heinous following mention of his name.

39. = "May His [i.e., God's] great Name be exalted and sanctified," the first few words of the *Kaddish* prayer that is recited by mourners

40. p. 355 of Reference cited in Footnote 1

41. P. 359 of Reference cited in Footnote 1

42. *Yaar HaKedoshim* (Hebrew) = Forest of the Martyrs, established in Israel as a memorial to victims of the Holocaust. See the following link: http://en.wikipedia.org/wiki/Forest_of_the_Martyrs

43. p. 369 of Reference cited in Footnote 1

[Page 381]

After the Liberation[1][2]

by Gorny Frum

Translated by Allen Flusberg

In August, 1944, my brother and I were liberated in a far-flung village not far from Warsaw.[3] The war was not yet over, Warsaw was still in the hands of the enemy, and in the extermination camps thousands of Jews were still dying on a daily basis; the heavy, dark clouds that had been obscuring the heavens had not yet been swept away.

After we had left the bunkers we decided to leave the village because of the enmity of the local peasants, some of whom were ready to murder us—so as not to leave behind any living testimony that might yet, with the passage of time, reveal their hooligan-like anti-Semitic behavior as active facilitators of the Nazis.

In this rather indeterminate situation we set out for Minsk Mazowiecki (our father's birthplace), where we joined a group of about 25 men who had been rescued from bunkers that comprised a kind of ghetto.[4] The war was still continuing. In the distance one could see giant flames that we thought must be burning within the capital city of Warsaw, engulfed in fire. The sound of cannon was also quite easily audible.

Along the roads the Russian tanks were traveling in the direction of Warsaw. Large military legions marched through the town, among them a significant number of Jewish soldiers.[5] I recognized one of these Jewish soldiers as a fellow townsman: Leon Tinski[6], a grandson of Herna Lent. While he was around he would visit us often, each time bringing us food, a little each time. But after a short time the brigade he was in was called to the front and he disappeared. We never saw him again.[7]

Each day brings more earth-shaking news: we hear that part of Pomorze[8] has already been taken by the Russian army. With our last few pennies we buy a newspaper in order to know what is going on. All sorts of thoughts are going through our minds: possibly Dobrzyn is already liberated. I am already imagining my upcoming visit. Perhaps I will find someone I know there: a survivor from our extended family, neighbors or friends. Maybe I will be able to find out the fate of those precious, prominent Jews, among them my father, whom the Nazis arrested on Rosh Hashana.

The war ended in April, 1945. After much preparation, I was ready for the trip. I made sure to take along enough food for several days. Because of the danger facing Jewish travelers, I wrapped my head in a red, flowery kerchief that made me look like a Christian. Rumors were going around that Jews were being beaten and murdered—thrown from trains. But even in this situation I had prepared myself for my journey to Dobrzyn.

I travel in a freight train, and the journey takes six days. Finally I reach the Kowalewo station[9], from which I proceed to Golub on foot. Along the way I walk along with a group of young Polish men who are returning from incarceration[10] in Germany. They are joyful for their good fortune; they sing as they march along. They are back on their own terrain, on their way home to their parents and friends.

Just then the castle of Golub appears before my eyes. My heart begins pounding and I feel dizzy as I approach my beloved town, which I left five-and-a-half years earlier together with my mother and sisters. I recall the cold winter day when the Nazi beasts chased us, beaten and broken, out of the town, together with the other Jews of Dobrzyn. And today I am going back there alone, lonely and exhausted, after having gone through the seven sections of Hell.

Now I have reached the built-up section of Golub; with measured steps I walk along the streets that will take me to the bridge leading to Dobrzyn. I don't recognize the passersby that I see along the way; clearly they don't know me, either. With a feeling of despair I cross the bridge and go straight to the town square. It is Tuesday, a market day, but it almost doesn't feel like it at all. Only a few meager shops are serving the small number of peasants who have come from the surrounding area; gone is the tumult and commotion of the thousands who used to come here on market day. The dozens of shops, filled with all kinds of merchandise, and the stands in the square with various items for sale are no more. The handicrafts of the Dobrzyn tailors and shoemakers that were renowned throughout the entire region are not here. I turn onto *Die Goldene Gass*[11], the center of Jewish commerce in Dobrzyn. Dreadful! Barely a single house left standing; the street looks like a plowed-up field. I keep going and come to *Die Lange Gass*[12]. From far away I notice a group of children playing and laughing. As I get close to them they fix their blue eyes on me.[13] From there I turn into *Die Shul Gass*[14], where all the religious institutes and institutions used to be, such as the synagogue, the *beis medresh*[15], the Alexander *shtibl*[16], the *Talmud Torah*[17], the *Beis Yaakov Ulpan*[18], the Community Board and the slaughterhouse. I think back to my childhood, when I studied in *Beis Yaakov* in the class of our beloved, unforgettable teacher, Gutmorgen of blessed memory. I look for some traces of the synagogue, but unfortunately all has vanished. Only small mounds, ruins, greet me from all sides.

Overcome by grief, I simply cannot hold back my tears.[19] My heart in pain, I wend my way in the direction of the Jewish cemetery, where I believe I will be able to find my grandparents' graves, and there bewail the great destruction. But I can't find the iron gate that stood at the entrance to the cemetery. I notice two shepherds nearby. When I ask them where the Jewish cemetery is, they reply as follows: "Here, on this very spot where you are standing, there was once a cemetery. Nowadays shepherds come here from far away for the good grass, to graze their flocks here."

Mournfully I sat down on a rock, thinking: Even the graves of our dear ones, on which I would have poured out my tears, are also gone.

Downcast and dejected, I bemoaned the ebullient town—with its precious Jews—that had once existed, the Jews who for generations had woven colorful lives, and the beautiful young people who had been so full of hope. Now it was all gone.

I stood up and recited a tremulous *kaddish*[20], a lament over the plowed-up earth where the bones of our beloved and faithful once rested.

And now I understood that there was nothing more for me here. My heart was filled with a deep sorrow as I dragged myself back to the town, taking for the very last time a long look at the ruins of the town, where not so long ago an intensive Jewish life had flourished.[21]

When I got back to the town square a woman recognized me. She was a former neighbor of ours, who once worked for us as our *shabbes goye*[22]. She cried out hysterically, "Manya, you are still alive!" And immediately I was surrounded by a large number of Polish women from the adjoining houses, crossing themselves as if they had just seen a creature from another world.

They put on a pretense of pity for the destruction of the Jews, but the true inner expression that could be read on their faces was the very opposite, gladness and satisfaction.

My neighbor invited me into her home. I tried to decline, but finally I did go in. Inside the apartment I noticed several items that had once belonged to my parents.[23] I turned my gaze away from them.[24] As I drank the glass of tea that she served me, I felt as if I was being served a beverage tainted with poison. Here, too, I felt the horrible tragedy that had befallen our people.

With hurried steps I went back to the train station to distance myself from everything that had once been so dear to me.

Rushka Frenkel-Kahn, Daniel Itche's daughter. Died in New York. [25]

Translator's Footnotes

1. From *My Town: In Memory of the Communities Dobrzyn-Gollob*, edited by M. Harpaz, (published by the Dobrzyn-Golub Society, Israel, 1969), pp. 381-384. This article is written in Yiddish.

2. A version of this article written in Hebrew appears on pp. 164-167 of the reference cited in Footnote 1. The Hebrew includes a statement that the article has been translated from Polish. Additions appearing in this Hebrew version are listed in several footnotes below.

3. For a description of the author's experiences during the Holocaust period 1939-1944 see G. Frum, "Seven Sections of Hell," pp. 149-160 of the reference cited in Footnote 1.

4. Hebrew version adds: "They had been concealed by Polish farmers."

5. Hebrew version adds: "They come to visit us, bringing along food."

6. Hebrew version has: "Lieutenant Leon Tinski"

7. Hebrew version adds: "He vanished without a trace in the chaos that prevailed at that time."

8. The province of Pomerania, incorporating much of what was formerly West Prussia.

9. Kowalewo is about 12km northwest of Golub

10. Hebrew version adds "in work camps".

11. *Die Goldene Gass* = Golden Street, or Street of Gold

12. *Die Lange Gass* = Long Street (the Yiddish name), called Piłsudskiego Street in Polish

13. Hebrew version reads: "As I approach them my eyes cloud over: the children are blond and blue-eyed." i.e. she can tell they are not Jewish.

14. *Die Shul Gass* = Synagogue Street, at the end of which the main synagogue stood

15. *Beis medresh* = study hall for religious studies

16. Alexander *shtibl* = prayer house (small synagogue) used by the Alexander Hassidim

17. Talmud torah – older boys' religious school

18. *Beis Yaakov Ulpan* = girls' religious school

19. Hebrew version reads instead: "I am weeping inside, but I am making an effort to suppress my tears."

20. *Kaddish* = prayer recited by mourners

21. Hebrew version adds: "And now the houses and streets were filled with murderers and collaborators."

22. *Shabbes goye* = Gentile woman who was employed to regularly come by and perform critical tasks for Jews on the Sabbath, tasks otherwise forbidden to Jews according to Jewish law. A typical task might be the stoking up of a previously lit fire that was being used to warm the home. See the following link: http://en.wikipedia.org/wiki/Shabbos_goy

23. Hebrew version adds: "The Gentile woman's daughter had been trying to hide them just as I was coming in."

24. Hebrew version adds: "And what value do these items have compared to all the precious things I have lost?"

25. From p. 384 of reference cited in Footnote 1.

[Page 385]

Memories[1]
by Joseph Dratwa
Translated by Allen Flusberg

The 1926 Gypsy pogrom in Dobrzyn, which resulted from a blood libel against the Jews, is one of my early memories that engraved itself deeply in my mind. Although I was only a small boy in 1926, I already understood the danger that confronted the Jews, particularly in the small towns of Poland where they did not have adequate moral and physical protection. The favorable verdict that the Polish court reached with respect to the accused Jews—with Mr. Avrohom Flusberg the principal accused—stirred up the anti-Semitic circles in our little town, which immediately began a campaign to suppress Jewish business by picketing Jewish shops. Attacks against Jewish passersby also became common occurrences. Meanwhile, the inciting sermons given by the local priest every Sunday during church services supplemented the anti-Semitic passion and led to ceaseless persecution of the Jews in the town.

The economic situation continued to become more acute, causing a large number of the young people to look for a place to live far from home. As members of *Hashomer Hatza'ir*[2], Chaim Lord and I traveled to Rovno[3] for *hachshara*[4]. After we got there the war between Germany and Poland broke out[5], and Rovno was occupied by the Russians[6].

The roads around Rovno were threatened, with danger lurking over each and every step. Nevertheless we decided to travel to Vilna, which at just that time had been ceded to Lithuania[7]; we believed that from there it would be possible for us to get to Palestine.

Meanwhile the Russian-German war broke out[8], and we began wandering from town to town to avoid falling into the hands of the Germans. Finally I arrived in Russia, where I was interned in a camp. I underwent not a small amount of suffering in the several years during which I was imprisoned in the camp. When the Russians freed us, in the year 1943, it was with the purpose of establishing a Polish army that would have to fight together with the Russians against Germany. I allowed myself to be mobilized because I felt a strong desire for revenge, knowing already then of the complete annihilation of Polish Jewry.

Pursuing the fleeing German army, which was retreating in disorder and terror from the occupied territories of Poland, we arrived in Lublin. Not far from there, in the extermination camp of Majdanek, the terrible image of the great tragedy was exposed before our eyes. Only then were we able to properly appreciate the frightful destruction!

After a few days in Lublin, our military forces continued onward in the direction of Warsaw. We took the city without meeting any serious resistance by the enemy. Then, while taking a walk along the Vistula River in Warsaw, I met Leib Miller[9]. He was a political officer in the Polish army, very removed from Jewish nationalism, but after a long discussion on the age-old Jewish problem he agreed with me that the only solution for the Jews was—Palestine. Later, in a battle with the Germans in the forests of Bydgoszcz[10] he was taken prisoner, together with his entire unit. His fellow soldiers sold him out, and the Germans, finding out he was Jewish, immediately shot him.

After several weeks of expanding the fighting to a final offensive, we left Warsaw. There were serious battles on the way to the Oder River, but the German army was retreating incessantly. As we approached the Oder we began preparing for an offensive against Berlin. By then the German army was broken and beaten down; resistance was weak, and the city fell after a short battle in the streets. We saw and understood that this was the end of the war. The Jewish soldiers in the Polish-Russian army immediately began taking an interest in and searching in the surrounding camps for acquaintances, friends or relatives. My comrades went to a women's camp in which, after a short inquiry, they found a woman named Dratwa who who originated from Pomorz[11]. They immediately told me about her. When I got together with her I felt a cold sweat, and the two of us were paralyzed with shock: she was my sister. Right away, when I told my commanding officer about this turn of events, he suspected me of being involved in a Jewish scam[12]. But once he was convinced it was true he gave me permission to stay with her.

The path to a tranquil, pleasant life was still far enough away. After I was freed I traveled with my sister to Dobrzyn, but we found no one there. From Dobrzyn we went to Lodz. There we met many members of *Hashomer Hatza'ir*. Together with some of them I was transported to Germany and from there to Israel. On the way the British interned us in a camp in Cyprus. With the establishment of the State of Israel I arrived in Israel and participated in the War of Independence. And only then was I able to build up my own home.

[Page 388]

Moishe Hersh Szmiga and his wife

Translator's Footnotes

1. From *My Town: In Memory of the Communities Dobrzyn-Gollob*, edited by M. Harpaz, (published by the Dobrzyn-Golub Society, Israel, 1969), pp. 385-387.

2. A socialist-Zionist youth movement that encouraged immigration to Palestine and settling in *kibbutzim*

3. Równe, Poland; now Rivne, in Ukraine, a town about 700 km southeast of Dobrzyn

4. Training in farm work to prepare for moving to an agricultural settlement in Palestine

5. September, 1939

6. After a pact with Germany, the Soviet forces occupied what had been eastern Poland

7. The Soviets ceded the city of Vilna (now Vilnius), which had been in Poland, to Lithuania, which for a short period (until being incorporated into the Soviet Union in August, 1940) continued to retain some independence, thereby providing some opportunity to escape from Europe.

8. June, 1941

9. A fellow native of Dobrzyn

10. A city in Poland, about 80 km west of Dobrzyn

11. Pomorz = the province of Pomerania, which incorporates much of what was formerly West Prussia. There are places in this province that are only 30km away from Dobrzyn.

12. i.e., in a concocted story to obtain leave from the military

[Page 390]

Personalities

[Pages 390-394]

Reb Yaakov Leyb Graner

By Esther Graner-Rabbe

Translated by Pamela Russ

Donated by Steve Bolef

My father Yaakov Leyb was an eminent, respected man in town, always surrounded by friends and family, met by every person who needed a favor; and he mainly granted these favors in a discreet manner (*matan beseser*). In community matters he was one of the most active people. He was also one of the first followers of Dr. Herzl even before the First Congress, and together with others, he – still in those years – founded the Zionist Organization in Dobrzyn. My father had the position of chairman, and in a short time, he was able to attract other friends, mainly from the older generation. He had to overcome many challenges from the religious circles that said they would only go to Israel with the help of the Messiah (*Moshiach*), and he who goes to Israel to settle before that is a heretic. In conflict with the *chassidim* (religious Jews) was the well-known Zionist community activist Reb Yitzchok Moishe Ofenbach, whom my father came to help, and who later was at the head of the Zionist Organization. With his enthusiastic and persuasive speeches that he gave each *Motzoei Shabbos* (Saturday night after the end of Sabbath) he convinced many of the *chassidic* circles to believe in Dr. Herzl's national, political thought and movement. Reb Yitzchok Moishe, with his broad, community-minded stature, established a Zionist youth circle and later established the club "*Hatchiya*" that served as a gathering place and also for evening courses for the youth to learn Hebrew. My father was always the right hand man of Reb Yitzchok Moishe and helped him in his devoted daily Zionist work. Still at the end of the previous century, my father organized a circle of Hebrew readers, subscribed to the "*Hatzefira*" and other Zionist newspapers for the town.

[Page 391]

Reb Yaakov Leyb Graner, OB"M

And whoever was interested in knowing what was happening in the Zionist world came to Reb Yaakov Leyb Graner. Many times there were debates in our house on many different subjects. The house was always filled with visitors who my father welcomed warmly, and he discussed all kinds of worldly issues with them. My home, as I remember, was never sad – but on the contrary, was always joyous. Groups of people would sit with a glass of tea until late into the night. There were also some Jews in town for whom reading a newspaper was a difficulty. For them, my father set aside a few hours during the daytime to read them the newspaper. That's how he would sit on the steps of his flour factory, a quorum of ten men (*minyan*) around him, and their ears perked to hear how Reb Yaakov Leyb reads the newspaper about the daily news. Of greatest interest to them was the "Political Letters" from Itchele in the paper "Haynt" (today). The letters were published each Sunday. The excitement around Itchele's commentaries on the political letters was enormous. They would discuss these with appropriate critique of the writer. It is noteworthy that these were Jews without a livelihood, and who barely had bread in their homes. And that's how they spent their years, with the hope of a better tomorrow.

[Page 392]

My father also played a significant role in community life in Dobrzyn. He wanted and was able to accomplish a lot, but with communities in small towns it was not easy to agree on things. And so the struggle in community issues was always sharp and bitter. For a long time, my father supported the city and then he undertook to renovate the synagogue that had been terribly neglected for a long time. In his time, the *shul* was redone almost like new. They changed the benches, chairs, and podiums, extended the women's section, and most important of all, brought painters from Plotsk – not ordinary painters, but artistic painters who painted permanent historical scenes on walls and ceilings – scenes such as: Mother Rachel's Tomb, Absalom's Tomb, the Tower of David, the Tombs of the Patriarchs, the Western Wall, and many other historical places. There's likely not even one person from Dobrzyn who doesn't carry these beautiful images of these artistic paintings in the Dobrzyn synagogue in his mind. Foreigners who visited this synagogue marveled at the artwork. Our synagogue was also prominent in the surrounding towns, and this was the pride of those from Dobrzyn.

The women of the *Ezras Noshim* (women's assistance committee) fulfilled their obligation and helped sew the curtain that covered the ark where the Torah was kept, and also made special drapes. They prepared the "opening day" of the synagogue with great splendor. That Shabbos, they brought in a famous cantor along with his choir from Lodz who sang the "*Lecho Dodi*" of the Friday night prayers, and the next day his prayers were filled with song; along with the help of the choir they created a holiday spirit in the town. The joyous event was tremendous and each person felt as if it was his own house that was being presented as new.

At the time when he held the position of supporting the city, my father also organized the cemetery that was without a fence for scores of years. The animals had broken through the flimsy wooden fence and ate the grass that was on the graves. Since there was no money in the fund, the community borrowed a sum of money, bought lots of bricks and cement from the brothers Mendel and Avrohom Hirsh Cohen, and built a tall fence (wall) that was visible from quite a distance. When the fence was built, the neglect ended and the Jews in the town had much nachas (pride) from Reb Yaakov Leyb Graner's accomplishment.

[Page 393]

Also, the *bais medrash* was fixed. The walls were painted, a new oven was built so that the yeshiva boys that learned there in the cold winter days should not suffer from the cold, and also so that the congregants should be warm when they come to pray.

My father organized a small guest house (*hachnosas orchim*) that was located not far from the street where the synagogue was. It was a tradition in Poland that the Jewish poor people, or "goers" as they were called, would go from town to town, and in each place would have the opportunity to spend two days and two nights in the guest houses where they would have a place to eat and a place to sleep. Along with that, they were permitted to collect alms from the congregants in the synagogue and from those learning in the *bais medrash* for those two days that they were in town. After those two days, they would receive a sum of money from the community fund, then they would leave and continue with their journey. Amongst them sometimes were also women and young children. For years they were homeless, practically like gypsies, but by the end of the 1920s the number of "goers" had diminished and after that it stopped completely. It is worthwhile to note that the phenomenon of the Jewish wanderers in these towns, especially in Poland, was a direct result of the difficult economic situation after World War I. It is also worthy to note that if the "goer" would have to leave town on a Thursday, then he would be kept over the Sabbath and they would send him for meals to the home of a wealthy man. What incredible compassion did Dobrzyn model for the many surrounding towns.

***

In the general destruction in Poland, much of the wrath was poured out onto the Jewish community of Dobrzyn. All the holy places, such as the *shul*, the *bais medrash*, and all the other community institutions were destroyed. The cemetery was demolished and the streets were paved with the tombstones. About 90% of the population died in the killing camps and some in the vast wasteland of Russia. This is how the story of the dear, beloved town of Dobrzyn ended, after being in existence for many generations, and after bringing forth many dedicated Jews, among them my father Yaakov Leyb

Graner, and all who remember him, know what he accomplished for the town and for her Jewish population.

[Page 394]

But, all is not lost for the Jews (*lo alman yisroel*). Our greatest comfort is that with our own hands, we built a Jewish state. And Jews all over the world are proud of their country. We owe much thanks to our parents who raised us in the spirit of love for Israel. My father also belongs to them – he raised his children with this same spirit, and in that atmosphere an entire generation of Jews was raised in Dobrzyn.

"May his soul be bound up in the bond of everlasting life"

Lignica

[Pages 395-396]

Bunem Zaklikowski, of Blessed Memory[1]

by Shimon Yosef Platnerz (USA)

Translated by Allen Flusberg

In this essay I would like to recount several factual anecdotes that reflect on the personality of Bunem Zaklikowski, his great virtues and his good nature.

Once when he and I had run into each other in the street, he asked me whether I would be willing to stay overnight at a sickbed—not alone, it should be understood, but together with someone else. When I found out that the sick person was one of my cousins, I realized who was acting like the real relative here.

The needs of the poor classes of the town gave him great concern. He was unable to rest whenever he became aware that one or another family was in need of help, and he would use any means available to ease their situation. For this purpose he put together a drama group that would give theatre performances, with the proceeds donated to help the indigent.

The entire town knew him, and he was everyone's friend. When aid was urgently needed for someone, no matter whom, he immediately knew whom to ask for it; and it was rare that anyone would turn him down. If it ever happened that a politically persecuted comrade had to be transported to Golub,[2] Bunem was the point of contact. He was also the first to lay the cornerstone for an unauthorized library during the era of the Russian regime.[3] Later, during the German occupation, the library was legitimized and became an important cultural center for a large number of the residents of the town. He was respected by all the parties for his devotion to the town and for his ceaseless interest in those who were in distress; it did not matter to him which party they belonged to.

As leader of the "*Poalei Tziyon*", he often had to polemicize against party opponents, but in this capacity, as well, he was honest and frank, without any kind of demagoguery.

Under his leadership, the "*Poalei Tziyon*"[4] grew and expanded its ranks, becoming one of the most important parties in the town. We who were on his staff learned a great deal from him, and we think back upon his dignified figure with respect.

For personal reasons he left the town and moved to America. There he married and established a fine home and a good livelihood. But his character did not change, and he renewed his party activity in the vast city of New York. He also maintained his link to his comrades in the old country as usual once he was in New York, and in spite of the distractions of earning a living he always found time to work for the community.

His home was open to friends and *landsleit*[5], and his face would always glow whenever he greeted a friend who came from the Old Country.

The capacity of his energy was amazing; it was like an inexhaustible spring. That is what Bunem Zaklikowski was like in Dobrzyn, and for many years also in America: a dedicated comrade, a friend, a person active in the community, always with a smile on his face; and as such we shall always remember him.

Bunem Zaklikowski[6]

Translator's Footnotes

1. From *My Town: In Memory of the Communities Dobrzyn-Gollob*, edited by M. Harpaz, (published by the Dobrzyn-Golub Society, Israel, 1969), pp. 395-396.

2. Prior to World War I, Golub, which was located on the other side of the Dreventz river, was in the German Empire, while Dobrzyn was in the Russian Empire. Sometimes political refugees from the Russian Empire were smuggled across the river to Golub. See the following articles in this volume: p. 415 of Y. Lipka, "Memoirs Dedicated to My Father, R. Feibish Lipka," pp. 404-438 of reference cited in Footnote 1; p. 270 of S. Aleksander, "The Grassroots Jews of Dobrzyn," pp. 270-272 of reference cited in Footnote 1; and p. 402 of M.

Sonabend, "My Beautiful, Loving Mother, of Blessed Memory, the Dobrzyn Rebbetzin," pp. 401-402 of reference cited in Footnote 1.

3. See Y. Wrzos, "The Struggle for Education in the Town", pp. 300-304 of reference cited in Footnote 1.

4. *Poalei Tzion* = Workers of Zion (Hebrew), a Zionist Marxist-socialist organization and party (Labor Zionists). See the following link (retrieved August, 2015): http://en.wikipedia.org/wiki/Poale_Zion

5. *Landsleit* = people hailing from the same town or area

6. From p. 395 of reference cited in Footnote 1.

[Pages 397-401]

The Rabbi of Dobrzyn[1]

by Mendel Sonabend

Translated by Allen Flusberg

My beloved father, Rabbi Yehudah Leib Sonabend z.l.[2], was born in Dobrzyn on the Dreventz River in the Plock Province. He was descended from an extended family of rabbis, religious prodigies and Kabbalists. His father, R.[3] Rephoel z.l., a textile merchant with a keen mind, was the brother of Rabbi Avrohom Sonabend, the Rabbi of Nieszawa[4]. Rabbi Yitzchok Meir Bornstein, the Rabbi of Gostynin[5], was the rabbi's brother–in–law, and Rabbi Yissochor Groibard z.l., the Rabbi of Bendin[6], was his cousin.

Right after his wedding, my father was appointed Rabbi of Janow[7], a town in the province of Plock. Three years later, he received a letter of appointment from the community of Dobrzyn. The election held for the position of Dobrzyn Rabbi turned into a feud, an extremely bitter struggle, between the Ger[8] Hassidim and the Aleksander[9] Hassidim. The *Rebbe*[10] of Ger, a world–renowned, prodigious scholar who was known as the *Sefas Emes*, after the name of the book he had written, backed my father's candidacy; but the Aleksander *Rebbe* supported his own grandson for the position. The controversy between the two Hassidic groups knew no bounds. At the very last moment, the other residents of the town decided to back the Ger Hassidim, and my father won the election. Afterwards the Aleksander *Rebbe* wrote a letter to his followers, instructing them to accept the election results as the finger of God[11].

My parents arrived at my father's inauguration as Rabbi of Dobrzyn in an elegant carriage—drawn by four white horses—that belonged to my grandfather, R. Mordechai Globus. A large crowd of Dobrzyn Jews had been waiting on the outskirts of the town to greet him. In a festive atmosphere they escorted him to the synagogue, where he was received with great pomp and ceremony. The synagogue was packed. The cantor and the choir sang "*Boruch Habo*"[12]. My father gave a heartfelt sermon that was well received, and the Aleksander Hassidim congratulated him and wished him long life.

In his apartment there was a room in which the religious court met for adjudication. All four walls of the room were covered with shelves filled with books on Jewish law: *Mishna*[13], Talmud, *Poiskim*[14], Responsa, etc.; it had been a gift from my grandfather, R. Mordechai Globus, z.l. In the room there was a long table with two long benches and a tall chair. When adjudicating, my father would sit on this chair to listen to the claims of the two sides. Cases of property disputes[15], divorces, *chalitza*[16] and the like would routinely be brought before him. For disputes he would announce his verdict only after the litigants indicated their agreement to abide by it by grasping the end of a handkerchief that my father would extend to each of them[17]. Aside from these cases, individuals would also come to him to pour their hearts out about their troubles and to discuss personal family matters.

During the period of thirty-four years that my father was the Dobrzyn Rabbi, he dedicated himself entirely to studying and to writing innovative Torah commentaries[18]. When he passed away after a short illness, his last, dying wish was that the yeshiva[19] students should be well taken care of. Throughout his life they had all been his students, taught by him, and he had practically raised them all.

My father had a deep affection for his yeshiva students. Twice a week he would go for a walk with them in the nearby woods. He loved the students like his own children. Delving with them into complex Talmudic passages, he would reveal to them interpretations that they had never heard before.

He would teach his students some of his Talmud lessons from memory, according to his own unwritten commentary. Shortly before his death he put this commentary of his into writing. He made several copies to distribute to his students in order to make it possible for them to learn these lessons by heart. These commentaries of his were accepted and became popular in scholarly circles.

Aside from being a great, God-fearing scholar, he was also highly educated. He was known as a gifted speaker who was capable of influencing his audience; his sermons on ethics would always arouse a great deal of enthusiasm. Among many of the town's residents he was truly venerated. Families whose personal lives were fraught with difficulties, and others who strayed from the path of virtue, found their way back under the Rabbi's influence.

My father often wrote in Hebrew and had a special love for this language. He particularly enjoyed reading "*Shirei Tifferet*," written by the well-known Hebrew poet N. Z. Wesel[20].

He passed away after a short illness, 34 years after becoming Rabbi of the town of Dobrzyn, the town in which, as stated above, he had been born.

My grandfather, R. Rephoel Sonabend, was also a highly regarded Talmudist who was active in the community. He, too, was born in Dobrzyn and died there. As a child he had already displayed prodigious abilities. He wrote a book criticizing the rabbis and scholars for their negligent attitude towards the ordinary, plain people, and for not providing them with a proper education.

Perhaps there will be someone out there who will greatly expand on the biography of the Sonabend family; and may he be rewarded[21] for it.

A group of people hailing from Dobrzyn in the Forest of the Martyrs[22]
Sitting on the left: **Kasriel Isaac, z.l.**[23][24]

A reception for Moshe Yaakov Katchor, and wife, of New York

Center: **Moshe Yaakov**

Left: **his wife, Chana Chaya**

Right: **his brother–in–law, Yaakov Rimon**[25]

Translator's Footnotes

1. From *My Town: In Memory of the Communities Dobrzyn–Gollob*, edited by M. Harpaz, (published by the Dobrzyn–Golub Society, Israel, 1969), pp. 397–400. A parallel article in Hebrew with the same title, and by the same author, appears on pp. 51–54 of this volume. It overlaps with, but is not identical to, this Yiddish article.

2. z.l. = contraction for *Zichroinoi Livrocho* = of blessed memory

3. R. = *Reb*, similar to English "Mr."

4. Nieszawa, Poland is located ~50km south of Dobrzyn.

5. Gostynin, Poland lies 100km south of Dobrzyn.

6. Będzin, Poland, located approximately 400km south of Dobrzyn.

7. There are several towns named Janow in Poland. The reference is probably to a town that is located 120km south of Dobrzyn.

8. Ger = a Hassidic group that had many adherents in Dobrzyn

9. Aleksander (or Alexander) is the name of a Hassidic group that had many adherents in Dobrzyn. See the following link (retrieved May, 2015): http://en.wikipedia.org/wiki/Aleksander_(Hasidic_dynasty)

10. *Rebbe* = religious spiritual leader of Hassidic group

11. "finger of God" (quoting Exodus 8:15), i.e. God's will, but with a hint of a wrong that cannot be undone.

12. *Boruch Habo* (Heb., literally "may he who has arrived be blessed") = welcome.

13. *Mishna* = the concise book of Jewish Law written down in Hebrew in ~200CE. See the following Web site (retrieved May, 2015): http://en.wikipedia.org/wiki/Mishnah

14. *Poiskim* = authors of post-Talmudic literature settling Jewish law (literally adjudicants).

15. *Din Torah* (Hebrew) = judgements made according to Jewish civil law

16. *Chalitza* = ceremonial rejection of levirate marriage by the brother of a deceased, married man whose wife had not borne him any children. The widow is permitted to remarry after the *Chalitza* is completed. See the following Web site (retrieved May, 2015): http://en.wikipedia.org/wiki/Halizah

17. Grasping the handkerchief is considered a form of acquisition or agreement, similar to an agreement by handshake in Western societies.

18. *chidushei Torah* (Hebrew)

19. Yeshiva = religious seminary

20. Naphtali-Hirz (or Naphtali-Zvi) Wesel or Wessely (1725-1805), was a German-Jewish Hebraist. His epic poem *Shirei Tifferet* (= poems of glory), describes the exodus from Egypt, with an emphasis on the greatness and humaneness of Moses. See the following Web site (retrieved May, 2015): http://en.wikipedia.org/wiki/Naphtali_Hirz_Wessely

21. Heb. *Tovoi olov berocho* = may he receive a blessing

22. Forest of the Martyrs = a forest on the outskirts of Jerusalem, dedicated to the victims of the Holocaust and the rebirth of the Jewish State. See the following link (retrieved May, 2015): http://en.wikipedia.org/wiki/Forest_of_the_Martyrs

23. From p. 398 in reference cited in Footnote 1.

24. Sign in Hebrew in the photograph reads "Dobrzyn".

25. From p. 400 of reference cited in Footnote 1.

[Pages 401-402]

My Beautiful, Loving Mother, of Blessed Memory, the Dobrzyn Rebbetzin[1][2]

by Mendel Sonabend
Translated by Allen Flusberg

The Dobrzyn *Rebbetzin* was the daughter of Mr. Mordechai Globus. During her youth she studied in the Plock *gymnasia*[3] together with someone who later became greatly renowned as a Zionist leader—Nahum Sokolow[4].

My mother read and wrote fluently in four languages: Yiddish, Polish, Hebrew and German. Her writing was that of a natively intelligent, well–read woman. She read the classical Polish, Yiddish, Russian and German literature. She also read the secular press, and in the period of the Dreyfus trial she read the reports written by Max Nordau[5]. She had a great appreciation for music and art.

She was also a good housekeeper who ran her home tastefully. She set the tone in clothing for herself, for the children, and for our father, the Rabbi, modestly and with much esthetic taste. She was active at home, despite the fact that we had a sturdy housemaid working for us. And in our home everything glistened; anything that we needed was there. She never complained and was always cheerful, with a smile on her face. Very seldom did anyone hear her sigh. In those days the income of the rabbi of a small town was very limited, yet nothing was lacking in our home. We children would often wonder how she did it all.

Sometimes when she was in pain she kept it to herself, neither wishing nor allowing herself to express it. She was always ready to help anyone who was in distress. That was what my mother was like: a loving, tender soul; no one ever heard a mean word out of her mouth.

As I go back in time to distant memories I have of her, I recall a particular Sabbath eve when she had just placed the silver candlesticks on the table and lit the candles. She covered her gleaming eyes with tender hands and then waved her hands in a circle around the slender flames. She recited the blessing with divine holiness, blessing the God of Abraham, Isaac and Jacob in a spasm of sobs. At that moment I sensed her noble character: the courageous woman, the Jewish mother who had just quietly pleaded for health and good fortune not only for herself, but for everyone else. That was the first time I had ever seen her cry, and as a feeling of sadness came over me and I wished to calm her, she stroked me, saying: "Get dressed, my child, soon your father will return from the synagogue; he will greet us singing '*Sholoim Aleichem*' as he welcomes the Holy Sabbath." At that moment the door opened and our father greeted us with a warm "*Gut Shabbes*"[6]. Two guests came in with him, and right away he began to recite "*Sholoim aleichem, malachei hasholoim*"[7], as he usually did.

The candles were burning brightly and the table was set. My mother served the fish and at the same time wished the guests good fortune on their trip— these were two Russian Jews who were about to travel to America after crossing the border to Golub[8]. After dinner my mother took out some warm underwear and woolen socks and gave them to the guests, saying: "Take these things and put them on, my fellow Jews, it is winter, and it is cold outside…"

My father refilled the glasses with wine and drank a "*lechaim*"[9] with the guests, wishing them a safe trip. When the guests were leaving our house, my mother was still quietly saying: "May they only be safe—may they only be safe."

———

Translator's Footnotes

1. From *My Town: In Memory of the Communities Dobrzyn–Gollob*, edited by M. Harpaz, (published by the Dobrzyn–Golub Society, Israel, 1969), pp. 401–402 (Yiddish). See also the English translation of the Hebrew version of this essay (similar but with some differences) by the same author, on pp. 179–180.

2. *Rebbetzin* = rabbi's wife (Yiddish)

3. *Gymnasia* = high school

4. Sokolow (1859–1936) was a Zionist leader and author. See the following link (retrieved June, 2015): https://en.wikipedia.org/wiki/Nahum_Sokolow

5. Nordau (1849–1923) was a Zionist leader and author. See the following link (retrieved June, 2015): https://en.wikipedia.org/wiki/Max_Nordau#Dreyfus_affair

6. *Gut Shabbes* = Good Sabbath (Yiddish)

7. "*Sholoim Aleichem...*" = Welcome, ministering angels of peace... (words of the Hebrew poem recited just before the Friday-night Sabbath meal, greeting the angels who have brought the tranquility of the Sabbath to the home).

8. Until 1920, the border between the Russian and German empires ran along the Dreventz River that separated Dobrzyn (in the Russian Empire) from Golub (in the German Empire). Smuggling people across the river border was common but somewhat risky, and this is likely what "crossing the border" is referring to here. See p. 415 of Y. Lipka, "Memoirs Dedicated to My Father, R. Feibish Lipka," pp. 404–438 of reference cited in Footnote 1; also p. 270 of S. Aleksander, "The Grassroots Jews of Dobrzyn," pp. 270–272 of reference cited in Footnote 1.

9. *Lechaim* = to life (Hebrew toast)

[Page 403]

Rivka Aleksander[1]

by Avraham Dor (Dobroszklanka)
Translated by Allen Flusberg

Without a doubt one of the most interesting figures in the town was Mrs. Rivka Aleksander, who was an important community volunteer in the social realm for many years. Members of her inner circle, who witnessed her tireless daily labor, knew what an asset she was and understood how much strength and effort she put into her sacred life's work.

The townspeople wondered where she found the physical strength and the means to deal with all the intricacies of aid. The word "*baflen*"[2] was quite foreign to her and practically did not exist in her vocabulary. She did everything with her own two hands: quietly, with humility and great modesty, and without any help from anyone.

In her later years, after her children in America insisted that she join them, she was actually depressed by the very thought that she was leaving behind widows and orphans who had no source of livelihood—that is what she told her friends and relatives who came to say goodbye before she left.

But even in distant America Mrs. Rivka Aleksander did not forget her duty. While she was still a "*greene*"[3] she set up a mechanism to send aid to the neediest of the town, and she continued her activity until she became bedridden.

With the deepest appreciation and greatest respect we here remind the Dobrzyners of the many years of charitable work accomplished by Mrs. Rivka Aleksander in support of victims of misfortune in our town.

Rivka Aleksander, of blessed memory, one of the most active community volunteers in Dobrzyn[4]

Translator's Footnotes

1. From *My Town: In Memory of the Communities Dobrzyn-Gollob*, edited by M. Harpaz, (published by the Dobrzyn-Golub Society, Israel, 1969), p. 403

2. *baflen* = delegating

3. *greene* = the American Yiddish term for a new immigrant (equivalent to greenhorn)

4. From p. 403 of reference cited in Footnote 1

[Page 404]

Memoirs Dedicated to My Father R.[1] Feibish Lipka[2]

By Yeshayohu Nosson Lipka

Translated by Allen Flusberg

1

Right on the border of former Germany, on the very bank of the Dreventz[3] River—facing the well-groomed German town of Golub, on the opposite riverbank—that is where my beloved town of Dobrzyn was situated. It was a community of more than two thousand Jews who had woven colorful lives there for many generations. It was a place that was modest and serene, delicate and tidy; a town pervaded by cordial warmth whose populace was devoted to one another.

On the Polish map the town took up quite a small area, but within the central Jewish circles of Poland it had made a name for itself as a place with a rich social life, one that embraced nearly all the Jewish parties that existed in Poland. There were Judaic scholars, intellectuals, communal leaders, leading personalities, as well as generally gifted people who contributed their skills to the town. Among them there were two I would like to mention with the greatest of respect: the founder of the Zionist organization, R. Yitzchok Moishe Offenbach z.l.[4]; and the leader of *Poalei–Tziyon*[5], Bunem Zaklikowski z.l.

*

My father, R. Yosef Shraga (Feibish) Lipka—or, as he was called in Dobrzyn, *Reb* Fahbish—was known, not only in Dobrzyn, but also in the entire region, as a Jewish scholar, one who was an expert in the Talmud and the *Poiskim*[6]. Moreover he had an excellent memory and was able to address a variety of questions on these subjects, where answers required true expertise. He knew the Hebrew language well and was acquainted with secular literature. In spite of his great knowledge he did not shut himself up in an ivory tower, but rather delved seriously into political–social problems, particularly Jewish ones.

Paying little heed to his own status as a Hassid, he was just about the only person in town who disseminated the idea of the Love of Zion[7] within Hassidic circles, among whom it was until then considered beyond the pale, anathema[8].

Since he was close with the Otwocker *rebbes*[9], he had the opportunity—which he utilized—via religious lectures, large gatherings, etc. to convince the Hassidim and the other pious Jews that it was not enough to recite, thrice daily, "May our eyes behold Your return to Zion"[10], thereby fulfilling one's religious obligation. Rather one should fulfil it in actual practice, recognizing that only the Land of Israel can complete the Torah of Israel. The Mizrachi Movement[11] is the proof that he and his close friends and colleagues were successful. Today this seems quite obvious, but many years ago it was not so simple and straightforward.

Among his friends were the well-known rabbi and religious-academy head, Rabbi Yitzchok-Yaakov Reines[12], also known as the Rabbi of Lida[13]; the Gaon of Kutno[14], Rabbi Yehoshue'le Trunk[15]; Rabbi Kowalski of Wloclawek[16]; Rabbi Brod of Lipno, and many others, z.l. And of course the rabbi of Dobrzyn, Sonabend, a warm and liberal person, who was especially lenient [in Jewish law].

[Page 406]

2

I recall the long discussions that my father would have with the Otwock *Rebbe, Rebbe* Menachem-Mendel[17] z.l., when he stayed over at our house. It appears that these very discussions had the proper effect, for at the end of each one I could see a look of spiritual pleasure on both of their faces, that of my father and that of the *rebbe*. The *rebbe* must have been thinking: Feibish is right, after all, with his proofs and clear statements. Several times my father remarked to me: "The *rebbe* is clearly interested, since he does want to hear all about it. That is his will, and it is one's will that leads one to faith." And one time, when the two of us had just left the *rebbe*'s bedroom, the *rebbe* called us back and said to my father: "Feibish, I see that it is the will of Heaven that I have been staying over at your house. I have been listening attentively to the idea of the Return to Zion. You are right: we have to shed the bitter burden of exile, and it our sacred duty to arouse our people to merit fulfilling, by their actions, the commandments that are dependent on living in the Land. Keep up the good work, Feibish." My father beamed with joy. And the same thing happened when the *rebbe*'s brother, R. Moshe'le[18] z.l., stayed over with us.

3

Not only was he propagandizing Zionism among the religious Jews, but also among the German Jews, most of whom were almost completely assimilated.

Russian–Polish Dobrzyn was separated from the German border town, Golub, by a bridge over the Dreventz River and a customs house for paying tariffs. And by the way in Golub there was a pharmacist named Riesenfeld, a warm Zionist and a very fine man. The walled city of Torun (Toyern in Yiddish) was a two– or three–hour train ride away from Golub. Since Torun was renowned for its excellent medical specialists, those who were ill came for treatment there from far and wide. There was a large medical diagnosis facility in Torun. When a sick person came to see a doctor, the doctor would send him to the facility, where he would be examined for all kinds of diseases, physical and psychological—not just the single malady he had come for. He would be poked, measured, weighed and thoroughly examined, and a report would be written up; only afterwards would the specialist take care of him. For those times this approach was a great accomplishment.

Naturally there were many doctors and professors there, and many of them were Jewish: Brandwein, Blank, Goldmann, etc. My father, who had recently been suffering from headaches, had gone to see Dr. Goldmann, a neurologist. Once, as I was entering my father's hospital room to visit him, I came upon the following scene: my father was sitting up in bed, surrounded by a quorum of doctors, as he lectured them about *Zionismus* (as Zionism is referred to in German). Several of them were nodding their heads, others were taking notes, and all had serious looks on their faces. My father finished to enthusiastic applause, and they said: "*Herr Lipka, wir müssen sich öfter zusammenkommen.*"[19] Afterwards almost all of them joined together and became active Zionists.

[Page 407]

4

One may ask: why should it have taken a religious, bearded, Ost Jude[20] clad in a long kapote[21] to convince them of the correctness of Zionism and to turn them towards this idealism? There was already more than enough literature on the subject: books, pamphlets, magazines; speakers etc. These were certainly educated people who themselves had acknowledged that they had heard of Zionism and had read about this movement. Here is the answer: first, my father had a unique approach: when he spoke he actually had something to say, and there was truly something to listen to. He had an outstanding talent to explain the most difficult subject in a popular, simple way, binding together the mind and heart—logic and emotion—and illuminating it all with humor. His scholarship and worldliness complemented one another. He gauged the intelligence of his listener and adjusted his words accordingly, drawing him slowly into the subject matter, and all in a convincing way. Anyone who had heard him speak once was drawn to him like a magnet to hear him again; and, to hear him, one needed no more than "R. Feibish will be speaking today in the synagogue, beis medresh[22], shtibl[23], or in the Zionist premises," and people came from all directions. He was tolerant to a fault. It did not bother him to speak to an audience of girls or of young people; nor did it bother him whether they did wear hats and caps or were bareheaded. He never criticized, and he always began with the words "My dear fellow Jews!"

[Page 408]

5

My father loved people and was democratic to a fault. "Tall" or "short", wealthy or poor: for him it was all the same. Just like everywhere else, our town had "*pani*"[24], those who considered themselves well-born, elite.. These people thought it would be improper to "lower" themselves, to be among "those kinds of people". My father found this attitude ludicrous. Whether in synagogue, in the *beis medresh*, in the *shtibl*, at festive occasions, or in business, he never bragged or was arrogant. "Nahum," my father would say, "let me have a sniff of your tobacco," as he put his finger into Nahum's snuffbox. "Aaron, let me try your glasses on," he would say as he sat down with the others in the *beis medresh*, on a bench with a long table, near the door, and he would converse and study with them. And all of this was natural for him, and sincere. One of the "*pani*" would have had a fit before "doing something like that."

Several Jews were employed in our sawmill, in our mill and in our lumber warehouse. Among them were some ardent Bundists[25]. Well, they would often have discussions with my father. He would ask them to first sit down comfortably, not like a boss with employees, but rather like a person with his equals. He would not notice even for a moment that this confounded them. And so these discussions would last for hours.

Like anywhere else, our town also had "certain elements". So…if someone was caught, he was put in custody and…beaten. My father would immediately intercede and stop the beating. "Do not judge someone until you are standing in his place,"[26] "All of Israel are bound together in friendship,"[27] and "Thou shalt love thy neighbor as thyself"[28] were for him the primary foundations of ethics. He helped dozens of needy people covertly, and he had the same attitude toward non–Jews. Intuitively sensing his sincerity and intimacy, people would come to him for advice about their problems. And indeed he helped them with both counsel and action. Had he had the desire to be a *rebbe*[29], he would have had many Hassidic devotees, and actually he was one in effect, unofficially. When someone addressed him as "*Reb* Feibish," or "*Pan*[30] Lipka", they were expressing themselves with respect and sincerity. But he was a modest man who shrugged off even the minimum "eighth part of an eighth of pride" that a learned scholar is supposed to have[31]. He fled from glory and honor, and he avoided the public sphere. Yet people chose to consult him specifically and to seek him out for his leadership.

[Page 409]

6

The local priest of Dobrzyn was friendly to the Jews. My father was a very close friend of his. For hours on end they would talk about religion, philosophy, world politics and municipal problems. Those were the days of the cooperative organizations: *spolkas*[32] *zgodes*[33], *swoj do swego*[34], and other afflictions. Of course my father would show him the disingenuousness of all these things. His influence helped: the priest began using his sermons to condemn all the incitements and libels against the Jews. The atmosphere in the town improved and became normal. The farmers from the surrounding areas avoided the *spolkas* and returned to the Jewish shopkeepers.

One day the priest informed my father that he wanted him to visit him the next day. What was the occasion? An important guest, a very learned priest who knew Arabic and Hebrew, was coming over, and the local priest wanted my father to have a conversation with him. I was very curious to hear a priest speak Hebrew, so I went along. As we entered the house, we saw a plump, broad–shouldered man sitting at the table, reading a book. Seeing us, he said, in a jesting manner, "*Dzien dobry, Maszku!*" (Good morning, Moishele). Now, we knew very well that for the Poles "Maszek" was a derogatory name for a Jew, an expression of contempt. "*Dzien dobry,*" we answered as we sat down.

Just then "our" priest came in. He went over to my father and said in a loud voice: "*Ah, dzień dobry, Panie Lipka*! (Good morning, Mr. Lipka.) We were just talking about you." The guest quickly stood up and said, "*Przepraszam bardzo* (pardon me very much) for insulting you by calling you Maszek. I didn't know that you were the *Pan Lipka* that my friend has been telling me so much about."

My father looked at him with a smile on his face and said: "I heard that you know Arabic and Hebrew. Well, all right, I don't really know any Arabic, but let me hear your Hebrew. Do you have a book in Hebrew?" "Certainly," he answered, taking a *Chumash*[35] out of his valise. My father stuck his finger between the pages and opened it; it opened to the section of Balak[36]. "Read," my father said, and the guest began to read: "And Balak the son of Zippor heard...", and continued on and on—correctly, without getting stuck, truly amazing! His pronunciation of Hebrew was excellent, and he immediately translated into Polish—precisely, effortlessly. My father tested him on other parts of the text, but the guest really did know it all; he was a true expert[37].

"Good," my father said, "Very nice. I must be honest with you, I didn't expect you to know it so well. But let me ask you, do you know who wrote the Pentateuch?

"What do you mean, who?" said the guest, astonished. "Why, Mojżesz[38], of course!" "Right, correct!" answered my father. "And we know that 'Maszek' is a corrupted, jesting form of Mojzesz. Could it have even occurred to you that you were insulting me by calling me Maszek? If not for that 'Maszek', there would not have been any Torah or religions. You would not have been a learned priest and would not have had such a nice, comfortable position. If not for that 'Maszek' you would be herding livestock today, mildly speaking." (My father did not want to overdo it, but both priests understood which livestock...) My father continued: "There was another great 'Maszek', Maimonides," and he went on, quoting in Hebrew, "From Moses to Moses there has not ever arisen anyone like Moses"[39]. (The guest understood this immediately.) "When you called me 'Maszek' you gave me the greatest compliment. This shows that in your fanatical hatred of Jews you are ignorant fools!"

The guest was stunned and, for a while, was lost in thought. Shaking my father's hand, he said: "No wonder my friend regards you with such high esteem. I learned a great deal today, and I will never forget it." Meanwhile, the priest of Dobrzyn was beaming, smiling from ear to ear.

[Page 411]

7

My father and my brothers conducted a great deal of business with the surrounding Sroros[40] (Pritsim[41], but the word "Porits" was almost never used in our parts). From them we purchased wooded areas, grain, cattle, and horses; and from us they would buy flour, wooden planks, and timber. They would also order stodoles (barns), stalls and other structures. We would prefabricate these orders in our huge courtyard, and then reassemble them on site. My father was never obsequious to the "Jasznie–Wielimadznies" (titled, gentry landowners); he told them the truth to their faces, and they respected him for it. Among them was a quite important nobleman, the Zbójno hrabia[42] (count in English), a conspicuous playboy, tall and well built. He liked to play chess with my father, and to discuss world politics, Poland and even Palestine with him. He strongly supported the idea that the Starozakonny[43] (the Jews) should return to their land. He said that all honest patriotic Poles should feel the same way. Other noblemen who were present when he said that would weakly mutter "tak, tak" (yes, yes). In their conversations, when they were doing business with us, they would be very careful to explicitly use the word zydzi—the polite, grammatically correct term, rather than zydy, the vulgar, disdainful form–for the plural of zyd, i.e. Jew.

During the German occupation of the First World War, the hrabia was so "broke" that he was compelled to sell off a large part of his famous "Zbójno forest", the largest forest in the vicinity. Here my father showed him and the other gentry that money is not everything to a Jew. Thanks to this count's liberalism and the favorable opinion of Jews that we knew he had, my father did not want to try to get a bargain from him. Instead he paid him the best price. We could have made a fortune from this transaction, but my father said that no treasure, no matter how great, could outweigh the value of making a good name for Jews—to encourage Gentiles to be friendly to the Jews. The hrabia never forgot it, and he publicized it among his noblemen friends.

[Page 412]

8

Now I would like to describe an interesting event that took place at the end of the spring of 1914. As always my father travelled to a spa, this time to Landek, in Silesia[44]. After the attack in Sarajevo[45], the guests in Landek who were foreign citizens were trying to get home before they would be interned. My father, too, boarded a train to go home. Two stops before Torun[46], the train he had taken was brought to a halt; all Russian citizens aboard were taken away to Stettin[47], and from there through Denmark, Sweden, Finland and Petersburg to Warsaw, a journey of several thousand kilometers. My father and I met up in Warsaw, where I was at that time, and together we took the train to Ciechanow[48]. There we hired a closed carriage, which brought us back to Dobrzyn along a very dangerous route.

Rumors about my father's long journey spread quickly in the town, and dozens of people came over to hear about his impressions of the trip. He also received an invitation from the German command headquarters in Dobrzyn. They were interested in finding out about the movements of the Russian troops, and also about what types of arms he had seen along the way. My father told them that he had seen many troops with a large number of weapons. They called him in several times, but were unable to obtain a clear statement from him; he was not a military man and did not understand much, if anything, about the nuances and fine points of weapons[49].

However, in the end the meetings with the German command did indeed bear fruit: my father and the commandant became good friends. Later this friendship brought a great salvation to the town:

The entire populace of the town had been brought to the town square with the accusation that someone had fired on the German soldiers in the town. The square was surrounded by armed soldiers. At a critical moment my father spoke to the commandant and convinced him of the innocence of the population. "Yes, it is possible," the commandant mumbled, and later gave the order that the populace should leave town. In this way the incident in the town square ended, thanks to my father's intervention with the commandant.

[Page 413]

9

Most of the members of my family were timber and grain dealers. During his early years my father studied in the Slonim[50] Yeshiva, where he received *smicha*[51], but he didn't wish to use the Torah as a *kardom lachpor boi*[52] and became a merchant. Later he built a sawmill as well as a large four-story [flour] mill. He was successful in business; after becoming very wealthy he turned everything over to my brothers and busied himself with Zionist propaganda. My brothers would consult him only for the most important transactions.

At that time he was elected in the Plock region as a delegate to the First or Second Zionist Congress. He then travelled to the Land of Israel for the first time, and upon his return he was ready to take the family on *aliya*. At home, within the family, we spoke about it very seriously, but in the meantime some problems came up and the plan was cancelled.

The German occupation created various problems in the town, and my father would in each case intervene with the German authorities—just as he did in the incident that took place at the beginning of the war, as mentioned above.

When the war ended my father again brought up the idea of *aliya* to the Land of Israel. It was after the Balfour Declaration, which had generated a great deal of enthusiasm in the town. We then owned a huge fortune, consisting of: an electricity station in the town, several estates, sawmills, a [flour] mill, houses, wood camps, forests, and other assets. My father's plan was to set up a factory in Israel that would manufacture orange crates; at the time orange crates were being imported from outside the country. But then another hindrance came up: the Russian–Polish War[53], which put my father's plans on hold. Still he didn't want to give up his life's dream; as he became more infirm with advancing age he decided to make the journey to Israel, where he would find his final resting place. Unfortunately, however, fate dealt him a cruel blow at the very end. He suddenly fell ill, and after several days he passed away at the age of 79.

With my father's passing, part of my world came to an end, as well. I was in a state of despair, feeling that I was done for, with no plans whatsoever for the future. It was then that my fate brought me to America.

[Page 415]
10

We were a large family with many branches, consisting of sisters, brothers, children, grandchildren, and even adult great–grandchildren. Among them were personalities who edified the Jewish community of Dobrzyn. There were also people who played a large role in the financial world, since they were owners of large industrial works, estates, forests, and various businesses.

The descendants of R. Feibish Lipka's dynasty studied in high schools and also in higher education. All were raised in the spirit of the Land of Israel, with Zionist leanings.

Already in the early 1920s some of his children and grandchildren immigrated to the Land of Israel. My brother Yaakov and his two sons started a business building houses in Tel Aviv. This brother was an expert builder who would join forces with the engineer in designing a building. His children helped out with the actual work. He wanted to create a livelihood for members of the extended family who would be immigrating in the future. But the 1926 crisis in the Land of Israel abrogated his building plans, and with a heavy heart he returned to Poland. Unfortunately my brother was not the only one; now, in 1963, I heard from Zipporah Cohen of Tel Aviv, who was here on a visit, that my brother Yaakov and several other members of my family who were in English Mandatory Palestine, as it was then known, had bought plots of land and were about to bring over the remaining family. But when Grabski reduced the tax rate a bit[54], and also because of the housing crisis, thousands of Jews, among them also my brother Yaakov and his children, went back to Poland and perished tragically in the widespread destruction.

11

Dobrzyn had approximately three thousand residents, of whom somewhat more than half were Jews. Most had a livelihood. On market days—Tuesdays and Fridays—the "*Tarek*" (the local term for town square, the marketplace) used to be filled with the farmers from the surrounding villages, one wagon right up against another. Jewish men and women would be buying and selling chickens, eggs, dairy products, grain, horses, cattle, etc. Jokesters used to tell the following story: once a Jewish man needed a rooster for *kapores*[55], and, holding up the chicken he had selected, but not knowing how to tell [whether it was male], he asked the lady farmer who was selling it, "*Czy to ja,' czy to ty*"[56] (is that me or you?)—[meaning,] a rooster or a hen. Oh, well...what jokesters can come up with!

The farmers, in turn, bought the following from the Jews: food supplies, fine fabric, haberdashery, shoes, boots, clothing, tools, etc. In Dobrzyn there were two [flour] mills, two sawmills, several shoe workshops, clothing workshops ("*tandetnikes*")—all in Jewish hands. There were also several bakeries (Shmuel Prum, with his famous "*kaiserkes*"— *lachmaniot*[57] in Hebrew), a soda-water and "*kvass*" factory, a chicory factory, a soap factory, a *lodownie*[58], etc. There were also several Jewish estate owners: We owned Grudza[59]; Moishe-Yaakov Kohn owned Zakrocz[60]; Rojna and Szmiga owned Szitna[61]; Zeinwel Yom Tov owned Cholewy[62]; Hersz Dobrzynski owned Dzalin[63]; and Florman owned Zarembe[64], a small estate. It was all legitimate—perfectly honest and legal.

Another source of livelihood, an open secret, was "*moilecherei*", a term used in Dobrzyn for smuggling (perhaps derived from the Hebrew word *moilich*, meaning bringing across or transporting). To legally bring merchandise into Dobrzyn from the German border-town Golub one had to pay customs tax. But that would not be any good! Citizens of both countries had documents called "*cartes*" that would allow them to cross the border. So they crossed and "*moilecht*" brazenly, as much as they wished. Mostly men's and ladies' garments, canned goods, liquor, chocolate, cigars, cigarettes, cameras, watches and dozens of other articles. When they were going across to Golub, the *moilechers* looked like slim young girls, but when they came back they looked like pregnant women carrying twins. Surprising? They would put on a few pairs of pants, vests (what would you expect, no vest?) and jackets; and on top of everything a *palto* (an overcoat). They would stuff the pockets of these garments with underclothes, ladies' bags, as well as the items mentioned above. They went back and forth this way several times a day. *Fonye*[65] the Thief would look the other way, his palm outstretched. Once *Fonye* made it look good: one day before the arrival of the government inspector (from Plock), the local inspector "captured" a couple of *moilechers*. Their brother *moilechers* compensated the captured ones until their *cartes* were returned to them. This was routine.

There was also another category of a political nature, which was called *ariber-shvartsn*[66]. Those who were smuggled across—among them non-Jews, as well—included people who did not wish to serve *Fonye*[67], political lawbreakers, and others who had their own private reckonings. Most of the time they were taken across the river at night in a *łódka* (a small boat). It often happened that they swam across the river during the daytime, although the *objeszczikes* (border guards) used to shoot at them and miss...It must have been set up in advance—what else?...

One should not think that Dobrzyn was a town consisting of only wealthy people, shopkeepers, and smugglers. Far from it. But since it was a border-town, smuggling was unavoidable. Besides, only a small number of Jews were involved in it. At the very least *Fonye* the Pig would benefit, and Jews would derive some livelihood thereby. In our town there were honest, hard-working, cordial people who labored physically: shoemakers, tailors, porters, wagon drivers, butchers, fishermen, carpenters, watchmakers, artists (incidentally, the Dobrzyn artist and monument mason was the brother of the renowned sculptor Enrico Glicenstein[68]); a tinsmith, a furrier, a rope maker, sausage makers, a barbecue lady, water carriers, musical bands, government teachers who were Jewish, and a *soifer*[69]— all cordial, warm Jews. Even the barrel-organ player and the Jewish thieves had a special Jewish romantic flavor, à la *Motke Ganef*[70]. Since my childhood I have felt some kind of gnawing, deep sympathy for these very people.

And on weekdays, very early in the morning, all these Jews would be the first to arrive at the *Beis Medresh*; they would pray with heart and mind, beseeching the Creator for health and livelihood, not only for themselves but for all of the Jewish people. There was a powerful sense of friendship and unity among the Jews of Dobrzyn. Kasriel Sonabend, may he rest in peace, the son of Rabbi Sonabend, would lead the prayer service with great fervor. It should be mentioned here that all the Jews of Dobrzyn at the very least knew some prayer-book Hebrew and, in their own simple way, understood what the words meant.

[Page 418]

12

Friday, in the mikve[71], a few hours before candle-lighting[72]. We youngsters have been fooling around the whole time. We are pouring buckets of cold water over each other's heads. Suddenly our fathers, already dressed, are shouting: "Get out! Go home!"

We jump out of the baths like roosters. We barely have a chance to dry ourselves, and still half wet we slip on our underwear and our shirts, which stick to our skin. Our skarpetkas[73] are wet, and in this state we drag ourselves home, home!

Our house was on the other side of town. The fact that we didn't get pneumonia could only have been because of the merit of the Sabbath. Mothers, you see, would not have let us go in that condition. Ah, you dear, warm, devoted Jewish mothers! They would have drunk up and kissed every toe on their children's feet.

13

The eve of Rosh Hashana. We are unpacking the Israeli wines. We youngsters are tearing the straw covers off the bottles and are turning them into "Land of Israel caps" that the Jewish colonists and shepherds wear. That picture of the two Jews on the bottles of wine always intrigued us children. These must certainly have been two of the spies, who are carrying a cluster of grapes on their shoulders[74]. And we think about it as we look at it and stroke it with such a warm feeling, somehow, of home and longing. And the pineapple, the *apfelsinen*[75] (oranges, *tapuchei–zahav* in Hebrew). The next day, in the *shtibl*, the special Torah–reading chant of "And it happened after these things…"[76]: the words and melodies are so drawn out and exotic. You can just see Abraham with Isaac, with the young boys who were left with the donkey, as they pace slowly and with difficulty through the sandy desert, until "On the third day he saw the place…"[77] So the fantasy weaves along, and before you know it we are going to *Tashlich*[78] at the Dreventz River. Gentile toughs[79] throw stones down at us from "Rokers Mount"[80], and we youngsters "storm" the mountain and chase them away.

[Page 419]

*

The eve of Yom Kippur. Quite early, people begin to *shlog kapores*[81]. For me this has always been a painful experience to endure. What do they want from these poor, unfortunate chickens? When I hold my chicken, how his little heart beats as I say "*Bnei Odom*"[82], and how sad his face is! Once I got so angry that I cut the cords off the birds' little feet and chased them away. My stepmother, who was very devout, was shouting, "Feibish, have a look, the *meshumed*[83] has been up to something again!" My father answered, smiling, "He probably put the chickens someplace so that they would live longer." It was getting late, so on that Yom Kippur Eve we *shlogged kapores* with money for charity[84].

And now an idea has occurred to me: why not write a list (a long one) of the names of all the enemies of the State of Israel on a piece of paper and *shlog kapores* with it? After the ritual you could burn the piece of paper. That would cover symbolism, appropriateness, and ceremony.

Then afterwards, around the time of *Mincha*[85], came the distribution of money in the various charity boxes. My father, wearing a white *kitl*[86], blesses me and all the grandchildren. In the *shtibl*, before *Kol Nidrei*[87], the fiery declaration: "By the authority of the Court on High and by authority of the court down below..."[88] As I see it, these few words reflect the essential perspective of the Jewish religion. Before accepting our sacred holiday, the day of introspection and reckoning, we proclaim: let not a single soul be rejected. Even the greatest sinner should not give up hope, since the relationship between one person and another is of the utmost importance. Etc. And after that, the lyrical-tremulous uplifting chant, the supreme ancient yet new Kol Nidre! After Maariv, my father and several other Jews remain in the shtibl and we say "*Shir HaYichud*"[89], a most beautiful religious poem. Then the next day the fast. The capable, determined little faces of the young children who want to do what the "big kids" are doing[90]. But after a while our spirits hang on the tip of our noses: we are inhaling smelling salts. And finally the blowing of the shofar, and we walk home slowly with unburdened hearts.

[Page 420]

*

After Yom Kippur and the Eve of Sukkos[91] we young children and my brother Mordechai-Mendel were busy erecting a large sukkah[92] that was big enough for all three families, many invited people, and just plain guests. We were banging, hammering, sawing, decorating the walls with beautiful rugs and hanging various fruits.

Plenty of *sechach*[93] was available. We had to just watch out that Lillis, the shrew—the mischievous goat—should not snatch it away. (We youngsters were rearing cattle and chickens, and we had given each its own nickname. The *shochet*[94] had no power over them.) Lillis, however, managed to grab a bundle of *sechach* with her mouth and fled, as if to say: "I am after all a Jewish goat, so let me also enjoy Sukkos." But Zagrai, the old dog, now saw his opportunity to demonstrate his loyalty, and in a way to settle scores with Lillis for the hard jab she had given him with her horns a while back. He caught her by the leg, and with a loud shriek she gave up the bundle of *sechach*.

The little roofs that were opened and closed by thick ropes wound on wheels were the pride of the sukkah[95]. And when my father and brothers were inviting the *ushpizin*[96], we kept looking at the door…oh, well, we thought, maybe next year.

*

[Page 421]

Purim. Last night we read the *megilla*[97] with its special drawn-out, up-and-down melody: "And it came to pass in the days of Ahasuerus…"[98] Stamping of the feet and noisemakers at the mention of Haman's name[99]. Delivering *shalach manos*[100] with the traditional white napkin over the plate. The actor in a Purim disguise with Aharon Tzukevich's (Aharon Shliepak) little song: "Happy Purim, kish kish kish; let us all eat some good fish; let us all have some good wine; ten pennies into the bottle!" Or: "Berl on the fiddle, Shmerl one the bass; play a little song for me; have along some gas." The older kids would put on long, white frocks with large blue stars of David, either sewn on or colored on, and they would collect money for the Jewish National Fund. It also sometimes happened that a large group of Gentile toughs[101] would attack these collectors of charity, who were barely able to rescue themselves. My nephew Yitzchok-Yaakov once split open a Gentile tough's head with an iron rod. People collecting money for *Mo'os Chittim*[102] would also appear at the Purim *Seudu*[103].

*

Passover Eve. The sense of spring. Something so proud. The heart is so joyful. We are washing, scraping, whitewashing walls, plastering ceilings, and *kashering*[104]. We take the Passover utensils down from the attic. The mysterious *B'dikas Chometz*[105]: husband and wife walk through all the rooms with a candle and feather in their hands, brushing crumbs of bread that they find into a large wooden spoon. A bunch of youngsters meet up on the mountain behind the synagogue, where they burn the *chometz*[106]. My father writes up the *Chometz* Sales Document in ornamental writing, reckoning out very precisely all that he was "selling" to the Christian flourmill supervisor, Plocharski.

The *Seder*. The tablecloth, white as snow, is laden with all the good food. The Passover wines from the Land of Israel. The silver cup for my father. The special Cup of Elijah, also silver. The crystal cups for the other adults, and for me the little glass with the ear-shaped handle. Everything is so clean and tidy. And the atmosphere is so joyful and warm. Father, dressed in a white *kitl*[1107], is on his recliner[1108]. I ask the Four Questions. The Haggada is read with a special narrative melody. The tasty dishes. (What else? The Haggada without kneidlach[1109]?) "Stealing" the *afikomen*[1110] and the negotiations between my father and me to "redeem" it. My price: a new little chalet; a new pair of shoes; new pants; a new hat; and "pocket money", as much as I desire. My father smiles amiably and accepts these terms. The few frightening, suspenseful minutes when the door is opened and we say "*shfoich chamoscho*"[1111]. Who else can so painfully understand it better than our unfortunate, martyred people, especially the generation of the last World War? For the other nations it was a war over power, but with respect to our people it was a cold-blooded campaign of eradication. Even as a child, since I began to understand what the Hebrew words meant, "*shfoich chamoscho*" was of primary importance to me. After that..."*Vayehi Bachatzi Halaylah*"[1112] and "*Oimetz Gvuroisecho*"[1113], the two artistic poems. The author reduces entire epochs and important historical events to two lines, and all so colorfully and dynamically. We sing "*El Bnei*", "*Echod Mi Yoideia*", "*Chad Gadyo*". My eyes...are...getting...heavy...Maybe because of the little glasses of wine, or because of the late hour...and I fall into a long, sweet sleep.

And afterwards an entire week of "playing" with nuts. Mostly *shlofkepl* and *bitch*. It often happened that when the little hole was full of nuts a "lapser", an awkward, tall creature with paws, came running over, put its two large paws into the hole and ran off with the nuts. Once, however, we played a trick on it: we filled the little hole with *kleister* (an adhesive) and mixed in a lot of India ink, which is very hard to get off. We covered it with nuts and "let" the creature grab it with his paws. He smeared his new holiday suit up and we laughed hysterically.

On *Choil Hamoied*[1114] children also used to go to the family to get "painted" eggs. The mothers used to cook them in onionskin, and they would come out colored.

[Page 423]

*

The eve of *Shovuos*[115]. Quite early we would go out beyond the town, looking for "reeds" near the water. We would cut them down, bring them home and place them in the windows. The next day, *Akdomus*[116] with its unique melody. And the idyllic and simple Book of Ruth. The tasty dairy dishes. The bewitching end of spring and beginning of summer weather! We youngsters get together and we all feel so good!

*

The Eve of *Tisha B'Av*[117]. We are all so sad and mournful. Nevertheless we youngsters tear up *kretz* (prickly thorns), and during the recital of *Eicha*[118] stick them into people's beards. Later, when we were somewhat older and understood the meaning of our national day of sorrow, and the sad, mournful *Eicha* melody had penetrated our souls, we recited the *Kinois*[119] together with the grownups. I don't know where the custom originated from, but on *Tisha B'Av* we young boys used to stick wooden swords into the graves of our dead family relatives. As for me, my young heart sank when I did this on my mother's grave, especially since *Tisha B'Av* was actually the anniversary of her death. The bystanders would look at me with compassion.

[Page 424]

14

The "going to recite *Krias Shma*[120]" to the women who were giving birth. We young *cheder* children are standing near the bed of a woman in labor, looking at the "*Shir Hamaalois*"[121] that have been hung around her bed to protect her against the *mazikim*[122], but in reality it is the goodies we will be receiving that are on our minds. We begin each group of two or three words in a loud, monotonous staccato, the way captured, hungry woodpeckers sometimes let out a refrain of "one–two–three". And we stretch our little hands out for the cookies, lollypops, raisins, almonds and nuts. We would be lucky if Mrs. Rusak, the midwife in the white coat, was there: she gave out double–size portions. It sometimes happened that a woman in labor asked, "Why the big hurry?" and made us start all over again.

*

That is what the holidays and customs of the Jewish town looked like. Idyllic, simple, warm. That is how we felt as children. We record it here so that our children, grandchildren and all their descendants, to the very last generation, should at least have an inkling of the past joy and pain in the little Jewish town. And that goes for us, the survivors, as well. So, one of these days try humming a *Kol–Nidrei* tune, an *Akdomus* melody or a *megilla* chant, and see if you don't get that feeling of yearning. And you will berate yourself: "Ah, where can one find the belief of yesteryear...and the faith, hard as stone, that comes with it?" After all, most of us are not religiously observant. And the tiny little inconsequential portion of This World that we capture, we fritter away, after all, because we are not even one tenth corrupt enough to be able to possibly utilize it completely. If so, let me at least warm myself with the small amount of faith of yesteryear, and meanwhile plan a future of belief. That is the fundamental basis of our existence...as a Jewish people in the State of Israel and in the Diaspora...

[Page 425]

15

R. Chatzkl was my first teacher. I don't remember his family name. From him I learned some fundamental Bible–Hebrew and began a bit of *Chumash*[123] and Rashi[124]. How glad he was that R. Feibish had entrusted his little boy to him! But I was in his class for only one term, because once I had caught on he was much too slow for me. While *Rebbi*[125] Chatzkl was still teaching Noah[126] to the other little boys, I was already up to Deuteronomy, having studied on my own.

R. Chatzkl had two sons. The elder of them, tall with dark hair, was serving in the Russian army. When he was home on leave, he would always sing for us in a long, drawn–out tone: *Poyechal Kossack*! The second son, Mechl, used to make skates for us out of a piece of wood into which he would force a piece of hard tin. The skates would be fastened onto our shoes with leather straps, but we fell down more than we actually skated. In order to hang on to their poor little bit of livelihood, the *Rebbetzen*[127] would often treat us to roasted potatoes.

Since my father loved me dearly and gave in to me, I ran around all summer, free as a bird. When once in a blue moon he ostensibly wanted to actually castigate me, he would say to me: "Yadush (undisciplined, 'Yatl'), what [mischief] have you now again been up to?" And his clever eyes gazed at me with such heartfelt warmth. There was one thing that I did learn very well: Hebrew from the book *Safa Chaya*[128] (the older among you readers probably remember this very book): *puzmak, ozen, ish tzaval*[129]. My "teacher" was (Yaakov?) Arda.

My second *rebbi*, from whom I learned Chumash–Rashi and *Posuk*[130], was R. Avrohom Gottlieb, a fine, good-looking man. He never beat us or slapped us around. While teaching, he would "make" cigarettes. He would lay the tobacco out on paper, spraying it a bit; then fill a metal tube containing little wrappers with the tobacco. He would close the tube, sticking one end into a "thimble". He would force a thin, metal pushing tool into the other end. He would do all this quickly, without even looking at his hands. Only rarely did a thimble tear. He would shear off the upper portion of the cigarettes and pack them into a textured little box. The man must have "stuffed" millions of cigarettes throughout his lifetime; nowadays it takes a machine half a day to do the same thing.

He was good at making models of the objects that he taught his students about. He made a miniature model of the Biblical Tabernacle in exact detail: the planks, the curtains, and even the clasps and sockets[131]. Everything was precise, in proportion, and properly scaled. He also made a model of the breastplate, the Ephod and the turban[132].

When he and R. Nisan (another one of my teachers) sat down to play chess (in Dobrzyn parlance, shoch[133]), it would take them days to finish the game. And no wonder, since it took them hours to make a move. They didn't rush each other. They drank tea and smoked; it was a true diversion for them.

We'd leave them to their chess game and off we'd go to play *palant*[134]. In this game R. Avrohom's son, Chaim'ye "Matchek", was an expert player, a daredevil[135]. He never missed the ball when he swung at it with the stick, and he would hit it a great distance, far away where no one would be able to catch it. And he struck the ball so gracefully and with such ease that even the Gentiles—for it was, after all, their national sport—would stop in their tracks in wonder. And not only did he hit the ball far, but also high, very high. Here in America, he would have been a first-class baseball player. He also had a good, sweet voice and sang well.

We used to make the ball out of old galoshes. We would cut the rubber into long, thin strips, and then wrap them together to form a large, hard core. If anyone would be hit in the head by it he might see stars...When someone did catch the ball the friction of the impact would chafe his hands.

My third—and favorite—teacher was R. Nisan Dembowicz. A worn–out, tall man. He was indeed strong as an oak[136], and strict! (We used to call him "Cossack", because he didn't let anybody, even the finest and wealthiest people, push him around.) With him I studied *Chumash*–Rashi, then *Posuk*, *Mishnayos*[137], *Gemoro*[138]; and even on the Sabbaths I had to study *Perek*[139]. With him you "had to" study and "had to" know. If not, then you felt the taste of Amalek. Amalek was a long leather strap, doubled over. Obviously Amalek was not to our liking.[140] So that led us to a *hovo nis'chakmo*[141] plot: how to get rid of it. Someone had heard that if you rub a lot of garlic onto leather and then strike it, it instantly bursts. He was ready to swear to it—amazing what a child can come up with! But this was all we needed to hear. The next day, when the teacher left the room for a few minutes, the two "*shtarke*"[142], Avrohom Moshe "Obal" (Tinski) and Hersh–Leib "Faife" (Glitzenstein) rubbed the Amalek hard with garlic, and volunteered to "provoke" the teacher. When we resumed class, "Faife" bleated loudly like a goat, and "Obal" bellowed like an ox. The teacher grabbed the Amalek as we waited for the miracle: Amalek was about to be sprung apart! But unfortunately it was the two victims who were nearly sprung apart. And they also had to wash the garlic out well.

But the amazing thing was that in spite of everything we really liked this teacher very much. Children want to have a disciplining authority over them. He was not only a good teacher, but he was also our spiritual leader. He inspired us to courage and valor: that we should not be afraid of the Gentile boys, that we should stand up to them and fight back, even when we were being beaten. This had a strong effect on us, and we did fight back.

During the winter, when the section of the Torah about to be read in synagogue was *Vayigash*[143], he would play out his fantasy, telling us what the "*midrashim*"[144] had to say about the meeting between Joseph and his brothers, the other sons of Jacob...Manasseh and Ephraim[145] were in Joseph's suite. One of them went over to Judah and the other to Simeon, and they planted a slap on the back on each of them. Judah and Simeon then called out to the other brothers: "Strange, that felt like a slap from one of us: it really hurt. But that's impossible—and we've been offended. Naphtali (the "hind that has been set loose"[146])! Go run through the streets of the city and then let us know how many houses there are here." When Naphtali returned, Judah let out a shout: "Get ready, brothers! Today all these houses will be smeared with Egyptian blood!" And meanwhile the hair on Judah's chest stood on end like steel spears. But of course Joseph understood everything they had said[147], and he ordered that they be surrounded by the bravest soldiers, the strongest charioteers and the fieriest horses. He disarmed them and locked them up in a fortress…And more and more fantasies of this kind. We young boys were sitting crowded together, listening with bated breath, and feeling lofty and strong. On that night we left our lanterns behind in the *cheder* and walked home with stones in our hands, ready to defend ourselves.

And needless to say, Judah Maccabee[148] as well. It appears (now, from my present perspective) that this teacher had gotten access somewhere to the First and Second Book of Maccabees of the Apocrypha[149], since he told us all of the stories of the Maccabees that appear there, in complete detail. And similarly he told us about King Solomon's greatness, as recorded in the Second Targum[150], and many other stories, all about valor.

Lag BaOmer[151] was truly special. We felt so secure around him as we marched into the woods with our bows and arrows and our knapsacks of food. There, in the woods, he told us in great length about Bar Kochba's heroic deeds[152], and his face glowed with passion…Afterwards he showed us how to defend ourselves with a stick, even against four simultaneous attackers. He said he had learned this in the military. He ran together with us in "vishtsiges" and showed us how to jump over a wide ditch, something that looked impossible to us. No longer was he just our teacher at that time, he was also a guide.

And he was also the *baal koirei*[153] and *baal tokeiya*[154] in our Otwock *shtibl*[155]. He also apparently thought a great deal of the commentary of the Malbim[156], because often he told my father: "The Malbim says this," or "the Malbim understands it this way," "the Malbim…", etc.

After something happened he established something new: a teacher came into our *cheder* to teach us Russian. This teacher had an unusual name: Krautwurscht. We were very proud and jealous when we heard our teacher conversing so easily and rapidly with him in Russian. This Krautwurscht set up the black tablet with chalk in diagonal lines quickly and precisely and wrote down words, which looked like they had been printed! We started with the book *Ruskaya Rietsh* (older readers probably remember: "*lapa, fila, kashka*").

After him my next teacher was Yosef–Elya, the "Little Stick". He had an innovation that was quite effective: if any student looked up from his *Gemoro* book, the teacher quickly grabbed him by the neck with the curved crook of his walking stick and pulled the boy's face down to the book. This idea must have come to him from goose herders, who used to do the same to geese that had wandered away from the "pack". With him we studied only *Gemoro* with commentaries. He had a mean temper, and learning from him was not satisfying. It was all pell-mell. A couple of months and that was it!

My last teacher was R. Chana Mendelson, "Shventi-yan". Why "Shventi-yan"? Because if someone was absent from *cheder* for a day, he would ask him the next day, in a hoarse, bass voice: "What kind of holiday was it yesterday, Shventi-yan?" He didn't use any "tools" to beat us. With him I studied *Gemoro* with *Toisfos*[157] and other commentaries. When we were reading Talmudic passages that were a bit "spicy" out loud, he would hurry us along, shouting, "So, keep going already, you *sheigetz*-like boy!"[158] We had "lost our place" and had to start all over again…We learned well from him and were very unrestrained, somewhat too unrestrained.

For a while all the teachers grouped together in a single *cheder*, a sort of *yeshivo ketano*[159], with classes and teachers—Saloman, Levinson, and others—for languages and secular subjects. Meanwhile the First World War broke out. My brothers' children and I then studied with private teachers in Plock and Warsaw. We were preparing ourselves for entrance to the Wlolclawek Jewish Gymnasia[160].

However, it was my father who was my very best teacher. During vacations on our estate, Grudza, we would wake up around 5am and study with great satisfaction until 8. In those few hours we "covered" more than would be done in an entire week of *cheder* study.

What a pity that *Girso deyankuso*[161] cannot suffice indefinitely. Apparently the statement "Thou shouldst contemplate it day and night"[162] is true, but concern about livelihood, family and health weigh very heavily…So why does it say "thou shouldst contemplate it" in the singular? Isn't the Torah meant for all the Jews? But the answer is quite simple. If all the Jews were studying constantly, who would be tilling, sowing, fashioning, building, etc.? It is the rabbis and spiritual leaders who should be busying themselves with Torah study.

[Page 430]

16

From the outside the Dobrzyn synagogue was not impressive. A not very high, but very wide and massive building—it was said that years back it had been a barrel factory—but inside, right near the entrance, before the pulpit, at the small incline to the women's section, there was a painting of the Tomb of Rachel, our matriarch. And flanking it paintings of the Tomb of Samuel and Absalom's Pillar. In other places, further into the synagogue, paintings of the Grove of Abraham, the Cave of Machpelah, Mount Zion, and other Biblical sites. Further in, next to the Holy Ark, from the beginning of the soffit to more than halfway up the wall, there hung plush, deep–red curtains. They were folded in a very natural way and covered over by a semicircular bow, which held them by flattened, gold–colored cord, with gold tassels at their end. It looked so natural you'd think you could go over to raise the curtain up or lower it a bit, or move it this way or that. But the masterpiece was the soffit. There, where the walls ended and the soffit began, one "saw" hundreds of artistic "knobs". A huge, eggshell–colored sheet was "fastened" to them; it contained paintings of thousands of delicate flowers, each within its own square. Approximately halfway along the soffit, way up, near the glass cupola, through which daylight penetrated, the sheet was folded into two large triangles. Each end was "fastened" to a large "knob". In the open, visible parts, Biblical fruits could be seen pouring out from one side as if from a cornucopia (horn of plenty): grapes, figs, dates, almonds, apples, pomegranates, etc. On the other, bare triangle, Biblical musical instruments were laid out in various poses: a harp, a violin (in another form), sitars, cymbals, tambourines, timbrels, fifes, trumpets, shofars, etc. It was a marvelous artistic masterpiece. It was said that the artists worked on it for almost an entire year. While the Torah was being read in our *shtibl*, I used to leave to go over to the synagogue and gaze in amazement at the masterpiece until the prayer service ended. Many times I came home with a stiff neck. But it was worth it! So pleasurable

[Page 431]

17

And now a little about the language of Dobrzyn. Because of the proximity to Germany, some words sounded strange, particularly their endings. When one wants to indicate a small or adorable item in German one adds the ending "chen". The Jews of Dobrzyn appropriated this ending, but transformed it into a combination between a soft, compressed "chof" and a partially smeared–out "yud", which together came out as "chye": a *meidchye*[163], a *yinglchye*[164], a *tishchye*[165], etc. The ending "chye" was also utilized for diminutive or beloved little people. For example: "Let's go to the Rusakchyen." "Let's ask Avrohomchyen." "Shmuelchye (Kohn), sing something!" And so on. The older people went even further and said "*meidelchyer*" and "*yingelchyer*". All right, this was going a bit too far[166].

However, there were also words that only the people of Dobrzyn used and only they understood. And here is a list of several of them:

"Shmeikpapchye": a cigarette or cigar holder, made of wood, Bakelite or amber.

"Shahnchye": the most distinguished, the best. For example: "He is the *shahnchye* of the family."

A "hohtchye": a membrane. When a lady wanted a fat chicken, she poked it and blew the feathers out to find out if it had a *hohtchye*.

"Tumbank": a checkout counter, where customers pay the shopkeeper (*dalpek* in Hebrew).

"Rithshahzenes": ice skates.

"Nahges" or "Ahngelaigte kloitskes": little dumplings made of potatoes or wheat flour.

"Ahnzaltsen": putting money into the pot during a game.

"Opkutern": winning money at a game of cards or dice, or in a "bones" game.

"Lapsen, tsilapsen": to steal, to snatch away fearlessly, to swipe.

"Chlihpsen, tsichlihpen": to steal silently.

"Plimp": a water pump. Who doesn't remember the *plimp* in the "torek"?

"Fledervish": a feathered wing of a slaughtered chicken, used for dusting around.

And here is a gem: "tsipronchye". Even if you had ten heads you would never figure it out. I'll even give you a hint: Two men are sitting in a synagogue and one of them says: "The 'tsipronchye' was as sweet as sugar today." So what's your guess, that it's marzipan? Not at all! You didn't figure it out! *Tsipronchye* is very simple: a young boy soprano[167]. So the sentence means that the little soprano's singing was a delight to the ear.

"Ziller": an attic.

And still more and more…

And that's it for Dobrzyn "philology".

[Page 432]

18

During the German occupation of World War I, Dobrzyn prospered greatly, both materially and in spirit. The town did not have the dreaded "*naszi*"—Russian, and "*wasze*"[168] —German, problems that the Poles threatened and carried out many times, helping the Russians rob, and shooting Jews as "spies". Dobrzyn was fortunate that from the moment the Germans first entered the town, the Russians never came back. After the well-known expulsion, the populace returned, and a very vigorous trade began. The Germans paid well for thousands of horses, cattle and grain. From Germany Jews bought soap, snuff, cigarettes and other items that were difficult to obtain in Poland at the time. Merchants arrived from far and wide. Several dozen poor families from various parts of Poland were housed and supported by the Dobrzyn Jews. The charity endowment of Dobrzyn was always full, there being no other city where the guests were covered as generously as in Dobrzyn. But Dobrzyn confirmed that "man does not live by bread alone." A wealth of social-cultural activities blossomed. Talks, discussions, presentations, lectures, debates were being conducted throughout the town. "Herzliya" and "HaTechiya"[169] were teeming with young people. The local *Poalei Tzion*[170] branch was animated by the energetic and intelligent Bunem Zaklikowski. So also the local branch of Bund. In the beautiful library there were meetings, conventions, planning, etc. Often there were theatrical performances. In "*Der Dorfsyung*"[171], the cantor's son, Yaakov Boruch Degala, outperformed even the *Kelmer Magid*[172], and it was a pleasure to hear and see it. This very talented young man would have gone very far here in America. People from Rypin and Dobrzyn would often get together. And as an aside, it should be noted that the young ladies of Rypin were quite charming; some were real beauties. Even today, although many of them are grandmothers, they still have their former charm and lovely features.

Who says that you have to give false compliments to be accepted? Here, in these few lines, I've gotten into the good graces of those spellbinding creatures, and with nothing more than the honest truth.

That's still nothing compared to the following: There was once a Jew who, when he was leading a prayer service in the synagogue, made a sacred, far-reaching benediction over women. When he got to "*mevorech hashonim*"[1173], he recited it slowly, very seriously, and ended it with an extensive chant of "*Boruch atto...mevorech hanoshim.*"[1174] Participants in the service who were nearby, and clearly heard what he had said, opened their eyes wide, shrugged, and cried out indignantly "*Mna! Mna!*[1175]" But shout as they might, the benediction had already risen way up high. I am almost certain that when that benediction, enunciated with naive innocence, reached the Throne of Glory, He Who examines our innermost thoughts smiled at it, so to speak...

Let's get back to the cultural–social business. We brought over lecturers, sermonizers and speakers such as Mileikowski, Itkin, Zerubabel, Hillel Zeitlin, Noach Prilucki, and others. The little town was flourishing culturally. How beautiful the charming little couples looked when they went out to sell the little blue–white flowers for the Jewish National Fund! The culturally rich Chanukah entertainments. The Purim festivities. The Passover and Sukkos *Choil–Hamoied*[1176] get–togethers with those from the nearby towns of Rypin, Sierpc, Lubicz, Lipna and others. So festive and cordial, so warm; a mixture of genteel romance and cultural refinement. How many entrancing words were murmured, and how many young hearts fluttered!

Ah, the town of yesteryear, the town that was! The walks on the main road behind the barracks and the brick factory, and from there down to the "*struga*"[1177], where you could catch tiny little fish, "kobzes", with your bare hands. "Going to Zarembe"[1178], a nearby small Jewish estate, and resting at the halfway point in the "zagoi" (a young little forest); the official excursions out of the town and the picnics. The *Hashomer Hatzair*[1179] that I established when it still had a very different character. The Dobrzyn Jewish "army": the scouts, which "Field Marshall" Shmuel Boruch Rusak led with iron discipline (don't touch it, Sh.! Don't erase anything![1180]) The Jewish firemen, with Hershel Lent as deputy.

The meetings in the synagogue and *beis medresh*! R. Yitzchok–Moshe Ofenbach, finely dressed, with a combed, grayish beard, starts the meeting with an extended "*Raboisai!*"[1181]; my father speaks, and smiling brightly he begins with "My dear fellow Jews". Hersh Isaac speaks emotionally. Avrohom Zudkewicz speaks briefly and to the point; and others and still others.

By the way, with respect to Hersh Isaac: he had good-looking, learned children. One of them, Yehoshua, was one of the very first students in the Haifa Technion. The oldest, Kasriel, devoted his entire life to developing a black rose, but I don't know if he ever succeeded. He and his brother, Aharon, had a large garden in Kutno; one of the daughters (Rurzka?) was a beautiful blond; and Yehuda drew quite well.

The meetings of the Dobrzyn Zionist *Vaad-Hapoel* in our house. Mendel Prum (Mendel "Shaigetz"[182]), a youngster compared to the other members but a good fellow, calls out: "And now we are going to select the permanent subordinates." Moshe Warszas, the very efficient secretary, smiles amiably.

The spontaneous appeal for *Keren Hayesod*[183]! Jewish women, daughters of Israel, gave away their most precious jewelry for the sacred objective. When the news came of the Balfour Declaration, I was in the Gymnasia room. Bochurski, the Hebrew teacher, walked in and recited the *Shehecheyonu*[184] benediction in a loud voice, as tears streamed down from his lovely grey eyes...and also from ours...Jewish Wloclawek was in upheaval! Joy and gladness![185] An exalted mood! I am imagining how Dobrzyn must be in jubilation. And afterwards the *hachshara*[186] activities.

I must take this opportunity to dedicate a few lines to an intelligent and much-neglected woman: Chana-Chaya Katcher, of blessed memory, a sister of the religious-lyrical poet Yosef Tzvi Rimon. There did not exist a single book that she hadn't read.

And this is how the social-cultural activities transpired in our town. The young, the old; the religiously observant, the modern; the wealthy, the plain people; each and every one did his part fully.

The constant voting confusion with the "slips of paper" of the various parties and of the little parties. The quarrels to "convince" the people, the voters. Each party wanted to rescue the Jews—what else?

[Page 435]

19

And More, and Still More Memories

Memories. They keep flowing as they emerge from the fog of the past.

Tu BiShvat[187]: Eating the stone–hard carob, dried out figs and almonds. It was simply a miracle that our appendixes didn't burst. Another miracle: stuffing ourselves during a "*Sholom Zochor*"[188] with salted, spiced chickpeas, and drinking up kvass and soda until our bellies ached.

Going home from *cheder* on winter nights while holding a lantern to avoid the deep mud.

The never–ending battles between us guys and the Gentile boys, using stones, nail–embedded sticks, whips, and strap buckles—until they begged us to let them alone.

The sleigh rides in the frosty winter nights! They would always remind me of Frug's "*Yiddishe Troike*"[189].

The days of summer, bathing in the Dreventz River, as naked as Adam.

Shivering on a cold night in the *sukkah*.

Going on the Sabbath for an "examination". How happy we were when the examiner pinched our cheeks, said "very good", and rewarded us with Sabbath fruit.

Carrying the *lulav* and *esrog*[190] through the streets. And how the *dayan*[191] would reverently poke himself in the belly with the lulav during the waving[192]. Still, saying "*Vetsidkos'cho*"[193] is not applicable.

Marching on *Simchas Torah*[194] with the banners, with the red apples and the candles that had been forced into them. Being called up to the Torah "with all the young boys"[195].

Playing "*Beiner* 21" on Chanukah; and the teachers and fine Jews with *kvitlach* on *Nitul*[196].

The "*Boruch Sheptorany*[197]". How strange both father and son felt afterwards. Father said, "*Oy vei*, no longer a father." And the son: "*Oy vei*, I've become a full–blown Jew. I'll have to be careful: from now on, all my sins will be on my own head."

Putting the *tsitsis* on a four–cornered garment[198].

Talking about exclusive clubs: the hours just before evening on the eve of a Sabbath or holiday in the synagogue, in the *beis medresh*, or particularly in the *shtibls*. Divided up in various groups, Jews were smoking enjoyably and conversing about everything: world politics, local affairs, worries, advice to one another, updates—until someone called out: It's time to start the Evening Service. And beginning with *Borchu*, everyone sang along the traditional dai-da-dai-ta, the dai-di-dam! And they ended with the loud, drawn-out "*HaMaariv Arovim!*"[199]

The Purim and *Simchas Torah* festive meals, fit for a king, that the brothers Mendel and Avrohom-Hirsh Kohn made in their house for the Alexander Hassidim. We drank until dawn, singing!

The funerals with the traditional "Charity rescues one from death"[200] and the jingling of the charity-box.

The blaring music of the wedding marches that proceeded to the outdoor *chuppa*[201] where the ceremony took place, usually in the synagogue courtyard.

During twilight in the *beis medresh*, between the *Mincha* and *Maariv*[202] prayer services: Jews are studying, talking, reciting *Tehillim*[203]. Suddenly a mother comes running in, a Jewish mother who is ready to sacrifice herself for her beloved child. In a heart-rending voice she cries out loudly: Jews, recite *Tehillim* for my child, who is dangerously ill. In the blink of an eye a grave silence descends on the entire place. The *shamash*[204] approaches the mother and asks her what illness her child has. Then he goes over to the Holy Ark and pulls the curtain open so quickly that the rings holding the curtain on the metal rod screech loudly. The heavens have split open! Only the gold-threaded embroidery on the Torah-scroll covers gleam out from the dark, sacred hidden place. The Jews—all the Jews: shoemakers, merchants, tailors, wealthy men, porters, teachers, and plain people—all of them, all recite *Tehillim* with such passionate humility that their prayer must, undoubtedly, at that very moment, reach all the way up to the Throne of Glory…and…proclaim…that the child should experience a complete recovery.

And still more and more memories that don't "connect" so easily after forty or fifty years. These are, however, the links of the long Jewish golden chain. Each link is an expression of an aspect of Jewish life, every generation in its characteristic manner. And thus the chain is extended, for the chain keeps going on…and it will continue until the end of generations!

[Page 437]

20

The first time that I was going with my father as a *sędzia* (magistrate) in the Polish *sąd* (court). The uplifting feeling of respect for the Jew!

Putting *tefillin*[205] on for the first time. My first cigarette. My first shave. My first meeting with the Otwock *Rebbe* together with my father. My first time in a Jewish Gymnasia.

The first punch in the chin that I gave a Gentile who was picking on an elderly Jew. I knocked him down and he was bloodied; he got up and ran away. And it was all because of R. Nisan's influence.

My first day in an exclusively Polish Technical University in Bydgoszcz (formerly Bromberg). Hundreds of eyes shoot piercing glances at me; I and the only other Jewish young man, who was from Kutno, return the piercing glances with contempt and stubbornness …And still more "firsts" and other memories.

And…my…first…day…away…from…Dobrzyn…for…real….

Such are my memories about myself. The events unravel and come back together, wrapping themselves up like a ball of thread. The ball gets larger and larger. It rolls away faster and still faster…until it disappears somewhere in the endless misty emptiness…

[Page 438]

21

I have described life in the Jewish town of Dobrzyn. The memories and feelings of a little Jewish boy who is just starting to read Hebrew, as he becomes a *Chumash*–Rashi–*Posuk* boy, then a big boy who studies *Gemoro*, and then finally a *Gymnasia* student. There were hundreds of thousands like me. I have written up the depth and creativity of a Jewish community. This all might have been more or less the same for at least a thousand cities and towns throughout Poland, Lithuania, Ukraine, the Baltic lands and even Western Europe. There were dozens, even thousands of R. Feibishes, hundreds of thousands like our family, and millions of Jews like those of Dobrzyn.

Six million! Six million martyrs who were so cruelly cut down, one third of our people! There are no words to describe the great disaster. When the prophet Jeremiah cried out "For your ruin is as vast as the sea; who can heal you?"[206], he could not have foreseen that even worse could befall our people. But it did happen, and the world, with few exceptions, didn't lift a finger to stop the destruction. Each and every time there was another excuse. Unlike the past, today we are more informed; our "friends" and "great" people have after all reacted, and we Jews have always been the scapegoat for the sins of the entire world.

Of course we cannot bring the Six Million back to life, but the prophet Ezekiel's Vision of the Dry Bones[207] will come true when we will all be united again in our own country, free from foreign rule and oppression, defended by our own strength: a nation like all other nations, in our land Israel.

Bluma Lipka, wife of Mordechai Lipka[208]

Henik Lipka, a son of Mordechai and Bluma Lipka[209]

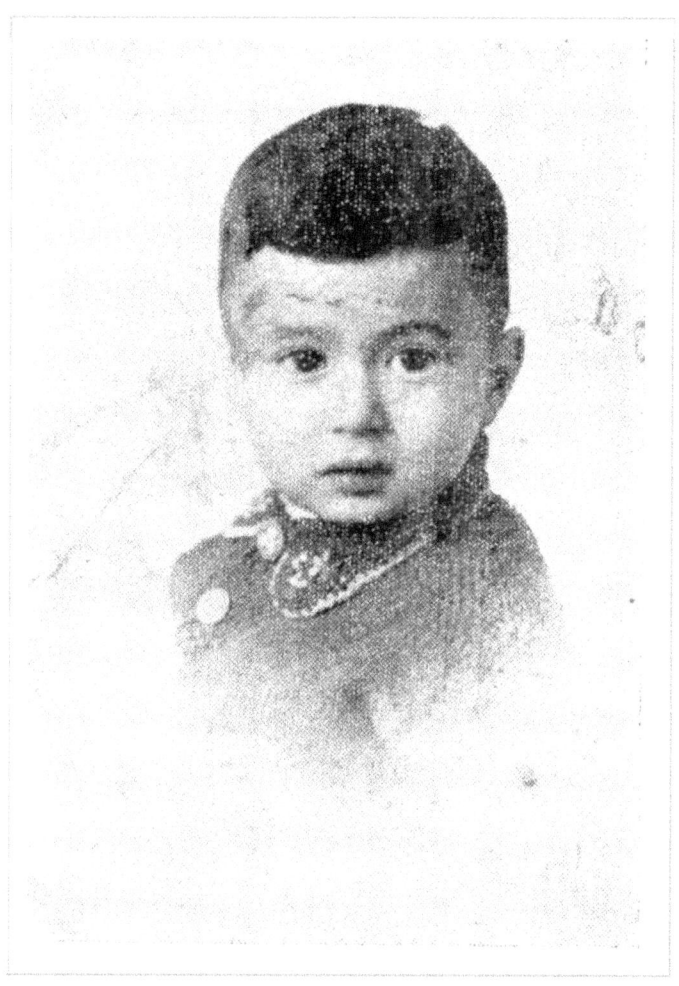

Jerzik Hirsz, a grandson of Mordechai Lipka[210]

Rorzka (on left) and Henich (center), children of Bluma and Mordechai Lipka[211]

Translator's Footnotes

1. R. = *Reb*, an honorific roughly equivalent to English "Mr."

2. From *My Town: In Memory of the Communities Dobrzyn–Gollob*, edited by M. Harpaz, (published by the Dobrzyn–Golub Society, Israel, 1969), pp. 404–438.

3. Polish: Drwęc

4. z.l. = contraction for *Zichroinoi Livrocho* = of blessed memory

5. *Poalei Tsion* = Workers of Zion, a Zionist Marxist–socialist organization and party (Labor Zionists). See the following link: http://en.wikipedia.org/wiki/Poale_Zion.

6. *Poiskim* = authors of post–Talmudic literature settling Jewish law (literally adjudicates).

7. Love of Zion (Hebrew: *Chibas Tsiyon*): a movement that promoted Jewish nationalism in the Land of Israel, predating the Zionist Movement by about 20 years. See, for example, the following link: http://www.yivoencyclopedia.org/article.aspx/Hibat_Tsiyon

8. Yiddish: *treif posul, rachmono litslon* (literally: forbidden evil, may God save us from it)

9. Otwock (pronounced Otvotsk), a town in Poland, ~30 km southeast of Warsaw. Simcha Bunem (~1851–1907), a Hassidic *rebbe* (religious spiritual leader of a Hassidic group), who was a scion of the Hassidic Vurke dynasty, settled there for a while, but moved to the Land of Israel in 1905. See the following link (retrieved May, 2014):
http://www.yivoencyclopedia.org/article.aspx/Vurke_Hasidic_Dynasty.

10. "May our eyes behold Your (i.e. God's) return to Zion": a sentence from the Jewish silent prayer (*Amidah*) that is recited in the three daily (Morning, Afternoon and Evening) Services.

11. Mizrachi = a religious Zionist movement

12. Reines (1839–1915) was a member of the *Hovevei Tsion* (Lovers of Zion) movement (see Footnote 7). See the following link:
http://en.wikipedia.org/wiki/Yitzchak_Yaacov_Reines.

13. Lida, Belarus, lies ~150km west of Minsk, Belarus, and ~200km northeast of Bialystok, Poland.

14. Kutno, Poland is located ~60km north of Lodz.

15. Yehoshua Trunk of Kutno, 1821–1893, who supported the immigration of Jews to the Land of Israel. See, for example, the following link:
http://www.hevratpinto.org/tzadikim_eng/126_rabbi_israel_yehoshua_tronk.html.

16. Yehuda Leib Kowalski (1863–1925), who was a leader of the Mizrachi movement in Poland

17. Menahem–Mendel Kalisch, a son of Simcha Bunem of Otwock (see Footnote 9), succeeded his father as *rebbe* of Otwock. He died in 1919.

18. Avrohom–Moshe Kalisch was Simcha-Bunem's son and Menahem-Mendel's brother.

19. German for "Mr. Lipka, we must get together more often."

20. *Ost Jude* (German) = Eastern European Jew

21. *kapote* = kaftan

22. *beis medresh* = study hall

23. *shtibl* = prayer house, small synagogue consisting of a single prayer room

24. *pan* = sir or gentleman (Polish), i.e. the genteel

25. Bundists = followers of a socialist/Marxist organization that supported cultural autonomy for the Jews within the countries of Eastern Europe, rather than a homeland in Palestine. It also favored Yiddish, rather than Hebrew, as the cultural language of the Jews. See the following links (retrieved May, 2014):
http://en.wikipedia.org/wiki/Bundism;
http://www.yivoencyclopedia.org/article.aspx/Bund.

26. Maxim of Hillel, a 1st–century BCE rabbi (Pirkei Avot [Ethics of the Fathers] 2:4)

27. *Chaveirim kol Yisroel* (Hebrew), from Sabbath blessing of New Moon in Jewish prayer book; see also Babylonian Talmud Hagiga 26a.

28. Leviticus 19:18, which Rabbi Akiva (early 2nd century) referred to as a major principle of the Torah (Bereishit Rabba on Gen. 5:1).

29. *rebbe* = Hassidic spiritual leader, who heads a group of Hassidic followers and gives them personal, individual advice.

30. *Pan* = Sir, Master (Polish). See Footnote 24.

31. Babylonian Talmud, Sotah 5a.

32. *spółka* (Polish) = partnership

33. *zgoda* (Polish) = agreement or accord

34. *swoj do swego* (Polish) = his to his (literally), i.e. keeping trade to within our own kind

35. *Chumash* = Pentateuch

36. The section of Balak starts from Numbers 22:2 and continues to Numbers 25:9.

37. Yiddish reads "*er hot geyocholt mit a groiser yud*" = he *yocholt* (was capable) with a large "y"

38. Mojżesz (Polish) = Moses

39. a well–known Hebrew maxim in which the second "Moses" refers to Moses Maimonides

40. *Sroros* = noblemen, landed gentry

41. *Pritsim* = noblemen, landed gentry (plural of *Porits*)

42. Count of Zbójno; there is a village with this name about 115km south of Dobrzyn

43. *Starozakonny* (Polish) = (literally) Old–Faith Believers, a euphemism for Jews that was used to avoid the more pejorative terms based on *żyd*.

44. Landek, Poland, presently near the southern border of Poland, is located ~400km south of Dobrzyn. In 1914 Silesia was part of the German Empire, while Dobrzyn was in Poland, part of the Russian Empire.

45. The attack referred to is the assassination of Archduke Franz Ferdinand of Austria in June, 1914, which led to the outbreak of World War I.

46. In 1914 Torun (presently in Poland) lay within West Prussia, which was itself part of the German Empire. The distance from Torun to Dobrzyn is only

~40km. The train ride would ordinarily have continued from Torun to Golub, West Prussia, from which the passengers would have disembarked and walked over a bridge across the border to Dobrzyn.

47. Stettin = Szczecin, Poland, which in 1914 was called Stettin and was in the German Empire. It is located ~450km west of Dobrzyn.

48. Ciechanow is located ~100km north of Warsaw, and ~100km east of Dobrzyn.

49. Yiddish: *hilchois gevehr*, literally "the rules and regulations of arms", *hilchois* being the Hebrew/Yiddish word for detailed religious rules and regulations, as in *hilchois shabbes* = the laws of the Sabbath.

50. *Slonim*, currently in Belarus, lies ~500km east of Dobrzyn.

51. *smicha* = rabbinical ordination

52. *kardom lachpor boi* (Hebrew) = a means of making money (literally, a spade to dig with). The expression derives from Pirkei Avot 4:9.

53. 1919–1921. See the following link (retrieved September, 2014): http://en.wikipedia.org/wiki/Polish%E2%80%93Soviet_War

54. The reference is to Władysław Grabski, the treasury minister of Poland in the 1920s. See the following Web site (retrieved June, 2014): http://en.wikipedia.org/wiki/W%C5%82adys%C5%82aw_Grabski.

55. *Kapores* (Hebrew: *kaporois* = atonements), a ritual carried out on the day before Yom Kippur (Day of Atonement), in which a Jew would wave a purchased chicken around his head, reciting "...let this chicken be my atonement (*kaporosi*)...." Males would wave a rooster, while females would wave a hen. The chicken would be slaughtered, and either the meat or its monetary value given to charity. See the following link (retrieved June, 2014): http://www.chabad.org/holidays/JewishNewYear/template_cdo/aid/989585/jewish/Kaparot.htm

56. *Czy to...* (Polish). The Jew who is the butt of the joke apparently had a very limited Polish vocabulary.

57. *lachmaniot* = rolls

58. *lodownie* (Polish) = ice maker

59. Possibly the Grudza that is located ~7km southwest of Dobrzyn was the site of this estate.

60. Possibly the Zakrocz that is located ~30km southeast of Dobrzyn was the site of this estate.

61. On Szmiga and the Szitna estate see "The Synagogues and Shtiebels in Dobrzyn", pp. 264–269; also Dzialdow and Sanger, "Religious Life in Dobrzyn," pp. 284–291, both in reference cited in Footnote 1.

62. There is a village with the name Cholewy ~180km southeast of Dobrzyn; perhaps this is the location of the estate referred to.

63. See p. 345 of Rosenwaks, "My Bundle of Troubles in the Russian Military", in reference cited in Footnote 1. About 10km south of Dobrzyn there is a Dzialyn that is possibly the site of this estate.

64. Written "Zaręba" in Polish, it is located about 2km south of Dobrzyn

65. "*Fonye*" is a colloquial term for Russian and for the Russian regime. Here it refers to the Russian border inspectors who collected customs tax.

66. *ariber–shvartsen* = smuggling people across a border

67. in the military

68. Glicenstein (1870–1942) was a famous sculptor who was born in Turek, Poland (200km south of Dobrzyn). He eventually settled in Rome, Italy, where he changed his name from Chanoch to Enrico; and he died in New York. See the following Web site (retrieved June 2014): http://en.wikipedia.org/wiki/Enrico_Glicenstein.

69. *soifer* = a scribe who writes and corrects Torahs and other handwritten scrolls

70. *Motke Ganef* (Motke the Thief) was a 1923 Yiddish novel written by Sholem Asch. It depicts, somewhat romantically, the lives of Jews living outside respectable society: Jewish circus performers, thieves, pimps and prostitutes.

71. *mikve* = ritual bath. It was customary for men to go there before the Sabbath.

72. Lamps or candles are lit shortly before sunset Friday evening, i.e. prior to the beginning of the Sabbath. They provide illumination for the first few hours of evening, when lighting or adjusting a fire is forbidden.

73. *skarpetkas* (Polish) = socks

74. The reference is to the spies sent out by Moses to Canaan, who "cut a vine with one cluster of grapes and carried it on a double pole…" (Num. 13:23)

75. *apfelsinen* (German) = oranges

76. The story of the "binding of Isaac," beginning with Gen. 22:1.

77. Gen. 22:4

78. *Tashlich* (Hebrew) = casting, a Rosh Hashana ritual in which Jews symbolically cast their sins into a body of water.

79. Yiddish: *shkotsim*, a term of derision

80. Rokers Mount overlooked the Dreventz River. See map on pp, 8–9 of reference cited in Footnote 1.

81. *shlog kapores* = conduct the ritual of *kapores* (see Footnote 55).

82. *Bnei Odom* (Hebrew) = human beings, the first two words of the introductory prayer (based on Psalms 107) to the *Kapores* ritual.

83. *meshumed* (Hebrew) = apostate (literally); here it means rascal, with a suggestion of heretical behavior

84. Since the second half of the 20th century, that is the way most observant Jews conduct this ceremony: with money rather than live chickens.

85. *Mincha* = afternoon prayer service, conducted in the early afternoon on Yom Kippur Eve

86. *kitl* = a loose white robe worn on Yom Kippur

87. *Kol Nidre* = prayer chanted by the cantor at sunset, at the beginning of Yom Kippur, nullifying in advance any personal vows that might be taken by members of the congregation within the coming year. See the following Web site (retrieved July, 2014): http://en.wikipedia.org/wiki/Kol_Nidre

88. Ending with, "...we declare it permissible to pray with sinners." See the previous footnote.

89. *Shir HaYichud* (Hebrew) = Song of Unity, a liturgical poem that some recite on the night of Yom Kippur

90. i.e., fast; children are not obligated to fast until the age of 12 or 13.

91. *Sukkos* = one–week festival of Tabernacles, beginning 5 days after Yom Kippur

92. *sukkah* = tabernacle, temporary dwelling where all meals are eaten during the festival

93. *sechach* (Hebrew, literally cover or thatch) = plants, often reeds, used to form a sparse roof for the sukkah. This roof, designed to provide shade from the sun but no protection from rain, is a critical component of the sukkah.

94. *shochet* = ritual slaughterer

95. When it rains there is no obligation to eat or dwell in the sukkah. The little roofs are lowered into place to cover the *sechach*, keeping the sukkah dry during rain. They are cranked open when the rain ends.

96. *Ushpizin* (Aramaic: guests) are symbolic guests that are invited into the sukkah: Abraham, Isaac, Jacob...See the following Web site (retrieved September, 2014): http://www.myjewishlearning.com/holidays/Jewish_Holidays/Sukkot/At_Home/The_Sukkah/Ushpizin.shtml.

97. *megilla* = handwritten scroll of the Book of Esther, read out loud to the congregation in synagogues on Purim

98. First verse of scroll (Esther 1:1)

99. Customary noisemaking during the *megilla* reading to symbolically blot out the name of Haman, the villain of the Book of Esther who sought to have all the Jews exterminated.

100. *Shalach manos* = gifts of portions of food to friends and relatives, a Purim custom fulfilling Esther 9:22, "a day of...sending portions of food to one another".

101. Yiddish: *shkotsim*. See Footnote 79.

102. *Mo'os Chittim* (Hebrew) = money for wheat (literally), i.e. charity for the poor, originally to provide them with requisite provisions for Passover (which occurs four weeks after Purim)

103. *Seuda* = special festive meal of Purim, held on the afternoon of the holiday

104. *kashering* = cleaning and scouring eating utensils, in this case to rid them of any leaven and thereby make them suitable for use on Passover

105. *B'dikas Chometz* = ritual search for *chometz* (leaven) on the night before Passover Eve

106. The ritual burning of *chometz* (leaven) takes place on the morning of Passover Eve.

107. *kitl* = loose white robe, tied at the waist, worn by the leader of the Seder (see also Footnote 86.) See the following Web site (retrieved August, 2014): http://en.wikipedia.org/wiki/Kittel

108. Recliner to fulfil the custom of reclining at the Seder as a symbol of freedom

109. *kneidl* (plural *kneidlach*) = soup dumpling (also known as "matzah ball"), a traditional staple of Passover

110. *afikomen* = a portion of matzah set aside to serve as the last dish to be eaten at the Seder meal. Since the *afikomen* is an integral part of the ritual, the Seder cannot continue until it is consumed. In many families the children "steal" it and hold it hostage to trade it for gifts—one of the many traditions that have been introduced over the centuries to keep the children awake and involved throughout the entire Seder.

111. *shfoich chamoscho* = Pour Your wrath [onto the nations who do not know You, for they have devoured Jacob...] (Psalms 79), which is recited with the front door open to express the atmosphere of freedom during the Seder.

112. *Vayehi Bachatzi Halaylah* = "And it came to pass at midnight", a poem recited at the first Seder

113. *Oimetz Gvuroisecho* = "Your numerous mighty deeds", a poem recited at the second Seder (outside Israel), in place of *Vayehi Bachatzi Halaylah* (see previous footnote).

114. *Choil Hamoied* = Intermediate (Days 3–6 outside Israel) of Passover, when most forms of labor are permitted by Jewish law

115. *Shovuos* = Pentecost, celebrated on the 50th day after the first day of Passover.

116. *Akdomus* = Introduction, a liturgical poem, written in Aramaic as an introduction to the Ten Commandments. It is recited in the synagogue on the morning of *Shovuos*. See the following Web page (retrieved August, 2014): http://en.wikipedia.org/wiki/Akdamut.

117. *Tisha B'Av* = the 9th day of Av (corresponding to July–August), the anniversary of the destruction of both the First Temple (in 586BCE) and the Second Temple (in 70CE), commemorated as a fast day

118. *Eicha* = Lamentations, the Biblical poems lamenting the destruction of the First Temple

119. *Kinois* = medieval poems of lamentation, recited on *Tisha B'Av*

120. *Krias Shma* = Recital of the verses beginning with "Hear, O Israel…the Lord is One" (Deut. 6), which express the foundation of the Jewish faith

121. *Shir Hamaalois* = "A Song of Ascents" (Ps. 121), a page with the psalm written on it, together with various charms. See, for example, the following Web site (retrieved August, 2014): http://www.sichosinenglish.org/books/healthy-in-body-mind-and-spirit-2/41.htm.

122. *mazikim* = injurious demons

123. *Chumash* = Pentateuch

124. *Rashi* = a concise commentary on the Pentateuch, written in Hebrew by Rashi (an 11th century scholar who lived in Troyes, France), and commonly taught to beginning students together with the text.

125. *Rebbi* = teacher of little children

126. Noah is the second section of the Book of Genesis.

127. *Rebbetzen* = the wife of the *Rebbi* (teacher)

128. *Safa Chaya* = (Hebrew) "The Living Language"

129. Hebrew words for stocking, ear, and soldier, respectively.

130. *Posuk* (Hebrew) = verse (literally), term used for the Prophets, the 2nd section of the 3 sections (Torah, Prophets, and Writings) of the Hebrew Bible

131. Following the detailed description in Ex. 36 of how the Tabernacle (the portable sanctuary used by the Israelites after the Exodus from Egypt) was constructed

132. The priestly garments, as described in some detail in Ex. 39.

133. By contrast, the Yiddish word for chess is pronounced "shach"

134. *Palant* is a Polish sport, similar to stickball and baseball. See for example the following Web site (retrieved August, 2014): http://www.ghs-mh.de/traditions/topics/health/sports_pl.htm.

135. Yiddish: *mazik*

136. In Yiddish, *demb* = oak

137. *Mishnayos* = sections of the Mishnah, the concise book of Jewish Law written down in Hebrew in ~200CE. See the following Web site (retrieved August, 2014): http://en.wikipedia.org/wiki/Mishnah.

138. *Gemoro* (or *Gemara*) = literally "study by tradition" (Aramaic), the detailed analysis and discussion of Jewish Law based on the Mishnah and additional traditions, completed in Babylon ~500CE, and written in a mixture of Hebrew and Aramaic. The Mishnah and *Gemara* are the two components of the Talmud. See the following Web site (retrieved August, 2014): http://en.wikipedia.org/wiki/Gemara.

139. *Perek* = Pirkei Avot (Ethics of the Fathers), one of the books of the Mishnah, describing the chain of tradition and listing ethical teachings and maxims of the early Rabbis.

140. In Jewish tradition, Amalek is the name given to the arch–enemies of the Jews throughout the ages, as based originally on Ex. 16:8–16.

141. *Hovo nis'chakmo* = "Come, let us deal cleverly..." the words of Pharaoh, conceiving a plan to enslave the Israelites in Egypt (Ex. 1:10)

142. big, strong boys

143. *Vayigash* = "And Judah approached him [Joseph]" (Hebrew), a section spanning Gen. 44:18 to 47:27.

144. *midrashim* (plural of *midrash*) = (Hebrew) the exegetical works of interpretation of the Biblical narrative, written by the rabbis of the Talmudic period

145. Manasseh and Ephraim were Joseph's sons.

146. hind set loose = As a result of this metaphoric name for Naphtali (Gen. 49: 21), Naphtali was viewed by the Midrash as a fast runner.

147. since, unbeknownst to his brothers, he understood the Hebrew they were speaking to each other

148. The hero who led the Jews of Israel in the Maccabean rebellion against Syrian–Greek religious oppression (165BCE), which ultimately led to the political independence of Judea.

149. In that period the Apocrypha was essentially unknown to the vast majority of observant Jews, and very little of the narrative of Maccabees I and II had made it into the midrashic works

150. Second Targum ("*targum sheni*" = second translation), a translation of the Biblical Book of Esther into Aramaic. The translation incorporates midrashic stories, particularly about King Solomon. See the following Web site (retrieved August, 2014): http://en.wikipedia.org/wiki/Targum_Sheni

151. *Lag BaOmer* = the 33rd Day of the Omer count (of the 50 days between Passover and Pentecost), a minor holiday celebrated with archery and outings to forests. See the following Web site (retrieved August, 2014): http://en.wikipedia.org/wiki/Lag_BaOmer

152. Bar Kochba has been enshrined as a hero for the (unsuccessful) rebellion he led in Israel against the Roman Empire in 135CE.

153. *baal koirei* = the person who every Sabbath chants the appropriate section of the Torah as he reads it from a Torah scroll, a difficult task that requires memorizing and practicing, since the words are written with no punctuation, no vocalization marks, and no chanting notes.

154. *baal tokeiya* = the person who sounds the shofar (ram's horn) on Rosh Hashana, a task requiring much practice and some talent.

155. Small prayer-room synagogue used by the Otwock Hassidim. See Footnote 9.

156. Malbim = acronym of **M**eir **L**eibush **b**en **Y**echiel **M**ichel (Weiser), a 19th-century rabbi who wrote a creative, widely read Biblical commentary. See the following link (retrieved August, 2014): http://en.wikipedia.org/wiki/Malbim.

157. *Toisfos* = literally: Additions (Hebrew), commentary on the text of the Talmud, written mostly around the 12th century, and printed as a gloss in most editions of the Talmud, together with the commentary of Rashi. It's in-depth analysis resolves inconsistencies between texts appearing in different parts of the Talmud. See the following Web site (retrieved August, 2014): http://en.wikipedia.org/wiki/Tosafot.

158. *Sheigetz* = derogatory term for Gentile, here suggesting uncouthness. The entire quotation is written in the pronunciation common to that part of Poland.

159. *yeshivo ketano* = a more advanced, high-school level school for religious studies

160. *Gymnasia* = high school

161. *Girso deyankuso* (Aramaic) = what is learned in youth. This refers to a statement in the Talmud that what is learned in youth is not forgotten as easily as that which is learned later in life (Babylonian Talmud Sabbath 21b; Rashi's commentary on it).

162. Joshua 1:8

163. little girl (compare German *Mädchen*), the Yiddish word for an unmarried young woman being "*moid*"

164. little boy, the Yiddish word for boy being "*yung*"

165. small table, the Yiddish word for table being " *tish*"

166. "*meidel*" and "*yingel*" already being the Yiddish diminutive of "*moyd*" and "*yung*", respectively, so the additional "chye" or "chyer" was superfluous.

167. *tsipor* being the Hebrew word for bird.

168. Polish: *nasze i wasze* = ours and yours, from the Polish motto "for our freedom and yours", which refers to exiled Poles fighting in foreign armies with the anticipation of achieving independence for Poland. See the following Web site (retrieved August, 2014): http://en.wikipedia.org/wiki/For_our_freedom_and_yours.

169. *HaTechiya* (Hebrew) = the revival or renaissance, the name of a local Zionist club (see E. Tzala, "Pain and Suffering in the Second World War," p. 356 of reference cited in Footnote 1).

170. See Footnote 5.

171. *Der Dorfsyung* = "The Village Youth", a dramatic play by Leon Kobrin.

172. *Kelmer Magid* = the fiery Preacher of Kelme (town in Lithuania). See the following Web site (retrieved August, 2014): http://www.jewishgen.org/yizkor/lita/Lit1427.html#Page1437.

173. *mevorech hashonim* (Hebrew) = Who blesses the years (yearly seasons), a prayer requesting properly seasonal weather. *Shonim* = years. One of the benedictions of the *Shmoineh Esrei* (Eighteen Benedictions), it is recited by the prayer–service leader on weekdays during his repetition.

174. That is, he transposed the letters of the last word, *hashonim*, pronouncing it *hanoshim* (=the women), so that it came out "Blessed are You, Lord our God, King of the Universe, Who blesses the women".

175. *Mna* (Hebrew) = deny

176. See Footnote 114.

177. *struga* (Polish) = stream

178. See Footnote 64.

179. A socialist–Zionist youth movement that encouraged immigration to Palestine and settling in *kibbutzim*

180. Apparently a request made by the author to the editor

181. *Raboisai* = Gentlemen

182. His family name meant "religiously devout", while his nickname meant Gentile.

183. *Keren HaYesod* (literally "The Foundation Fund"), a Zionist fund founded in 1920 to support the establishment of a Jewish State in Palestine. See the

following Web site (retrieved June, 2014):
http://en.wikipedia.org/wiki/Keren_Hayesod.

184. *Shehecheyonu* = "Who has granted us life" (Hebrew), a benediction that might be recited spontaneously by someone who has lived to attain a long-sought goal: "Blessed are You, Lord our God, King of the universe, who has granted us life, sustained us and enabled us to reach this occasion." See the following Web site (retrieved September, 2014):
http://en.wikipedia.org/wiki/Shehecheyanu.

185. *Simcha veSasson* (Hebrew), paraphrasing Esther 8:17

186. *hachshara* (Hebrew) = Training in farm work to prepare for moving to an agricultural settlement in Palestine

187. *Tu BiShvat* = 15th day of the month Shvat (corresponding to January–February), a minor holiday that commemorates the New-Year's Day for fruit-bearing trees in Israel

188. *Sholom Zochor* (Hebrew: welcome, male) = celebration on the Friday night following the birth of a boy

189. *Yiddishe Troika* (= Jewish Three-Horse Sleigh), a song, with lyrics written by Shimon Frug, about riding in a horse-drawn sleigh. See the following Web site (retrieved August, 2014): http://www.polishjewishcabaret.com/2013/02/a-yiddishe-troike-di-yidishe-troyke.html.

190. *lulav* = palm branch, *esrog* = citron. These two species are grasped by hand together with two others, willow and myrtle branches, on the holiday of Sukkos to fulfil the commandment of Lev. 23:40.

191. *dayan* = judge in Jewish religious court

192. The four species are ritually shaken or waved during certain parts of the morning prayer services of Sukkos.

193. *Vetsidkos'cho* (Hebrew, literally 'and your righteousness', from various verses in Psalms, also quoted in the Jewish prayer book): a euphemism for hypocritical piety

194. *Simchas Torah* = Rejoicing of the Torah, a holiday immediately after *Sukkos*, commemorating the end and beginning of the yearly cycle of reading the entire Torah

195. Customarily on *Simchas Torah* all the young children receive a common "aliyah" (being called up to the Torah to recite a benediction of thanks for receiving the Torah).

196. *kvitlach* = pieces of paper; *Nitul* = Yiddish euphemism for Christmas. See the following Web site (retrieved August, 2014) for an explanation:
http://www.slate.com/articles/life/faithbased/2009/12/holy_night.2.html.

197. *Boruch sheptorany* (Heb.: blessed is He who had freed me): a blessing recited by a father when his son reaches the bar-mitzvah age of 13. The father has

been freed of responsibility for the actions of his son, who is now considered responsible for himself.

198. *tsitsis* = strings tied with a traditional, fixed pattern of twists and knots on each of the four corners of a ritual garment that is worn daily in fulfilment of Num. 15:38.

199. "*Borchu*" is recited by the prayer leader at the beginning of the Evening Service, and "*HaMaariv Arovim*" is recited by him at the completion of the first paragraph of the service.

200. Based on Prov. 11:4.

201. *Chuppa* = canopy for wedding ceremony

202. *Mincha* and *Maariv* = afternoon and evening services; the time between these two prayer services is usually short, hence many of those who attend these services remain in the synagogue between them.

203. Psalms, sometimes recited as a prayer for the ill

204. *shamash* (often pronounced "shammess" in Yiddish) = beadle, person whose job it is to run the synagogue on an everyday basis

205. phylacteries, worn during morning prayers by men starting at age 13

206. Lam. 2:13, the Lamentations scroll being attributed to the prophet Jeremiah

207. Ez. 37

208. From p. 405 of reference cited in Footnote 1

209. From p. 410 of reference cited in Footnote 1

210. From p. 417 of reference cited in Footnote 1

211. From p. 422 of reference cited in Footnote 1

[Page 439]

The "Dreamer" Who Did Not Live to See His Dream Fulfilled[1]

by Shmuel Meiri–Minivski

Translated by Allen Flusberg

History tells us of individuals who, with their numerous activities in various social spheres, laid the foundations for lofty ideals that supported the progress and development of the human race. With their spirit they lit a beacon, penetrating the fog that encompassed them.

Perhaps this is the correct meaning and significance of Our Teacher Moses, the great hero: Moses the leader, the lawgiver; the struggler whose aspirations were so diversified but self–consistent.

Adolf Riesenfeld (Avrohom son of Pesach) belongs to this very category of people. He was born in the year 1878 in Silesia. Although he was raised in a village, where he lived among Gentiles, he never forgot his Jewish brethren.

One could discern the love he had for his persecuted people in his daily life, in his speech and in his writing. He always used the expression "my people", the people to whom he was bound heart and soul.

Riesenfeld was endowed with specific qualities that earned him the love and admiration of thousands of Jews who either knew him personally or had heard of him.

He was known as Riesenfeld the pharmacist, but he was also a leader and a prominent man who was active in the community and headed the Zionist Movement of Golub. He provided—in the full sense of the word—for dozens of families in need. He was a physician—though he had no diploma—who would help the ill; he was a writer, a speaker, and a dedicated family man. This is the type of person that Riesenfeld was.

I can still see his tall, dignified figure with the sympathetic smile on his lively face, a smile he retained even in difficult moments of doubt and sorrow.

I recall him also in his daily, tireless labor in the Zionist movement to which he devoted a major portion of his time, primarily to imbue the plain people of the Diaspora, who did not have a very deep understanding of their destiny, with the concept of Zionism.

He was always ready with advice, even when it was associated with material help, and it goes without saying that he often filled prescriptions for free for the needy.

Riesenfeld's home was known as a gathering place for people active in the community, both young and old, who would come together to discuss community and party matters. In these discussions his final say, backed up by clear logic, usually won the day.

Riesenfeld stayed in close written contact with several Dobrzyn townsmen who were living in America. Under his influence they provided respectable sums of money for the needy of the town. Whoever has read his letter to Jacob Fogel[2], written several days before the outbreak of the war—concerning the sorrowful situation of dozens of families who had remained with nearly no means of support, and the difficult state of most of the Jews in general—is able to sense the pained heart of this great person and dedicated Jew, as well as his fear for the fate of his destitute fellow townsmen.

Zionist activity was an integral part of his life. Immediately after the Balfour Declaration he undertook a series of presentations in both private and public circles, first in Dobrzyn–Golub and thereafter in other cities and towns, among them Danzig. His fluency in cultured German made an impression on his audiences.

He took part in several Zionist Congresses, which he attended accompanied by his wife, and later also by his daughter, Ruth. There he made the acquaintance of many Zionist leaders, among them Motzkin, Gruenbaum, Ussishkin and also Chaim Nachman Bialik[3].

His reports from Israel aroused great enthusiasm in his audiences, primarily after his visit there during the opening of the university in 1925. His deeply felt faith in Zionism, which he foresaw as the future of the Jewish people, gave him the courage and energy to plant these thoughts in the hearts of the Jewish masses who attended his lectures to hear his impressions of the Land of Israel.

Through an extensive correspondence with Zionist activists, he inspired intense activity to raise funds for the Zionist cause.

With his unwavering labor he served as an example for thousands of Jews; every Jew who found himself in his circle was exposed to and experienced the influence of his dynamic, lofty personality.

Riesenfeld, the people's friend, the dedicated father and parent, the follower of the German classics by Goethe and Schiller, never once imagined the great depth to which the German people could sink in their hatred of the Jews. As a result he never envisioned the approach of the horrific Destruction.

Jewish tradition reigned within Riesenfeld's home and family, and if he was forced to open the pharmacy on the Jewish Sabbath it was only because of the law that pharmacies were not to be closed on Sabbaths and Jewish holy days, and not even on any Christian holidays. But on Rosh Hashana[4] and Yom Kippur[5] we would see him in the congregation, praying in the synagogue that was located near the bridge, among his brethren Jews whom he loved so much.

Everyone found his enthusiasm for Zionism quite remarkable, knowing as they did that he came from an assimilated family; it was a riddle. It was known that he grew up among Gentiles. He was raised among them, and he was imbued with German patriotism within their educational institutions. But as soon as he came in contact with the Eastern European Jews, he changed his attitude completely and dedicated his life to the Jewish national movement.

From a rational perspective it is a bit difficult to analyze the factors that led Riesenfeld to make this drastic turn. But undoubtedly emotional factors must have been involved—influences that were not completely clear even to him, and certainly not to the rest of us.

It is our sacred duty to immortalize the name of this lofty individual, who more than most others devoted his life to the Jewish people in the Land of Israel; yet he himself did not merit seeing the dream of many years come true.

In the history of our people his name will be recalled as one of the first pioneers who laid the foundation for the development of the State of Israel.

Translator's Footnotes

1. From *My Town: In Memory of the Communities Dobrzyn–Gollob*, edited by M. Harpaz, (published by the Dobrzyn–Golub Society, Israel, 1969), pp. 439–442. This Yiddish article appears to be a shortened and slightly modified version of the article, written in Hebrew, appearing on pp. 193–200 of this volume. See the footnotes there.

2. Jacob Fogel, a native of Dobrzyn, had immigrated to the US in April, 1939.

3. Bialik (1873–1934) was a Zionist poet and author who wrote in both Yiddish and Hebrew. See the following link (retrieved May, 2015): http://en.wikipedia.org/wiki/Hayim_Nahman_Bialik

4. Jewish New Year

5. Day of Atonement

[Page 443]

From Home to Home
Translated by Allen Flusberg

From Home to Home[1]

Altstein [Altsztajn], Hershl and family

Altstein, Leib and family

Altstein, Shimon and family

Offenbach, Yaakov and wife, perished

Orbach, Mendel. A grandson was rescued. He lives in America.

Altstein, Yaakov and family. A son lives in Argentina.

Ordau, Esther and children

Eizik, Hersh and family. A daughter lives in Israel.

Eizik, Kasriel. Died in Israel.

Eizik (Eshel), Yehoshua. Died in Israel.

Eisenberg, Nisan Wolf and wife.

Eisenberg, Chaim Leib and family, perished.

Altman and family

Alterowicz, Elya Leib and family. 3 sons in America.

Arnob, Binyamin Aharon

Arfa, Binyamin and family

Arfa, Kalman and family, perished.

Arfa, Shimon.

Blumenthal and family.

Brana, Moshe Mendel and wife.

Brana, Mordechai and family.

Brana, Akiva and family

Berkman, Meir, wife and sons perished. 2 daughters and 1 son live in Israel.

Blechner, Yitzchok and wife

Balaban and family. A son lives in America.

Bielawski, Fishel and family perished. Two daughters live in Israel.

Burtke, Hersh Boruch and family perished. A son was rescued. He lives in Canada.

[Page 444]

Britzman and family.

Budziner, Shimon and family perished.

Budziner, Moshe Chaim and wife. Died in America. 2 sons live in Detroit, America.

Berman, Hersh Ber and family. Oldest daughter Chaya Shifra Bielawski died in Israel.

Goldbrach, Levi Zalman and family.

Gerlitz, Yosef Chaim.

Goldman, Yosef and wife. Their sons Avrohom and Shimon Leib perished. Their daughter Esther died in Israel.

Glitzenstein, Mendel and family.

Gurfinkel, Yisroel and family.

Gold, Zalman and family.

Golomb, Wolf and family

Gonsher, Yechezkel and family perished; a son was rescued. He lives in Israel.

Greber, Michael (the kavran [undertaker or gravedigger]) and his wife.

Greber, Avrohom and family

Gutglas, Menashe and family, perished.

Gutmorgen, Yechiel Meir and wife.

Goldberg Shmuelik, wife and children perished; a son and a daughter live in Israel.

Gorni, Mendel, wife and daughter perished; 2 sons died in America; 1 son, Yaakov, lives in America.

Gotlieb, Avrohom and family. Part of the family perished.

Gonsher, Yosef Binyomin and family

Goldring, Nosson and family

Geller, Shimon and family

Groner, Shimon and family

Dratwa, Yisroel and family

Dobroszklanka, Shmuel and family

Dobrochowski and family.

Dzabete and family.

Dobroszklanka, Zalman and family.

Dobrzinski, Hershl and wife.

[Page 445]

Dragan, Eliyohu and family

Dragan, Moshe and family

Dzaldow, Eliyohu and family perished. A son rescued. He lives in Germany.

Dratwa, Yosef Yitzchok and family

Digala, Leib, the cantor, and family

Dratwa and family, perished. A son and a daughter were rescued. The son lives in Israel, the daughter in America.

Dobrzynski, Itche

Dibow, Yaakov and family

Hertzke, Shlomo and wife

Hertz, Leib and family, the *dayan* [ritual judge]

Hartbrot, Mordechai and wife

Hartbrot, Hersh, perished in France

Holtz, Mendel and family

Horowitz, Noach and family; the children live in America

Horowitz, Itche Meir and family, perished; a daughter, Rivka, lives in Israel

Hirsh and family

Waldenberg, Yehoshua Meir, wife and children; two sons are alive, one in New York, the other in Canada

Waldenberg, Yehuda Asher and family

Waldenberg, Moshe Leib and family

Weissmel, Mendel and family; two sons died in America, one lives in Chicago

Weissmel, Yosef Eliyohu and family

Weissmel, Yosef Chaim and family, perished

Wuzszus, Moshe and family. A son, Yaakov, lives in Israel.

Wuzszus, Avrohom and family. A daughter rescued. She lives in America.

Wuzszus, Yechiel Meir and family. A son lives in Israel.

Warshawski, Berish and wife Mindel

Wiur, Mordechai and family

Zelkowicz, Azriel and family

Zilberman, Shmuel Yitzchok and family

[Page 446]

Zilberman, Yechezkel and family

Zissholtz, Yechiel and family

Zelig, Shamash and wife

Zaklikowski, Esther Malka

Zaklikowski, Eliezer, perished

Zaklikowski, Leibish and family

Zaklikowski, Berish and family

Zilberstein and family

Zatok and family. The children live in Canada.

Zilberstein and family

Chaskel, Mordechai and family. The sons live in America

Chaleva, Zeinvil Yom Tov and wife

Chaleva, Meir Nata and family

Teitelboim, Meir Henech, wife Chana Malka and family

Turkewicz, Yehuda and family

Tinski, Yaakov and family. A son Tuvya lives in France.

Topol, Zalman and wife

Topol, Henech and family

Topol, Asher and family

Topol, Hersh, Dr., died in France.

Jendzejewicz, Avrohom and family, perished.

Januar, Chaim and family. A daughter in Israel.

Japuncik, Yaakov, the *treger* [porter], and family

Juricze with her daughters

Jospe—*hachazzan* [the cantor] in Golub—and his family

Lewinson, Shlomo and family

Lurie, Eliezer and family

Lipka, Wolff and family

Lipka, Avrohom Yitzchok and family. A son Leib lives in Israel.

Lipka, Moshe and family

Lipka, Aharon and family

Laks, Hersh Wolff and wife. A daughter lives in Israel.

Lipshitz, Yechiel Meir and family

Lipshitz, Shimshon and family

Lipshitz, Aharon and family

[Page 447]

Lipshitz, Leib and family

Lipsztat, Leibl and family

Levin, Lemel and family

Lipski, Shlomo Yosef and family

Lenet, Hershel and family

Lichtenfeld, Yitzchok and wife Sarah Vechne

Lipka, Yitzchok and family. A grandson is in Israel.

Lenet, Mendel and family. Two sons were rescued. They live with their families in Israel.

Lord, Yisroel and family. A son, Chaim, lives in Israel.

Lipka, David and family, perished

Lesznik, Yitzchok and family, perished

Lipka, Moshe from France, perished; his wife Bayla and a son live in France.

Lipka, Shimon and family

Landsberg, Manus Melamed and famly

Landsberg, Yosef, the son of Manus Melamed, perished with his entire family—his wife and six children

Lewinson the teacher and family, perished.

Lidzbarski and family

Lipka, Yosef and family

Lipka, Mordechai and family

Layzerowit, Bat–Sheva the daughter, perished; a son lives in America

Levin, Avrohom and family

Levin, Zalusz and family

Miller, Daniel and family

Miller, Chashke and children

Mishke, Shmuel and family

Miller, Chaim Ber and family

Makowski, David and family

Maszkowicz, Hirsh Isaac and family

Miller, Israel and family

Memel, Yehoshua and family

Manke, Nisan Mordechai and family

[Page 448]

Mendelson, Chane the *melamed* [teacher of small children], and family

Maluchna and family

Memel, Itze and family

Motil and family

Munter, Salamon family

Maszkewicz (Mishigye) and family

Nagurski, Leib and wife; their son died in New York

Neuman, Mendel and family. A son Shlomo died in Israel.

Nusboym, Mendel and family. Their son Hersh was killed in an accident in Chicago.

Nawolski, Binyomin Isser and family

Nawolski, Perel

Nawolski, Yehoshua and family

Sawe, Pinchas and family

Smuzszik, Hersh Leib and family

Skop, Osher and family. A daughter lives in Israel.

Smuzszik, Fishl Boruch and family. A son was rescued and lives in Israel.

Smuzszik, Issachar and family

Sapirstein, Zanvil and family

Salamon, Abba Yosef and family

Salamon, Mordechai and family

Skurnik, Yochanan and family

Suchedol the tailor and family

Sawe, Shimon and family

Sawe, Zalman and family

Engler, Kalman and family, perished

Freilich, Levi Yaakov and family. A daughter lives in Israel, a second daughter in Australia.

Pieniek and family

Freilich, Nachman

Prum, Shmuel and wife. Three sons live in Mexico.

Prum, Mendel and family, all perished.

Fogel, Eliyohu and family. A son lives in America.

Piechatka, Betzalel and family

[Page 449]

Furgacz, Avrohom and family

Furgarcz, Pinchos and family

Pieniek, Tuvya Wolff and wife

Pieniek, David and family

Pilat, Shlomo and family

Platniarz, Asher and family

Platniarz, Yechiel Meir and family; one daughter lives in Israel and the other in New York.

Frenkel, Leib and family

Friedman, Sina and family, perished

Fuks, Wolff and family

Freilich, Zalman Leib and family

Pozmanter, Shlomo and family

Pozmanter, Moshe and family. A daughter lives in America.

Postolski, Yosef and family

Fisher and family

Pincewski, Henech and family

Plansker, Avrohom and wife

Prager, Shaul and family

Prager, Nachum, died in Germany.

Fuleder, Sandel and wife

Friedman, Shmuel Yitzchok and family

Plocker [Plotzker], Aharon and family

Poznonski, Simcha and family

Pszuk, Chana and daughter Dina

Carnabroda [Tzarnabroda], Efraim and wife

Carnabroda, Aharon and family

Carnabroda, Eliyohu and family

Cudkewicz [Tzudkewicz], Avrohom Hersh and family

Tzarna, Chana and family

Tzarna, Yechiel Yosef and family

Tzarna, Ozer and family

Cala [Tzala], Yoel Michel and family. A son lives in America.

Cirklarz [Tzirklazh], Feivel and family

Kadish the teacher, and family

[Page 450]

Kanicer [Kanitzer] and family

Kahn, Ozer and family

Krajanek, Rephael and family

Kahn, Rachel Leah and children

Kristal and family

Kadecki [Kadetzki], Yitzchok and family

Kive, Parnes and family

Kahn, Aharon—cigarette factory in Golub

Kadecki, Yaakov and family

Kadecki, Simcha and family

Kahn, Daniel Itzes and family. 2 sons and a daughter live in America.

Kahn, Yosef and wife

Kszeczanowski, Chaim and family

Kszeczanowski, Aharon and family

Kszeczanowski, Meir and family

Kszeczanowski, Itcze and family

Kahn, Daniel and family

Klein, Leib and family

Kahn, Moshe Yaakov, his wife and three sons

Kristal, Gershon and wife

Kristal, Ber and family

Kristal, Yaakov and family

Kuzak, Shmuel Gavriel and wife

Krajanek, Reuven and family

Krajanek, Yisroel and family

Kutner, Nisan the melamed [teacher of small children] and family

Kufeld, Kalman and family

Kufeld, Mendel and family

Kufeld, Boruch and family, perished

Kufeld, Shimon and family, perished

Kozak, Bunem and family, perished

Krantz, Yitzchok and family

Kahn, Zalman Shaya and wife. Their son Ozer Ber perished in an automobile accident in Israel.

[Page 451]

Keller and family, perished; one son lives in Israel and another in America

Kirstein and family, perished

Kukawka and family, perished

Kahn, Meir and wife, the parents of Mendel and Avrohom Hirsh

Kahn, Yitzchok and family

Kive, M.A. and family

Kufeld, Yaakov Yehoshua and family from Zaremba

Kowalski, Fishl and family, perished; two daughters in Israel

Kaczer, Chaim Yitzchok and family

Karpa, Yisroel Shimon Melamed and family

Karpa, Mendel and family

Karpa, Yosef and family

Rebe, Zelig and family

Ruina, Shmuel Moshe and family

Ruda, Yosef Chaim and family

Rapaport, Wolff and family

Rusak, Yitzchok and wife Sonya

Ruine, Hillel and family

Ragenstein, Lipman and family

Ragenstein, Nicha

Ragenstein, Shaya and family

Rukman and family

Rapaport, Yedidya and wife

Ruina Yosef Chaim and family

Rebe, David and family

Ryz, Kalman and family; two sons—Leib and Yitzchok—recently died in America; two sons—Avrohom Moshe and Yaakov—live in America

Ryz, Yisroel Asher and family

Rosen, Nachum and family. Two daughters live in America. A son Avraham passed away in Israel.

Rapaport, Avrohom Shlomo, his wife and children with their families live in Israel.

[Page 452]

Riesenfeld and family

Rirzow, Chaim and family perished; a daughter lives in Israel

Rosenman and family

Rapocki and family (the son-in-law of the tailor Groner)

Szlachter and family, a son Moshe Szlachter

Shmuel and family—grain merchant of Golub

Shilski and family

Szajnbart, Yisroel Yaakov and family

Szlachter, Moshe Aharon and family

Szlachter, Yosef Mendel and family

Szlachter, Meir and family

Szlachter, Shimon and family

Szlachter, Moshe and family

Szlachter, Leib and family

Szmiga, Moshe Hirsh and wife

Szmiga, Yitzchok Yaakov, perished

Szmiga, David and family

Sova, Zalman and family; a son lives in Israel

Stolzman and family. A son lives in America

Sova, Henich perished

Shurek, Lazel. Two daughters live in America

Szajnbart, Chananya and family, perished

Shlomo, Zalman (Shochet) and family

Szimanski and family

Szajnbart, Yitzchok and family

Sperling, Chaim Yoel and family

Sperling, Moshe and family

Sperling, Binyomin and family
Sperling, Yosef and family
Stencel, Avrohom Chaim and family
Szmiga, Zelig and family
Szlachter, Avrohom Mendel and family

[Page 453]

List of Those Who Passed Away in Chicago

Dratwa, Yitzchok Moshe

Dratwa, Rose

Harris, Bayla

Harris, Sholom

Weissmel, Leib

Weissmel, Yakir

Weissmel, Nisan Mordechai

Weissmel, Asher

Weinshenker, Oscar

Weinshenker, Penny

Waldenberg, Avrohom

Waldenberg, Yosef

Waldenberg, Max

Silberstein, Moshe Hersh

Silberstein, Elke

Silberstein, Meir

Silberstein, Joseph

Jordan, Itzi Meir

Jordan, Chana

Landsberg, Moshe David

Luster, Max

Luks, Avrohom

Luks, Shmuel

Luks, David

Lichtenfeld, Beinish

Lichtenfeld, Chana

Lefkowitz, Ike

Lefkowitz, Feige

Lefkowitz, Freddy

Lefkowitz, Julius

Lipka, Shmuel Yitzchok

Lipka, Taltze
Levinson, Chune
Miller, Shlomo
Laks, Mordechai
Laks, Tzipora
Nusbaum, Avrohom
Nusbaum, Beila
Nusbaum, Hersh
Surgal, Aharon
Surgal, Sheine
Surgal, Avrohom Moshe
Solomon, Avrohom
Solomon, Yetta
Fuks, Wolff
Fuks, Feige
Fogel, Boruch
Fogel, Penny
Fogel, Chaim
Fogel, Asher Leib
Pierce, Deborah
Pierce, Wolff
Fisher, Luzer
Fisher, Feige
Paczecha, Phillip
Kahn, Anshel
Kahn, Bertha
Kahn, Avrohom
Kahn, Ike
Kahn, Manny
Kirshenbaum, Moshe Aharon
Kirshcnbaum, Hudes
Kirshbaum, Alye
Kirshbaum, Meir
Klein, Shmuel Zeinwil
Kantor, Avrohom

Kantor, Freida
Kesler, Taltze
Frantz, Efraim
Frantz, Rela
Frantz, Alex
Rapaport, Moshe
Rapaport, Benjamin
Rapaport, Yitzchok
Rapaport, Meir
Rosen, Yehoshua
Rosen, Lipshe
Ruina, Alye
Shlesinger, Avrohom Boruch
Shlesinger, Hinda Rivka
Shlesinger, Chaim Yakir
Shlesinger, Simcha Bunem
Cohen, Hanchye
Freida, Gorny

[Page 454]

List of Those Who Passed Away in Israel

Offenbach, Braina

Offenbach–Vinkor, Shoshana

Isaac, Katriel

Eshel (Isaac), Yehoshua

Bilewski, Chaya Shifra

Berkman, Chana

Berkman, Yaakov

Berman, Mira Plotniarz

Goldberg, Mordechai

Granat, Ephraim Eliezer–Rimon

Granat, Esther–Chana Rimon

Granat, Yosef Tzvi Rimon

Granat, Yechiel Bunem Rimon

Dobrzinski, Asher

Dobroszklanka, Yeshayahu

Dobrechowski, Ham

Dobrechowski, Hans

Hartbrot, Shlomo

Vizelberg, Esther–Goldman

Yalowski, Dov

Yeshiwitz, Dov

Fogel, Nisan

Zudkewitz, Tzadok

Czernobrody, Chana

Czernobrody, M.

Rosen, Chaya

Rosenwaks, Yitzhak

Rosenwaks, Chana

Rosen, Avraham

Rusk—from Kfar Shmaryahu

Ryz, Shmuel Hersh

Shivak, Tova nee Lipka

Sperling, Yehuda

Cohen, Fogel

Cohen, Avraham Hirsh

Cohen, Ozer Bar

Minski, Yehoshua Chaim

Minski, Chaya Leah

Minski, Yechiel Shimon

Chana and Gronem Lichtenstein

*

List of Those Who Passed Away in England and in Germany

Prager, Nahum, in Germany

Gottlieb, Hirsh Asherk in England

Lichtenfeld, Azriel Alye, in England

*

Commemoration of Parents and Relatives

As a sacred memorial to our dear parents, sisters, brothers and family:

Platniarz, Yaakov Leib

Platniarz, Aidel

Platniarz, Yeshayahu

Platniarz, Mordechai

Platniarz, Yisrael

Platniarz, Leah

Memorialized by:

Their only son and brother, Hershel Platniarz in Cleveland–Ohio, America

*

[Page 455]

As a sacred memorial to our parents, sisters, brothers and family:

Platniarz, Tina

Platniarz, Asher

Platniarz, Manya

Platniarz, Hinda Leah

Platniarz, Yechiel Meir

Platniarz, Yisrael

Silberstein Platniarz, Michle

Silberstein Platniarz, Eliezer

Silberstein Platniarz, Malka

Silberstein Platniarz, Chana

Silberstein Platniarz, Libe

Silberstein Platniarz, Shimon

Memorialized by:

Their children, Sidney and Michle Platner and children, Chicago:
Sam and Betty Platner and children, New York.
Beatrice and Leo Platner and children, New York.
Genya and Yisrael Platner and children, Israel.
Charna and Mur Platner and children, New York.

*

As a memorial to our dear, beloved parents, sisters, brothers and relatives who perished in the Holocaust:

Dratwa, Lipman and wife Shoshana—our parents

Dratwa, Avrohom

Dratwa, Leah

Dratwa Hersh Yaakov

Dratwa, Feige

Dratwa, Miriam—(siblings)

Dratwa, Yosef Yitzchok (uncles)

Memorialized by:

Dratwa, Yosef and family (Israel)

*

As an everlasting memorial to our dear parents, siblings and their families

Parents:

Alexander, Meir Mendel. Died in 1925 in New York.

Alexander, Rivka. Died in 1953 in New York.

Son: Hersh Eliezer. Died in 1962 in New York.

Daughter-in-law: Feige, died in 1968 in New York.

Memorialized by:

Shlomo Alexander and family, Alex Alexander and family,
Moshe Henech Alexander and family, and our sister Bina and family.

[Page 456]

As an everlasting memorial to our dear parents and grandparents:

Yerachmiel and Rosa Katcher

Abraham Shlomo and Nitzi Katcher

Yehoshua and Molly Katcher

Shmuel Gedalia and Rita Katcher

Abba Libowitch and Esther Chana, nee Katcher.

*

As a memorial to our parents and sister:

Daniel Kahn–Itches and his wife Feige Leah;

daughter: Rosa Frenkel–Kahn.

Memorialized by:

Tzipora and Nathan Warszoi; Judith Orbach–Kahn; Leo Kahn, his wife and children; Oscar Kahn, his wife and children.

*

In memory of our parents, sisters, and relatives together with their families:

Sova, Zalman and Bilhah

Sova, Bendet and family

Sova, Pinchas, Michal and their children

Sova, Yitzhak Yaakov and his family

Choronazitz[2], Amram and his wife Devorah, nee Sova, and their children

Lichterz and his wife Bracha, nee Sova, and their children

Tzernobroda, Eliyahu, his wife Feige, and children (brother-in-law)

Beldiger, Avraham, his wife Sarah Rivka (uncle)

Beldiger, Aharon, Yaakov, Yosef and their families (cousins)

Kaczor, Lipman and his wife Elka (uncle and aunt)

Lifschitz, Aharon, Arye, Rachel Leah, and Chana—cousins

Memorialized by:

Sova, David and his wife Chana and their children (Israel)

*

To the memory of my departed parents, as well as my sisters and brothers who perished in the Holocaust:

Azriel and Rivka Dobroszklanka

Leib Dobroszklanka

Zalman and Malka Dobroszklanka

Toibe Dobroszklanka

Feivil Dobroszklanka

Yetta Gutglas, her husband and their children

Memorialized by:

Sheindel Rapaport, Avraham Dor–Dobroszklanka, Tzesha Berger–Dobroszklanka, of Israel.

Bella Bresler– Dobroszklanka, of France.

[Page 457]

As an everlasting memorial to our parents, brothers and sisters and their families,
the virtuous martyrs who died and perished in the Holocaust. Their burial place is unknown:

Our parents: Zalman Rosenwaks (Zalman Hassid) and his wife Tzipora, who died in Dobrzyn.

The brother: Avraham Yaakov and his wife Chana and their son Chaim, his wife and their children.

Our sister: Miriam Rosenwaks–Arnow, her husband Binyamin Aharon, who perished together with their children: Yisrael Hersh, Yaakov Yehoshua, Meir Neta, Yechiel, Tzerka.

Our brother: Yitzhak Rosenwaks and his wife Chana, who died in Israel.

Memorialized by:

Feige Rosenwaks–Maimon and her husband Yechezkel
Zahava Peres–Rosenwaks and their children, Yehuda and Chava Rosenwaks and their children
Michale Herzog–Rosenwaks, her husband and children
Yehudit Golan–Rosenwaks, her husband and children
David Shoshani–Rosenwaks and his family
Rivka Gavrieli–Rosenwaks and her family

*

In memory of my parents and sisters:

Avraham Rothman and his wife Adele

Moshe Rothman and his wife Gendl

Avraham Rothman and their children: Frimet, Yosef and Rita.

Memorialized by:

Tuvya Rothman of Rehovot, Israel.

*

In memory of my parents, brothers, sisters and relatives who passed away and perished in the Holocaust:

Zaklikowski, Meir and his wife Esther Malka—our parents who passed away.

Zaklikowski, Hersh and his wife Ita, nee Zik, who came from Lipno, and their children:

Yosef Meir; Yaakov…missing

Esther, nee Sentor, the wife of Yaakov…perished

Bunem and his wife Hila, nee Tzlekownik…perished

Yeshayahu and his wife Itka, nee Korewa, who came from Rypin, and their child Moshe…perished

Shlomo and his daughters: Reizl, Marta, and Ilonka…perished

Leib, the son of Meir and Esther Malka, and his wife Mindl, nee Warshawski…passed away

And their sons: Bunem and Eliezer…passed away

[Page 458]

Sheinberg, Mindel, nee Zaklikowski, her husband Meir and their three daughters.

Memorialized by:

Menahem Zaklikowski and his wife Chaya, nee Lofta, Tel Aviv; Chana Dimant, nee Zaklikowski and her husband, Jerusalem.

Szmiga,[3] Moshe Hirsh and his wife Yente…passed away
Szmiga, Yitzhak Yaakov and his wife Feige…perished
Their son David and his wife Leah, nee Szimanski and their children, Yisrael and Moshe Hirsh…perished
Hartbrot, Hirsh and his wife Rozha, nee Szmiga…passed away
Holtz, Mendl and his wife Sara Devora…perished
Bertza Holtz and his wife and their two children…perished
Shlomo Holtz and his wife Nechama, nee Eisenberg, and their two children…perished
Aharon Holtz and his wife Eva, nee Motil, and their two children…perished
Yisrael, Rachel, Feige and Luba, the son and daughters of Mendel and Sara Devora Holtz

Memorialized by:
Yechiel and Golda Lofta, nee Szmiga, of Argentina.

*

In memory of our parents, brothers and sisters who perished in the Holocaust:

Shmuel and Masha Goldberg—parents

Lipa Friedman and his wife Bella, nee Goldberg—my sister and brother-in-law and their children

Chaya and Munik Yosef Chmielnicki and his wife Sara, nee Goldberg—my sister and my brother-in-law, and their children: Rachel and Avraham; Yaakov Moshe, Yosef Gershon—my brothers—and my sister Rachel.

Feige Toibe Goldberg, my wife's mother

Yoachim Goldberg, Feige Toibe's son

Yosef Postolski, my uncle, and his children: Avraham Natan, Gershon, Feige, Leibl

Hersh Natan Bergman, my uncle, and his wife Rivka and their children: Shmuel, Luba and their children

Yoel Braun and his children: Chana Sara, Motl, Yosef Gershon

And our brother Mordechai Goldberg, who died in Israel in 1937

Memorialized by:

Yehoshua Goldberg and his wife Liza; Leizer Postolski and his wife Beracha, nee Goldberg

*

As an everlasting memorial to my relatives who perished in the Holocaust in Poland:

Rebe, Isser, his wife and two children

Rebe, Anshil, his wife and one child

Rebe, Avraham, his wife and one child

[Page 459]

Rebe, Frimet, with her husband D. Rothman and two children

Rebe, Gucze, with her husband A. Goldbojm and one child

Yaakov and Liba Ofenbach

Avraham and Michle Nroine[4]

Chana Puleder

Memorialized by:

Esther Rebe Groner of Chicago, America

*

As a memorial to our dear parents and siblings:

Yosef Alterowicz (father)

Tzerl Alterowicz (mother)

Yitzhak Leib Alterowicz (brother)

Beila Alterowicz–Rosenberg (sister)

Moshe Rosenberg (brother–in–law)

Nicha Alterowicz–Margolis (sister)

Avrohom Margolis (brother–in–law)

Avrohom Alterowicz (brother)

and all the others of the family

*

Names of members that are no more with us. May they rest in peace![5]

New York

1. Harry Alexander
2. Sol Bartkey–Brooks
3. Julius Brown
4. Al. Davidson
5. Joe Flamenbaum
6. Jack Freilich
7. Gerstein
8. Milton Goldfeder
9. Greenberg
10. Irving Gursky
11. Charles Katcher
12. Morris Katcher
13. Klapman
14. Aharon Lefkowitz
15. Sam Leshnick
16. Max Leshnick
17. Newman
18. Dr. Luis Posmer
19. Plucki
20. Rosenzweig
21. Ruina
22. Joe Rosenbaum
23. Ben Zacklow

24. Irving Shoenbart

25. Ben Gutglas

26. Goldfeder

27. Leo Rogenstein

28. Ros Frenkel (Cohen)

29. Irving Cohen

30. Nachum Flato

31. Morris Katcher

32. Chana Chaya Katcher

Translator's Footnotes

1. From *My Town: In Memory of the Communities Dobrzyn–Gollob*, edited by M. Harpaz, (published by the Dobrzyn–Golub Society, Israel, 1969), pp. 443–459. Note that the beginnings of sections are denoted by large asterisks (*).

2. Possibly a printing error of "Hurynowicz"

3. A new section appears to begin on this line, although there is no asterisk to indicate it

4. Possibly a misprint of "Groine".

5. There was no need to translate this section, which was printed in English on p. 459. It has been reproduced here for completeness.

[English Page 3]

My Home Town
By Walter L. Field

Dobrzyn our Shtetl was muddy and dark,
With cobbled stone streets and dogs that bark,
A fast flowing river, but not a park

Houses and shops were built of wood;
Some were sturdy, straight they stood;
Others were leaning, tipping but good!

Winter was cold, the river frozen white;
Summer was hot, with flies to fight;
Spring meant life, a lover's delight.

Horse power was used in place of steam.
Logs from the woods floated down stream.
Traveling was done by coach and team.

Feather covers were used not to freeze;
Teeth were pulled with howl and squeeze.
Snuff – an aid to bring on a sneeze.

Beinkes and herbs, health to restore;
Hot poultice and Shmaltz to heal a sore;
The midwife was first the baby to adore.

[English Page 4]

Constant attention the gossips gave
To every person from cradle to grave;
The slightest rumor and they would rave!

Peasants and merchants on market days
Displayed their wares in stalls and bays:
Produce on wagons, baked goods on trays.

A Kopek a herring, five a bread;
Very few Jews could afford a spread!
But no one went hungry, so people said.

Families were large and mothers were tired;
Fathers worked hard for the little acquired;
Faith in the "hereafter" kept them inspired.

With hardly a look, very little to say,
Daughters found mates the Shadkhan way,
While parents struggled the dowry to pay.

The Badhan as clown came in with a bang;
At every wedding he danced and sang
And told stories using Yiddish slang.

[English Page 5]

A boy's day began with prayer and cap,
in Heder he learned by the Rebes strap;
Many hours were spent the Bible to tap.

Girls and boys went walking for fun;
Behind fences caressing was done;
If ever discovered, oh, did they run.

Life was centered around Mikvah and Shul,
Balabatim chose men, the Kehillah, to rule.
Each Shtetl had a rich man, a wise man, and fool!

Widows were protected and orphans taught;
For the poor, shelter and food were sought;
With tears and prayers, epidemics fought.

The help from the Hevras was always free;
Wherever the need, there they would be;
Their readiness to serve, a Torah decree.

Shabbes in our Shtetl, a joy to describe;
Holiness and peace enveloped the tribe;
The Kiddush wine all eager to imbibe.

[English Page 6]

Winter, summer heat or icy raw,
Everyone in Shul on the Sabbath you saw;
Hallah and Tzulent an unwritten law.

Old and young dressed in style
And on the Sabbath walked for a while,
The pious man and wife in single file.

On Passover, a king was every trader;
For freedom's cause each a serenader;

Matzos and wine graced the poorest Seder.

On Torah and Talmud the pious were reared;
God they loved, Gehinnom they feared;
Some displayed Payot, others the beard.

Yihus claimed those of the Rabbinic line;
The learned were always invited to dine;
To help a bright student, few would decline.

The Hasidim, dressed in unique attire,
Assembled and prayed as one huge choir.
Their devotion to their Rebe one had to admire.

[English Page 7]

In matters of faith the Rov led;
His word was law when Traif he said;
He taught Torah and eulogized the dead.

Life in our Shtetl, though not always serene,
Yet when the peasants weren't drunk or mean,
The place looked peaceful – a pastoral scene.

[English Page 8]

My Mother's Legacy
by Walter L. Field

A woman of valor, where can one find?
To choose my mother, I would be inclined;
Dobrzyn, our town, had few of her kind.

Everyone in our Shtetl knew her by name;
The rich she humbled, none would she shame.
All sought her advice, such was her fame.

Respected and loved by young and old,
She fed the hungry, sheltered the cold;
Ask Sarah V., the perplexed were told.

To father she was like a lighted beam
That lit his way o'er road and stream;
They were Heavenly matched, a blessed team.

A mother of six – helpmate and wife,
She met the demands of family life;
Her presence was peaceful, a stranger to strife.

Sabbath to us was a great delight;
Our home was cheerful, the table bright;
Many candles she lit on Friday night.

[English Page 9]

God she implored to be her guide;
In men of torah she would confide,
Ask their blessing, pray and decide.

To seek knowledge the young she inspired;
Men of learning she greatly admire;
Of helping students, she never tired.

For the tired and sick her help knew no end;
Troubled souls she would try to mend;
Neighbors for guidance on her would depend.

Heaven claimed her – early indeed;
Serving the poor had been her creed;
Her legacy – love for the good deed.

[English Page 10]

Walter F. Field is the author of More Truth Than Poetry, published in 1954, and A People's Epic, published in 1963. A People's Epic is the first complete history written in rhymed verse. The book has been acclaimed by Zalman Shazar, President, and David Ben Gurion, former Premier of the State of Israel, Professor Salo W. Baron, historian, the late Rabbi Morris Adler, spiritual leader of Congregation Shaarey Zedek, Detroit, Michigan, and many others. Mr. Field's main aspiration is to make the Jewish youth aware of their great heritage and to that end he devotes his time, energy and means. A civic leader for over a quarter century, Mr. Field in private life is a paint manufacturer and President of the Mac–O–Lac Paints Inc., Detroit, Michigan.

[English Page 11]

Those Terrible Days...
by Pozmanter H.

Terrible times have come upon us. In Sept. of 1939, when Hitler's forces reached us, I lived in a small town named Dobrzyn. I lived there with my parents, two brothers and three sisters. My mother, Malka, a native of Dobrzyn, a woman of deep understanding and charm. Her pallid features were illumined by typically sad Jewish eyes. My father, Moshe Pozmanter, inherited many of his finer attributes. He was always smiling, always full of life. He created and radiated happiness wherever he appeared, and was the life and soul of any company in which he formed himself. He was a devoted husband, father, and in the bosom of his family, he radiated warmth and glow.

A harsh and bitter period of persecution began. Decrees were issued at lightning speed, one after the other, stupefying the Jews. After three months the town began an absolute liquidation. All the Jews of the town, including us, were cruelly murdered, in cold blood. We got transferred. My father and two brothers went together with Jews from Dobrzyn, they were assembled and shot, their bodies burned.

My mother and sisters and I were in Ghetto Minsk M. On July 24, 1942, the ghetto was liquidated. Hundreds of Jews were sent by the railway wagons to Treblinka where they were murdered. I was the only one who succeeded in escaping, and I found myself in Warsaw Ghetto. On Sept. 6, 1942, I was sent, among many others, to Maidanek death camp: a number were murdered and a number were sent to Aushwitz death camp.

[English Page 12]

Lajb Ryz

Lajb Ryz (Leo) of 96–98 Oxford Road, Reading Berks, England, passed suddenly away on September 6, 1968 in San Francisco, being on a visit to the U.S.A.

He was born on January 18, 1902 in Dobrzyn, the son of the late Kalman and Lejna Ryz. In the year 1920, he left for Germany and married in 1933 Ilse Ascher, whom he became to know, since he arrived in this country.

Like thousands of other Jewish friends, he was sent to a Concentration camp in 1938, and only through the help of his former neighbros from Dobrzyn, the late Mr. and Mrs. J. Lichtenfeld and Mr. and Mrs. Ch. Lichtenfeld, an affidavit was granted for the whole family. They left in June 1939 for England with very little money and bare essentials. During the war he volunteered for warwork and afterwards worked his way up as a tailor and a successful businessman.

Many friends will remember him as a very kind, quiet man. He left a widow, a daughter, and two sons. The business is carried on by his wife and married son.

His whole life was dedicated always first to his wife and family and then to himself.

May his dear soul rest in peace.

The funeral took place September 11, 1969 at Bushy Cemetery, London, England.

[English Page 13]

The Kristal–Brown Family
by Samuel Abraham Meiri

Jewish tradition and a devotion to Zion were deep rooted in our family and have inspired us to this day. There, in our shtetl Dobrzyn, which was "muddy and dark with cobbled stone streets…and fast flowing river…" my father and relatives used to dream of a better life and of a happier future in their Old Country – Eretz Israel….

Only few of our dear relatives turned the dream into reality – leaving Dobrzyn in order to begin a new life in Israel. Others left for the U.S.A., where they succeeded in building for themselves a safe and wealthy home. But many of our dear relatives remained in the Shtetl and were brutally persecuted, among the Six Millions, during the terrible Holocaust. Great is the loss and deep is the sorrow of which only a prophet could have given vent to…. Therefore we feel a greater need of belonging, a deeper need of family ties…which is by no means less important in our technological world. The need of identification and self–concept becomes much more urgent in or modern world, especially for Jews in the Western World and in the U.S.A., where they enjoy prosperity and safety.

We can, therefore, hardly over appreciate the important work done, for many years, by Telly Spurling and Ira M. Kay – publishing a Family News Circle for the purpose of preserving and promoting family identity. We all join in their hopes "that the accomplishments of past and present generations may serve as an inspiration to those yet to come…"

Being a shoot of the same deep rooted Kristall–Brown tree, I am deeply moved by their devotion to the family. It makes me remember my mother and grandfather in the Shtetl Dobrzyn, their pious ways of life, their unshaking belief in God and in their People….

[English Page 14]

Jennie (Sheina) Kristal–Danzinger

And I am happy to feel that the same characteristics are symbolized in many of our large family, of which Sidney Danzinger and his wife Gloria are very prominent personalities. His devotion to Israel was shown, once again, by rising to her help during and after the Six Day War. Not only did he raise a very great sum of money of his own, but urged his fellow industrialists of the metal branch to come to the help of Israel. "Once more" – he old them in his moving appeal – "The valiant fight of the people of Israel has proven that a man desperately fighting for his own piece of land, his own home, his own live stock, and his own chosen way of life can withstand seemingly impossible odds... However, this small country of Israel cannot exist under the economic strain placed on it by the drains of mobilization ... unless we Americans – of all denominations – come to their immediate help."

[English Page 15]

This love for Israel and its people he inherited, undoubtedly, from his mother Jennie (Sheina) Kristal–Danzinger of Dobrzyn, God bless her soul, who did not cease hoping, till her last day, to visit the Holy Land of which she used to dream from the days of her childhood.

She brought up her four children in an orthodox way of life, trying to make them merciful and faithful Jews. A true daughter of the Kristal–Brown family, of whom we may rightly say, "Strength and honor are her clothing; and she shall rejoice in time to come."

[English Page 16]

Isaac Ryz
by Yehuda Rozenwax

Trying to describe Isaac Ryz, I come to remember my cousin's family, the large family of Kalman Ryz. Kalman, the head of the family, had died before the Second World War, but his wife Lejna and their eleven children – Shmuel Hersh, Beila, Esther Frieda, Leib, Yeta, Hendel, Abraham Moshe, Beina Jacob, Isaac and Meir, lived in Dobrzyn till the War. One son only – Abraham Moshe, immigrated to the U.S.A., where he is still living. All the others were terribly persecuted, with all the Jews of Poland, only three of them survived.

Kalman's family was a typical liberal Jewish family. The head of the family possessed a hat shop, where he worked together with some of his elder children. It was a prospering business. The energetic children helped their father. They also took part in all youth activities, being members of Youth Movements.

I left Dobrzyn 45 years ago, when Isaac was only nine–ten years old, a very happy and animated boy. I came to know him better only five years ago, when he visited Israel with his family. He toured all parts of the country, happy to find it built up and prospering. I can hardly describe his happiness in meeting his relatives and many friends here.

Being familiar with all those hard and terrible years he passed during the war: the escape to Russia where he was detained and sent to Siberia, till the day he was freed and immigrated to the U.S.A. – I was indeed happy to see him so very energetic and full of life.

He invited his relatives and all his friends to a party in a hotel, where he and all those present there recalled memories of Dobrzyn, remembering the Shtetl, its happiness and sorrow.

It was an evening to remember. He was so happy. His eyes glittered. He started to sing remembering, undoubtedly, himself as a member of the synagogue's choir in the shtetl.

That evening had a very deep impression on him. He promised us to visit Israel again. In his letters to me he expressed his longing for his old friends.

[English Page 17]

The Jewish Partisans
– Objective and Subjective Difficulties
by Shalom Cholawski

Introductory Remarks

In the time at my disposal it will be difficult to bring support by way of quotation to what I have to say or even to indicate the sources. This is because of the great volume and also duplication in the Holocaust literature and in the testimonies that have not yet been published.

Every underground movement springs up in the nation concerned like a plant in its natural soil. The Jewish partisan movement was deprived of the basic conditions necessary for fighting underground movement.

I shall describe the conditions briefly.

The objective difficulties:

- our being a national, urban minority, out of touch with nature, with no acquaintance with warfare or how to acquire it.
- the lack of arms prevented many Jews from joining partisan units.
- the absence of assistance from abroad.
- the "normal" antisemitism of the vast majority of the local populations became intensified with the retreat of the Soviets from the Eastern areas and was further inflamed by the Nazi propaganda.
- the time factor worked against us to a fatal extent. The great extermination swept over White Russia and the Ukraine before the partisan movement was organized there.
- the complete isolation that cut off the ghettos from one another (apart from a few instances).
- the absence of a non-Jewish underground, particularly in the forests, prevented contact between the Jews in the ghettos and the partisans in the forests.
- in the areas of Poland that were sparsely forested but infest with antisemitism the assistance given by the anti-Nazi non- Jewish

undergrounds was extremely limited. In a few places help was given in hiding Jews on the "Aryan" side, but almost never were they brought to the partisan units.

[English Page 18]

Understanding and assistance for the Jews on the part of weak Armia Ludowa did show itself in a number of cases, but this came late and was not very effective. The Armia Krajowa underground movement in Poland was strong, but the great majority of its members were hostile to Jews and part of them were no less brutal in their conduct than the Germans, and only a few of them gave help to Jews.

- in many places the men between 16 and 60 years of age were liquidated in the first "Actions".

- in the Soviet areas conquered by the Germans the exterminations came without warning. The Jews there had not heard of the German havoc in the occupied parts of Poland.

- getting from the ghetto to the forest was full of danger and the vast majority of those who tried were killed. When larger groups made their way to the forests (as in Tuchin or Lachova) they were wiped out either before they got there or in the forests by the hostile local population.

- in the forests the Jews met yet more torments. In addition to their principal enemy, there lurked also for the Jewish partisan the local population, most of whom were hostile and the anti-semitic partisans. The hatred of the population was directed at him as a partisan, as a representative of the Soviet authority, and as a Jew.

- this attitude prevented the Jews from the ghettos and the labor camps and also those who were wandering through the villages from joining the partisans.

- the fact that the partisan organization was territorial, not national, even though at the beginning without any antisemitic intention, involved considerable implications for the Jews. The disbanding of the independent Jewish units was a heavy blow to the Jewish susceptibilities and purpose of the Jewish partisan.

[English Page 19]
The Subjective Difficulties:

- the concept of the sanctity of life that was deepened by the torments inflicted on an isolated and persecuted minority. This concept inhibited the underground which faced so many dangers with such little hope of survival.

- the illusion that after all the Germans would not exterminate all the Jews confused the people in the ghetto.

- the Jews had no faith in the forests or in the farmers of the vicinity.

- the Judenrats: one of the principal inhibiting factors was the opposition between the underground organizations and the partisans on the one hand and the Judenrats on the other. It took different forms in different ghettos. In quite a number of Judenrats the members gave assistance to the underground and some even belonged to it. In many, however, among the largest of the ghettos, the confrontation widened the distance and so sharpened the attitudes as to make for open hostility between the two sides.

- the absence of a fighting tradition.

- in the choice between death in the ghetto and death in the forest most chose the first.

- the close family ties in the ghettos constituted an understandable human factor, but the fear of being deported prevented escapes to the forests.

- the dispute within the ghetto underground between those who favored struggle "within the walls" and those who favored struggle in the forests. Moral authority was on the side of the former.

- the collective responsibility which the Germans imposed on the ghetto acted as a most powerful deterrent to the underground's organization and activity.

- apart from in a few places, the Jewish partisans did not have any centralized spiritual leadership.

[English Page 20]
Summing Up:

The Jewish partisan movement in Europe was deprived of the basic conditions required for military struggle. Round their necks hung the heavy millstones of Jewish difficulties which were the sequelae of the Holocaust –

None of the Jewish fighters in Europe had the advantage of area – even the smallest – where they could wage a struggle in normal condition of warfare- conditions which the others had.

In spite of the handicaps that we have enumerated, the partisan movement endured thanks in the main to the remarkable spiritual strength with which the Jewish fighter in those days was imbued.

The Relationship Between the Jewish and the Polish Underground in Nazi-Occupied Poland

by Michael Borwicz, Paris

- State of research.

- Clandestine activities of individuals.

- Initiatives of Polish clandestine movements. Problem of chronological succession pertaining to the two branches of resistance, their respective transformations and their mutual correlation of effects.

- The anti–Jewish pre–war heritage.

- The impact caused in 1939 by a large proportion of Jewish soldiers in the Polish Army and the effect of their willingness to fight and their devotion.

- Prisoners of war.

- The Soviet occupation of Eastern Poland (1939–1941); (a) its consequence for those territories; (b) its reflections on the situation during the ensuing years.

- Contacts of Jews with Polish underground organizations following the Polish debacle of 1939.

- "Caritas" and Christians of Jewish origin during the ghetto period.

- The exodus of Jewish leaders from German–occupied territories to foreign countries and to the Soviet zone of occupation.

[English Page 21]

The vacuum left behind as a result:

- The disappearance of Jewish organizations, societies and institutions in the Soviet Zone of occupation (of Eastern Poland).

- Ghetto confinement as a factor of estrangement.

- The attitude of the Polish underground press to the Jewish cause.

- Infrequent contact of Jewish organizations (active in the ghettos) with Polish underground movements: (a) the P.P.S.; (b) the "Harcerz" scouts; (c) military personnel, etc.

- During the preparations for armed resistance in the ghettos.

- During the fighting in the ghettos and camps.

- Contacts with the free world.

- The Jewish Coordinating Committee and the Jews underground after the liquidation of the ghettos.

- The Jewish Relief council.

- The problem of Jewish forest "gangs".

- Jews with "Aryan" identification papers present in almost all Polish underground movements: (a) those having joined through the mediation of Polish activists; (b) those having joined directly; (c) those having joined as Jews (particularly physicians); (d) Census problems and statistical evaluation.

- The antisemitic military organization N.S.Z.

- The Polish Warsaw uprising.

- Vacant spots in up–to–date research.

- Deeply rooted misconceptions.

- Methods of research and research problems.

The Yishuv's Traditional Help to Jews in the Time of Holocaust
by Yehuda Slutsky

1. The British White Paper of May 1939 severely limited the help that the Yishuv could give to the Jewries of the occupied countries. Even before that, the Zionist Movement had lost the great historical opportunity of "redeeming" the Jews of Europe. This must be blamed on the failure of the British royal Commission's recommended plan of 1937 for the establishment of a Jewish State in part of Palestine.

[English Page 22]

2. For the first three years of the war the Yishuv did not realize the dimensions of the Holocaust, though it was realized that the disasters in Europe would destroy Jewish public life and that hundreds of thousands of Jews would perish from hunger, disease and the sword. The Yishuv and its responsible institutions saw their principal duty to take active participation in the war effort. Thirty thousand men and women of the Yishuv volunteered for various formations in the British Army in spite of the refusal of the British authorities to grant them national or political status.

3. The Yishuv's efforts to assist the refugees by way of immigration, both legal and "illegal" were met by the savage opposition of the British. "Illegal" immigration dropped after the "Patria" and "Struma" disasters. Attempts to make contact with the Jewish refugees in Soviet Central Asia were not successful.

4. It was when the first clear news of the dimensions of the Holocaust and its real nature (the systematic extermination of the Jewish people) was received in Palestine at the end of 1942 that the Yishuv was aroused to help the Jews of Europe in every possible way. The **Magbit Hahitgaysut** (Mobilization Fund) for some years already engaged in the collection of money for the Yishuv's security purposes and for assistance to families of soldiers, became the **Magbit Lehitgaysut Vehatzalah** (Mobilization and Relief Fund). In neutral Istanbul the Vaad Hatzalah (relief committee) which was composed of representatives of the Jewish Agency, the Aliya Foundation, the Histadrut and other bodies, extended its

operations. It made contact with Jewish individuals and with youth groups in occupied Europe, sent money and food parcels, made efforts though bribery and other ways to have repressive decrees abrogated or deferred. The Committee's activities helped in halting the expulsion of the Jews from Bulgaria and in saving Jews in various occupied countries by bribery, the provision of forged documents, etc.

[English Page 23]

5. Towards the end of the war the **Vaad Hatzalah** and the Aliya Foundation renewed their efforts to transfer Jews from Europe to Palestine. The smuggling of Jews from Occupied Europe to Turkey began in a small way and later in large numbers by ship from Rumania to Turkey. About 5,000 Jews were so saved. A total of 52,000 Jews immigrated to Palestine during the war years, which means to say that not all the 75,000 immigrations certificates permitted under the White Paper were utilized, due to deliberate and sustained efforts by the British to hinder the immigration.

6. The Jewish soldiers from Palestine were active in all the liberated countries. Apart from the decisive part played by them immediately after the war in connection with the Jewish survivors in Europe (a subject that is not part of this paper), there is their wartime help to the Jews of Cyrenaica, Tripolitania and Italy. With their help communities were reconstituted; Jewish schools opened; food and clothing provided. They organized the move to Palestine of Jews whom they provided with military uniforms and forged army documents.

7. The most impressive manifestation of the Yishuv's determination to come to the help of the Jews in the occupied territories is to be seen in the chapter of the **parachutists**. Thirty-two of them reached Europe, of whom seven met their death on their mission. It has to be said that their actions, like those of the Ghetto uprisings, had symbolic rather than practical significance. In Hungary and especially Rumania, however, they fulfilled a most valuable purpose in their encouragement of the Jewish youth in the final months of the war when those countries had been liberated by the Soviet Army to emigrate to Palestine.

Conclusion: The time has not yet arrived for a full evaluation of the Yishuv's activities in extending help to their brethren in the European exile. It is our task to gather the source material. A first conclusion that the researcher has to draw is that whatever was done was little in relation to the dimensions of the Holocaust. It was too little and it came too late.

[English Page 24]

The Uniqueness of Jewish Martyrdom During the Holocaust
by J. Gottfarstein

1. The command of sanctifying the Divine Name, in the light of Halacha.

According to the Rambam, the words "I will be hallowed the children of Israel" in Chapter 22, Verse 32 of Leviticus indicate a positive command calling for unconditional self–sacrifice. Thus, the Rambam in the 5th Chapter of his rules on the Fundamentals of the Torah, in Rule 1, lays down: "the entire of the Divine Name, as it is said, "I will be hallowed among the children of Israel".

This command is applicable everywhere and at all times and should be observed by males and females, and whoever violates it and does not sanctify the Divine Name when necessary has not only made this positive command in–effective, but also infringed on the express prohibition of not profaning the name of the Holiest...and the sin of profaning the name of the Lord is an extremely grave one, for have not our late sages already stated that there can be no forgiveness, not even on the Day of Atonement and not through repentance nor suffering but only through death according to the last chapter of Yoma ("Sefer Hahinuch", 268,6).

This positive command, this command to sanctify the Divine Name, according to Jelinek, contains the whole Torah in a nutshell. We may add that it also serves, no doubt, as a foundation, not only for the Jewish people's existence, but also for its destiny, since it appears that the Jewish nation has been created for the sole purpose of sanctifying and thereby glorifying the Divine Name throughout the world, as expressed by the Paitan in his words, "Israel is responsible for His righteousness, Israel is responsible for His holiness, Israel is responsible for His exaltation". Or, in the words of the blessing contained in the Kedushah, "From generation to generation shall we pronounce Thy greatness, and all eternity shall we sanctify Thy Holiness".

[English Page 25]

2. **Definition of the concept "Holiness" and "name", especially as appearing in expressions as; Sacrificing oneself for sanctification of the Name.**

3. **Manifestations of Sanctifying the Divine Name, in the history of the Jewish people:**

   a. Abraham as the prototype of sacrifice on behalf of the Lord; the "binding" of Isaac;

   b. Hanna and her seven sons;

   c. the Hasmonean revolt;

   d. the Jewish wars against the Romans; Massada;

   e. the Bar–Kochba revolt;

   f. the ten victims killed on orders of the King;

   g. Jewish sanctification of the Divine Name during the Middle Ages;

   h. the Chmelnitzki persecution;

   i. the death of Potocki as an outstanding example of Jewish martyrdom.

4. **Heroism inspired by martyrdom and by the will to prove the holiness of the God of Abraham, Isaac and Jacob through an act of heroism containing the elements of courage and tremendous devotion to the point of death.** (a few examples).

5. **Three commands which the Jew is obliged to observe even at the price of his life.**

The number of the slain during the Jewish wars against the Romans was so great that our sages were compelled to define and restrict the question for the fulfillment of which command a Jew is forced to go as far as giving away his life rather than fail to comply with it, and under what conditions, whether being faced with the alternative of renouncing his faith or not, in public or privately, he is obliged to choose a martyr's death and renounce life, even though the Torah says, "He shall live by them", meaning "He should not die by them" as it is said, "He should rather be killed than transgress the law".

a. serving other Gods and everything thereby involved;

b. incest (with all its implications);

c. murder.

[English Page 26]

6. **Definition of the above three grave offenses.**

7. **Deadly peril suspending all other commands.**

8. **"Deadly peril" does not apply at the time of forced conversion".**

9. **The problem of the Marannos during the Inquisition.**

10. Denial of the possibility to sanctify the Divine name, during the Holocaust period, which found its expression in the following forms:

    a. by the scheming and trickery of the Nazi persecutors and murderers who even deprived the Jews of their historic right to sacrifice their lives on the altar of God by their free choice, and who denied to them the alternative of choosing between abandoning their faith and death;

    b. by the stratagems of the Nazis to subject the Jew to total persecution, not only his body but his soul as well;

    c. by applying ruthless torture against rabbis and Jewish leaders;

    d. by closing down the schools in the ghettos;

    e. by timing deportations and exterminations subsequently taking place in the death camps, so that they fall on Sabbaths, Jewish holidays and Rosh Hashanah and Yom Kippur.

11. Notwithstanding all this, many Jews – often even such Jews as were not traditionally observant – found ways and means for creating conditions enabling them to sacrifice their lives for the Divine Name in the full meaning of the word, in the spirit of the Halacha and the historic purport of the expression. A number of examples and documents corroborate this statement.

12. Manifestations of Jewish martyrdom in the Jewish partisans units (a few examples).

13. Rabbis, Rebbes and Yeshiva students calling for armed rebellion (a few examples).

14. The Hassidic resistance movement (a few examples).

15. Manifestations of Jewish martyrdom inspired by spiritual heroism both in the Ghettos as well as in the extermination camps and even in the face of the crematoria (a few examples).

[English Page 27]

16. Jewish women in sacrifice and heroism (a few examples).

17. Jewish children sanctifying the Divine Name (a few examples).

18. God, Torah and Israel are One

This well–known and instructive adage of the Zohar obliging all Jews to love the Lord, the Torah and the People of Israel, found a subconscious echo among the Jewish masses during the Holocaust, and this gave many Jews the strength and courage to rise up in active rebellion against the enemy, or to resist him passively. From time to time, the expressions of this adage manifested themselves, one way or other, as reflected in the saying, "For on account of You, we have been killed all day long".

a. by sacrificing one's life for the name of God, in the direct meaning of the expression (a few examples);

b. by preventing the desecration of the Torah and its commands (a few examples);

c. by sanctifying the people of Israel (a few examples);

d. by sanctifying life and disclosing the fervent will for the preservation of life so as to live up to see the day of the horrible enemy's defeat.

19. **The sanctification of the Divine name has seventy faces** (a few examples from the Responsa Literature during the Holocaust follow).

20. Jewish martyrs who died purposefully in order to take vengeance on the persecutors of the Jews (a few examples).

21. Martyrs among all the categories of the Jewish population (a few examples).

22. The Halachic rule: every Jew killed in our days for the only reason of being Jewish, is holy.

23. The process of martyrdom among the survivors of the Holocaust.

This process is not yet completed and will be concluded only the the day on which Ezechiel's vision of the ingathering of the exiles and a total redemption of our nation and land will come true.

[English Page 28]

Doresh Tou – Dobrzinsk
List of Officers:

Alex Alexander	President
Sidney Dubin	Vice–Pres.
Max Goldfeder	Treasurer
Julius Sobel	Fin. Sec'y.
Nathan Schaeffer	Rec. Sec'y.
Sidney Dubin	Cemetery Chairman
Irving Schoenbart	Trustee
Sam Plotner	Trustee

[English Page 29]

If I forget thee, O Jerusalem,
let my right hand forget her
cunning.

If I do not remember thee,
let my tongue cleave
to the roof of her mouth;

If I prefer not Jerusalem
above my chief Joy!

[Pages 443-452]

List of names - Golub-Dobrzyn, Poland
Transliterated by David Sosnovitch
Edited by Ann Harris

Note: Page numbers listed here are the page number in the original Yizkor book, not this translation. This list does not appear in the original Yizkor Book and was apparently added in the on-line translation with additional information not in the original book. The translation of these ages, 443-452, from the original book are translatied above, starting on page 557 of this book.

Family name(s)	First name(s)	Sex	Marital status	Father's name	Name of spouse	Additional family members	Remarks	Page
Offenbach	Yaakov	M	Married					443
Offenbach		F	Married		Yaakov			443
Eisenberg	Haim Leib	M				and family		443
Arfa	Kalman	M				and family	See also Additions to Holocaust Necrology	443
Berkman	Meir	M	Married					443
Berkman		F	Married		Meir			443
Berkman		M		Meir				443
Bielowski	Fishel	M				and family		443
Bortke	Hersh Baruch	M				and family		443
Budziner	Shimon	M				and family		444
Goldman	Yosef	M	Married					444
Goldman		F	Married		Yosef			444
Goldman	Avraham	M		Yosef				444
Goldman	Shimon Leib	M		Yosef				444
Gonsher	Yehezkel	M				and family		444
Gutglaz	Menashe	M				and family		444
Goldberg	Shmulik	M	Married			and children	See also Additions to Holocaust	444

Surname	Given name	Sex	Status		Spouse/Family	Notes	Page
Goldberg		F	Married		Shmulik and children	Necrology See also Additions to Holocaust Necrology	444
Gorny	Mendel	M	Married				444
Gorny		F	Married		Mendel		444
Gorny		F		Mendel			444
Gotleib	Avraham	M			and family	some of the family survived	444
Dzaldow	Eliyahu	M			and family		445
Dratwa		M			and family		445
Hartbrat	Hersh	M				perished in France	445
Horowitz	Itshe	M			and family	See also Additions to Holocaust Necrology	445
Weismel	Yosef Haim	M			and family		445
Wrzos	Avraham	M			and family		445
Zaklikowski	Eliezer	M				See also Additions to Holocaust Necrology	446
Jendzejewicz	Avraham	M			and family		446
Lent	Mendel	M			and family		447
Lipke	David	M			and family		447
Leshnik	Yitzhak	M			and family		447
Lipka	Moshe	M	Married			perished in France	447
Landsberg	Yosef	M		Manos	and family of 6 children	See also Additions to Holocaust Necrology	447
Levinson		M			and family	teacher	447
Leizerowit	Bat Sheva	F					447
Smozhik	Fishel Baruch	M			and family		448
Engler	Kalmen	M			and family		448
Prum	Mendel	M			and family		448

Friedman	Sina	M			and family	449
Koppeld	Baruch	M			and family	450
Koppeld	Shimon	M			and family	450
Kazak	Bunam	M			and family	450
Keller		M			and family	451
Kirshtein		M			and family	451
Kokavka		M			and family	451
Kowalski	Fishel	M			and family	451
Riszaw	Haim	M			and family	452
Szmiga	Yitzhak Yaakov	M			See also <u>Additions to Holocaust Necrology</u>	452
Sawa	Henich	M				452
Sheinbart	Hannanya	M			and family	452

INDEX

A

Alberg, 112

Aleksander, 41, 85, 92, 98, 106, 211, 231, 237, 272, 273, 353, 355, 367, 375, 376, 377, 379, 383, 384, 385, 407, 408, 496, 497, 501, 504, 505, 506

Alexander, 6, 16, 23, 29, 33, 44, 59, 94, 106, 237, 256, 347, 353, 363, 367, 383, 480, 483, 501, 535, 576, 584, 612

Alterowicz, 367, 557, 583

Altman, 557

Altstein, 557

Altsztajn, 557

Altyna, 270

Anchi, 130

Anders, 72, 154, 158, 166, 168, 292, 295, 297

Anders army, 72, 154, 158, 166, 168, 292, 295

Anielewicz, 103, 109

Arfa, 349, 557, 613

Arnob, 557

Arnow, 417, 579

Asher, 136, 137, 165, 252, 312, 378, 394, 559, 560, 563, 566, 568, 571, 575

Auerbach, 251

B

Balaban, 213, 218, 557

Barszewski, 348, 349

Bartkey, 584

Baum, 135

Beldiger, 577

Ben Tzvi, 254

Ber, 413

Berger, 578

Bergman, 582

Berka, 171

Berkman, 557, 571, 613

Berman, 224, 378, 380, 558, 571

Beryl, 16, 18, 83

Bialik, 13, 111, 114, 161, 162, 209, 211, 554, 556

Bielawski, 48, 198, 199, 224, 225, 376, 380, 476, 558

Bielewski, 105

Bielowski, 117, 413, 613

Bilewski, 571

Binem Bich die Zodektes, 444

Birkenau, 190, 191

Blank, 509

Blauzeg, 349

Blechner, 557

Blumberg, 375

Blumenthal, 557

Bolef, 196, 229, 402, 489

Bornstein, 229, 497

Borochov, 118, 119, 388, 389

Bortke, 613

Borwicz, 602

boy scouts, 54

Brana, 557

Brandwein, 509

Braun, 216, 217, 394, 407, 582

Brauns, 215

Brenner, 250, 256

Bresler, 578

Britzman, 558

Bromberg, 16, 95, 96, 536

Bronstein, 184, 185

Brooks, 584

Brown, 215, 217, 260, 584, 594, 596

Broyn, 444

Budziner, 558, 613

Bulka, 441, 444

Bunim, 203, 207, 267, 281, 282, 368, 376, 383

Burtke, 558

C

Cala, 563

Carnabroda, 563

Chaleva, 560

Chamand, 444

Chaskel, 560

Chatzkl, 524

Chmelniecki, 17, 30

Chmielnicki, 582

Cholawski, 598

Choronazitz, 577

Chossid, 48, 379, 380, 417, 419

Cierklorsz, 400, 489

Cirklarz, 564

Cohen, 83, 196, 399, 413, 476, 491, 516, 570, 572, 584

Cudkewicz, 563

Cudkiewicz, 349, 354

Czarniecki, 2, 5

Czernobrody, 571

D

Danziger, 216, 218

Davidovicz, 347, 351

Davidson, 584

Degala, 129, 130, 420, 531

Degola, 187, 363

Dembowicz, 526

Digala, 559

Dimant, 581

Dobraszklanka, 112, 117, 177, 186

Dobrechowski, 571

Dobrochowski, 558

Dobroshklanka, 50, 59

Dobroszklanka, 77, 87, 129, 138, 139, 142, 193, 264, 265, 274, 312, 316, 318, 326, 370, 476, 505, 558, 571, 578

Dobrzinski, 75, 558, 571

Dobrzynski, 136, 400, 517, 559

Dobzhinsker, 379

Dor, 50, 77, 87, 129, 134, 139, 142, 144, 186, 193, 230, 264, 274, 312, 313, 316, 318, 320, 326, 370, 476, 505, 578

Dragan, 559

Dratwa, 331, 332, 378, 444, 461, 475, 485, 486, 558, 559, 568, 576, 614

Drogen, 373

Dubin, 612

Dzabete, 558

Dzaldow, 559, 614

Dzialdow, 48, 89, 237, 349, 350, 375, 378, 412, 419, 543

Dzialynski, 2

E

Eisenberg, 557, 581, 613

Eizberg, 198

Eizik, 557

Engler, 457, 562, 614

Epstein, 323

Eshel, 134, 135, 237, 274, 275, 276, 277, 325, 557, 571

Even–Shayish, 202, 207

F

Fajwel, 95

Fein, 102, 110, 152

Field, 40, 532, 586, 589, 590

Fin, 65, 612

Fisher, 563, 569

Flamenbaum, 584

Flato, 584

Florman, 105, 110, 289, 298, 301, 517

Flusberg, 1, 2, 6, 7, 8, 13, 15, 40, 44, 50, 58, 64, 68, 69, 70, 73, 77, 95, 97, 98, 110, 116, 120, 129, 132, 135, 145, 147, 148, 159, 161, 162, 163, 170, 175, 188, 189, 193, 198, 202, 209, 212, 219, 224, 227, 230, 238, 249, 258, 261, 264, 267, 269, 272, 274, 278, 281, 284, 286, 289, 296, 299, 302, 304, 307, 312, 314, 316, 318, 321, 323, 326, 328, 334, 339, 341, 342, 347, 349, 354, 355, 359, 361, 363, 370, 375, 378, 384, 385, 387, 390, 394, 397, 407, 413, 420, 422, 426, 430, 453, 476, 478, 485, 494, 497, 502, 505, 507, 553, 557

Fogel, 87, 112, 117, 142, 195, 247, 312, 313, 314, 397, 554, 555, 562, 569, 571

Frager, 400, 444

Frajlich, 270

Frantz, 570

Freida, 112, 214, 216, 570

Freilich, 192, 377, 562, 563, 584

Frenkel, 56, 482, 563, 577, 584

Frenkiel, 164, 349

Friedman, 563, 582, 615

Fuchs, 199

Fuks, 563, 569

Fuleder, 563

Furgacz, 563

G

Gallikus, 4

Gasior, 349

Geller, 558

Ger, 29, 106, 159, 207, 224, 226, 237, 349, 353, 363, 367, 376, 378, 383, 497, 501

Gerstein, 584

Getzel, 159

Glitzenstein, 135, 526, 558

Globus, 41, 42, 497, 498, 502

Golan, 147, 170, 173, 248, 579

Gold, 62, 69, 99, 107, 172, 174, 483, 558

Goldberg, 87, 117, 142, 189, 318, 320, 417, 422, 558, 571, 582, 613, 614

Goldbojm, 583

Goldbrach, 378, 558

Goldbruch, 270

Goldfaden, 38

Goldfeder, 345, 408, 584, 612

Goldfinger, 176, 379

Goldman, 98, 558, 571, 613

Goldmann, 509

Goldring, 558

Golomb, 394, 558

Gonsher, 377, 558, 613

Gorni, 97, 558

Gorny, 112, 175, 193, 394, 478, 570, 614

Gotleib, 614

Gotlieb, 558

Gottfarstein, 607

Gottlieb, 394, 525, 573

Grabski, 516, 543

Granat, 133, 135, 143, 202, 205, 206, 207, 219, 221, 249, 267, 281, 282, 283, 334, 337, 361, 571

Graner, 312, 390, 391, 402, 489, 490, 492, 493

Grayevsky, 204, 250

Greber, 558

Greenberg, 584

Groibard, 497

Groner, 80, 270, 387, 558, 566, 583

Grosman, 270

Gruberd, 41

Gruenbaum, 241, 248, 554

Grunem, 23

Gur, 16, 22, 29, 41, 92, 94, 98, 106

Gurfinkel, 160, 270, 349, 558

Gurfinkiel, 349

Gursky, 584

Gutglas, 558, 578, 584

Gutglass, 364

Gutglaz, 139, 613

Gutmorgen, 269, 377, 378, 480, 558

H

Hachshara, 81, 82, 89, 107, 134, 271

Hakoach, 80, 82, 87, 89, 142, 312, 313, 318, 320

Halevi, 145, 146, 228, 251, 252, 256, 335, 340

Harpaz, 5, 7, 12, 13, 29, 40, 48, 54, 68, 72, 75, 87, 97, 106, 114, 118, 126, 130, 134, 143, 146, 147, 157, 162, 168, 174, 188, 191, 195, 201, 206, 211, 217, 222, 226, 228, 236, 247, 255, 260, 263, 266, 267, 271, 273, 277, 280, 283, 285, 288, 295, 298, 301, 303, 306, 311, 313, 315, 317, 320, 322, 325, 327, 332, 337, 340, 341, 346, 353, 358, 360, 362, 367, 374, 382, 389, 393, 396, 401, 412, 418, 421, 424, 429, 451, 476, 483, 488, 496, 500, 504, 506, 540, 555, 585

Harris, 568, 613

Hartbrat, 614

Hartbrod, 20, 126

Hartbrot, 80, 133, 136, 137, 397, 559, 571, 581

Hashomer Hatzair, 71, 80, 89, 98, 99, 100, 101, 104, 106, 263, 278, 280, 296, 308, 311, 314, 315, 532

Hassid, 21, 23, 44, 47, 48, 133, 138, 207, 224, 264, 272, 377, 379, 390, 419, 507, 579

Hassidim, 22, 33, 37, 41, 44, 45, 49, 56, 59, 78, 88, 92, 98, 130, 159, 202, 203, 208, 224, 231,

242, 264, 267, 347, 375, 376, 379, 483, 497, 508, 535, 549

Hassidism, 23, 202, 208, 363, 376, 378

Hechalutz, 80, 81, 82, 89, 312, 313, 318, 320

Hertz, 18, 375, 559

Hertzke, 27, 559

Hirsh, 79, 80, 83, 167, 198, 230, 231, 232, 233, 236, 267, 268, 272, 289, 316, 377, 379, 380, 384, 400, 444, 491, 535, 559, 561, 565, 566, 572, 573, 581

Holtz, 102, 117, 318, 378, 559, 581

Holz, 125

Horowitz, 159, 269, 559, 614

I

Isaac, 6, 22, 133, 134, 135, 138, 199, 209, 222, 256, 272, 316, 400, 415, 417, 460, 499, 502, 519, 533, 544, 545, 561, 571, 597, 608

J

Jagiello, 3

Jalowski, 399, 400

Januar, 272, 560

Japuncik, 560

Jendzejewicz, 560, 614

Jordan, 568

Jospe, 560

Juricze, 560

K

Kaczer, 565

Kadecki, 269, 270, 271, 564

Kadish, 564

Kahn, 236, 482, 564, 565, 569, 577

Kalischer, 16, 29

Kalish, 207, 376, 383, 385

Kanicer, 564

Kanitzer, 564

Kankowalski, 444

Kantor, 569

Kariv, 252

Karpa, 272, 565

Katcher, 203, 219, 221, 222, 426, 444, 533, 577, 584

Katchor, 500

Katz, 444

Kaufering, 471, 478

Kay, 215, 594

Kazak, 615

Keller, 565, 615

Kesler, 570

Khmelnytsky, 30

Kipnis, 81

Kirschner, 391

Kirshenbaum, 569

Kirshtein, 615

Kirstein, 460, 565

Kive, 564, 565

Klapman, 584

Klein, 78, 564, 569

Kohn, 44, 48, 83, 138, 198, 230, 231, 232, 233, 234, 235, 236, 272, 342, 344, 349, 351, 377, 379, 384, 391, 444, 517, 530, 535

Kokavka, 615

Kook, 204, 219, 222, 252

Kopernik School, 178, 179, 180, 181

Kopland, 166

Koppeld, 615

Korczak, 103, 109

Kowalski, 23, 166, 508, 541, 565, 615

Kozak, 565

Krajanek, 361, 564

Krantz, 387, 565

Kristal, 212, 215, 216, 217, 261, 564, 594, 595, 596

Kristall, 594

Krulik, 394

Krystal, 430

Kszeczanowski, 99, 104, 105, 564

Kufeld, 564, 565

Kufler, 379

Kukawka, 565

Kutner, 78, 313, 564

Kuzak, 151, 564

L

Lahav, 102, 108, 278, 280

Laks, 79, 267, 268, 560, 569

Landau, 196, 229, 391

Landberg, 444

Landsberg, 29, 313, 561, 568, 614

Lansburg, 471

Lasher, 444

Layzerowit, 561

Lefkowitz, 568, 584

Leizerowit, 614

Lenet, 561

Lent, 58, 63, 64, 444, 479, 532, 614

Leshnick, 584

Leshnik, 614

Lesznik, 162, 561

Levin, 398, 561

Levinson, 83, 528, 569, 614

Lewin, 350

Lewinson, 560, 561

Lewiston, 96

Lewkowicz, 379

Lezkovski, 335

Lichtenfeld, 78, 85, 113, 115, 397, 448, 449, 561, 568, 573, 592

Lichtenstein, 15, 48, 412, 419, 572

Lichterz, 577

Lidzbarski, 561

Lidzberski, 112

Lifschitz, 577

Lignica, 493

Lipka, 65, 79, 87, 101, 105, 133, 134, 139, 142, 176, 179, 196, 197, 211, 229, 284, 388, 390, 428, 476, 496, 504, 507, 509, 511, 512, 516, 537, 538, 539, 540, 541, 560, 561, 568, 572, 614

Lipke, 6, 614

Lipman, 142, 444, 565, 576, 577

Lipshitz, 560, 561

Lipski, 350, 561

Lipstadt, 59, 165, 166

Lipsztadt, 379

Lipsztat, 561

Lodzki, 29, 237, 367

Lord, 10, 40, 89, 98, 110, 251, 311, 315, 485, 547, 550, 551, 561, 607, 608, 610

Lozar, 102

Luks, 568

M

Lurd, 406

Lurie, 560

Luster, 568

Luzzatto, 252, 257

Mages, 13, 36, 41, 56, 90, 93

Makowski, 164, 561

Manke, 561, 562, 581

Mapu, 111, 114

Markish, 111, 114

Maszkewicz, 562

Maszkowicz, 561

Meir, 52, 56, 95, 99, 104, 105, 110, 124, 128, 159, 167, 218, 230, 236, 261, 270, 272, 336, 372, 376, 377, 378, 379, 383, 394, 396, 399, 497, 549, 557, 558, 559, 560, 563, 564, 565, 566, 568, 575, 576, 579, 580, 581, 597, 613

Meiri, 93, 212, 238, 261, 262, 263, 553, 594

Melamed, 35, 80, 83, 93, 94, 312, 313, 363, 561, 565

Memel, 561, 562

Menashe, 87, 105, 110, 117, 139, 142, 558, 613

Mendelson, 394, 528, 562

Mileikowski, 532

Milifyes, 444

Miller, 160, 378, 379, 397, 400, 486, 561, 569

Minisewski, 212

Minivski, 238, 261, 553

Miniwski, 93, 262

Minski, 572

Minsky, 379

Mishke, 561

Moti, 227

Motzkin, 241, 248, 554

Muller, 349, 350

Munter, 562

N

Nagurski, 562

Nawolski, 562

Neuman, 562

Newman, 336, 584

Nobleski, 444

Nordau, 209, 211, 241, 247, 502, 504

Nowalski, 394, 399

Nusbaum, 569

Nusboym, 562

Nussbaum, 166, 470

O

Ofenbach, 489, 532, 583

Offenbach, 76, 79, 99, 101, 199, 278, 286, 507, 557, 571, 613

Oranienburg, 470, 471, 477

Orbach, 557, 577

Ordau, 557

Otwock, 37, 77, 88, 133, 134, 203, 207, 267, 363, 368, 383, 508, 527, 536, 541, 549

P

Paczecha, 569

Patchek, 444

Paznewski, 61

Peretz, 111, 114, 130, 149, 209, 211

Perger, 78

Piaskowski, 95

Piechatka, 562

Piechotke, 378

Pieniek, 176, 179, 180, 181, 182, 193, 194, 391, 399, 401, 413, 562, 563

Pierce, 569

Pilat, 563

Pilsudski, 52

Pincewski, 563

Pinczewski, 116, 399, 401

Pinkus, 335

Plansker, 563

Platner, 575

Platniarz, 563, 574, 575

Plocker, 391, 563

Plotner, 612

Plotniarz, 359, 361, 388, 392, 571

Plotnirsh, 346

Plucki, 584

Posmer, 584

Postolski, 563, 582

Postolsky, 95

Pozmanter, 176, 349, 563, 591

Poznonski, 563

Prager, 378, 563, 573

Prilucki, 532

Prince Dobrzyn, 3

Prum, 98, 112, 117, 166, 175, 193, 397, 447, 478, 483, 517, 533, 562, 614

Pszuk, 563

Pszuwieszewski, 80

R

Rabbi Brod, 23, 196, 508

Rabinowitz, 114, 250, 252, 256, 401

Ragenstein, 565

Rapaport, 565, 566, 570, 578

Rapocki, 566

Rappaport, 112, 397

Rashish, 81

Rebe, 142, 565, 582, 583, 587

Rebi, 166

Reines, 249, 255, 508, 541

Riesenfeld, 87, 99, 107, 115, 171, 199, 238, 239, 240, 242, 244, 245, 246, 248, 349, 354, 423, 509, 553, 554, 555, 566

Rimon, 36, 135, 136, 143, 202, 203, 205, 206, 219, 249, 254, 258, 260, 267, 281, 282, 283, 334, 337, 339, 340, 341, 361, 500, 533, 571

Rirzow, 566

Riszaw, 615

Riz, 152

Rogenstein, 584

Rojna, 48, 75, 78, 194, 517

Rosen, 101, 105, 326, 566, 570, 571

Rosenbaum, 241, 248, 328, 329, 332, 584

Rosenman, 566

Rosenthal, 159

Rosenwaks, 62, 73, 120, 132, 138, 144, 147, 155, 170, 173, 224, 248, 270, 302, 303, 323, 325, 330, 342, 430, 446, 450, 476, 544, 571, 579

Rosenzweig, 584

Rothman, 580, 583

Rozenwaks, 44, 47, 379, 380, 397, 419

Rozenwax, 13, 90, 597

Rubashov, 399, 401

Rubenstein, 23, 348

Ruda, 99, 107, 198, 199, 200, 398, 400, 565

Rudzink, 160

Ruina, 231, 565, 570, 584

Ruine, 565

Rujna, 117

Rukman, 565

Rusak, 400, 523, 532, 565

Rusk, 80, 112, 571

Ruska, 441, 444

Russ, 402

Rytov, 241

Ryz, 163, 565, 566, 571, 592, 597

S

Sachs, 397, 398, 399

Salamon, 562

Salomon, 349

Sanger, 48, 89, 237, 375, 379, 412, 419, 543

Sapersztajn, 350, 357, 577

Sapirstein, 562

Sawa, 615

Sawe, 562

Schaeffer, 612

Scheinbart, 391

Schlachter, 151, 391

Schlechter, 95

Schoenbart, 612

Schwab, 250, 256

Sentor, 580

Sforim, 111, 114, 240, 247

Shaigetz, 533

Shamash, 126, 349, 368, 560

Shapira, 56, 269

Shazar, 399, 401, 590

Shedletzky, 188

Shefer, 391

Sheinbart, 615

Shevikowski, 272

Shilski, 566

Shivak, 572

Shivek, 284, 285

Shleifstein, 102, 108

Shlesinger, 359, 361, 388, 570

Shliepak, 521

Shlomo, 27, 117, 133, 136, 137, 184, 250, 252, 350, 355, 375, 378, 391, 397, 407, 444, 559, 560, 561, 562, 563, 566, 569, 571, 576, 577, 580, 581

Shmuel, 18, 23, 80, 93, 152, 166, 167, 199, 212, 216, 217, 229, 238, 261, 263, 284, 335, 377, 380, 384, 397, 447, 517, 532, 553, 558, 559, 561, 562, 563, 564, 565, 566, 568, 571, 577, 582, 597

Shneour, 173

Shochetman, 23

Shoenbart, 584

Sholom-Aleichem, 110, 111, 113, 115

Shperling, 70, 80, 87

Shulsinger, 346

Shurek, 566

Silberstein, 568, 575

Siskind, 100, 256

Skop, 562

Skurnik, 562

Slutsky, 604

Smozhik, 614

Smuzszik, 562

Smuzyk, 394

Sobel, 612

Sokolow, 209, 211, 502, 504

Solomon, 34, 256, 263, 527, 549, 569

Sonabend, 41, 43, 78, 79, 80, 92, 193, 209, 264, 266, 375, 389, 496, 497, 499, 502, 508, 518

Sonnabend, 400

Sosnovitch, 613

Sova, 566, 577

Sperling, 100, 215, 289, 296, 301, 304, 306, 311, 566, 572

Steinman, 204, 250

Stencel, 567

Sterling, 142

Stolno, 4

Stoltzman, 160, 453, 460, 473

Stolzman, 566

Suchedol, 562

Surgal, 569

Swedes, 4

Szaijnbart, 425

Szajnbart, 566

Szeinbart, 87, 142, 229

Szimanski, 566, 581

Szlachter, 71, 270, 566

Szmiga, 75, 82, 89, 231, 237, 348, 354, 377, 384, 410, 412, 487, 517, 543, 566, 581, 615

Sztetyn, 349

T

Techursh, 23

Teitelboim, 378, 560

Tidhar, 334, 336

Tinski, 363, 365, 366, 405, 479, 483, 526, 560

Tinsky, 395

Toib, 347, 375

Topol, 87, 560

Trunk, 508, 541

Tschenstochau, 420, 421

Turkewicz, 560

Turkewitz, 87

Tzala, 424, 453, 461, 473, 474, 550, 563

Tzarna, 563

Tzernobroda, 577

Tzidkewicz, 391

Tzudkewicz, 563

Tzudkovich, 296

Tzukevich, 521

U

Ulstein, 151, 152

Ussishkin, 241, 248, 554

V

Vinkor, 278, 286, 571

Vizelberg, 571

W

Waldenberg, 52, 105, 372, 379, 399, 559, 568

Warsaw Ghetto, 103, 189, 293, 414, 591

Warshawski, 342, 343, 344, 559, 580

Warszawski, 116, 398

Warszoi, 577

Weinshenker, 568

Weismel, 614

Weissmel, 559, 568

Weizmann, 220

Wier, 444

Wiur, 559

Wolff, 22, 113, 115, 267, 268, 284, 453, 473, 560, 563, 565, 569

Wrzos, 116, 376, 378, 397, 400, 496, 614

Wuzszus, 559

Y

Yaakov, 17, 19, 21, 23, 30, 36, 37, 46, 48, 75, 82, 93, 96, 97, 101, 105, 114, 117, 129, 130, 135, 166, 190, 198, 199, 202, 203, 205, 207, 208, 219, 222, 231, 249, 252, 255, 260, 267, 269, 270, 272, 281, 330, 331, 334, 337, 339, 341, 348, 365, 366, 376, 377, 378, 379, 380, 390, 391, 394, 397, 399, 400, 410, 413, 430, 444, 448, 449, 475, 476, 480, 483, 489, 490, 492, 500, 508, 516, 517, 521, 525, 531, 557, 558, 559, 560, 562, 564, 565, 566, 571, 574, 576, 577, 579, 580, 581, 582, 583, 613, 615

Yakir, 398, 431, 444, 568

Yalowski, 321, 571

Yanuar, 349, 378, 379

Yavetz, 202, 207

Yendziewicz, 379

Yeshayahu, 264, 265, 571, 574, 580

Yeshayowitz, 137, 430, 431

Yeshiwitz, 571

Yom Tov, 517, 560

Yosef, 16, 18, 37, 83, 87, 100, 136, 138, 144, 190, 194, 198, 199, 200, 202, 203, 231, 249, 250, 251, 253, 254, 256, 258, 260, 270, 272, 279, 280, 349, 350, 367, 377, 378, 392, 398, 399, 400, 448, 449, 453, 473, 494, 507, 527, 533, 558, 559, 561, 562, 563, 564, 565, 566, 568, 571, 576, 577, 580, 582, 583, 613, 614

Z

Zabytski, 118, 212, 216, 217, 224, 261, 375, 378, 380, 382, 389, 408, 558, 561, 564, 565

Zacklow, 584

Zaklikovski, 398

Zaklikowski, 102, 349, 399, 400, 411, 444, 494, 495, 507, 531, 560, 580, 581, 614

Zaremba, 60, 61, 565

Zatok, 560

Zbicki, 404

Zeidner, 379

Zeitlin, 249, 255, 532

Zelig, 560, 565, 567

Zeliger, 250, 255

Zeligfeld, 81

Zelkowicz, 559

Zeromski, 80

Zerubabel, 532

Zilberman, 444, 559, 560

Zilberstein, 560

Zisshoif, 394, 396

Zissholtz, 349, 394, 396, 444, 560

Zudkevitz, 59, 61, 63, 148, 156, 289, 294, 295

Zudkewicz, 70, 72, 397, 533

Zudkewitz, 80, 87, 100, 301, 311, 571

Zudkiewic, 117

Zygmunt, 2, 3, 5

Zylberberg, 349

Appendix: Additions to Holocaust Necrology, Extracted from Articles in Yizkor Book

By Allen Flusberg

Family name(s)	First name(s)	Sex	Marital status	Father's name	Name of spouse	Additional family members	Remarks	Original Yizkor Book Page
ALTYNA	Bina	F						213
ARFA	Kalman	M				and family	Administrator of *Poalei-Tzion* organization. See Note 1.	264-269; 443
ARNOW	Miriam (nee Rosenwaks)	F	married	Zalman ("Zalman Hassid")	Binyamin Aharon	6 children		58; 457
ARNOW	Binyamin Aharon	M	married		Miriam (nee Rosenwaks)			457
ARNOW	Yisrael Hersh	M		Binyamin Aharon				457
ARNOW	Yaakov Yehoshua	M		Binyamin Aharon				457
ARNOW	Meir Neta	M		Binyamin Aharon				457
ARNOW	Yechiel	M		Binyamin Aharon				457
ARNOW	Tzerka	F		Binyamin Aharon				457
BELDIGER	Avraham	M	married		Sarah Rivka			456

Family name(s)	First name(s)	Sex	Marital status	Father's name	Name of spouse	Additional family members	Remarks	Original Yizkor Book Page
BELDIGER	Aharon	M				and family		456
BELDIGER	Yaakov	M				and family		456
BELDIGER	Yosef	M				and family		456
BERGMAN	Hersh Natan	M	married		Rivka			458
BERGMAN	Rivka	F	married		Hersh Natan			458
BERGMAN	Shmuel	M	married	Hersh Natan		and children		458
BERGMAN	Luba	F	married	Hersh Natan		and children	nee Bergman	458
BERMAN	Hersh Ber	M					taught classes in Large Ger Shtiebl	285-291
BLAUZEG	Yoel	M					Dentist. See Note 1.	244
BRAUN	Yoel	M	married					458
BRAUN	Chana Sara	F		Yoel				458
BRAUN	Motl	M		Yoel				458
BRAUN	Yosef Gershon	M		Yoel				458
CHMIELNICKI	Yosef	M	married		Sara (nee Goldberg)			458
CHMIELNICKI	Sara (nee Goldberg)	F	married	Shmuel	Yosef			458
CHMIELNICKI	Rachel	F		Yosef				458
CHMIELNICKI	Avraham	M		Yosef				458
COHEN		M	married				Deported from Warsaw Ghetto to a death camp.	318
COHEN		F	married				Deported from Warsaw Ghetto to a death camp.	318
COHEN	Ita	F					Deported from Warsaw Ghetto to a death camp.	318

Family name(s)	First name(s)	Sex	Marital status	Father's name	Name of spouse	Additional family members	Remarks	Original Yizkor Book Page
DEGALA?		M	married				p. 73 states cantor of town executed ~Sep 1939 near Golub fortress; pp. 118, 432 indicate town cantor was named Degala. But see Note 3.	73; 118; 432
DOBROSZKLANKA	Leib	M		Azriel				456
DOBROSZKLANKA	Zalman	M	married	Azriel	Malka			456
DOBROSZKLANKA	Malka	F	married		Zalman			456
DOBROSZKLANKA	Toibe	F		Azriel				456
DOBROSZKLANKA	Feivil	M		Azriel				456
DRATWA	Yaakov Henich	M					"baal koreh" (=Torah reader) in Large Ger Shtiebl	285-291
DRATWA	Lipman	M	married		Shoshana			455
DRATWA	Shoshana	F	married		Lipman			455
DRATWA	Avrohom	M		Lipman				455
DRATWA	Leah	F		Lipman				455
DRATWA	Hersh Yaakov	M						455
DRATWA	Feige	F		Lipman				455
DRATWA	Miriam	F		Lipman				455
DRATWA	Yosef Yitzchok	M						455
DZIALDOW		M					See Note 1.	264-269
DZIALDOW		F					See Note 2.	264-269

Family name(s)	First name(s)	Sex	Marital status	Father's name	Name of spouse	Additional family members	Remarks	Original Yizkor Book Page
DZIALDOW		F					child of woman named Dzialdow. See Note 2.	264-269
ENGLER	Nachman	M					soldier in Polish army; shot by the Germans as a Jewish POW, ~1939	359
FLUSBERG	Mordechai Elya (Elly, Eliahu)	M	married		Esther Leah (nee Lesznik)		Photograph: p. 139. Tasked with calling men up to Torah in Large Ger Shtiebl. 59 years old, "an ill, broken-down man". See Note 1.	264-269; 137-138, 288.
FLUSBERG	David	M		Mordechai Elya			Photograph: p. 139. See Note 1.	137-138
FRAJLICH	Esther	F						213
FRENKIEL		M					executed ~Sep 1939 near Golub fortress	73, 264-269
FRIEDMAN	Lipa	M	married		Bella (nee Goldberg)	and children		458
FRIEDMAN	Bella	F	married	Shmuel	Lipa	and children		458
FRIEDMAN	Chaya	F		Lipa				458
FRIEDMAN	Munik	M		Lipa				458
GANSIOR	Yosef Binyomin	M					Age 60. See Note 1.	264-269
GOLDBERG	Yosef Gershon	M		Shmuel			shot dead by Germans in Warsaw when he could not fit into a truck headed for Auschwitz	161-163; 458

Family name(s)	First name(s)	Sex	Marital status	Father's name	Name of spouse	Additional family members	Remarks	Original Yizkor Book Page
GOLDBERG	Yaakov Moshe	M		Shmuel			executed by hanging after he was caught trying to escape from a death camp	161-163; 458
GOLDBERG	Shmuel ("Shmulik")	M			Masha			444, 458
GOLDBERG	Masha	F	married		Shmuel			444, 458
GOLDBERG	Rachel	F		Shmuel				458
GOLDBERG	Feige Toibe	F						458
GOLDBERG	Yoachim	M					son of Feige Toibe	458
GOLDBOYM	Gutshe (nee Rebe)	F	married		A. Golboym	1 child		459
GOLDBOYM	A.	M	married		Gutshe	1 child		459
GOLDBROCH	Hillel Ovadya	M					gabbai (sexton) of Large Ger Shtiebl	285-291
GOLDBROCH	Hinda	F						213
GOLDBROCH	Yente	F						213
GROINE	Avraham	M	married		Michle			459
GROINE	Michle	F	married		Avraham			459
GRONER	Tultza	F						213
GROSMAN	Sara	F						213
GURFINKEL	Chana (nee Flusberg)	F			Mendel			213
GURFINKEL	Mendel	M			Chana		*a shochet* (ritual slaughterer). See Note 1.	138, 213, 264-269
GURFINKEL	Avrohom	M					See Note 1.	264-269

Family name(s)	First name(s)	Sex	Marital status	Father's name	Name of spouse	Additional family members	Remarks	Original Yizkor Book Page
GUTGLAS	Yetta (nee Dobroszklanka)	F	married	Azriel		and children		456
GUTGLAS	Azriel	M	married		Yetta	and children		456
GUTMORGEN	Yechiel Meir	M			Pasya		chairman, Agudas Yisroel	285-291
GUTMORGEN	Pasya	F			Yechiel Meir		headed Bais Yaakov girls' school	285-291, 214
HOLTZ	Mendl	M	married		Sara Devora			458
HOLTZ	Sara Devora	F	married		Mendl			458
HOLTZ	Bertz	M	married			wife and 2 children		458
HOLTZ	Shlomo	M	married		Nechama (nee Eisenberg)	2 children		458
HOLTZ	Nechama (nee Eisenberg)	F	married		Shlomo	2 children		458
HOLTZ	Aharon	M	married		Eva (nee Motil)	2 children		458
HOLTZ	Eva (nee Motil)	F	married		Aharon	2 children		458
HOLTZ	Yisrael	M		Mendl				458
HOLTZ	Rachel	F		Mendl				458
HOLTZ	Feige	F		Mendl				458
HOLTZ	Luba	F		Mendl				458
HOROWICZ	Elyakim (Itshe) Meir	M	married		Bayla Frumit (nee Flusberg)			213; 445
HOROWICZ	Bayla Frumit (nee Flusberg)	F	married		Elyakim Meir			213, 443

Family name(s)	First name(s)	Sex	Marital status	Father's name	Name of spouse	Additional family members	Remarks	Original Yizkor Book Page
HOROWICZ	Yaakov	M		Elyakim Meir				213
HOROWICZ	Avraham Yosef	M		Elyakim Meir				213
HOROWICZ	Hinda	F		Elyakim Meir				213
HOROWICZ	Baruch Mendel	M		Elyakim Meir				213
HOROWICZ	Sheina	F		Elyakim Meir				213
HURYNOWICZ	Amram	M	married		Devorah (nee Sova)	and cihldren		456
HURYNOWICZ	Devorah	F	married		Amram	and children		456
KACZOR	Lipman	M	married		Elka			456
KADECKI	Chana	F						213
KATCHER	Zalman Boruch	M	married		Tsirl	5 children		329
KATCHER	Tsirl	F	married		Zalman Boruch	5 children		329
KATCHER	Avrohom Yisroel	M	married		Miriam	5 children		329
KATCHER	Miriam	F	married		Avrohom Yisroel	5 children		329
KATCHER	Zisl	F						329
KOHN	Oizer	M					Age 64. See Note 1.	264-269
KOHN	Mendel	M					Court alderman, parnas (chief administrative officer) of community	285-291
KUFLER	Yaakov Yehoshua	M					gabbai (sexton), Aleksander Shtiebl	285-291
LANDSBERG	Yosef	M	married	Manos		wife and 6 children	Photo, p. 36	447
LEWIN	Lemel	M					See Note 2.	264-269
LICHTERZ		M	married		Bracha (nee Sova)	and children		456

Family name(s)	First name(s)	Sex	Marital status	Father's name	Name of spouse	Additional family members	Remarks	Original Yizkor Book Page
LICHTERZ	Bracha (nee Sova)	F	married			and children		456
LIFSCHITZ	Aharon	M						456
LIFSCHITZ	Arye	M						456
LIFSCHITZ	Rachel Leah	F						456
LIFSCHITZ	Chana	F						456
LIPKA	Ruchtza	F					killed in Minsk Mazowiecki ghetto, 1942	150-160
LIPSKI	Shlomo Yosef	M					See Note 2.	285-291
LIPSZTADT	Leibl	M					executed ~Sep 1939 near Golub fortress	73
MAKOWSKI	Avraham	M					led "musaf" prayer service in Large Ger Shtiebl. (May be identical to Yisrael Muller, Note 1.)	285-291
MILLER	Yisroel	M						
MILLER	Leib	M					Became political officer in Soviet Polish army. Taken prisoner by Germans in battle in forests of Bydgoszcz, 1944, and executed when he was found to be a Jew.	385
MINIVSKI	Sarah Leah	F					trainee in the Shomer Hatzair	209

Family name(s)	First name(s)	Sex	Marital status	Father's name	Name of spouse	Additional family members	Remarks	Original Yizkor Book Page
MINIVSKI	Esther Devora	F					trainee in the Shomer Hatzair	209
MINIVSKI	Fraydl	F	married			husband, 2 little children	nee Minivski	209
MULLER	Yisrael	M					See Note 1. (Distinct from man with same name, Note 2.)	264-269
MULLER	Yisroel	M				wife and 10 children	See Note 2. (Distinct from man with same name, Note 1.	264-269
NUSSBAUM	Yitzchak	M					Last seen Nov, 1944, on train leaving Auschwitz for Germany at Gliwice (near Auschwitz)	376
OFENBACH	Yaakov	M	married		Liebe			459
OFENBACH	Liebe	F	married		Yaakov			459
PIECHOTKE	Yisroel Meir	M						285-291
PIENIEK	Sali	M	married				murdered by SS men Dec 24 1942 in Minsk Mazowiecki ghetto	150-160
PIENIEK	Ruth	F		Sali			young girl, murdered by SS men Dec 24 1942 in Minsk Mazowiecki ghetto	150-160
PIENIEK		F	married		Sali		perished in Treblinka	150-160
PIENIEK		F					nee Pieniek; sister of Sali. Perished in Treblinka	150-160

Family name(s)	First name(s)	Sex	Marital status	Father's name	Name of spouse	Additional family members	Remarks	Original Yizkor Book Page
PIENIEK	Franya	F					shot dead by Germans after digging her own grave in Minsk Mazowiecki ghetto, 1942	150-160
POSTOLSKI	Yosef	M	married					458
POSTOLSKI	Avraham Natan	M		Yosef				458
POSTOLSKI	Gershon	M		Yosef				458
POSTOLSKI	Feige	F		Yosef				458
POSTOLSKI	Leibl	M		Yosef				458
POZMANTER	Moishe	M	m		Malka	2 sons murdered with him	See Note 1, based on pp. 264-269. English p. 11: "assembled and shot"	264-269; English 11
POZMANTER	Malka	F	m		Moishe	2 daughters murdered with her	murdered in 1942 in Treblinka	
PRAGER	Shoul	M						285-291
PULEDER	Chana	F						459
REBE	Isser	M	married			wife and 2 children		458
REBE	Anshil	M	married			wife and 1 child		458
REBE	Avraham	M	married			wife and 1 child		458

Family name(s)	First name(s)	Sex	Marital status	Father's name	Name of spouse	Additional family members	Remarks	Original Yizkor Book Page
RIESENFELD	Adolf Abraham	M	married		Johanna		Photograph: p. 194. Pharmacist of Golub and Zionist leader. First town victim of Germans, taken away by Germans Sep 1939	145-148; 193-200; 452
RIESENFELD	Johanna	F	married		Adolf Abraham			193-200; 452
ROINE	Shmuel Moshe	M					*mohel* (performed circumcisions)	285-291
ROSEN	Nachum	M	married			and family		451
ROSENWAKS	Gela	F						213
ROSENWAKS	Avraham Yaakov	M	married	Zalman ("Zalman Hassid")	Chana	7 children		457; 58; 145-148
ROSENWAKS	Chaim	M	married	Avraham Yaakov		wife and children		457
ROTHMAN	Frimet (nee Rebe)	F	married		D. Rothman	2 children		459
ROTHMAN	D.	M	married		Frimet (nee Rebe)	2 children		459

Family name(s)	First name(s)	Sex	Marital status	Father's name	Name of spouse	Additional family members	Remarks	Original Yizkor Book Page
RUDA	Yosef Chaim	M	married		Rivka		Photograph: p. 172. Escaped from Dobrzyn to the countryside in 1939. Died of illness while hiding out in a farmer's house.	171-173
RUDA	Rivka	F			Yosef Chaim		After husband's death reached Warsaw, where she testified about her experiences.	171-173, 451
RUDA	Esther Yehudit (Yudka)	F		Yosef Chaim				171-173
RUDA	Pinchas	M		Yosef Chaim				171-173
RUDA	Perl Leah	F		Yosef Chaim			was living in Kutno before war broke out	171
RUDA							was living in Vienna before war broke out. Caught after Germans took Vienna and sent to a concentration camp, where she perished.	
RYZ		F	married			2 sons and 5 daughters	mother of essay author Yitzhak Ryz (pp. 140-144)	140-144
SANGER	Nentshe	F	married	Mendl Kohn	Nathan Sanger			285-291

Family name(s)	First name(s)	Sex	Marital status	Father's name	Name of spouse	Additional family members	Remarks	Original Yizkor Book Page
SANGER	Yitzhak Dov	M		Nathan Sanger				285-291
SANGER	Meir	M		Nathan Sanger				285-291
SAPERSZTAJN	Mendl	M					See Note 2.	264-269
SHAFRAN	Avrohom	M	married		Perl, nee Katcher	5 children		329
SHAFRAN	Perl	F	married	Katcher	Avrohom	5 children		329
SHAMASH	Itzik	M					See Note 1.	264-269
SHEINBERG	Mindl (nee Zaklikowski)	F	married		Meir	3 daughters		458
SHPERLING	Moshe	M	married		Feige			73
SHPERLING	Feige	M	married	Zudkewicz	Moshe			73
SHPERLING	Reizel	F		Moshe				73
SHPERLING	Tzipora	F		Moshe				73
SOCHACZEWSKI	Nesanel	M					a *shochet* (ritual slaughterer), originated in Czechoczinek	285-291
SOLOMON	Mordechai	M					Chairman of Social Institutions of town. See Note 1.	
SOVA	Zalman	M	married		Bilhah			456
SOVA	Bilhah	F	married		Zalman			456
SOVA	Bendet	M	married			and family		456
SOVA	Pinchas	M	married		Michal	and children		456
SOVA	Michal	F	married		Pinchas	and children		456
SOVA	Yitzhak Yaakov	M				and family		456
STOLTZMAN	Avrohom	M	married		Rochel			380
STOLTZMAN	Rochel (nee Tzala)	F	married		Avrohom			380
SZLACHTER	Neche	F						213

Family name(s)	First name(s)	Sex	Marital status	Father's name	Name of spouse	Additional family members	Remarks	Original Yizkor Book Page
SZLECKA	Henye	F						213
SZMIGA	Yitzchok Yaakov	M	married		Feige		taken away by SS men, autumn of 1939, and apparently executed. Photo with wife and grandchild on p. 316.	264-269; 458
SZMIGA	Feige	F	married		Yitzhak Yaakov			458
SZMIGA	David	M	married	Yitzhak Yaakov	Leah (nee Szimanski)			458
SZMIGA	Yisrael	M		David				458
SZMIGA	Moshe Hirsh	M		David				458
SZTETYN	Meir Henich	M					See Note 1.	264-269
TEITELBOIM	Meir Henich	M	married		Chana Malka		taught classes in Large Ger Shtiebl	285-291, 446
TINSKI	Leon	M					soldier in Soviet army; disappeared at end of war	381
TZALA	Shloime	M					shot by SS officer on a street of Bydgoszcz	362
TZALA	Shoul	M						380
TZALA	Avigdor	M						380
TZALA ?	Mechel	M					uncle of essay author Alya Tzala (p. 354). Perished in Treblinka.	366
TZERNOBRODA	Eliyahu	M	married		Feige	and children		456

Family name(s)	First name(s)	Sex	Marital status	Father's name	Name of spouse	Additional family members	Remarks	Original Yizkor Book Page
VINKOR		F				several sisters of Shoshana Offenbach (nee Vinkor)		224-226
WALDENBERG	Yehoshua	M					head of Jewish community of Dobrzyn	285-291
YANUAR		M		Chayim			First son of Chayim Yanuar. See Note 1.	264-269
YANUAR		M		Chayim			2nd son of Chayim Yanuar. See Note 1.	264-269
YANUAR	Chayim	M						285-291
ZAKLIKOWSKI	Eliezer	M					See Note 1.	264-269; 446
ZAKLIKOWSKI	Hersh	M	married	Meir	Ita (nee Zik; originatd in Lipno)			457
ZAKLIKOWSKI	Ita (nee Zik; originatd in Lipno)	F	married	Hersh				457
ZAKLIKOWSKI	Yosef Meir	M		Hersh			"missing"	457
ZAKLIKOWSKI	Yaakov	M	married	Hersh	Esther (nee Sentor)		"missing"	457
ZAKLIKOWSKI	Esther (nee Sentor)	F	married		Yaakov			457
ZAKLIKOWSKI	Bunem	M	married	Hersh	Hila (nee Tzlekownik)			457
ZAKLIKOWSKI	Hila (nee Tzlekownik)	F	married		Bunem			457

Family name(s)	First name(s)	Sex	Marital status	Father's name	Name of spouse	Additional family members	Remarks	Original Yizkor Book Page
ZAKLIKOWSKI	Yeshayahu	M	married	Hersh	Itka (nee Korewa; originated in Rypin)			457
ZAKLIKOWSKI	Moshe	M		Yeshayahu				457
ZAKLIKOWSKI	Shlomo	M	married	Hersh				457
ZAKLIKOWSKI	Reizl	F		Shlomo				457
ZAKLIKOWSKI	Marta	F		Shlomo				457
ZAKLIKOWSKI	Ilonka	F		Shlomo				457
ZISSHOLTZ	Yechiel	M					Municipal councilman. See Note 1.	264-269
ZUDKEVICZ		M					See Note 1.	264-269
ZUDKEVITZ	Avraham	M	married				Fled to Warsaw, where he died of a stroke in 1942	230
ZUDKEVITZ		F	married		Avraham	2 sons, 2 daughters	all perished in Treblinka	230
ZYLBERBERG		M					A chazzan (cantor). See Note 1. Also Note 3.	264-269

NOTE 1

One of 230 men taken out of synagogues by Germans on 1st day of Rosh Hashana (Sep 14, 1939), loaded into trucks and taken away, initially to Bydgoszcz (pp. 244, 138). Possibly executed in forest near Inowroclaw, 40km south of Bydgoszcz (p. 364).

NOTE 2

Among 35 most distinguished families of Dobrzyn (~100 people) taken away by Germans on Nov 6, 1939 in transport of 3 trucks (men, women, children), driven away in unknown direction; no one knows what became of them (p. 244).

NOTE 3

The "cantor of the town" could have meant Degala, but alternatively it could have referred to Zylberberg.

[Page 173]

R. Yitzhak Moshe Offenbach[1][2]

Avraham Dor (Dobroszklanka)

Translated by Allen Flusberg

As far back as the early 1920s I already knew R.[3] Yitzhak Moshe Offenbach. He was then a middle-aged man of average height, adorned with a full beard: a splendid patriarchal, illustrious figure. He was a respectable merchant who dealt in processed leather; but the most important part of his life was his communal activity.

It was in communal work that he invested most of his time and vision. He was active in all of the town's public institutions, serving for many years as chairman of the Zionist *Histadrut*[4]. The townspeople considered him an inspiring spiritual leader whose opinion everyone eagerly sought out. It would be difficult to describe the cultural life of Dobrzyn without viewing him as a central figure, someone who, with wisdom and energy, encouraged others to be actively engaged and inspired them with his noble spirit.

[Page 174]

I recall in particular the lectures he gave every Sabbath in the auditorium of the "Abba Yosef" school. These lectures attracted a large crowd, and many a time the small lecture hall was unable to hold all those who came to hear him.

R. Yitzhak Moshe Offenbach, chairman of the Zionist *Histadrut* of Dobrzyn

More than anything else he liked to lecture about Herzl and his era. He would very skillfully describe the enormous contribution made by the seer of the Jewish State to the development of the Zionist idea. With sincere excitement and great ardor he would count out, one by one, the laudable actions of the great Zionist leader. The audience could sense how much he admired Herzl and how committed he was to his ideas. Indeed, how profound and important his influence on us young people was, and how much he contributed to enhancing our Zionist education.

His educational ability would reveal itself even more after his lecture ended, when the audience began asking questions, whether to clarify some detail or dispute what he had said. How patient he was as he answered everyone's questions; he would reply good-naturedly and cordially, his words revealing his affection for those gathered there.

His presentation on the 20th of Tammuz, the anniversary of Dr. Herzl's death, was considered a special event in the life of the town. He would colorfully describe the deeds of the great Zionist leader and the revolution that he initiated in his people's thinking. With much enthusiasm he demanded that his listeners follow in Herzl's footsteps, striving to fulfill his aspiration, for it was only this fulfillment that could guarantee the continued existence and prosperity of our people.

[Page 175]

R. Yitzhak Moshe Offenbach was one of the founders of the *Hatechiya*[5] Club and played an important role in its activities. The club was located in Sperling's house, opposite the fire station auditorium, and it served as one of the most important Zionist institutions in Dobrzyn. Among the important activities that took place in this club was the teaching of the Hebrew language. The Hebrew course met four evenings a week and was taught by some of the best educators in town, among them: R. Shaul Blum (son-in-law of R. Nisan Melamed), Yaakov Bezura, and others.

Mrs. Breina Offenbach

At this moment an image of R. Yitzhak Moshe comes back to me. I see him seated at one of the Hebrew classes, near the teacher, Bezura, leaning back in his chair as he cups his ear. A smile appears on his face when he hears students giving the correct answer to a question, all in Hebrew. It is as if this noble, dedicated man senses he is experiencing his reward.

Very soon after the Balfour Declaration, a branch of *Keren Kayemet*[6] was established in Dobrzyn at his incentive; and very quickly this branch became well known for its ability to collect contributions. This institution excelled not only in collecting money to be transferred to the head office in Warsaw, but also in extensive Zionist activity.

How happy R. Yitzhak Moshe was when, with glowing eyes, he escorted the first pioneers of the town who were about to immigrate to the Land of Israel. I, too, was one of these pioneers; and I recall to this very day the stirring well-attended party that was made in our honor. He passionately repeated words of encouragement to us, explaining that as the very first we would pave the way for the many others that would follow.

For many years he headed the Zionist activity in the town, providing his advice and guidance to the movement as he toiled incessantly, his devotion unlimited. Many absorbed his passion and joined the Zionist movement, viewing him as its leader. From among them he chose trustworthy aides who served as deputies and followed in his path.

He also educated his own children in the spirit of Zionism, planting in them his great love for the Land of Israel. And indeed, most of them immigrated to the Land while he was still alive; and the others, together with their mother, after he had passed away.

However, he himself was not fortunate enough to fulfil his own aspiration, to immigrate to the Holy Land and settle there. He passed away in the Polish Diaspora as the dark clouds began gathering over Polish Jewry.

To this very day the image of his noble figure and the memory of his praiseworthy actions accompany those who hail from the town.

Translator's Footnotes

1. From *My Town: In Memory of the Communities Dobrzyn-Gollob*, edited by M. Harpaz, (published by the Dobrzyn-Golub Society, Israel, 1969), pp. 173-176.
2. See also the following biographical article written by Offenbach's daughter: S. Vinkor (Offenbach), "My Father's House", pp. 224-226 of this volume.
3. R. = *Reb*, similar to English "Mr."
4. *Histadrut* = Jewish socialist-Zionist party in Poland
5. *Hatechiya* = the revival
6. *Keren Kayemet* = Jewish National Fund, an organization that purchased and developed land in Palestine for the settlement of Jews there. See the following link: http://en.wikipedia.org/wiki/Jewish_National_Fund